T0277895

Praise for Thomas Suárez

"A *tour de force*, based on diligent archival research that looks boldly at the impact of Zionism on Palestine and its people in the first part of the 20th century. The book is the first comprehensive and structured analysis of the violence and terror employed by the Zionist movement, and later the state of Israel, against the people of Palestine. Much of the suffering we witness today can be explained by, and connected to, this formative period covered thoroughly in this book."

—ILAN PAPPÉ, ISRAELI HISTORIAN AND AUTHOR

"This is archival history that has been intentionally forced down the memory hole..." **—JONATHAN COOK, JOURNALIST**

"[B]elongs in the top 5 most invaluable books on the history of modern Palestine ... [it] is Palestine's Yad Vashem."

—DR. VACY VLAZNA, *COUNTERCURRENTS*

"[A] book that really does get to the heart of the Zionist soul—a very dark place indeed." **—MIKE PARKER, *TRIBUNE* MAGAZINE**

"Should be added to the essential sources for researchers on this issue, as well as required reading for university courses on the Palestine/Israel Conflict." **—ELAINE HAGOPIAN, *ARAB STUDIES QUARTERLY***

"It proves beyond doubt that Israel is not the perpetual victim of Arab violence that it claims to be, but has been the aggressor throughout the history of the conflict." **—DR. DAVID GERALD FINCHAM, *MONDOWEISS***

Other books by Thomas Suárez

Writings on the Wall [Olive Branch Press, 2019]

State of Terror [Olive Branch Press, 2017]

Palestine Sixty Years Later
[Americans for Middle East Understanding, 2010]

Early Mapping of the Pacific [Charles E. Tuttle, 2004]

Early Mapping of Southeast Asia [Charles E. Tuttle, 1999]

*Shedding the Veil: Mapping the European Discovery of
America and the World* [World Scientific, 1992]

Contributing author

*En el archipiélago de la Especiería: España y Molucas
en los siglos XVI y XVII* [Desperta Ferro Ediciones, 2021]

"Cartography and the Making of the Philippines from Antiquity to Now,"
in Carlos P. Quirino's *Philippine Cartography* 1320-1899 [Vibal, 2018]

"Early Portuguese Mapping of Siam," in *500 Years of Thai-
Portuguese Relations* [Thai Ministry of Foreign Affairs, 2011]

"Genesis of the American West: The Cortes Map," in *Mapping the
West: America's Westward Movement* 1524-1890, ed. P. Cohen
[Rizzoli, 2002]

PALESTINE HIJACKED

HOW ZIONISM FORGED AN
APARTHEID STATE
FROM RIVER TO SEA

THOMAS SUÁREZ

OLIVE
BRANCH
PRESS

An imprint of Interlink Publishing Group, Inc.
www.interlinkbooks.com

First published 2023 by

OLIVE BRANCH PRESS
An imprint of Interlink Publishing Group, Inc.
46 Crosby Street, Northampton, Massachusetts 01060
www.interlinkbooks.com

Copyright © Thomas Suárez, 2023
Portions of this book first appeared in *State of Terror* by Thomas Suárez.

All rights reserved; no part of this publication may be reproduced,
in any form or by any electronic or mechanical means, without the
written permission of the publisher, except by a reviewer who
may quote brief passages in a review.

Library of Congress Cataloging-in-Publication Data available

ISBN 978-1-62371-819-0

Printed and bound in the United States of America

To request our complete 48-page, full-color catalog, please call us toll free at
1-800-238-LINK, visit our website at
www.interlinkbooks.com, or send us an email:
info@interlinkbooks.com

"The growth of Fascism in Palestine
at a time when the liberated nations will put it into its grave
is a tragi-comedy."

—*Physicist Wolfgang Yourgrau, a German Jew
who knew anti-Jewish violence
by both the Nazis and the Zionists,
in the journal* Orient, *February, 1943*[1]

C O N T E N T S

Dedicated to the youth of Palestine,
who from their parents'
unwavering struggle for freedom
will build a future of their own choosing

Acknowledgments

The origins of this book lie in research inspired by the author, academic, and lecturer Dr. Ghada Karmi, without whose expertise, encouragement, and assistance it would doubtfully exist.

I am indebted to the many people who helped me along the way in research that ultimately informed this book: Laurence Dreyfus, Nancy Elan, Yosef Grodzinsky, Rashid Khalidi, Francis Manasek, Joseph Massad, Nancy Murray, my brother John Suárez, and my daughter Sainatee Suárez. My gratitude goes as well to Lama Alhelou, Michele Cantoni, Emily Dreyfus, Mirene Ghossein, Tony Greenstein, Elaine Hagopian, Massoud Hayoun, Fred Pragnell, Rona Sela, Mathilde Vittu, Rawan Yaghi, as well as the Trustees of the Lancaster City Museum (UK), and the entire always-helpful staff of the National Archives in Kew.

Three eye-witnesses to events in the 1940s and early 1950s who are no longer with us kindly shared their first-hand knowledge and insight during my early research. Ex-Haganah member Hanna Braun met with Nancy Elan and me in London in 2007, and her experiences both pre- and post-statehood inform the book beyond the scope of documents. "Max" Maxwell, Sgt Maj, 16 Field Security Section, Intelligence Corps, was present after the Irgun's Austrian train bombing of August 1947, and shared his detailed account of the incident. Ted Steel was part of the British occupation during the last years of the Mandate, and spent an afternoon sharing recollections and photographs. On July 22, 1946, he delivered documents to the British headquarters in the King David Hotel and, breaking with his routine of heading straight to the canteen, left the building. As he did, it blew up. He awoke later in an oxygen tent. My thanks to Camilla Saunders for making our meeting possible.

I am grateful to my publisher, Michel Moushabeck, not just for his efforts regarding the present book, but for his and Interlink Publishing's decades of service to society with books that truly matter. Interlink's remarkable roster has always furthered the open exchange of ideas and knowledge, each in its own way a tool toward a better world. My great thanks to the entire Interlink staff, with special thanks to Pam Fontes-May for her expert assistance.

To my mother and my late father I owe everything, not least of which was growing up with their sense of universal fairness, of healthy skepticism, and of searching for truth beyond the headlines, that has led me to all that has mattered in my life.

Finally, my partner Nancy Elan was my constant alter-ego, perceptive critic, and idea tester. In the midst of my early research toward the book, its topic proved unexpectedly prescient when her activism in the Palestinian cause led its adversaries to come knocking at the door of her professional life.

Introduction

> "Jews ... cannot be as entirely English in thought as the man who is born of English parents ... There is no use disguising this fact. To me it seems impossible to separate religion from nationality in Judaism."
> —*Norman Bentwich, Zionist advocate who would become attorney-general of Palestine, 1909*[2]

This is a book of history written to influence the present. It is written in the belief that knowledge of the past will contribute toward today's collective efforts to bring peace to all of Palestine, from river to sea. History has the power to pierce the opaque narratives that hide the truth to perpetuate injustice.

The prevailing narrative of Israel-Palestine is of a complex, even irreconcilable, collision—conflict—between ancient enemies. What history and ongoing reality expose is however something vastly simpler: the single story of a racial-nationalist settler movement—Zionism—determined to ethnically cleanse a land for itself.

This of course is no revelation. It is what Palestinians have been saying since they were first displaced by Zionist settlers in the late nineteenth century. It is what outside observers warned of since the turn of the twentieth century, and what witnesses such as Moshe Menuhin have been chronicling since the 1950s. Expanded scholarship in the 1970s added documentary backbone to what should have long been self-evident from Israel's behavior, and in the subsequent two decades historians such as Ilan Pappé scoured Zionist archives that laid to rest any lingering doubts that the "conflict" was in truth settler-colonialism wrapped in elaborate mythology.[3]

Anti-Jewish persecution was the professed motivation of political Zionism's architects, and a Jewish state its solution. For the victims of pogroms in Europe and Russia, the attraction to Zionism was unquestionably sincere. What history makes plain, however, is that the driving motivation of the Zionist movement itself was not Jewish safety and dignity, but an ethnically-predicated settler state for which persecuted Jews were its renewable fuel.

As the settler project progressed, so did its addiction to this "fuel" and the need to ensure that its wells would never run dry. Palestine's history of religious tolerance was erased from the common memory as Palestinian opposition to ethnic domination was framed as antisemitism.[*]

Palestinians fought alongside the Allies in World War I against the Ottoman occupation of their land. The Palestinians had been promised liberation[†]; but upon victory Britain instead replaced the single Ottoman occupation with *two* simultaneous occupations, British colonialism facilitating Zionist settler-colonialism. Whereas the British occupation was one of traditional empire, the exploitation of the land and its strategic geographic position, the goal of the Zionist occupation it enabled was one of outright dispossession.

Messianism

Zionism flourished by rewriting turn-of-the-20th-century European ethnic supremacism as a messianic script, transforming Palestine into a Biblical theme park for the script's—the narrative's—stage. Palestine's privileged turf in the collective Judeo-Christian mindset was exploited to seduce fundamentalist Christians, including those

---

[*] The term *antisemitism* is problematic, historically and linguistically, but as it remains the dominant term for anti-Jewish bigotry, I use it in this book.

[†] The promise of Palestinian liberation was part of Britain's Hussein-McMahon Correspondence of 24th of October, 1915. Britain then secretly negotiated its 1916 Sykes–Picot Agreement contradicting that promise, rumors of which Britain dismissed as Turkish propaganda.

in positions of power, to believe that they were living the Prophecies themselves, the beginning of the end of the world.

Yet however brilliant as marketing, that script would have been received with incredulity at best, were it not for a confluence of circumstances. Western powers saw the movement as symbiotic with their own imperial designs. Anti-Jewish bigots supported Zionism because it offered an easy way to send Jews to a ghetto far from their own shores without stigma. And finally, World War I brought new opportunity as Zionists exploited British notions of Jewish power to claim that they could assure Allied victory ... if only Foreign Secretary Lord Balfour would sign the 1917 Declaration now known by his name.[4]

Palestinian rights subjugated to Zionism
Despite the Balfour Declaration's evasive allusion to equal rights, the British imposed institutional superiority for the settlers—what today would be called apartheid rule. Zionist leaders across the spectrum, from the allegedly "moderate" Chaim Weizmann to terrorist leaders like Menachem Begin and Yitzhak Shamir, uniformly demanded Jewish supremacy in Palestine and denounced any suggestion of non-Jews' participation in democracy.

In justification, they variously claimed that non-Jews ("Arabs") are inferior people and so do not deserve a voice in civil affairs; that Jews were a majority in a Biblical realm two or three thousand years ago, and that "they" never gave up "their" claim and thus are Palestine's exclusive electorate; that Jews are a nationality, by blood, and thus Jews worldwide are Palestine's voting public; that even a world-wide Jewish vote counter to Zionism would be void, since Zionists know what is best for Jews and must preserve Zionism for future generations; and that the Zionist claim to rule Palestine is not subject to norms applicable to the rest of the world.[5]

Language
Language as a weapon rather than as a tool of communication—its power to spark a message past linear reasoning and plant a conclusion by stealth—is a coveted perk of statehood. As much as control of

land, control of language is why Zionism needed statehood, and why it continues to fight to prevent Palestinian statehood.

Statehood gifted the Zionists an Orwellian inversion of language under whose shadow today's so-called conflict is informed. From the podium of statehood, Zionist terrorism became Israeli self-defense, and Palestinians attempting to step foot on their own land became infiltrators or terrorists. Armed Israelis invading Palestinian land, commandeering non-Jewish families' homes and expelling their inhabitants, were now "settlers" or "immigrants." Palestinian land seized and depopulated was not stolen, but annexed, and Israel pressured the media to refer to its illegal settlements as "Jewish neighborhoods," CNN among those acquiescing. Biblical and Hebrew nomenclature, and indeed the Hebrew language itself, were themselves exploited as weapons of expropriation, seamlessly woven into secular news coverage to make the absurd seem self-evidently true.[6]

Even the concept of Arab Jews has fallen victim, severed into two seeming opposing identities. Jews were as integral to the cultural landscape of Arabian lands as Christians and Muslims, but Zionism enforced a strict dichotomy between Jews and all others in Palestine, as European colonialism has done to some extent throughout the Middle East and North Africa. The false imagery of Jew *versus* Arab became another subliminal weapon informing the issue of Israel-Palestine.[7]

Terrorism

Ethnic depopulation is, by definition, deliberate violence against civilians—that is, terrorism. It is immaterial whether it is accomplished through outright annihilation, by expelling the land's people through pogroms, by expropriating all means of livelihood and thus starving them out, by commandeering their aquifers, through laws ethnically engineered for the purpose, or simply by making life so miserable for the wrong ethnicity that they leave "of their own accord."[8]

As Israel's narrative would have it, Zionist violence during the British Mandate was not terrorism, because it targeted the British occupation. Overlooking the irony that it was upon that same British occupation that the settlements' claim to legitimacy was founded, civilians inconvenient to Zionist aspirations were always a target, whether Palestinian, British, or Jewish.

Above all, it erases the more than three-quarters of a million civilians ethnically cleansed by Zionist terror in 1948, ethnic expulsion that continues today. Finally, since Zionism depended not just on the transfer of non-Jewish Palestinians *out* of Palestine, but also on the transfer of Jews *into* Palestine, hundreds of thousands of people in Europe, North Africa, and the Middle East became fair game for Zionist violence *because* they were Jewish. The fact that the Zionists' goal also required targeting the very British colonial establishment that had weaned it, is irrelevant.*

Zionist militias enjoyed wide support among the settlements, especially among the youth indoctrinated into their cause. The British, forever lamenting the very tragedy they continued to facilitate, were unable to control the Zionist terrorism ravaging Palestine and powerless to dampen the terror organizations' lucrative fund-raising in the US, Britain, and France. Though best remembered by the iconic Irgun and Lehi (Stern Gang), the Jewish Agency's Haganah was little different, and by early 1948 this official militia—soon to be the Israeli Defence Forces (IDF)—terrorized the non-Jewish population with barbaric depopulation campaigns that surpassed the abilities of the Irgun or Lehi.

Palestinians also committed terror attacks, and this book's focus on Zionist and Israeli terror must never be misinterpreted as excusing Palestinian violence against innocents. This book follows the *causes* and *driving force* behind the present tragedy; it is not an inventory of every incident of violence. Its coverage of Zionist violence during the several years leading up to the 1947 UN decision to partition Palestine, though by no means complete, will at times read like such

---

* Because of its widespread acceptance in the US, mention should be made of the construct that what we call Palestinians were Arabs who flocked to Palestine due to improvements brought by Zionist settlers and British colonization, and so have no claim to their own land. The World Zionist Organization tried to make such a claim, advocates like Churchill repeated it (page 303, below), Joan Peters gave it new life in her book *From Time Immemorial*, and it was further popularized by Alan Dershowitz (*The Case for Israel*). Beyond its historical absurdity, the claim is applied only to non-Jewish Palestinians, not to the influx of Zionist settlers who did indeed come to Palestine under the British occupation and with massive external financing.

an inventory. An understanding of the relentlessness of the terror, and the inability of the British military to dampen it, is key to an understanding the of UN's behavior in 1947 and the catastrophe it enabled.

Palestinian terror occurred principally during the uprisings of the late 1920s and late 1930s after years of being institutionally discriminated against for the benefit of the Zionists, and after non-violent resistance—diplomacy, entreaties, strikes, boycotts—proved futile. The British response to Palestinian terror was brutal: suspects were summarily hung, hundreds of houses of innocent people demolished, and Palestinians were used as human shields.

Any people attacked, will resist; and among any group there will be people who will resist in extreme ways, especially when denied any means of self-defense. A state or political movement cannot claim self-defence when putting down the resistance to its own violence—otherwise all aggression would self-justify. It was British and Zionist terrorism that dictated the course of events in Palestine between the world wars, Zionist terrorism that dictated events during the war and pre-state years, and it is Israeli state terrorism that has dictated events since 1948.

As the critical years 1940-1947 will illustrate, the virtual absence of Palestinian violent resistance changed nothing. Throughout the war and post-war years leading up to the partitioning of Palestine, the British remarked on Palestinian restraint in the face of increasing Zionist attacks. In contrast to their previous treatment of the Palestinians, the British avoided strong measures against the Zionists for fear of unleashing a revolt they could not control, as well as the propaganda windfall it would afford the Zionist movement, especially in the United States.[9]

As the British exit was assured in late 1947 by the UN's proposal to partition Palestine into a Zionist and Palestinian state, the terror militias focused their cross-hairs onto the sole remaining obstacle to seizing all of historic Palestine: the Palestinians themselves.

Emotionally scarred, vulnerable Jewish survivors of the war in Europe were indoctrinated in Zionist-run DP camps (displaced persons, refugees) and in the settlements with the message that

Palestine was their only hope of survival, but that it was inhabited by the heirs to their German tormentors, hardening the war's survivors against soul-searching when, barely three years after the defeat of the Nazis, they razed village after village because of people's ethnicity.

British documents state explicitly what is overwhelmingly supported by the cumulative evidence: that UNGA Resolution 181, the partitioning of Palestine, was a capitulation to Zionist terror. The UN feared that backing a single, secular democratic state would unleash a new and unprecedented wave of Jewish terrorism (as they called it) that would not be confined to Palestine. Resolution 181 was also a fraud: Its advocates were fully aware that the Zionists backed Partition only to extract the single prize of Israeli statehood and disregard the rest.[10]

The US Truman Administration bullied Resolution 181 into passage well aware that the Jewish Agency's acceptance of it was a pragmatic chess-move within the walls of the UN. For the Zionists, Partition was a necessary inconvenience to achieve statehood—which in turn was the one weapon powerful enough to defeat Partition.

The Palestinians, fully aware that the proposed Zionist state would be merely a beachhead to further conquest and expulsion, refused to endorse Partition. That did not negate their right to their half of the deal, but no effort was made by the international community to enforce it or to prevent the ethnic cleansing that any informed official feared was imminent. The British, whatever limited control they exerted slipping away precipitously, washed their hands of the catastrophe they had created and—to use their own word—evacuated.

By the time the Armistice Line established a cease-fire at the end of 1948, Israel had seized and ethnically cleansed not just the 56.5% of Palestine that the United Nations had designated for the state, but fully half of the Palestinians' portion as well. This Line was not a redrawn Partition—it did not give Israel the extra land it had seized—but Israel hurriedly settled new immigrants on that Palestinian territory, rather than on Israel's side of Partition, in order to make the theft appear irreversible. Thus in January 1949, the eminent *New York Times* correspondent Anne O'Hare McCormick declared the two-state solution dead due to Israeli aggression.[11]

Meanwhile, the terror gangs' leaders moved on to key positions in the new Israeli government. The most notorious of them, Menachem Begin, went to New York and openly fundraised for the violent takeover of the rest of Palestine.

Crowded into that remnant of Palestine were the people Israel had ethnically cleansed, both from its own side of Partition and from the Palestinian land it occupied to the Armistice Line. Destitute, the refugees were captured or killed on sight if caught trying to reach their homes, if only to pick their harvest or retrieve hidden savings. Israel flouted the UN's demands to desist even as it sought—and won—membership in the world body.

By the mid-1950s, two events might have ended Israeli aggression. One, its violence against its neighbors had become so serious that Britain made plans to neutralize the entire Israeli air force and key Israeli military and communications installations. Secondly, Israel was caught targeting British and US citizens in a botched false-flag operation, the so-called Lavon Affair. But cynical geopolitics took precedence: instead of attacking Israel, Britain joined forces with Israel and France to attack Egypt, creating the Suez Crisis.

Sources

I have relied chiefly on declassified source documents in the National Archives of Great Britain (Kew). Their many authors certainly had their own biases; but they were also professionals, bureaucrats, and firsthand observers, recording clinically and commenting candidly.

For Zionist records I have used the terror organizations' own words when possible, transcripts of meetings, Jewish Agency documents, and the works of Israeli scholars who have scoured the limited Zionist archives made available, principally Ilan Pappé and Benny Morris. I supplement these with documents from US intelligence and from existing scholarship on the topic. Interviews with two eye-witnesses to events provided additional corroboration.

My original intent had been to check the Zionist Archives for any newly-declassified material not yet tapped by Israeli scholars, with the help of an Israeli archivist and translator. But Israel began resealing some records and prevented the unsealing of others due for release, while a "Malmab unit" has been searching the country's archives to remove evidence of war crimes.[12]

Jewish terrorism was the term commonly used during the Mandate, but when not quoting or paraphrasing a source, I have preferred the more accurate *Zionist terrorism*. When referring to the native people of Palestine, I have preferred the obvious term *Palestinians* rather than the broad ethnic term *Arabs*, which was—and is—misused as a tool of expropriation, painting the natives of Palestine as nomadic blurs in a great Arab mass who should be happy to vanish into that mass.[13]

Any quotes not specifically identified are from British Colonial, Foreign, or War Office records as cited in the relevant endnote. Other than quotes, spellings of Palestinian villages and Jewish settlements are modern when their identity is clear, otherwise spelled as cited in the source documents. All emphasis within quotes (underline, italics, uppercase) is original.

Tom Suárez, London, May 2022

A selection of lesser-known source documents cited in this book are online at the author's document website, paldocs.net, *or via* thomassuarez.com.

1

Zionism, Messianism, and Marketing

"Zionism is a kind of intoxication which acts like an epidemic.
It may, and presumably will, also pass away like one.
But not overnight."
—*the political theorist Eduard Bernstein, writing in the
German socialist journal Die Neue Zeit, 1914* [14]

Palestine was a popular destination in the nineteenth century. People from myriad walks of life came as tourists, pilgrims, adventurers, writers, and as hopeful immigrants—all at a time when various nations jostled for political, religious, economic, and strategic interests in the Levant and greater Middle East.

Beginning in the early 1880s, Europeans who championed the new ethno-nationalist movement of Zionism began arriving in Palestine. In principle, the movement was to serve an urgent and noble purpose, offering victims of European and Russian anti-Jewish persecution a route to safety and dignity. Zionist ideology, however, made the land exclusionary, effectively excising it from the shared inheritance. For the people of Palestine who had lived, loved, and died on the land for millennia, including Palestine's Jews, the settlers were seen not as immigrants, but as usurpers.

Zionism's leaders, however, made a starkly different claim: they were neither settlers nor immigrants, but as Jews they were the actual sovereigns of the land, returning home after a two-millennia absence.

Through the decades to come, from mainstream leaders like David Ben-Gurion and Chaim Weizmann* to the fanatical terror gang Lehi, the ideological pronouncements of the settler project were couched in the language of messianism. Zionism was building the final Kingdom, the Biblical Third Temple, a resurrection rising from the ashes of the fabled Second Temple and Solomon's Temple. Zionism's battles, its enemies, its conquests, its tragedies, were Biblical, and its establishment of the Israeli state in 1948 was sold as the resumption, the reconstitution of the Biblical realm. As Ben-Gurion put it, "the Bible is our mandate" to take Palestine.[15]

Zionism's imagery touched deep into the collective cultural subconscious of much of the Christian world. In the United States, Christian fundamentalists were seduced by this opportunity to believe that they were living the prophecies themselves, the beginning of the end of time.

"Are we not witnessing," US Congressman Albert Rossdale testified in 1922 in support of the Zionist colonization of Palestine,

> the truth of the words of the prophets of the return of Israel, the assurance of whose restoration gleams through the whole vista of prophecy?[16]

Fast-forward a century, and the need for "the Jewish people [to] go back to their homeland [in order for Christ to] come back to the earth" is among the reasons voiced by US lawmakers for legislation prohibiting US citizens from boycotting the Israeli state.[17]

Marketing Zionism

Like other European settler movements, Zionism had to sell itself. Its marketing challenges were however novel, because its narrative was reversed from that of traditional settler movements. Instead of colonists settling faraway lands and spreading the faith, Zionism had

---

* Israel's first Prime Minister and President, respectively. Weizmann was the main constant figure of influence to span the years from the Balfour Declaration to the Israeli state. Ben-Gurion was the dominant figure in the post-war years and is considered Israel's "founding father."

to sell the opposite story: that Jews were already foreign settlers in the European countries they now inhabited. They had gone there involuntarily from Palestine two thousand years ago, and now wanted simply to go back to where they came from, a covenanted people returning to a land to which they'd never been, yet had never left. And in contrast to Europe's Christian colonists settling in Africa, Asia, the Americas, and the Pacific, the Zionists had no interest in spreading their faith to Palestine's (actual) natives who, as the script read, had somehow moved in during their absence.[18]

Thus to sell its product, what would become the Israeli state, Zionism inverted the historic relationship between religion and colonialism, between Bible and sword. By sailing to the Holy Land, the settlers were sailing to the final page of the Old Testament in order to begin the page's overleaf.

Branding was crucial. The other-worldliness of the name *Israel* would clinch the messianic narrative and place the state apart from all others. The very sound of the name summons imagery of that place exalted in the some of the most profound music and art of the Western canon and beyond, celebrated in Negro spirituals, sung with reverence in the finest Christmas carols, and invoked with adoration every Sunday at Christian mass, that place in the *Book of Genesis* that was seemingly created by God. Who would challenge such a name hard-wired with veneration into our cultural womb?

The branding of Israel was equally important for another, practical reason: as Ben-Gurion would explain in private, without it, the state would never attract enough Jewish settlers.

Palestine was the principal piece of the imagery, the stage itself. There could be no ingathering (as it was called) except to the actual soil of the Hebrew lands in the Bible. Other locations were considered as stepping stones to Palestine, never as substitutes. Proposals like Argentina, Uganda, the Sinai, or Cyprus were what Zionism's founder, Theodor Herzl, called "auxiliary colonization" that would only attract "a few thousand proletarians" and—the key point—"serve no political end." In contrast, "the very name of Palestine," Herzl argued, "would attract our people with a force of marvelous potency." Only in Palestine could Zionism's messianic narrative play out.

Herzl tried to buy Palestine from the occupying Ottomans in exchange for settling their foreign debt (1896), and when that failed he tried to get it as payment from Germany for helping that country to extend its suzerainty to the Middle East (1898). The exercise continued after his death until his followers found a willing state sponsor—Britain, as it happened.[19]

As Zionism's salespeople looked to the heavens to claim their divine right of return, they turned to the ground below to corroborate their Biblical story and their connection to it. So effectively were archaeology, mythology, nomenclature, divine right, the collective Western subconscious, and genetics fused in the service of Zionism that today, when Israel designates Levantine archaeological sites as Israeli national heritage sites, subliminally, the ancient ruins are not just those of a realm from antiquity; they are the living heritage of the Israeli state and its settlers. Israel's leaders visit these sites and speak as though the stones awaken in them a distant memory, an intrinsic familiarity, like one returning to his childhood home and clearing cobwebs from a faded photo album.

The militarization of the Hebrew language

Deep under those ancient cobwebs—under what Herzl called "the musty deposits of two thousand years" since the Roman conquest—lay another piece of the imagery of the ingathering: language. Clearing away two-millennia worth, Herzl dug through Arabic, brushed aside some Greek and a bit of Latin, and found Aramaic. But digging down through a few more centuries, he unearthed the right answer: Hebrew, the language to be resurrected and promoted as the settlers' native tongue. No mere historical society re-enacting pages from the past, the settlers learned the language of the Biblical realm because Zionism required that they be its people.[20]

Although by the second decade of the twentieth century the lack of a common language in the settlements had become a serious problem, there was wide resistance to reviving an ancient language as the remedy.

German was a popular candidate. Dr. Paul Nathan, a prominent Jewish leader in Berlin, made an extensive trip through the Middle

East in 1907 with the aim of improving the educational systems among Jewish communities. Seven years later, he returned to Palestine on behalf of the German Jewish National Relief Association, as plans were made to establish a technical institute in Haifa. But in what language would the Institute operate? An impassioned dispute was underway as to whether it should be a language that was already widely spoken in the settlements, such as German, versus Hebrew. Nathan argued that knowledge of Hebrew was fine, but that it is an utterly impractical language for a discipline like engineering.

What shocked Nathan more than the illogic of Hebrew for the sciences were the tactics of those insisting on it. In a pamphlet published in January 1914, he charged that the settlers were carrying on "a campaign of terror modeled almost on Russian pogrom models" to enforce the use of Hebrew. Nor was this terror confined to the Jewish settlements: Nathan accused them of stirring up discord with their "arrogant Zionist activity" and "overwrought Jewish nationalist chauvinism," including against "the Mohammedan and Christian populations."

But the push for Hebrew was fierce. The Actions Committee of the Zionist Organization branded Dr. Nathan part of "an anti-Zionist alliance, which finds no methods too base to use in fighting Zionism." Why Hebrew? Because "our children must know that they belong to an ancient civilized race." Hebrew, however, was being treated more as a tool of political Zionism than as a venerable ancient language. The imagery of the messianic ingathering would have a cosmetic flaw if its native tongue were any of the living languages being spoken in the settlements: German, Polish, Russian, Ladino, Yiddish, or the Arabic of many indigenous Palestinian Jews.

Annie Landau, a paramount figure in Jerusalem education during the first half of the twentieth century, taught Hebrew—but drew the ire of the Zionists for teaching English as well. This however paled next to the outrage she caused for slighting another symbol of Zionist sovereignty: music. In March 1919, she refused to stand for what was called the Zionist national anthem, *Hatikva*, at the inauguration of a new music school. Furious, *Haaretz* compared her to Dr. Ya'acov Israel de Hahn, a critic of Zionism whom the newspaper called "antisemitic scum," whom Ben-Gurion denounced as a traitor, and whom the Haganah would soon assassinate.

Hebrew remains an important subliminal dimension of the imagery for Israel's sponsor states. A settler in Hebron fresh off the plane from his native United States, speaking acquired Hebrew or flaunted by Hebrew settlement signs, is intuited as more native than the Arabic-speaking actual native whose house or land he is commandeering and whose family has lived there for a thousand years.[21]

Legal precedent made a brief resurrection from Herzl's musty deposits of two thousand years. When in Tel Aviv in 1938 Talmudic scholar Jacob Melnik was caught married to three women, each unknown to the other two, he successfully argued that it was the Torah, which contains no prohibition against polygamy, that was the law in effect. Not even a Talmudic ban on polygamy changed matters: the defense successfully argued that "a Talmudic law is not as strong as one in the Torah." Melnik won twice, in both the District Court and the Court of Appeal. The not-guilty verdict elicited controversy and misgivings, but nonetheless was said by the defense to have "forestalled a social upheaval in the Jewish National Home."[22]

At the UN's 1947 sessions deliberating Palestine's future, Ben-Gurion testified that Palestine belonged to the Jews because *they* never gave up *their* claim to it from Biblical times—three thousand five hundred years ago, to use his figure. Even if the UN accepted the extraordinary claim that he was the descendant of a particular ancient Middle Eastern people, the argument itself would have been laughable, indeed delusional, had his audience's mindset about Palestine not also lay under Herzl's musty deposits of two thousand years.

We still see Palestine through the eyes of the medieval mapmaker. Post-Crusades *mappaemundi* typically flaunted Palestine at the center of the earth, a symbolic location even when the presumption of a spherical earth made any notion of geographic centrality symbolic as well. It is not happenstance that the first Western printed map of certain date based on actual observation was of Palestine, printed from a woodblock in the northern Germany city of Lubeck in 1475.

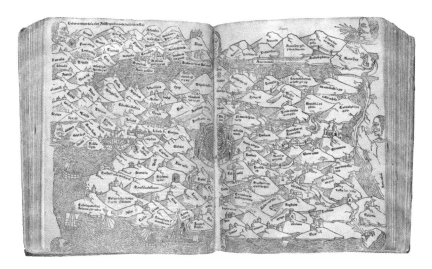

Palestine, in the *Rudimentum Novitiorum*, Lübeck (Germany), 1475. Woodblock, with inserted moveable type. Anonymous (perhaps the printer Lucas Brandis), based on the reports of Burchard de Mont Sion, a German priest and Dominican friar who spent a decade in Palestine, 1274 to 1284. East is at the top. This is the first European printed map of certain date based on actual observation. It extends from Damascus and Sidon on the north (left), to the Red Sea on the south (right). (Library of Congress).

Even during the scientific revolutions of the sixteenth to eighteenth centuries, most European cartographers presented Palestine in a Biblical framework despite their appetite for the latest geographic data. That mindset still informed the Palestine Exploration Fund's British surveyors in the nineteenth century.

Biblical nomenclature increasingly became a weapon of aggression rather than mere chauvinism. "Is it not absurd to turn the Hills of Judea, Samaria and the Galilee over to non-Hebrew ownership?" Irgun Commander Menachem Begin asked UN representatives in 1947, the circular reasoning eliciting no recorded protest. "Do not the names themselves bear evidence to whom they rightfully belong?" Today, when Israel calls the occupied West Bank *Judea and Samaria*, or when it assigns Hebrew or Biblical names to new settlements it builds over the remains of Palestinian villages it depopulated, they sound like they are part of the Israeli state and always have been.[23]

Zionism and the idea of Jews as a nationality-race

Zionism's advocates invariably treated Jews as a monolithic "nationality," defined above all by the so-called ingathering back to Palestine. From Ben-Gurion to the Irgun and Lehi, the previous two millennia of Jewish life were discarded as barely relevant to Jewish history. In 1919, Christian Zionist Colonel Richard Meinertzhagen, Chief Political Officer of the (British) Egyptian Expeditionary Force, went so far as to claim scientific interest in "re-establishing a race after a banishment of 2000 years," as though an ancient tribe's DNA had been frozen for two or three millennia and Palestine was the petri dish where a bolt of lightning would bring it back to life for the fascination of anthropologists.[24]

When that precipitous bolt of lightning struck in 1948, Israel's leaders anointed their creation "the Jewish state," not in the sense of Judaism and the state, but Jews *as* the state, a tribal definition altogether distinct from one of a national religion in the sense of other nations.

As a result, the nationality of Jewish citizens of Israel is not Israeli, but *Jewish*—by Israeli law and upheld in its Supreme Court. Any acknowledgment of a national identity or individual voice among world Jewry would undermine Israel's premise of ethnic (Jewish) nationalism.

The irony of Zionism selling its ethnic-nationalist project in the wake of the Allies' defeat of racial-nationalism in Europe was repeatedly noted at the time, including by people who knew Nazi—and Zionist—fascism firsthand. It was, as Wolfgang Yourgrau put it in this book's epigraph, "a tragi-comedy."

Like the Germany that Jews fled during fascist rule, the Israeli state defines Jews by ethnic descent, accords itself the right to define its genetic parameters, and seeks to protect its perceived purity through laws prohibiting what it considers to be mixing-of-blood—in Israel's case, marriage between a Jew and a non-Jew. Since national self-determination in Israel is by its own laws "unique to the Jewish people," Israel as such would soon cease to exist without such race laws (discussed further in the Postscript, page 368).

Zionism freed nationalism from the constraints of geographic borders, making ethnicity itself the frontier. Ethnicity and state were made one and the same.[25]

The nature of Zionist settlement and land acquisition

Zionist settlement was not immigration *per se*, but the extra-national-ization of land, resources, and labor, excised from the shared Palestinian inheritance. In 1919, Baron Edmond de Rothschild, a principal early funder of the settlements, made this explicit: the settlers' success in displacing the Palestinians from their land "had been shown when the original Zionist colonies were established," that is, since he began financing those settlements in the 1880s.[26]

A firsthand glimpse of the pioneering Zionist settlers came from the Jewish essayist Ahad Ha'Am (Asher Zvi Ginzberg). Visiting Palestine in 1891, he reported of the settlers

> suddenly they find themselves in unrestricted freedom and this change has awakened in them an inclination to despotism. They treat the Arabs with hostility and cruelty, deprive them of their rights, offend them without cause and even boast of these deeds; and nobody among us opposes this despicable and dangerous inclination...

Yitzhak Epstein, speaking at the Seventh Zionist Congress in Basel, 1905, warned of land purchases that uproot and dispossess:

> We must not uproot people from land to which they and their forefathers dedicated their best efforts and toil. If there are farmers who water their fields with their sweat, these are the Arabs ... Can this type of land acquisition continue? Will those who are dispossessed remain silent and accept what is being done to them? In the end, they will wake up and return to us in blows what we have looted from them with our gold![27]

Intensively cultivated Palestinian lands, such as one described by a visitor in 1882 as "a huge green lake of waving wheat," were acquired by the Jewish National Fund (JNF), usually from absentee (or alleged) landlords living abroad who began registering land as theirs to take advantage of the high prices being offered.

As with Zionist immigration, its purchases of land were not land sales as commonly understood. The sales would have been illegal in

Britain or the other countries endorsing Zionism, because they were for the purpose of racially segregating the land *in perpetuum*—severing it forever from the country for anyone but a particular ethnicity.[28]

Zionism and antisemitism

In its early decades, few Jews wanted anything to do with Zionism. Most wanted equality in their home countries, not a new ghetto far from home. "The idea of founding a modern Jewish State," the Berlin correspondent for the *London Standard* reported after the First Zionist Congress in 1897,

> which goes by the name of Zionism, finds little favour in Germany, except among the Anti-Semites. The *Kölnische* calls it one of the greatest Utopias of our time; and the *Frankfurther Zeitung* sums up an article on the subject as follows:— *In short, the degeneration which calls itself Anti-Semitism has begotten the degeneration which adorns itself with the name of Zionism.*[29]

Zionism's violence against Jews was articulated by activists like *Jewish Chronicle* journalist and historian Lucien Wolf. Wolf had at first been open to Herzl's ideas as a remedial scheme, but after digesting the "inner meaning" of the settler movement, in 1903 he condemned Zionism as "a comprehensive capitulation to the calumnies of the anti-Semites." He could, he wrote in the London *Times* that year, conceive of no more serious setback for the Jewish struggle for equality than the Zionist scheme.[30]

Many resented Zionism's treatment of Jews as a race apart—they'd had enough of that from bigots—and *antisemitic* might well have been the epitaph that buried Zionism along with Herzl. But Herzl fought back, claiming worldwide Jewish allegiance and crowning Zionism as the standard by which good Jews and bad Jews are distinguished.

"No true Jew can be an anti-Zionist," Herzl decreed, "only Mauschel is one" (*Mauschel* is an offensive word for a religious Jew). "Merely to look at him," this father of Zionism said of such Jews, "let alone approach or, heaven forbid, touch him was enough to make us feel sick." They are, Herzl wrote, a hideous distortion of the human character, something unspeakably low and repulsive … We'll breathe more easily, having got rid once and for all of these people who, with furtive shame, we were obliged to treat as our fellow tribesmen…[31]

The Zionists would successfully wield extra-national claim over Jews long after the establishment of the Israeli state. In the 1980s, during former Lehi bigwig Yitzhak Shamir's second term as Israeli Prime Minister, Russia finally allowed Jews to leave; most wanted to go to the US, and the US welcomed them to its shores. Shamir, furious, called them "defectors" and successfully coerced US president Reagan to close its doors in order to force them to go to Israel, where they were needed as place-holders for the state's expansion into the West Bank.[32]

Zionism handed antisemites a way of sending Jews elsewhere, and at times even discreetly marketed that as a selling point. "It is very significant that anti-Semites are always very sympathetic to Zionism," Claude Montefiore, President of the Anglo-Jewish Association, testified in 1917 in opposition to British endorsement of Zionism. "It is no wonder." Gertrude Bell, the English writer, traveler, archaeologist, and spy, observed the same fondness for Zionism among anti-Jewish bigots in France: "The French are anxious to establish Jews anywhere [i.e., support Zionism] if only to have an excuse for getting rid of them."[33]

2

"With a stroke of the pen..."

"With a stroke of the pen, almost, England could assume to
herself the active support of the Jews all over the neutral world."
—*Edgar Suarès, banker and president of the
Alexandrian Jewish community, January, 1916.*[34]

In 1905, Prime Minister Arthur James Balfour blocked the
immigration of Jews fleeing pogroms in Czarist Russia, citing
"the undoubted evils that had fallen upon" Britain from these people.
Twelve years later (1917), as Foreign Secretary, he signed another
document that would direct Jews away from Britain: the Declaration
known by his name, sixty-seven words addressed to Baron Rothschild
that quickly became the claimed legal basis for turning Palestine into
a Zionist settler state. It read:

> His Majesty's Government view with favour the establishment in
> Palestine of a national home for the Jewish people, and will use their
> best endeavours to facilitate the achievement of this object, it being
> clearly understood that nothing shall be done which may prejudice
> the civil and religious rights of existing non-Jewish communities
> in Palestine, or the rights and political status enjoyed by Jews in
> any other country.[35]

The document's calculated ambiguity allowed it to be treated like a mystical codex whose inner meaning was to be forever beyond reach, and thus to be divined by Zionism's prophets. Asked three decades later, an exasperated Foreign Secretary Ernest Bevin responded bluntly:

> I am sorry that I cannot give an accurate definition, and Balfour is dead.[36]

By putting its "viewing with favor" into action, Britain would serve three overlapping functions for the Zionists over the next three decades:

1. The core purpose was for Britain's patronage to give the Zionist project and its settlements perceived legitimacy, political recognition, and semi-autonomy.

2. Thus the second function of the British was to use its military might to suppress the Palestinian resistance to their dispossession.

3. As the Zionists had advertised it, the "national home" would then grace Britain's Empire. Instead, the Zionists waged a massive terror campaign to oust them from Palestine, and it was in that very process of being ousted that the British performed their final, wholly unanticipated function: transforming the Zionists from occupiers to the occupied, from settlers into natives. The bloody uprising against the British colonizers enabled the Zionists to replace the Palestinians as the people perceived to be under occupation, and so to spin their 1948 war of conquest and ethnic cleansing as an indigenous emancipation struggle, a "war of independence." In perfect efficiency, this Act Three left the Palestinians offstage altogether.

Act One began in London.

The Great War, the Zionists, and the Balfour Declaration

When World War I began in late July 1914, the Zionist movement was in need of a breakthrough to elevate its three decades of settlement in Palestine to a recognized political feature of the land. A half year into the war, in January 1915, Liberal Party MP Herbert Samuel distributed a paper to the Cabinet proposing what he called "the restoration of the Jews" to Palestine. This so-called restoration faced an obstacle: as Samuel explained it, the settlers might not at first be able to "command obedience" from people of the land, "Mahommedans of Arab race." Britain, however, had the military power to secure that Palestinian "obedience" on behalf of the Zionists—if it were to add Palestine to its Empire as war booty. And what nation would not want to add such a jewel to its collection?

So far, empire and prestige were the lure. Samuel made no mention of any alleged ability of the Zionists to reciprocate in any substantive way at present—only the benefit of "the devoted gratitude of a whole race, whose goodwill, in time to come, may not be without its value."[37]

By early 1916, the story evolved. The war was not going well for the British, and so it was of great interest when they were told that "the Jewish Race" could turn matters around for them. The price tag? Palestine.

Balfour would become Foreign Secretary in December, but at the time it was Sir Edward Grey. Grey received a letter dated the 27th of January from Sir Henry McMahon, then High Commissioner in Egypt, detailing a "conversation with Edgar Suarés, a prominent Italian businessman and Head of the Jewish colony in Alexandria." Suarés advised the British that they were "making a great mistake" in their handling of the war.

> It was clear that England had not, in the present struggle [World War I], the sympathy of the Jewish Race, and he feared that the indifference or hostility of the Jewish Race had been a deadweight against us during the past 18 months of the War and would continue to retard every step we took towards victory.

How to get rid of that "Jewish Race … deadweight" stymieing British progress in the war? If only Britain could assure Jews about Palestine, it would secure

> the support of the whole Jewish and German-Jewish Community in America … What the Jews in America were waiting for was only the knowledge that British policy accorded with their aspirations for Palestine.

Suarès was "distressed to see England throw away" this "golden opportunity" to turn the war around to its favor, which would take barely more than "a stroke of the pen." The simple promise of Palestine "would instantaneously change the indifference or hostility of American Jews" to the Allied war effort "to active enthusiasm."[38]

Telegraphic instructions from Foreign Secretary Grey were sent to Paris on the 11th of March 1916, discussing the "suggestion … to the effect that if it were possible to come to some arrangement with the Jews in regard to Palestine completely satisfactory to Jewish aspirations," it would have "very far reaching consequences." The goal was to use the "Zionist idea … in such a manner as to win the sympathies of the Jewish forces in America, the East and elsewhere."[39]

When the Persian-born British financier, arms dealer, and journalist James Aratoon Malcolm met with the influential Mark Sykes (of the Sykes-Picot Agreement that carved up the Ottoman Empire among Britain, France, and Russia) in the autumn of 1916, Sykes was depressed over "the general bleak outlook" of the war—"the military deadlock in France, the growing menace of submarine warfare, the unsatisfactory situation which was developing in Russia." The solution, Malcolm suggested, was "to make American Jewry thoroughly pro-Ally" in order to influence the US government to enter the war—and the way to do that was to give Palestine to the Zionists.

If Malcolm is to be believed, he was a direct influence on the events leading to the Declaration. Three decades later, one month after the establishment of the Israeli state, he wrote to Weizmann at the Hotel Meurice in Paris to remind him of "that fateful Saturday evening in October [1916] in Addison Road [when you, unlike some of your] incredulous friends, manfully asked and accepted my advice … I sincerely want you to recall what my friends were able to accomplish in 1916 and 1917."[40]

The British were receptive to the gibberish intimating the globally powerful Jew, and honed the Declaration with input from Zionist leaders. Rothschild and Weizmann succeeded in getting the British to delete a phrase protecting "Jews who are fully contented with their existing nationality and citizenship," since their settler project would claim *Jewish* nationality. Other deliberations involved the messianic *re-establishment* of a home for the Jewish *race*, versus the final text's *establishment* of a national home for the Jewish *people*.[41]

As they finessed the wording, opposition was diverse and eloquent. Claude Montefiore described as "intensely obnoxious" the invention that Jews constitute a nationality. The Zionist claim that antisemitism was eternal, he condemned as "a libel upon (1) the Jews and (2) human nature." For the true well-being of Jews, emancipation and liberty throughout the world "are a thousand times more important than a 'home.'"

Edwin Montagu, a (Jewish) MP and member of the Cabinet, viewed "with horror" the idea of "Jewish Nationalism," that Jews constitute a "race world-wide." Fully aware of what the Zionists planned, he condemned the premise that Jews in Palestine should be "invested with certain special rights in excess of those enjoyed by the rest of the population." He was particularly baffled by his government's zeal to please the Zionists in the midst of the Great War, and—clearly not a believer in notions of Jewish power—baffled that it had to do with US participation in the fighting.

> Now will you forgive me for saying that if I am right in thinking that Jews of British birth are in the main anti-Zionist ... what can be the motive for our Government, in the midst of its great preoccupations and perplexities [World War I], doing anything in this matter? To help the Allied cause in America was one of the reasons given in the Cabinet discussion.

Presciently, he dismissed French support for the Zionists as "characteristic of the anti-semitic trend of opinion in that country," and in an articulate three-page statement bluntly charged his own government with antisemitism for rallying around the "mischievous political creed" of the Zionists.[42]

Weizmann, outraged, dismissed Montefiore and Montagu as "Jews who by education and social connections have lost touch with the real spirit animating the Jewish people," and so spoke only for themselves, no matter their numbers. He and Rothschild, not having "lost touch," spoke for Jews world-wide. Sykes as well warned against anti-Zionists and their "pacifist tendencies," such as Lucien Wolf "and those who think like him."[43]

Montagu continued his offensive when the Cabinet met on September 3. The phrase "the home of the Jewish people" for Palestine was presumptuous and prejudicial, he argued—and how was it proposed to get rid of the land's people "and to introduce the Jews in their place?"

Lord Curzon voiced the same. "What is to become of the people of this country…? They and their forefathers have occupied the country for the best part of 1,500 years," but would now either be expelled or left "to act merely as hewers of wood and drawers of water" to the settlers. Or, as Lawrence of Arabia asked in a letter to Sykes: "Do the Jews propose the complete expulsion of the Arab peasantry, or their reduction to a day-labourer class?"

More opposition was voiced by a "deputation of Jews" who came to protest a segregated "Jewish Regiment" that the War Cabinet had sanctioned under Zionist pressure. Some 40,000 Jews, the deputation noted with pride, had served with distinction in the British forces without the Zionists' segregation.[44]

In an intriguing reference with no further details, Weizmann and Rothschild wrote to Balfour on October 3 to remind him that it had been with British approval that their "extensive propaganda for a Jewish Palestine" had been carried out. They asked Balfour for help at the next Cabinet meeting in countering the troublesome Montagu, and assailed the "assimilated Cosmopolitan Jews" of "Haute finance" who deny that Jews constitute "a separate group" from other people, and "to whom Judaism is a mere religious formula."

The Cabinet, indeed, was nervous about the Zionists, not Montagu or the Jewish deputation or Montefiore. The Acting Secretary of State for Foreign Affairs reported that the Foreign Office had been "very strongly pressed for a long time past" by the Zionists.

> It would be of most substantial assistance to the Allies to have the earnestness and enthusiasm of these people enlisted on our side. To do nothing was to risk a direct breach with them, and it was necessary to face this situation.

And so it was decided that the War Cabinet would explain to US President Wilson that "His Majesty's Government were being pressed to make a declaration in sympathy with the Zionist movement," asking his advice on the matter. Wilson's response was cautious: perhaps just a statement of "sympathy provided it can be made without conveying any real commitment [because] things are in such a state of flux."

On the 15th of October, Chief Rabbi Joseph Hertz, at odds with British Jews for his support of Zionism, repeats the call to remove from the draft the clause protecting the rights of Jews who are fully content with their existing nationality and citizenship, as others had.

He expresses approval of the draft's vague clause about protecting the rights of the Palestinians themselves—but what is remarkable is his reason. He approves because of his religious obligation to the Palestinians as *foreigners* in the land, the treatment of "the stranger that dwelleth with you," citing Leviticus 19:33-34: modern wording, *when a foreigner resides among you in your land, do not mistreat them.* The settlers were the *you*, Palestine was *your land*, and the Palestinians were the *foreigners* not to be mistreated.

With the advantage of twenty years' reflection, key players behind the Balfour Declaration testified about it at the 1937 Peel Commission, convened to address the ongoing upheavals in Palestine that Zionist dispossession had caused in the interim.* The story remained unchanged: promised "Jewish influence" in the Great War was cited as *the* reason for their support for the Declaration twenty years earlier (none said whether they actually believed that the Allied victory was the result of the "Jewish influence").

---

* While much of the Peel Commission's proceedings has long been available, the full record of the "secret" testimony of witnesses was only formally declassified in 2017. "These copies … will, no doubt, be of considerable value to the historian of the remote future"—so wrote J.M. Martin, secretary to the Peel Commission, in an annotation dated 1/2/40 on the blank front leaf of copy FO 492/19. Eight decades later, we are now in that "remote future." Martin states that 30 copies of the secret proceedings were printed, and that "the Commission didn't even allow the witnesses to retain copies of the record of their own evidence." On the same day, a second annotator confirmed that "10 spare copies only will be retained by the Library," though in 1968 it was noted that "only 3 copies now held." These correspond to FO 492/19, FO 492/20, FO 492/21; the author has checked all three.

David Lloyd George, prime minister when the Declaration was signed, testified that "the Zionist leaders gave us a definite promise" that "they would do their best to rally Jewish sentiment and support throughout the world to the Allied cause ... if the British government were to declare their sympathy for a Jewish administration of Palestine."

It was important to "rally Jewish sentiment," he explained, because in 1917 "there were no American divisions at the front ... in the trenches ... and we had every reason at the time to believe that in both countries the friendliness or hostility of the Jewish race might make a considerable difference."

Winston Churchill testified the same. Zionism was embraced because "it was a potent factor on public opinion in America" from which "we gained great advantages in the war."

But Horace Rumbold, who had been Britain's ambassador in Berlin for the five years ending with Adolf Hitler's rise to power in 1933, and who is remembered for his unvarnished warnings of Hitler's ambitions, asked whether Zionist policy is worth "the lives of our men, and so on." And did it follow, he asked Churchill, that having "conquered Palestine we can dispose of it as we like?"

Churchill replied to that and similar questions by repeating the deal with the Zionists: "We decided in the process of conquest of [Palestine] to make certain pledges to the Jews."

The head of the commission, William Peel, was skeptical of this reasoning. He asked Churchill if it is not "a very odd self-government" when "it is only when the Jews are a majority that we can have it."

Churchill never addressed the question, insisting instead that "we have every right to strike hard in support of our authority." Yet when Peel pointed out that the Zionists were the cause of the present ethnic tensions, that "even the old [indigenous Palestinian] Jews who used to get on so well with the Arabs have now been roped into the hatred of the Arabs," Churchill did not deny this. "It is a serious situation," was his reply.

Reginald Coupland, a historian, remarked that the "average Englishman" would wonder why the Arabs were being denied self-government, and why we had "to go on shooting the Arabs down because of keeping his promise to the Jews."

Peel, similarly, asked Churchill if the British public

> might get rather tired and rather inquisitive if every two or three
> years there was a sort of campaign against the Arabs and we sent out
> troops and shot them down? They would begin to enquire, 'Why is
> it done? What is the fault of these people?… Why are you doing it?
> In order to get a home for the Jews?'

"And it would mean rather brutal methods," added Laurie Hammond, who had worked with the British colonial administration in India. "I do not say the methods of the Italians at Addis Ababa," referring to Benito Mussolini's Ethiopian massacre of February 1937, "but it would mean the blowing up of villages and that sort of thing?" The British, he recalled, had blown up part of the Palestinian port city of Jaffa.

Peel agreed, and added that "they blew up a lot of [Palestinian] houses all over the place in order to awe the population. I have seen photographs of these things going up in the air."

When Peel challenged Churchill's remarks and questioned whether "it is not only a question of being strong enough," but of the ethics of "downing" the Arabs who simply wanted to remain in their own country, Churchill lost patience.

"I do not admit that the dog in the manger has the final right to the manger," he countered, "even though he may have lain there for a very long time." He denied that "a great wrong has been done to the Red Indians of America, or the Black people of Australia," by their replacement with "a higher grade race."

Weizmann's arguments at the hearings were of the same sort. He ridiculed the Palestinians' desire for independence as "a crude imitation of the material side of European nationalism, very crude," and mocked them for fearing "that we shall come and sweep them out of the country."

Britain gives away Palestine

When Balfour's "stroke of the pen" was applied to the Declaration on November 2, 1917, giving away a land Britain did not own, it was treated as legal and authoritative by its supporters—US Judge Joseph

Proskauer called it "the law of the world"—despite its equivocalness and Britain's lack of any right to the land.

Members of the British Cabinet were the first to be confused by it and, asking for clarification, were assured that the Declaration did *not* mean the establishing of "a Jewish Republic or any other form of state in Palestine or in any part of Palestine."[45]

Weizmann, while maintaining the moderate public demeanor that was his hallmark, was pushing to create that very Jewish Republic. He demanded that Jewish settlers be accorded special privileges over the Palestinians, and that the British authorities must lie about the scheme in order to discredit protest.[46]

Meeting with British Major-General William Thwaites on the 14th of February 1919, Weizmann wanted

> to be able to give an assurance to the Jews throughout the world that Mr. Balfour's assurances are going to materialise and a Jewish country will be established in, say, one or two years.

This "Jewish country" was by 1920 or 1921 to occupy all of historic Palestine and then expand further. Yet this precipitous transformation of Palestine was spoken of as a modest demand.

> He [Weizmann] does want to push extravagent claims for territory—the Jordan [River] as an eastern frontier would suffice as a commencement.

With the ink from Balfour's pen barely dry, what had been little more than a spiritual home was in truth a Zionist state river-to-sea "as a commencement." Meanwhile, the Zionist Organization made proposals to remove non-Jews from the region, and the words *Jewish Commonwealth* replaced the Declaration's *national home*.[47]

"Now what is a Commonwealth?" asked an exasperated Lord Curzon.

> I turn to my dictionary, and find it thus defined: 'A state.' 'A body politic.' 'An independent community.' 'A Republic' ... What then is the good of shutting our eyes to the fact that this is what the Zionists

are after, and that the British Trusteeship is a mere screen..? And the
case is rendered not better but the worse if Weizmann says this sort
of thing to his friend but sings a different tune in public.[48]

Another of Weizmann's supporters who helped him "sing a different
tune in public" was Colonel Richard Meinertzhagen, who stated
plainly that the Palestinians were not being told the truth:

the people of Palestine are not at present in a fit state to be told
openly that the establishment of Zionism in Palestine is the policy
to which H.M.G. America and France are committed.[49]

Instead, a statement was composed using "the most moderate language" that denied "that immigration spells the flooding of Palestine
with the dregs of Eastern Europe." Moreover, the Palestinians were
explicitly and repeatedly assured, as the Cabinet had been, that this
so-called national home would never lead to a Zionist state.

Writing to Balfour from Tel Aviv on May 30, 1918, Weizmann
justified the lies as all propagandists for settler projects have: by
dehumanizing the land's native people.

The Arabs, who are superficially clever and quickwitted, worship one
thing, and one thing only—power and success ... [The British know]
the treacherous nature of the Arab [who would] stab the Army in
the back [and who] screams as often as he can and blackmails as
much as he can.[50]

He fought the threat of democracy by dismissing Arabs as too
inferior to be its participants. For self-determination in Palestine to
include the Palestinians would be, in his words, to "level down the
Jew politically to the status of a native." Repeating the pejorative use
of *native*, he claimed that those who object to giving Jewish settlers
special privileges denied the Palestinians were "looking on the Jews
as so many natives" and were "not conversant with the subtleties and
subterfuge of the Oriental mind."

After noting that German agents foster notions of the ruthless, wealthy Jew, "the financier, the exploiter, the stock-broker," Weizmann then complained, betraying no awareness of the irony, that "the British have been strengthened in such views" by the "rich Jews of Egypt" who are "shining examples of Jewish capitalism." He doesn't hesitate to identify the cause of his dislike of Egyptian Jews: they "are opponents to Zionism…"[51]

Weizmann was in Palestine at the time as head of an Inter-Allied Zionist Commission organized by the British. On April 28 he gave what the War Cabinet described as "a carefully worded speech" in which he again denied that Zionism heralded any move towards a state. But behind the scenes, he continued to behave (as British records put it) "as if he were sovereign of the country" or "a sort of uncrowned King of Palestine," signing a "treaty" on Palestine's behalf with Emir Faisal (later Faisal I of Iraq) the following January 4 (1919), two weeks before the Paris Peace Conference opened, where Faisal led the Arab delegation.[52]

As Weizmann sealed his personal deal with Faisal, he continued to complain to the British that "the Jews were not receiving that consideration which they had expected in a country which was to be their national home." Rothschild as well pushed for Jewish settlers to be treated more "distinct from the other citizens of Palestine," in order to demonstrate that Britain "really intended to make Palestine the Jewish National Home." The British had already outlawed anti-Zionist publications, excluded the Palestinians from their country's civil affairs, and would impose draconian censorship on the Arabic press. Weizmann now pressed to have Arab iconography removed from the region—complaining, for example, that "on the postage stamps in use an Arabic inscription appears." He pushed to have Hebrew recognized as the official language of Palestine even though, as the British governor of Jaffa commented, the settlers were having "to sit down and learn their supposedly native tongue."[53]

The Paris Peace Conference
On the 18th of January 1919, all attention shifted to Paris, where the Peace Conference began the business of settling post-war agreements and the terms for the defeated Central Powers. On the 27th of

February, Weizmann handed the Conference a list of proposals from the World Zionist Organization, arguing that the Balfour Declaration had already given it the authority to do so.

In response, several prominent US Jews composed an articulate rebuttal to the Zionists, delivered to US President Wilson by California Congressman Julius Kahn on March 4. "For the very reason that the new era upon which the world is entering aims to establish government everywhere on principles of true democracy," the paper read, "we reject the Zionist project." They wrote in disgust at Zionism's reduction of Jews into a nationality, and warned that "no Jew, wherever he may live, can consider himself free from the implications of such a grant." Pretenses that Palestine's native people had nothing to fear were patently disingenuous: the Arabs deserve "neither condescension nor tolerance, but justice and equality."[54]

On March 21, the British held a meeting to discuss the proposals Weizmann had submitted, but more importantly to discuss what had been deliberately *excluded* from the WZO submission. Among the nine attendees were Weizmann, Baron Rothschild, T.E. Lawrence, and Gertrude Bell.

Whereas the proposals Weizmann submitted to the Conference repeated the guarantees that "existing non-Jewish communities" in Palestine would suffer no loss of civil or religious rights, and that "there shall be no discrimination among the inhabitants ... on the grounds of religion, or race," in private he and Rothschild treated the outright ethnic cleansing of non-Jewish Palestinians as indispensable to their plans. In Rothschild's words, he proposed "a comprehensive emigration scheme" to ship non-Jews to Egypt and Syria. Neither Lawrence nor Bell objected.*

> Miss Bell and Colonel Lawrence agreed and Miss Bell added that there was scope in Mesopotamia [Iraq] for such emigrants.[55]

---

* Gertrude Bell was anti-Zionist and had opposed the Balfour Declaration. It is surprising that she and "Lawrence of Arabia" were ready to push Palestinians off their land, but Edward Said's *Orientalism* may be relevant: they were "agent-Orientalist," whose Orient was "held in check by the White Man's expert tutelage."

Discretion was necessary: their plans could obviously not be voiced at the Conference, but would be dealt with only after the Mandate was settled.

Meanwhile, the objects of the planned ethnic cleansing were already suffering Weizmann's "equality" and appealed for their rights. On the 24th of March, the Jaffa Moslem Christian Committee sent a telegram addressed to the British Prime Minister, Lloyd George, in Paris:

> What fault have we Palestinian Arabs committed … Release us from the Zionists greed which is increasing from day to day … Were we liberated by the Allies from the Turkish yoke to be put under the Zionist yoke?[56]

Even Balfour was getting nervous. In a letter to Weizmann in Paris dated April 3, Balfour spoke of his "considerable anxiety" over "reports reaching me from sources which I know are unbiased that your adherents there [i.e., the settlers] are behaving in a way which is alienating" the sympathies of others.

Weizmann replied that there was perhaps some "undue exuberance" among Zionists that was nonetheless understandable, and stated categorically that Zionist intentions were "scrupulously regardful of the non-Jewish elements of the Palestinian population." He instead blamed the Palestinians' "purposeful and organised misunderstanding … which is as much anti-British as it is anti-Jewish," and mocked "the continued talk of a 'Jewish State' when such a claim has been authoritatively repudiated…."[57]

King-Crane Report

Among the participants in the Paris Conference was Charles Richard Crane, heir to the Crane plumbing parts fortune who was considered knowledgeable on Middle East affairs. That summer (1919), President Wilson sent Crane and Henry Churchill King, president of Oberlin College and professor of mathematics, philosophy, and theology, to survey the post-war, post-Ottoman Middle East first-hand.

Both men reached the Middle East "with minds predisposed

in [Zionism's] favor," as they put it, but that pro-Zionist mindset did not survive "the actual facts in Palestine." Their landmark 1919 King-Crane Report should have been indispensable to the architects of Palestine's future, but it was suppressed until late 1922, when Wilson supplied a copy that was picked up by the *New York Times*. The paper published the Report in its entirety on December 3-4, with its own introduction lamenting that the world had not seen it three years earlier, before a course had all but irrevocably been charted for the Middle East.

> The world is askew today because facts have been concealed or perverted. If in 1918-1919 the world had seen the international situation, stripped of all camouflage, with every secret treaty opened and every national condition made clear, it would have insisted on a totally different outcome of events.

The suppressed Report, indeed, corroborated the Palestinians' core allegation: that contrary to the Zionists' public protestations, they intended to purge non-Jews from the land.

> The fact came out repeatedly in the Commission's conference with Jewish representatives that the Zionists looked forward to a practically complete dispossession of the present non-Jewish inhabitants of Palestine...[58]

Zionist assertions that a claimed Biblical prerogative outweighed the Palestinians' right to self-determination were dismissed outright. The claim

> submitted by Zionist representatives, that they have a 'right' to Palestine, based on an occupation of 2,000 years ago, can hardly be seriously considered.[59]

The Chief Administrator in Palestine, H. D. Watson, reported essentially the same. Dismissing religion as driving the Palestinians' opposition, he wrote that

The people of the country, the owners of the land [who] have looked with eager eyes to the peaceful development of their country and the better education of their children—for their own benefit, and not for the benefit of peoples of alien nationality … The great fear of the people is that once Zionist wealth is passed into the land, all territorial and mineral concessions will fall into the hands of the Jews whose intensely clannish instincts prohibit them from dealing with any but those of their own religion, to the detriment of Moslems and Christians. These latter, the natives of the soil, foresee their eventual banishment from the land…[60]

Britain, he warned prophetically, "will lose the lives of many of her sons in a war which will be fought, against the principles of the League of Nations, in forcing upon a small country a population of aliens." And it was force, Sergeant Major J. N. Camp wrote from Jerusalem with obvious frustration, that would be necessary:

If we are to carry out any sort of Zionist policy we must do so with military force, [so] before you publish your mandate for Palestine with its conditions, for God's sake let us know, not your policy, but your method of putting it into effect … if we are to proceed with energy, then send us more troops.[61]

The public lie was carefully guarded. Weizmann's friend Colonel Meinertzhagen, writing to Balfour from Cairo in September of 1919, reassured the Foreign Office that "the determination of H.M.G. to establish Zionism in Palestine … is still withheld from the general public." He warned against "contact with the local (Palestinian) Jew," who are "the least representative of Jewry or Zionism," and corroborated, indeed boasted, that ethnic cleansing was the plan. The "acknowledged superiority of Jewish brains and money," he declared, will force Palestinian "land-owners and business men to realise their impotence to withstand eventual eviction."

Most revealing is the adjective he used to describe the Palestinians' objection to their domination by the Zionists, "against the minority ruling the majority": for them to object was "fanatical."[62]

From the moment Balfour signed his name, Weizmann behaved as though the British were already the heirs to the Ottomans in Palestine. But this was not yet the case, and the buried King-Crane report showed that it was the United States that the Palestinians themselves wanted to assume stewardship of their land. They viewed the US as the sole great power whose history in the region was not yet tarnished by hypocrisy, and admired its system of representative government.

Fear of such a representative government in Palestine being considered at the Paris Conference prompted the Zionist Organization to publish a "case for a British Trusteeship" (London, 1919), which argued that democracy does not take into account "stages of civilisation or differences of quality" of the public.[63]

The Zionists vs Laws of Occupied Enemy Territory

Upon Britain's conquest of Palestine in late 1917, it was subject to the Laws of Occupied Enemy Territory, which state that the status quo of the land must not be altered. The occupying power was simply a caretaker—unless and until Britain were made the mandatory power by post-war agreements and the League of Nations. The Chief Administrator of the military occupation, Major General Sir Louis Bols, took that task seriously, but found himself stymied by Weizmann's impatience. "It is no use," he said, to tell the Christian and Moslem natives of Palestine that the law is being observed, because "facts witness otherwise." Despite their denials, the Zionists "will be satisfied with nothing less than a Jewish State and all that it politically implies."

Bols brought his concerns to the British Cabinet, warning of the "untenable" situation that would befall Palestine "if the policy outlined by Dr. Weizmann in Cannon Street were followed."[64]

There were nonetheless limits to what Weizmann could do until, in his words, "the mandate for Palestine has been granted." In mid-1919 he tried but failed to get the British to replace part of its military presence with a Zionist militia comprised of thousands of "Jewish young men" from "the Russian army, mountain Jews of the Caucasus, Galician [and] Polish prisoners of war," among others.[65]

But a year later, Weizmann prevailed. The British Mandate did not and could not begin until July 1922, but on June 30 of 1920 Britain

Left-to-right: Edmund Allenby, Faisal I of Iraq, and Lawrence of Arabia.
Falastin, 27 June 1936. Accompanying text reads:
???!!!
— Faisal: What happens in Palestine ???
— Lawrence: Dreadful !!! Shameful !!!
— Allenby: Humiliating !!!
— Faisal: Long live the Mandate...

prematurely ended military rule and replaced Bols with Weizmann's hand-picked first High Commissioner of Palestine, Herbert Samuel, the same who had first raised the idea of a Zionist Palestine with the Cabinet five years earlier.

This change also allowed existing Zionist militias to be organized into the settlements' official militia, the Haganah. Although allegedly defensive, anti-Zionist Jews soon joined the ranks of what the Haganah defended against. On June 30, 1924, it assassinated Dr. Ya'acov Israel de Hahn as he left the synagogue on Jaffa Street in Jerusalem—the sixth recorded Zionist assassination attempt, and the first by the Haganah.

Despite Britain's two-year jump-start on the Mandate, Weizmann still expressed irritation over the slow pace, while Churchill, then government minister in charge of the colonies, stressed all that had been done to please him. In a Cabinet paper dated August 1921 and marked *secret*, Churchill confirmed that "in the interests of the Zionist policy, all elective institutions have so far been refused to the Arabs"—that is, a "democracy" denied the majority indigenous people. He lamented the drain on Britain's economy for the garrison there, which he estimated at £3,319,000 for 1922, "almost wholly due to Zionist policy." But despite all this, "Dr. Weizmann and the Zionists are extremely discontented at the progress made."[66]

Churchill was an active voice in the public deception. Even after Britain was appointed the mandatory power and the "national home" became official policy of the League of Nations, he still denied that it heralded "the subordination of the Arabic population ... as appears to be feared by the Arab delegation." But the Arab delegation was no more skeptical than the British Cabinet, which complained that

> the entire Mandate is built on the fallacy of attempting to reconcile the irreconcilable, [being] the creation of Jewish privileges with the maintenance of Arab rights.[67]

Whatever Zionism's success in isolating the public narrative from actual intentions, it could not hide that the situation was untenable. In July 1920, Anstruther Mackay wrote in the *Atlantic Monthly* that

> The theory that the Jews are to come into Palestine and oust the Moslem cultivators by "equitable purchase" or other means is in violation of principles of sound policy, [and] to this might be ascribed by future historians the outbreak of a great war between the white and the brown races, a war into which America would without doubt be drawn.

Similarly, in November 1922, the British *Daily Express* complained that

> Doctor Weizmann is inducing us now to remain in Palestine ... up to the day when we sink up to our necks in a catastrophe which will no longer be in our power to rectify or correct.

By 1926, Weizmann had grown dissatisfied with "Jewish privileges" being limited to Palestine and (according to him) Jordan. He now wanted to extend the Zionist project into Syria and the Hauran region, fully as far as the Euphrates River. On June 21 he met with Sir John E. Shuckburgh, assistant understate secretary of the Colonial Office, to promote the idea, in which the Euphrates would be siphoned for irrigation of the Zionist settlements. Britain remained neutral on this extension of Zionism to land under French occupation.

As Weizmann pushed for more, Palestinian resistance elevated from entreaties and diplomacy to strikes, boycotts, and by the late 1920s, violence, most notoriously the August 24, 1929 massacre of sixty-seven Jews in Hebron, sparked by a false rumor.

Racializing of schools and playgrounds

When the wealthy businessman Sir Ellis Kadoorie of Hong Kong died in 1922, he willed his money to various cross-cultural causes, and one-third of his residuary trust "to the British Government for the purpose of building a School or Schools to be called after

Political cartoon-map mocking William Ormsby-Gore, Under-Secretary of State for the Colonies, from the Palestinian newspaper *Falastin*, June 27 1936.

The Whole Object!!!
«The Whole Object of His Britannic Majesty's Government is that both Arabs and Jews should live together in peace and amity......»
(from Colonial Secretary's speech broadcasted)

The prominence of Jaffa reflected ongoing tensions between the British and the people of that city. Two days after the cartoon's publication, the British blew up part of the ancient city on the orders of Ormsby-Gore.

my name in Palestine or Mesopotamia [Iraq] as the said British Government shall think fit."

What the British government "thought fit" was to use the funds for "the erection and endowment of a single school which would be open to the boys of all communities in Palestine" and which would "promote mutual understanding and co-operation between the Jewish and Arab communities." The director of education in Jerusalem welcomed the inter-community project, calling it "an opportunity of bringing Jews and Arabs together on common ground."

The settlers, however, protested that this "legacy left by a Jew" should not also benefit non-Jews, and so Herbert Samuel decided to make two segregated agricultural schools. The Arab school was then further diminished in 1936 when some of its land was given to the Jewish National Fund, by definition making it unavailable to the Palestinians in perpetuity. After statehood, the Israeli government successfully lobbied Britain for maintenance funds from Kadoorie's estate even though all non-Jews had either been ethnically cleansed or placed under martial law.

Similarly, when Bertha Guggenheimer died in 1927, she left behind a trust fund of one hundred thousand dollars for Palestine "with special reference to playground needs," among whose projects was a new playground in Safad (Galilee). But the settlers blocked Palestinian children from the playground, and protests from Mrs. Guggenheimer's representatives that this violated the philanthropist's intent were ignored. The presence of Arab children, the settlers maintained, was "corrupting" to Jewish children—indeed it was against "Jewish ethics" and the Torah itself.[68]

Land acquisition

The expropriation of land and labor, and thus of ethnic cleansing, were integral to Zionism from its beginnings. Herzl himself had proposed starving out the indigenous people by getting control of the local labor market and then denying them employment—but he cautioned that this had to be "carried out discreetly." By 1907, new Zionist immigrants, among them the young David Ben-Gurion, organized boycotts in order to starve non-Jews from the land.

The boycotts were imposed against the wishes of traditional, and typically indigenous Jews. When in 1924 the ban on non-Jewish labor was used to stop Orthodox Jews from employing Palestinians to milk their cows on Saturdays, they took their grievance to JNF director Menachem Ussishkin. If our cows are not milked they will become ill, they explained, but it is a sin for us to do it ourselves on the Sabbath. In response, Ussishkin, who would facilitate major land acquisition by the JNF, told them that the Zionist prohibition on Arab labor "is more sacred than Saturday."

Race laws became further institutionalized with the founding of the Jewish Agency in 1929. The Agency's constitution specifically denied land and labor to all non-Jews in perpetuity, and stipulated penalties for disobedience.

As the more conscientious British officials on-the-ground complained to no avail in the 1930s, the JNF enforced "only Jewish labor" regulations in open violation of Mandate laws forbidding discrimination based on race, religion, or language.[69]

In 1930 Sir John Hope Simpson, who became known for his involvement in refugee issues, warned that land purchases by organizations such as the JNF meant that the

> land became extra territorial. It ceases to be land from which the Arab can gain any advantage either now or at any time in the future. Not only can he never hope to lease or cultivate it, but, by the stringent provisions of the lease of the Jewish National Fund, he is deprived forever from employment on the land.[70]

This, Simpson continued, is the reason Arabs dismiss the Zionists' professions of good will. He refuted a justification for Zionist land expropriation, then already prevalent, that the settlers made the desert bloom where Arabs had left barren land.

> It is, however, unjust to the poverty stricken fellah who has been removed from these lands that the suggestion should continually be made that he was a useless cumberer of the ground and produced nothing from it. It should be quite obvious that this is not the fact...[71]

It is ironic, he continued, that this charge is made even as Zionists spend vast foreign capital to acquire the most fertile land, evict Arabs from it, and facilitate cultivation for Jews only. Yet poor productivity plagued early Zionist settlements, and some land tilled by Palestinians fell into disuse *because of* its acquisition by Zionists, with consequences such as a plague of field mice that tormented both communities.

Inflation caused by the Zionists' rampant land speculation also forced Palestinians off their own land. The resulting sharp rise in prices plunged smaller farmers into such debt that they could only extricate themselves by, ironically, selling their plot.

In his 1932 report on the problem of non-Jews "displaced from the lands which they occupied in consequence of the lands falling into Jewish hands," Lewis French, director of the Department of Development, pointed out the misunderstandings created by the term "surplus lands." There were none in Palestine, save for "a few insignificant areas in the hills, temporarily abandoned because the owners have lost their cattle or other simple resources and are too much indebted to be able to replace them."

Reporting from Nazareth in January of 1935, Archer Cust corroborated French's assessment.

> Thus the Jewish National Home is being established by the combined compulsion of the bayonet and the bribe... To-day the purpose of the Jews, a large proportion of whom, though they may not outwardly admit it, have now accepted the Revisionist* creed that aims in fact ... at the conversion of Palestine into a Jewish state to include ultimately Trans-Jordan as well, is to prevent the introduction of any form of popular representation until at all costs and by any means a Jewish majority is secured

thus rendering the indigenous population irrelevant—a tactic which "all fair opinion must hold such circumstances deeply repugnant."

---

* Major branch of the Zionist movement founded by Irgun-founder Ze'ev Jabotinsky that advocated maximal territorial aims on both sides of the Jordan.

"I should hate to think," Assistant Under-Secretary for the Colonies Sir Charles Parkinson wrote the same year in reference to the settlers' destruction of Palestinians' livelihoods,

> that ten years hence our successors … should say that perhaps in 1935 if we had had the courage we might have saved the situation."[72]

"Ten years hence" came and passed. In 1936 Weizmann pushed to acquire another million dunams (1,000 km²) of the Palestinians' remaining irrigable flat land for the Zionists.[73]

Weizmann met with Benito Mussolini in February 1934, hoping that a relationship with the fascists might serve as leverage in the Jewish Agency's demands on the British. "When we reach the stage of practicalities," he asked the Italian dictator, *practicalities* an apparent reference to the coming showdown for the Zionist seizure of Palestine, "can I count on your support?" To which Mussolini replied "Certainly."[74]

Zionism vs the anti-Nazi boycott

Hitler's rise as Chancellor in January 1933 quickly led to calls for an international boycott of German goods and services. There was resistance—the (Zionist) UK Board of Deputies of British Jews, for example, opposed the idea—but revulsion over the news from Germany led to a million-strong show of support throughout the United States on the 27th of March. In New York alone, fifty-five thousand people crowded in and around New York's Madison Square Garden as prominent Jewish and Christian leaders demanded that Hitlerism be given the same treatment "we gave the Ku Klux Klan," as former NY governor Smith put it.

The boycott hit Germany hard and fast. Within a few months, it had all but bankrupted its shipping and trans-Atlantic passenger travel industry, which had been an important source of foreign capital for the Reich. Heavy machinery exports plummeted to half their 1930 levels, and the same fate befell Germany's once-lucrative medical industry. Foreign endowments fell fully 95%, hurting not just the national purse but also the unquantifiable element of academic respectability.

Perhaps the most humiliating act of boycott came in June from Arturo Toscanini. This most celebrated conductor had been scheduled to conduct at the world's most celebrated opera festival, Bayreuth, and his high-visibility announcement of cancellation in solidarity with Germany's oppressed left German authorities bereft of stock rebuttals. "For once," as the *NY Times* reported it, Germany could not invoke the excuse of "Jewish machinations." His snuff proved more than artistic: as the newspaper *Boersen Zeitung* conceded, only Toscanini's presence could have assured the festival's financial success.[75]

When the composer Richard Strauss broke Toscanini's boycott and raised the baton for Wagner's *Parsifal*, his intervention did nothing to ameliorate Toscanini's injury to the Reich's international veneer.

As the boycott movement solidified in March, Sam Cohen, director of the Hanotea citrus company in Netanya, was in Germany proposing to the Reich Economics Ministry a scheme to circumvent it to their mutual advantage. The idea was that German Jews with sufficient capital would emigrate to Palestine and have their money, which they would otherwise forfeit, used to purchase German goods and equipment. The Reich would get desperately needed capital, Hanotea would get a cut, and the émigré would salvage part of his capital. Cohen's scheme worked; and though small in scale, it provided a blueprint for a larger boycott-breaking operation by the Zionists.

Encouraged by Germany's Gestapo, Foreign Office, and Interior Ministry, Jewish Agency representatives such as Chaim Arlosoroff, head of the Agency's Political Department, went to Germany to negotiate that vastly larger deal with the Nazis, what became known as the Haavara Transfer Agreement. German Jews would deposit Reichmarks into the Anglo-Palestine Bank—what would become Bank Leumi—and eventually receive 42.8% of it in Palestine. Part of the rest financed the Jewish Agency's settlements, with a fee going to the Haavara company itself.[76]

For Germany, it was also a propaganda win: the boycott-breaking deal had been made by Jews.

Two days after Arlosoroff returned to Palestine from Germany, he was assassinated on the beach at Tel Aviv. Majority suspicion (but never proof) fell on the Revisionist Abba Ahimeir and his short-lived terror group Brit HaBirionim ("Alliance of the Thugs"). Brit HaBirionim was sympathetic to the Italian fascists and would influence the ideology of Lehi.

On December 23, Germany announced its new laws classifying Jews in the same category as "criminals and enemies of the state." As it did, in New York a crowd of about 3,000 heard Zionist Labor leader Berl Locker and head of the Jewish Labor Committee B. C. Vladeck argue for and against the Haavara Agreement—"frequently interrupted by volunteered rebuttals, cheers, whistles and boos," as the *Jewish Telegraphic Agency* reported it.

Haavara's supporters argued that boycott might fail anyway, whereas the deal with the Nazis would save some Jews. Yet the Jewish Agency's profit from the deal was never put into buying the freedom of Jews who didn't have the minimum assets necessary, but was used to finance the settlements.*

Amid massive opposition, the Haavara scheme was adopted in Lucerne by the World Zionist Organization in 1935 at the Nineteenth Zionist Congress. Its supporters justified breaking the boycott by saying that they did not wish to take "political positions" that might compromise the settler project in Palestine:

> Zionism must concern itself exclusively with the building of the National Home in Palestine, and cannot afford to take political positions against individual states.

For the Zionists, a key attraction of the deal with the Nazis was its restriction of Jewish evacuation *only* to Palestine. In 1937, four years into Haavara, the Nazis still wooed a contact in the Hagana, Feivel Polkes, with the lure that they would pressure Jewish groups in Germany "to oblige Jews … to go exclusively to Palestine, and not to other countries."[77]

---

* Brenner (*Zionism in the Age of the Dictators*) states that between 1933-1939, fully 60% of the money invested in Zionist settlement came from breaking the anti-Nazi boycott. He also cites statistics demonstrating that Jews in no danger, coming from Britain, the Americas, Africa, and Turkey, were given preference over European Jews "because they were Zionists, and primarily because of their youth and training."

Polkes met with Adolf Eichmann in Berlin and claimed that he could supply intelligence on the British, French, and Italians, as well as help the Nazis secure a source of oil—in exchange for channeling Jewish emigrants (only) to Palestine. He welcomed Eichmann at Haifa's port when the Nazi official visited Palestine in October 1937, but had only got so far as to give him a tour of a kibbutz when the British learned of his presence. Expelled from Palestine, Eichmann went to Egypt, accompanied by Polkes.

Nazi files captured by the US at the close of World War II shed some light on what Eichmann learned from his Haganah host. "In Jewish nationalist [i.e., Zionist] circles," Eichmann reported, "people were very pleased with the radical German policy," since it helped achieve "a [Jewish] numerical superiority over the Arabs." It was however difficult to get German Jews to stay in Palestine once there, as most wanted to go elsewhere. To prevent this, "those Jews coming from Germany, after taking away their capital, should be put in a communal settlement."

The Hagana's records on Polkes are closed.[78]

The Peel Commission

It was also in 1937 that the Palestine Royal Commission, established the year before to investigate the causes of unrest in Palestine, issued its report (see also pages 30–32). In stark contrast to the buried 1919 King-Crane report, the Peel Commission (as it is better known) accepted Zionists' claim of an ancient Jewish nationality with extra-legal Biblical entitlement. Zionist settlers, the Commission's extraordinary reasoning read, "mean to show what the Jewish nation can achieve when restored to the land of its birth."

Framed thus, the Commission proposed a Partition plan that gave vast Palestinian tracts to the settlers and required the forcible transfer of 225,000 Palestinians and 1,250 Jews—a ratio of 180 to one. Yet, in a premonition of today's peace talks, the Commission presented this as though it were the Zionists that were sacrificing: "Jews," the Commission lamented, "must be content with less than the Land of Israel they once ruled," both *Land of Israel* and, especially, *they* left begging explanation.[79]

Although the Zionist establishment welcomed the Peel Commission's implicit promise of racially segregated statehood, it rejected the plan because it did not give them all of Palestine. Ben-Gurion, speaking to the media after the hearings, invoked the Bible as Jews' unassailable legal title to (all) Palestine, and ridiculed the "Arabs" as being "busy with politics."[80]

Offering the Commission his explanation as to why the Palestinians were against Zionist colonization, Ben-Gurion continued in the fashion of Weizmann: it was their "intolerance, which is inherent perhaps in them ... in their education and upbringing. It is different levels of culture."[81]

In his diary, Ben-Gurion fixated on the Peel Commission's proposal of ethnic segregation, underlining "forced transfer," and "really Jewish." He then elevated his four underlined words beyond even the Biblical: Couched in a tribal use of *us* and *we* that transcended even the Peel Commission's messianic *they*, he wrote that transfer "will give us something [ethnic purity] we never had ... neither in the period of the First Temple nor in the period of the Second Temple." Ben-Gurion believed, or at least wanted us future readers of his diary to believe, that he believed, that we are indeed entering the epoch of the Third Temple, and he is its prophet.[82]

Major British papers published a news photograph on October 21 showing, so the caption read, Arabs rioting in Jerusalem over the Peel Commission's proposals. By the time the story was proven fraudulent (the indistinct photograph had already been circulated four years earlier), it had served its apparent purpose of reinforcing Arab stereotypes, and provided the Nazis with anti-British propaganda.[83]

The Palestinian Uprising

The Peel Commission did far more to vindicate Palestinians' fears than address the causes of unrest. The uprising continued—lacking any coherent plan or methodology, the few rising leaders were violently eliminated, and the chaos often an excuse for bandits and extortionists rather than a liberation struggle.

The British response to Palestinian terror was indiscriminate punishment on a massive scale. In June 1936 British Under-Secretary of State for the Colonies William Ormsby-Gore ordered the wholesale destruction of a swath of Jaffa because

> the old town of Jaffa presented an extremely serious problem to the police and military authorities … a warren of tortuous and narrow covered streets, where blind alleys and cul-de-sac make the operation of police or troops an extremely hazardous enterprise … neither police nor soldiers could effectively penetrate into it.

British troops blew up about 230 Palestinian homes in the city, leaving about 6,000 people homeless. Chief Justice Sir Michael McDonnell sided with Jaffan petitioners against the attack, calling it "a singularly disingenuous lack of moral courage." He was dismissed from his post.

When a lone Palestinian assassin murdered a British official in 1938, the British responded by leveling much of the town from which he came—Jenin. Reports of the norms of the British anti-terror operation in Palestine paint a consistent image of its own unstrained terror: "just kill, kill, kill innocent and guilty alike," as policeman Raymond Cafferata recorded it.

Early in the revolt, Britain began systematically using Palestinians as human shields, a practice not repeated in response to the Zionist terror of the 1940s. The practice is recorded as early as September 24, 1936, when the Nablus mayor, Sulayman Tuqan, was used as a human shield by the local British garrison. In another instance the British tied him to the top of truck.

Palestinian human shields were particularly useful on trains. In one tactic, the British forced hostages onto a separate, single-axle extension on front of the trolley, or onto the bonnet (engine section) of trucks to discourage would-be saboteurs. Yet saboteurs would not necessarily know they were there, and so some hostages sang as loudly as they could as the vehicle moved. Some were tied in place; if any tried to escape, they would be shot.

When the same tactic was used with trucks, the fact that trucks are not bound to tracks allowed the ritual to become yet more depraved. In the words of a Manchester Regiment private, after finishing the run

Two photographs of Palestinian hostages used by the British as human shields, forced to remain on a single axle extension in front of the train. The extraordinary upper photo (dated 1938) was taken from inside the locomotive such as is visible in the lower photo (1936-8). (upper photo courtesy of the King's Own Royal Regiment Museum, Lancaster, KO638.01)

the driver would switch his wheel back and to make the truck waver and the poor wog on the front would roll off ... if he was lucky he'd get away with a broken leg, but if he was unlucky ... nobody bothered to pick up the bits ... we were the masters...

Another method was to seize Palestinians for what were called "mine-sweeping taxis." As described by a colonial official in the Galilee,

the car is filled with them, lashed together and with little room to move. On most occasions they are put in at the point of a revolver and there they stay from about 2100 until about 0430.[84]

The Zionist militias
Whereas the Palestinian terrorists were loose bands of guerrillas operating in the country districts, the Zionist terrorists were

organized militias operating from within urban centers and enjoying the protection of those populations. Records of Zionist gangs' early violence are sparse, "owing no doubt," the British surmised, "to the heavy penalties by which Jewish members of the organisation are bound to secrecy." The terror had first been assumed to be the work of isolated Jewish fanatics, but by the time of the Palestinian uprising of 1936-1939, the British were aware of the highly organized nature of the Zionist militias. The following summary attempts to draw a brief outline of the violence during those years.[85]

Palestinians shot three Jews on April 15, 1936; one survived. Two days later, the Irgun shot dead two Palestinians "while they were sleeping in their hut in one of the plantations of the Jews in the colony of 'Ramataeem,'" as the newspaper *Falastin* reported it. Palestinian shoeshine boys and peddlers were attacked on April 18, and on April 19 rumors of the murders and beheadings of Arabs in Tel Aviv set off an anti-Jewish rampage in Jaffa by unemployed Palestinians. Nine Jews were killed. As with the 1929 anti-Jewish massacre in Hebron, the number would have been higher had local Palestinians not hidden would-be Jewish victims. The next day (April 20) the Irgun shot "two Arabs riding a camel west of Tel-Benyamin," killing one, and murdered a plantation worker. Irgun records cite further anti-Palestinian attacks without details.[86]

Jaffa, summer 1936. As the British Royal Engineers dynamited sections of Jaffa, one of the dynamiters poses with the corpse of a cat blown up with the just-demolished building behind him. (Library of Congress)

Passenger trains joined the Irgun's anti-Palestinian targets by August 17, 1936, when it attacked the Jaffa-Jerusalem line with grenades and gunfire at the bridge at Shlush Street in Tel Aviv, causing (as the Irgun put it) "great consternation among Jaffa Arabs." Palestinian beach-goers remained a favored target for the next decade; the terror gang murdered some in March 1937, as well as agricultural workers in the Hefer Valley.

Irgun bombings of Palestinian cafés are first documented in April 1937 in Haifa, and bombings of Palestinian buses are recorded as early as September of that year. Rehavia was hit on March 6, Yazur on March 22, Jerusalem on May 20, with further attacks on July 7 and October 20.

On November 11, the Irgun threw a bomb at a group of Palestinians on Jaffa Street in Jerusalem, "near the garage of the 'National Bus Co.,'" and that month it attacked cafés in Jerusalem with semi-machine guns and grenades. Palestinian vehicles in the Galilee region were attacked in December, and on December 27 the Irgun opened fire on a Palestinian bus on the Tel Aviv–Jerusalem Road.[87]

Escalation of Irgun bombing

The attacks became more sophisticated in 1938. "Two sacks containing bombs were found on the Iraq Petroleum Company's workers' train from Haifa," the British reported on April 11. A Palestinian sergeant removed the canvas sacks from the train and placed them in the Company's terminal site, where they exploded, killing two people and seriously wounding a third. As police rushed to the scene, news came of a similar sack discovered on another train in the vicinity. That carriage was evacuated and uncoupled, and a bomb expert was summoned. In the meantime, a sergeant and two constables, hoping to protect the train, threw the sack out the window. As they did, it exploded, killing two of them.

The British appear not immediately to have known who was responsible, until the Irgun took credit for placing what it called "clock mines" on the trains carrying Palestinian workers. Four more people were killed that day by Irgun bombs near Kiriat Haim.[88]

The Irgun attacked what it called "mob rioters" on April 17. Four days later, a faulty grenade foiled their attempt to blow up a Palestinian bus. "Reprisals against groups of Arabs" followed on May 17 in Jerusalem and on the Hebron-Jerusalem Road. More "mob rioters" were attacked on May 23, this time in the Tel Aviv

1938

area, and further attacks against Palestinians in Haifa were said to be in response, strangely, to the British trials of three Irgun members.

The Arab market in Jaffa was bombed on June 26, and on the fourth of July five more Palestinians were killed and twenty wounded in an Irgun attack on the Arab quarters (what the Irgun called "concentrations of Arabs") in Jerusalem. The gang attacked Palestinian buses in the Ramle area on July 5.[89]

What happened on July 6, 1938 was the urgent topic when the British ship HMS *Repulse* anchored in Haifa Bay two days later. The District Commissioner came aboard and explained the situation on shore:

> A large bomb had been thrown on Wednesday afternoon [July 6] in the Arab market, and had exploded causing a large number of casualties, and these had increased to about 120 before order was restored.[90]

As reported in *Falastin*, the terrorists had

> slipped up to the roof of a shop in the entrance to the bazaar market near the Aloon market and threw a bomb on a crowd of Arabs and it exploded with a terrible noise near the shop of the Jewish money changer who was killed with his son … the sight of [the many victims] was harrowing, this one moaning, that one in pain.[91]

The attack, the British report said, "must almost certainly have been committed by Jews of the Revisionist party." They were correct—it was the Irgun, whose records cite both this and a similar bombing "in the Old City of Jerusalem" that day.

On July 7 Irgun militants from Kfar Saba took up positions on the Tel Aviv–Haifa highway "to attack Arab traffic," but they hit Indian visitors from Tanzania instead, mistaking them for "Arabs."[92]

Early proof of the Zionists' radicalization of children came the next day, July 8. A bomb "tore apart a bus filled with Arab countryfolk" (as the *NY Times* reported it) by the Jaffa Gate, killing four Palestinians immediately and wounding thirty-six, the blast so strong that it shattered a nearby vegetable market. Taking responsibility for the bombing, the

Irgun boasted that it had caused "great consternation in Arab quarters." The British took four Jews into custody for the crime, among them the alleged bomb-thrower—a twelve-year-old schoolgirl.[93]

In an attempt to prevent further attacks, the British imposed a curfew and assigned a platoon to safeguard each of Haifa's five police districts—yet the Irgun pulled off an even deadlier terror attack on July 15. Disguised as an Arab porter, the bomber placed a booby-trapped cucumber can in the middle of Haifa's Arab market, killing what was described as "scores" of Palestinians and wounding many. Again three days later, a bombing by Jewish militants killed eleven Palestinians and seriously wounded three.

In Haifa, "just when the situation in the town seemed to be getting back completely to normal," a captain in the Royal Navy reported on July 25, Zionist terrorists threw a bomb into the (Arab) melon market, the same as the July 6 attack. The time chosen—six o'clock in the morning—ensured maximum civilian casualties. The bombing "did a terrible amount of damage, causing the death of 45 Arabs, wounding 45 others, and killing 3 horses and 9 donkeys."

The massacre made plain the terrorists' invulnerability: early morning grocery shoppers might have thought the situation was safe, since "no more public place could have been chosen," situated by Kingsway, the Seamen's Institute, the headquarters of the landing parties, "and within easy sight of the Central Police Station."[94]

The next day (July 26) might have been deadlier yet. One of the Irgun's most venerated "martyrs," Jacob Rass (Yaacov Raz or Ras), tried to deposit "a particularly loathsome time-bomb in the Old City of Jerusalem," as British records put it. Dressed as an Arab, Rass hid the device in a barrow of vegetables and was wheeling it into the market when suspicious onlookers exposed the bomb and handed him over to the British. According to the Irgun, he committed suicide to avoid revealing secrets under torture.

The Irgun inhabited an imagined Israel that had been interrupted two thousand years ago but which they were now reawakening from dormancy. The gang exploited Old Testament passages to encourage what it called "right-thinking Jews" in the murder of Arabs—for example, Moses summarily executing an Egyptian after making certain that no one would see it. When the militia extolled Rass and other fallen Irgun heroes as having "saved the honor of Israel more than once during years and enlarged the number of Arab deaths," the *Israel* it referred to was a single concept, ancient and future."[95]

Évian Conference

As the Irgun bombs of July 1938 exploded in Palestine, representatives of thirty-two nations met in Évian-les-Bains (France) at the behest of US President Roosevelt to discuss shared responsibility for the resettlement of the Jewish targets of Nazism. Even though Nazi intentions were terrifyingly clear, the international community failed to rise to the urgency of the danger—in part because the Zionist movement failed as well. The Board of Deputies of British Jews viewed "mass emigration [to various countries] as no solution to Jewish troubles in central Europe," and the Zionist Organization of America adopted a resolution insisting that Palestine be the Conference's answer to the emergency.

Ben-Gurion, too, was lackluster in support for Évian's success. Open safe haven for Jews, he (correctly) argued, would weaken the Zionist project. Not even *Kristallnacht* changed his priorities: Speaking in December 1938, the month *after* that terrible night heralded the beginning of the Holocaust, Ben-Gurion assailed attempts to save Germany's Jewish children unless it was to Palestine. Rather than see all the children escape safely to England, he argued that it was better to let half of them be slaughtered at the hands of the Nazis in order to get the surviving half to be settlers in his colonial project.

Although this oft-quoted statement has been excused as hyperbole, an ex-Haganah member whom the author interviewed stated that Ben-Gurion repeated, and meant it. His actions, indeed, speak for him: Ben-Gurion assailed that very attempt to save Jewish children then in progress, the *Kindertransport*, for which Britain placed no limit and waived all visa requirements, and which saved about 10,000 children.[96]

3

Spared the War, Palestine battles itself

"[The democratic principle] does not take into account the fact
that there is a fundamental qualitative difference between
Jew and Arab." —*Chaim Weizmann, May, 1918* [97]

"The fundamental difficulty over Palestine was that the Jews
refused to admit that the Arabs were their equals."
—*Ernest Bevin, April, 1948* [98]

The crushing of the Palestinian uprising was one of a confluence of events in 1939 that shaped the future of Palestine.
Britain issued the White Paper that spring in an attempt
to put limits on Zionist settlement and land expropriation.
The Irgun opened its US front, run by Hillel Kook under the
pseudonym Peter Bergson. And of course, in late 1939, World War
II broke out. [99]

The Second World War dramatically strengthened Zionists'
ability to commingle safe haven for Jews with a settler ethnocracy in
Palestine. The incomprehensible horrors of the Holocaust engendered
such unqualified empathy for persecuted Jews, that it was easily
co-opted to the Zionist argument, even as Zionism put itself before
Jewish salvation.

Fear of a Nazi victory led the Irgun and Haganah to moderate
their terror at the outbreak of World War II. Not all Irgun members

agreed, however, and in 1940 a splinter group formed under Avraham Stern, just as the Irgun had been formed as a splinter group from the Haganah in 1931. The Stern Gang, as it was commonly called, or more formally Lehi (*Lohamei Herut Israel*), was the most fanatical of the three major organizations, claiming to be (as the Chief Secretary in Jerusalem put it) "the inheritors of the purest traditions of ancient Israel." Lehi made little distinction between the Allied and the Axis powers, and therefore saw no reason to restrain its terror during the war. "Sensible Jews," the group reasoned, "may well look to remain in a relatively good position in Palestine after a German victory." [100]

Lehi and the Italian fascists

Soon after parting ways with the Irgun, Stern hoped to thrust his new, minuscule and barely-known group to victory in the contest to usurp Palestine, above the Irgun, above the Jewish Agency, and above the British, by enlisting the Italian fascists to his cause. Perhaps the very idea that a band of breakaway Irgun militants could have much to entice Mussolini, himself joined in the "Pact of Steel" with the Nazis, should have seemed odd to Stern.

He nonetheless negotiated via a contact whom he believed worked for the Italian consul. This much was correct; but unknown to Stern, the contact also worked for the Irgun. Learning of Stern's plans, the Irgun took over the "negotiations," posing as the Italians in order to secure a signed document to embarrass its rival.

The result was the *Jerusalem Agreement 1940* which "must be ratified not later than the fifteenth of September in the year 1940" with the signatures of the Italians and the "Provisional Jewish Prime Minister" (presumably Stern himself).

The Irgun never got its trophy, however. "Some hitch," a British Security Officer wrote, "the nature of which is not known," kept the document from being signed by Stern.

The intended Lehi-fascist pact offers good insight into the gang's thinking. It provided that Italy would help Lehi overthrow the British in Palestine, establish Lehi as the land's sovereign ruler, and then transfer all Jews there. In the first of its twenty clauses, Italy "solemnly declares … the sacred right of the Jewish nation to create anew an independent and sovereign Jewish State." The second clause is the most relevant to our topic:

> The first party [the Italians fascists] undertakes to assist the second party [Lehi] with all the means in its power to liquidate the Jewish Diaspora by transferring the Jews in countries under its influence and those of other countries with whom it is under agreement to Palestine.

In other words, after helping Lehi oust the British from Palestine, the fascists would help Lehi destroy ("liquidate") all possible Jewish communities outside of Palestine and transfer their populations to Palestine—implicitly with or without their consent. Clause 3 simply states that the Italians "will provide the second party with all the means necessary for the execution of Sections 1 and 2."

Among the Italians' several benefits in the deal was clause 11, in which Lehi "declares that the Mediterranean is an Italian sea and that only the first party [Italy] has the right to an absolute rule over it." The Palestinians are not mentioned at all, suggesting that they are to become part of what the Agreement refers to as "the Arabs" in "the Arabian countries." After the *Jerusalem Agreement*, Stern made two unsuccessful attempts the following year, 1941, to forge an alliance with the Nazis.[101]

These "pro-Axis terrorists," as the London *Times* referred to Lehi, sought, in their own command group's words, to "clean the city streets from every person who wears a uniform," referring to the British. In truth, anyone seen as an obstacle was vulnerable, and most victims of Zionist assassinations (i.e., targeted killings of specific individuals) were Jews.[102]

A passenger arriving at Palestine's Lydda airport from Germany on February 22, 1939 aroused the suspicion of an immigration officer, and so the officer put the man under guard and left to make inquiries by telephone. He returned to find that the mysterious passenger had escaped, and the passport he had used was that of a Jew killed by Palestinians five months earlier, the photograph replaced. Four days later, Ben-Gurion rallied the Yishuv with what the British called a "manifesto … to the Jews of Palestine." The next day (February 27) "outrages were committed by Jews in all parts of the country" against Palestinians, this still three months before the White Paper that became Zionists' new justification for terror attacks. Thirty-eight Palestinians were killed and forty-four injured.

When the Va'ad Leumi (General Council of Palestinian Jews) met the day after that, even those considered moderates "spoke in the militant and uncompromising tone previously used only by the followers of Jabotinsky," new-found support for the more radical Revisionist movement echoed by such media as the Labour daily *Davar*.

In May, the man who had vanished from Lydda Airport was caught boarding a flight for Haifa using a phony identity card. He was David Raziel, Commander in Chief of the Irgun, and presumed architect of the February 27 attacks. Raziel met his end in Iraq two years later, working with the British to foil a pro-Axis revolt (pages 76-77, below).[103]

The White Paper

May
1939

The text of the proposed White Paper was to be aired in Palestine on the evening of May 17, but a half hour before the scheduled broadcast the wires connecting the wireless transmitters at Ramallah with the Jerusalem studio were cut. The British made emergency arrangements in Ramallah and were able to broadcast an hour and a half late. As they did, "about 1,000 Jews" sacked the District Commissioner's Office. An hour later, "five unknown Jews [succeeded in] overpowering two Jewish watchmen" at the Immigration Department in Jerusalem and "distributed a number of incendiary bombs throughout the building." Four of the nine devices exploded.

Rioting continued the next day as one thousand settlers mobbed Zionist Square while others stoned non-Jewish traffic. That evening, "youthful Jewish extremists" broke windows, looted shops, stoned police, shot one dead, and set fire to a post office in Mea Shearim Quarter, gutting it. Zionist assassinations of unsympathetic Jews continued with the execution of a police corporal on May 3.[104]

"Three Jews opened fire from a car on a group of Arabs near the Eastern Station Haifa" on the 25th, as a British Dispatch described it, and "in the early hours of May 29 a party of unknown Jews" raided the Arab village of Biyar Adas. They shot ten Palestinians, of whom five—four women and a man—died on the spot.

The attackers, who were "dressed in European clothes and talking Hebrew," planted a Zionist flag in the village and fled by motor car. "An unknown Jew" assassinated a Jewish police constable and a (Jewish) civilian who was speaking with him.

Early that evening, the Irgun bombed the Rex cinema in Jerusalem. Casualties included thirteen Arabs, three Brits, and two young Jews, a boy and a girl who (as the Irgun justified it) had gone to the cinema "to enjoy themselves in the company of Arabs." The bombing was intended to be more lethal: half of the four devices had failed. In Jerusalem the next day (May 30), two Palestinians in an Arab bus were shot "by unknown Jews."[105]

On June 2-3, Irgun bombs killed fourteen Palestinians and injured thirty-five in attacks on the Arab market near Jaffa Gate, and in indiscriminate mining of Palestinian villages' orchards, roads, and footpaths. Communications were sabotaged, as simultaneous explosions in telephone manholes in three sections of Jerusalem destroyed 175 telephone wires, affecting 1700 lines, and telephone booths were bombed in Jerusalem, Tel Aviv, and Haifa.

June 1939

When the murder "of an Arab by a Jew" in Jerusalem on June 7 "took place close to and in full view of a number of other Jews," the witnesses did nothing to stop the murder and "then refused to give evidence to the Police." In Tel Aviv that day, the telephone lines were bombed again, as was a railway line near the city. On the night of June 8, "upwards of a dozen simultaneous explosions of time-bombs destroyed five electric supply-transformers and plunged a third of Jerusalem in darkness."[106]

The next morning, a teenage Jewish girl "who is reported to have been dressed like an Arab woman, was arrested at 9:30 A.M. just after she had put down a basket containing a time-bomb set to explode at 11 o'clock among a crowd of Arabs*." That "crowd," the intended victims, were women and children waiting to visit their husbands and fathers in Jerusalem's central prison.

The capture of the unexploded "highly lethal" device was, as the *NY Times* saw it, "the first time that incontrovertible evidence has been obtained to show the long-suspected Jewish origin of the bombing of Arab crowds." The arrest of the girl further vindicated fears that children were being indoctrinated by the Zionists.[107]

Post offices and postal workers now joined the roster of targets. Packages rigged with bombs, including what was described as an "envelope mine"—a letter bomb, likely by an Irgun operative soon to break away with Lehi—were now a threat. The first exploded in the Central Post Office at about a quarter to nine on the evening of June 10. As police investigated, three Jewish additional police, and a private, became casualties of a second bomb.

In the morning, a postal worker clearing the debris found a suspicious heavy package; he alerted a constable, but before the constable had a chance to investigate, it exploded, killing him and injuring eight postal employees. The good news that morning was the failure of an assassination attempt against the Mayor of Jaffa.[108]

Between June 12-13, coffee houses were bombed, the post office on Herzl Street was mined and destroyed, all telephone kiosks in Tel Aviv were bombed or otherwise sabotaged, and the Tel Aviv train station near Beth-Hadar and a Palestinian house in Jaffa were both set afire.

When on the night of June 12 five Palestinians from Belad es Sheikh (Haifa) were rounded up "and shot in cold blood outside the village," the "Jewish wireless later boasted of this crime as a Jewish achievement." The road to the Arab village of Fejja was bombed, as was a Public Works Lorry, killing one Palestinian and wounding thirteen, at least one of whom soon died from his injuries.

The most deadly attack of those forty-eight hours was in Tiberias,

* A 1945 report by R. Newton in TNA, FO 371/45382 states that: "in 1938 a Jewish girl still in her teens had been arrested with a bomb which was to have been exploded in a public place in Jerusalem." I have assumed this to be a mis-dating of this 1939 incident.

where Zionist militants planted a land mine that killed seven Palestinians and wounded fifteen. More Palestinians were killed on June 15, and British records cite continued unprovoked, random violence against Palestinians by the Jewish settlers, both by sniper fire and bombs—what the General Officer Commanding (G.O.C.) summarized as continuing "sabotage and a number of direct terrorist attacks on Arabs by Jewish extremists."[109]

Haifa was the scene of the Irgun's next major market bombing. Ethnic tension in the city, the British said, was "maintained by explosion of a large Jewish bomb in vegetable market on June 19 which killed 21 and wounded 24 Arabs" on the spot (British figures rarely address the survival of the wounded). As in previous market bombings, the blast was set at the busy hour of six o'clock in the morning to maximize civilian casualties, half of whom were women and children. Lest the Irgun leave any doubt that civilians were indeed its intended targets, in its next radio broadcast the terror group bragged that they had killed far more than the British acknowledged—fifty-two Palestinian market-goers dead and thirty-two wounded in that one bombing. Three Palestinians were murdered and three wounded in Lubya village (Nazareth) the next day.

When the day after that (June 21) a Jewish man was gunned down in Kiryat Motskin (near Haifa), the British might have first assumed that he was a victim of Palestinian retaliation, but quickly learned otherwise: a "secret Jewish wireless broadcast" announced that he had been executed as a "traitor."[110]

Three days later (June 24), a Palestinian constable was assassinated in Haifa and more communications were sabotaged. Four Palestinians were hit by a bomb thrown at them in Haifa on June 26, two police inspectors were assassinated by a land mine outside their house in Jerusalem, and when the British put up posters in Tel Aviv condemning terrorism, all were torn down. *With blood and fire Judea will rise* typified the graffiti painted on the walls in their stead. On the morning of June 27, the Syrian Orphanage was bombed, wounding six Palestinians, including a boy left in serious condition.

The next day, the Military Commander in Jerusalem reported a particularly "flagrant case" of the Jewish settlers "aiding and abetting terrorism": When a Palestinian man, attacked by a Jewish settler west of Nahalat Shimon quarter, managed to wrest the gun from his assailant, the "Jews from the neighbourhood … instead of assisting in the capture of the would be murderer," freed him and reunited him with his gun.

Anti-Palestinian terror continued the next day (June 29) with "the killing and wounding of a number of Arabs in six separate shooting attacks by Jews this morning." Thirteen murdered and four wounded was the British tally of that morning's anti-Palestinian violence.[111]

"An Arab was shot dead this morning" again on June 30, the *Times* reported. Later that day, a Palestinian bus was attacked in Jerusalem, and a bomb "of Jewish origin" exploded in an Arab café on Mamilla Road, with eleven casualties.

That the Irgun maintained a state of fear through the randomness of its civilian victims is apparent in a fragment of an Irgun diary seized by the British, covering one week from June 26 to July 4, 1939:

June 26: At 5:30 A.M. our men fired on an Arab carriage in the vicinity of Beit Shearim. Four Arabs were killed and one wounded and died later. On the same day, a short time after this, our men fired at four Arabs on the way of Ness Ziona to Rishon le Zion. Three Arabs were killed and one wounded. At 8:20 an Arab was killed by our men at Mea Shearim quarter, Jerusalem.

June 17: At 7:00 a bomb thrown by our people exploded near the Shneller School [the missionary-run Syrian Orphanage] in Jerusalem. Six Arabs were wounded.

June 28: At 5 A.M. our men wounded an Arab on the Nebi-Samuel Road. At noon a bomb was exploded in a lane opposite the Anglo-Palestine Bank, Haifa. At 2:30 P.M. an Arab was killed in Jurianno Square, Haifa. At 7:20 P.M. a bomb exploded in a house in Wadi Salib Quarter, Haifa.

June 29: A few minutes past 5 A.M. our men opened fire on two Arabs on the Petah-Tikva–Rosh-Ha-Ayin Road. Two killed and the third badly wounded. At the same time our men shot two Arabs at km 78 on the Haifa-Jaffa Rd. One killed and the other badly wounded. At 5:30 A.M. an Arab was shot and killed on the Jaffa–Tel Aviv Road. At 5:30 A.M. shots were fired at an Arab cart near Sha'araim. Four Arabs killed and one badly wounded—died later. At 6:15 A.M. two mines exploded under a train between Acre and Haifa. Railway tracks were demolished. A locomotive and three coaches derailed. There were no Jews on this train. At 6:30 A.M. an Arab was killed near the Sheik-Munis orange grove. [Added at the end of the casualty tally for the day:] One of the wounded died.

June 30: At 8 A.M. an Arab was killed by our men at Mea Shearim market, Jerusalem. On the same day a bomb was placed by our men at an Arab cafe in the corner of Mamillah Road and Julian Street exploded. Twelve Arabs were wounded. In the afternoon shots were fired at an Arab bus going from Liftah to Jerusalem. On the same day an Arab who had been wounded on June 29 by Rishon Le Zion died.

[*The month of July opened with two days* [Saturday-Sunday] *of respite from Jewish terrorist attacks,* the British reported on the 3rd. But then Jewish *outrage succeeded outrage.*]

July–
Aug
1939

July 3: At 5:20 P.M. a bomb exploded in the Arab cafe "Edmond" on Kingsway, Haifa, 200 meters (656 ft.) distance from the police station. Official communique said one Arab killed and forty-two wounded.

July 4: At 5:30 A.M. a bomb was thrown at a truck carrying Arab workers [British records: "near Rehavia quarter of Jerusalem … the Jews escaping to Rehavia"]. Three Arabs were wounded. Two Arabs were shot in Jaffa Str. near the Sephardi orphanage. One Arab was badly wounded.*112

---

* The British record attacks on July 3 & 4 that are sufficiently similar to attacks dated

As the Irgun recorded the week, there is no suggestion that it was atypical.

The same gang murdered five Palestinians and wounded eight on July 20, all "casual pedestrians" in the Jaffa and Tel Aviv area, and bombed the Lydda-Kantara Railway. "Jews demonstrating … against cancellation of immigration decree" killed seven Palestinians and wounded six on July 22, and thirty-nine Palestinians were killed and forty-six wounded in another terror attack three days later.

When on August 2 Jerusalem's new Broadcasting House was bombed, a Palestinian engineer was killed, as was "a South African Jewess [May Weissenberg, who was] the organizer of the English Children's Hour." The British, correctly, suspected the Revisionists: the attack is confirmed in Irgun records. What the British did not know was that May Weissenberg was the Irgun's inside plant at the station, "mortally wounded by mistake," as the gang put it. The bombing rendered the new station unusable; operations were moved to Ramallah.

No group claimed credit for the attempted bombing of a cricket match in Haifa on August 5, likely targeted because one of the teams was the Haifa police. Smoke led to the discovery of the large, smoldering bomb, which malfunctioned when its timing device triggered it at 5:00 p.m. More attacks went similarly unattributed, such as the bombing of the cutter *Sinbad* on August 9, killing a police sergeant.

The Irgun hit an Arab bus in Tiberias with a "clock mine," but on August 18 botched the assassination of a Jewish officer by the name of Gordon, who then fled Palestine. It was more successful on August 26, assassinating Police detective Ralph Cairns and Inspector Ronald Barker in Jerusalem, as well as bombing the Arab market in Jaffa that day.

The Palestinians had one break. There had been a series of bombings of Palestinian houses, but when one bomb failed to explode, police dogs were able to follow the scent to the origin, a nearby Jewish settlement.

---

the 4th & 5th in the Irgun records that I have assumed they are the same rather than risk duplication. As the British tended to be more clinical with details such as dates, I have used them here.

Among the cities where the Irgun had established a visible presence was Geneva. The August 1939 issue of The *Irgun Press*, "distributed only in Geneva" (in English), ended with a warning to dissenting Jews,

> the Jews of the Ghetto, who are weak and faint-hearted and not strong enough for this revolutionary period … Our fathers fought against Rome, against Babylon and against Hellas; the Irgun has taken over the sword of Bar Kochba* … May God Help Us! Freedom or Death!

It happened that on the 15th of the month H.G. Daniels, The *Times* correspondent in Geneva, was approached by a man identifying himself as a member of the Irgun, giving the name "Yardany." In his (apparently unpublished) interview, Daniels noted that the Irgun is cell-like in structure ("each member knows only his own immediate chief on whose orders he acts"), and that the group is

> a pretty extensive secret organisation throughout Palestine formed on Nazi lines. Its purpose is to be in readiness to take action against the Arabs … the organisation has plenty of money at its disposal [and] has the support of the population, without which it could not continue … his organisation works only among the youth of Jewry, and abandoned the "oppressed" Jews as hopeless … the ultimate aim was to seize control in Palestine at some future date [and] to colonise Palestine and Transjordan.

In the event of war in Europe, Irgun recruits were to "shape their actions" with Palestine as the objective, a point that confused the correspondent at the time.[113]

World War II broke out two weeks later. In Palestine, the Jewish Agency made a show of support for the British war effort and said that "a system of registration for service of all Jews between 17 and

---

* Simon bar Kokhba led a rebellion known by his name against the Roman Empire in Judea, 132–136 AD.

50 is now in progress." A year later, by September 1940, the British conceded that the Agency's "so-called registration at the beginning of the war was purely a political gesture." The Agency, rather, was interested only in a segregated "Jewish army" that would further its territorial claims to Palestine.[114]

Control of labor as a method of dispossession

Palestinians developed the Jaffa orange trade in the nineteenth century, and were exporting 38 million oranges by 1870, a dozen years before the first Zionist settlers stepped foot on the land. Zionist racialization of land and labor gradually locked Palestinians out of their own trade, and even as the year brought an excellent orange harvest, the settlers' drive to exclude non-Jews continued. Groves such

Jaffa orange culture. Packing oranges, 1900-1920.
(Library of Congress)

as at Nes Siyona (Ness Ziona) were sabotaged for using non-Jewish labor against the orders of the Labour Exchange (Histadrut). Grove owners who hired Palestinians were assaulted and any non-Jewish workers forced off the grounds. Packing sheds were burned down if their groves employed any non-Jews. From the retail end, Tel Aviv shops selling "Arab goods" were vandalized.[115]

Histadrut officials "considered that they were immune from arrest" for their violence against non-Jewish workers and any that employ them, and so the British detention of some of its officials under Emergency Regulations came as a shock to the settlements. Protests against the arrests ranged from "a spate of appeals" to the brutal murder of a (Jewish) constable involved in the detentions.

But the Histadrut refused to end its systemic starving of non-Jews off the land, offering instead to slow down the process, to "retain such Arab labor as is now in their employ" and eliminate non-Jews by attrition.[116]

As the dispossession of the Palestinians continued through such tactics by the settlements' recognized institutions, the terror gangs continued their more direct methods. The Irgun in particular continued to be

> responsible for the indiscriminate slaughter brought about by setting bombs in places frequented by Arab crowds and for waylaying and murdering lone Arabs,

as the High Commissioner put it. Their "systematic campaign" against the police continued as well, especially in Tel Aviv, where Zionist militants planted incendiary bombs in police vehicles and murdered Jewish constables.[117]

Both the Eden and Orient Cinemas were bombed on March 4, and the same day the printing equipment of the newspaper *Haboker* was attacked for refusing to print a Zionist manifesto. Zionist terrorists beat a Jewish policeman to death with iron bars on March 13 for his part in the arrest of militants, and another (Jewish) policeman was "shot dead in Haifa by Jewish terrorists" on June 26. *Pum*, the Hagana's assassination department, murdered four Jewish soldiers in May as "traitors to the Jewish cause," as the British described it. *Traitor* was also the Hagana's own epitaph for a Sephardic Jew it assassinated on May 3.

Printing presses serving German Jewish immigrants in their native tongue were hit by arson, one on March 30, another on April 8. Two Egged buses were set afire by the Irgun or Lehi on August 15, and violence continued against shops selling Palestinian goods or produce. Jews refusing payment to the Jewish National Fund were threatened, and when two Jews resisted a special tax imposed by the Jewish Agency (*Kofer HaYishuv*, "Jewish Settlement Ransom"), their cars were bombed. Lehi, new and short of finances, devoted much of its efforts to robbery, while remnants of Arab robber gangs raided both Arabs and Jews; one attacked a Jewish milk truck on 26 March, killing the assistant driver.

On May Day 1940, the Jewish Agency is reported to have instructed Jewish Czech subjects "not to register their names for military service" in the Allied struggle, because Palestine is their national home and "they should fight only in her defence."

Italian warplanes attacked Haifa on July 14 and 15, and again on September 6 and 8-9 in the Tel Aviv–Jaffa area. On their last raid the fascists dropped white, pink, and yellow propaganda leaflets in Arabic promising the Palestinians liberation; these, according to the British, were ridiculed by their intended converts. More Axis raids followed on September 21 and 26.[118]

The *Patria* and the *Struma*

The most deadly single terror attack to hit Palestine unfolded in
Nov
1940
November 1940, when the British transferred the passengers from three illegal immigrant vessels, the *Pacific*, the *Milos*, and the *Atlantic*, onto the ship *Patria* for the trip to Mauritius where, whatever the hardships, there were facilities for the refugees and they would be safe from the war. The last refugees were put aboard on November 24. At about 9:15 the next morning, a powerful explosion (or two in quick succession) ripped open the vessel and "almost at once," a British committee headed by Supreme Court judge Alan Rose reported, "the ship listed to starboard and within fifteen minutes

of the explosion she had heeled over completely" in Haifa port. An estimated 267 people were killed and 172 injured. More than 200 of the dead were Jews fleeing the war in Europe; about 50 were crew and soldiers.[119]

"Much protestation of innocence" came from both the Irgun and the Jewish Agency. Suspicion at first fell on the Irgun, but the bombing was soon proven to be the work of the Agency's Haganah under the authority of future Prime Minister Moshe Sharett (then Shertok).

This saddled the Jewish Agency with a public relations nightmare. While the hope was obviously to cripple the vessel rather than sink it, inescapably, the Agency was willing to accept refugee deaths as sacrifices for the settler state, especially as most of the DPs were trapped in its lower level and could drown even if the explosion didn't kill them.

The answer—which would become a recurring theme—was to blame the DPs. The Jewish Agency circulated the story that it was the refugees themselves who blew up their ship. It was a mass suicide.

Sharett argued behind Agency doors that mythicizing the *Patria* disaster into a tragic legend of heroism and sacrifice would serve the Zionist cause, both then and for historians in the decades to come. Future Israeli Minister of Defense Pinhas Lavon was not convinced, but agreed that there is no "necessary link between the legend and the truth."

The Yishuv's media embraced the lie. Articles proposed epic plays and poetry to immortalize the victims as willing suicide heroes who, with a logic that is never addressed, sacrificed themselves in the hope that in the future some might live. The exploitation of the *Patria* dead was also a windfall for Zionism's appetite for Biblical tie-ins: the *Patria* was a modern-day Masada.*

The lie was still being spread in print nine years later by the author and journalist Arthur Koestler :

---

* According to Roman historian Josephus (first century A.D.), in ca. A.D. 73-74, 960 Jews holed up on the Masada, a high, steep mountain plateau by the Dead Sea, committed suicide or killed each other on the approach of Roman troops.

> The passengers blew up their ship. They had reached their journey's
> end. They were not even threatened with deportation back to Europe;
> only to a tropical island [Mauritius] without hope of return.[120]

Catastrophe struck several of these immigrant vessels before even reaching Palestine. The SS *Salvador* capsized in the Bosphorus in 1940 with the loss of 350 lives, and more than twice that number perished in the *Struma*.

The *Struma* was originally a two-masted sailing vessel registered in 1830 in Macedonia, later fitted with a small engine. The Revisionists placed ads in the Romanian press for the voyage, and prospective passengers, wary over the fate of the *Salvador*, were reassured with claims that proved largely fictitious. In early February 1942 the frail vessel, dangerously overcrowded and beset with constant engine trouble, reached Istanbul through the Black Sea carrying 10 crew and 781 immigrants.

When Palestinian landing permits promised by the organizers proved to be non-existent, the British attempted to facilitate the transfer to Palestine of the vessel's children aged 11-16. This, too, failed.

Britain claimed to know that the Gestapo had been behind some of these immigration vessels, that Reich agents were aboard, and thus that the vessels represented a security threat. Whatever the case, Turkish authorities towed the *Struma* back through the Bosphorus Strait into the Black Sea, where its engine failed again. The vessel drifted until sinking with the loss of all aboard save for one nineteen-year-old refugee. The likely cause was a Russian torpedo.[121]

The Jewish Agency seized upon the *Struma* tragedy to reinforce its calls for Jews *not* to join the Allied struggle against the Nazis. The argument was that [1] Palestine was the natural home of all Jews; [2] no Jew should fight except in defense of that home; and [3] they should fight only as a segregated "Jewish army," which would be a *de facto* recognition of a Zionist state. The idea, which dated from World War I, was now being pushed by Ben-Gurion and would culminate with the creation of the so-called Jewish Brigade in 1944.

Recent German immigrants to Palestine were outraged by Zionism's exploitation of the horrors they had just fled, including its manipulation of the *Patria* and *Struma* tragedies. Among those giving voice to this outrage was the prominent journalist Robert Weltsch, who had been editor of the twice-weekly Berlin newspaper *Jüdische Rundschau* until it was banned by the Nazis in 1938. In a speech in Tel Aviv in 1942, Weltsch railed against "this small group of fascist Zionists in Jerusalem, London and America"—mentioning Ben-Gurion and Shertok by name—who "poison our youth ... we Central European Jews have nothing to do with it."

Of the Jewish Agency and the drowned refugees of the *Patria* and *Struma*,

> it is an injustice to the dead [to] misuse this terrible tragedy for a political demonstration. We say it openly that we would have been happy if the *Struma* people had landed in Mauritius. But the Jewish Agency wanted them only for the National Home. It rejected all other possibilities of saving them. This was a very great crime ... The victims on the *Patria* were the fault of the Jews [blown up by the Hagana]. It is incomprehensible why the Jewish Agency should link these two incidents together.

Weltsch warned that the Jewish Agency was naive to the horrors of Nazism. The Zionists

> have not yet understood that the enemy seeks the destruction of the Jews ... We who have been here only a few years, we know what Nazism is.

Instead, the Zionist establishment takes "part in the crash of European Jewry only as spectators," fighting the British and keeping Jews from joining the Allied struggle while getting comfortable and rich from their political project in Palestine. Recent immigrants from Germany and Central Europe know the truth in Europe but have no representation in the Zionist politic. If they did, "we would have demanded that the Yishuv should put itself at the disposal of Britain for the fight against Hitler and Nazism." But

They do not want to fight against Hitler because his fascist methods are also theirs … They do not want our young men to join the [Allied] Forces … day after day they are sabotaging the English War Effort.[122]

The Farhud: pogrom in Iraq

Violence against Jews erupted in Iraq on the first two days of June 1941, when the British retook control of the country following a two-month-old coup by a nationalist Iraqi political faction, the Golden Square. Though aligned with the Axis, it was principally concerned with ridding Iraq of the British; and although the pogrom appeared to be instigated by the victims' non-Jewish countrymen, it was not typical of life for Iraqi Jews. Oddly, Lehi reported in its *Communique* that "Churchill's Government is responsible for the pogrom in Baghdad," and the same allegation came from an Iraqi Jewish witness to the violence, who wrote that the pogroms were a British false-flag operation designed to justify the return of British rule to the country.

British documents declassified at this author's request strongly suggest this as well. The UK government has however refused to declassify another ten-page, eight-decade-old archive that holds the answer to the question, on the grounds that even in redacted form it might "undermine the security of the country [UK] and its citizens."*

The clues that *have* been declassified involve Amin al-Husseini, the infamous Mufti who is best remembered for his overtures with the Nazis. When in 1921 votes were cast for the new Mufti of Jerusalem, al-Husseini came in last among the four candidates, but Herbert Samuel over-rode the count and appointed al-Husseini in the belief that he would be advantageous to the Mandate—which he was, until he joined the rebellion that began in 1936. He went into hiding to escape arrest, fled to Beirut in October 1937, and in October 1939 slipped to Baghdad, then under nominally independent pro-British rule.

---

* The archive at issue is in two parts. Part 1, CO 733/420/19, was released as a result of the author's 2014 FOI request. Despite its documents being heavily redacted, it leaves no doubt that the British conspired to create instability in Iraq in order to justify their renewed control. The British government however refused this author's 2018 request for access to the second half of this file, CO 733/420/19/1, which covers the critical time period through to June 1941.

1941

British plans to retake control of Iraq were already in progress five months before the Golden Square coup. In November 1940, with the Mufti ensconced in Baghdad, the British discussed

> possible action against [the Mufti, and] it was decided that the only really effective means of securing control over him would be a military occupation of Iraq … We may be able to clip the Mufti's wings when we can get a new Government in Iraq. F.O. [Foreign Office] are working on this.

Propaganda to justify the proposed coup was also being discussed. High Commissioner Harold MacMichael suggested "that documents incriminating the Mufti have been found in Libya" that can be used to embarrass him among his followers. But the idea was nixed by others who, knowing that "there was no truth in the statement," felt it would not work.

Notwithstanding suspicions of British involvement in the anti-Jewish violence, Zionist activity to pressure Jews to emigrate from Iraq to Palestine began about this time.[123]

Back in Palestine, the terror groups' noose around the settlers tightened. Records covering a two-week period in the summer of 1941 offer a glimpse into how the Irgun dealt with three people refusing "donations":

> June 28: A bomb was thrown at the house of a Mr. Zweig of Ramat Gan, a first warning for an unpaid demand for £P.200;* there would be no second warning.

> July 3: A Mr. Rosner of Tel Aviv was abducted and taken to Ramat Gan, where he was tortured on account of his refusal to pay £P.400. Eight days later a bomb exploded outside his house in Tel Aviv.

---

* As a reference to the value of the £P, in 1929 a schoolteacher earned a minimum of £P60 and a maximum of £P340 per year. (*Report by His Majesty's Government … Palestine and Trans-Jordan… 1929*, 65)

July 6: A bomb was thrown at the house of a Mr. Dankner in Petah Tiqva, who was ordered to pay £P.400. Six days later his business premises at Petah Tiqva were wrecked by a bomb.[124]

1941: Zionist goals reaffirmed by key leaders

To be treated as most secret is the red ink heading accompanying a transcript of a meeting of twenty people held in London on September 9, 1941. Present were Weizmann (who had called the meeting), Ben-Gurion, three of the Rothschilds, other Zionist leaders such as Selig Brodetsky and Simon Marks (of Marks & Spencer), and the prominent non-Zionist industrialist, Robert Waley Cohen.

Discussing the path to the proposed Jewish State, the conversation ran along the lines of George Orwell's still-to-be-written *Animal Farm*, in which all animals are equal, but some are more equal than others.

Anthony de Rothschild began by stressing that there would be no "discrimination … against any group of its citizens" in the Jewish state, not even "to meet immediate needs," as equality and non-discrimination were principles "for which Jewry has always stood." Weizmann and Ben-Gurion also assured the skeptics: "Arabs" would have equal rights.

However, Weizmann's "equality" included the transfer of most non-Jews out of Palestine while permitting "a certain percentage of Arab and other elements" to remain in his Jewish state, the in-sinuation being as a pool of cheap labor. Anthony de Rothschild's vision of equality and non-discrimination was equally compelling: equality "depended on turning an Arab majority into a minority," and to achieve this, there would be "no equal rights" for non-Jews.

Cohen found the scheme dangerous "for everyone concerned," submitting that the Zionists were "starting with the kind of aims with which Hitler had started." Cohen did not stop there: he suggested that if a state with equality for everyone were indeed intended, the state should be named with a neutral geographic term such as *Palestine*, not a religious name that denoted "one the basis of race or religion."

Lewis Bernstein Namier, who had worked as political secretary to the Jewish Agency a decade earlier, refuted Cohen: he argued that if the state had a non-Jewish name, "they would never get a Jewish majority," acknowledging the use of messianism as a calculated strategy. Ben-Gurion and Weizmann agreed, adamant that the state must have a Jewish name.

Ben-Gurion clarified that his Jewish state was not based on Judaism, but on "the fact that they happened to be Jews." Weizmann, asked about borders of his settler state, Weizmann continued in the same surreal manner. He replied that he would consider the Peel Commission's Partition plan, but that "the line [the partition, Israel's border] would be the Jordan." This was nonsensical: the Jordan was the Commission's eastern border for *both* states, and so Weizmann's partition meant 100% for his state, 0% for the Palestinians—that is, no partition. He went further still: he would "very much" like to "cross the Jordan" (take Jordan along with Palestine).

At the end of the meeting Weizmann sought to put his proposals into effect officially in the name of all Jews worldwide. Those against his proposals were, in his word, *antisemites*.[125]

"Anti-Semitic" was also the word the Irgun used a mid 1941 pamphlet to describe any "plan to begin the settlement of Jews outside Palestine," as the gang also railed against Jews fighting with the Allies for "a war not theirs."

Contradicting apologists who attributed their terror to the desperate plight of Jews in Europe, the Irgun clarified that its attacks "were not acts of despair and not acts of revenge," but calculated campaigns of terror, "acts of persons who believe that the Jewish Kingdom will be created by force." Jews who believed otherwise were "Jews of the Ghetto, who are weak and faint-hearted and not strong enough for this revolutionary period."[126]

The year 1942 began with almost three weeks without a major attack, but this ended on the 20th of January. Police received an anonymous tip about an explosion at 8 Yael Street in Tel Aviv, so five policemen were dispatched to investigate. Outside, they saw no evidence of damage, and so they entered the house to investigate. The bombs that ripped the house apart once they were inside killed four of them

1942

on the spot, the fifth surviving only because twenty-nine sticks of gelignite failed to explode. All but one of the victims were Jewish. One was to testify against Lehi members for the murder of two bystanders, both Jewish, during a robbery.

This "cold blooded act of terrorism," the War Office wrote, was not the first time Lehi had used the trick of luring people into a house rigged to explode.

After Lehi assassinated three more police officers the following month (February 1942), the British caught its leader, Avraham Stern. Stern got no further—he was shot dead by the officer who captured him, Geoffrey Morton, when he tried to escape (some allege, not without reason, that Morton simply executed him while no one was looking). Morton himself proved difficult to assassinate—Lehi tried on May 1 by planting a massive mine on a roadside where his car would be passing, but Morton's driver veered to the middle of the road to overtake a bicyclist just before the lethal spot. The car was not directly hit and all the occupants survived the blast.[127]

Hiking parties, walking tours

Compiling meticulous, comprehensive intelligence about the Palestinian areas was essential to the Jewish Agency's ultimate aim of conquering Palestine. To this end, surveillance teams were organized posing as hiking parties or walking tours. The British were slow in understanding their actual purpose, despite noting their propensity for traveling in "Arab areas." By April 1942, it is clear that they had become commonplace: even if oblivious to their purpose, the authorities had frequently warned the Agency against the practice, "but to no avail."

> Parties of Jews consisting mainly of men and women and of students arrange extensive walking tours, frequently through Arab areas. A popular journey is to the Dead Sea. It practically invariably means taking a route through an area of Palestine that is completely Arab...

That month, one "walking tour" was recorded only because of an accident during what was presumed merely to be "illegal training."

A party consisting of 156 men and women aged 15-27, having "completed that theoretical part of a course of pre-military training held by the HAGANA, proceeded to the Dead Sea hills in order to carry out practical training."

What was described as an "exercise" was to commence at 4:00 A.M. on April 9. About fifteen minutes before the hour, a group preparing breakfast was oblivious to a sack with hand grenades close to the cooking fire. Six of the "hikers" were killed and ten seriously wounded in the blast.

Several hours later, "thirteen Jewish Youths and five girls" returning from the Dead Sea and well-armed, were stopped by the police near Nablus.[128]

At about eight o'clock on the morning of April 22, 1942, as Assistant Inspector General of Police M. J. McConnell drove away from his Jerusalem residence, wires connecting a bomb to his steering column and chassis snapped. A few minutes later, his Palestinian servant noticed something strange on the ground. He picked it up, and a moment later he was dead.

Three hours later, a child noticed a peculiar object on the side of the road near the house of the Inspector General. The child, fortunately, drew the attention of a passing constable to this second Lehi car bomb of that morning that had broken loose of its wires and failed to kill its intended victim—this one containing seventy sticks of gelignite and six-and-a-half pounds of rivets. Police dogs followed the scent to a nearby Jewish suburb (Rehavia), there losing the trail. Had either of the assassinations succeeded, evidence pointed to a grander terror attack awaiting the funeral. A further Lehi assassination attempt on the first of May also failed.

When on May 19 police attempted to seize an armory of illegal weapons at Givat Haim, 500 settlers convened to block them, and rather than precipitate a confrontation, the police left.[129]

The Biltmore Program

May's most consequential news was in New York, where a meeting of Zionist leaders led to the so-called "Biltmore Program" after the name of the hotel where the conference took place. Authored by Ben-Gurion and endorsed by Weizmann, the Biltmore platform demanded the complete and unconditional surrender of all of Palestine to the Zionists. The goals of the Revisionists were now those of mainstream Zionism.

Biltmore was publicly denounced by several prominent rabbis and *NY Times*' publisher Sulzberger. Judge Proskauer, though a devoted Zionist, was branded "a traitor to his race" by American Zionist leaders Stephen Wise and Abba Silver for resisting the Biltmore's extremism. Most significantly, opposition to it led to the creation of the American Council for Judaism.[130]

As Biltmore made Revisionist policy mainstream, the ranks of Lehi, specializing in assassinations, grew slowly, while the ranks of the Irgun and its large-scale destruction, swelled. Irgun recruitment records show that during a one-month period between July-August of 1942, it admitted "680 youths and girls" into the organization "after the rejection of the medically unfit."[131]

Intolerance for non-Zionist Jews continued to tighten, and with it intolerance for any Jew using his or her native German rather than Hebrew. *Orient*, a German language weekly published by the German writers Arnold Zweig and Wolfgang Yourgrau—or, as US Intelligence described it, "published by German Jews of the old liberal type"—was being suppressed by the Zionists' Council for the Propagation of the Hebrew Language. Zweig was a well-established writer, a friend of such intellectuals as Thomas Mann, Bertolt Brecht, and Sigmund Freud. Yourgrau was at the time a relatively unknown social psychologist, physicist, and journalist.[132]

When on May 31, 1942 Zweig and other German-speaking Jewish immigrants attempted to hold a meeting of the Anti-Fascist League in Tel Aviv's Esther Cinema, it was violently broken up by thugs that included the sons of Jewish Agency officials. To read the *Palestine Post*, it was Zweig's fault:

> However much sympathy may be due to those who … are unable to speak to Palestine Jews in their own language [sic, i.e., Hebrew],

the use of German in public is unconditionally to be denounced … Mr. Arnold Zweig should have known better than to rouse the resentment and anger of undisciplined youths.

Blumenthal's Neueste Nachrichten was a German language daily authored by Jewish immigrants and produced by the Aliyah Hadashah (New Immigrants Party). It reflected a softer form of Zionism than the orthodoxy of the Jewish Agency and the terror gangs. On the evening of June 12 (1942), the newspapers were burned, and a few hours later, at eighteen minutes after midnight on the 13th, Blumenthal's printing press was blown up. The blast was so strong that it injured five people in an adjoining building and started a fire that spread and seriously damaged a neighboring house.

Two weeks later—on June 27—the paper's office on Rehov Ahad Ha'am in Tel Aviv was set ablaze, causing extensive damage and completely destroying the contents of the store room.[133]

Meanwhile, threats against *Orient* continued, as well as against its advertisers, printers, and distributors. After its bookbinding shop was set on fire, Yourgrau tried to continue printing in Jerusalem. This was short-lived: the new printing shop was blown up.

"In Jerusalem," Yourgrau later recalled,

> I found a well-qualified printer, who neatly brought out our badly roughed-up mouthpiece. One evening—it was February 2, 8:30 p.m., 1943—I received a call informing me that our printing shop was destroyed by a bomb. Twenty minutes later I found a scene which was reminiscent of a medieval destruction technique. Several bombs must have been placed at various points inside the shop. The detonation was so violent that the people in the neighborhood mistook it for an aerial bombardment by the Nazis and tumbled into the air raid cellar … The Hebrew press, interestingly, failed to report the destruction of our printing premises and took, so to speak, no notice of us.

All other printers, whether in the settlements or Arab, were warned that the same fate awaited them if they printed *Orient*. Determined to tell his readers why the journal could no longer exist, he found one Christian-Arab printer who agreed to print the cover, while he resorted to stenciling to print the contents. "We brought out our first issue in April 1942," he reminisced, "and our last in April 1943.[134]

A meeting between Revisionist and Agency representatives said to have taken place about this time produced the following summary of "the enemies of Jewry":

- the foremost enemy were non-Zionist Jews;
- second was "the democracies and their Atlantic Charter";*
- and lastly, "Arabs."

Addressing these in reverse order, Palestinians were third only at the current stage. The British already foresaw the Jewish Agency's tactical reason for fueling an alleged "Arab problem" that would never end, and an intelligence officer noted the "self-centred and patronizing attitude" to the Palestinians that "make any protestations on the part of the Zionists of desire for good relations with the Arabs seem very unreal." The Irgun had already begun the task of morphing the Palestinians into Hitler, plastering posters warning that "Arabs" were "making vigorous underground preparations to destroy the last of our people's hope."[135]

As for democracy, on October 4 (1942) Ben-Gurion, in Jerusalem between trips to the US and England, told Jewish Agency leaders that although Hitler had made Jews suffer, he also "revive[d] in assimilated Jews the feeling of Jewish nationalism, [and] we have exploited this feeling in favor of Zionism." Democracy, however, threatened to undo it. Ben-Gurion warned that Jewish nationalism is

> slowly disappearing again because the democracies, in contrast to the dictator states, recognize the Jews as people having full rights of citizenship … [and so] in America there now exists a strong movement away from Zionism.

Fully 85% of America's Jewry, he warned, were "assimilationists," a setback he blamed again on America's "democratic attitude." Another

---

* The Atlantic Charter of August, 1941, was an agreement among the Allies of post-war goals; principal among them were no territorial enlargement or territorial changes made against the wishes of the people, and self-determination. It became the basis for the United Nations.

Agency speaker agreed, condemning the democratic countries and their Atlantic Charter as enemies of Jewry, an echo of the September meeting in London.

Opposition to Zionism among Jews had always plagued the movement, but now Ben-Gurion moved to oust any Agency members he considered insufficiently Zionist, in particular anyone who voted with the socialist Hashomer Hatzair and their acknowledgment of Palestinian national rights.

Meanwhile, Weizmann met with the political theorist and philosopher Isaiah Berlin in England, telling him that Jews are incapable of establishing roots anywhere but in Palestine, and that the "Arabs [need to] be told firmly" that they will never have a state.[136]

World War II and recruitment from Palestine

British pamphlets fell from the sky over Haifa on the first day of November 1942, urging people to enlist in His Majesty's Forces against the Axis powers. By the end of the year, about 9,000 Palestinian Arabs had enlisted with the Allied forces, notwithstanding reluctance to join a battle that would not bring them their own freedom. As the Haifa advocate Elias Koussa reminded the High Commissioner in an eloquent fourteen-page response to the pamphlets, Palestinians had flocked of their own accord to join the British in the previous world war, but Britain then betrayed its promise of liberation.

Jews enlisted despite recruitment being hampered for quite a different reason: Zionist leaders' continuing determination that Jews enlist only as an exclusively Jewish army that would further the cause of Zionist statehood, not as equal soldiers in the common front.

The Jewish Agency maintained its opposition to Jews joining the Allied struggle against the Nazis even though the present month—November of 1942—brought hard news of the death camps. Hebrew newspapers were "flooded with reports on Nazi atrocities on the Jews in Occupied Territories, most of them appearing with black-bordered columns." One or two of the papers took up the theme that "[n]ow is the chance for Jews to join the Army and go to the rescue of our bretheren [sic]," and into December, Nazi atrocities remained "the main item in the Hebrew newspapers almost every day."[137]

Lehi invoked the Old Testament to continue its preaching against Jews joining the Allied struggle. "The Jewish youth does not want to enlist in this Gog and Magog War," a Lehi broadcast said in December of 1941—the two Biblical monsters a reference to the Allies and the Axis—"because it is not the war of the Jews," not one for their "national interests [a Zionist state]." The Biblical stage the ever-present prop, Lehi decried that "a foreigner [i.e., the British High Commissioner] is placed on the seat of King David."[138]

The Jewish Agency continued to compromise the Allied struggle by what the War Cabinet described as "a large-scale arms stealing racket" from the Allied forces. "Organised by the Jewish authorities [it was] directly undermining the war effort" against the Axis. This "racket," the War Cabinet lamented, was draining Allied resources "as if they were paid by Hitler himself."[139]

Solomon Schonfeld's rescue effort

In rescue as well, Zionism failed European Jewry during their most desperate hour. In response to the horrific revelations coming from Nazi-held territory, a joint Declaration issued by eleven nations condemned "in the strongest possible terms this bestial policy of cold-blooded extermination." The Declaration was read to both UK Houses of Parliament on December 17 (1942), and to this backdrop British Rabbi Solomon Schonfeld, a primary figure in the 1938 *kindertransport*, redoubled efforts to arrange safe passage for Jews in Axis territory to England. "In view of the massacres and starvation of Jews and others in enemy and enemy-held territories," Schonfeld gathered support for a motion "to declare its readiness to find temporary refuge in its own territories or in territories under its control for endangered persons…."

Inertia for the project grew quickly. By early 1943, Schonfeld had 177 British MPs ready to support the measure, in addition to Archbishops, Bishops, Peers, and the Episcopate of England and Wales.

It was at that point, with passage of the rescue effort in sight, that Selig Brodetsky, president of the (Zionist) Board of Deputies of British Jews, assisted from the United States by Stephen Wise, president of

1943

the World Jewish Congress, intervened and scuttled it—this despite Wise's having just held a press conference in the US capital to spread the alarm that the Nazis planned the extermination of European Jews.

Schonfeld, trying to save his project, told the Board of Deputies that they should make the project *their* idea and take full credit for it. But vanity was not the problem—the sole reason was that the safe haven was not in Palestine. Brodetsky's mentor, the Zionist leader Lavey Bakstansky, reinforced the message: he admonished Schonfeld's close associate, Marcus Retter "in no uncertain terms," for attempting a rescue not directed to Palestine, and made explicit that they would do whatever was necessary to squash UK Parliamentary support for it.

In the end, the Zionists created what appeared as an internecine battle among Jews questioning the very seriousness and urgency of the horror in Europe, making rescue seem futile among members of Parliament who had the influence and desire to help.

Meanwhile, during the second half of April (1943) representatives of the UK and US met in Bermuda to discuss the issue of Jewish refugees already liberated by the Allied forces and those who remained in Nazi-occupied Europe. Nothing substantive came of the effort, other than affirming that the defeat of the Nazis had to be highest priority.[140]

Zionist officials sent not a single emissary to the ghettos of Poland, yet posthumously conscript the victims of the Warsaw Ghetto Uprising, like those of the *Patria*, as a mass suicide in the service of the settler state. Few ghetto fighters lived to speak for themselves, but one who did, Marek Edelman, condemned Zionism and refused to endorse the Israeli state as the heir to, or moral outcome of, the Holocaust. He was marginalized, and his account of the Uprising, *The Ghetto Fights*, was silenced in Israel.[141]

Rescue, Ben-Gurion preached, was not Zionism's top priority; the top priority was furthering the Zionist state, what he referred to as "internal action." The "Jewish Conference is alive," the December 11, 1943 *Jewish Daily Forward* complained, only when it concerns Palestine, "and it is asleep when it concerns rescue work." As Haganah member and future Israeli politician Eliezer Livneh would later explain, "the rescue of Jews was not an aim in itself, but only a means."

Yitzhak Gruenbaum, head of the WZO's Palestinian Rescue Committee, was emphatic that rescue must take second-place to Zionism. Amid reports of the death camps,

> a mood swept over Eretz Yisrael, that I think is very dangerous to Zionism, to our efforts for redemption, our war of independence. How is it possible that in a meeting in Yerushalayim [Jerusalem] people will call: *If you don't have enough money [for rescue] you should take it from the Keren Hayesod [a fund for building the state], You should take the money from the bank, there is money there.* And this time in Eretz Yisrael, there are comments: *Don't put Eretz Yisrael in priority in this difficult time, in the time of destruction of European Jewry.* ... I said: *no!* And again I say *no* ... we have to stand before this wave that is putting Zionist activity into the second row. I think it necessary to say here Zionism is over everything...[142]

Referring to those pushing for rescue as "pleaders," Gruenbaum invoked Zionism's unfailing companion, messianism, to explain why the settler project was more important than saving Europe's condemned Jews. "Whenever Jews underwent a disaster," he argued, "our ancestors saw the footsteps of the Messiah. Our history does not extol the pleaders ... But history extols the Messiahs, that made heroic efforts for the redemption of the nation."[143]

That "redemption of the nation" meant what the repeated "Messiahs" suggests: the reestablishment of the imagined Biblical kingdom, *not* post-war rebuilding. When in March of 1943, the British announced post-war reconstruction plans formulated by the Palestine War Supply Board, the Jewish Agency reaction was at first divided; but since Ben-Gurion saw reconstruction as an obstacle to Zionism, he "urged the Jewish community to adopt an attitude of non-cooperation." The Jewish Agency's active opposition to post-war reconstruction brought the resignation of a Dr. Werner Senator, its only remaining moderate, non-Zionist member. By the war's end, Jewish Agency opposition to Reconstruction would extend to European Reconstruction, though this was voiced publicly only by fringe groups.[144]

On New Year's day of 1943, "a Jew whose integrity ... is not open to question" approached high-placed British authorities in great secrecy. Code-named Z, he was "profoundly disquieted" by the direction of the Zionist movement.

> It was accordingly Z's earnest plea that Government should act now before the movement grew too strong; he instanced the parallel development of the Nazi movement.

Settler youth, Z reported, were being enlisted *en masse*, with the greatest esteem placed on what Z called "S.S. Squads" after the Nazi death squads, a reference to the Hagana's elite fighting force, the Palmach.

Z, as it turned out, was J.S. Bentwich, Senior Inspector of Jewish Schools, ironically the brother of Norman Bentwich, former attorney-general of Palestine.[145]

Another first-hand source was Henry Hunloke, a former Conservative MP who kept close contact with Jewish Agency officials. He reported that month that the Haganah was preparing to secure the Zionist state by force, but "as a feeble conscious saver for the outer world they will say that the British were unable to protect them and their settlements." Hunloke—who a year later would fall under suspicion of compromising intelligence to a Jewish mistress—said that the Jewish Agency "make one think that they have picked the strangest parts of Nazism, Fascism, Communism with a spicing of Tammany Hall* as the system best suited for the control of Jews in Palestine." Those with more moderate views are tolerated only until they become influential.

"From a tender age," children are brought up to have one aim only, the fulfillment of Zionism, and children have walked out on their parents when the parents try to instill some moderation on that aim. The system "is closely akin to that adopted by the Nazis," and as history has shown, "in a comparatively short space of time, such

---

* "Tammany Hall" is a reference to political patronage, graft, and corruption in the US Democratic Party in New York in the second half of the nineteenth century through the first quarter of the twentieth.

teaching is very hard to eradicate." Mutilated bodies are found with labels tied to them stating: "This is what happens to an informer."

Immigration, Hunloke reported, was the ever-present focus, with Poland, Russia, and North Africa looked to for new settlers. But the Jews of North Africa were difficult: they "are not Zionist-minded," and so "propagandists are at present being trained in Palestine" to recruit them. "The [Jewish] Agency at the moment are exerting every effort to Zionise Jews in various North African territories," and "any method will be adopted" to achieve Zionism's political goal. Among these methods, he speculated, could be to "stir up anti-Semitism ... in order to force Jews ... to come to Palestine."[146]

Dr. Arieh Altman, chairman of a delegation of the New Zionist Organization (NZO, a Revisionist group founded by Jabotinsky), said much the same: anti-Semitism must "form the foundation of Zionist propaganda." Keeping alive the specter of anti-Semitism, Dr. Altman argued, would persuade Jews in Britain or America to emigrate to Palestine.

The lure of Zionism for bigots should not be overlooked: "non-Jewish support [for Zionism] in America could also be increased by emphasising the advantages" of the settler project in "reducing the number of Jews" coming into the US.[147]

The Irgun in the United States during the war

Zionism's need for perpetual anti-Semitism was the essence of Irgun-founder Ze'ev Jabotinsky's message when he preached that Zionism must remain in a permanent state of emergency. In the 1940s, his son Eri was working with Peter Bergson's US organization as it attained, in the words of Israeli Defence Minister and Knesset member Moshe Arens, "unparalleled influence in many circles of American society as well as in the U.S. administration and in Congress." Some light on their operation is preserved in a letter, intercepted and copied by the British, from Eri to a friend in Jerusalem.

Jabotinsky explains to his friend that they were operating under the name Committee for a Jewish Army,* and that in January 1942,

---

* Full name: Committee for a Jewish Army of Stateless and Palestinian Jews.

Bergson "hit upon a new idea."[148]

> We bought a page in the 'New York Times' and advertised the
> Committee for a Jewish Army just the way you would advertise
> Chevrolet motor cars or Players cigarettes. The full page
> advertisement created a sensation. A coupon under the advertisement
> asked the public to send in their names and a contribution to cover
> the expenses [similar images on page 288]. The results were so
> encouraging that we have since kept up a campaign of full page
> advertisements throughout the country. The advertisements have
> appeared in New York, Philadelphia, Washington, Chicago and Los
> Angeles at regular intervals. Other cities like Detroit, San Francisco,
> Houston (Texas), and others, have had one or two advertisements
> each. The results were astounding.[149]

The Committee boasted as its National Chairman Colorado Senator
Edwin C. Johnson, whom posterity remembers for an incongruous
Senate diatribe against the actress Ingrid Bergman for an extramarital
affair. The Committee, posing as a "non-sectarian, non-partisan,
American organization," composed a letter addressing only venerable
principles and sent it to one hundred men taken out of the *Who's
Who*. Ten replied. New stationery was then printed containing the
names of those ten prominent men (as though they were part of the
organization), and a second letter was sent to a thousand people. This
procedure was repeated several times.

Among their other tactics of self-promotion was the hijacking
of a religious day, what he described as "the most beautiful act of
sabotage that I have ever witnessed … Everyone got the impression
that the fasting, the mourning, the pious demonstration in the
synagogues … were all a part of the Jewish Army business." But he
is now, Jabotinsky tells his friend, "active in a new field: the saving of
the Jews of Europe," and this banner served the terror organization's
fund-raising for the next few years.[150]

Their various newspaper ads and publication *Memo* boasted
long lists of supporters and testimonials. Among the articles *Memo*
reproduced were overtly racist anti-Arab pieces by such then-popular

names as Dorothy Thompson and George Sokolsky. The Committee's own anti-Arab material painted the Palestinians with the mufti brush and alleged, ironically, that "Arabs" did not want democracy. Readers were encouraged to send money and to sign their petition demanding the creation of a Jewish army "based on Palestine."[151]

Full-page Irgun fund-raising ads simultaneously exploited antisemitism and dismissed any answer to the catastrophe in Europe other than a Zionist state in Palestine—the two were mutually reinforcing. Although "five million people are condemned to die," the Irgun warned in a 1943 *NY Times* ad, it quickly assured the reader that "America is not asked to open HER doors to the uprooted Jewish millions," but exclusively Palestine's doors. The New Zionist Organization of America used the same appeal to anti-Semitism: In a three-quarter page *NY Times* ad, it threatened that without a Jewish state in Palestine, "America will face increasing pressure to open her doors" to Jewish DPs. "It will be difficult for her to refuse."[152]

This tact did not take into account those in the US who might be quite happy to welcome Jews as their neighbors. For those people who fail to support Zionist aims, Irgun propaganda targeted their reputations: they were depicted as "lacking in humanitarianism, failing in Christianity, anti-Semitic, and by implication pro-Nazi."[153]

War-time intelligence on fascism in Palestine
At a time when the horrors of racial-nationalism in Europe were all too apparent, parallels to the variety evolving in Palestine were increasingly noted. Britain's War Cabinet warned that the Jewish settlers were becoming "more and more regimented on totalitarian lines," so that "any Jew who openly opposes the 'party line' is in personal danger."[154]

A report by US Intelligence in the Middle East, dated June 4, 1943, described "Zionism in Palestine" as

> a type of nationalism which in any other country would be stigmatized as retrograde Nazism. Indeed, the very same doctrine of blood and soil is being inculcated. It permeates the main Jewish systems of education.

As with so many other observers at the time, US intelligence wondered if Zionists "would have got further towards rescuing the unfortunates in Axis Europe, had they not complicated the question by always dragging Palestine into the picture."

Antisemitism, it reported, was essential to Zionism; and whereas "assimilated Jews in Europe and America are noted for being … stout opponents of racialism and discrimination," Zionism has instead bred "a spirit closely akin to Nazism, namely, an attempt to regiment the community, even by force, and to resort to force to get what they want."[155]

The fate of the German language weekly *Orient* was cited as an example. The journal's January 1943 issue condemned the "Yishuv Nazis" and their "super-Zionism," which it said were as bad as the super-nationalism of the German Reich; and in a February issue, the physicist Wolfgang Yourgrau attacked "the totalitarian monster" gripping the Jewish settlements, "even in the ranks of the Left parties."

Kiosks were bombed for selling non-Hebrew papers to Jews, and cafés and cinemas were bombed if they did not stay closed through to the end of the Sabbath. Anti-Gentilism was rife: "Tel Aviv barely tolerates other than Jews," the US report stated, "where they even object to the use of the cross on Red Cross ambulances passing through the town" (because of its Christian symbolism).[156]

Its authors assailed "the crude conception" being spread of the Palestinian people as "a nomad tent-dweller … with a little seasonal agriculture," as being "too absurd to need refutation." Citing the Palestinians' priority for education and interest in modern agricultural techniques, the report noted the irony that it was from them that Zionist settlers had learned the cultivation of Jaffa oranges. Indeed whereas the Palestinians were self-sufficient, the Zionists settlements exist on massive external financing, and should Jews overseas ever tire of supporting the settlers, "the venture will collapse like a pricked balloon."

The conclusion of this early US intelligence report was however premature. Now that the world "has seen the lengths to which the Nazi creed has carried the nations," it reasoned, the Zionists "are due to find themselves an anachronism."[157]

In late 1943, a campaign of meetings, plays, and songs was launched to encourage people to have more children, which was one of the Irgun's six "Commandments"—while a parallel campaign more aggressively sought to maintain Jewish "purity" by preventing friendships between Jews and non-Jews, presaging the Israeli state's laws against such "mixed" marriage.[158]

It is at this point that the Irgun began to dismiss the ongoing war against the Nazis as a reason to moderate its violence. As Begin would later explain, in late 1943 and early 1944 "it became obvious" that the Allied effort would not in itself lead to what he called a "Hebrew Nation" on both sides of the Jordan, and so their terror in Palestine resumed without regard for how it impacted the struggle against fascism.[159]

The sale of Palestine fails

The close of 1943 brought the rambling end of a four-year attempt to create a Zionist state by purchasing the entirety of Palestine for twenty million British pounds, payable to Saudi Arabia's Ibn Saud—who would have become Palestine's ultimate absentee landlord.

It was Churchill who had come up with the idea, and in the fall of 1939 suggested it to its obvious champion, Weizmann. The go-between for Ibn Saud was already in place, despite his opposition to Zionism: Harry St John Bridger Philby, explorer, writer, Arabist, and Colonial Office intelligence officer who since 1929 had been trying to make some accommodation between the Zionists and the Arab world—what had become known as the Philby Plan. Weizmann, meanwhile, sought support from President Roosevelt.

Yet by 1943, when Weizmann thought that the scheme might indeed work, he regretted limiting his "purchase" to the land west of the Jordan River (i.e., all of what is now Israel and Palestine). In December he wrote to Sumner Welles, who had just retired as Roosevelt's Under Secretary of State, hoping to add Transjordan to the tab. Limiting the purchase to the land west of the Jordan, he complained, would cut "our heritage … down to the bone."

There was another reason, Weizmann confided in Welles, that he wanted Jordan: owning the land east of the Jordan would help in the ethnic cleansing of non-Jews from Palestine—"facilitate transfers of population," as he put it.

In the end, however, Ibn Saud expressed great insult that Weizmann expected to "buy" him to betray the Palestinians. The deal was dead.[160]

A relative quiet of late 1943 was the calm before an ever-deadlier storm building from 1944 to statehood. After five bombs exploded in the truck park of Steel Brothers in Jaffa on the night of January 28-29, pamphlets dropped at the scene accused the firm of being "parasites of the foreign [British] government." The Irgun claimed responsibility for the attack in a letter to the Hebrew Press.

Jan–Feb 1944

Lehi, too, had been quiet, as many of its key people had been captured. But on October 31, some twenty Lehi operatives in the Latrun Detention Camp slipped to freedom through a 176 foot long tunnel they had bored. After three months' preparation, the terror organization was back in business.

St. Georges Cathedral—where Israeli whistleblower Mordechai Vanunu would sequester himself after his release from prison in 2004—was its target on February 3. At 3:00 in the morning, alerted by a Palestinian taxi driver, police found the bombers planting an electrically triggered device (an "infernal machine," as they described it) in the Cathedral wall. They escaped, murdering a Palestinian civilian who had assisted the police.[161]

Imaginative security-defeating tactics enabled the Irgun to bomb the Immigration Offices in Tel Aviv, Jerusalem, and Haifa. In Jerusalem, the building's guard was distracted with cries for help from a staged street attack. In Tel Aviv, a sympathetic locksmith supplied a key to an adjoining building, by which four Irgun operatives carried sacks of explosives over the roof. The ruse in Haifa was the most colorful: a decoy "couple" passed in deliberate view of the guard's post, then slipped into a nearby doorway and staged a wild sex encounter whose loud moaning was too much for the guard to resist investigating—at which the actual bombers slipped past, blowing up an air raid shelter and demolishing the building. The Irgun claimed credit for all three attacks, and in a pamphlet declared that its violence was a holy battle ... a sacred war, and God will help us ... The Jewish movement ... to establish its sovereignty over the entire land ... is based on our historic right, as we are the descendants and legal heirs of our forefathers, who lived in and governed this country for thousands of years .... [as Hebrews we are] the only persons to have the right to represent this country ... all non-Jewish bodies holding this country ... are our mortal enemies.[162]

The chief rabbi of Egypt reacted angrily to the ongoing "criminal, crazy actions" of the Zionists, while the Hebrew daily *Haboker* acknowledged that "we are living through a period of almost official admiration for underground activities," and the Irgun warned newspaper editors not to oppose them.

The Jewish Agency and the American Zionist organizations, meanwhile, financed a world-wide campaign to abrogate the White Paper, which they spun as "anti-Bible," and framed any impediment to funneling Jews *only* to Palestine as the final genocide—"before it is too late to save even the remnant," as the Jewish Agency put it.

Foretelling what would become the *modus operandi* of the Israeli state, British Political Intelligence in the Middle East (PICME) speculated that Zionists "would welcome if not actually provoke Arab reaction" to the terror, "in order that they might use the argument of self-defense against the Arabs as further justification for their own illegal acts." The Palestinians themselves, it noted, remained tolerant.[163]

On the night of January 14-15, the Irgun bombed government buildings in Jerusalem, and Lehi murdered two more police officers, Inspector Green and Constable Ewer. Lehi's successes continued with two more police assassinations on the 16th, but it failed twice on the 24th. The bomb that Lehi buried outside the garage of the Deputy Superintendent of Police exploded as he drove out, but he survived inside the wrecked vehicle. Similarly, when Lehi operatives connected wires to detonate their roadside bomb some sixty meters (200 ft) away, the targeted car blew up, but its four occupants, which included two inspectors and a sergeant, all survived their injuries, shock, and deafness.

A third roadside device was discovered before it was tripped. The British analyzed it: a cocktail composed of five hand grenades made in the United States, plus thirty-three sticks of gelignite, ammunition, nuts, and bolts. Further bombings struck the Income Tax Offices in Tel Aviv, Haifa, and Jerusalem on February 26-27. The Irgun posted pamphlets in Haifa claiming responsibility.[164]

Political Terrorism Rises in Palestine, read the headline to a February 26 *NY Times* article about "terrorist activity … in favor of extremist Jewish nationalist demands." The paper's publisher, Arthur Sulzberger, was among the prominent American Jews opposed to those extremist demands and who refused to finance the Irgun's operations. In response, Bergson's solicitations for money now distinguished between the "Hebrew nation" and the "Hebrew race." Jews could contribute to help save "stateless Hebrews from oppression" without considering themselves "Hebrew nationalists." The move appears to have helped Irgun coffers: later that year (1944), an informant for the British reported that "Bergson's group of racketeers known as the 'Hebrew Committee of National Liberation' [have] succeeded in collecting large sums of money by posing as refugee organizations and exploiting gullibility of American public."[165]

Hiking parties increase

It is around this time that the Jewish Agency's reconnaissance expeditions begin to figure more prominently in British records. Photographs of Palestinian villages taken by the hikers were processed by a secret photography lab fronting as an irrigation company, and mapping was led by a Hebrew University topographer who, as it happened, also worked as a cartographer for the British. Information collected included topographic location of each village, its access roads, quality of land, springs, main sources of income, socio-political composition, religious affiliations, names of the village leaders, ages of individual men, and an index of its hostility toward the Zionist project—everything needed to determine "how best to attack" the villages, in the words of one such hiker. Once these basics were tallied, details were expanded to encompass husbandry, cultivation, the number of trees, quality of fruit groves, average land holding per family, number of cars, names of shop owners, members of work-shops, and the names of the artisans and their skills. When 1948 came, the Zionist armies already had photographs, maps, plans, and meticulous statistics about the villages and villagers they would erase.

These hiking parties also served two immediate needs: the data collected enabled the Haganah to conduct more accurate simulated assaults on Palestinian villages, and the hikes themselves camouflaged movement to and from hidden military training settlements, such as Ayelet HaShahar. Three such intelligence-gathering groups were discovered spying on Palestinian villages during the first week of February, 1944.[166]

March
1944

March was marked by Jewish protests over a new Palestinian restaurant in Jerusalem. The problem was the name: "Palestine Restaurant." As reported in the then-popular paper *Hatzofeh*, an Arab business' use of the name *Palestine* was "a deliberate insult to the Jewish public."

March also brought a new spree of assassinations of policemen. One was shot in the back by Lehi in Tel Aviv on the 2nd, Jewish constable Zev Flesch was murdered on the 13th in Petah Tikvah, more constables were murdered on the 15th and 18th, and there were further attacks on police on the 21st.

The 23rd was the deadliest day of the month for policemen—eight were murdered by the Irgun in Tel Aviv, Haifa, and Jaffa—but Jaffa's toll would have been much higher had a bomb not been discovered in the air raid shelter below police headquarters. Everyone was evacuated before several explosions ripped through it, completely demolishing one end of the building. All three cities' CID (Criminal Investigation Department) offices were blown up by bombers using such guises as doctors and barbers.[167]

Thanks to an unexpected informer—an ex-Irgun member named Jankelis Chilevicius—the police had fifty Irgun members under arrest within the week. However, "Zionist institutions and Yishuv generally," High Commissioner MacMichael reported, "have given no (repeat no) assistance in suppressing these political fanatics partly, no doubt, through fear, but also because, to some extent, they sympathize with them." Support for terrorism was reinforced by the Jewish Agency's "intense Nationalist drive … for years past through the education of the young, and platform propaganda." The "terrorists regard themselves as the chosen instruments" of Zionist goals. Both the Agency and the terrorists exploit the world's

> sympathy for Jewish suffering, and humanitarian urge to do everything possible to relieve it, and [the resulting] readiness to make every possible concession to [the Zionist] viewpoint.[168]

Responding to charges that the Agency shielded terrorism, Ben-Gurion accused the British of conspiracy: he claimed that the British deliberately failed to catch the Jewish terrorists so that they could punish all Jews in Palestine. The Jewish Agency, meanwhile, was mandating terms to the British to secure its cooperation against terror—conditions that the British found "to say the least of it, amazing," and tantamount to a "condonation of crime." The terms required that the British agree neither to search for terrorists nor to search the settlements for arms, and in exchange, the Agency would share information if it wished to.

Despite the chaos, Zionism's British supporters continued to boast that Zionism is "a virtual gift to the Empire," in the words of the Anglo-Palestinian Club, and that the British Empire's strength "is in direct proportion to the extent of Jewish immigration."[169]

In the US, the Democrats had been the traditional guarantors of Zionist support, but the Irgun now began playing that party off against its rival Republicans, forcing a competition for more vocal support. The NZO's "Resettlement Committee" was busy enlisting the US to endorse "the transfer of [non-Jewish] populations" out of Palestine. According to a NZO letter seized by the British en route to Irgun member Abraham Abrahams in London—who later would emerge as a key figure in domestic terrorism in Britain—the organization's plans for forced transfer now had the endorsement of four hundred "important representatives of American public opinion," perhaps garnered through Eri Jabotinsky's list.

The Republican Party, hoping to one-up the Democrats, announced its demand for unlimited Jewish immigration into Palestine, and in the UK the Labour Party outdid both US parties, issuing a declaration for the (implicitly compulsory) transfer of the non-Jewish population out of Palestine.

Labour's April resolution, formally adopted at the party's annual December conference, read in part:

> But there is surely neither hope nor meaning in a 'Jewish National Home', unless we are prepared to let Jews, if they wish, enter this tiny land in such numbers as to become a majority... [and so] for transfer of [non-Jewish] population. Let the Arabs be encouraged to move out, as the Jews move in.

Labour further proposed ethnically cleansing non-Jews from parts of Egypt, Syria, and Jordan for the Zionists: "Indeed, we should reexamine also the possibility of extending the present Palestinian boundaries" into those countries. Notwithstanding the polite language of Palestinians being "encouraged to move out," the meaning was clear: in the words of Gaza District Commissioner WR McGeagh, it was a declaration "in favour of the compulsory transfer of the Arab Population of Palestine."

The Palestinians were, in MacMichael's words, "genuinely shocked" that "the chosen representatives of a large segment of the British public" could advocate removing them from their homeland for the benefit of the settlers. They were also alarmed at the Zionists' obvious influence: until now, Palestinians who "had been inclined to regard Zionist propaganda abroad with little more than irritation, are now thoroughly alarmed at what they regard as this new manifestation of its effectiveness."[170]

April–July 1944

Lehi used a grenade to kill a sergeant on the first day of April (1944), attacked two constables the 5th, and failed in an assassination attempt on two British constables at the Northern Police Station in Tel Aviv on the 9th despite the use of firearms and explosives. Only one of several police assassination attempts in Tel Aviv the next day was successful.[171]

Palestine's Jewish civil servants were particular targets of Lehi. A pamphlet the gang distributed in May included a Black List of

Jewish policemen, and one on the list was already assassinated on the 10ᵗʰ with gunshots and a bomb.

Mortars and "rearguard action" were used against the Police Fort on May 17, and in the evening "some 40 armed Jews from the coastal area" hijacked the broadcasting station in Ramallah and ambushed the police when they arrived, but the attack was disrupted by the happenstance appearance of an Arab taxi that ran their blockade. The attackers questioned the station operator in Hebrew without success, then shot up the control desk and two aerials.[172]

That same evening, about thirty Jews described as wearing khaki shirts and shorts placed wooden boards studded with nails on the road. As a taxi with three Palestinians came to a halt from blown tires, the attackers ignited explosives under the vehicle, knocking it off the road. Although the occupants survived the blast, the Jews fired on them as they fled, hitting two of them.

Nail-studded boards was the method *du jour*. Some hours later, at about 2:30 A.M. on May 18, a police patrol northeast of Lydda returned fire to six attackers, damaging their truck, whereupon they slipped into the darkness. Shortly afterwards, two more trucks came from the same direction, stopped, and "about eighteen persons of both sexes got out and ran away." In all three trucks the police found gelignite and boards studded with nails, as had been used earlier to disable the Palestinian taxi. The attackers acquired the trucks by commissioning their owners for work outside of town, who on arrival were "attacked, removed from their trucks and bound."

Gelignite bombs, grenades, tommy guns, and automatic pistols were the method on the night of July 13-14, as two Palestinians were killed and a Jewish constable critically wounded in the bombing of the District Police Headquarters and Land Registry Offices. The militants entered dressed as police, then shot the guards as others in plain clothes carried in the explosives. The Irgun "boastfully claimed" responsibility. The next day (July 15), the gang hijacked an explosives truck and murdered a constable. More bombings followed on July 28.[173]

"It cannot be denied," the Commissioner's Offices in Jaffa reported that month, "that the recent outrage of the Irgun Zvai Leumi has increased their reputation enormously amongst Jewish youth," and further successes would "considerably enlarge their field for recruits." The Chief Secretary in Jerusalem, similarly, reported that a large segment of the settlements' youth "looks upon these terrorists as the *Kanaim* [holy warriors] of modern times." Palestinians continued to die in Zionist attacks, and this "has inevitably increased Arab hostility towards everything Jewish."[174]

Zionism vs Allied successes

Setbacks to the Nazi armies during the summer of 1944 caused some concern that Zionism would suffer a setback in turn. "In political circles," the Chief Secretary in Jerusalem wrote, "there appears to be some tendency to fear that Nazi oppression will end before it has been possible to obtain permission for large numbers of Jewish refugees to enter Palestine on that account." Similarly, MacMichael reported that Agency leaders were trying to "utilize all remaining vacancies" of the White Paper's 75,000 permits quickly, in order to create an immigration crisis "while the refugee problem is still acute."

Ben-Gurion as well appeared to be addressing the Nazi setbacks when, lecturing in Tel Aviv on April 2, he warned that the defeat of the Axis would not end the threat against Jews—indeed the Allied victory against the Nazis would make matters *worse*, bringing "mounting anti-Semitism" and "many other countries" ready to enact "Hitler's solution."[175]

The Jewish Brigade

Ben-Gurion's biggest success of the summer of 1944 was Churchill's creation of the Jewish Brigade, under intense pressure from the United States but against the overwhelming advice of Churchill's own military.[176]

The alleged rationale for an all-Jewish army was that it would afford Jews dignity in the fight against the Nazis. British generals, however, argued that a segregated brigade was strategically inefficient and only exacerbated the struggle against the Nazis. Jews, they noted, already served in the British military along with everyone else.

What, in truth, was the push for a segregated Jewish army? The military view was that the Zionists wanted a Jews-only army for two reasons unrelated to the Nazis: one, to claim that the segregated Jewish army had been a *de facto* acknowledgment of a Jewish nationality (and thus of a Jewish state); and two, to have the British create a professionally trained Zionist army to be better prepared to take Palestine by force after the war. And so this Brigade ostensibly created to participate in the fight against ethnic nationalism in Europe, was in truth created to help install ethnic nationalism in Palestine.[177]

Writing eloquently against the Brigade, the noted Russian-born American philosopher and legal scholar Morris Cohen warned that "the complete moral bankruptcy of racialist nationalism [i.e., which Zionism adopted] has been made obvious by Nazi Germany" and condemned as "anti-Semitic [the] contention that the Jews are a foreign national group everywhere except in Palestine."

A Memorandum to the War Cabinet said much the same. The Zionists' true purpose was a state based on ethnic supremacy:

> It is clear from both the public and private utterances of the Zionist leaders that … they do not want a joint Jew and Arab state. They want a purely Jewish state, and they are determined to get it, by any means in their power. That is the motive underlying the agitation for a Jewish army … [The Palestinians] will have no share in the government of the country—that will be reserved entirely for Jews. We must face the fact that this is their conception, and that they will accept no other.

Sixty-two US rabbis signed a press statement condemning the idea of a segregated Brigade—it would, they said, further "add to the unhappy plight of our stricken people."

By late January 1944, however, Internal War Office correspondence concedes that "we can no longer use the argument that an implication of a Jewish state would be a prejudgement," because "the writing is on the wall" that there will be such a state (*Surely Babylon*, another penciled in).

Weizmann wrote to Churchill on the 9th of February, imploring him to "give the Jews their national name, emblems, and military organisation." He linked this to the question of "Jewish participation in the war effort" with the usual stipulation that Jews would not enlist as equals, but only as Jews, and only with other Jews.[178]

As the Jewish Brigade was formalized in the summer of 1944, the expansion into Lebanon and Syria of the yet-to-be-established Zionist state was being pursued. An emissary of the Jewish National Fund was sent that summer to the Lebanese and Syrian governments "for extensions of the Fund's activities to those territories," as MacMichael put it, while Ben-Gurion boasted to the Jewish Agency that after taking Palestine by force of arms, "if the country be too small, we shall expand its boundaries."[179]

Aug–
Sept
1944

On August 8, MacMichael left Jerusalem for Jaffa, his vehicle escorted by police fore and aft. At a sharp bend on a cliff the little entourage was ambushed with US-made grenades and gunfire by about twelve Lehi members disguised as a surveying party. The driver was shot in the neck and lost control of the vehicle, but an officer next to him grabbed the wheel and directed the car to a bank. Another passenger was shot in the lungs, while MacMichael received minor bullet wounds. This was the gangs' seventh assassination attempt on MacMichael, and their last chance: it was his final day on the job.

Police followed the assailants to Givat Shaul settlement, where they were blocked by the settlers from apprehending them, just as police had been blocked from apprehending Lehi members said to be hiding near a settlement at Beit Dajan three days earlier.[180]

This was the continuation of a long pattern of the settlers protecting terrorists. Such were the "severe disorders" greeting any attempt by the police to pursue terrorists into the settlements that a year earlier, MacMichael himself, though considered a hardliner, decreed that no further searches of Jewish settlements would be made, for fear of all-out rebellion.

With this brazen assassination attempt, however, the British put renewed pressure on the Jewish Agency for cooperation. The Agency responded with the offer to ask for volunteers to help the British. At the same time, "open and almost boastful pronouncements regarding the achievement of maximum Zionist aims in Palestine" were coming from the settlements. As for the Palestinians, MacMichael wrote that they "are showing increased concern at the audacity and strength of the Jewish terrorist organization, which they fear will ultimately be used against themselves."[181]

Coordinated attacks on August 22 against the Jaffa Divisional Police Headquarters and two Police Stations on the Jaffa–Tel Aviv border took two officers' lives. After mining and booby-trapping approach roads and rail crossings to kill or delay first responders, three separate parties, each about a dozen men, attacked with bombs, grenades, and sub machine guns.

An attack on the Eastern Police Station on September 27 killed one, and ten were injured when the militants blew up their truck with a land mine. Four police stations—Haifa, Qalqilya, Beit Dajan (Beth Dagon), and Qataa (Qatara)—were attacked the next day, "planned and executed by a force estimated to have been at least 150 strong and armed with bombs and automatic weapons." Four Palestinians were murdered in the attacks. Lehi assassinated Police superintendent J.T. Wilkin in Jerusalem on September 29.[182]

A £P100,000 Irgun theft of textiles on October 6 was used in part to finance a bunker for the terror group's commander, Menachem Begin, whom the Haifa police chief described as "a ruthless thug who made Al Capone* look like a novice." Palestinians continued to be attacked by "bands of Jewish youth" on the seashore, while Tel Aviv was "buzzing with a rumor that His Majesty's Government is going to bring in partition."[183]

Oct 1944

Partition, again

The War Office, indeed, was secretly discussing Partition by late 1943. This much is not surprising—the British needed a fig leaf to extricate themselves from the chaos they'd empowered. What is remarkable is that already in November 1943, the War Cabinet is already suggesting that the Palestinians—what it refers to as the "Arab residue"—would

---

* Infamous Chicago gangster who was imprisoned in 1932.

be merged into one of the "adjoining Arab states." Four years to the month before the UN's Partition Resolution, some British planners are already talking about a partition that they never intend to come to pass. This co-existed with the presumption of partition as legitimate, forming two states.

The British withheld the news that they'd settled on Partition as their escape because it could not spare the troops to handle the violent reaction it expected. They were keenly aware that the "extremists dominating the [Jewish] Agency" would resist Partition "with the forces at their disposal—forces which past experience and recent intelligence (on the HAGANA) has shown to be both fanatical and well disciplined."[184]

Rumors of partition spread quickly. The implacably messianic Weizmann condemned the rumors with the lament that "Pharaoh once offered us to make bricks without straw"—the word *us* ensuring that twentieth-century European Jewry had been plucked out of the Old Testament but had left the page about the Pharaoh dog-eared. It was however the British on the ground who proved to be the prophets, worrying that Partition would cause the "extremist Jewish element" to "raise the excuse of Arab outrages" in order to take whatever portion of the land is allotted to the Palestinians.[185]

Allied struggle impeded by Zionist violence

Throughout the war years, Zionist violence was an encumbrance on the battle against the Axis power, both because of the manpower and resources diverted to dealing with the attacks, and because of the Zionists' pilfering of Allied arms and munitions. As a British report from October lamented, relentless Jewish terrorism is the "sabotage of the general effort of the United Nations* in their life-and-death struggle against the worst enemy that Jewry has ever known."

Hoping that the specter of a Nazi victory would move the Zionists to stop the terror, the British beseeched the settlers in

---

* "United Nations" here refers to the Allied Nations, not the UN, which was established in late 1945.

print and over the airwaves:

> Palestine … has enjoyed five years of virtual immunity from the horrors of war … Palestine has however been the scene of a series of outrageous crimes of violence by Jewish terrorists, acting with the deliberate intention of bringing about by force developments favourable to the realization of political aims … These events are proceeding side by side with the bitterest phase of the critical fighting between the United Nations and Nazi Germany.[186]

Yet the British on the ground reported increasing "numbers of Jewish young men and women who are becoming infected with the gangster virus [providing] recruits for the terrorist organisation" in order to force the "maximalist aims [of] a Jewish state covering all Palestine and ultimately Trans-Jordan." Youth are nurtured by the

> propagandist nature of much teaching in Jewish schools, the Youth Movement (unpleasantly reminiscent of the Hitler Youth), and the totalitarian organisation and regimentation of the Yishuv by the agency of the Histadruth, etc. These things constitute the negation of free thought and speech.[187]

The Palestinians, meanwhile, "are losing their lives, here and there, in small numbers, at Jewish hands in the course of terrorist operations." As reported by the Jerusalem District Commissioner's Office in October,

> The killing of Arabs by Jewish terrorists, and the distribution of Arabic copies of notices by the Irgun Zvai Leumi threatening that the hands of any Arabs raised against the Jewish [Zionist] cause would be cut off is creating an atmosphere of tension and hatred comparable with that of [the Palestinian uprising of] 1938-39.[188]

The Irgun posted pamphlets in principal Arab towns announcing that it was the Palestinians' "new government," and warning in what the British described as "offensive terms" that they must not interfere with its operations.

Yet the Palestinians maintained their collective refusal to respond in kind. As the Chief Secretary of Lydda District reported,

> It is noticeable that the continuance of Jewish terrorist outrages has not so far provoked the Arabs to retaliation...[189]

When the moment was right, the War Office predicted, the settlers would increase their violence to elicit a reprisal. There was evidence that

> whatever course the Zionist leaders may adopt, they will deliberately provoke Arab reaction to it, in order to increase the justification for the use of force in 'self-defence'.[190]

Two days after a Palestinian policeman from Gaza was murdered, "a party of about sixty Jews from a neighbouring settlement chose to pay a visit to Gaza and parade through the streets," yet the Palestinians resisted the taunt. Their restraint, the British observed, was largely due to their awareness that they would "be playing into the hands of Jewish propagandists." Similar remarks came independently from the Chief Secretary in Jerusalem in October: "not even the deeds and propaganda of Jewish terrorism" have driven the Palestinians to respond in kind.[191]

Jews with political sense "draw a parallel" between Zionist militancy and "the rise of Nazism, and express the fear that the groups are gaining an increasing number of adherents amongst the youth." Jewish terrorism "is becoming so much a part of the every-day life of Palestine that the average Jew is showing little interest so long as he is left undisturbed himself." Yet the British continued to fear that forceful attempts to stop the terrorism would unleash retaliation from "Zionist circles both within and without Palestine" that it could not control.[192]

Hiking parties continued their surveillance preparing for the coming reckoning. Twenty-eight hikers from the Emek settlements scouting the lands east of Jenin were stopped on October 23, followed five days later by two more parties totaling thirty hikers. More such surveillance teams were recorded by the Commissioner's Offices in Nablus, which noted their cameras and anti-personnel grenades. Arab

Legion* soldiers arrested yet more hikers in Galilee District but, as described by the Galilee District Commissioner, the soldiers diffused the incident by "entertaining the hikers to dinner and immediately releasing the insolent Jews on arrival at the camp."[193]

Walter Guinness, 1ˢᵗ Baron Moyne

November 6 brought the first Zionist assassination outside of Palestine. As Lord Moyne, the British Minister of State in the Middle East, reached home in Cairo at 1:10 that afternoon, two Lehi operatives jumped out from hiding. *Don't move*, one demanded in what Capt. Andrew Hughes-Onslow, who had exited the Packard saloon car, described as "English, without any noticeable trace of accent." One thrust the barrel of his gun into the open window and shot Moyne three times, firing "separately and slowly." The driver, who had gone to open the car door for Moyne, lay dying on the ground. The killers escaped on bicycle as per their plan but were spotted by a policeman on motorcycle. Both were captured.[194]

Nov
1944

Moyne, heir to the brewing firm Guinness, was a target because of his criticism of political Zionism. Two years before his assassination, he succinctly pinpointed the Palestine problem in the House of Lords:

> The Zionist claim has raised two burning issues: firstly, the demand for large-scale immigration into an already overcrowded country, and, secondly, racial domination by these newcomers over the original inhabitants.

To charges of antisemitism and innuendos of Nazism, Moyne replied that

> If a comparison is to be made with the Nazis it is surely those who wish to force an imported regime upon the Arab population …

---

* The Arab Legion was an army formed and led by the British in 1920 to defend the Transjordan region occupied by Britain after World War I. It played an important role in the fight against the Axis powers in World War II under Sir John Bagot Glubb, the British soldier and scholar who commanded the Legion from 1939 to 1956, when it became the Jordanian army.

[the] proposal that Arabs should be subjugated by force to a Jewish regime is inconsistent with the Atlantic Charter, and that ought to be told to America.[195]

Lehi cited two further reasons for his murder: to demonstrate its policy of personal terror as a warning to others, and to use a high-profile assassination to promote its demands on the global stage.

A massive media effort by American Zionists to depict the assassins as "martyrs" and grant them a reprieve failed, even after garnering support from US politicians and figures as public as Arturo Toscanini. The two were tried and hanged.[196]

With Moyne's assassination, the Jewish Agency found itself under international pressure to demonstrate that it was acting against the terror. In a campaign commonly remembered as "the season," the Haganah employed what the British called "unconventional attempts to extract information" from Irgun members—though Moyne's assassins were Lehi, and the cooperation was viewed as "largely political," an opportunity to eliminate "persons obnoxious to the Agency on party grounds." As MI5 put it, the Agency fought terror "when it suited their political book."

Ben-Gurion and Weizmann publicly expressed outrage at Moyne's assassination, while maintaining non-cooperation. Rabbi Fishman (Yehuda Leib Maimon), future Israeli MP, persevered in the view that "under no circumstances should we permit co-operation with the Government" in fighting terrorism, and Yitzhak Gruenbaum, who would become first Interior Minister of Israel, described Moyne's assassins as "nothing less than national partisans." Palestine's chief Ashkenazi Rabbi Herzog declared that handing over terror suspects to the authorities was against Biblical Law.

When in 1975 Egypt returned their bodies to Israel, the two assassins were hailed as "heroic freedom fighters," given a state funeral, and laid in state in the Jerusalem Hall of Heroism. In 1982 Israel issued postal stamps honoring them.[197]

4

Fascism: Axis falls, Zionism rises

> "The weeks and months following the collapse of the Hitler
> régime will be a time of uncertainty in Europe and even more so
> in Palestine, and we must exploit this period in order to
> confront Britain and America with a fait accompli."
> —*Ben-Gurion, speaking in February, 1943* [198]

United States President Roosevelt died on April 12, 1945, before the Allied victory against the Nazis was complete. The new president, Harry Truman, took office on the eve of that victory—and on the eve of plans by the Jewish Agency to exploit the post-war fatigue and confusion. He inherited the Zionists' "Nazi type of gangsterism" in Palestine, to quote Lord Moyne's successor, James Grigg, and their shift of focus from London to Washington, DC.

Sharett's opinion of Truman was likely typical among the Jewish Agency: he was a malleable, "naive diplomat," and as the British observed, the Zionists "feel that their influence in the U.S.A. is sufficiently strong to keep the new president on the right lines." [199]

At least two years before the Allied victory, Ben-Gurion was looking ahead to exploit its aftermath to further Zionism's goals by force. As recorded by the British:

> Mr BEN GURION and other extremist leaders have on several
> occasions warned the HAGANA that the fight for the Jews will

begin when the war against GERMANY ends, and have urged them, citing the occupation of VILNA by the Poles after the last war as a precedent, to exploit the confusion and war weariness of the post war period [to create] a fait accompli.

In preparation for exploiting that post-war weariness, Ben-Gurion fixated on the urgency for human facts-on-the-ground. In a war-time article entitled "The Time Factor in Zionism," he called for

a large immigration, the transfer of masses of people to Palestine … We must consolidate every one of our existing positions. Every area of land already in our possession must be settled immediately … we must bring in immigrants from all possible countries by every means.[200]

To learn what the Irgun was planning, Ex-Irgun informant Jankelis Chilevicius was now secreted to the United States to infiltrate the Bergson organization. Code-named Y 32, he trusted only a certain Catling, a member of the Palestine Police, to confide his identity, and so Catling went to the US to get Y 32's report in person.

Meeting in New York on the first day of October, Y 32 told Catling that the Irgun "has plans far advanced for a full-scale Jewish up-rising in Palestine, scheduled to begin some two or three months after Germany is defeated." Palestine would be "denuded of British troops, and a fair number of Jewish [Brigade] troops [would be] back in Palestine." The Irgun and Lehi would seize key positions: the Ramallah Broadcasting Station, Jerusalem General Post Office, Secretariat, and the government offices in Jerusalem, Haifa, and Tel Aviv.

"Should troops be used against them," he reported of the Irgun's thinking,

the propaganda value of a wail that British soldiers were killing Jews in their own homeland would turn world opinion in their favour.

More worryingly, Y 32 told Catling that "Jews in the armed forces are heavily involved"—that there are Zionist plants in the British military.

Independent confirmation of a planned post-war blitz came from a Cairo prison cell six months later (April 1945) when Yacov Meridor, a former Irgun commander, boasted to a prison warden that he "must be in Palestine by V-Day" to take part in the plan, because "it will be the greatest day in Palestine's history."[201]

Thus when in the early afternoon of May 7, the BBC broadcast announcing the unconditional surrender of Germany was heard in Haifa, Palestine entered a new dynamic. Bands of Jewish youth celebrated the two mornings following the Allied victory by parading through the Wadi Salib Arab quarter in Haifa with Zionist flags, taunting the Palestinians until being stopped by the police.

May–
Aug
1945

Coordinated mortar attacks the Irgun had planned for the night of May 13 were foiled, but not its campaign of telegraph pole bombings: fifty-seven were hit on May 14-15. A malfunction largely spared the telegraph route north of Hadera: only six of the many bombs ignited. On May 16, militants bombed the Lydda Police Station and Tel Aviv Police post, and tried to bomb PMF Camp Sarona but the device exploded outside. Two more mortar bombs missed the Jaffa police station, and more than 200 telegraph poles were found rigged with explosives, most near Lydda.

The communications blitz continued with the destruction of lines on the Tel Aviv–Jerusalem road on May 17, the Haifa-Lydda road on May 18, near Givat Shaul and Mikve-Israel on May 21, and the sabotage of government lines on May 22. The next day bombs severed oil pipelines belonging to the Iraq Petroleum Company in two places near Indur in Galilee District, and the pipelines were bombed again on May 25 near Haifa. Police in Sarona were attacked on May 26, and mortars loaded with incendiary projectiles were discovered in a nearby orange grove.

There was, however, a noteworthy act of resistance: on May 13 a truck containing four mortars, detonators, gelignite, and "73 anti personnel blast" was apprehended by members of the Kfar Hassidim orthodox settlement near Haifa and turned over to police. Meanwhile, reconnaissance hiking parties discovered in the Nablus area "provoked comment but no incidents" among the Palestinians.[202]

When in response to the escalation in sabotage the British again pressed Sharett for cooperation, he now "admitted that the majority of the [Jewish] community was not necessarily so opposed to these activities as to make them willing to assist in their suppression." Weizmann continued to argue against Partition, and continued to do so as if he were an oracle for the Scriptures:

> The choice made by destiny cannot be undone. Palestine is the Jewish people's birthplace, and it gave birth to no other. It owes its place in history to the Jews and to no other people … the curse of homelessness must be lifted from the entire race.

Teddy Kollek, a future mayor of Jerusalem, began to figure importantly as a source for the British. Known as "Scorpion," his mission was enigmatic, sometimes behaving as a diplomat or go-between, as if seeking credibility with the British in order to contain the most serious suspicions about the Jewish Agency. He is believed to have informed against the Irgun and Lehi, whether independently or on the Agency's behalf.

In the summer of 1945 Kollek spoke about the relationships among the three terror organizations, that "there can be no question" of cooperation, that neither the Irgun nor Lehi "was willing to lose its identity" to the Haganah. While it was true that the militias coveted their individual identities, the evidence already suggested that, as a British defense report described it, "the Hagana will have a lot of its dirty work done for it, without carrying any responsibility," by having the Irgun carry out attacks which the Jewish Agency then "condemns." In a few months, an intercepted telegram would prove Haganah-Irgun collaboration was already in progress, and by the following June the Irgun would be openly cheering its collaboration with the Haganah and Lehi.

While Kollek was being cautiously courted by the British, the Jewish Agency sought to ingratiate him in London as without political investment. He was a true friend of the British who "has lots of Arab friends"—to quote the draft for an article the Jewish Agency considered planting in the gossip column of one of the major London newspapers.[203]

Kollek was probably the source of a tip that led the British on June 13 to discover a loaded triple mortar battery behind the YMCA at Jerusalem, "aligned in the direction of the King David building, the saluting base area for the King's birthday parade."This break followed a day in which they thwarted a mortar attack apparently intended to destroy the government printing press in Jerusalem, but failed to stop the Irgun(?) from blowing up a bridge on the Bejaz line and exploding more pamphlet bombs.[204]

On July 13, "a lorry containing 500 lbs of high explosives intended for use in a quarry was ambushed in daylight by ten armed Jews near Petah Tiqva." Constable Wilde, escorting the truck, was murdered, and the explosives vanished, raising the suspicion that Temporary Additional Constables (TAC) were themselves Irgun or "had been squared by them."

Police dogs followed the scent to the orange groves of Givat Hash Shelosha settlement near Petah Tiqva. As had become routine, when the settlers refused to cooperate, the British authorities ordered the police to call off the search because "any attempt to search the Jewish settlement would lead to severe disorder."[205]

Two of the policemen nevertheless continued to hunt for their colleague's murderers and the stolen explosives, but were again stopped by their superiors. In frustration, they wrote to the British government recounting the inexplicable end of their investigation. "Two of the under-signed," the letter summarized,

> were in the search which, after discovering ample evidence, was called off, for no accountable reason, when on the point of discovering more, and better, evidence.

Several policemen reported this calling-off of the pursuit of Zionist terrorists, and many complained bitterly of the severe restrictions placed on their right to defend themselves against the Zionists. In each case, their superiors cited two reasons for overriding their concerns: fear of an insurrection from the Zionists if the terrorists were pursued into the settlements, and fear of handing them a propaganda windfall in the United States.[206]

Lehi joined forces with the Irgun on July 23 to bomb the railway bridge on the Haifa-Cairo line near Yavne. The collaboration continued two days later when the combined terror groups blew up a five-span girder bridge on four stone piers on the main Kantara-Lydda line near Yibna, between Gaza and Lydda. Police dogs traced the scent to three Jewish colonies—again in vain. Another government vehicle carrying explosives vanished to an Irgun hijacking the next day.[207]

In the US, the Irgun's Bergson Group had so woven itself into American life that on the first day of August a retiring US Senator, Guy Gillette, became the new president of the terror organization's American League for a Free Palestine, and chief political adviser to its so-called Hebrew Committee of National Liberation.

In Palestine, "a large party of armed Jews," numbering "between 30 and 90, including several women," attacked an explosives store on August 13, stealing 450 lbs of gelignite, fuses, and detonators. Joseph Davidescu, formerly with military intelligence, was assassinated on August 22 as he chatted with a neighbor at the kitchen table.

Twenty-four years earlier, Davidescu had been convicted of perjury for protecting a Zionist arms-smuggling ring, but Lehi had now suspected him of gathering intelligence on them.[208]

Meanwhile the Zionists' own intelligence-gathering hiking missions intensified with the Allied victory. In the north, the district commissioner's office in Nablus reported that

> apprehension has been aroused there by the activities of large Jewish walking parties, who, it is claimed, were equipped with pistols and cameras. It is popularly believed that the role of these parties is to "spy out the land".

And in the south,

> In Beersheba Sub-District anti-Jewish feeling which has in the past been comparatively mild has recently become much intensified. The chief reason for this is the large number of Jewish hiking parties which have been operating lately in the Negeb and which as regarded

by the Arabs as foreshadowing further infiltration and settlement.*[209]

Out of their office at 55 W 42nd Street in Manhattan, in September the United Zionists-Revisionists of America now advocated a further method to exploit post-war vulnerability: the group issued the first calls for the boycott of Britain, economically devastated by the war against Hitler, until it accedes to their demands.

Sept
1945

After a failed robbery of the Palestine Discount Bank in Tel Aviv on September 2 by "a party of Jews" (Irgun), British officials, nervous over rumors that terror attacks were planned for mid-September, arranged another meeting with Teddy Kollek. "Despite the lull at the present time," Kollek told them, "the N.M.O. [Irgun] particularly were very active indeed … generally putting their house in order." Enlarging their dwindling stockpile of explosives was high on their to-do list, explaining the recent rash of such thefts.

The Irgun and Lehi were "feverishly training new recruits, particularly in such fine arts as shadowing," and the Irgun was perfecting its new 40 kilo (88 lb) mortar known as "V.3."—presumably the type discovered behind the YMCA on June 12. More accurate and with a longer range, the gang was planting them in pre-arranged positions for use at later dates. Due to political deliberations underway in London, the Jewish Agency told the Irgun and Lehi to "pedal slowly," and so the two militias were likely to engage only in robbery during the coming few weeks.[210]

Irgun-Lehi collaboration was corroborated by Irgun documents seized five months later, on February 28 1946, during a British raid on 45 Zichron Moshe Street (Jerusalem). One document codified an Irgun-Lehi agreement to carry out attacks in Palestine "or outside, if necessary," and celebrated their first joint operation, the destruction of the bridge at Yibna (presumably the July 23 sabotage), "the results of which have been described by news agencies and broadcasting systems throughout the world as an attack on one of the most vital roadways of British imperialism by units of the National Military

---

* This report from the Gaza District Commissioner refers to "a separate report [that] has been submitted to you on the subject" of the hikers, but which the author has not been able to locate.

Organisation [Irgun] and Stern Group [Lehi] under their respective commanders."[211]

Five pamphlet bombs "of a larger size than hitherto exploded in various parts of Jerusalem" on September 15, injuring nine people (all Jewish), as the Irgun also shot dead a constable in an attempted robbery. A bridge was bombed four days later, as was an armored car escorting diamonds. Another constable was murdered outside the Tel Aviv Post Office on the 28th.[212]

September's most disturbing news came with the British intercept of a message sent by Moshe Sneh, head of the Hagana, to the Jewish Agency's London office. It again proved the Agency's direct hand in terror, and suggested that Kollek's informing on the Irgun and Lehi was competition control rather than terror control. The message spoke of causing a "serious incident" that would be merely a warning of "much more serious incidents" to come if the British failed to heed the Zionists' demands, incidents that would involve an Irgun-Lehi alliance and "threaten the safety of all British interests in the country."

With September's surrender of Japan ending the war, Weizmann turned to reparations and demanded that they go directly to the Jewish Agency. His argument went as follows: The victim of the war was "the Jewish people as a whole"; that what happened is "without parallel in the history of mankind"; and that the Jewish Agency is "the [sole] representative of the Jewish people" (to this last point, a Foreign Office official penciled in *we do not admit this—nor do many Jews*). Weizmann also proposed that the assets of ordinary Germans in Palestine (presumably excepting German Jews) be tapped for reparations, which the Foreign Office thought a "monstrous suggestion."[213]

Oct–Nov
1945

"Immigration from all sources by all means" was the unanimous battle cry at a mass meeting at the Jewish Centre on October 8 in which once-moderate factions now demanded the immediate creation of a Jewish state in all of Palestine. Thus the Jewish Agency was all the more furious when the next day Hebrew University president Judah Magnes lambasted the "growing trend towards totalitarianism amongst the Jews" and denounced the pressure, "particularly in America, to yield to Zionist totalitarianism which seeks to subject to its discipline the entire Jewish people." In response, the Agency smeared Magnes with a Nazi allusion, characterizing his words as akin to "praising the Germans at the time of Dunkirk."[214]

The night of Magnes' speech, Palmach operatives broke into the Athlit Clearance Camp, where immigrants were held pending immigration permits. After murdering a constable and raiding the depot, they freed all the immigrants—minus eleven, who they bound, gagged, and left.

When the British arrived, one of the gagged victims—identified as a Christian woman—was dead, suffocated. The eleven had "presumably refused to participate in the escape," the British report read, whereas the Hagana's Sneh put the number they'd tied up at thirteen and dismissed them as "illegal immigrants" (meaning that all eleven were Christian?). The victims were smeared as Magnus had been smeared: Sneh charged that they "had maintained contact with the Nazis." In a message to a contact in London, he described the Athlit attack as a "great success!"

In the new post-war dynamic, the Jewish Agency's protection of those responsible was no longer just the threat of bedlam if terrorists were pursued into the settlements. When police tried to enforce a road check in the area, they were ambushed "by Jews armed with rifles, sub-machine guns and grenades," killing a constable on the spot and seriously wounding another. In the hills about seven hours later, a police detachment detained nine suspects en route to Meshek Yajour, but while their identities were being established, a "party of 100 Jewish men, armed with pick halves, arrived on the scene" from that Jewish colony and forced the police, who had been forbidden from using firearms, to free the suspects.

At about the same time, police pursuing terror suspects in the Montefiore quarter of Tel Aviv, not related to the Athlit incident, "were attacked by a mob of 150-200 Jews who threw stones" and blocked them, while more settlers were bused in from nearby quarters to stop the police from taking away three suspects.[215]

The Irgun raided an army camp on October 11, seizing hundreds of rifles, guns, grenades, and ammunition. On the 16th, "at about 10:30 A.M. a number of unknown Jews attempted to hold up an Army truck at the Salameh railway crossing," apparently having learned that the truck carried £14,000 in soldiers' pay. A second Irgun attempt further up the road left one casualty, a fourteen-year-old Palestinian bystander.

In the south, a large number of hiking parties were operating in the Beersheba region (Negev), while in London Azzam Bey, the secretary-general of the Arab League, received a "final summons" from "the Messiah" (probably Lehi) threatening "woe to all Arabdom" should he in any way question the "return [of the] Israelites."

In Palestine, High Commissioner Viscount Gort gathered three Jewish Agency officials—Dr. Joseph, Mr. Kaplan, and Mr. Ben Zevi—and "warned them solemnly and with emphasis" to help end the terror. The three appeared little impressed, replying only that they would continue to take their instructions from their superiors.[216]

Lord Gort, a veteran of both world wars, turned to one R. Newton, a Hebrew-speaking former resident of the settlements. "Violence and intransigent nationalism," Newton testified, "was fostered by the Jewish educational system," and by "the incitement and hysteria fostered systematically among the Jewish youth in Palestine. This education and political propaganda has produced youths and girls who were ready to use murder for their political ends."[217]

Thus a prerequisite for peace in Palestine, Newton said, would be "the re-education of the Jewish youth." As for the Palestinians, they "did not wish for violence and indeed it was only the intense Zionist propaganda" that led them to "a renewed interest in politics," with "a growing number of young [Palestinian] men who were interested in social and economic matters and were more up-to-date in their ideas" than the established figures from old prominent Arab families.

Europe's persecuted Jews were "being used as a political weapon to gain control of Palestine, [and any] declaration of a policy unfavourable to extreme Zionism" would be met with terror. Jews "who were against political extremism … were exposed to intimidation [and] had no political influence."

Independently, a British report that month noted an example of such intimidation: an American Jew in Nathanya named Cliansky was ostracized, both his sons were fired from their jobs, and he was evicted from his synagogue to shouts of "he is defiled."

The Jaffa District Commissioner noted the same post-war change. "Until recently," he wrote in October, the settlers "deprecated the resort to force," while refusing any assistance to stop it. Now, "it is no exaggeration to say that the whole of the Jewish urban community is in sympathy with the saboteurs."[218]

It was the Jewish Agency itself that was the ringleader of the next blitz, "a series of concerted attacks" during the night of October 31—November 1 that "was made by armed Jews on Palestine railway system, culminating with a full-scale attack on the railway station and goods yard at Lydda" in which several people were killed. Lehi, independently, "caused serious sabotage" and one fatality at the Haifa refinery. Railway tracks were severed in 242 places, and police naval vessels were bombed, two sunk at Haifa and one at Jaffa.

An intercepted telegram proved that the Jewish Agency enlisted the collaboration of both the Irgun and Lehi for the operation. A testament to the planning involved, the telegram reported that

> in the all the activities, no one [i.e., of the saboteurs] was hurt, stopped or arrested," and bragged that "500 explosions [sabotaged the railways] from the Syrian frontier to Gaza, from Haifa to Samakh, from Lydda to Jerusalem … The activities have made a great impression on the country. The authorities are bewildered.

Kol Israel radio announced that the country-wide sabotage "serves as a warning to the Government of the White Paper [Britain]."

In the daylight following the night of carnage, the police discovered a bomb that had failed to explode, raising hope that police dogs could follow the scent to the terrorists' hideout—which they did. A small patrol under a Mr. Gould followed the canine sleuths to Ramat Hak Kovesh settlement. As they approached, the settlement's school bells rang and "a large part of the population turned out at the gate to bar his progress."

Gould explained that they were interested only in detaining a suspect in the night's attacks, and that "it was wrong of them to harbor a terrorist." As he made his appeal, the crowd threatened him with stones, fresh supplies of which were brought to the scene in boxes, and "considerable parties" of reinforcements, principally from Kefar Saba settlement, soon arrived "on foot and in transport of all kinds."

Facing choreographed mayhem and a propaganda bonanza in the US media, and quite possibly the loss of their lives, the little patrol turned around and left—"once again," as the British put it.

The vast sabotage of the railways and the civilian dead "failed to elicit even the usual formal expression of deprecation" from Zionist leaders. Instead, the "dominant note was satisfaction at the display of organisation and the strength of the Yishuv's armed forces"—this reference to the three terror gangs as the "Yishuv's armed forces" an early acknowledgment that they would coalesce into a state army, the Israeli Defence Forces (IDF).

As those "armed forces" continued preparations to seize Palestine, Kol Israel radio continued the necessary dehumanization of the Palestinians: they were "ignorant people [who] have done a great deal of harm to themselves in trying to stand in our way." Preparations to remove those "ignorant people" also continued: the British confiscated more documents from an Egged bus containing detailed surveillance about Palestinian villages, more fruit from the hiking parties.[219]

Yet the Palestinians' reaction to the violence and taunting, as recorded in a mid-November British report to the British Minister in Beirut, continued to be "general dissatisfaction but NO disposition to violence" [capitalization original].

Native Jews of the Levant states, the report continued, are "apprehensive of Zionism." They "show solidarity with local Arab population [and] regret [the] inclusion of pro-Zionist America in Enquiry Commission," a reference to the Anglo-American Commission of Inquiry, newly-formed to advance a solution to the Palestine question.[220]

Politicians of that pro-Zionist America were now demanding that Britain admit an additional 100,000 Jews into Palestine immediately—an electioneering gimmick, charged Foreign Secretary Ernest Bevin. "Any other alternative to relieve suffering unless it was founded upon Palestine policy alone," he complained, "was rejected by the United States Government and by the Jews."[221]

In early November, the Haganah announced the conscription of all Jewish boys and girls aged 17-18, what the *Palestine Post* referred to as "national service," with no exceptions. Previously, conscription had applied only after leaving school.

The 14th and 15th of the month heralded a new round of violence. The district offices in Tel Aviv were attacked for the third time in five years, destroying two floors along with many of their documents. Emergency crews attempting to reach the burning offices were stoned. A curfew was imposed but proved meaningless: cars were overturned, a military truck set afire and burned out, part of a railway line torn up, Arab buses stoned, and several buildings wrecked and looted. After partially destroying the Post Office, the crowd attempted to burn it down.

When the police, under heavy stoning by a crowd of about 5,000, attempted to charge the crowd with batons, the crowd advanced against them instead and forced the police to retreat. Haganah leader Sneh, meanwhile, was baiting the Palestinians in an address to a large crowd in Jerusalem. The army camp at Rosh-HaAyin was raided on the 22nd to replenish supplies.[222]

On the night of the 24th-25th, "Jews opened fire with automatic weapons, rifles and hand grenades" at Sidna Ali coast guard station. Three of four bombs exploded, seriously damaging the building. Similarly, the coast guard stations at Givat Olga "was surrounded by Jews who opened fire with automatic weapons and grenades," who then "succeeded in placing gelignite charges against building which wrecked it."

This time, the British decided to risk the propaganda and mayhem to get the bombers. When the settlers stopped the police from any investigation, the police persevered. Prepared for such a possibility, "large crowds [of] Jews [then] poured in from surrounding country" on buses to block them. Still the authorities did not give up, now forcing their way into Rishpon settlement with tear gas, guns, and batons. There they discovered a man badly injured by a grenade, presumably one of the attackers, along with 175 lbs of the explosive ammonal, twenty sticks of gelignite, grenades, military uniforms, and clothes stained with sea water.

Immediately, the Jewish Agency turned the capture of one bomber into a public relations bonanza. The US media accepted the Agency's announcement that the British had "forcibly entered three peaceful labor agricultural settlements [and] wantonly beat hundreds men and women ... without any reason ... intimidating the Jews of Palestine into submission," who the more melodramatic media referred to as the "Children of Israel."[223]

First signs of US loan as pro-Zionist leverage

Dec
1945

In what must have seemed to the British a consummate irony, the Jewish Agency now sought to exploit the debilitating debt Britain incurred fighting the Nazis—a debt that only a loan from the US could relieve, but that Zionist influence in the US could hold hostage—to force Britain to capitulate to its demands. An informant code-named Circus was present at a mid-December secret meeting of the Jewish Agency Executive, at which Ben-Gurion stressed that "our activities should be directed from Washington and not from London ... Jewish influence in America is powerful and able to cause damage to the interests of Great Britain," with the post-war loan the threat.

Zionism's appeal to antisemitism remained another key to manipulating the Americans. The tactic was repeated at a mid-December meeting of the Jewish Agency Executive:

> Propaganda in America is to be increased, and is to include an approach to the Americans on the lines that if they do not wish an influx of European Jews as immigrants to the United States, they would be well advised to support the Zionist claim to Palestine.[224]

This appeal to antisemites was no surprise—the previous July, the British Embassy in Washington had reported that "the average citizen does not want them in the United States, and salves his conscious by advocating their admittance to Palestine."[225]

Circus also repeated the Jewish Agency's determination that any "differentiation made between the problem of the Jew and that of Political Zionism" had to be stopped. Of this, Bevin was well aware, and so when in a public speech on November 13 he distinguished between Jews and Zionists, the fallout was swift and vicious. A worldwide smear campaign ensued, and Bevin became an assassination target.

Distrust of Reconstruction continued as well, lest conditions in Europe "be improved sufficiently to induce Jews to resume residence there" rather than emigrate to Palestine, as Haifa district commissioner A.N. Law saw it. To counter any such inclination, Circus reported that the Agency "decided to increase propaganda measures among Jews in Camps and other countries in Europe." Emissaries were being sent from Jerusalem, London, and New York with the goal that "85% of the Jews in Europe [i.e., not limited to DPs] can be persuaded" to emigrate to Palestine.

R. Newton corroborated the Jewish Agency's opposition to Reconstruction, testifying that

> They were not interested in Jewish rehabilitation in Europe. They were afraid that with the improvement of conditions in Europe the pressure on Palestine would subside.[226]

As the British observed Christmas on December 25, the Irgun raided the army camp at Beth-Naballa. This attack failed in its goal, the "requisition of weapons," but the setback lasted only two days. December 27, indeed, proved to be a prelude to what was to come in 1946, the year that marked Britain's effective loss of control to the Zionist militias.

A "serious Jewish terrorist attack" began at 7:15 that evening, when Police Headquarters Jerusalem was "attacked by armed Jews" in a "savage and ruthless" manner that "will be viewed with horror by all the civilized nations of the world." After "Jews armed with automatic weapons and explosives" killed two police and blew open the door to a building opposite Police Headquarters in order to gain access to its balcony, "other Jews laid explosives at one corner of the Police Offices" under cover of fire from the balcony and blew it up. Ten people were buried under the rubble. Five were still alive when pulled out.

A policeman named Flanagan was on his way to the hospital in answer to an emergency call to donate blood when he learned of the ongoing attack. He rushed to assist but was murdered by the militants, as were a Constable Hyde near Zion Cinema, and a policeman Nicholson.[227]

Two minutes into the Jerusalem siege, District Police Headquarters in Jaffa were "heavily attacked by armed Jews in the Jaffa/Tel-Aviv Road," the first of coordinated attacks on two police stations and two military barracks intended to prevent reinforcements from reaching the scene. A Palestinian telephone operator was killed in the attack, which wrecked the ground, first floor, and telephone exchange.

About three minutes after the Jaffa attack began, "the Jews cut through the wire fence" of the R.E.M.E. Depot at Levant Fair in Tel Aviv, and "murdered in cold blood an unarmed British soldier L/Cpl. R. Symons. The Jews then lobbed a grenade through the window of a room in which a number of men were asleep." Ten people were killed in the day's carnage, and eleven wounded.

"The attacks," an Irgun *Proclamation* announced, "were carried out with zeal and heroism by all the fighters according to predetermined plan."[228]

When in the aftermath of this newest terror the British made yet further appeals to the Jewish Agency, Ben-Gurion and Sharett "disassociated themselves from the murderous attacks" but reiterated that the terrorism would not stop as long as Britain stood in the way of Zionist nationalist ambitions. Sharett went so far as to state this publicly, telling reporters that "any appeals to Jews to obey the law would fall on deaf ears" unless Zionist demands were met.

It was the British instead that offered an olive branch. In an attempt to secure cooperation, they authorized another 1,500 Jewish settlers a month (the White Paper quota had been exhausted in December). The overture was without effect.

The end of the year brought the news that Transjordan had been granted independence. This elicited a dual reaction: publicly, Zionist leaders like Sharett condemned Jordanian independence, claiming that the land had been promised to them as part of the Jewish state; but privately, they calculated that it was a lucky turn of events, because it would be much easier for them "to infiltrate into a weak but independent Arab State" (as British sources put it) than wrest Transjordan from British control.

And so in anticipation of future claims on Jordan, Jewish Agency propaganda began referring to Palestine as "Western Palestine," and Haganah Commander Sneh made clear in an interview for the *New York Post* that he spoke of "both banks of the Jordan." Year-end rumors of Partition within Palestine received the same split reaction: publicly, they were condemned, but pragmatists "would even welcome partition," since Partition would mean statehood, and statehood would enable "infiltration and expansion"—that is, partition was a tactic, not an end.[229]

None of this was happening fast enough to satisfy the fanaticism the Zionists had nurtured. Sneh warned Sharett that the Haganah was so "anxious for action" that 250 Palmach members had defected to the Irgun. Ben-Gurion helped contain the impatience by reassuring the Jewish Agency Executive that he "would never agree to Agency assistance to the Administration and police in stopping Irgun activities."[230]

Documents seized from Sneh's flat show that the Agency did more than cooperate with the Irgun: it actually helped finance the terror gang. Jewish Agency treasurer Eliezer Kaplan is the likely author of this penciled comment to Sneh :

> But if they really do free us from all expenditure on illegal immigration
> it will enable us to increase the allocation to the Irgun.[231]

Another document, a four-page plan of action clipped to a letter to Ben-Gurion and copied to Sneh, stressed that the "final solution" in Palestine will be determined by "the relative forces on the spot," not by Partition. The point is then restated more bluntly: "seizing control of the country by force of arms." Conscription into the Yishuv's military "will be backed when necessary by physical force," and the Agency's rule over Jews would be absolute, with a supreme body that "can impose on any [Jewish] person, group, or enterprise any duty or prohibition it finds necessary" to achieve Zionist goals. Its powers over Jews would extend "beyond the 'legal' boundaries."[232]

5

"Subordinated to a Single Cry"

"The unfortunate Jews of Europe's D.P. Camps are helpless
hostages for whom [Israeli] statehood has been made the only
ransom … Admitting that the Jews of Europe have suffered
beyond expression, why in God's name should the fate of all these
unhappy people be subordinated to the single cry of statehood?"
—Arthur Hays Sulzberger, publisher of the New York Times,
both in a speech and in print, 1946 [233]

"**P**owers beyond the legal boundaries" certainly characterized
Zionist leaders' attitudes in the long-awaited post-war
confusion that was now theirs to exploit. As the world picked up
the pieces from the global cataclysm, the once-only opportunity
it presented Zionism brought heightened campaigns of terror to
Palestine, the first Zionist bombings in Europe, new efforts to
preserve Jewish "racial purity," accelerated recruitment into the
militias, tightened repression of the Yishuv, and new methods of
control over the war's Jewish survivors.

Control over Europe's Jewish DPs, what Newton had referred
to as "exploiting the situation of the Jews in Europe," was necessary
to prevent them from emigrating anywhere other than to Palestine
or opt to remain in their own countries—which "under no circumstances," Sharett lectured to the Jewish Agency Executive, should
be permitted. An Intelligence Summary from April of 1945 quotes

Eliyahu Dobkin, then head of the Jewish Agency's Immigration Department, as saying that terrorist methods would be used to force European Jews to move to Palestine after the war, and that the sinking of the *Patria*—which killed about 267 people—would be "eclipsed" if necessary to make Jews *in* Palestine *stay* in Palestine (which was the goal of the *Patria* bombing). "We should not treat this danger lightly," Ben-Gurion said of the possibility that the war's Jewish survivors might not want to go to Palestine.[234]

This, however, appears to have been the case. The best estimate available is that immediately after the war, only fifteen percent would have willingly opted to go to Palestine despite years of Zionist propaganda. An actual emancipation of Europe's Jews would have crippled the Zionist project, and so campaigns to stop it included the isolation and coercion of the survivors themselves, the sabotage of international safe haven for them, and the forced removal of Jewish orphans from their adoptive European families.[235]

Influencing Jewish survivors required that they first be segregated from other DPs. The Truman Administration acquiesced to Zionists' demands that this be done, despite misgivings among many that it echoed Nazi behavior. Even the pro-Zionist Churchill was uncomfortable with the forced segregation: he wrote to Truman that the Control Commission "have endeavored to avoid treating people on a racial basis," noting that "within these camps were people from almost every race in Europe and there appears to have been very little difference in the amount of torture and treatment they had to undergo." But with Jews now segregated from all others, Jewish Agency "relief workers" could now set about indoctrinating them into the Zionist cause.

The Irgun as well was active in the camps—MI5 reported "ample evidence of the existence of Revisionist and Irgun cells in Displaced Persons camps in both the British and American Zones" in Europe. The groups' influence would become more visible with the bombings by Jewish DPs of European trains and hotels in 1947.[236]

Many Jewish DPs resisted the Zionists message, and so where persuasion failed, uncooperative DPs were shunned, their rations reduced, and in some cases subjected to violence. When a Jewish survivor in the Bergen-Belsen DP camp began to voice the opinion that many countries, not just Palestine, be open to them, she was physically attacked and "dragged down the steps." Men who refused to join the militias were sometimes beaten. DPs were trained to organize mass *aliyah* (immigration to Palestine), and those who resisted the Zionist indoctrination quickly learned to pretend otherwise.[237]

Anglo-American Commission of Inquiry

An urgent object of the indoctrination was to train the DPs to give fanatical *only-to-Palestine* statements to the Anglo-American Commission of Inquiry. Thus when in early 1946 the AACI visited the Jewish DP camps, they were greeted by prominently displayed Zionist flags and notices reading *Our answer to the Anglo-American Commission—Palestine or death*. "Everywhere," the Committee reported, "Jews shouted or chanted, 'to Palestine, to Palestine,'" and threatened "waves of suicide" if denied this.

There is no way to know to what extent the DPs were successfully indoctrinated, versus pretending to be a convert in order to survive life in the Zionist-run camps. In 1945, one unconverted Jewish survivor compared life under the Zionists to that of Spanish Jews at the close of the fifteenth century, who had to follow their beliefs in secret and pretend to have converted to Christianity:

> [We] live here like the Moranos once lived in Spain!*

The difference in numbers between the indoctrinated versus "Moranos" is immaterial to its effect on the Committee. When asked what alternatives to Palestine they might consider, they repeated *en masse* that there was only one alternative: mass suicide.

Even when the United States, long the favored destination, was raised as an option, the DPs refused fearfully, saying that they would not be safe there. Publicly, the Committee claimed that they had no idea "how the Jews in the camps had got this idea."[238]

---

* From a letter written in Hebraico-Yiddish, to a friend in New York. Grodzinsky, *Shadow*, 134.

However, if the Committee was shocked by the DPs' fanaticism, *Palestine* was the answer the Committee's American members had hoped to hear. When Britain first approached the US about such a Commission to find solutions to the crisis, the US

> agreed in principle to the formation of a joint Committee, but wished to shift the emphasis in its terms of reference from the general problem of Jewish displaced persons to the particular question of their entry into Palestine, and indeed tried to eliminate any reference to countries of possible settlement other than Palestine.[239]

Military training became part of the DPs enforced program, and by late 1946, MI5 reported that "para-military training in Jewish camps appears to be an everyday occurrence." Bergen-Belsen, a DP camp "of some 11,000 Jews," had become "a semi-autonomous state" that defied the Allied authority. Some survivors however escaped the camps and settled in Europe, heightening Jewish Agency fears that peace was damaging the Zionist project.[240]

Rabbi Herzog and adopted Jewish orphans

Orphans of Jewish background adopted by European families were another crack in the Zionist narrative. For Yitzhak HaLevi Herzog, Ashkenazi Chief Rabbi of Palestine since 1937, the solution to these children was to forcibly remove thousands of them from the adoptive families that had saved them when their parents perished years earlier. Armed ex-Jewish Brigade soldiers helped in the removals when necessary.*

---

* This summary of Herzog's trip is taken from a transcript of his report to the Vaad Leumi Executive, by "a usually reliable source" and marked "secret" (TNA CO 537/1705). This author has relied on two separate documents to corroborate the accuracy of the transcript. Principally, Trafford Smith, who was supportive of Herzog's removal of the children, heard about the trip from Herzog himself shortly after his return. Afterwards, Smith read this transcript and commented on it, but made no mention of inaccuracies. Grodzinsky's research (in *Shadow...*) complements the transcript (which he had not seen). More generally, Eliyahu Dobkin of the Jewish Agency, in an address to the Mapai Executive on May 1, 1946, discussed the "problem" of Jewish children in Christian families. Articles in the *Palestine Post* and *NY Times* support the basic idea of the transcript, and none contradict it.

Rabbi Herzog made a six-month tour of Europe in 1946 "to organise the rescue of Jewish children" from their adoptive homes, where they were faced with "spiritual destruction." Ten thousand children was the general number he cited in February as his goal. After a supportive meeting with the Pope in early March, he spoke of eight thousand children in Christian homes and monasteries, and that he hoped "to bring these children back into the Jewish fold." The "Jewish fold" did not mean Jewish homes *per se*, but Palestine: the plan was to place them in other homes "until they could come to Palestine," because "only Palestine could give them" relief from their "mental and spiritual shock."

Herzog's problem was that too few Jews in Europe shared his views, and upon reaching Europe he confronted fierce resistance by local Jewish organizations. The *Œuvre de Secours aux Enfants* (OSE, a French-Jewish humanitarian organization) had a list of 600 Jewish children growing up in Christian homes, but the relief organization was not interested in making the children orphans for a second time. Herzog lambasted OSE for doing "nothing … to take the children away" and used his power to circumvent them. He succeeded in removing 250 children from their homes.[241]

Next, finding himself up against a French resistance, Herzog "met the Prime Minister of France* from whom [I] demanded promulgation of a law which would oblige every family to declare the particulars of the children it houses" in order to forcibly expose those children who were Jewish so they could be taken away—quite a Kafkaesque twist on Passover for these children who had just been spared the Nazis. He however "had to satisfy myself for the time being with 1,000-1,500 children" taken from their homes and put in a Talmudic school until they "can be transferred to Palestine."[242]

Switzerland as well proved difficult for Rabbi Herzog because of the influence of what he called Jewish "assimilants," particularly a Mr. Bloch who was Chairman of the Jewish Community. But Herzog prevailed—Bloch was forced to resign, after which Herzog

---

* Presumably meaning the Chairman of the Provisional Government, in 1946 either Félix Gouin or Georges Bidault.

"approached Government circles" to extricate 600 children from their homes. He worried, however, that "Swiss Jews cannot be relied on" to perform the kidnappings, and so suggested that "a special committee be sent from the Yishuv" (i.e., from Palestine) to insure that the children are taken away.[243]

In Belgium, Rabbi Herzog again faced the obstacle of a "Jewish committee … composed mainly of assimilants." The Committee knew of 400 families who had adopted Jewish orphans, but it was not interested in his demands to "rescue" them, and so Herzog went to the Prime Minister, the Crown Prince, the Catholic Cardinal, and the Minister for Justice, and won legal backing to force them to hand over the list of children.

When the horrified Jewish committee still refused to divulge the information, Herzog had "considerable pressure" put on the committee, after which it "supplied me with names but withheld addresses." He appealed to the authorities for "full legal assistance" to force the Jewish committee to divulge the addresses so the children could be pulled from their homes and shipped to Palestine.[244]

In Holland, the situation was particularly frustrating for Herzog, because "during the war, the Dutch treated the Jews very well." It is too upsetting to remove the children, the Dutch told him, as "attachments have been formed between them and the families." Herzog nonetheless appealed to the government for "the necessary legislation" to forcibly remove the children.

Poland was more of the same. Despite meeting with Edward Osóbka-Morawski, Prime Minister of the provisional government, Herzog left frustrated that he could only remove half of what he believed to be the country's 4,000 Jewish orphans. Great Britain was worse still: the rabbi failed "to win over the Jews there in support of my work," because the "assimilants there do not show much understanding." Jews, he warned in summary, "must not be exposed to the tactics of non-Zionist Jewry."[245]

In Herzog's view, these Jewish "assimilants" were condemning the children to a fate more terrible than death. For a Jew to be raised as a Christian, he said in justification for his kidnappings, is "much worse than physical murder."

Reaction to Herzog's kidnapping project was mixed. John Gutch, who had just survived the King David Hotel bombing, condemned it.

> It illustrates only too clearly the fact that Zionist Jews are not in the least interested in the happiness and comfort of Jews … a Jew who seeks to find a home and happiness elsewhere [than Palestine] is regarded as a renegade from the Zionist cause … Such bigotry and callousness are difficult for us to appreciate.

Trafford Smith of the Colonial Office was typical of those who defended Herzog. He argued that "it is understandable that Jewish religious leaders should wish to keep as Jews the few children left to them." Even Smith, however, added that "it is tragic in the extreme that the sufferings of these children should be still further prolonged" in order to "preserve them for Jewry."

The problem with defenses such as Smith's is that—as history repeatedly demonstrated—the children were not being "preserved for Jewry," but for Zionism. At the same time Herzog was "rescuing" Jewish orphans from their non-Jewish families, Zionist leaders were sabotaging *Jewish* adoptive homes for young Jewish survivors, for the single reason that those homes were not in Palestine. In August 1945, Jewish activists in Britain asked their government to allow one thousand Jewish child survivors still without homes to emigrate to England. Among the organizers were those who had run the *Kindertransport* in 1938 that had saved the lives of many Jewish children. Britain agreed, and the first three hundred children were flown to England, where they were received by members of Jewish youth movements, teachers, and nurses knowledgeable about refugee issues. They were united with their adoptive Jewish families and received excellent attention from the local Jewish community, enjoying frequent visits by community leaders and rabbis.

But when word of the transport reached Zionist leaders, they stopped it. The remaining 700 child survivors were left to remain in the orphanages, on display to garner world pity for opening the gates to Palestine until they could be shipped there as facts-on-the-ground.

Even as doctors reported the desperate condition of the camps, and the shortage of food, heat, and medical attention, Ben-Gurion sanctioned the use of force to stop the evacuations to Jewish homes in Britain. A similar rescue program was sabotaged in France.[246]

The actual driving force was not saving Jewish children from a Christian home "much worse than physical murder," as Rabbi Herzog explained it, but gathering ethnically-correct settlers.[247]

Some of the children were in their mid-teens and, fully understanding what was happening, wrote letters to the Zionist leaders who had taken control of their lives. The teenagers explained that they had lost any hope that their parents were alive, that they had been offered new lives in England and the opportunity to study in London, and asked that they not be blocked from this new life—but to no avail. As further insurance, some Jewish children were forbidden from seeking out family members who survived the war, for fear that ties in Europe might be reestablished. The Jewish Agency's Eliyahu Dobkin lamented the "grave dispute" caused by non-Zionist Jews over the "exodus" of the children.[248]

The Roosevelt refugee program vs the Zionist "pet thesis"

What might have been the most important resettlement program of the entire post-war period was stopped by Zionist leaders in the United States. When President Roosevelt proposed his plan "for the easy migration of the 500,000 beaten people of Europe" to his friend Morris Ernst, co-founder of what would become the American Civil Liberties Union, he explained that if Britain would open her doors, he could get the US to do the same.

Ernst went to London on Roosevelt's behalf in February of 1944, when the second Blitz hit. The British accepted Roosevelt's proposal, agreeing to provide for 150,000 refugees if the US would reciprocate. Roosevelt was excited:

> 150,000 to England—150,000 to match that in the United States— pick up 200,000 or 300,000 elsewhere [in the Americas and Australia], and we can start with half a million of these oppressed people.[249]

But the rescue program was dead within a week. "The dominant vocal Jewish [Zionist] leadership of America won't stand for it," Roosevelt told Ernst, after making a sarcastic quip about Stephen Wise.

Ernst, bewildered, began to lobby influential Zionist friends on behalf of freer immigration, but facing an "often fanatically emotional vested interest in putting over the Palestinian movement," he was "thrown out of parlors" and accused of treason. Ernst:

> Jewish leaders decried, sneered and then attacked me as if I were a traitor ... I was openly accused of furthering this plan of freer immigration in order to undermine political Zionism.[250]

In the end, a half million European refugees were denied the option of new homes in modern, safe countries because of what Ernst called the Zionists' "pet thesis"—that Jews must be blocked from going anywhere other than Palestine.

Jan 1946

When an explosion on New Year's day of 1946 brought the police to 84 Dizengoff Street in Tel Aviv, it proved to be an accidental blast from Lehi explosives, exposing their hideout in the cellar of the building. There the British found a small arsenal that included revolvers, grenades, bombs, "a very considerable quantity of chemicals and laboratory equipment, Army, Police, and RAF uniforms."

More interesting were the documents found there. Some suggested imminent targets: a plan and photographs of the court in Jerusalem, of the Jerusalem railway station, and the government printing press. Other papers showed that Lehi nurtured contacts (described as "involuntary informants") with police, government officials, and watchmen, while agents ("active informants") were sought among soldiers, seamen, technical specialists, radio and telephone operators, and factory owners. Lehi activities outside Palestine were pursued through foreign Jews and agents sent abroad. Training and meetings took place at synagogues, schools, stores, flats, factories, workshops, offices, orange groves, and packing sheds.

Lehi assassinated the officer who filed the report.[251]

The Yishuv's Recruiting Centre made a New Year's announcement repeating calls for "all girls and boys born in 1928" to report. Five hundred new recruits had joined this "Jewish Brigade Group" the previous month (December 1945), and another two to three hundred would be added shortly.

The main Jewish Brigade was the subject of news from Europe: it was believed "not unconnected" with "the recent seizure of 40 tons of [Allied] arms in the S. of France." The Brigade was increasingly a problem in Palestine as well: "the evidence is clear," British Commander in Chief Sir Bernard Paget reported, that Jewish (ex-Brigade?) soldiers in the British forces were "a menace to security" to the extent of murdering fellow soldiers and police, confirming Y 32's warnings. Since there was no way to distinguish Zionist plants from Jewish soldiers, Paget pushed to have all Jews released from service "as early as possible."[252]

On the second day of 1946, pamphlet bombs exploded in Tel Aviv and Haifa announcing that the attacks six days earlier, December 27, had been a joint Irgun-Lehi operation. But the militias were running short of cash, and so January 12 was devoted to fundraising. At 10:10 that morning, the Irgun—aided, according to Circus, by the Palmach—blew up the Haifa-Jerusalem passenger train as it passed about two miles north of Hadera, the blasts overturning "engines, coaches, and the majority of the wagons." As the crippled train reeled to a halt, "fire was opened at the train from both sides by party of some 70 Jews, including women, armed with rifles and Tommy guns." The militants had learned that the train carried £P 35,000 in railroad staff salaries, and the train's guards, even "after extricating themselves from the wreckage," could not prevent the robbery by such a large armed mob.

The attackers used pepper to obscure the scent of their escape, causing investigators to lose the trail half-way between the station and Hadera. ("Am concerned," Sir Alan Cunningham, who had assumed the position of High Commissioner after Lord Gort, wrote in an understated cypher telegram, "that such a large sum of Government money has fallen into the hands of the terrorists.") Meanwhile in Jaffa, the Irgun's armed robbery of the Arab gold exchange of £P 6,000 brought its one-day bounty to £P 41,000.[253]

At about 8:00 P.M. on January 19, an employee at the Jerusalem Electric Corp called the Power Station to report that the padlock and chain to the Sub-Power Station in Musrara Quarter had been cut through. Shortly he "was held up by an armed Jew [who] ordered him to leave the premises," whereupon the plant was bombed by "five Jews [including a girl]." Next, radios went dead as the Palestine Broadcasting Service was knocked out by four explosions, and

> other parties of armed Jews, including girls, were taking up positions in St. Paul's Road, Queen Melisande's Way and adjoining small streets … three or four Jews [were] lying in the road manning a Bren gun … About eight girls were crouching against a wall [with arms, and] the Jews were wearing battle-dress and steel helmets, some of the girls blue shirts and khaki shorts.[254]

After the Bren gun party opened fire on a military patrol, "a confused period followed" with explosions from grenades, incendiary bottles, and mines, the collective shrapnel causing injuries far from the blasts. Roaming militants shot the Deputy Superintendent of Police in both legs on St. Paul's Road; one leg had to be amputated. Two groups of assailants, one about fifteen strong, the other about eight, slipped in and out of alleys.

At about 9:30 P.M. the Assistant Superintendent of Police attempted to neutralize one of the mines, but it was booby trapped: the explosion killed him and injured another.

Upon the arrival of the military, the roaming gang members turned to sniper fire from streets and rooftops. They shot dead a student at the Middle East Centre of Arab Studies, and hijacked a taxi by shooting the driver in the head.

The Irgun and Lehi jointly claimed responsibility for the evening of terror.[255]

British anxiety over their inability to distinguish Zionist plants among Jewish personnel took another turn for the worse when the Givat Olga Coastguard Station blew up on the night of January 20-21. The police were baffled, because there had been no attack—the structure just seemed to blow up of its own accord. They discovered that the "workmen" who had rebuilt the structure after it was bombed two months earlier (November) were Palmach plants, and had simply imbedded the new bomb into the reconstruction.

As recorded by Cunningham, the explosives were "planted in the building with the assistance of Jewish workmen engaged in repairing the damage caused in the previous attack by armed Jews." The new blast demolished the tower and injured seventeen people, at least one of whom died of his wounds.

The radar station at Mount Carmel was also attacked that day but, in the Hagana's words, "the activity failed. The members were not taken out." Firing caps used in the failed Haifa bombing were "of local manufacture and defective," the British found, and—a rare event—the booby trap on the device had been defeated. Haganah Commander Sneh sent a letter to British headquarters congratulating the bomb expert who had outwitted the device's tamper-proofing.

January closed with an odd success and an odd failure. On January 25 "twenty armed Jews" (Lehi or the Irgun) stole £6000 of an unusual bartering commodity: yarn. But three days later, seventeen Irgun members were defeated by an unexpected enemy: mud. In what must have served as fodder for British jokes over beer that night, the militants commandeered forty machine guns and more than five hundred Sten guns in a raid on the RAF base in Akir, but then their stolen truck sank in newly-ploughed ground during the retreat and had to be abandoned. They escaped by jeep.[256]

The trio of militias remained active in February. The Irgun raided the RAF base in Tel Aviv on the 3rd and the Haganah attacked the Safad police station and its sentry on the 5th. Lehi hit the military camp at Agrobank on the 6th, murdering three (Jewish) civilians and two servicemen, including a doctor, and wounding several. As was their habit, the militants mined the approach road to blow up anyone coming to the victims' aid.

Feb
1946

Some of the arms stolen by Lehi were used by the Irgun in an attack on a railway workshop in Haifa on the evening of June 17, testifying to the current cooperation between the gangs. Indeed, in its newsletter *Herut*, the Irgun praised "this glorious week" of "united action of all three organisations [and] the support of the entire, united Jewish youth."[257]

Haifa's Superintendent of Police at the time was Raymond Cafferata, who seventeen years earlier had helped protect victims of Hebron's 1929 anti-Jewish riot but whom the gangs had since accused of cruelty in his treatment of Jewish terror suspects. As a vehicle escorting Cafferata passed on Mt. Carmel Road just outside Haifa at about 8:25 on the morning of February 15, both Lehi and Irgun assassins were in position waiting for him. A truck blocked the road as he approached, and "Cafferata was about to slow down when his British police escort noticed tommygun concealed under raincoat of Jew nearby," as a telegram from Cunningham read. Cafferata's driver successfully accelerated around the truck. Another truck appeared and chased after him, "firing heavily," but the police engaged the truck and Cafferata escaped. The hunted Superintendent returned to England, where Irgun assassins allegedly tried, but failed, to find him.

Several important British public figures were joining the Lehi-Irgun assassination lists, with Foreign Secretary Bevin still a particular target, the murder to be carried out in England by operatives connected with a Revisionist newspaper printed in Manchester, or during the Foreign Secretary's visit to Egypt.[258]

Another Lehi hideout was discovered on February 18 in a penthouse at No. 3 Hashomer Street in Tel Aviv. Among the articles found there were a "U.S.A. type transmitter" set to the frequency normally used by Lehi, "U.S.A. type earphones," and "U.S.A. type speech amplifiers."

Two days later, as the appearance of more hikers unnerved the Arab Legion, the R.A.F. radar station at Haifa was bombed by the Palmach, exactly a month after the previous attack. Several people were severely wounded in the extensively damaged facility. The Palmach was active again the following evening, bombing police stations at Shafa Amr, Kefar Vitkin, and Sarona, leaving four women and one child in shock amid the wreckage. Electricity to the entire town of Jenin was sabotaged the next afternoon (February 22) in preparation for an attack on the village's police station, but the station had a back-up generator and the attack failed.

Forty to fifty thousand settlers and Jewish Agency officials turned out in Tel Aviv on the 24th to honor four Palmach militants killed in attacks a few days earlier. Among the crowd were several high Jewish Agency officials, including Ben-Gurion himself, who (as British records put it) did not "normally care to associate themselves publicly with terrorist activities." The dead were buried as "national" heroes.[259]

"It is the extremist tail that wags the dog," as the High Commissioner put it. The Jewish Agency, through its constant propaganda, "have so inflamed Jewish young men and women that terrorist organizations have received a fillip both in recruits and sympathy." In a situation to be mirrored by the future Israeli state, the Agency created such hysteria among the settlements that it forfeited even the option of moderating terrorism, instead "being forced to greater lengths of extremism" by its own hyperbole.[260]

American "refugees" given DP permits

In the United States in the last week of February, Zionist organizations announced an extraordinary initiative: they would "recruit young American Jews as emigrants to Palestine," using the available British permits intended for European Jewish DPs. Healthy Americans made better colonizers than the downtrodden survivors of the war. The project had the "full support" of the Zionist Organization of America (ZOA) and leaders such as Abba Silver.

Thus every American Jew sent to be a settler in Palestine deprived a European Jewish DP of that opportunity, an opportunity that the same organizations claimed to be the DPs' only hope of survival. Some of the US citizens using the DPs permits would soon bomb the *Empire Lifeguard* (pages 233–235, below).[261]

About fifty Irgun members "dressed in Battle Dress or as Arabs" attacked three RAF airfields on February 25: Lydda, Petah Tikvah, and Qastina. British records say that sixteen aircraft were destroyed and five damaged beyond repair, but the Irgun dismissed these figures, claiming that it destroyed fully "25 four-engine heavy bombers and a number of fighter planes." One of the leaders of the attack, Dov Cohen, was in the British Commandos.

Palestinian fears that the Jewish Agency's hiking parties were surveillance missions to prepare for their ethnic cleansing were substantiated two days later, after the British repelled an assault on the Arab Legion Camp at Jebel Canaan. They traced the attackers to Birya Settlement, where aside from the expected stockpile of weapons and explosives, they found a cache of documents that were "full details of Arab villages, giving the population, water supply and the number of stock carried," notes about reservoirs, water wells, bridges, police stations, telegraph poles, the height of fences, topographical information, numerous sketches and maps, and a "diary of hiking trips."

The diary covered the period of March 4 through April 19 of the previous year (1945), during which eleven of these reconnaissance hikes were conducted by this one settlement. The teams averaged five members selected from a pool of nine. Other papers detailed the security and secrecy measures of this group, which described itself as "an integral part of the Alef," an Irgun-Haganah alliance (*alef* is the first letter of the Hebrew, Arabic, and other alphabets).[262]

The first major attack of March vindicated the military's warnings that they had trained the Jewish Brigade only to return to Palestine as conquerors. At Sarafand Military Camp on March 6, ex- Jewish Brigade soldiers who were "located inside the camp facilitated the entry" of fourteen Irgun disguised as airborne troops. They seriously wounded a female welfare worker as they took captives. Two days later, a Jewish (Brigade?) corporal was part of an Irgun operation transporting a cache of gelignite, demolition charges, detonators, automatics, stens, and suits of battle dress.

Attacks on two bridges and a transformer planned for March 25 were foiled, though road mines and road blocks had already been set to delay emergency vehicles' access. Routine harassment continued after midnight by "4 Jews disguised as Arabs on the sea shore at Bat Yen, south of Jaffa." Sukreir station was bombed on the 27th.[263]

A brief, relative lull in the sabotage was observed when the Anglo-American Committee arrived, but widespread sabotage again crippled the railway infrastructure on April 2. Block houses and bridges between Yibna and Arab Shukreir were attacked, the line was

"Demolished Rail Car." From *Palestine Pamphlet Terrorist Methods With Mines and Booby Traps.* Headquarters, Chief Engineer, Palestine and Transjordan. December, 1946.

bombed on either side of the Yibna Railway Station, "and bridges there and at Arab Shukreir were seriously damaged." Tracks leading to the station were mined, local telephone lines cut, policemen injured, patrols blown up, the Na'aman bridge near Acre demolished, and the railway stations at Yavne and Ashdod hit. Trains were "attacked and burnt out by Jews," injuring five people, one seriously, and railway lines were cut in several places near Mishmar Hayam Colony.

At Na'Amin Bridge south of Acre, Jews dressed as Arabs held up a police guard while about 20 armed Jews blew up the bridge. Just after 10:00 that night, the militants attacked the Isdud Railway Station between Majdal and Yibna, murdering a policeman and bombing a railway engine. Further attacks were thwarted on April 3 when the British tracked "some thirty armed Jews" south of Bat Yam at about 8:30 in the morning, some disguised as Arabs, and three hours later another group of about thirty was discovered by air reconnaissance. Among the weapons they carried were Bren, Sten, and Tommy guns, and "48 locally manufactured grenades." The Haganah attacked the Haifa-Lydda train on April 5 and stole 6,000 rounds of cannon shell.[264]

Just after midday on April 13, "six men in the uniform of the Jewish Brigade, using W.D. vehicle," robbed the Army Convalescent

Depot at Nathanya. About forty minutes later, "between ten and fifteen armed Jews disguised as Italian 'collaborators'" attacked the Army Leave Camp in Nathanya (a separate report read "20 men in Italian P.O.W. uniforms"). All were Irgun. To make good their escape, they bombed the bridge between Nathanya and Kfar Vitkin on their exit, the blast injuring the crew of a police car. One of the attackers was apprehended near the bridge with an anti-personnel bomb.[265]

When a "British sergeant" in battle dress appeared at the Ramat Gab (Gan) police station on April 23, he had important news to report: "Arabs" had been caught stealing from the nearby military establishment. "British soldiers" then appeared at the police station with the "Arab prisoners." Once inside, the collective sergeant, soldiers, and Arabs proved to be an Irgun Trojan Horse. They quickly seized the building, but as they did the (Jewish) wireless operator slipped into the wireless room and bolted the door. The attackers blew it open, but too late—the distress message had already been understood. Military and police reinforcements soon approached, but in their escape the attackers murdered a Palestinian TAC, wounded two other constables, and made off with an assortment of weapons and seven thousand rounds of ammunition.

Simultaneously, the Irgun attacked the Tel Aviv Railway Station. Four bombs exploded and rocked the waiting room, but "one Jewish terrorist was injured while igniting bombs and captured."[266]

At about 8:45 on the night of April 25, Irgun operatives threw an anti-personnel bomb into the Airborne Division's car park in Tel Aviv. As it exploded, a group of 20-30 "armed Jews in civilian clothes" murdered "anyone they saw" under cover by heavy fire from accomplices in adjoining houses. After killing the sentry, they entered the park, "shone torches on the occupants asleep in the tents and killed them out of hand," and finished by killing two more people in the car park.

Two signals from militants planted in nearby houses appear to have been confirmation of success and the order to withdraw: a bugle sounding twice, and a light flashing on and off three times in an upper window. As had long been the Irgun's standard practice, it had mined all approaches, which "seriously hampered the bringing of medical assistance to the casualties."

Irgun notices posted in the morning read: *With their aims achieved our people withdrew with their arms and booty … All our fighters returned to base safety. Fatal casualties were inflicted on the Enemy.* For the British, it was "a premeditated and vicious attack obviously designed to cause the maximum casualties." Sniper fire and vehicle bombings continued.[267]

British nerves were rattled by a near-disaster on May Day of 1946 when explosives were discovered on the HMS *Chevron*, rigged to blow up by the ship's magazine. "The ship was carrying thirteen Jewish naval ratings [non-commissioned sailors] from Alexandria to Haifa for discharge," a telegram from Cunningham read, and when they were found onshore one had a detonator sewn into his clothing, and others had explosives similarly concealed. (Seven months later, HMS *Chevron* would rescue about 800 Jewish immigrants shipwrecked on the small Greek island of Syrna.)[268]

May 1946

Seemingly meaningless attacks against civilians were, the British surmised, youthful recruits getting hands-on practice. On May 14 ten armed settlers held up a café in Petah Tiqva to steal a jeep, but being unable to start it, they set it ablaze, while four others stole a jeep in nearby Tel Aviv by shooting the driver in the leg. The pros were back the next day, stealing 100,000 small-arms ammunition from a special RAF train en route from Acre to Wadi Sarar (Nahal Sorek). An armed bank robbery in Nablus on May 20 was, the British suspected, the work of the Irgun, and Irgun records confirm this. Mortar fire targeted a police post in Nathanya two days later.[269]

"Malkhut Israel"

On June 6 Lehi militants freed an imprisoned colleague as he was being escorted to a clinic for medical attention, wounding two people. The patient was no ordinary Lehi operative, but Israel Eldad, a key assassin who in two years would be party to the murder of Count Bernadotte. Today, an Israeli settlement near Herodion in the (Palestinian) West Bank is named in Eldad's honor.

June 1946

As was likely typical among Lehi then, and indeed the more fundamentalist settlers today, Eldad's goal was not the Israeli *state*, but a *kingdom* of Israel born of Biblical mythology. He saw the Israeli state "as the bridgehead of *Malkhut Israel*," the re-establishment of the Biblical realm itself in all its perceived ancient splendor. He set out three requirements to achieve this: [1] population: "the return to Eretz Israel of the entire Jewish People ... either of its own free will or under external duress ... by reason of race and blood"; [2] land: "the boundaries set out in the Divine Promise ... from the Euphrates to the Nile"; [3] characteristics: a revival of "the principles of faith and prophecy."

June 10 brought a trio of coordinated attacks on passenger trains. In all three, "armed Jews, disguised as Arabs [were] distributed along the train with about 1 or 2 in each coach." About 6:30 that Monday evening, a train coming from Jerusalem to Jaffa was stopped at a predetermined spot, about 3.8 km (2.4 miles) from the Tel Aviv station by one of the "passengers" pulling the communication cord. In coordination, thirty armed Jews—twenty-five men and five women—converged on the train, forced everyone off, and blew it up, completely gutting five coaches and wounding a TAC.

Roughly simultaneous with that attack, a girl planted for the purpose pulled the communication cord on a train bound for Jerusalem from Lydda as militants on the line waved a red flag for the train to stop. About fifteen more met the scene by truck, drenched the five coaches in petrol and set them ablaze, completely destroying them.

An hour after these two attacks began, roughly 7:30, a train traveling between Lydda and Haifa was also stopped by a "passenger" pulling the communication cord. One (real) passenger described the attacking party as consisting of "four men and four girls, all below the age of 25, the girls approx 16 years." One of them pulled an explosive charge out of a luncheon basket and detonated it in the locomotive, but the militants then left, probably unnerved by the more exposed location and fear that word of the first two bombings had already spread.[270]

When early the next morning a Palestinian railway employee discovered an explosive charge of about 50-60 lbs on the line southwest of Lydda, he followed the device's electric cable to a nearby orange grove, surprising its three authors, Irgun or Stern militants dressed as Arabs. The bomb would have blown up the night train from Kantara, which was due to pass the spot a half hour later. More explosives rigged on the main line near Hadera went undetected and exploded, severing the track.

In Tel Aviv, an explosion led to the discovery of sixty-four homemade bombs at 57 Mizrahi "B" St., most primed and packed in cases. The District Officer in Haifa was seriously injured in an assassination attempt two days later, and a bomb thrown into Cafe Central in the Arab market area that evening left two casualties.[271]

The British received a report of a meeting of the Haganah in which the socialist group Hashomer Hatzair demanded to be consulted before any Haganah action, and to guarantee that it would not collaborate with the Irgun. When the reply was unsatisfactory on both issues, "a member of Hashomer Hatzair rose" and replied that

> a Nazi is a Nazi, be he a Jew or otherwise, and it is a false sentiment of the Jewish people to condemn Nazism and condone Jewish fascism.[272]

Foreign Secretary Bevin laid bare his exasperation with the US Administration's continuing acquiescence to the Zionists in a speech he gave in Bournemouth on June 12. His speech had already abandoned all decorum in advocating "for a Palestinian and not a Jewish or Arab state," and for saying that a Jewish state "may set you [Jews] back for years"—but the outrage against that was drowned out by the furor over his charge that American support for Zionism was largely fueled by antisemitism.

> Regarding the agitation in the United States, and particularly New York, for 100,000 Jews to be put into Palestine, I hope it will not be misunderstood in America if I say, with the purest of motives, that that was because they did not want too many of them in New York.

Bevin's remark elicited venomous indignation, with Senator Robert Wagner accusing him of antisemitism for his "echo from Nazi dogma [which] will not be excused or forgotten." The American Federation of Polish Jews called Bevin "a disciple of Hitler."

Bevin had however merely pulled the veil off what had long

been an indispensable part of the Jewish Agency's strategy. A week after Bevin's speech, on June 19, Shertok repeated assurances to the Jewish Agency Executive that the Americans could be relied on to support a Zionist state because of the "American fear" of Jews "opening the gates of New York."[273]

A night of blitzed bridges

Paralyzing attacks hit roads and rail bridges at or near the Palestine frontiers during the night of June 16. Among the worst hit was the Yarmuk bridge on the Hijaz railway between el Hamme and Samakh, which was irreparable, with reconstruction estimated to take more than a year. As Cunningham reported it to Secretary of State for the Colonies G.H. Hall,

> It is composed of three spans, the center one being fifty metres in length passing over a deep gorge. The tops of the two pillars supporting the girders were blown up in such a way that the center span collapsed completely to the bottom of the gorge…

The same night, "the railway bridge at Az Zib, north of Acre, was blown up by a large party of Jews," but one powerful charge apparently ignited prematurely, as "remains of the bodies of six dead Jews were found near [that] railway bridge … it appears that one charge blew up whilst it was being placed in position." Six haversacks filled with gelignite were discovered on a road bridge nearby. The main bridge at Wadi Gaza was also hit, but being of ferro-concrete construction it did not collapse and was thought to be repairable. Nearby Bedouin were attacked by the saboteurs.[274]

Road bridges fared no better. The Allenby Bridge "was blown up after a determined attack lasting about forty minutes by a party of some twenty armed Jews," and the nearby frontier control building was bombed. The pier on the Palestinian side of the Jordan was destroyed, and "as a result of the demolition of the pier," the Palestinian end of the bridge's center span "weighing approximately 200 tons is now resting on the river bank."

Police dogs trailed the Allenby Bridge attackers to Kivutsat Ha

Hugim Jewish settlement. They were met by men and women "lying down on the ground with legs arms interlocked" as women attacked the soldiers with sticks.

Bombs sent the Palestinian end of the bridge at Jisr Sheik Hussein collapsing into the river, destroying the entire structure. The bridge at Jisr Sheik Hussein was completely destroyed by a bomb that left the Palestinian end in the Jordan. At Jisr Banat Yacoub (Northern Frontier), the bridge on Damascus Road crumbled into the river, "so badly twisted and bent" from a bomb "that it must be regarded as a total wreck."

When a bomb was discovered on the bridge at Jisr Damiya near Jiftli, a specialist from the Royal Engineers attempted to save the structure. The device exploded as he struggled to disarm it, killing him and wrecking the bridge as intended.

The nocturnal blitz continued with the bombings of the bridge and culvert on the road north of Metulla, and the road bridge at Wadi Gaza. To hamper relief efforts, the militants accompanied their night of region-wide destruction with a series of diversionary bombings.

This blitz bore all the hallmarks of the Irgun or an Irgun-Lehi collaboration—but it proved to be the handiwork of the Jewish Agency's Haganah, which had yet more planned for the next evening.[275]

A good evening to miss a concert
Two journalists sympathetic to the Jewish Agency—one named Simon who worked for United Press, and Erich Gottgetreu of Associated Press (described in a cipher telegram two weeks earlier as a "Jewish journalist in close touch with Jewish Agency"), had tickets to attend a concert by the Palestine Orchestra (forerunner of the Israel Philharmonic) on the night of June 17. Neither went: when the day came, someone at the Agency "suggested" to both that it was a good evening to stay home.

At about 9:30, as the concert progressed without them, about thirty militants used grenades and automatic fire to break into the Palestine Railways workshops at Haifa Bay and set bombs. "After several loud explosions … searchlights from Mount Carmel went into action and night planes were sent out to investigate … Explosions continued till late night" and the fires raged until sunrise. Vital railway machinery was destroyed, crippling railway maintenance and thus making subsequent terror attacks on the railways all the more serious.

The approach to the workshop had been mined to target first responders, and so the Haifa Municipal fire engine that rushed to the scene was blown up, leaving several firemen injured in the wrecked vehicle.

Obviously, the Jewish Agency knew in advance that it was a good night for two journalists to stay home.

A document found with Shertok twelve days later contained a dismissive of statement about victims, reminiscent of Sneh's "illegal immigrants" comment at the Athlit Clearance Camp incident the previous October.

> Among the killed and wounded in the events at the railway workshops was an appreciable number of new immigrants who did not even know Hebrew properly.

Further incidents of sniper, grenade attacks, and bombings dotted the evening of the railway workshop bombing. The next day (June 18), the Haganah extolled the attacks, boasting on Kol Israel (radio) that the government was no longer in control in any part of Palestine: the militias wreaked havoc even "in the purely Arab parts of the country" and fully to the borders.[276]

That afternoon at 1:20, "twelve Jews armed with tommy-guns" drove up in four taxis and two light trucks to the Officers' Club in Tel Aviv's Hotel Hayarkon. After cutting the telephone lines and suspending traffic, they "went round the dining room inspecting shoulder tabs" and seized five senior officers. Two who attempted to resist were struck on the head with lead piping. Elsewhere at about 3:15, "armed Jews drove up in a taxi" and tried to abduct two more officers, but settled for shooting them in the legs when they successfully resisted. An eighth officer was abducted in Jerusalem; he managed to slip his bonds and escape from the house on Moshe Street where he was being held.

When word of the kidnappings reached London, military

officials argued that talks with the Jewish Agency about raising the immigration quota should be suspended pending their release, but government officials, in deference to the United States, refused.

The saga ended on July 4 when the three remaining kidnapped men were chloroformed, put in a coffin-esque wooden box, and dumped on the corner of Shedal and Rothschild Street in front of "hundreds of passers-by," none of whom, the British complained, "apparently considered the occasion worthy of note, and no information was obtained from them."

In the evening of the day of the kidnappings (June 18), a train driver came across red flags on the tracks near Kafar Jindis, two miles north of Lydda. But the driver was savvy to this Irgun ruse—he kept going as a bomb blew up under the train and Irgun fighters fired on it from the sides.[277]

Sharett exuded confidence when he addressed an extraordinary session of the Jewish Agency Executive the next day. Their political influence in the US, he assured the members, will "suffice to compel the President to act energetically and quickly" for the Zionists, and the US knows that "the threats of the Arabs are worthless and that their military potential is nil … We shall exploit to the maximum the American pressure on the British government," emphasizing the US' "pre-election period" and "Great Britain's dependence on the U.S.A." for its post-war loan. Sharett continued to speak of Europe's Jewish DPs as Agency property: they must be permitted no future other than Palestine.[278]

Another diamond heist on June 26 by "some 30-40 Jews" (probably Irgun), most 20-21 years of age, raised speculation that these robberies were sometimes pulled off as insurance scams in (likely involuntary) collusion with the owners.[279]

The British, meanwhile, had new indications of the Agency's surveillance abilities: they intercepted a letter, dated June 27, from the Jewish Agency in Washington to Eliezer Kaplan in London, containing details of a private meeting of the Anglo-American Committee three days earlier.[280]

Training in Europe

Both the Irgun and Lehi were active in Italy, which had become a final way-station for the refugees' presumed destiny in Palestine. "Training kibbutzim" and "training camps" supplemented the UNRRA camps, and America's Joint Distribution Committee (JDC) made Hebrew the official language of the schools it established and of the refugee camps' weekly newspaper.[281]

A weekly periodical, *La Risposta* ("the response"), began publishing in Florence under the Irgun emblem, advocating terror and the establishment of a "Jewish government" outside of Palestine. The editor, Corrado Tedeschi, had worked for the Psychological Warfare Branch and published a translation of a violent Irgun pamphlet that originated in the US. On June 22, the English-language *Rome Daily American* carried an interview with a Lehi member who "threatened the British Ambassador in Italy and various other Government officials with assassination when their activities became inconvenient to the Jewish cause, and described in highly coloured detail the training given in Rome to Jewish terrorists."[282]

Irgun recruitment in Austria (US Zone) was accelerating with what the British described as the terror gang's "considerable activity" among Jewish DPs. Polyglot Irgun leaflets encouraged Jewish youth to "join the Crusade for a great and independent Palestine." In Salzburg-Parsch, a DP camp was now named "New Palestine" and organized into Zionist nationalist associations. As reported in the intelligence summary *Mitropa*:

> Those in the Badgestein [Bad Gastein] contain a core of fanatical Palestinian nationalists who are organised into units of the Irgun Zvai Leumi. These Jewish fanatics are a constant security problem.[283]

At Pocking, in the US Zone of Germany, a similar but smaller group of about 250 members carried out regular drills with the objective of reaching Palestine by any means necessary. The streets of Prague were plastered with Irgun posters enlisting support for the "Jewish struggle in Palestine," concluding with "Glory to Russia, America and Czechoslovakia," the last of these a major arms conduit for the coming Israeli state.[284]

Operation Agatha

Telephone lines throughout much of Palestine went dead at 3:45 on the morning of June 29. A massive blitz to nip terrorism, code-named Operation Agatha, had begun. The British considered Agatha "a declaration of war against the Jewish extremist elements" and extraordinary efforts had been made to keep it secret: US President Truman was notified only seven hours before it began, a timing that would marginally satisfy diplomacy while "ensuring that the message does not arrive in the White House until it is too late for leakage to be of any consequence."

But despite the extreme precautions, "a large degree of surprise has been lost" due to "a leakage through military channels of part of the original plan." That leakage included "the black list of names of those to be detained" which, to the Brits' palpable unease, was reproduced and "plastered all over the walls of Tel Aviv." Should the document "find its way to America," the British worried, it might have "the most unfortunate results for us."[285]

Moshe Sneh, for one, had been tipped off and slipped away, and when British soldiers seized the Jewish Agency offices, it was "apparent that a number of documents had recently been removed from safes." Nonetheless, the documents still there made "clear that the Agency ran an elaborate espionage organization" and that "the Jewish Agency offices were the center of a vast organization for the theft of Top Secret diplomatic, military and police documents," including police personnel and Weekly Intelligence Summaries. Six secret reports from British intelligence organizations were found, as well as a note to Ben-Gurion that read: "Attached herewith a report from American Intelligence. It is interesting because it reveals the opinion of the State Department."

Jewish Agency possession of these US documents likely explains why the Agency's US representative, Stephen Wise, had begun pressuring Truman to dissociate US policy from his own State Department—which the US President did, dismissing the "rumors" that Wise raised, and "loyally and wholeheartedly" assuring him about his support for "Jewish immigration into Palestine."[286]

Officially, Agatha "did not specifically include a search for arms," any such search being "purely incidental." Whether this was indeed the case, or whether it was to protect informants and minimize the risk that targeted settlements would get advance warning, one settlement, Mesheq Yagur, was searched. Three major and about thirty smaller caches were uncovered, despite the elaborate methods devised to conceal them. Of the major cache,

> The ventilator shaft of the store room was identical with the central prop of the childrens see-saw. Entrance into one of these stores was effected after a paving stone with a small trolley beneath it had first been lowered by a worm and wheel and then pushed aside along a ramp.

The smaller caches "were skillfully hidden" as well,

> their entrances being disguised beneath paving stones, or rubbish, or behind sliding panels in rooms. Two were found in the cow shed, one in the nursery and several built into the masonry of culverts.

The weaponry found "were most diverse in type, varying from German 80 mm mortars to Polish detonators, and grenades concealed in beer cans." Much was from Britain and the US, and many were of unknown origin, lacking any of the usual identifying markers, apparently "made in PALESTINE or by private contract in some other country" by makers "anxious to hide their identity." Some probably found their way to Palestine via the many thefts by Zionist gangs from US arms supplies in Europe; it was known, for example, that ex-Jewish Brigade personnel had concealed "huge quantities of war materials" in hut partitions and elsewhere in a shipment from a US army camp to Palestine.[287]

The Haganah suspected that the discovery of arms in Mesheq Yagur was not luck, and suspicion turned to two Jews, named Freund and Papanek. Papanek was a Czech who had lived in Yagur settlement before the war, and then returned to fight in the Czechoslovak army, despite pressure from the Jewish Agency not to do so. After being discharged he moved to Haifa, where he shared a residence with Freund.

Papanek was visiting friends in Yagur when the British raided the settlement, and the (apparently coincidental) timing led the Haganah to believe that he had tipped them off. On July 3, Haganah operatives chloroformed and abducted them both, then chloroformed and moved them again the next day. Freund was released a week later, but Papanek was tortured, beaten, and burned on various parts of his body, including his penis, in order to elicit his "confession." He was found guilty of "high treason" by the Haganah "tribunal," the "High Court of the Underground Movement" and sentenced to death.

His luck changed suddenly: en route to his execution, his captors came to a military check point and had to hide him, at which he escaped. The British safely repatriated him to Czechoslovakia, while Kol Israel announced that a "Jewish people's court" had banished him.[288]

Zionism, terrorism, and the "purity of Jewish blood"

Increasing normalization of terror as a means, combined with the belief in Jews in racial terms and the determination to preserve its "purity" for the coming Jewish state, crystallized into a new terror organization, Otsray Ha Magifa. Meaning "the stoppers of the epidemic," it fought against the "epidemic" of friendships between Jews and non-Jews, the ultimate fear being that such a friendship might produce a child. Its vigilantes disfigured a disobedient Jewish girl with acid, leaving her blind in one eye.

The same word—*epidemic*—is now invoked by the Israeli state's vigilante groups, such as *Fire For Judaism* and *Love of Youth*, that patrol Israel and the settlements to catch, and stop, "mixed" dating.[289]

The King David Hotel

The terror gangs reacted to Agatha with a spectacular sneer at British impotence. The British were still assessing the results when on July 22 the Irgun, under the helm of future Israeli Prime Minister Menachem Begin, blew up a wing of Jerusalem's King David Hotel. Executed with the approval and cooperation of the Hagana, the attack was timed for when "the maximum number of people were in the building," as a British report gloomily observed. It was "mass murder," wrote

July 1946

Cunningham, "obliterating a complete cross-section of the public service": the ninety-one dead included forty-one Palestinians (the British themselves using the word *Palestinians* rather than *Arabs*), twenty-eight British, seventeen Jews, two Armenians, one Russian, and one Egyptian. Sixty-nine people were injured.[*]

British records describe how Irgun operatives disguised as Arabs entered the hotel and removed the reception clerk as other Irgun "Arabs" rounded up the remaining hotel employees in the basement. Milk cans filled with 500 lbs of high explosives were delivered to the hotel basement through the passage to *La Regence* Restaurant and placed directly under the cafe, timed to explode at about half past noon, the lunch hour. Security became aware of the intruders but, according to the British War Office, other Irgun "Arabs" then launched a diversionary bombing between the hotel and the YMCA and then fled in a saloon car. An Irgun *Communique* later called this a "warning bomb."

The Haganah immediately acted to protect the bombers. As recorded in written orders seized by the British that had been in the possession of Sneh, at 11:00 that night it issued a General Order that included:

• If the army comes to your settlement looking for the bombers, the Mukhtar (settlement head) will express disapproval of the bombing and declare that no terrorists are there.

• If the army searches, "there must be no co-operation with the searchers."

• If the army nonetheless discovers an arms cache in a settlement, wait until the army has left and is at least a kilometer (0.6 mile) from the settlement, and then attack it.

• "Suspects must not sleep in their usual dwellings."

• "The Special Detachment men will be given false names."

---

[*] However improbable, according to what the British called a "reliable report," representatives of the Irgun, Lehi, and Haganah had met the day before the King David bombing, July 21, in the Sderoet Chen area of Tel Aviv, to plan the bombing and decide who would carry it out. Menachem Begin, Nathan Yellin-Mor, Moshe Sneh, and Itzhak Ish-Shadeh (Feldman) were present. "At this meeting, lots were cast as to which of the three organizations … should fall the task" of bombing the hotel. TNA, KV2 2251, pencilled "25a"

The day after this iconic terror attack of the Mandate period, "[Jewish] youths plastered all walls and shops in Tel Aviv" with broadsides extolling the bombing. Of the Hebrew press, only the Hashomer Hazair published an unqualified condemnation of the bombing. An intercepted message "from a leading member of the Hagana" stated that there would be a civil war among Jews if they were to oppose the terror. A week later, an informant alleged that Sneh knew about the attack in advance, but that "the 'Jewish Resistance Movement' as a whole were authorized to disclaim responsibility."[290]

Following international condemnation, the Irgun defended the bombing by claiming that it had made phone calls to the hotel giving warning to evacuate. This is a diversion: No one, beginning with the operators receiving such calls, would simply wait inside the building if they knew they were about to be blown up. The onus cannot be put on the victims to have known that these particular claims were credible.

The author interviewed a survivor of the blast who was in the building delivering papers to the British offices during the time the warnings calls were allegedly being made, who was friendly with one of the telephone operators, and who was inside until the end, reaching the exit as it exploded. He had heard of no such calls. The British, to be sure, were keenly aware of the hotel's value as a political target: security precautions at the building, according to a document dated exactly seven months before the bombing, "are all that can be taken without declaring open war and going into a state of siege."[291]

The King David bombing endures as the iconic terror attack of the Mandate years, and history books falsely cite it as the most deadly. The 1940 bombing of the *Patria* was three times deadlier, killing about 267 people, and the two atrocities are identical in the claim that only infrastructure, not people, were the targets.

Of the attacks in which the killing was the acknowledged purpose, at least one of the Irgun's bombing of Palestinian markets killed more (July 6, 1938, about 120), and the Zionist armies' coming slaughter of villages such as Deir Yassin—still during the Mandate—would also kill more people than the King David attack.

Why, then, the status of the King David attack as the defining image of pre-state terror? The answer would seem to lie in the adaptability of this bombing to the Zionist narrative: unlike the more deadly terror attacks, the building itself can be explained as a military target, since it housed the seat of the British colonial administration.[292]

"We will continue to go our way," the *Voice of Fighting Zion* announced after the King David bombing, "the way of sufferings, the path of war." The Hebrew daily, *Davar*, stated that not only would the attack "not alter ... the political struggle of Zionism," but this struggle for "the secret plans of Zionism" will be "even more terrible and bitter." In its newsletter *Herut*, the Irgun referred to their terror campaign as the "third world war." For the Palestinians, the bombing reaffirmed the fear that (in the words of a British report) the "Government could not protect Arab lives and property from Jewish terrorists."

In comic irony, Brig. Iltyd Clayton joked that the way Zionists are extolling terrorism, we might one day even see Menachem Begin head the Zionist Organisation—scarcely imagining that Begin would become Prime Minister of the Israeli state. "Will nothing," this veteran of both World Wars wrote,

> ever convince people at home that in dealing with political Zionism we are dealing with something based on sentiment, on lust for power and I believe hatred for the West, and that it is fundamentally unjust........[293]

The King David outrage prompted another massive anti-terror operation, this one code-named Shark. On the morning of July 30, twenty thousand troops, mainly from the 6th Airborne, cordoned off Tel Aviv and screened 100,000 residents with instructions to "watch particularly for: (a) Bogus women. (b) Bogus sick." Over the next four days, the Operation led to the discovery of five arms caches. Tel Aviv's Great Synagogue, 110 Allenby Street, proved to be the hiding spot for a large weapons cache, counterfeiting equipment, and according to some reports, $1,000,000 in counterfeit Government bonds. Another large weapons cache was discovered behind a hollow wall in the washroom of a technical school. The Palestine Potash Company, which since 1929 had been extracting lucrative potash from the Dead Sea as Israeli companies do today in Palestine, was also discovered to be secretly doubling as an arms depot.

But the Irgun boasted that Shark missed the big prize: Menachem Begin, who was actually screened by the British but slipped through "with the help of false papers."

In the aftermath of the King David bombing, the British decided to go public with eight telegrams between Jerusalem and London that they had intercepted during the previous few months, supplemented with statements from Lehi's publication *Hamaas*, the Irgun's *Herut*, the Hagana's Kol Israel radio broadcasts—and an informant, as best as could be done without unduly risking his life.

The telegrams proved the Jewish Agency's collaboration with Irgun terror, indeed that Ben-Gurion himself wielded the baton on its podium: "The Jewish Agency and 241* policy" regarding planned Irgun attacks were "to be put into effect on receipt of instructions from BEN GURION in America."

For the British, the intercepts provided

> irrefutable evidence of the complicity of the Jewish Agency in terrorism … [Ben Gurion, Sharett, Sneh, Joseph, and others], under the cover of their positions in the Jewish Agency, have been for long engaged in directing, planning and organising sabotage of all kinds throughout the country and also in directing [broadcasts which] praised the terrorist acts of sabotage and murder in the highest terms and have poured forth a stream of perverted propaganda of a standard imitated from NAZI GERMANY. It is further revealed that, under the direction of those high officials, the HAGANA and PALMACH have assisted the STERN and the N.M.O. [in their attacks].[294]

Although the British continued to fear that taking stronger action against the terror would (as they put it) "alienate the Americans," it was hoped that the evidence would help justify any future raids on

---

* "241" referred to the number of alleged terrorists held under emergency regulations.

Jewish Agency offices and settlements. It was first condensed into a type-written *White Paper of Evidence*, and then published by the Colonial Office in July as a pamphlet entitled *Palestine Statement of Information Relating to Acts of Violence.*

Nervous about the response, the British prepared responses to foreseen criticism. The evidence is flimsy. Why were Weizmann and Eliezer Kaplan, both implicated in the documents, not detained? Why action was not taken sooner, with evidence already in hand?

Yet not even everyone in the House of Commons agreed on the interpretation of the evidence. Richard Crossman, a staunch Zionist who served on the Anglo-American Committee (ironically at Bevin's recommendation) and who had even advised the Jewish Agency against anti-terror cooperation with the British, isolated chosen passages to argue the opposite. As for the Jewish Agency itself, a "jumble of alleged telegrams" is how it dismissed the revelations.[295]

Other British members of the Anglo-American Committee proposed abolishing the Jewish Agency because of its direct involvement with terrorism. When word of this leaked out, Weizmann warned of the consequences with more apocalyptic theater: abolishing the Agency would mean the destruction of the "Third Temple" and the last hope of Jews "throughout the world."[296]

The Irgun, and to a lesser extent Lehi, continued to enlarge their ranks with defectors from the Hagana. Three reasons for disaffection were cited: anger at the Hagana's betrayal of some Irgun agents to the British (though according to the British, this betrayal was tactical, for the Agency's benefit); anger at lax security that had allowed the British to seize documents and "acquire a great deal of information on the organisation"; and "disgust at Agency denials of association with HAGANA and all it has accomplished."

The Irgun, meanwhile, was winning considerable clout, claiming for example that Britain's commuting of two terrorists' death sentences and other concessions were "done with the sole purpose to calm American opposition [fostered by the Irgun's US branch] against the American loan to Britain." To stem the exodus to its rivals, the Haganah promised "stronger activity in the future."[297]

August began with the bombing of rail tracks near Petah Tiqva. The next morning, the people of Salzburg, Austria, woke up to a city "plastered with posters in ten languages" encouraging young Jews to enlist in the Irgun and go to Palestine, what the British called the continuing "deliberate and highly organised plan" to force the creation of a Zionist state by exploiting "the sufferings of unfortunate people."

> Herded into over-crowded and unseaworthy ships, with insufficient food and in conditions of the utmost privation and squalor, they are brought across the Mediterranean inspired by a conviction, which has been instilled into them, that this is their only road to safety.[298]

Instilling that conviction required maintaining the terror of a war that had never ended and whose only relief would be a Zionist state of (literally, geographically) Biblical proportions. In London that month, *The Jewish Struggle* published a cartoon showing Prime Minister Attlee and Bevin gleefully destroy Jews' last hope of survival by symbolically taking a scissor (i.e., Partition) to a map of Palestine and Transjordan.[299]

When a Red Cross ambulance arrived at the Government Hospital in Jaffa on August 11, five hospital orderlies—or so they were dressed—emerged and asked for the ward where two injured Irgun members were recovering. The sentry became suspicious and called for reinforcements. A gun battle ensued, but the five impostors escaped in their stolen ambulance.

A change in British policy on August 13 threw new fuel into the terrorists' fire. Until then, illegal immigrants were not denied landing in Palestine, but were held in the Athlit Clearance Camp until they could be released under the current quota (now in excess of the White Paper) of 1500 per month. Since this policy presumed unlimited Zionist immigration, it was seen as prejudicial to a decision on the future of Palestine, and so the new policy required that above-quota immigrants be taken to DP facilities on Cyprus. Exceptions were made for the sick, children, and pregnant women.

Among several incidents on August 16, Lehi bombed a Tel Aviv flour mill because its owner refused demands for "contributions." On the 21st, three Haganah swimmers placed bombs on the vessel *Empire Rival* in Haifa harbor, blowing a hole in it eight by three feet.

At 20:00 Palestine time on August 29, Britain announced the commutation of death sentences for eighteen Lehi terrorists, following repeated intelligence warnings of a surge in terror and assassinations should the sentences be carried out. August also brought calls for a Jewish atomic fission facility in Palestine.[300]

Sept
1946

Ben Hecht's pro-Zionist play *A Flag is Born* was launched by Peter Bergson in the United States in September. With a cast that included Marlon Brando and Paul Muni, the play raised money for the Irgun, whose terror it romanticized. In a brilliant stroke of marketing savvy and irony, Bergson wooed American progressives to his ethnic supremacist cause by refusing to perform in segregated (black/white) venues. Hebrew University president Judah Magnes, who was in the US at the time, assailed the play's glorification of Jewish violence; in response, Hecht ridiculed "Jews in fancy dress with frightened brains."

Bevin, frustrated by the worsening situation, called for a London Conference between Arab and Zionist leaders to discuss Palestine's future. Arab states agreed to attend, but Palestinian representatives did not—they maintained their right to self-determination and thus saw nothing to discuss. The Jewish Agency refused to attend because Britain would not accept its preconditions for attendance.

Among those preconditions was global control over which Jews would be allowed to attend. When challenged on this point at a press interview, Golda Meir (then Meyerson) pursued non-sequiturs and finished by stating that the Jewish Agency was the "spokesman for Jewry."

Other preconditions set by the Agency appeared to Prime Minister Attlee to be "an obvious manoeuvre to put the Arabs in the wrong and to avoid a position where the Jews would have to come out for partition"—this reflecting a tactic used by Ben-Gurion in which Partition would be exploited but never advocated (see *Outline of Zionist Policy*, page 256, below).

The Jewish Agency also insisted that Bevin share Britain's proposals in advance of the Conference. Bevin refused. "If, for instance," he wrote, "it leaked out that we were willing to consider partition, the Jews, having got us to that point, would, I am certain, change their tactics and put pressure on the United States for the whole of Palestine."

Thus, representatives of Arab states were the only attendees to this London Conference. Palestinians boycotted it peacefully; Zionists boycotted it with fury.[301]

"This is our protest against the London Conference," the Irgun scowled in a type-written statement taking its share of credit for a three-day bombing blitz that began on September 8—a "Day of Bomb Outrages in Palestine, Terrorism on Eve of Conference in London," as the *Times* headline read. After blowing up some bridges, the militants bombed a signal box near Haifa, wrecking the building and killing a Palestinian child nearby.

Bombings of the railway system continued throughout the night. Communication lines between Palestine and Transjordan were blown up; a bomb at a railway bridge near Haifa exploded as attempts were made to remove another bomb; a level crossing near Haifa Oil Refineries was bombed; three oil pipelines were cut and oil set ablaze; the Lydda-Jerusalem railway line was bombed between Bittir and Jerusalem; and the main Haifa-Kantara line was destroyed in several places in a series of bombings.

Six explosions near Tarshiha (Acre) incapacitated the Haifa-Beirut line, while more bombs discovered there and on the Lydda–Tel Aviv line were discovered and detonated, sparing lives but not the infrastructure they rigged. The British continually hunted for more bombs to avert further attacks.[302]

Sergeant Killed by Jews is how the *Times* headlined Lehi's assassination in Haifa on the morning of September 9 of Sergeant T. G. Martin in retaliation for his capture of Yitzhak Shamir of the terror gang's high command, despite the future two-time Israeli Prime Minister's attempt to camouflage himself as a bearded orthodox rabbi.

That evening, "Jews dressed as soldiers" drove in two taxis to the Food Control Office. After killing the guard, they were engaged by the local Haifa security officer, Major Desmond Doran, who was on his balcony where he had been dining with his wife. The militants—all Lehi—demolished Doran's house with a mine, burying the couple and at least one other person under the rubble. Doran survived briefly. The cornucopia of bombings continued, targeting communications, transportation, and anyone maintaining public order. Relief workers remained a particular target: an ambulance assisting the wounded was blown up north of Hadera.[303]

When a jeep patrol sent to investigate explosions at Caesarea, Tulkarm, and Petah Tiqva was halted by mines, it was a trap: a sergeant exited the vehicle to investigate and was shot dead. A series of incidents began fifteen minutes later: bombs thrown at a jeep passing Ramat Hadar, numerous roads south of Rehovot mined, bombs on the railway between Lydda & Kafr Jinnes, explosions on Petah Tiqva Road, and attacks near Kefar Vitkin.

A trolley carrying civilians near Ras El Ain was bombed and blown off the tracks, and a railway was blown up in the Hadera-Zichron-Binyamina area. Civilian trains near Battir and near Qalqilya were targeted with bombs, as was a railway by a culvert near Rehovoth. The Greek monastery in the outskirts of Jerusalem was the site of more violence.

In response, eight thousand British troops were sent to Tel Aviv and nearby Ramat Gan, but what Cunningham called the "outrages by Jewish terrorists" continued. Irgun boasts of its anti-Conference terror occupied its September 11 broadcast of *Voice of Fighting Zion*, while Lehi used its *Bulletins* to catalogue its own contributions. The tallies followed the expected divisions of the two terror gangs' philosophies: the Irgun had carried out the bulk of the mass destruction, while Lehi had focused on narrower targets and assassinations.

The Irgun hit the Ottoman Banks in Jaffa and Tel Aviv on September 13, killing two people during a diversionary attack on Central Police Station in Jaffa. Arriving in jeeps at the main thoroughfare of Bustrus Street in Jaffa, the militants threw petrol cans which hit pedestrians as they burst into flames. Simultaneously, another group attacked the police station at the other end of the street.

A broadcast by Kol Israel announced that the attacks were a joint Irgun-Lehi undertaking, and in London *The Jewish Struggle* reported that the organizations had "raided banks in various towns in Palestine" and killed four Arabs. An attempt to bomb the railway near Qalqilya was thwarted on September 18, but the next day militants enriched themselves with "a daring daylight robbery" (as the British recorded it) of an entire conference of Diamond Exporters in Tel Aviv.[304]

At ten minutes to one o'clock on the afternoon of September 20, the Eastern Railway Station in Haifa was bombed, wrecking much of the structure as well as railway cars and nearby shops. Three days later an oil train on the Haifa-Kantara line north of Hadera was ambushed, bombed, and attacked with automatic fire. "One third of the train was derailed by remotely controlled charges of high explosive … the attackers opened fire on the train guards and attempted to ignite the oil with incendiary bullets." A guard was killed in an attack on a bridge on the Lydda-Jaffa branch, and on September 27 "a mob of about 400 Jews" stoned a Palestinian bus in Jaffa.

Dogs, already used for tracking, were now proving their ability to find hidden objects that their handlers' metal detectors missed. The trained dogs indicated a "find" by scratching the dirt and then sitting or lying down on the suspect area, and if accurate were rewarded with meat. At Ruhama, a dog named Dumbo found a hidden wireless transmitter, and a dog named Rex sensed something strange at Dorot. Digging out the area indicated by Rex, his humans discovered a wooden trap door three and a half feet underground, concealing a large cache of light and heavy machine guns, machine Carbines, mortars, and sundry other military equipment.

Dumbo and Rex got meat.

Acting on a tip, the British scouring Haifa harbor on September 29 found "an ingenious contrivance" of arm and springs that would have held its 50 lbs of explosives firmly against the side of a ship refueling at the jetty at Haifa Oil dock. Its likely intended targets were British destroyers refueling there. As with the attempted destruction of the HMS *Chevron* four months earlier, the explosives were positioned to ignite the vessel's ammunition magazine.

When on the Haifa–Tel Aviv Road the next evening a jeep was hit by a small mine, the driver was able to keep the vehicle moving as the bombers jumped out from hiding and showered it with gunfire.

Later that evening, militants drew up in a car alongside a British officer on motorcycle and shot him dead with automatic fire.[305]

A new plan to end the carnage, and the Mandate, was proposed in late September by a committee represented by seven Arab states, the Arab League, and the British government. It outlined a democratic Palestine with a government made up of Jews and Arabs of all religions, with both Arabs and Jews free to become head of state. Its authors were confident that the plan was consistent with international principles of self-determination. Lest the US be unaware of it, Bevin personally handed US Secretary of State Byrnes "the proposals for a democratic State as set out by the Arabs." But Zionists rejected the plan outright, adamant they would accept nothing less than a Jewish state in all of historic Palestine.[306]

Musa Bey Alami, who after the 1948 expulsions would work with Palestinian refugees to make the desert in the Jericho area bloom, visited Bevin in late 1946. Bevin described him as "frank and honest and extremely helpful." He blamed Zionism and the Balfour Declaration for destroying centuries of peaceful coexistence among the region's Jews, Christians, and Muslims, but stressed that there was no point looking back. The settlers were a reality and Palestinians wanted to live at peace with them—but as equals. He saw "this movement into Palestine" as merely "a spear-head," and Partition as merely a tactic.[307]

Zionist "persecution of Jews" and "intimidation is complete"—so warned "a Jew before an audience at a dominion club" and noted in War Office records. Zionism's course, the speaker continued, "is potentially disastrous to Jewry and to the peace of the world as a whole." Like other witnesses, he compared the Hagana's conscription of teenagers to Hitler's Youth Movement.

> Every boy of 16 years of age must join the Hagana. If he declines, his life at school is made unbearable and professional training and openings are withheld from him. If parents object, they are encouraged to deceive them in secret obedience to the 'call.' Even children 10 years old are enrolled in political parties—and this, eighteen months after we all believed we had destroyed Hitlerism for all time.[308]

Speaking "from first hand knowledge," even Orthodox Rabbis fear for their jobs and their lives, should they speak out. It is fundamentally "difficult to reconcile the pleas" to force open Palestine's door when safe haven elsewhere is thwarted by the Zionists. Zionism was never predicated "on the sufferings of our people," but on political objectives, on making the DPs "propaganda pawns of Zionist Power Politics."[309]

"Despair," a British report agreed, was exploited "to swamp the country [Palestine] with a Jewish majority." Any relief for the suffering of Jewish DPs, other than Palestine, was shunned.

There were in fact "large numbers of Jewish refugees in Europe [who] are seeking to emigrate to other parts of the world where living conditions are surer and more attractive than Palestine," British intelligence reported separately in September, and so "to combat this 'regrettable' trend," propaganda and "a species of black-mail" are waged "to keep the flame of zionism alive." Through "the exploitation of human misery and despair ... the Jewish remnants are being actively incited to embark on stinking unseaworthy hulks" in a promise that the Zionists cannot keep.[310]

On the last evening of September, a jeep returning to Tel Litwinsky from Nathanya was ambushed with a Molotov cocktail and sprayed with automatic fire, hitting a girl in her back. Near Peta Tiqva, a man from the First Parachute Brigade was gunned down from a passing car.

Then a new tactic appeared, probably the work of Lehi: a sign bearing the single word *MINES* was placed on the side of the road next to six objects—which turned out to be shoe boxes. When a vehicle stopped at the sight of the warning, it was ambushed and the occupant murdered. The British interpreted the "shoe box" murder as confirmation of reports (and, soon, Lehi broadsides) that Lehi was widening its tactic of personal terror.[311]

October heralded a heightened Lehi campaign of assassination favoring off-duty personnel. On the 1st it assassinated a senior NCO of the Airborne Division, and tried but failed to kill the occupants of a jeep on the Haifa–Tel Aviv road. In Tel Aviv the next day, the Irgun blew up the house of a (Jewish) woman who refused to finance them.

Oct 1946

On October 6, two British RAF personnel who had just arrived in Palestine that day were gunned down with automatic weapons, leaving one dead on the spot and the other in critical condition. The method was Lehi's signature: the operatives shot their victims in the back and instantly disappeared "into a conveniently placed Jewish quarter," as the British put it. The heightened assassination campaign was accompanied by further deaths through "a steady stream of road mining."

A key dimension to the terror in Palestine during the post-war, pre-state period is almost completely missing from this book's account: the terror against the Palestinians themselves. The British did not keep record of the violence by Jewish settlers against Palestinians, except occasionally to confirm that it continued. An attack that evening (October 6) in which "an Arab was stabbed in the back by Jewish youths on the Tel Aviv sea front" gives some indication: it was described by a British Intelligence Summary as being "typical of many that have occurred" against Arabs by Jews.[312]

Commentary during those years suggests that the Palestinians as a whole believed in the integrity of the Allied powers to do, ultimately, what was just. It was also widely believed that their collective refusal to retaliate would prevent their tormentors from obfuscating the situation with claims of self-defense.

On the 8th, Palestine saw renewed "widespread road and rail mining operations … by Jewish terrorists." In one incident, the worst was averted: although a bomb exploded as a train passed about 30 miles south of Haifa on the Haifa-Kantara line, that bomb was merely the detonation charge for a much larger bomb that failed to explode. The road to the Government House in Jerusalem was mined, a Palestinian civilian was hit by a land mine in the Sheikh Jarrah quarter on the Mount Scopus Road, and a Palestinian car was bombed in Tel Aviv.

A "prepared charge of considerable size" was electrically detonated on the Jerusalem-Jaffa Road, blowing up a truck and killing two of its five occupants immediately, severely wounding the others. The attackers then waited on the side for the first responder, which happened to be a policeman: they killed him as well, and then disappeared into Givat Shaul settlement. Three more roads were mined, causing at least one more casualty, another Palestinian civilian. People were maimed by mines between Jaffa and Beit Dajan, and more mines were discovered on the roads between Petah Tiqva and Wilhelma (now Bnei Atarot), between Tel Aviv and Petah Tiqva, and east of Kirbot-Beit—"main traffic arteries mined throughout the country," as the Irgun described its day's accomplishments. Lehi claimed responsibility for a series of attacks on October 9 in which it paralyzed major roads with mines, attacked a train on the Haifa-Kantara line, and exploded a bomb on the Jerusalem-Jaffa road, killing two and injuring six.[313]

"A large gang of armed Jews raided a Military Training Depot" at about 1:00 AM on October 11, stealing various guns, grenades, and bayonets, along with three trucks. The owner of the Yahalom Diamond Company had refused to pay Lehi "subscriptions," and so on the 13th the gang staged a robbery that yielded the entire wages of the workers. It mined roads "in many sectors" on October 14, wrecking at least one vehicle, with casualties. When the Pal Central-Haifa cable went dead that night, the break was traced to Yarkona, where "about 8 Jews" were attaching a bomb to the end of the cable by way of a pull igniter, to kill the repairmen sent to fix it.

This heralded a new trend. Two days later (16th), Lehi sabotaged the main telegraph cable between Haifa and Tel Aviv and booby-trapped the broken ends with mines, which exploded as intended when the repairmen arrived.

Anyone who helped keep Palestine a functioning society now had to fear. When the next day Inspector Bruce, condemned by a "Hagana court," was assassinated on Jaffa Road in Jerusalem, "none of the Jewish occupants of the street" who witnessed it, the British complained, "will throw any light on the matter."

Extensive mining of the roads during the night of October 17-18 left the British uncertain as to who was responsible. Although road mining was typically Irgun, they suspected Lehi because the night's array of bombs seemed calculated to kill, and only secondarily to wreak wider havoc. Their suspicion is borne out in Lehi records that cite road-mining in four regions, and an attack on an army motor transport. Lehi was widening its scope.

The same militia blew up an army jeep (Lehi described it as a truck) near Rishonlezion on October 20, choosing a site near Beit Dajan between an ice factory and a cold storage building. Inside the vehicle, which was "reduced to a mangled wreck," the two occupants were found alive, "severely injured" with serious burns and multiple abrasions. Its routine destruction continued, such as the severing again of the Haifa–Tel Aviv cable. The next day, the militants destroyed "two heavy mountain wagons" of a train near Jerusalem, attacked an army truck near Haifa, and blew up a jeep near Rishon Le Zion, seriously injuring two.

Bombs derailed a train on the Jerusalem-Lydda line on October 22. An army truck was attacked near Haifa on the 23rd, and three checking posts were bombed in Jerusalem on the 24th, killing two and injuring eleven. A bridge near Hadera was bombed, and the Jerusalem-Beirut and Jerusalem-Cairo cables were cut.

Lehi buried several bombs during the day in various key locations, but the British, suspicious that multiple assassinations were planned, made last-moment changes in personnel's locations. The worst attack in store for the evening was averted when a "diabolical" shrapnel bomb "of formidable dimensions" malfunctioned.[314]

Ever-more confident that Partition would be imposed, the Jewish Agency expedited the establishment of new outposts in the Negev and southern Palestine, and the Hula area in the north, in order to secure regions that it predicted would lie on the Palestinian side. As Cunningham put it, the Agency was planting "further Jewish outposts in an area at present unlikely to be allotted to them in any scheme of partition," regardless of cost; for example spending some £30,000 to lay a 25-30 km (15-19 miles) water pipeline to establish two new outposts deep in a region it was confident would not be given to them.

The specter of Partition led former US Senator Guy Gillette, now in his second year in the employ of the Irgun's US operation, to place large messianic advertisements in the press directed at the recently formed United Nations. The "fate of the Hebrew," the notices read, "has long been the barometer of civilization," the "oldest unfinished business in history." The only way to "finish history's business" was to hand Palestine over to the Zionists.[315]

When the ZOA held its annual convention on October 26, President Abba Silver categorically condemned any discussion of Partition—*Silver demands all of Palestine*, as the *NY Times* headline put it—and he demanded an "aggressive and militant line of action" to get it. Silver stressed "that the Zionist movement must stand on the proposition that it is not an immigration or a refugee movement but a movement to rebuild the Jewish state for the Jewish nation"—hence the Zionists' enthusiasm for giving Americans immigration permits intended for the war's Jewish survivors.[316]

Lehi killed two soldiers on October 29 in an attack on a truck near Wilhelma, east of Tel Aviv, what is now just northeast of Ben-Gurion Airport. The Irgun was active as well: its bombers blew up vehicles on the Haifa-Jaffa road, then escaped to the settler colony of Gan Hayim, while others blew up a Palestinian civilian truck and a British military vehicle in the Sheikh Jarrah area of Jerusalem, killing two immediately and leaving four in serious condition, then disappeared in the direction of nearby Jewish quarters.

The bombing of the British Embassy in Rome

Zionist bombings made their European debut on the night of October 30 with the bombing of the British Embassy in Rome. This, however, was merely the nightcap to a busy day in Palestine. It began at 5:45 in the morning when "Zionist extremists" (as the *NY Times* referred to them) blew up a truck in Jerusalem, killing two soldiers and injuring seventeen, four seriously. The blast was so strong that it set fire to the truck behind it, destroying its cargo of blankets and bedding, plunged a truck over an embankment, and overturned a Palestinian truck bringing grapes to the city market. One of the victims was hurled thirty yards.*

Elsewhere, the Haifa-Lydda train was derailed, a truck was "ensnared by a wire mesh across the road," a jeep was blown up causing two casualties, and a truck was destroyed by an electrically detonated mine, killing two. A large cache whose explosives paraphernalia

---

* Lehi boasted of a similar attack on October 27 that is probably a mis-dating.

The front (top right), back (top left), and inside (bottom) of a leaflet seeking to influence British soldiers in Palestine, 1946. [TNA, CO 733/456/10]

included detonators for acid bombs, was discovered at Givat Shaul in a shack near a biscuit factory.[317]

At about three o'clock that afternoon (October 30), a green taxi pulled up to the Jerusalem railway station. A girl exited the taxi carrying three suitcases loaded with high explosives, walked into the booking hall, and abandoned the suitcases. As she ran back, she shot at a Palestinian civilian who had become suspicious and tried to stop her. Once in the taxi, her accomplices fired at the station precinct as it sped off.

A police sergeant dragged one suitcase outside and destroyed it by detonating it with a revolver. He returned to repeat the procedure on the other two, but the next one exploded, killing him and destroying the waiting room, station master's office, booking office, and military transport office.

There are two curious footnotes to this attack. The *Palestine Post* printed a Haganah claim that it had sent a member to remove the explosives, but that he was too late and was killed in the cross-fire between the police and the taxi gang. But the Haganah knew that such suitcases were booby-trapped, and only the Palestinian bystander is mentioned in other reports.

A more curious enigma is that the British captured four of the attackers, while a fifth, known as Yanai (but whose actual name was Hans Reinhold), disappeared. The Irgun suspected that he was an informer, and the following May (1947) its operatives tracked down the man they believed to be Yanai in Belgium and tried, unsuccessfully, to assassinate him.[318]

So end the daylight hours of October 30. That night, four months after Zionist gangs used the Italian media to threaten attacks on its soil, the Irgun destroyed the British Embassy in Rome with suitcase bombs detonated by timer. The explosion shattered windows through-out a wide area and severely damaged the 350-child Handmaids of the Sacred Heart, a school run by nuns across the street. Reports conflict regarding the several casualties, but one man who happened to be passing the building when the bombs detonated was "so badly hurt that it has been impossible to question him." With no immediate claim of responsibility, the media suspected Communists as well as Zionists, and the Communist Party in turn blamed Fascists.

But Irgun posters soon appeared claiming responsibility, and four days later (November 4), several American correspondents in Rome received a "Communiqué the Supreme Command of the I.Z.L. [Irgun] in Eretz Israel" taking credit for bombing of the Embassy.

> [We] will continue to fight the British enslavers, the attack against the British Embassy in Rome is the opening of the military campaign of the Jews in the diaspora … May God be our aid I.Z.L. published in the Diaspora 2nd November 1946.[319]

Jewish refugee centers in southern Italy were, according to the British, "exceptionally well-organised strongholds of extreme Zionism." Four UNRRA (United Nations Relief and Rehabilitation Administration) camps in the heel of Italy were "an extreme Zionist enclave on Italian territory … believed to be full of hidden arms," but the Italian authorities "are not unnaturally afraid of the political consequences of provoking a row with UNRRA."

The Anglo-American Committee became aware of the camps' radicalization when it visited them the previous February—indeed certain members woke up to slashed tires. But the Rome bombing forced authorities "to bring under proper control the camp and admin. machinery," which was suspected of financing terror by selling UNRRA rations on the black market. As always, the British worried about upsetting the Americans, "since otherwise we may have them, as well as the Jewish terrorists, against us." Both the British and the Italians avoided searching the Jewish camps for fear of violent resistance and the exploitation of it to the US audience.[320]

Seven weeks after the bombing, the Italian press reported the results of the initial Italian investigation. Several DPs from the refugee camps, including one from the camp in nearby Ostia, had set up a bogus correspondence bureau in an office near the Embassy. Operatives arrived from Palestine with instructions how to carry out the attack, the order allegedly "hidden in the sole of a shoe." After the attack, the Irgun office moved elsewhere with all its equipment, but the police seized two suitcases full of documents and propaganda, which included instructions for the use of explosives written in German and translated into Hebrew. The principal suspects escaped, apart from one who was killed by Italian police in the attempt.[321]

Five years later, Israel lobbied Britain to pressure Italy not to pursue the terrorists, claiming that doing so would "evoke memories of past bitterness." The result was a token trial *in absentia* of eight suspects, all living in and protected by the Israeli state. On April 17, 1952 the Rome court sentenced ringleader Moishe Deitel to sixteen months' imprisonment, and seven other bombers to a maximum of eight months, these nominal sentences then forgiven. As the *Daily Express* summarized it,

> Light sentences, automatically wiped out by amnesties, were imposed
> today on eight Jews accused of blowing up the British Embassy in

Rome in November 1946. None of the eight appeared, and it was said that they were living in Israel.[322]

It is about the time of the Rome bombing, October-November of 1946, that the British began systematically under-counting casualties in terror attacks—or so Lehi claimed. "The enemy has <u>for the first time</u>," their *L.H.I. Bulletin* bragged,

> been issuing fake lists of casualties. We know for certain that on several occasions the casualties suffered by the British were higher than those 'officially' disclosed.

Meanwhile in London, *The Jewish Struggle* mocked Yehudi Menuhin and Bronislaw Huberman for performing in Royal Albert Hall, comparing them to the *Moshke* who danced and sang for his oppressors in seventeenth century Poland. The juxtaposition of the two famous violinists was curious: ten years earlier, Huberman, along with Felix Galimir, had founded the Palestine Orchestra, precursor to the Israel Philharmonic; and Menuhin was the son of Moshe Menuhin, who after attending Yeshivas in Jerusalem and the ultra-nationalistic Gymnasia Herzlia in Tel Aviv became an articulate and impassioned critic of Zionism. Galimir, a native of Vienna, joined the Palestine Orchestra in early 1937 after being fired from the Vienna Philharmonic because he was Jewish, but emigrated permanently to New York by the summer of 1938.[323]

Britain itself becomes a target

Substantive threats of Zionist terrorism on Britain's home soil date back at least to early 1944 (Irgun) and 1945 (Lehi). Even the radically pro-Zionist Winston Churchill incurred Lehi's wrath by condemning its assassination of Lord Moyne, and so was cited as a target by May 1945 and continued to be a target of Lehi letter bombs.

In the fall of that year, reports warned that both Lehi and the Irgun would infiltrate Britain by posing as merchant seamen and service personnel in ships reaching British ports from the eastern Mediterranean. More warnings of maritime infiltration followed quickly: the British learned that agents for Swedish and Norwegian vessels in the Greek port of Piraeus were willing to arrange passage for individuals as crew members, and Zionist operatives would exploit this to enter Britain. January of 1946 brought the first confirmation of specific Lehi plans to assassinate Bevin, and the roster of targets widened in February.

In August, British intelligence reported that five Irgun/Lehi cells would go to London if the death sentences of eighteen Lehi operatives were confirmed, contributing to the commutation of their sentences on the eve of the London Conference. Several British officials, including Colonial Secretary Arthur Creech Jones, received death-threat letters claiming to be from Lehi, dated from Barcelona but postmarked from Lisbon. Most threatened that the "execution" of the "stinking British pigs" will "soon take place by silent and new means." Meanwhile, in what the British called "one more victory for the pressure groups," the US granted Moshe Sneh an entry visa, and so he and Ben-Gurion reportedly left France for New York on an American aircraft on August 28.[324]

In the hours after the Rome attack, the early morning hours of October 31, a truck was blown up two miles south of Petah Tiqva, killing two and seriously injuring two. Another truck tripped and detonated a road mine near Ir Ganim Colony (Haifa), and a police mobile patrol was attacked north of Tel Aviv.

Nov
1946

November began with a mine detonated under a goods train on the Haifa-Kantara Line between Hadera and Binyamina, damaging a bridge along with the train. Nonetheless the British, ever fearful of violent backlash from the settlements, initiated what the *Times* called an "official policy of turning the other cheek."

An attempt to sabotage an oil pipeline near Kishon Bridge at Haifa on November 2 was foiled—the bomb was discovered strapped to the pipeline, removed, and detonated. Near Jaffa, a truck was blown up and burnt out, injuring ten, three seriously. Electrically detonated explosives hit a culvert, a truck was ensnared and forced off the road by a wire mesh stretched across the road north of Petah Tiqva, a road bridge was blown up on the main Haifa–Tel Aviv Road near

Telmond, and vehicles were attacked near Hadera and in Jerusalem. In the north, the settlement planned for the Hula region was founded, a fact-on-the-ground towards pre-empting Partition.[325]

Jews continue their terrorist activity, the Jaffa-based *Falastin* reported the next day, as militants blew up a train on the Haifa-Kantara line south of Qalqilya, killed two Palestinians, injured eleven soldiers, and blew up a train on the Lydda–Tel Aviv branch line near Battir village. When the Jerusalem-Beirut telegraph cable was sabotaged again, engineers were unable to locate the underground break; fully eight kilometers of the cable had to be replaced.

The saboteurs bombed oil train no. 57 on the Haifa-Kantara line near Qalqilya on November 5, and then attacked the train and the railway blockhouse. A car was blown up on Beit Dajan Rishon le Zion Road, the railway was bombed near Kiryat Haim, two mines were electrically detonated under a train on the Haifa-Kantara line, and telephone wires were cut again. A military train traveling on the Haifa-Kantara line was mined by the Irgun on the 6th, and Lehi bombed the Cairo-Haifa train on the 7th, derailing two coaches, then bombed the tracks at both Neane and Petah Tiqva on the 8th.[326]

More sophisticated railway bombs were making their debut. In a November radio broadcast, the Irgun claimed credit for the devices' increasing sophistication, their "military experts" having developed a new type of railway mine that cannot be dismantled and is capable of paralyzing any railway system. According to the broadcast, the device automatically regulates itself to destroy both heavy and light trains. The newer devices could be completely buried and were better booby-trapped to kill anyone who might discover them. They worked as planned: two people were killed and several injured when the first one was uncovered.[327]

Nerves were given a reprieve by what a Captain in Airborne Field Security described as "an amusing anti-climax" regarding a Palestinian man whose house lay within what had become a Divisional Training Centre. He was "long-established" and the British were loath to evict him. Enjoying the rare opportunity to relax security and trust a civilian, they simply gave him a key to the military gate and made it his responsibility "for seeing that it is secured" when he returned home every day from his field, which lay outside the camp.[328]

In the morning of November 9, police received an anonymous phone tip about a hidden arms cache in an abandoned house. Four officers were sent to investigate. Shortly after entering, the booby-trapped house blew up, killing all four men—what Lehi explained as its retribution for the police "tracing Hebrew arms."

Four train incidents between the 5th and 8th of November intrigued 317 Airborne Field Security for their sophistication and planning. Most interesting was the bombing and attack of an oil tanker on the 5th, "probably the largest single ambush of its kind, involving not one, but three separate charges, and two entirely separate detonating circuits."

> The operation had been carried out by eight persons during the night, and great energy had been expended in burying the charge and flax, which was, on the whole, well camouflaged. The party had been well equipped and prepared for the job in every detail… Then, when all was ready and prepared to catch the first train, the main body withdrew, and left two no doubt innocent-looking people to press the button. Even if they had been caught at the scene, it would have been difficult to have convicted them.

Working the night trains had become so hazardous that the drivers struck, leading the saboteurs to shift focus back to the stations. The El Ain railway station was the principal target on the 10th. Four Jews dressed as police entered the station and planted suitcase bombs in the station master's office while they held the station master at gunpoint, then left. One Palestinian was killed and several people injured in the attempt to remove the bombs, and the station was completely demolished. The Jerusalem-Beirut telegraph cables were cut again, and 80 meters (260 ft.) of rail were destroyed on the Haifa-Lydda Line.[329]

Terrorists Say 'Nothing Can Stop Us' screamed the headlines of London's *Daily Herald* on November 11, as their war to bring Palestine to its knees forged ahead. The railway station at Rosh

Ha'Ayin was destroyed, the railway line near Qalqilya was bombed, two coaches were sabotaged near Tel Aviv, telegraph lines were hit, and a railway trolley was attacked near Jerusalem.

England: the domestic terror threat, but no poisoned wells

In England, Scotland Yard locked its gates as Parliament opened with "detectives on the watch for [Jewish] terrorists who might have smuggled themselves into the country mixed with Remembrance Day crowds in Whitehall." A primary suspect was a 32 year old woman who was said to be "the fiancée of a prominent member" of the Irgun. According to news reports, she entered on a British passport but, according to Lehi, a fake one: Lehi's *L.H.I.-Bulletin* of December 1946 claimed the passport used by "Mr. Irgun's fiancée" had been "issued by the L.H.I. [Lehi] passport department."[330]

The British media's nervous coverage of the domestic Zionist terror threat was treated by the militias as proof of their success, an unease compounded by the continuing "security problem presented by the presence of suspect Jewish terrorists in His Majesty's Forces." Lehi gave itself credit for an "England in Terror" and claimed responsibility for two attempted bombings of the Colonial Office. The gang also suggested—enigmatically—that Jews had attempted to poison water wells, as if to bring to life the medieval antisemitic lie.

"In Middle Ages," Lehi wrote in its *Bulletin*, "many slanderous rumours were spread about Jews," notably "that Jews poisoned wells of Christians." Jews, Lehi said, had good reason to do so, but couldn't, because Jews "were not a living organism in those days." But they are today, and although not the cause of the panic in London, "Jews were involved in this affair" of poisoned wells.

But which affair? Although poisoned wells would soon become a reality in Palestine at the hands of both the Haganah and the settlers, there is no evidence of this in England. Lehi, rather, was probably referring to the foiled poisoning of German water supplies by the *Nakam*, a terror group composed in part of Jewish Brigade soldiers. Nakam allegedly planted operatives in the water filtration plants of five cities—Munich, Berlin, Weimar, Nuremberg, and Hamburg—ready to poison the water for the indiscriminate murder of Germans on a massive scale. The delivery of the poison was foiled, though Nakam killed a few hundred German detainees by having an operative secure employment at the bakery that supplied their bread, then lacing it with arsenic.[331]

At this time in the United States, the Political Action Committee for Palestine—formed the previous February by a soon-to-be-infamous Rabbi Baruch Korff—was especially active, and its media propaganda rivaled Bergson's. Britain, one of Korff's newspaper ads said, was not merely as bad as the Nazis: it was worse. Britain was running "concentration camps" for Jews that "are even worse than the Nazi German concentration holes … where millions went to their deaths." No one could "remain Christians" and accept the "torture, suffering and murder of 6,000,000 Jewish men, women and children," the wording nearly suggesting that the Holocaust was ongoing and being conducted from London.

Like Bergson, Korff seduced bigots with the lure of fewer Jews, and threatened everyone else with being smeared as antisemitic or un-Christian. Korff went further: Christians had to fear not just for their reputations, but for their very lives, because Britain is "a malignant cancer from which no people eventually will be safe." Whichever incentive applied, there was a solution: pressure the US government to cancel its post-war loan to Britain unless it cedes to Zionist demands.[332]

Palestine's epidemic of railway terrorism kept trains limited to daylight hours and preceded by a special armored car. A dawn patrol combed the railways every morning for bombs, a job known as the "suicide patrol." The patrol not only risked happening upon booby-trapped bombs, but also being ambushed by the bombers themselves. At five o'clock in the morning of November 13, Irgun operatives ambushed the workers on one such "ramshackled hand-propelled car" looking for the militia's bombs, murdering all six—four Palestinians and two British.

Later that day a locomotive and three wagons were hit by electrically detonated mines, and an electrically controlled bomb was detonated on St. George's Road in Jerusalem, both incidents with serious injuries. Lehi was busy as well, assassinating two policemen in the course of the day. Two days later, bombers used a remote-controlled mine in a culvert to blow up a trolley patrolling the line at kilo 44 on the Haifa-Lydda Line near Benyamina, with several casualties.

Despite being well aware of the trail of corpses left by Irgun bombs, railway workers still tried to protect the trains. At 5:20 in the morning on November 17, a worker discovered a bomb on the Haifa-Kantara line near Kafr Sirkin and tried to move it away from the tracks, but the Irgun's anti-lifting device worked as intended. The explosion killed him and injuring another man. A second mine was discovered fifty-five minutes later (6:15) on the narrow gauge track near Haifa.

At about 6:45 a third mine exploded under a train on the Haifa-Kantara line between Rehovoth and Yibna—but in what the British described as "a most astonishing incident," it was faulty and did not blow up until the seventeenth wagon of the thirty-one wagon train. Probably in fear of the traditional militia attack coordinated with the bomb, the driver continued on, the fifteen derailed wagons destroying a mile of track as they were dragged along. A fourth bomb was found on the Jaffa-Lydda branch outside Tel Aviv.

The worst attack came in the evening, when bombers blew up three civilian vehicles and one British vehicle on the Haifa-Jaffa road—the blast so loud that, according to *Falastin*, it "was heard to resound in Jaffa and Tel Aviv." Three policemen in their twenties and one RAF sergeant, all returning from the cinema, were killed instantly, and six people wounded.

Again on the 18th, despite a keen awareness of the militants' predilection for booby-traps, the safety crew who discovered a bomb on the Haifa-Kantara thought first of protecting the trains. The device outwitted them as well, killing four and injuring six, one blinded in both eyes.

The use of multiple, hidden anti-tamper triggers on a single device, the British were learning, was among the Irgun's new fetishes. As the day wore on, a pressure mine on the Lydda-Rehovot line derailed a train and injured the driver, a mine was detonated under a train on the Lydda-Jaffa branch, and a rail trolley that was checking for bombs was blown up. Further bombings were spoiled when militants were discovered laying road mines near Givat Shaul.[333]

"A complete shut-down of railway traffic" hit Palestine—so boasted the Irgun of the day's sabotage on the 19th. One person was killed and others injured while attempting to neutralize a bomb at Kfar Sirkin; a constable was murdered in Tel Aviv; a mine was detonated under a train on the Haifa-Kantara line; and more mines were discovered on the same line, as well as on tracks near Benyamina and near Battir. An attempt to blow up a police car failed, and in Jerusalem a land mine shattered windows without known casualties. Cunningham decried "the continuance of terrorism with its almost daily toll of lives," while a small group of enraged British policemen rebelled with their own anti-Jewish rampage in Tel Aviv, resulting in an anti-British feast in the media.[334]

At 8:00 on the evening of the 20th, two "juveniles, riding bicycles" shot and gravely wounded 22-year-old Shimon Azzulai as he was walking with his wife and their baby, in what was judged a political crime: he was in possession of a British passport and was contemplating leaving for London in a week. In Jerusalem, the Income Tax office was destroyed by an Irgun bomb, killing a (Jewish) policeman and wounding ten people.

Constable Moshe Ben Bezalel was assassinated on the 21st for refusing to cooperate with Lehi, as railway tracks were sabotaged on the Jaffa-Lydda line. Fifteen meters of track were blown up near Petah Tiqva on the 23rd, and a military vehicle was attacked near Beit Dajan on the 25th. On November 30, roads were mined in several parts of Jerusalem and a police billet in Mustashfa was hit by bombs, gunfire, and grenades. *Jerusalem rocked by bombs, gunfire in revived terror*, the *New York Times* headline said. *Jews are attacking Jews*, the (London) *Times* reported.[335]

"This is murder and nothing else," a mother wrote to the government on the first of December after her son was killed, one of the many letters that reached members of Parliament from parents, spouses, and siblings protesting their loved ones' murder at the hands of the Zionists.

Dec
1946

What right have our Sons, who went bravely to fight for their Country, having been taken from their studies, their homes, and everything that was dear to them, and suffered without complaint, be murdered now in such a cause…[336]

"We must get these terrorists under control," wrote another.

… Will you please get our youth out of Palestine before they all get blown to smithereenes.[337]

When the Council of Christians and Jews met in London early that month, it adopted a resolution condemning "Jewish terrorism," and the Archbishop of Canterbury leveled blame at the United States: "I do not think that we can possibly feel that from across the Atlantic there has been much to help the relieving of this situation." Cunningham was more direct: he complained of the militants' increasing confidence deriving from the "effective pressure which Zionists in America are in a position to exert on American Administration…"[338]

Analysis of the various explosive devices and booby-trapping was collected into a restricted pamphlet printed in Jerusalem for British personnel. It gave "a brief summary of present-day methods employed by Jewish Terrorists with mines and booby traps." Devices that had been recovered were analyzed and illustrated. The book warned, however, that every device encountered must be treated anew. "Take nothing for granted … Having discovered one means of firing, look for a second—and a third; they are seldom used singly."[339]

When printed in December, the debut of a new type of bomb already made it out-of-date. On the 2nd of the month, "the first electrically detonated road mine to be fired in broad daylight," killed all four people in a jeep on Latrun-Jerusalem road at 11:45 in the morning. The bomb was

a departure … from previous road mines, in that a single charge of ammonal, packed with rivets, was exploded to cause a shrapnel effect similar to that of the German "S" mine. The bodies were in an appalling state. This mine has only one advantage over the previous twin charge of HE, in that it inflicts more serious and sickening casualties on its victims.

Rocks and broken glass were scattered over the ground above the bomb in order to increase the effect. At least two more people were killed and three seriously wounded in continuing attacks over December 2-3, with the bombs placed on, or dug into, the camel track by the edge of the road, the detonating wire tailed off into the nearby terrain.

One gang member was injured in a militia's thwarted attempt to steal funds from the Polish Refugees Committee on the 3rd. His accomplices brought him to (and held up) the hospital for an operation—and then took him away.[340]

Two or three hours after leaving a Tel Aviv repair shop on the morning of December 5, a three-ton truck appeared at Sarafand Camp, driven by what was described as a tall, fair-skinned Jew, who produced identification and a work ticket. After a couple of minutes working inside the truck, he "tinkered with the engine," then told the sentry he was going to the NAAFI*—and left. The blast from the explosive-laden vehicle killed two people on the spot and wounded twenty-eight, including five civilians, demolishing nearby medical and operational buildings. Separately, a grenade and firearms attack on the Mustashfa police station seriously wounded a constable, and the GOC's residence was attacked with grenades.

Bombers' carelessness averted what could have been the worst attack of the day. As the British recorded it, "a terrorist motor convoy … consisting of a truck with over 400 lbs of explosives and two taxis in line astern" was proceeding down Street of the Prophets in Jerusalem for an attack on Air Headquarters. The militants in the second taxi were about to lay mines by the Police Billet as a diversionary attack when they ran over a traffic island, detonating the mines they were transporting and killing two of the bombers. Aware that the explosion had likely alerted the British, the other militants

---

* The Navy, Army, and Air Force Institute was a canteen service for the British.

stopped, booby-trapped their vehicles, and fled. The British, indeed quick to the scene, correctly assumed that any attempt to disarm the vehicles would be deadly. They had no choice but to explode the rigged vehicles (two taxis and a truck) where they were. The explosion caused extensive damage to nearby Palestinian houses.

A few days after the failed attack, three Halifax aircraft left the airfield and risked dangerous weather conditions to drop food, clothing, and medicine to intended illegal settlers shipwrecked off the island of Syrina. In gratitude, the Jewish Agency gave the Flight Commander three crates of beer, but the gratitude was short-lived: although Britain brought the injured, women, and children to Palestine independent of quota, it brought the uninjured men to Cyprus to await their turn, for which the Agency warned of retaliatory terror attacks.[341]

December brought a lull in significant bombing of the railways—the result of a business deal the Irgun and Lehi struck with Jewish citrus interests that needed the trains at this point in the harvest cycle. Both gangs issued pamphlets assuring the public that the railway terror would resume once the citrus season ended.

High-profile attacks on the British also entered a brief, relative lull with the opening of the Zionist Conference in Basel on December 9. The terror groups were not, however, inactive. "During the lull," British intelligence reported, "the Jews have turned their attention to Arabs and to unpopular Jews." Two days after the Conference began, in the village of Salameh—a village that would be leveled and erased by the Zionist armies in a year and a quarter—the Haganah kidnapped two Palestinian children and shot the mukhtar who tried to help them.

Palestine Arabs Schedule General Strike As Protest Against Zionists' Terrorism, the *NY Times* headline read, as Palestinians organized non-violent resistance that the War Office described as "orderly." Cunningham as well remarked on the Palestinians' continuing restraint, but worried that "further Jewish provocation" would risk "isolated acts of retaliation."[342]

Not coincidentally, a "well-informed Jewish contact" told the British that Zionist leaders were spreading the propaganda that "the only real solution to the Arab problem in Palestine" (to which was inserted *[sic]*), is a transfer of Arabs out of Palestine, and a transfer of Middle Eastern and North African Jews into Palestine.[343]

Zionist violence against uncooperative Jews continued, with four attempted assassinations of Jewish civilians by the Zionist gangs recorded within a ten-day period in December. Three were over refusal to fund the Irgun, beginning with one on the 6th without details. Two days later, Selig Kunin of Nathanya found an explosive charge fixed to the exhaust manifold of his truck, and on the 18th a Mr. Jacobson of the Rehovot area was about to drive his new American car when he saw a bomb with a burning fuse under it.

The fourth incident was not directly about money and suggests that Zionism's anti-Jewish violence was under-reported, as fear kept victims from coming forward. Hayim Klear, a resident of Nathanya, had publicly denounced "terrorist methods and policy," and so on the evening of December 8, his car was blown up. But after an initial report to the police, something reversed Mr. Klear's attitude: he suddenly refused to speak about the matter, moved to "an unknown address in Tel Aviv," and the bombing was now officially listed as an "accident." In another instance, one Yerovcham Wardiman, a prosperous cinema owner, "departed hastily for the USA" after refusing the Irgun's extortion. As a local informant remarked, Zionist terrorism was a "profession" devoid of any alleged "ideal."[344]

December 24 brought the end of the Basle Conference, and an end to the lull in violence. When in Rehovoth that evening, "a gang of approx 80 young Jews, under control of a leader," went on a rampage against uniformed personnel, the Jewish Special Police made no attempt to stop them—whether out of fear or solidarity. A "gang of 10 Jewish youths" then set upon four soldiers, but were stopped by the Palestine Policemen. The following day, Christmas, militants blew up a truck, killing two people and injuring twenty. Another Irgun(?) diamond factory robbery followed on the 26th, and the Divisional Police Headquarters in Rehovot was attacked on the 30th.

Jews are not Zulus, Lehi railed in a crop of new pamphlets that appeared in the last week of December accusing the British of treating Jews like "natives"—echoing complaints from across the Zionist spectrum. In response to Britain's flogging of a teenager convicted in the deadly bank robbery spree of September 13, Lehi kidnapped and flogged four British army personnel on December 29: one abducted from Rishon Cafe (Cafe Theresa in Rishon LeZion), one from Hotel Metropole (Nathanya), two from Hotel Armon (Tel Aviv).

"Palestine's regime of terror," the *NY Times* reported, now "threatens to assume increasingly serious proportions."[345]

6

The Partition scam

"There is no serious difference between the [Irgun and
the Jewish Agency] over Partition. The policy of the Irgun
is to insist publicly on the whole of Palestine and transjordan
as a Jewish State; but at a recent meeting of Irgun leaders it
was agreed that the Irgun would secretly agree [with
the Jewish Agency] to the principle of Partition as
a temporary expedient..."
—*British Colonial Office, February 11, 1947* [346]

And so began the fateful year of 1947, the year when the British officially bequeathed to the Palestinians the catastrophe they had enabled.

The year brought an "even greater reluctance than formerly" of the Jewish Agency to cooperate against terror. British-trained ex-Brigade soldiers returned to Palestine and joined the militias, some having engaged in assassinations in Europe, others having assisted in the removing of Jewish orphans from their adoptive homes. Still others were in the United States, "endeavouring to influence U.S. public opinion," as the Colonial Office reported it, "through Veterans' Organizations and through individuals," under the guidance of Shlomo Rabinowitch, who would become Commander of the Israeli Air Force.

When the British renewed attempts through diplomatic channels to stop the terror fund-raising in the US, word leaked out and the overtures were publicized as "British pressure" against Jewish "philanthropic organizations." The American Council for Judaism, meanwhile, warned of the consequences of Americans being "drawn into supporting directly or indirectly a racial-nationalist Jewish state in Palestine," contrary to the high principles which Americans espouse. The "self-imposed ghetto" that Zionists sought, "using a gun and forcing themselves into another land," will cause terrible harm to Jews.[347]

In Palestine, "recruits for the Irgun are said to be coming in fast," British intelligence reported, as students became captive audiences to Irgun coercion "after the silencing of the teacher by overpowering him or by other means." Among the terror gang's kinder recruiting methods was to commandeer the projection room of movie theaters to show their propaganda films.[348]

In a massive assault on the second day of 1947, the gangs used flame throwers against people, buildings, and vehicles in Jerusalem and the Galilee. Tel Aviv's Citrus House, which housed the British army headquarters, was the Irgun's missed trophy of the day, and the attack exposed that some Jewish Settlement Police were working with the militia. According to the British,

Jan 1947

> At 1800 hours on 2 Jan the Jewish ghaffirs [corporal rank] at the gate of CITRUS HOUSE told the sentry that they were being relieved. This was NOT in fact true, but they then disappeared, and nine minutes later three Jews, carrying flame-throwers, and armed, two with TSMGs and one with a pistol, opened fire…[349]

The choreographed attacks on Citrus House proved too ambitious. Under cover of fire from a neighboring building, "flame-throwers [reached] the northern perimeter wire" of the building, while a coordinated "stream of oil was directed towards the vehicle park" to be ignited by the flame throwers—but the flame throwers failed to hit the oil. The *NY Times* reported that "forty or more terrorists on the roof of a building opposite Citrus House" opened fire on the House's third floor with machine guns and small arms, "but this was the wrong floor and they merely hit the kitchen help." At least one of the day's wounded soon died.

Among those less seriously wounded was a "Jewish NAAFI girl," one Rosa Hirsch of Tel Aviv, who imprudently exclaimed: "My husband told me not to go to Citrus House tonight." Her husband had already slipped away when police went to question him.[350]

In Jerusalem, grenade attacks against the Syrian Orphanage and the RAF Unit failed to cause serious damage, though the Orphanage would be less fortunate in two months' time. Grenades were thrown at a military billet and into the Air Ministry Works Dep't Yard, and a road mine exploded in the Sheikh Jarrah area. In Hadera, the Corps of the Royal Electrical and Mechanical Engineers Camp was attacked, seriously wounding a Palestinian, and the Fire Brigade was attacked. Two jeeps were blown up. A Bren gun carrier was destroyed by a road mine near Haifa, killing one person and wounding four. Near Kiryat Haim colony, a military camp was attacked with bombs and automatic weapons. A taxi was blown up by a mine on the Haifa–Tel Aviv Road, and another mine targeted two Sixth Airborne Division vehicles. In Tel Aviv, a police billet and military post were attacked with mortar bombs and automatic fire and a police armored car was blown up, with casualties in both. Several explosions rocked the city's streets.[351]

A new type of shrapnel mine was used "most effectively" by the Irgun in the day's attacks (January 2). Mimicking Lehi's latest device that debuted exactly a month earlier, the Irgun was producing this newer, more lethal device in two sizes, one with eighteen pounds of explosives and eighteen pounds of scrap metal, the other with twenty-four pounds of explosive and twenty-two pounds of scrap metal. That evening, one such mine blew up between two jeeps.[352]

Early the next morning, another of the new shrapnel mines hit a vehicle near Petah Tiqva, while a third missed a "civilian lorry near the cold storage depot" between Rishon and Beit Dajan, the site of three previous attacks. At 7:20, yet another of the new mines blew up a jeep, putting three people in the hospital. The next day (January 4) bombs blew up a police truck on the Jerusalem–Bethlehem Road and a truck in Haifa.[353]

January 5 brought the attempted bombings of a mail van at 5:15, and a civilian bus three hours later. The Irgun attacked the railway station at Hadera the next day and blew up a military vehicle on the Lydda–Petah Tiqva Road near Petah Tiqva. The body of Israel Levin was discovered in a garden in Tel Aviv, executed by Lehi the previous Saturday evening (Dec 28) for alleged collaboration. Levin was said to be about to leave for Italy on behalf of the British.[354]

Italy was still a busy spot for the Irgun as well, as it threatened to "attack nerve centers" unless the Italian government accepted Zionist demands. On the 10th, pamphlet bombs exploded in eight major Italian cities, though these were amateurish in production and most of the pamphlets were destroyed in the explosions. Two men planting the bombs in Milan and Padua were caught; both were from the Zionist-run DP camps. A series of Irgun bomb threats against US and British interests in Italy caused havoc, but none materialized.[355]

As the Zionist Organization of America allocated $800,000 for a new propaganda campaign (roughly ten million dollars in 2022 value), Ben-Gurion returned to Palestine from what was called a "peace mission" to Europe. In a goal-setting broadcast from Tel Aviv on January 11, he made no reference whatsoever to the problem of terrorism.

Lehi, meanwhile, hijacked a Chevrolet utility vehicle from its owner. Vehicle theft in Mandate-era Palestine was often more than the crime itself, but preparation for an attack. The next day, Sunday the 12th, the vehicle was driven to the District Police Headquarters in Haifa, now filled with explosives. The driver ran away and guards saw the fuse, but time and fuse were too short—the vehicle exploded as they were evacuating the area. Two British and two Palestinians were killed immediately, and among the sixty-two wounded were several with life-threatening injuries. As Lehi claimed credit and bragged that "there were no casualties among our men," its gang members murdered a railway guard near Haifa.

When the next day the British again confronted Ben-Gurion about the continuing terror and the Agency's complicity, he gave a curious reply: if the Agency used "physical force [to stop the terror, it] would result in Jewish leaders being killed by themselves." Whatever his motivation for the odd admission, it reinforced the "civil war" warning in the previously intercepted Haganah text: the Zionist movement's tactics had succeeded in creating such a psychosis among the Yishuv as to make the movement self-perpetuating beyond the lives of its architects.[356]

The Agency was expanding its intelligence-gathering antennae of informants and wiretapping. Eating and drinking establishments patronized by British soldiers were fruitful venues for its extensive network; indeed some of these popular meeting places were specifically designed as eavesdropping operations.

At least by mid-1946, the British had been aware that the Haganah was employing women spies to consort with British troops in order to extract information—"when discretion and restraint invariably weaken," as they put it—as well as Jewish sex workers who were unwilling spies but were exploited to gather intelligence from the right customers.

When the British found that "some Jewesses … employed as business bait by the manager of the Armon Hotel in Nahariya" were "remarkably well-versed" in sensitive intelligence, pressure was applied to have them removed from the hotel employ. This proved futile: the women continued in the espionage trade without the convenience of the hotel because, as the British would learn, the gangs left them little choice (pages 251, below).[357]

High-profile kidnappings

Jewish terrorists struck again tonight, the *Daily Telegraph* reported on January 26, "when they broke into the home of Mr. H. E. Collins, a British banker, beat him insensible, chloroformed him and carried him off in a sack." He was, in fact, in the flat of a (Jewish) friend on Mamillah Road in Jerusalem, who could not summon the police until she was released by the abductors about forty minutes later, at 5:50 PM. British media were struck by the terrorists' choice of Collins because he was an official in a bank owned and operated by British Jews.

The most brazen kidnapping came the next day, January 27, when Judge Ralph Windham was abducted right from his court room in Tel Aviv by eight armed Irgun operatives, four of whom were listening to the proceedings inside the court. Telephone communications had been severed, and all other offices in the building were held under the gun.

It is at this point that British officials publicly acknowledged that no one in Palestine was safe against Zionist terror, and that British women, children, and non-essential civilian personnel must be evacuated. Three days later, High Commissioner Cunningham ordered this evacuation, "Operation Polly."

The Irgun confirmed that they held the two high profile figures as hostages to force Britain to stay the execution of convicted terrorist Dov Gruner, scheduled for the next day, the 28ᵗʰ—a strangely Machiavellian demand on the Irgun's part, given that Gruner would ultimately refuse a life-saving appeal that the British wanted to give, and that this "suicide" was allegedly at the Irgun's instructions.[358]

Palestine Jews Given Ultimatum (Daily Telegraph) and *Ultimatum Gives Jews 48 Hours to Free Britons* (News Chronicle) were typical of British headlines as the fate of the hostages remained unknown. It was however the militants' ultimatum, not Britain's, that decided the issue: the British stayed Gruner's execution, and the two hostages were freed. The government led the media to believe that Gruner had appealed to the Privy Council, but this was a lie so as not to appear to have caved to the terrorists. In fact, he had refused to do so.

When after the abduction Collins regained consciousness from the chloroform, he found himself bound, blindfolded, gagged, and covered by a sack, being frogmarched over rough terrain to a cave with a mud floor and water that dripped continuously overhead. His burns from the chloroform were so severe that it was impossible for him to eat. An Irgun doctor tried to stitch his head wound, but his captors' treatment continued to be what he described as "brutal and coarse." If Gruner were hanged, his captors explained, so would he.

After the stay of Gruner's execution, Collins was forced to sign a statement saying that he had been well treated. He was then blindfolded and led over stones and ditches for about a half hour and abandoned. Collins never recovered; he died from the chloroform.

Judge Windham was hidden in an outhouse and given a copy of Arthur Koestler's newly-published Zionist novel, *Thieves in the Night*. In contrast to Collins, he was not gratuitously maltreated.

When the British combed two suburbs of Jerusalem in an attempt to find the kidnappers, alleged to be members of a "Black A Squad," the Jewish Agency denounced the search, saying it "alters the situation beyond all expectation."[359]

On the day of the would-be execution, the House of Commons listened to Arthur Creech Jones explain why Britain was powerless against the kidnappings. Jones had credibility: he had been imprisoned as a conscientious objector during the First World War and had directed a rescue of hundreds of Jews from Czechoslovakia after the Munich Agreement was signed. Jones told the House of Commons that

> The suppression of terrorism demands the active participation of the whole Jewish community and also direct cooperation by the Jewish Agency, which I regret has not been forthcoming.[360]

Schools remained the prime venue for the Irgun's recruitment of youths between the ages of fifteen and nineteen, with teachers powerless to protect their students. Behind closed doors, the Va'ad Leumi spoke of the terror groups' "domination and coercion, intimidation and threats, the extortion of money and use of force against teachers and pupils, policemen, drivers and others," yet like the Jewish Agency, refused to challenge it. JNC chairman David Remez, future Knesset member, acknowledged that they

> compel Jews to join them and help them against their conscience. People are compelled to subscribe money and assistance against their will ... Pupils in the schools and youth movements are also compelled by beating and threats to join these organizations. Headmasters and teachers are also similarly constrained."[361]

Exasperated with the open secret that the Jewish Agency was itself part of the terror network, the British decided to call its bluff: they challenged the Agency to live up to its claim to be the nascent government of a civilized nation-to-be. On February 3 they "invited the Jewish Agency and the Va'ad Leumi to call upon the Jewish community for their assistance in bringing to justice the members of the terrorist groups who had been guilty of murder and other crimes over a considerable period." Such, the British pointed out, would be the behavior "of any civilised state." The Agency's response was that to do so would be "contrary to Jewish political interests."[362]

Independently, the Archbishop of New York asked the same question: how will the Jewish Agency, failing to control terrorism now, control it in its own state? He wrote of the

> deep and growing indignation over the treacherous and cruel outrages [and] world-wide Jewish propaganda. Justifiable anger is felt not only against the actual terrorists, but also against the reckless and unscrupulous support which they receive from Jews in the United States and elsewhere.[363]

The diplomatic correspondent of the *Daily Telegraph* summed up the situation thus:

> The inflation of Jewish claims from a modest spiritual home to a Jewish state, which they were seeking to enforce by terrorism, had driven the Arabs to the point of exasperation.[364]

The *Times*, reflecting not just Palestinian fears but what was self-evident from the Agency's behavior, put it this way: statehood would not be geographically finite, but instead "give Jews a bridgehead capable of indefinite expansion."[365]

The next move in this "indefinite expansion" came on February 7 when hundreds of Haganah militiamen "roared south in a truck convoy today and founded three new Jewish settlements near the Egyptian border," the latest installment in the Jewish Agency's tactic to scupper any coming Partition. In Samaria (the British report using the Biblical name, now part of the West Bank), more hikers continued their intelligence-gathering in preparation for the

Feb 1947

final showdown everyone assumed was imminent. Expansion into Lebanon remained a goal as well: Uriel Heyd, a Jewish Agency official then in London with Kollek, discussed with fellow official Eliahu Epstein (Eilat)—who in a year would become Israel's first US ambassador—the goal of absorbing "the Lebanon" into Israel.[366]

In an admission through which the coming UN proceedings and Partition Resolution must be viewed, the British now state plainly what had been obvious for three decades: that the Zionists will not honor any partition of Palestine. Partition was for them a "temporary expedient."

The ensuing deliberations over partition and its precise configuration were acted out in full expectation that it would never happen. In the end, not just the Zionists, but Britain and the United States as well would be party to the charade.

Refugees vs settlers of convenience

With the war over and the Palestinian reckoning approaching, the Jewish Agency's preferred immigrants were increasingly non-refugees from safe countries, because they make better colonizers than the desperate survivors of war. Where the desperation and misery that typified the wartime's nightmarish voyages was missing, it had still to be maintained by theatre.

The British reported "ample proof" that after a voyage of strict discipline and cleanliness, "an atmosphere of poverty, misery and filth is encouraged" for the final two days before interception or beaching. There is "a considerable discrepancy between the picture painted" by the Agency's propaganda of the weak, desperate survivor arriving in its vessels, and the Europeans and Americans it often selects instead, the young and healthy who "will make ideal colonizers." The overcrowded vessels served to confuse "the two entirely different issues of displaced persons in Europe, and the Jewish population of Palestine."

When the illegal immigrant ship *Merica*, said to have been financed by the Irgun's "Bergson Boys" in the US, reached Haifa on February 9, "it was noticed," the British commented, "that a large number of the passengers, both male and female, had worked themselves into a state of hysteria, and were obviously playing to the gallery of numerous press reporters." The passengers, all of whom "were in a disgusting state of filth and squalor," attacked the British with broken bottles and tins, injuring several soldiers. But according to what Airborne Field Security judged a "reliable source," "a reasonable state of hygiene was maintained" during the voyage, but about a day before reaching land, "orders were given to convert the ship into a veritable pig-sty" for propaganda value. The report tallied with others received about the camps in Cyprus.[367]

On the night of February 11, the Irgun used Molotov cocktails to burn down two youth clubs of the Hashomer Hatzair. This and other incidents, Air Headquarters Levant reported, "confirm the belief that the active intervention by Jews to wipe out terrorism must inevitably involve civil war."

On February 13, Dov Gruner's sister arrived in Palestine in a failed attempt to persuade her brother to sign the appeal to the Privy Council that would save his life. In Haifa port that day, the Haganah bombed and sunk two vessels.

In Jerusalem on the 18th, Lehi blew up two vehicles by remote control mines, one near the Jerusalem Zoo with five casualties, the other on Haifa-Jaffa Road opposite Gan Hayim Colony. These mines probably evaded detection by being disguised as kilo stones (distance markers), as the following day (February 19), two mines disguised

Lehi bombing of a civilian car (foreground) and police car (background, left). Photo stamped 6th Airborne Div, May 1947.

as such were discovered on the main Gaza-Rehovot Road, attached to electric detonating sets in a nearby orange grove.

More mines exploded in Haifa outside the Moriah Cinema, two army trucks on Mount Carmel were bombed, the airfield at Ein Shemer was attacked by mortar and arms fire, and oil pipelines near Afula (Haifa) were sabotaged. A female Irgun member with what was described as an American accent telephoned correspondents to claim credit on behalf of the organization—though the British were grateful that the "Afula sabotage cell" appeared to be poorly trained and its botched job did not cause a serious loss of oil. Shoddy work also minimized the damage to the airfield: "not one of the Irgun's major technical achievements," the British reported upon examining some mortars found fixed on the airfield. Continuing sabotage of the pipelines strained oil supplies, with some leaks only later discovered to have been caused by explosives.

The last day of February heralded a bloody March, with the bombing of the Haifa Shipping Agency on the third floor of Barclays Bank leaving two dead and seven seriously injured, some with fractured skulls. "The incident was carried out by two Jews dressed in khaki uniform, carrying army packs, who walked into the building in a leisurely manner, talking to each other." Both of the dead were Jewish, leading Lehi to publish the story that two "Hebrew clerks" had been forced "by the enemy officers" to remove the bomb.[368]

The curious case of the *Ulua*

At 10:45 that morning, the illegal immigrant ship *Ulua* ran aground at Ras El Kurum. Less than two hours later, before any announcement of the inelegant landing had been made, the British were perplexed to see printed posters rallying the Yishuv to action against the British for having imprisoned all 1,350 of the *Ulua's* passengers who, the posters said, had jumped into the water after the vessel had beached—not at Ras El Kurum, but at Bat Gallim.

As it turned out, the plan was indeed for the ship to beach at Bat Gallim, but a miscalculation had brought it to Ras El Kurum, where the prepared script of "hundreds of refugees jumping into the water" did not take place. The pre-made posters condemning the scripted incident had however already been disseminated at the agreed hour. The British, suspicious of a curiously well-informed *Hamashkif* reporter, offered to bring her to the scene, but betrayed no hint of what had happened. "Tears came into her eyes" when she realized that they were not heading to Bat Gallim.

As had become commonplace, among the *Ulua's* "European refugees" were elective settlers from the United States.[369]

The United Zionists-Revisionists of America published full-page ads in March calling for the total boycott of Britain, which was the "successors of Hitler's extermination camps" and "had callously decided to let the tragic remnants of European Jewry continue to rot in concentration camps" in order to turn them into "degenerate slaves of a police state." In Palestine, Irgun broadsides now threatened worldwide hell until its demands were met, and civil administration in Palestine, British officials admitted in private, was "a besieged garrison."

March 1947

The first day of March lived up to the phrase. It began fairly typically, with the bombing of a vehicle on the main road between Rehovot and Rishon Lezion at 8:35, another blown up by a land mine on the Haifa-Jaffa Road at 11:15, killing two people, and bombs thrown at the Rehovot Police Stations. There was one break: a mortar hidden in an orange grove failed when the first bomb exploded in the barrel.

Next, at 3:20 P.M. the Goldschmidt Officers' Club in Jerusalem was bombed in a well-planned attack, killing fourteen people immediately, of whom ten were civilians, and injuring sixteen. As the militants ploughed their truck through the building entrance, one exited the vehicle under the cover of automatic fire from five locations: two points in the Yeshurum Synagogue, the Jewish Agency grounds, Pikovsky's printing press, and an unidentified point. The militant who had slipped out of the truck planted a phosphorus bomb while others threw a suitcase bomb through a side window and planted more bombs against the building. The attackers escaped as a big explosion "destroyed the South end of the building, which collapsed burying a number of occupants."[370]

There were several witnesses to the bombing of a jeep by a shrapnel mine disguised as kilo stone in Haifa. The bombed vehicle continued down the road with its dead driver, hit a pile of stones, turned a complete somersault, burst into flames and was completely gutted. Three of the occupants were dead on the spot; later reports refer to all four dead.

Two of the eye-witnesses were a Jewish couple who "were sweeping up broken glass quite calmly" when 317 Airborne Field Security reached the scene about two minutes later, but "as usual, neither had seen anything." Another was a Palestinian, who supplied a description of the assailants to police. But there were other eye-witnesses unknown to the British at the time: "a party of young Jews" including a woman who, some months later, was with a man in 317 Airborne. The woman

> told a member of this section that she had witnessed [the bombing of the jeep on March 1], and volunteered information, whilst in an intimate mood, which exactly confirmed the description of the operators which had been obtained [from the Palestinian man] … [W]hen the saboteur ran past within a few feet in HERZLIYA Street, she said "Look, he's the one that did it." "Shut up," said her escort, "and mind your own business." The party then walked into a nearby cafe, as they had originally intended to do, while the bodies of the British soldiers were lying, as yet undiscovered, by the side of MOUNTAIN Road.

At 6:45 that evening, "six armed Jews" laid explosives at the naval car park in Haifa, wrecking fourteen vehicles. Two minutes after that attack began, a road mine exploded under two vehicles at Khirbet Beit Lid, and at 7:00 a truck was hit by a land mine at Kiriat Haim on the Haifa-Acre Road. Ten minutes after the hour, eight mortar shells were fired into a military camp near Khirbet Beit Lid, killing one and injuring three. After a half hour reprieve, at 7:45 another land mine exploded on the Haifa-Jaffa Road near Petah Tikva, followed fifteen minutes later by three separate attacks. Old stock appears to have been used up on an attack on a truck at

Kiryat Motzkin—it was, as the British put it, "of the pre-shrapnel period types."

At a quarter to midnight a scout car was blown up by a land mine on Rehovot Gaza Road, adding three more dead and one more seriously wounded to the day's tally. At least twenty-three people died and twenty-five injured in the day's terror attacks. Thirteen of the casualties were civilians.[371]

The next day (March 2), as martial law was declared in parts of Palestine, a "Bedford 3 tonner" was blown up by an electrically detonated mine at a roundabout near Hadera. The chaos continued on March 3-4, as nine people—five British and four Palestinians—were injured, five critically, in continuing Zionist attacks. Three men were seriously hurt when their army truck was blown up near Rishon le Zion, and civilian workers were hurt when their truck was hit by an electrically detonated mine near Ramle. A canteen at a military camp in Haifa was hit by grenades thrown from a stolen taxi, a camp near Hadera was hit by automatic and small arms fire, and "armed Jews" raided the booking office of Orion Cinema in Jerusalem.

On March 5, pedestrians were injured by grenades thrown at a CMP vehicle and into a Jerusalem street. A civilian vehicle going between Rishon and Le Zion was blown up by a road mine, killing one person and injuring another. "An unknown Jew" placed a russet-brown suitcase in Haifa's Municipal Assessment Office, which then blew up—"as suitcases are wont to do in Palestine," the Security officer added bitterly. The next day, two grenades that failed to explode were analyzed: they contained rivets and American TNT. Successful blasts that days caused injuries but no deaths.[372]

In the US that month, full-page ads by the United Zionists-Revisionists of America, based at 55 West 42nd Street in New York, pushed for a boycott of Britain to stop what it called the British "war of extermination on the Jewish people" waged by the "successors of Hitler's extermination campaign against Jewry."

London bombing

Meanwhile in Britain, authorities monitoring domestic Zionist terror suspects were getting increasingly nervous about attacks in London. The suspects' careful language, however, left little to act upon. What, for example, to make of a suspected terror cell's tapped telephone conversations of February 21, involving the transportation of some object to Britain by small plane? And that "even then, we have to carry it around ... have to bring it from the landing spot" and wait for a reply from Palestine "as to whether they want it done?"[373]

The concern was vindicated when on March 7 a bomb exploded at the Colonial Club and Colonial Welfare Department, 6 St. Martin's Place, causing "considerable structural damage" and injuring several people. That evening, an unnamed man from France left his hotel near Victoria Station with a case and visited Abraham Abrahams, co-editor of the New Zionist party organ the *Jewish Standard*, in his private flat. British surveillance recorded a conversation between Abrahams and his wife shortly before midnight, in which he skirted around explaining to her why he must keep the visitor's case, pending his return. Yes, it has a false bottom, he conceded, but only "some papers from abroad" were hidden there.[374]

"Circumstantial accounts" of how the Colonial House bombing was accomplished came a few days later in France, when Lehi claimed responsibility. Robert Misrahi—who was a protégé of the anti-colonialist, but ironically pro-Zionist Jean-Paul Sartre—allegedly wore a coat with explosives sewn inside it. Lehi explosives artist Yaacov Eliav, who was perhaps responsible for the development of the letter bomb used in a wave of Zionist attempts on public figures, probably made the device.[375]

As the Colonial Club was bombed, a staff car on tow on the Haifa-Jaffa Road near Hadera was blown up. The next day (March 8) a military camp in Haifa and a police camp at Sarona were both hit with grenades. Coldstream Guards in Tel Aviv were attacked by heavy small arms fire, killing one guardsman. Two armored cars were blown up, and two policeman in civilian clothes were shot, killing one immediately. Grenades thrown at a patrol in Jerusalem seriously injured three people, and heavy small arms fire hit Police Headquarters in Jaffa. Attacks continued into March 9 as one person was killed and six injured when a camp near Hadera was hit with automatic fire and bombs. A police truck was attacked near Khirbet Beit Lyd, and telephone lines in Haifa and Upper Galilee were sabotaged.[376]

"The whole Zionist community is allied in spirit with the terrorists," the *NY Times* reported on March 9. "A prominent Zionist official privately acknowledged," the reporter continued, "that Irgun Zvai Leumi, with its bombs and guns, and not the Jewish Agency, was dictating the policy of Palestine Jewry, [and] once their deeds are done the terrorists melt back into the population. They are not betrayed to the authorities."

What the *NY Times* reporter did not know was that the British, noting the correlation between the terror tactics of the Zionists and those of the defeated Axis powers, now sought the help of "a small number of Officers who have both technical and psychological knowledge of terrorism, having themselves been engaged in similar operations on what may be termed the terrorist side in countries occupied by the enemy in the late war."[377]

The Syrian orphanage in Jerusalem was the target of a grisly attack on March 12. Early that morning, the terrorists blasted a hole through the orphanage's twelve-foot wall and then made a diversionary attack while bringing in three fused sacks of gelignite. When the first sack detonated it "rocked every building in the vast Orphanage [and] threw many of the boys from their beds." The blast "was followed by the sickening sound of falling masonry as a large part of the interior of the building collapsed, burying the occupants beneath the dust and debris. Many were injured and one person succumbed to his injuries almost immediately." The full intended carnage was averted: an armed and uninjured British official chased the bombers and prevented them from detonating the other two sacks of gelignite.[378]

Elsewhere in Palestine that day, a military camp near Karkur was attacked with grenades and fire arms, an Arab truck was targeted with a mine on Gaza Road near Rishon LeZion, a WD vehicle was blown up by road mine near Saron, and vehicles were attacked near Tulkarm and on Haifa-Jaffa Road.

The citrus shipping season was now over, and with it the deal the Irgun and Lehi had struck with Jewish citrus growers to spare the railroads from terrorism. On March 13 the gangs used an electrically detonated mine to blow up a goods train south of Jerusalem, near Beit Safafa, killing its Palestinian engineer and injuring its Palestinian fireman. North of Lydda, bombers hid near the scene as they watched their five contact mines blow up an oil train, knocking nineteen of the train's cars off the tracks and destroying 500 yards of track. They then jumped out from hiding and sprayed the train with gunfire for fifteen minutes. In Tel Aviv, the Toelet Ashrai Bank was robbed, presumably for arms money.

On the 14th, a branch of the main crude oil line running from the Iraq Petroleum Company's fields to the Haifa oil docks was bombed by four Irgun operatives. "The choice of targets," the British noted, "and the placing of the charges shows a fair theoretical knowledge on the part of the saboteurs," though insufficient explosive was used to cause a major incident. Near Beer Yaacov, two mines were detonated under a freight train on the Lydda-Gaza line. The Irgun demolished the Officers Club and a food depot in Hadera on the 15th.[379]

The Irgun's next choice of pipeline target was as savvy as the last: it bombed the crude oil feed near Kfar Hussedini (Haifa) on the 16th, causing considerable loss of oil. Its separate bombing of a military vehicle left four casualties.

Another incident that day was not routine: the bombing of the Jewish Agency press room and tourist agency on Jerusalem's Ben Yehuda Street, for which no group took credit. It was a strange target—but in retrospect, might be explained by an event two days later and at the distance of a thousand miles. A "representative of Jewish Agency in Romania" called on the British Consulate "to read out a statement he had been instructed to make by the Jewish Agency Palestine" expressing "sincere condolences" to the families of its terror victims. Although no connection between the two events is noted at the time, perhaps the "condolences" were originally to have been made on Ben Yehuda Street, at British pressure, and to the outrage of the Irgun? The Irgun blamed the "Nazi-British Rule," which would fit the theory.

A jeep was hit by a mine in Tiberias that day (18th), while a second mine was amateurishly prepared and failed to explode. The British continued to note a trend of shoddy work from the Irgun, which they attributed to their arrests of many of the gang's better operatives, leaving some jobs to the inexperienced.[380]

One constable was killed and six injured on March 19 by a bomb thrown near Zichron Yanqov Police Station in Haifa. At 2:45 the next morning, a remotely detonated bomb missed its targets, a sergeant and three constables. "Six armed Jews" robbed the Palestine Discount Bank on the 24th, "apparently assisted by members of gang already in the building." When three days later, "a grenade was thrown by Jews at the car of a party of police," the police managed to throw the grenade out of the car, but the explosion injured two pedestrians. The attackers continued with gunfire and a flash bomb.

At 9:05 the next morning (28th), "five young Jews youths dressed as Arabs" drove a truck to the Acre Beach area. Two remained in the truck as cover while three got out and walked to "a carefully reconnoitered point" where seven oil feed pipes ran together above ground, laid explosives under each, rushed back to the truck, and drove toward a level crossing to escape. "As luck would have it," the War Office reported, "the barrier was down and shunting [re-railing of train cars] was taking place." They abandoned the truck and fled. The blast came a few minutes later, first igniting oil and benzine, and after about fifteen minutes the heat of the fires caused two further explosions.* "This is correct sabotage technique," the War Office concluded warily, "and indicates forethought and attention to detail."[381]

The Irgun was nonetheless still short of competent help. In Kiriat Haim (Haifa area), its operatives bombed the water supply line valve and inspection chamber—an odd target, which while costing the British P£1000 to repair did not interrupt the water supply. The explanation began to emerge six days later, at two-thirty in the morning on April 3. "A party of Jews entered a house at Kiryat Haim near Haifa and beat up a Jewish civilian," and in the course of the

---

* The Irgun claims to have sabotaged oil pipelines near Afula and near Haifa on the 29th, but I have assumed this to be a misdating for the 28th.

day as many as sixteen more Jews "were similarly beaten up," three so seriously that they were hospitalized. Pressed for an explanation, they explained that the Irgun had sent them to sabotage an oil pipeline, but they blew up the water main by mistake. The beatings were punishment, and the day they were beaten up, new operatives did the job correctly, sabotaging oil pipelines near Kfar-Hassidim. Meanwhile, the routine attacks continued, such as the assassination of an officer and police inspector on horseback on March 29.[382]

The most colossal of all the Zionist oil sabotage, indeed the most catastrophic attack ever to hit Palestine's coast, came on the last day of March, with Lehi's bombing of the Shell-Mex oil tanks. The blasts rocked the entire Haifa coastal area, destroying about 20,000 tons of oil, disrupting oil supplies, and causing huge fires that raged for three weeks. A quarter-mile of Mediterranean waterfront was devastated. Taking credit for the attack, Lehi noted in its *L.H.I.-Bulletin No. 5* that its fighters had successfully penetrated the heavily guarded zone "and returned safely to their bases, without loss." No longer just the assassination virtuosi, Lehi now rivaled the Irgun and Haganah in the field of sheer destruction.

The coast in flames must have been a shocking and foreboding sight to those aboard the illegal immigrant ship *San Filipo* as it approached Palestine that day. The vessel was so dangerously unseaworthy that the British had already rescued a third of its passengers during its voyage. Spinning these latest settlers' arrival in bluntly messianic terms, the Jewish Agency called the *San Filipo* passengers "Palestinian subjects returning home [who] had owned Palestine for thousands of years."[383]

With one hundred thousand British troops in Palestine impotent against Zionist terror, public servants and victims' families continued to write to the government in despair. One former constable's letter typifies the exasperation of those charged with maintaining public safety:

> We keep hearing the postponement of [convicted Jewish terrorists'] execution ... Did we do that with the Arab? No, his house was burned, Arabs were hanged by the dozen [but] there seems to be

a feeling that we are afraid of the Jews. It is a well known fact that you will <u>never</u> get any co-operation from the Jewish people in your efforts [to stop terrorism] … we accuse you of [not carrying out your duty and] being influenced by American and Jewish propaganda.[384]

Creech Jones replied.

> First there are very considerable differences between the Arab disturbances of 1937-1939 and the Jewish terrorist organizations of to-day. The Arab insurgents were loosely-knit bands of guerillas operating in the country districts whereas Irgun Zvai Leumi and the Stern Gang, the terrorists active today, are secret societies of well-trained saboteurs, some thousands strong, buried in the heart of an urban population.[385]

"During the Arab disturbances," Jones continued, "the Police and the Army did enjoy this co-operation to some extent, and were able to track down the guilty parties." In contrast, Jewish community institutions made the decision "to withhold all aid in this matter [and] the Security Forces have been confronted by the stolid refusal of the Jewish civilians to give what information they may possess … the Jewish Institutions have maintained their attitude of non-co-operation."[386]

"It is a situation," Cunningham wrote from Jerusalem, "in which a policeman is shot [by a Jewish terrorist] and lies wounded in the street beside a bus queue, no member of which will lift a finger to help him." The British are powerless against the terror without the "aid of a still functioning civil power."

> The placing of explosives against the walls of a building under covering fire [a tactic of Zionist gangs] was a method successfully used by the Germans in 1940 against the strongest fortifications in Europe … The chances of its succeeding are plainly improved where, as in Palestine, the law-abiding members of the community for purely political reasons have combined in deciding not to distinguish themselves from the members of the attacking forces, who thus

emerge from within a civilian population at any moment with full initiative and every operational advantage.[387]

April
1947

April brought what should have been very good news for Jewish DPs, when US Bill H.R.2910 was introduced in Washington DC. The bill was to provide immigration to the United States for 400,000 displaced persons from Germany, Austria, and Italy over a four-year period, as non-quota immigrants. The State Department supported the admission of Jewish DPs, and the bill was championed by the (non-Zionist) American Council for Judaism. Yet none of the famously proactive, Zionist lobbying organizations demonstrated any support for the bill, and it died.[388]

On the first day of April, as fires raged along the Haifa coast from Lehi's attacks on the oil supplies, two Lehi dressed as Arabs entered a railway control box near Nahariya (Galilee), murdered the sentry "propped up against a wall," and stole weapons. Four constables escaped attempted assassination, while a civilian was murdered in the course of a botched assassination of a sergeant. In Cyprus the next day, the Palyam, the sea force of the Hagana's Palmach, bombed the British freighter *SS Ocean Vigour*.

"In broad daylight" on April 3, "and in full view of the local Jews," militants set up an explosive device on the corner of Mountain Road in Haifa. While being "calmly witnessed by a number of local Jews taking breakfast in flats overlooking the scene," they blew up a ration truck, seriously injuring two. The next day, as the *Empire Rival* left Haifa for Port Said, it was bombed for the second time.[389]

British intelligence had long been concerned about the radicalizing of Jewish youth at the hands of the Revisionist organization Betar and its North London premises. This "militant Jewish Youth Movement," as Percy Sillitoe, then Director General of MI5 described it, "bears a striking resemblance both in general structure and character to the Hitler Youth Movement." Children under ten were in a section called Shoalim (MI5 spellings), those aged ten to sixteen in Betar Zeirar, and sixteen to twenty-three in Dargat Halegion.

Among Betar's protégés was the Irgun terrorist Dov Gruner, whose execution the British continually delayed in fear of the repercussions. When Gruner's execution was stayed in late January, Churchill knew that it was not, as the media had been told, because Gruner had appealed, but to win the release of the Irgun's hostages, H. E. Collins and Judge Windham. ("Is it not a very serious thing," he asked Arthur Creech Jones, "to turn aside from the normal process of justice because of threats of murder by terrorists launched against hostages who they have taken?") By April, however, the British ran out of ways to avoid handing the Irgun a martyr. He was an engineered martyr: the militia, led by Begin, saw that Gruner would be more powerful for the settler state if executed, and so allegedly convinced him not to cooperate with the reprieves that would spare him, to ensure that he is put to death—which, on April 16, he was.[390]

His impending "martyrdom" had already led to heightened security when on April 11 Gilberte Elizabeth Lazarus (aka Betty Knut), the young but battle-seasoned granddaughter of the composer Alexander Scriabin, reached England. Immigration believed her story: she had come to visit one Chun Chan Yeng at Trinity College whom she had met in France. Four days later, feigning the need for the loo, she got past the guards at the Colonial Office with a substantial bomb concealed in her coat. She deposited it in the lavatory, wrapped in copies of the *Evening Standard* and *Daily Telegraph* ("firmly right-wing," a Scotland Yard investigator later mused).

As she left, a cleaning woman named Lizzie Hart saw the package and, having no clue as to what she held in her hand, did exactly the wrong thing: she began removing the wrapping paper. The next instant, however, passed without catastrophe. The bomb was not booby-trapped and, as Scotland Yard later explained, "one of the hands of the watch was pressed too close against the face—and the watch stopped before it reached zero hour." The watch bore a fingerprint on record with the British, that of Lehi bigwig Eliav. Its tolamite bore the trademark of the explosives factory of St. Martin de Crau, France, and would later match explosives discovered in the Paris residence of Rabbi Baruch Korff after his thwarted aerial attack on London.[391]

"The bomb planted by our fighters in the British Colonial Office in London was perchance discovered before it exploded," Lehi conceded in the June issue of its *L.H.I.-Bulletin*. Lehi had, nonetheless, "penetrated into the heart of the Empire," and the chief of Scotland Yard was unable to keep his public promise to "arrest within 48 hours" the female terrorist. Lazarus had, indeed, slipped back to France.

As Britain hunted for the terrorist, bomb and death threats continued to rattle its Embassies and Consulates throughout the world—in Chicago, Athens, Bogota, Buenos Aires, Santiago, and Tunis.[392]

In Palestine in mid-April, as the last fires from the March 31 Shell-Mex attack were extinguished, roads themselves were set afire: the Irgun doused mined roads with gasoline and ignited them at the presence of a mobile patrol. Attacks were now so numerous that many merited only cursory mention in British records, such as a bomb that was discovered and diffused at Jerusalem's Eden Cinema on April 16.

On the 18th, "eight Jews drove up in a truck" to No. 61 Field Dressing Station in the Nathanya area, a building flaunted by two prominent Red Cross flags. They "shot the British sentry dead and laid explosive charges" at the facility, blowing up the medical inspection room adjoining a ward of sick people. The Irgun claimed responsibility.

Militants assassinated a policeman in Tel Aviv, killing a civilian in the process. Military dispatch riders in Haifa were targeted from a saloon car on Herzl Street, and others were targeted on King George Avenue. The Irgun claims it mined a train near Rehovot that day. Random military personnel were the targets of sniping from a commandeered taxi in Haifa on April 19.

On April 20, an Arab Legion truck was blown up by a land mine on Acre-Haifa Road near Kiryat Motskin. A Red Cross depot was bombed, leaving many casualties, and two road mines were uncovered in Haifa, one with a considerable amount of Italian explosives, partly buried in a heap of asphalt. At Ramat Zev, a land mine blew up a Sherwood Foresters truck, injuring four, and in Jerusalem another kilo stone mine was exposed.

Four people were injured, one quite seriously, when a bomber threw an explosive device into the Camp Cinema at Nathanya Convalescent Depot as the audience of about 200 was leaving. The next day (21ˢᵗ) a military truck was blown up by a mine on the Khirbet Beit Lid Haifa Road.³⁹³

Although April 22 brought minor failures for the militants—the police freed three people the gangs had kidnapped, and three bombings failed—these disappointments were dwarfed by the day's great success: the bombing of the Cairo-Haifa train at Rehovoth, killing eight people on the spot and leaving six wounded, three seriously. As described by a survivor, the train

> was mined and wrecked by Jews [while] travelling at reduced speed along an embankment with orange groves on either side… Suddenly, there was a terrific explosion. The air became dense from smoke; there were sounds of shattering glass and of woodwork being reduced to splinters and debris was flying in all directions. The coach in which I was travelling was blown off the rails by the force of the explosion… The scene along the track was an unforgettable sight, [with] two compartments blown to bits, [a coach] down the embankment, [another] telescoped by the sixth car, in which more casualties had occurred… For some distance the track had been torn up, rails were buckled and twisted into odd shapes… Troops were moving the bodies to the side of the track and covering them with blankets, the injured were being given first-aid treatment, passengers pinned in the wreckage were being released with the aid of crowbars, pick-axes…³⁹⁴

The next morning, a furious High Commissioner Cunningham called in Ben-Gurion. After the Jewish Agency leader professed his condemnation of the attack but refused the Commissioner's plea for cooperation, Cunningham asked if his refusal was especially strange given that the UN was currently reviewing the Palestine situation. Ben-Gurion replied with "a flood of polemics" and told Cunningham that the British "were still bound to interpret the Mandate as the Jews see it." Meanwhile, two more trucks were blown up on the Lydda–Petah Tiqva Road, with four casualties, the assailants reinforcing the blasts with automatic weapons.³⁹⁵

The attacks raised new questions in Parliament about protecting the railways against Jewish terrorism. Counter-terrorism measures already in place before April 22 included "frequent examination of lines, patrols, guards and restriction of traffic to hours of daylight," and "curfew prohibiting all movement outside built-up areas is imposed as the situation demands." It was conceded, however, that the terrorists' "use of remote-control electronically detonated mines makes it most difficult to take effective precautions against sabotage."[396]

Aside from the usual scattered attacks, April 24 brought two odd incidents. Five armed Jews entered a Tel Aviv hotel "and inquired whether any Britishers were present." The front desk obviously complied, because a British businessman guest was abducted—but then released "on finding that he was a Jew."

The second odd incident, in Haifa, could be described as macabre irony. Lehi had booby-trapped a house to kill the policemen whom they would summon to investigate on some invented pretext. But the plan went afoul: a Haganah operative entered the house and was blown up instead.

The next morning (25th) at about 8:55, a Post and Telegraph vehicle was stopped by a Jew dressed as a Palestinian constable, at which eight militants appeared and abducted the driver and a postal employee. They were taken to the Benei Braq area, held under guard, and later abandoned, still bound.[397]

While British records do not make the connection, it was surely this vehicle that Lehi used for a brazen attack on Sarona camp that began an hour and twenty minutes later, at about 10:15, when two of its operatives dressed as employees entered Sarona in such a vehicle. The guards were at first suspicious but found nothing irregular, and the men's passes appeared to be in order. These "workers" parked the van between two buildings containing the Telephone Exchange Office and Company Office, then returned to the gate carrying a ladder and wire, saying they needed to repair the telephone cable outside the perimeter.

The explosion followed quickly upon their exit, shaking the camp and destroying both offices. According to the British, five people were killed immediately and sixty injured, some seriously, but Lehi scoffed at these figures. The dead, it bragged, numbered "much more than the number officially disclosed," and added that before "our fighters all returned safety to their bases," they rigged more heavy charges of explosives.[398]

Haifa was spared a bombing that day when the device triggered prematurely, killing the operative. Another attack failed in Jerusalem, when the bomber was caught depositing a mine in a tree. The usual sorts of minor incidents continued: hand grenades thrown at vehicles, hijacked taxis, and the like. On the 26th, A.E. Conquest, chief of the CID in Haifa, was assassinated by Lehi.

The next morning, three separate attacks occurred within a twenty-two minute period. The first came at 10:30, when a remote-controlled explosive device was triggered under a goods train on the Lydda-Jaffa line near Tel Aviv. Fifteen minutes later, another goods train was targeted on the Haifa-Kantara Line near Benyamina. At eight minutes to eleven in the morning, the Ramleh railway station was blown up and completely destroyed. A civilian was injured the next day by a grenade thrown at a CMP vehicle in Jerusalem, and on the 30th, a large land mine found buried on Jaffa Road in the outskirts of Jerusalem was safely dismantled; it consisted of two four-gallon petrol cans containing a large quantity of explosives and rivets.[399]

May's routine terror was overshadowed by the successful defeat of security at the Acre Prison on May 4. The operation began when "a party of armed Jews, some of whom were wearing British military uniforms," entered the Acre market in British military transport. Explosions and gun fire broke out immediately in various localities, with four huge blasts near the old Turkish baths abutting the prison.

May 1947

This attack was more than a blow to British security; it deepened the soul-searching in London because it advertised just how little control Britain actually retained in Palestine. Three days later, officials were groping to explain to the House of Commons and the British public how such a heavily fortified facility "can apparently be attacked with impunity." Indeed Cunningham's dispatch about the attack was an admission that "the civil and military authorities are quite unable to put down [Jewish] terrorism."[400]

Yet the most revealing aspect of Cunningham's report was that the British government feared publishing it. They feared doing so because it necessarily addressed "the general political background in

Palestine which is, in effect, a most severe castigation of the Jewish community and its leaders," and this might cause repercussions, "especially in the American press."[401]

On the same day as the prison break, mines were laid on roads over a large area, and a truck was blown up near Kiryat Haim. The shops of five Jewish merchants who refused to fund the Irgun were gutted with incendiary bombs on the 8th. Four days later, two constables were murdered and a workmen's train was sabotaged.

Calls for a Palestinian resistance to the ever-increasing Zionist terrorism were now heard, and even talk of an "Arab awakening," but the Palestinians, British intelligence observed, "appear no keener to disturb the peace than hitherto."

In the New York suburb of Lake Success, the fledgling United Nations grappled with the Palestine debacle. Representatives of the Arab League objected to the "Zionist plea to the United Nations to base a solution for the Palestine controversy on the homelessness of Europe's displaced Jews" (May 9), while the Irgun filed a claim to turn all of Palestine and Transjordan over to them for a Jewish state (May 14). As they did, they bombed a cinema at Sarafand camp and a railway line north of Hadera.[402]

Both Arab and Jewish passengers were the targets of an attempted train bombing near Bat Gallim on the 15th, as they were employees of an army depot in the vicinity of Haifa. The bomb was positioned to send the train crashing down an embankment, but the alert driver saw something irregular ahead and was able to stop the train before triggering it.

A mine discovered on the Haifa-Beirut line near Acre exploded while being dismantled, killing two officers and injuring three, one seriously. Another mine on the Lydda-Jerusalem branch was discovered in time, and one on a railway near Tel Aviv failed. Near Rehovot a goods train was blown up, and the next day a constable was killed and others injured by a remote controlled shrapnel bomb in Haifa.[403]

Even Irgun-seasoned readers of the *New York Herald-Tribune* and the *New York Post* were likely taken aback by May's full-page appeals to finance terror in Palestine. The ads, in the form of an open letter by the playwright Ben Hecht (see illustration, page 288), abandoned any pretense of military targets, celebrating even the bombing of trains. In what would otherwise be seen as vile antisemitism, he states that US Jews take joy at the terror—all except for the "rich Jews," whom he ridicules.*

> Every time you blow up a British arsenal, or wreck a British jail, or send a British railroad train sky high, or rob a British bank, or let go with your guns and bombs at the British betrayers and invaders of your homeland, the Jews of America make a little holiday in their hearts ... Brave friends, I can imagine you wondering, "If the Jews of America are behind us why don't they help us with their support and money?" It so happens that a certain small percentage of the Jews of America are not behind you yet ... Unfortunately, this small percentage includes practically all the rich Jews of America...[404]

Yet Hecht's call to terror was not off the spectrum of mainstream views—it was supported by the popular columnist Walter Winchell. The British once again lodged protests with the US for allowing the terror fund-raising on its soil, but Truman replied that it was better not to "inflame the passions," while the relevant government agencies replied that even revoking the Irgun's tax-exempt status "would stir up more trouble than it would be worth." When Orme Sargent, head of the Foreign Office, asked Ambassador Douglas if the US might not be unhappy if such calls to murder appeared in the British press targeting the US, Douglas as well refused any action against the Zionists.[405]

A New York City government worker reported that "higher ups [in the city's government] frequently stretched" regulations on behalf of Revisionist causes, otherwise strictly enforced. When a new front, the Palestine Relief Committee, began sending large sums of money to Palestine, the nature of these remittances "raised eyebrows" even within New York Mayor William O'Dwyer's particularly pro-Zionist

---

* Ben Hecht's views changed in later years, as evidenced in his 1961 book *Perfidy* about the 1954–5 trial of alleged Nazi collaborator Rudolf Kastner trial in Jerusalem.

(indeed pro-Irgun) City Hall. Nonetheless, the city's accountant was told not to record the identity of the money's recipient in Palestine "for obvious reasons," and the Committee's purpose was officially recorded as "the dissemination of public information for Palestine."[406]

There was a spurt of resistance that appeared in Palestine at this time from a Jewish organization called the Anti-Terror League. It accused the militants of "using the same methods" as the Nazis, and "will therefore cause to the Jews the same fate like the Nazis did suffer." The British, probably correctly, believed its members to be from the socialist Hashomer Hatzair. The League appears to have had no identifiable influence, an obscure footnote.[407]

A failed attempt to kill four police in a CID car on the morning of May 20 was followed by a more successful raid. At 8:15 that evening,

> a number of armed Jews entered an Arab café and searched the occupants. On leaving they placed a mine in the building and fired a number of shots killing one Arab

and wounding the rest, three seriously. Rather than the usually fatal attempt to challenge the booby-trapping, the military destroyed the bomb *in situ*, completely wrecking the Palestinian café.

Roughly forty-five minutes after the café attack began, about twenty-five "armed Jews entered Arab Sarwarkeh Encampment near Petah Tiqva and opened fire on the inhabitants, killing one Arab," and planted a land mine as they left to blow up first responders. The long-ubiquitous bombings of vehicles continued, such as a convoy targeted in Tel Aviv by a remote controlled device.

In Paris two days later (May 22), the arrest of five young Lehi members brought a new clue to the bombing of the Colonial Office in London on April 11. One of the five, Jacques Martinski, had bomb-making materials believed to be related to that attack.[408]

Two train stations and two railway lines were bombed on May 27: Ramle Station (which was destroyed), a station near Zichron Yaacov, the Haifa-Kantara line near Benyamina, and the Lydda-Jaffa line near Tel Aviv. The next day, an attack on the IPC oil dock and office in the Haifa port area was largely thwarted.[409]

Zionists' battle for Europe's Jewish DPs was being challenged by groups such as the Bucharest-based Jewish Democratic Front, which claimed that the Jewish Agency's envoys convinced Jewish families to sell their worldly possessions in order to leave, only to find they are left penniless and abandoned in neighboring countries.

But Haganah envoys, using relief work as a cover, accelerated their campaign to persuade "these uprooted individuals that their only hope for a decent future is to turn Zionist," in the words of British intelligence. A May telegram from the Foreign Office described the situation as

> a racket largely organised and financed by Zionists in the United States, themselves in no personal danger, who are persuading the Displaced Persons of Europe by false promises to sell all their property and belongings and embark in search of a "land flowing with milk and honey," whereas in fact they will be herded in over-crowded, unseaworthy vessels without regard to conditions or safety of life.[410]

The Haganah quoted a figure of $200 as the cost of "transporting one refugee across the Mediterranean" to Palestine, of which $40 was getting the person overland through Germany, $10 was bribes, and $150 was everything else: loss of ship, indemnity, and insurance. The finances and accounting were dense, with several people investing, and no paper trail. In but one example of these opaque dealings, a Greek national who was "a procurer of women in Alexandria" backed such a settler voyage by paying harbor dues owed in Britain by a Swedish shipping company. The Agency's campaign to displace North African Jews was also bearing fruit: a Hagana-sponsored ship arrived in Palestine carrying not European DPs, but North African Jews.

The British at this time received intelligence that a vessel filled with European immigrants has set out on a propaganda mission: to arrive at Palestinian shores "for the benefit of the Fact Finding Commission (UNSCOP) and the 60 odd journalists who will accompany" that UN committee. The vessel renamed the *Exodus* was en route.[411]

Gilberte Lazarus

June
1947

Meanwhile in France, explosives guru Yaacov Eliav and the energetic Gilberte Lazarus set out on a new sabotage mission, this time in Brussels. Their luck, however, ran out at the Belgian border on June 2, where suspicious officials pulled them aside and found fourteen sticks of explosives "secreted on the person of the woman" (in her girdle). Under her suitcase's false bottom were detonators, pencil batteries, and six letter bombs "identical with those dispatched to Britain from Turin," corroborating British suspicions that the letter bombs mailed from Italy originated in France. Eliav was carrying more of the batteries, but allegedly managed to dispose of a watch that would have proven incriminating for its similarity to the watch used in Lazarus' failed Colonial Office bomb.[412]

The ranks among the terror gangs ran the gamut from self-serving, opportunistic leaders to the traumatized survivors of the war who were their easy prey. Gilberte was born in 1926 to poet Ariadna Scriabin and Daniel Lazarus—like her famous grandfather, a composer. After a failed second marriage, Ariadna began a long friendship with poet Dovid Knut. They visited Palestine in the latter half of 1937, became dedicated Revisionist Zionists, and in 1940 married. Mother and daughter converted to Judaism, and Ariadna grew extreme in her Revisionist politics, remembered for uncompromising statements about ridding Arabs from "our land."

And so when Gilberte, who was living with her uncle in Paris, announced that she wanted to convert to Catholicism, Ariadna was furious. She had her daughter brought immediately to Toulouse where, with the help of a rabbi, convinced her to remain Jewish and indoctrinated her into Revisionist causes. And so Gilberte, at age fourteen, was already active in the resistance movement her mother and Knut established, *La main forte* (The strong hand), which became the *Armée juive* (Jewish army).

Ariadna was ambushed and murdered by the Vichy regime's *Milice française* while en route to an *Armée juive* appointment in Toulouse in July 1944, two weeks before that city was liberated. Gilberte, separately, had been injured by a land mine.

Her indoctrination to Lehi began about a year before her arrest, when she received an anonymous phone call to meet in the *Café de la Paix* in Paris concerning a "Jewish resistance" organization. Under the gang's grooming, battlefields blurred; enemies blurred; the war had not ended. Well-seasoned in the tasks requested of her, she was given rendezvous points and descriptions of contacts—sometimes a man, other times a woman—and instructions to transport a case. Usually she did not know its contents.

She was a complicated prisoner: both a terrorist and a war hero. The *Exodus* affair also helped turn public sympathy in her favor, as it would for vastly less sympathetic characters like Rabbi Korff. She served eight months in a Belgiun prison and was fined £8. By August 1948, at age 22, Gilberte Lazarus was in Israel working as a reporter for a French newspaper.

Lehi threw a cafè party for her on the 24th. "They are a Stern Gang patent, you know," she told reporters about the deadly letter bombs that caused her arrest. She expressed regret that none of them reached their intended recipients, as "we are still at war with Britain." But the murder of Folke Bernadotte the following month appears to have been a reckoning; she parted ways with Lehi.

Lazarus moved to Beersheba in the early 1950s and opened its first nightclub, *The Last Chance*. Whether she intended the name as a reference to the city's southern location, and/or to her final hope for a normal life, it would also prove autobiographical. She died of a heart attack at the age of thirty-seven.[413]

Two days after she and Eliav were arrested at the Belgian border, on June 4, an envelope bearing Italian stamps reached the home of Harold MacMichael, the retired High Commissioner who had returned to England nearly three years earlier. He began to open it, but stopped short upon seeing two pieces of cardboard between which were "a quantity of material with the appearance of toffee" and wires. MacMichael was experienced enough to appreciate, in that instant, that he was fortunate still to be alive: carbon paper often obscured the interior, and even unfolding the plain white paper surrounding it might already have completed the circuit to the detonator. His was one of several Zionist letter bombs that reached various British

Failed Lehi letter bomb, c1947. In this oblique view, the explosive sac occupied the central dark area, and the two cylindrical objects on the right are the detonators. The batteries had connected to the wire on the far left, via the triggering mechanism in the center foreground. On the far right is the fold and part of the cover. [Actual letter bomb held by TNA, EF 5/12. Photograph Tom Suárez]

officials in England in early June, among them Ernest Bevin and future Prime Minister Anthony Eden.

A bomb intended for MP Arthur Greenwood was misdirected and reached a different Arthur Greenwood, the owner of a laundry in Gypsy Hill. The laundry owner proved savvier than some MPs—he was suspicious and alerted the police. One MP's secretary began opening an envelope for her boss, but sensed heat and thrust it into a pail of water kept handy for the event.[414]

Winston Churchill was among the intended victims of a new rash of more potent letter bombs that began arriving on June 7, twenty of which originated from Turin. Other recipients included the Admiral of the Fleet Lord Fraser and the Postmaster General. One reaching Nairobi was caught in time and analyzed: it was similar to those sent from Italy, consisting of slabs of gelignite sandwiched between two pieces of cardboard, with detonating wires fastened by small nuts.[415]

President Truman, whose pro-Zionist influence would prove decisive in Palestine's future, also received Irgun letter bombs that summer. When one senior mail room worker was called back from vacation because of a backlog resulting from the Palestine question, it was not from volume, but because some letters reaching the president's mail room "had obviously been intended to kill."[416]

UNSCOP hosted by a spy network

The British wanted to get out of Palestine and turned to the UN for an exit. To this end, the UN appointed the United Nations Special

Committee on Palestine (UNSCOP) to examine the situation and recommend a solution.

Unknown to the Committee, the Jewish Agency prepared for its arrival in Palestine with an elaborate spy ring, manuscript records of which were found among other Haganah papers uncovered by the British in Jerusalem after the fact, on August 3rd. Some of the words used were euphemisms, such as the word "hotel" which the British believed to mean the Jewish Agency, but these appeared not to be intended as code.

The ring comprised three networks: a "drivers network," "waiters network," and "theater network." Five spies were needed for the drivers network, but a sixth was recruited to displace a Committee driver who happened to be Palestinian. The other five drivers "supplied information daily on the movements of the Committee members their meetings etc.," the manuscript notes read in translation, but "to our regret the drivers had not too much understanding [i.e., English?] and therefore they did not utilize fully their special position." Further limiting their effectiveness, most of the cars had a glass partition between driver and passengers, making listening difficult. One driver spy, however, accompanied a Committee member on a likely fruitful trip to Beirut. The waiters network, similarly, "operated for the purpose of tracing the meetings of the Committee's members with various persons."

By far the most productive, however, was the all-female theater segment of the spy ring. "Through full cooperation of the general labor exchange [Histadrut?] we were able to engage 5 house attendants at Kadima Building."* Just what these "theater girl spies" did while serving the (all-male) UNSCOP cast is not elaborated, but two qualifications were cited: they had to be educated and, most importantly, they had to be "daring."

Finding suitable candidates was difficult:

> The time allowed for procuring these girls was very short—we
> succeeded in pushing in three suitable girls and two others on

---

* Beit Kadima was a building complex in Jerusalem built by the British two years earlier for the families of British officers, but which was used to house the entire UNSCOP Committee while it was in Palestine.

recommendations by close persons—but they proved insufficiently daring and their educational standards was much less than that of the first three.

The three better-educated and "sufficiently daring" girls

proved their great importance. They brought considerable and first rate material. Through them we received among other things Bancz's letters and reports, Sir Abdur's and Sandstrom's questions as [and?] also Hood's telegram to his government. The three girls showed great devotion, understanding and a great deal of risk which must be recorded.*

There is no record of the sort of risk and daring the young women employed to secure their considerable intelligence prizes, nor any way to know whether any excessive hospitality might have influenced the mens' subsequent decisions. Although the two "insufficiently daring" girls were less productive, they "did not prove an obstruction and their material was emptied and brought by the first three."

After the mission, the Agency faced "the lack of an expert stitching group [?] of Secondary and high education which knows the English language thoroughly." The "machinery staff" pitched in for the stitching, but "it was only after the completion of the examinations at the University that we succeeded in recruiting a number of female students for this work."[417]

UNSCOP held its first public hearing in Jerusalem on June 17. This was the committee that would decide Palestine's fate, yet most of its members were, according to the *NY Times* reporter Elbert Clifton Daniel (who would later marry the daughter of then-President Truman), "obviously unaware of some of the simplest facts about the country [Palestine]" and were "groping for information." Jewish Agency officials like Sharett were there to supply that "information"

---

* "Bancz" is Ralph Bunche, who was then assistant to UNSCOP, and would soon be principal secretary of the UN Palestine Commission; Sir Abdur is Abdur Rahman, representative from India; Sandstrom is Justice Emil Sandström, representative from Sweden; Hood is J. D. L. Hood, representative from Australia.

to UNSCOP, and its liaison officers maintained a close association with the Committee throughout its visit.

As would happen at the UN in November, only India's Sir Abdur Rahman attempted substantive debate, which Sharett "sidestepped," to use the *NY Times'* word. Seated around a horseshoe-shaped mahogany table in the auditorium of the Jerusalem YMCA, Sharett stated bluntly that the Jewish Agency would never accept equality ("unity") with the Palestinians, justifying the discrimination to UNSCOP with the argument that "Palestine owes its existence to the fact that it is the birthplace of the Jewish people." Denying the ethnic cleansing that he thought his audience feared was soon to come, he made the remarkable claim that "not one single Arab village has disappeared from the map of Palestine" due to the Zionists—which, if reporter Daniel's assessment was accurate, some members may have accepted as fact.

A far more honest meeting took place in secret a week later. Carter Davidson, another American journalist in Palestine covering the Committee's visit, was approached in secret by a man bringing a message from Irgun Commander Menachem Begin: Begin wanted to arrange a clandestine meeting with Committee members. Davidson conveyed the request to Committee chairman Sandström; Sandström agreed. On June 24 Davidson and three Committee members, Mr. Sandström, Dr. Victor Hoo, and Dr. Ralph Bunche, "went for a stroll" and met a pre-arranged taxi. They were driven to a darkened street and left there. Then "a pretty girl approached, mentioned the pre-arranged password and took us on a circuitous walk" to a second taxi that drove them for fifteen minutes through an unlighted route to the meeting place with Begin and two of his aides.

"The peace of the world," Begin vowed to the UNSCOP representatives, will be threatened if Partition is approved and "the Hebrew homeland" not returned in its entirety to "its rightful owners." Lest there be any doubt as to what this homeland encompassed, it is "the territory which stretches between the Mediterranean and the desert East of the Jordan and from Dan to Beersheva."

Why not simple democracy in Palestine? the Committee asked. Yes, Begin agreed. But three thousand years ago the land had a "Jewish State," and so Jewish blood, worldwide, now constituted the citizenry of Palestine. All Jews, worldwide, were its electorate. What if, despite his methodology, Jews worldwide still did not vote as he wished? Begin replied by enlarging the dimensions of his Jewish electorate from the geographic to the temporal: Such a vote would be illegitimate, he explained, because the Jewish nation belongs equally to Jews of all generations to come, and therefore no majority of "this generation of Jewish people" mattered if it voted contrary to Zionist interests.

The meeting with this most wanted of terrorists was kept out of the Committee's report and not acknowledged until Davidson revealed it in the *NY Times* a month later. A formal transcript of it was produced by the Jewish Legion, but the first transcript was fourteen type-written pages by the "Diaspora Headquarters of the Irgun Zvai LEUMI by Authority of the High Command in Eretz Israel" of the "Irgun-Unscop Conference."[418]

UNSCOP's presence brought only a modest lull in Zionist violence. The Air Ministry Works Dept compound on the grounds of the Italian Hospital in Jerusalem was bombed on June 3, and trains on both the Haifa-Kantara and the Lydda-Jaffa lines were blown up on the 4th. Both the Athlit Railway Station and the IPC pipeline northeast of Jalama were bombed on June 5, causing extensive damage in the former and the loss of 800 tons of crude oil in the latter.[419]

At about 5:00 PM on the 9th, the telephone line at Gal Gil swimming pool at Rammat Gan went dead. Seven "Jews armed with T.S.M.G.S. and revolvers" entered and abducted a sergeant and constable. As they threw two smoke bombs to hide their escape, one witness saw "ten men and one girl" pull the captives into a (stolen) truck. The Haganah issued a statement ordering the Yishuv not to give information about the kidnappings to the British, but rather to "the Yishuv's Security Institutions."

At noon the next day, the British cordoned off Qiryat Shaul settlement and recovered the two men, whose captors had told them that their fate was dependent on the outcome of ongoing trials of accused Irgun members. Among the weaponry uncovered were a Thompson submachine gun and "U.S.A. pattern grenades." The terror gangs attacked the Reuters office in Tel Aviv on June 12, and that evening staged bombings as warnings to uncooperative Jews, one a wine merchant, the other the owner of an ironmonger shop who was accused of buying milk from Palestinians.

The Irgun, meanwhile, had been busy boring a tunnel to Army HQ in Tel Aviv's Citrus House from the basement of a neighboring building. Citrus House had long been in the Irgun's cross-hairs—their complicated attack on January 2 failed to cause the destruction intended—but the 250-300 foot tunnel would give them a deadly advantage. As was their practice, the gang booby-trapped their handiwork to kill any unwary snooper, and so when at about 11:00 on the morning of June 18 a Haganah operative, Zeev Weber, came across the tunnel, a bomb detonated, killing him. The explosion was heard outside and alerted the British.

The Jewish Agency made great play out of their fallen hero saving British lives. Although saving British lives was a happenstance consequence, it was nonetheless true. British representatives attended the funeral in respect.[420]

On June 22, "four men and a girl" attempted to kill an Assistant Superintendent of Police with an iron pipe in Jerusalem's Jordan Book Shop. That evening a small bomb blew up in a porch of the English Girls School on Shabatai Levy Street in Haifa, "to deter Jewish mothers from sending their daughters to a 'foreign' school," as 317 Airborne Field Security interpreted it. A Sten gun and ammunitions factory discovered on June 20 proved to be "one of a chain of such factories" maintained by the Hagana. Two days later, an attempt to kidnap the Frontier Control officer in Jerusalem was foiled.

When on the evening of the 24th, a small explosion was heard in the garden of a house near the Salvia Hotel opposite the Jerusalem Military Courts, the British, well aware of the terrorists' penchant for baiting police into a booby-trapped house, did not enter until daylight. Their suspicion of being lured into a death trap was vindicated: inside they found a mattress, but careful not to disturb anything, they attached a rope and pulled it from a safe distance outside. The explosion demolished the entire wall. A drawer of a table also proved to be booby-trapped.[421]

On June 25, militants burst into the Jerusalem flat of an UNSCOP liaison officer and struck him on the head with a pipe. He resisted his attackers' attempts to chloroform him long enough to run outside and signal a passing military vehicle, foiling the abduction, though the assailants shot the driver as they fled.

Meanwhile, in Devon (Britain), the theft of explosives from two quarries heightened domestic terrorism concerns, as wiretaps strongly suggested that the explosives were destined for bombings in Britain in the Zionist cause.[422]

On the Sabbath, June 28, Lehi drove a taxi ("borrowed in the usual manner") to the Astoria Restaurant on Haletz Street in Haifa and sprayed it with automatic fire, killing an officer and wounding two before the assailants sped off upon return fire, then escaped by foot when the British punctured the taxi's tires, leaving behind two grenades. The restaurant was known to be crowded with British officers on Saturday evenings, and the "Jewish proprietress [was] well known for her reasonable outlook" on the Palestine issue.

In Tel Aviv on the Allenby Road, four British officers were gunned down from behind, the signature Lehi method. One survived. During the night, a bomb detonated behind Jerusalem's Vienna Café without casualties. On Sunday, soldiers were attacked while bathing near Hertzliya, two presumed not to have recovered from their wounds.

Heedful of Irgun boasts of undefeatable boobytrapping, the British detonated a bomb discovered on the tracks between Kafrsanir and Athlit *in situ*, destroying sixty yards of track. Lehi, in the meantime, added an imaginative twist to booby-trapping: it began distributing pamphlets and banners that exploded if burned.[423]

Train bombing reaches Europe

The Irgun's infiltration into European DP camps had made Europe a new front in the terror. In May and again in June, Zionist-mentored DPs attempted to bomb trains on the main railway line between Berlin and Hanover, but the explosives were discovered before their intended deadly disasters.

The first traceable clues as to the source of the bombs came with a failed attempt on the Hanover-Hamburg express train on June 28.

The bomb was typical: thirty kilograms (66 lbs) of gelignite of the type used for quarrying, with an electrical detonator. The break-through in sleuthing came with the paper used as wrapping in the device. Part of the paper had Hebrew printing, which was traced to a publication called *Unsere Stimme* ("Our Voice") from Belsen Camp. This and other bits of paper wrapping placed the source of the explosives to a quarry at Bochum in the Ruhr, where the foreman's records, combined with separate investigations in Hanover, led to the arrests of four individuals, two in the vicinity and two in Munich.

"Although the terrorists were reluctant to give information," one of the four confirmed that the Irgun's European operation was headquartered in Paris, "with subordinate headquarters in Munich, the whole being supported by the United Zionist Revisionist Organisation."[424]

The first week of July was "marked by a number of assassinations and attempted assassinations of British soldiers," Lehi's retaliation for the disappearance of sixteen-year-old member Alexander Rubowitz on May 6. Evidence implicated one Major Roy Farran, who allegedly grabbed Rubowitz for posting Lehi broadsides and killed him in the process of a brutal interrogation. Farran maintained his innocence and was acquitted, but his behavior only reinforced suspicions, and Lehi continued to believe that he was guilty. Fifty-six years later, in 2003, the British declassified documents that substantially prove Lehi's allegation: a confession allegedly made by Farran to the Assistant Inspector General of Police, Bernard Fergusson.[425]

July 1947

The *Exodus*

July 18-19 brought Palestine to the headlines. The overburdened vessel *President Warfield* reached Haifa brimming with 4,515 Jewish DPs, unwitting actors on a grand stage that stretched from Germany to the Promised Land and with an audience as large as the world. Choreographed for the global media and timed for UNSCOP's visit, the vessel itself became the stage prop—its sponsors renamed it the *Exodus* for the obvious Biblical iconography, and Ben-Gurion extolled its passengers as even more heroic than the Jews who had rebelled and died in the ghettos of Europe. Yet Britain, as the story was spun, refused to allow these desperate survivors of fascism to disembark in their promised land, their final hope of survival. Britain found itself in its worst public relations catastrophe of the entire Mandate.

The British were not taken by surprise. Two years earlier, then-High Commissioner Gort, in conversation with informant R. Newton, already expected that the Jewish Agency might arrange "the arrival at Tel Aviv of a ship with illegal immigrants from Bergen-Belsen who would ostensibly be welcomed ashore," at which "the Palestine Police would thus be dared to take action, [and] the clash would be fully utilized for propaganda." The *Exodus* was the consummate theater of what Newton described as exploiting the "plight [of the persecuted] Jews in Europe … to gain control of Palestine."

Now having to choose between Zionists' "unscrupulous attempt to exploit the sufferings of unfortunate people, in order to create a situation prejudicial to a final settlement," or "unleashing a storm of atrocity propaganda" in the presence of the UNSCOP Committee and the global media, the British chose the latter.[426]

Ben-Gurion called the *Exodus* affair an "enormous, awesomely great spectacle," with *spectacle* the revealing word. He cried out against Britain's having "forcibly returned" Holocaust survivors "to the land of the Nazis." But this was a lie: it was he and the Jewish Agency that forced the survivors back to Germany. The Jewish Agency Executive sabotaged efforts to get the passengers true safe-haven elsewhere, such as in Denmark; and but for them, the Exodus passengers could at least have disembarked in southern France.

As described by Professor Idith Zertal, these survivors of the Holocaust were for that moment

> Zionism's trump card, and the greater their suffering, the greater their political and media effectiveness. Not only did the Zionist leadership make no effort to spare the refugees the appalling return to Germany; it actually took distinct steps toward preventing any solution other than Germany.[427]

Once the curtain fell on the Final Act of the *Exodus* show, its human cargo were quickly forgotten by Ben-Gurion. "It's over, finished," he quipped impatiently to an inquiry about them because, in the bitter words of one of the ex-*Exodus* passengers, "we are no longer a sensation."

In the years to come, Israel simultaneously exploited the Holocaust to shield the state against criticism of its own racial-nationalist policies and expansionism, while treating the survivors "with condescension ... as second class citizens," as one survivor put it. The state would systematically steal German reparation money intended for survivors who continued to live in poverty, and Ben-Gurion would frame them for atrocities he knew to have been committed by his military, in order to insulate the state (e.g., pages 322, 345 below).[428]

The return of the Exodus refugees to Europe

The *Exodus* passengers were split among three vessels for the return to Europe. A "British Officer of the Escort" of one, the *Runnymede Park*, was from the 6th Airborne and wrote an (unauthorized) account of the voyage.

"By no possible stretch of the imagination could they [the DPs] be called Zionists," but Palestine was the only choice they were offered in the Zionist-controlled camps. "They had all been told what to say" and would "repeat whatever political mumbo-jumbo" was required. They survived at sea at the mercy of "quite a little Nazi organization—complete with muscle-men, group 'führers,' and capped by Hitler himself, or so we called" *Exodus* leader Mordechai Rosman. The DPs lived in terror of the "organization." For example, an old woman who "came one morning in terror of her life" because her service to the ship's (British-run) hospital was branded by the onboard Zionist regime as "co-operating."

When the three vessels carrying the ex-*Exodus* DPs reached Port de Bouc in southern France, all were legally free to disembark there rather than continue to Germany. The *Exodus* script, however, required the imagery of the DPs being forcibly returned to Germany, and so "persistent Zionist threats and propaganda"—these the words not of the escort's often hyperbolic account, but of an official communiqué, confirmed by an announcement from the Haganah itself—were used to be sure the DPs did not disembark in France.

The 6th Airborne officer states that in response, the British "set up a secret disembarkation center in the [ship's] hospital" to smuggle out any *Exodus* DPs at Port de Bouc willing to risk "being torn to pieces in the holds" for endangering the *Exodus* narrative. One couple who escaped the *Ocean Vigour* in this manner naively returned to retrieve some belongings, "unaware that their secret had leaked out. They were set upon and would undoubtedly have been killed by the thugs detailed for the job" had eleven men not raced to their rescue. These eleven were then "attacked with tins of bully and broken-off bottles" by the Agency thugs, but successfully extracted the unconscious victims from their grips. Both survived.

Fearing that the incident would prove difficult to explain if the press learned of it, the Agency concocted the story that the two were Gestapo agents taken aboard to bring them to justice.

We also know independently of the onboard officer that the British, meanwhile, called the Jewish Agency's bluff. They appealed directly to Golda Meir and spoke as though the Agency would obviously want to spare the DPs from the horrific return to Germany. Why not send an Agency representative to Port du Bouc to remind the DPs that they are free to disembark there, in case they are not aware?

Meir scoffed at the suggestion. "No Jew," she said as if it were a reply, "could contemplate advising another Jew to proceed anywhere but Palestine."[429]

On the evening of July 11, two sergeants in civilian clothes, Mervyn Paice and Clifford Martin, met at the café Pinati in Nathanya with a friend, Aharon Weinberg, sat at a table near the orchestra and (as a British report put it) "consumed a quantity of beer." Conversation was, according to Weinberg, of a general nature, and the attitude of the other patrons was "mutely hostile." After leaving the café at about half past midnight, Weinberg decided to accompany the two non-commissioned officers as far as his home. Walking along Herbert Samuel Street near the café Rimon, "a dark saloon car passed and stopped in front of them, and some six Jews, armed with sub-machine guns and pistols, alighted." All three were abducted, blindfolded, and chloroformed. Weinberg was later abandoned in an orange grove, hands and feet bound. An intensive search for the two sergeants was stymied by false leads and (apparently deliberate) misinformation. Their fate remained unknown for three weeks, when their bodies were discovered hanging from trees (pages 236-237, below).[430]

Two trucks carrying military personnel on Tiqva-Lydda Road were targeted on July 16 with electrically detonated mines, killing one and injuring three, one seriously. On the Haifa–Tel Aviv Road north of Petah Tiqva, four were injured when an electrically detonated mine struck a jeep. A mine exploded in Jerusalem, injuring eight, and an electrically detonated mine hit a staff car on Haifa-Jaffa Road.

Near Kfar Bilu (Rehovoth) on July 18, a truck was blown up by an electrically detonated mine, killing a sergeant and injuring three others. Jerusalem was hit with scattered attacks by grenade, incendiary bomb, and automatic fire, wounding three, one (a civilian) seriously. Two constables in plain clothes were assassinated by Lehi the next day in Haifa, shot in the back as usual; a civilian was also killed. A truck was blown up in Jerusalem, wounding five civilians and three military personnel, and incendiary bombs were thrown at vehicles.[431]

When a bomb thrown at a British Constable in a main thoroughfare failed to explode, the Constable attempted to make an arrest, but then a "hostile crowd" assaulted the officer and made good the suspect's escape.[432]

More activity in London
In London that same day—July 19—British fears of continuing domestic Jewish terrorism heightened. Harry Isaac Presman, "prominent in Jewish circles in North London," owned two cars which he had kept in adjacent lock-up garages on Fairholt Road until two weeks earlier, July 6, when he told his chauffeur that one of the garages had been rented, and so one vehicle would now be kept at new premises he had acquired at the rear of Church Street.

The next day (July 7), Presman phoned Leo Bella, whom the British believed to be a "controlling figure" behind the plans for domestic terror attacks. The British were listening: Presman wanted to get back into the garage because "I had to leave some things in there, some of my chauffeur's things, and as he is rather nosey

I would like to have those things removed." Twelve days passed without the chauffeur needing access to the garage. But on July 19, wanting to wash both cars, he needed box-ends that had formerly been kept there. He went to the garage door and found that although the padlock was closed, it had not been put through both ends of the hardware. Opening the door, instead of box-ends he faced twenty-four hand grenades and twenty-three detonators. He alerted a mounted policeman. Although a stash of Irgun literature awaited the police in Presman's flat, Presman claimed ignorance: the garage was being rented from him.[433]

The morning after the garage hideout was exposed, Bella called Senior at the Waldorf Hotel and in what British eavesdroppers described as nervous, disguised language, told him that "something had happened." Then Bella, who owned an Auster aircraft and had been taking flying lessons, called his instructor in Cambridge, asked if it was good weather for flying, was told "yes," but then said he would not have his lesson today. British intelligence was aware that Senior, in the course of flights between England and France, was making unreported "emergency landings" in fields to collect or drop off unknown items. Bella was now very anxious that he deliver something to Senior at 11:30 the next morning (July 21), and this had something, unspoken, to do with the Auster.

Efforts turned to figures that British intelligence had already been following, in particular Leo Bella, Boris Senior, Abraham Abrahams, Chonel Poniemunski, Paul Homesky, Eric Prinz, Moyses Kaplan, Cyril Ross, and the South African Revisionist Israel Lifshitz. These men clearly assumed that they might be trailed and wiretapped, and behaved accordingly, speaking in what appeared to be plain language code. Poniemunski, suspected in the quarry theft of June 25, seemed to be toying with the police "to make them look foolish." He traveled frequently, but searches of his baggage yielded nothing damning—"about 10 small tins of surplus American contraceptives" on one inspection.[434]

Back in Palestine, July 20 brought more railway bombings and attacks by mortar, mines, and firearms. By 9:00 AM, five separate instances of bomb-rigged tracks had been discovered by the "suicide patrols." At noon, a bomb detonated in front of a goods train on the Haifa-Kantara line, and an hour later, an electrically detonated mine on the Jaffa-Haifa Road north of Hadera killed one person and seriously injured two more. A constable on duty at Mustashfa billet was shot from the roof of a neighboring house. Two police were shot in the back by three young Lehi militants as they walked down Hehalutz Street in Haifa. Both died on the spot.

It was in Haifa as well that the next day's attacks began. At 1:30 in the morning "Jews armed with machine guns and grenades" attacked a radar station, and two hours later "armed Jews" bombed a wireless transmitter, destroying it, and mined nearby roads. A jeep was blown up by an electrically detonated mine, killing one boy and injuring six. A Palestinian civilian was seriously injured by a mine, and roads were extensively mined. Iraq Petroleum Company pipelines near Affuleh and near Kfar Yehoshua (Haifa) were bombed, but another bomb in Haifa was discovered in time and destroyed. The next day (July 22) a military truck was hit by an electrically detonated mine, grenades were thrown at a Palestinian civilian truck, and shots were fired at an RAF vehicle, injuring two, one a civilian. A fire bomb was thrown at an RAF vehicle in Jerusalem, two civilians were burned by a fire bomb intended for a police car, and the Mustashfa Police Station was attacked. British records detail numerous further, daily attacks by sniper fire, bombs, mines, and hand grenades that failed to cause major injury but maintained the state of debilitating fear without relief.[435]

The strange case of the *Empire Lifeguard*

Terrorists Sink British Ship Landing 259 Jews at Haifa. So read the *NY Times* headline to a terror attack that was particularly revealing as to the mentality of those at the helm of the Zionist project, both in Palestine and in the United States—the Jewish Agency's bombing of the British vessel *Empire Lifeguard* on July 23. This was an attack that involved elaborate, costly, months-long preparation, and risked the lives of Jewish refugees while serving no possible practical benefit. The *Empire Lifeguard* was doing precisely what the Zionists wanted: bringing Jewish refugees (and American colonists) to Palestine for permanent settlement. There was nothing to be gained by the bombing, not even the false justification of the *Patria* bombing. Yet to taunt the British, the Agency risked the lives of all aboard to the accuracy of a detonator timer, the fickleness of the seas, and unpredictable maritime delays.

The bombing was carried out by settlers from the United States in collaboration with the Hagana, using British entry permits intended for European DPs. The American settlers had begun their voyage from Miami in another vessel, the *Hatikvah*, and boarded the *Empire Lifeguard* in Cyprus along with the war's DPs who were held there awaiting their turn for emigration to Palestine, which had now come.

The conspiracy required several people to smuggle aboard the large amount of explosives required. They hid the explosives in bags in the small of their backs, in shaving cream tubes, in a nurse's handbag, and even in a handicapped person's wheelchair. Haganah operatives in Cyprus taught one of the American settlers how to make the bomb; he is said to have concealed the pencil-shaped detonator in his anus.

The Haganah also taught the bomber to booby-trap the detonating timer so that no one would be able to thwart it once set—including him. While this was to stop anyone from foiling the attack if discovered, it also meant that if the acid ate through the delaying switch quicker than estimated, or if the vessel's arrival were delayed more than briefly, it would have become a suicide bombing.

And this, indeed, nearly happened. With its human cargo confined above the device, the vessel was stopped outside of Haifa for a medical check, its British captain unaware that they sat on a floating bomb.

The vessel made it to shore with insufficient time. The bomb exploded as the passengers were disembarking, blasting a hole in the hull six by three feet and igniting a raging fire in the engine room that took fire fighters both inside and outside the vessel to extinguish. Records of casualties are oddly contradictory.[*]

---

[*] Many sources, including pro-Zionist and the CIA, cite 65 dead and 40 injured, though these could be from a single source, copied and recopied. A telegram sent by Cunningham at 14:30 on the day of the bombing stated "believed no loss of life," and the *Palestine Post* (July 24 1947), among other media, reported no casualties. The author could not find a reliable, authoritative record.

The bizarre case of the Empire Lifeguard stands out as a testament to the mentality and values of all involved—the Jewish Agency, Hagana, and US Zionists. Terror for its own sake without thought of consequence, the lives of two hundred fifty nine people, most of them Jewish survivors of the war, were gambled for a jeer devoid of purpose*.[436]

British efforts to evacuate and care for the *Empire Lifeguard* immigrants were complicated by the militants' sniper fire, fire bombings, and road mining around Palestine. As the vessel sat crippled on the bottom of Haifa's twenty-foot deep inner harbor, a military truck was mined in Haifa, killing one and seriously injuring three, and another truck was blown up near Rehovoth, injuring nine, of whom two succumbed to their wounds. A school compound in Haifa used by the military was bombed, injuring one; a car park in the city was bombed, injuring three, and an ambulance was blown up by a mine on Haifa-Jaffa Road near Khirbet Beit Lidd, killing two and injuring two seriously. After the railway near Gaza was bombed, the British found an array of land mines, grenades, explosives, mortar bombs, and detonating sets left behind by the bombers that suggested that far more ambitious sabotage plans had been stymied.

July 24 brought three more bombings, one causing extensive damage to the Haifa-Kantara line near Zichron Yeaqov, as well as another Irgun or Lehi diamond heist, and an unsuccessful attack on an officers' mess.

The background terror was now incessant and escalating. The sum of relatively minor incidents, too numerous to catalogue, formed what Airborne security described as an "all out effort on the part of the Jews to co-operate in creating a wave of terror."[437]

That wave of terror hit Germany the next day, July 26, when "Irgun in the Diaspora" attacked a British train in Hanover. Although the British described the train as military, the Irgun attacked it in

---

* The Palmach's website, in its listing of the July 23 1947 *Empire Lifeguard* bombing, calls the vessel a "deportation ship." Although the vessel had in the past been used to bring unauthorized immigrants to Cyprus to await entry under quota, it was now bringing immigrants *to* Palestine, not away from Palestine, and would have continued to do so, but the British had to cancel further immigrant Cyprus-Palestine trips due to the fear of another bombing.

the belief that it was civilian, as it boasted that with their attack on the Hanover train they forced the British to "protect their civilian" installations worldwide.

The increased focus on civilian targets was apparent in Palestine that same day. Workers sent to repair a cable the militants had sabotaged were unaware that it had been booby-trapped. Two repairmen were killed on the spot, and eight injured.

"New measures are being adopted by the saboteurs," the War Office reported, "namely that of attempts against the lives of repair parties by the concealment of booby traps and mines."[438]

Arson attacks that day targeted the identity card office in Tel Aviv and a wooden railway bridge—that wooden bridge itself a temporary replacement for the original bridge that was destroyed in a previous terror spree. An attempt to blow up the Haifa-Kantara train near Nes Tsiyona was foiled.

July 27 brought more explosions and more casualties: a contact mine bombing on the Lydda-Jaffa line, a rail worker attacked upon discovering a mine on the line south of Hadera, and a convoy attacked in Jerusalem by grenades.

A time bomb filled with rivets exploded in the open air cinema at Tel Litwinsky on July 28, leaving eight casualties. Bombers targeted two vehicles by electrically detonating a mine on Gaza Road near Kfar Bilu, a grenade was thrown at W.D. vehicle in Jerusalem, and a police car was attacked by a mine and gunfire. The next day, a check-post at the Acre roundabout on the Haifa-Acre road was bombed and destroyed, a police car was targeted by grenade, and a mine blew up a considerable length of track on the Haifa-Kantara line near Athlit. Two people were killed and thirty injured on July 30 by an electrically detonated mine near Hadera. A bomb in the Romema Quarter of Jerusalem was successfully neutralized.[439]

The hangings of the kidnapped soldiers

It was in Jaffa that afternoon, July 30, that District Police Headquarters received an anonymous phone call about the two sergeants kidnapped on the evening of July 11. Police had already followed several tips without result, but the caller specified a precise map reference where their bodies would be found. At 7:40 the next morning, the last day of July, members of the Nathanya Jewish Settlement Police Patrol reported that two bodies had been seen hanging from trees in a government eucalyptus grove at Umm Uleiqa.

At 9:00 the British found the corpses of the two young men, aged twenty and twenty-one, as promised. The police surmised that the original intent was to hang the bodies in public display, but that this had proved too risky. They assumed that the Irgun had mined the area, and used mine detectors before approaching the hanging bodies. But again the Irgun was a step ahead—the police failed to consider that the militants might have booby-trapped the bodies themselves. When an Army Captain tried to free the first victim from its noose, the corpse blew up in his face.[440]

The discovery of the hangings was but the beginning of the troubles of July 31. Jewish mobs in Tel Aviv ransacked the Barclays Bank, the Post Office, and the Income Tax Office. An RAF vehicle was overturned and set afire by the crowd, a police car was stopped and stoned, a RASC driver was dragged from his vehicle by a mob who set fire to the vehicle and then prevented the Fire Brigade from extinguishing it. In Jerusalem, the Military Billet and Defence Post were attacked with automatic fire and bombs. A mine was electrically detonated under a train between Zikron Yaacov and Ben Yemdina, derailing the engine and wagon and damaging 50 meters (164 ft.) of track. More mines were discovered on the Jaffa–Lydda line and on the Haifa–Tel Aviv road.

Anti-Jewish riots in Tel Aviv and England

Although the sergeants' murders were statistically unremarkable in Palestine's daily tally, the shocking method and the symbolism were seized upon by bigots as vindication. That evening in Tel Aviv, vigilantes in the British military and police went berserk, murdering five people, and in England, news of the sergeants' executions ignited a five-day rampage. British Jews were assaulted, their windows smashed, and swastikas painted on Jewish businesses.

Britain's 1947 anti-Jewish pogrom is but one illustration of Zionism's self-fulfilling and self-perpetuating cycle of antisemitism.

The bigots who carried out the pogrom had accepted Zionism at its libelous word: Zionism represents Jewry. The resulting violence in turn assures Zionism's need for antisemitism as a permanent state of humanity.

Aug
1947

In print as well, the battles of anti-Semitism continued alongside those of radical Zionism. *The Jewish Struggle* extolled Zionist terror and threatened that "every community in the diaspora [will become] a centre of revolt." British authorities were even more concerned by a neo-Nazi paper, *The Protestant Vanguard*, and back in March of 1945 Parliament had held debates on the wisdom of forcibly suppressing it. Its publisher insisted on "the absolute right of any Briton to be anti-Jewish if he wants to be," and suggested to unhappy government officials they purchase from him *Protocols of the Elders of Zion* and other hate literature. In the United States, the Zionist terror gangs' fundraising continued, while the antisemitic periodical *Christian Patriots* attributed all wars since the French Revolution to a Jewish conspiracy.

If on the surface, the neo-Nazism of *The Protestant Vanguard* and the violent Zionism of *The Jewish Struggle* appear to be polar extremes, some people correctly saw both as forms of antisemitism.[441]

On August 2 the Irgun exploded pamphlet bombs in Petah Tiqva, injuring four people, and attacked a military patrol and the RAF Club in Jerusalem. The next day a bridge on the Haifa Kantara line near Rehovot was bombed, killing one Palestinian and injuring another.

In Europe that night (August 3), the Irgun bombed Vienna's Sacher Hotel by two suitcase bombs planted in the coal cellar. In Tel Aviv the day after that a bank cashier, a Sephardic Jew, was killed in a robbery of a Barclays Bank by "seven Jews and one Jewess, all armed." They were Hagana. A device set to bomb a post in Jerusalem was discovered and destroyed.[442]

Two armed men speaking Hebrew walked into the Department of Labour in Jerusalem the following day (the 5th), deposited a bomb, and left. After the building was evacuated, employees described the position of the bomb to police. Four police entered the building, located the bomb and, tragically, tried to remove it. The explosion killed three on the spot, seriously injured the fourth, and heavily damaged the building.

Two days later (the 7ᵗʰ) a mine on the Haifa-Kantara line between Ras El Ain and Qalqilya derailed nineteen oil wagons, and an electrically detonated mine near Hadera injured four in a military staff car. In the outskirts of Jerusalem, a grenade was used in an attempted assassination of the Bethlehem District Officer, two mines were discovered on the road near Petah Tikva, and near Gaza a length of the railway was blown up.[443]

One of the terror gangs' favorite devices, disguising themselves as Arabs, had been overused. As recorded by British officials that day,

> Arab Guards on the Ajami Police Station, Jaffa, challenged a man dressed as an Arab and leading a camel. The man ran away and was captured with the assistance of the public. He was found to be a Yemenite Jew and to be carrying a haversack containing a grenade and detonating device. In panniers on the camel were found two mines.[444]

Eight Jews (Irgun?) with automatic weapons robbed the Hasharon Cooperative Bank in Ramatgan on August 8. The Cairo-Haifa train was bombed by the Irgun the next day, killing the engineer, a Jew from Tel Aviv, and leaving two passengers critically injured. This attack was unusual in that it occurred on a plain with little place to hide, and two of the three bombers, aged fifteen and nineteen, were caught. The third escaped by spraying the scene with machine gun fire.[445]

On August 10, on the outskirts north of Tel Aviv near an Arab village, the Hawaii café, a "Jewish owned cafe in which an Arab has an interest" was attacked with automatic weapons and hand grenades. Four Jews and one Palestinian were killed on the spot, and eight people injured, three seriously. The British never determined who the five attackers were—did the Zionists target it because its Jewish owner worked with an Arab? Or did Arabs attack it because it was Jewish owned? Each side blamed the other, and in the "numerous stabbing, stoning, shooting and arson incidents" springing from the dispute, the dead included four Jews, four Palestinians, and one of unknown identity. Forty-eight Palestinians and twenty-three Jews were injured.

In Jerusalem on the day of the café attack, a tip warned of a bomb planted inside the Income Tax Office; it was evacuated in time before the device detonated. In Haifa, an attack was averted by a terrorist's carelessness: Lehi militants were transporting a small bomb in a taxi they had stolen "in the usual way" when, stopped at the Herzl Street crossing, one lit a cigarette. All three were found nearby with various injuries, one with a hand blown off. In Gaza, a military vehicle was attacked between Nuseirat and Julis.[446]

The bombing of the Naim Railway Line south of Gaza on August 11 was one success among a handful of failures. A bank robbery in Jerusalem (presumably for arms) was foiled, as was an attack on a Haifa post office with a rivet bomb. The next day police and military repelled an attacker at the Police Headquarters in Jerusalem, a phosphorus bomb was discovered on Ben Yehuda Street in Jerusalem, and a land mine on Jerusalem-Beit-Hakerem Road was found and safely detonated.[447]

Most importantly, the next attack also failed.

The Medloc train bombing

High in the Austrian Alps that night, August 12,[*] a Medloc train reached Mallnitz with 130 men and 40 women aboard, Allied troops and civilians of the Allied Commission for Austria, plus a crew of about five. The train had begun its journey at Hook of Holland late morning the previous day.

Leaving Mallnitz, it now continued toward Spittal at slow speed up a considerable gradient. About twenty minutes out of Mallnitz, near the Tauern railway tunnel, it proceeded onto a steep trestle. As it did, a bomb exploded underneath it—but not as intended. What would have been the most catastrophic Zionist terror attack after the *Patria*, twice as deadly as the King David bombing, failed.

"I was flung to the floor of the compartment," Commanding

---

* Irgun records in Kister cite two Irgun attacks on trains in Europe in mid-August of 1947, neither corresponding to this attack whose time and place are well documented. One is on August 13 "near Linz," which is roughly 165 km (100 miles) from the Mallnitz attack. The second is recorded as August 14 and simply "in Austria." The author has not been able to corroborate these attacks. (Kister, *Irgun*, 194 & 275)

Officer R. Wilson testified,

> and from that position the coach appeared to travel some distance in
> a series of bumps until finally coming to a standstill. On regaining
> my feet I found the coach considerably listed but I made my way
> along the corridor to the coach door, and avoiding the electric wires
> which hung over the coach, ascended to the track.[448]

Officer Wilson evacuated the passengers "to a point some 200 yards
in front of the train to a clearing on the track where a type of signal
box was located" and from which he signaled for help.

The attack was designed to be catastrophic—the bombers' choice
of this remote mountain pass was intended to plunge the train to the
depths below, with no survivors. As the report from the Carinthian
authorities summarized, the purpose was

> to derail the train and to cause it to fall into the deep Dösen-gorge,
> whereby the occupants of the train, about 175 persons, would have
> been killed.[449]

Their lives were saved by a happenstance failure. The bomb was in
two stages, an initial charge to be triggered by the engine's wheels,
which would detonate the main explosive and knock the locomotive
off the trestle, its weight taking the rest of the train with it. But
the initial charge exploded under the next car, the baggage van,
and the main explosive failed altogether.

A clock device incorporated into the mechanism suggests that
the Medloc train was the bombers' specific target. Despite its failure,
the device was not amateurish: in his report, the explosives expert
called to examine the remains wrote that the error that prevented
the main detonation was "the only primitive thing in the whole
arrangement." Significant parts of the device had come from the
United States.

However disappointed, the Irgun distributed handbills in the
Jewish DP camps claiming responsibility. It had least derailed an
Allied train, stopped travel on the route until the damaged tracks

Above: Medloc train carrying Allied troops and civilians, crippled following the Irgun's failed attempt to blow it off the trestle into the abyss on August 12, 1947. (Allied Commission for Austria, in *British Morning News*, August 17,1947, in TNA, FO 1020/1774)

Below: What the Irgun intended for the Medloc train is seen in this photograph of a 1946 Irgun train bombing on the Jaffa-Jerusalem line. Here the bomb exploded as intended under the locomotive, its weight dragging the rest of the train with it—in this case, only as far as the ravine, but the Medloc locomotive would have been blown off the trestle, dragging the entire train into the abyss with it. (*Report of The General Manager on the Administration of the Palestine Railways and Operated Lines:1946/1947*, Warhaftig's Press, Haifa)

were replaced, and most importantly kept the fear, and the need for expensive and laborious precautions, alive.

Four DPs were arrested for the attack, three from the US Zone, one from the British. The first to be caught, a seventeen-year-old member of the DP camp police who lived in the Bad Adelschloss Hotel in Bad Gastein (US Zone), confessed to being the lookout. Bad Gastein had become so infamous a stronghold of Zionism that Major General Harry Collins, commander of the US Zone in Austria, had months earlier forbidden British civilians from going there.[450]

Two and a half hours after the Medloc bombing, a "Red Devil" type bomb exploded outside the office of the Camp Commandant 138 BDE at Velden, Austria. Bombs threats had to be taken seriously and so false ones continued to be supplemental methods of disruption. The Hotel Sacher was evacuated at one such threat on August 15, the hotel that had been bombed twelve days earlier. A spate of bomb threats followed on August 19: against the United States Legation in Vienna, the Minister's residence, a power plant in the American zone, a "moving picture house" in the British zone, the plant where the British German-language newspaper was published, and once again the Hotel Sacher.[451]

Anti-terror policies were reassessed in the wake of the Medloc attack. The first on a list of eight recommendations was to "Get Austrians to move Jews to a camp as far as possible from our L of C [Lines of Communications]." Another was a change in the twenty-minute rule for when a pilot engine (used to check for bombs) should precede the train, as the set timing effectively told terrorists when the train would be coming. These pilot trains were an unrecognized drain on the Allies caused by the Zionists: each day they consumed about twenty-five tons of coal.[452]

US and British military personnel in Europe faced constant risk from DPs conditioned in the Zionist-run camps. Lucius D. Clay, commander in chief of US Forces in Europe and military governor of the US Zone in Germany, stressed the seriousness of this violence against Allied soldiers to members of UNSCOP when he met with them in Berlin on August 13. General Clay told the delegation that the

Jewish DPs from eastern Europe should be sent to Palestine quickly—not out of any affinity for Zionism, but because US personnel had been beaten, robbed, and killed by them, and that as a result of their "violent, asocial, and criminal behavior," anti-Semitism was growing sharply in US military units in the US Zones of Austria and Germany. Clay feared "severe spontaneous reactions on the part of other soldiers" if the situation were to continue, and his claims were reinforced by the Deputy British Military Governor, Sir Brian Robertson.

The Jewish Agency was well aware of the violence it had nurtured in the DP camps. Eliezer Kaplan, treasurer of the Jewish Agency, told Mapai* leaders the previous October that he had been "reliably informed" that US military reports submitted to Truman were "very pessimistic" about disturbances in the Zionist camps, and that the US feared having to use force to quell them.[453]

Some British officials now proposed boycotting the Jewish citrus crop pending Agency cooperation against terror, but this was shelved on four counts: British business interests, especially as much of the payment for the crops had been made in advance; the difficulty in determining the origin of the fruit; the fear that the action would backfire and be met with increased terrorism; and the surety that a boycott would play into the propaganda campaigns in the US.[454]

Near Petah Tiqva the day after the Medloc attack, two Jews shot a Palestinian dead from passing cars and left his body on the roadside. The next day, a Palestinian watchman at a factory in Ramat Gan was abducted by Jews; they stabbed him to death and threw his body into an orange grove.[455]

Two more Palestinian watchmen were stabbed to death by a gang of Jews near Jaffa on the 15th. One of the victims was thirteen years old. In Jaffa, three Jews vandalized a Palestinian shop and poured paraffin over its contents, but local (Jewish) residents intervened and stopped them from setting the shop ablaze. A bomb exploded under a goods train near Hadera, and Jews attacked a Palestinian on the Jaffa-Jerusalem Road, burning out his car.[456]

---

* Workers' party, merged with the Labour Party in 1968.

The bloodiest attack of the day was near Petah Tikvah, where "a party of 30-35 Jews in khaki shirts and shorts and armed with automatic weapons approached an Arab owned building in an orange grove near Petah Tikvah," as a British official recorded it. "As the Jews approached, they split up, several entering the building, and all firing indiscriminately." Four Palestinians were shot dead, and then

> the building was almost completely demolished by an explosion, probably electrically detonated. 3 males and 4 females are believed to be buried in the debris.

The dead bodies pulled out from the rubble confirmed the figure: five children and their parents, plus one further victim murdered outside, pushed the total dead to twelve. The Haganah claimed responsibility. Two days later, what was described as a gang of Jews seized a Palestinian man in a café in Tel Aviv near the Jaffa border, dragged him to an alley and stabbed him to death.[457]

The summer of 1947 thus marks the beginning of today's ongoing phase of the Zionist project, in which the Palestinians themselves remain the final obstacle to the so-called Jewish state, an ethnocracy in all of historic Palestine. Britain had nearly served its purpose. It had established the Zionist settlements as an autonomous part of the Palestinian landscape, and it had defended the settlements against the indigenous uprising as the Yishuv's own military strength grew to self-sufficiency. During the war years, Britain's value to the Zionists quickly diminished as it became instead the colonial oppressor against which they could posture their war of conquest as a native liberation movement.

Although the UN vote had yet to take place, there was no question that the Mandate would soon end. The British were reduced to a defeated co-conspirator now wanting only to extricate themselves as quickly as possible. In nine months, they would be gone, and in half that they would already be irrelevant.

In a twist, the coming reckoning also meant that the Irgun and Lehi found themselves in competition with the Haganah for international respectability as a path to power. The result was that both the Irgun and Lehi seized upon the Haganah's slaughter of Palestinians to posture themselves as the principled alternatives. Even as the Palestinians were increasingly all three militias' targets of choice, Lehi and the Irgun distributed pamphlets condemning the Haganah for murdering Arab "women and children who are beyond any political controversy," and denouncing as "traitors" any Jew who harmed any Arab.

The Hagana, similarly, accused the Irgun of needing a new *raison d'etre* now that a Zionist state appeared imminent, and assigned about a hundred members to "beat up in public known [Irgun] extortionists." Sharett went to the United States and told the media that the Jewish Agency was "trying to organize a campaign of enlightenment among Jews to open their eyes to the freak charlatan aspect" of Bergson (the Irgun's US branch).

A principal layer of this Hagana-Irgun power play was the increasing rivalry between Ben-Gurion and Begin, which would culminate with Ben-Gurion's burning of Begin's *Altalena* and its arms shipment in June, 1948, which Ben-Gurion would cleverly wield under the guise of principle.[458]

Early signs of a Palestinian backlash

Near Jerusalem on August 16, the militants exploded a time bomb in a games room at Tel Litwinsky, injuring six. Less dramatically but more significantly, Palestinians that day threw stones at a Jewish bus near Haifa. The following day, a Palestinian was attacked on the Tel Aviv sea front, and Palestinians fired three shots at a Jewish bus on the Jerusalem-Jaffa Road. In mid-August 1947, with the end of the Mandate in sight and Zionist violence escalating, the Palestinians' nearly decade-long refusal to reward Zionist terror was beginning to wear.

More clashes followed on August 18-19, and on the 20th a Jewish café owner was assaulted by six Jews because he employed Palestinians. A Haganah arms cache was discovered that day in a Jewish school—including sub-machine guns, 4,609 rounds of ammunition, and 401 hand grenades—and so the Agency spun the embarrassment by announcing that they had "<u>so</u> hoped [to use] these particular arms" to fight terrorism. Jewish snipers fired from rooftops at police cars, and a mine (Irgun?) on the railway line near Gaza was discovered and diffused. On the 21st a road mine near Nathanya injured two, one seriously. Just before midnight on the 26th, three Jews in Samaria District were injured when they challenged Lehi militants who had entered the village to distribute pamphlets. Lehi continued its threats against Jewish civil servants, and when a member of the gang was caught with a phosphorus bomb after a foiled raid on a Jerusalem bank that month, he was identified as the son of an Assistant Superintendent of Police.[459]

Baruch Korff

A particularly bizarre Zionist terror-funding scheme came to the fore in September of 1947. Rabbi Baruch Korff, a US citizen, was raising money to enact, in his words, "the greatest exodus since Pharaoh" by his organization, the Political Action Committee for Palestine. According to the Committee's money-raising ads in the *New York Post* in March, DC4 aircraft would make four round trips daily from "a certain port in Europe."

> The operation will be divided into two categories: (A) Planes carrying women and children will be directed to secretly designated make-shift landing fields in Palestine; (B) Planes carrying able-bodied men will be unloaded by Parachute

Sept 1947

to assist them. In a June interview in the *New York Sun*, Korff announced a new plan, more delusional than the first: he was going to drop Jews by parachute to Middle East waterways, where they would be picked up by waiting PT boats and smuggled into Palestine.

The money, in truth, was financing (to quote British intelligence) a "project for an air-raid on London" from France, "in the course of which leaflets were to be dropped in the name of the Stern Gang, together with high explosive bombs." For the task he hired an American pilot, Reginald Gilbert, but this was a bad choice: Gilbert informed the French authorities, and when on September 6 he and

Korff, accompanied by Judith Rosenberger (who some sources say slipped into Belgium when Eliav and Lazarus were caught) reached the Toussus-le-Noble airfield, they were apprehended.

The Korff saga led investigators to Lehi operative Jacques Martinski, who was previously involved with Gilberte Lazarus' unsuccessful attempt to bomb London's Colonial Office. When interrogated "in connection with the Jewish Terrorists proposed plan to drop leaflets and bombs on London," Martinski testified "that a man whose name he did not know, but whom he knew as a member of the Stern Group in Paris, had given him 10,000 francs to buy six fire extinguishers." Three days before the planned raid, Martinski took the six extinguishers and a heavy, padlocked case, the contents of which he claimed not to know, to a spot near Paris' Gare du Nord and handed them over to a contact with a private motor vehicle. The receipt for the extinguishers was found in Korff's room.

To the backdrop of *Exodus* sympathy, Korff was treated leniently and soon released. He later reappeared in the limelight as a vociferous defender of Richard Nixon in the midst of the Watergate scandal.[460]

Korff's was not the last London terror attack to be foiled. One agent working for Special Branch, Glasgow, learned of "Jews [in Britain who] are anxious to have the 'stuff' as soon as possible," preferably TNT, otherwise gelignite, to use "as a counter demonstration to what may happen in Palestine," probably meaning the UN decision. At 3:30 in the afternoon on September 3, a parcel slipped off a conveyor belt at the SW District Post Office and exploded, injuring two postal employees. What appeared to be part of a watch was found in the debris.[461]

When on September 9, the three vessels carrying the ex-*Exodus* passengers reached Hamburg, one of the DPs (or their minders) affixed a bomb to his ship, the *Empire Rival*, that would have torn a six-foot hole in its hull. It was discovered and safely detonated outside, though the blast broke about a dozen windows in nearby buildings.

The following day at Haifa, where the *Exodus* DPs had been refused entry two months earlier, four bombs exploded at the heavily-guarded Consolidated Refineries. Evidence suggested that sympathetic employees had facilitated the attack from the inside. Meanwhile, a terror group called Lameri, said in a British report to be "younger right wing elements in Palmach," distributed pamphlets claiming that "the Arabs" were preparing a revolt, likely to begin in October.

On September 26, three constables transferring money from the Barclays Bank in Tel Aviv to the Treasury in Jerusalem were murdered by ten or more Lehi members, netting the gang £150,000. Two more police were murdered in the chase. The Irgun, meanwhile, continued holding up cinemas to project its propaganda onto the screen for the edification of the audience, to the accompaniment of patriotic Irgun songs played from records.[462]

"An Arab constable at the front door blew his whistle, and the next moment he was blown to bits," the *NY Times* reported about a gruesome attack on District Police Headquarters in Haifa three days later, September 29, when the Irgun tried out a new massive tar barrel bomb which it said was "catapulted by a special mechanism from a lorry." Timed for the first day of the Feast of the Tabernacle, the explosion killed twelve people, both police and civilians, and injured fifty-four, thirteen seriously. Six of the dead were Palestinians, one a woman.

> Some of the small detachment of men on duty at the front door and in the orderly room were torn to pieces … Scarcely any structure in the immediate neighborhood escaped damage, [and] part of bodies were blown fifty yards across the Kings Way.[463]

"The general reaction" of the Jewish settlements to the massacre, according to a military report, "was one of admiration for the way the outrage was implemented and very little sympathy was reserved for the dead and wounded."

The more routine attacks continued. That same day, an explosion hit the rear of the Immigration Office in Jerusalem, and a rivet-type mine was detonated under a jeep on the Lydda–Petah Tiqva Road, injuring two. The bombers hid nearby and fired on those who came to investigate. On the 30th, what the military called "Jewish thugs"—the terminology part of a new tact to deny them any glamor associated with "terrorist"—exploded a mine beneath the Cairo-Haifa train, south of Haifa. A truck carrying ice was blown up in Rehovot on October 1, and the day after that a Parachute Brigade truck was mined about a mile north of Hadera.[464]

Oct
1947

At about 10:15 on the night of October 6, between fifteen and twenty militants approached two Palestinian tents, spread out into a semi-circle around them, and indiscriminately opened fire into the tents with 160 rounds—a prelude to the three-pronged assault, known as Plan Dalet, that would depopulate Palestinian villages in a few months' time. Neighboring Palestinians fled for safety, but the attackers killed two more in their escape.

Despite the increasing anti-Palestinian violence and scattered incidents of Palestinian backlash, the arrival of October failed to usher in the prophesied Palestinian revolt. Disappointment among Zionist leaders, whose plans to conquer Palestine in the name of self-defense required a Palestinian threat, was sufficiently visible that it was noted in a British military report for the fortnight ending October 10:

> The Jews continue to exhibit signs of anxiety because the lack of [Palestinian] disturbances shows unexpected control by the Arab leaders over the masses.

Whether or not the British were correct in attributing the lack of Palestinian reaction to "Arab leaders," there was, in fact, a Palestinian attack that month, but not directed against Jews. In what the British military described as "a token of disgust" at US behavior at the UN, an "Arab Committee of Struggle" claimed responsibility for a bomb that caused minor damage to the American Consulate on October 13—a one-off with no follow-up.

The Irgun tried a new ploy on October 18, inspired by Lehi's invention of explosive-laden pamphlets: it now displayed banners in Tel Aviv and Jerusalem rigged with explosives intended to blow up the worker sent to remove them. The two gangs were indeed in contact, meeting on the 23rd-25th of the month outside of Tel Aviv to agree on joint tactics to fight Partition.[465]

Testimony of a sex worker

Jewish sex workers continued to be exploited as an espionage network. In November, at great personal risk, one testified to the British.

Nov 1947

She and her colleagues did not cooperate willingly. They would be confronted by men identifying themselves as "Stern Gang Intelligence," though the British believed they were not Lehi, but were using the Lehi brand because it was even more frightening than "Haganah" or "Irgun." The Jewish state, the women were assured, was imminent. Upon its founding they would be tried for sleeping with the enemy, convicted, and executed—if not simply "shot out of hand."

Stern Gang Intelligence was however giving them the opportunity to save their necks by becoming spies, since they "have continual access to a large number of slightly inebriated and highly repressed officers and men," and thus to their information and their thoughts.

"As can be imagined," the British summarized, "the average night club hostess, cafe girl or prostitute falls readily and is able to furnish the organisation with an astonishing amount of personal and official information concerning the activities of British army personnel." Any one woman would mingle among different cliques of men, since they "work at one place or another according to the amount of custom they bring to the management."

A questionnaire was printed to guide the women in their task, one copy to be filled out after each patron. The form pressed the indentured spies to extract the expected military and personal information, and to use their conversation to identify any British who betrayed any sympathy with the cause and might be recruitable. The women were instructed to "exploit your activities to the full" to garner all information possible, to be clear and concise, and to "comply strictly with instructions." Separate from that clinical reporting, they were also encouraged to offer any comments and opinions that might prove insightful, but these were to be strictly confined to the "special remarks column." Every ten days, Stern Gang Intelligence would visit the women and collect their forms and replenish their supply.[466]

November also brought an astonishing announcement from the Jewish Agency: it was forming an elite "Mishmar Force" to stamp out terrorism. However suspect the opportunistic timing—just as the UN was deciding Palestine's future—the British nonetheless honored the Agency's request to remove police and troops from the area in order not to interfere with the work of this anti-terror unit, which the Agency said would be established within ten days.

No such force was ever established.[467]

Police remained targets even in the lead-up to the United Nations vote. A Jewish police corporal was assassinated at his home in Jerusalem on the 3rd, and a constable was seriously wounded at the city's Northern Police Station. In Tel Aviv, two police were shot from behind, left on the ground and ignored by the passing Tel Aviv public until the arrival of a British patrol twenty-five minutes later. Both died. After two suspects in a separate incident were brought to the Apak Police Station, "about ten Jews armed with pistols and sub-machine guns" overpowered the station and released their comrades. On the 12th, five CID personnel in Cafe Haas in Haifa were sprayed with bullets from a Thomson sub-machine gun, killing one and critically wounding three.

A tip that day led the British to a Lehi "criminal school" in a house in the Ra'anana area. The British burst in and "took the 'thugs' completely by surprise" despite heavily armed sentries in a nearby orange grove. Lehi "men and girls jumped from the windows and doors," attacking with a variety of firearms, grenades, and bombs, but were overpowered. Among the Lehi trainees were "children of tender years," of which "two Jewish youths and three girls were killed" in the battle.

Lehi's first reprisals came on November 13 and targeted civilians, police, and soldiers indiscriminately. Its assassins murdered four civilians as they left Haifa's Armon cinema, apparently because they were oil workers: three were employees of Shell Oil and the fourth worked for Socony (now Mobil). At the time of the killings, "the streets of HADAR," the British reported of that area of Haifa, "were crowded with Jews, tens if not hundreds of whom" must be able to supply information or even describe the murders. But the population appears "to be infected with the totalitarian ideology" and no help was received—though legitimate fear of informing must also account for some witnesses' silence.

Lehi was equally busy in Jerusalem that day. The gang threw a flash bomb and grenades into Jerusalem's Cafe Ritz on King George's Avenue while shooting two constables outside, killing five people and wounding twenty-three. Two soldiers walking in Colony Square in Tel Aviv, and two constables walking on Jaffa Road in Jerusalem, were murdered on the 14th.

In Britain, Town Clerks throughout the country received Irgun leaflets posted from Tel Aviv warning that any interference in the Irgun's plans, whether by the British or the Arabs, would bring a campaign of terror to British shores.

Meanwhile, the Hebrew Legion was formed in Britain, a group that MI3 (a defunct division of the British Directorate of Military Intelligence) described as "the Jewish equivalent of the Mosleyite toughs," a reference to the British racial supremacist and Nazi sympathizer. The Legion was an extension of the American Hebrew Committee of National Liberation.

The immigrant ship *Aliyah* beached in the early morning hours of November 16, transporting the Agency's favored settlers: not the downtrodden of Europe, but "some three hundred carefully selected young Jews, earmarked and trained for service with HAGANA."

At 4:30 in the morning on November 20, "a party of about 6 armed Jews entered an Arab house at Ra'anana" and executed four Palestinians whom Lehi accused of having tipped off the British to the location of its training school—wrongly, according to the British, who "denied that the Arab victims had been in any way connected with the discovery of the Stern training ground." A fifth victim died a few days later from his wounds. This time, some Palestinians retaliated, firing on "a Jewish bus" and a river boat, causing no deaths.[468]

The big news for Palestine came on November 29.

7

Statehood, the "Archimedean fulcrum"

"In my view the state, even if it is small,
is the Archimedean fulcrum."
—*Chaim Weizmann to Benito Mussolini, Rome, February 17, 1934.*
Weizmann's point to the fascist dictator was that a Zionist state in
part of Palestine would enable them to conquer the rest.[469]

On November 29, 1947, the United Nations General Assembly passed non-binding Resolution 181, recommending the division of Palestine into two proto-countries separated by ethnicity, the larger for the minority Jewish population, the smaller for the majority Muslims and Christians. A small central region encompassing Jerusalem and Bethlehem would remain an international zone administered by the UN.

The vote had been delayed while the Truman Administration used, in the words of Under Secretary of State Sumner Welles, "every form of pressure, direct and indirect," to "make sure that the necessary majority" would be secured.[470]

Resolution 181 was a capitulation to Zionist terrorism. UNSCOP had also proposed a single, federated state, which the Palestinians would have accepted despite concerns that, as recorded in British Cabinet papers, it did not "altogether close the door to eventual partition."

The Zionists, "on the other hand," would have begun "an intensification of Jewish terrorism" at such a decision—an intensification over the Zionist terror that had already brought Palestine to its knees and was now increasingly threatening Europe—making the single democratic state "not capable of being enforced."

Equally damningly, those deciding Palestine's future already assumed that the new Israeli state would disregard the Partition anyway—and, implicitly, that the Security Council would do nothing to stop it. The reason the UN awarded the Zionists such a disproportionately large land area under Partition was in the hope that it might simply *delay* what they already assumed would be Israel's further conquest:

> The desire for expansion might develop earlier if the Jewish State occupied a smaller area and would be felt more strongly if the Jews were dissatisfied with the frontiers.[471]

Thus the UN knew all along that even after capitulating to the terrorism in instituting partition with arbitrarily generous borders, Israel would still wage expansionist wars afterwards. Alexander Cadogan, a British statesman remembered for his opposition to appeasement of the Nazis, then the United Kingdom's representative to the United Nations, described the scheme as "so manifestly unjust to the Arabs," that it is difficult to see how "we could reconcile it with our conscience."

Exploiting partition as a tactic had always been the Jewish Agency's plan. When Partition was first seriously proposed a decade earlier, in 1937, Ben-Gurion assured the Zionist Executive that "in the wake of the establishment of the state, we will abolish partition and expand to the whole of Palestine." He wrote to his son Amos that

> The decisive question is: Does the establishment of a Jewish state [in only part of Palestine] advance or retard the conversion of this country into a Jewish country? My assumption ... is that a Jewish state on only part of the land [i.e., Partition] is not the end but the beginning ... Our ability to penetrate the country will increase if we have a state.*

---

* The accuracy of passages from this widely-quoted letter has been contested by the Zionist watchdog CAMERA. In response, the editors of the JPS undertook a fresh, critical translation of the full original letter, and it is from that translation

Adolf Eichmann, visiting the Zionist settlements in October of 1937, heard much the same from his host, the Hagana's Feivel Polkes: Once a state was secured, "then the borders may be pushed outward according to one's wishes."[472]

When in late 1941 Ben-Gurion left London for the United States, the British secretly searched his luggage and found a document entitled *Outline of Zionist Policy*, Ben-Gurion's blueprints for the future. In it he described how Partition would be passively exploited: it would be "an irreparable mistake" to *suggest* Partition, he reasoned, but rather, statehood should be extracted from the *offer* of Partition. That state must then be enlarged at least to the Jordan River, and into Transjordan if possible.

Perhaps most revealing, Ben-Gurion referred to Palestinians by the extraordinary phrase "Arabs who happen to be in Palestine"—the ethnic purity of his envisioned state was high on his to-do list.[473]

By 1944, opposition to Partition had "hardened throughout all shades of Jewish opinion," as the Chief Secretary in Jerusalem put it, and in December of that year the Inner Zionist Council and *Assefat Hanivcharim* (Yishuv Elected Assembly) passed resolutions that placed "special emphasis on the rejection of partition."[474]

"Can we really believe," the British Secretary of State for Foreign Affairs asked rhetorically that year,

> more particularly after reading the newest memorandum of the Jewish Agency, that the Zionists … will accept as final the frontiers as proposed? … It seems inevitable that [they] would fill their State up far beyond its capacity and so prove their need for more living space."[475]

One month before the UN vote, the *Jewish Standard* published a full-page disavowal of Partition. "Whatever might be signed or pledged by the few Zionist spokesmen at the United Nations," the *Standard* argued, would still be subject to the resolute opposition to Partition

---

that this extract is quoted. See "JPS Responds to CAMERA's Call for Accuracy: Ben-Gurion and the Arab Transfer," in *Journal of Palestine Studies*, Vol. XLI, No. 2 (Winter 2012), 245–250.

and the "struggle for the integrity of Eretz Israel" in all of historic Palestine. The "power and passion opposed to Partition" represent a force of Jewish public opinion "of uncompromising resolve."[476]

In London, *The Jewish Struggle* equated Partition with the final genocide of Jews and vowed that it would be fought to the end. In Palestine, *Voice of Fighting Zion* denounced Partition with virulent broadcasts, and Tel Aviv mayor Israel Rokach—part of the Jewish Agency mainstream—headed a movement dedicated to fighting Partition. In the US, the ZOA railed against the Jewish Agency for so much as discussing Partition.

Privately, however, even the Irgun and Lehi agreed with Ben-Gurion's pragmatism: Partition meant statehood, and statehood was the weapon to defeat partition and conquer the rest.[477]

One month before the UN approved Partition, the CIA warned that an Israeli state would never abide by Partition, indeed that not even "the more conservative" Zionists would honor Partition. Moderate Zionists would gradually take over all of Palestine west of the Jordan River, while the less moderate would fight to take over Jordan as well, along with parts of Syria and Egypt.[478]

Arab representatives at the UN believed the rightfulness of their case to be self-evident, stressing that they were neither asking for favors nor basing their claim on anyone's promises. Their right to independence rested, rather, on the

> high principles which [after the First World War] were to govern the organization of international relations and serve as the basis of the structure of modern civilization [and] the rejection of all ideas of conquest and recognition of the right of self-determination.

US intelligence officer Kermit Roosevelt (grandson of Theodore) agreed, testifying to the National War College in 1948 that "most of the Arab arguments for their case in Palestine are taken from American and democratic thought." Ben-Gurion asserted that such principles were trumped by Jewish exceptionalism. It did not matter, he told the UN, that their alleged ancestors had left Palestine "a considerable time ago," because "we did not give it up," the preposterousness of his *we* and *it* passing unchallenged. To Arab negotiators, the claim seemed so fantastic as to scarcely need rebuttal:

> What should then be said when an effort is made to set the clock of history back by twenty centuries in an attempt to give away a country on the ground of a transitory historic association?

Similarly, when Ben-Gurion repeated the argument that Jews would bring Arabs a more advanced civilization, Palestinian representatives could only say the obvious:

> Even if the premises on which this argument rests were true, [it would be] an immoral argument [which would] justify any aggression by the more advanced nations against the less advanced.

Roosevelt said much the same:

> If you are looking to determine the rights to a land on the basis of who could most efficiently develop that land, then you are going to have a pretty disastrous series of world shifts and revolutions. And if that was our theory, then on what grounds did we, for instance, oppose the Nazis?

Nor, Roosevelt lectured, was the premise true. The Palestinians had always been self-sufficient and had been removed from the land by settlers receiving vast outside financial backing with no expectation of having to repay it.

Only UNSCOP's Sir Abdur Rahman treated Ben-Gurion's pronouncements at the UN hearings with any seriousness. When Ben-Gurion stonewalled Rahman's questions with non-sequiturs about British atrocities, Sir Abdur stood fast, telling him: "We will not finish for two months if you go on in that way. I do not mind if we take two months or two years." Rahman, however, was not in charge. Ben-Gurion simply continued his oratorical obstructions until the compliant Chairman changed topics.

The Jewish Agency leader told the Committee that "the relations of the Jews of this country cannot be judged by a rule applied to other countries," and accused any who disagreed with him of Nazism. "There is only one reason that the people here say 'No, we will not let those Jews come back,'" he charged, and to identify that "one reason," he segued to the Nazis and murdered Jews. His messianic "come back" left unchallenged, he said that "Jewish right" to Palestine has existed for 3,500 years.[479]

A few days before the UN Partition vote, Tel Aviv mayor Rokach "significantly declared" (as Cunningham put it) to the Vaad Leumi that once statehood was achieved, his city would never be "the Jewish capital." It would be Jerusalem, directly scuppering in advance the Resolution they claimed to be endorsing.

The day before the vote, the CIA reinforced earlier warnings:

> Zionists in Palestine … will continue to wage a strong propaganda campaign in the US and in Europe … Even the more conservative Zionists will hope to obtain the whole of the Nejeb, Western Galilee, the city of Jerusalem, and eventually all of Palestine. The extremists demand not only all of Palestine but Transjordan as well. They [will not] settle for anything less, and will probably undertake aggressive action to achieve their ends.

UNGA approves Resolution 181

The moment the success of Resolution 181 was announced, "hysterical celebrations of victory" broke out in the settlements, as Cunningham described the euphoria. "Vast crowds of rejoicing Jews swarmed the streets," in the words of British intelligence, "dancing and singing … as though they had won a war—the scenes in Jerusalem were reminiscent of VE Day, and continued with staggering endurance for almost two whole days."

But these celebrations were not about having won a Zionist state in more than half of Palestine. They were, as Cunningham described it, because 181 was "a preliminary step to a Jewish state in the fullest extent of its historical [Biblical] bounds." The Yishuv envisioned "the present state only as a welcome forerunner of greater things … [they] are still not satisfied with its size [and] hanker after the whole."

Amid the celebrations, "young Jewish volunteers with money boxes swarmed through the streets of Haifa ... blackmailing the public into buying rapidly produced [Zionist] flags for large sums of money." In a second wave of this campaign, names were taken of those few who refused.

The various Hebrew media varied in tact, but their message was consistent: "The youth of the Yishuv," as the newspaper *Haboker* put it, "must bury deep in their hearts the fact that the frontiers have not been fixed for all eternity."

Meanwhile at the UN, Arab representatives—whose request to have the legality of Partition reviewed by the International Court of Justice had already been denied—took advantage of a twenty-four hour reprieve granted them to put forth a conciliatory alternative. They proposed, in vain, a single democratic nation with what the *Times* described as "a constitution similar to that of the United States."[480]

Scattered ethnic violence marked the first several days after the UN vote. There were bombings of Palestinian homes, cafés, bus queues, and a cinema, and there was more of the anti-Jewish violence that had begun to resurface by mid-August when the UNSCOP recommendations were formalized. Most Palestinians, however, appear to have resigned themselves to the new dynamics, and wanted simply to get on with their lives. Cunningham described "the initial Arab outbreaks" as "spontaneous and unorganized ... more demonstrations of displeasure at the UN decision than determined attacks on Jews."

The Arabs' main weapons, Cunningham pointed out, were "sticks and stones," and the unrest would likely have subsided had it not been that the settlers ratcheted up the provocation. Until then, "the Arab Higher Committee as a whole, and the Mufti in particular," wanted non-violent resistance—boycott—and "were not in favour of serious outbreaks." The British military cited several cases "of Mukhtars of Arab villages visiting the adjacent Jewish settlements and insisting that they want to remain on friendly terms with their Jewish neighbours."[481]

Palestinian violence against the British occupation, which had ceased by 1939, did resurface on a small scale, though the British security forces reported that it "should not be considered ... part of a deliberate plan, and in many cases the Mukhtars have apologized profusely for damage and casualties ... the Arabs as a whole are loath to start hostilities."

About 1,300 Palestinians in Gaza—Muslims and Christians, men and women—demonstrated peacefully on December 5, carrying banners that read "Down with Truman and Down with Partition." Near Khan Yunis, 3,000-4,000 Palestinians demonstrated for four hours and then sent a delegation to speak to the police. A thousand Palestinians walked in peaceful procession in Kefar Saba against Partition.[482]

The Jewish Agency's defiance of Resolution 181 was visible within a week of the vote. As the Tel Aviv mayor had promised, the Agency announced that "a number of 'national institutions,' including the Chief Rabbinate," would not be in Israel at all, but illegally in Jerusalem, in the UN-administered international zone.

British intelligence reports in mid-December already acknowledge "the illegal appropriation of land in PALESTINE by the Jews in order to est[ablish] new settlements" on land designated for Palestine, and that Ben-Gurion was collaborating with "an Arab ruler," King Abdullah of Jordan.

A scant two weeks after Resolution 181, still well before the 1948 war, the British already reported outright that the state promised to the Palestinians would doubtfully ever be, that

it does not appear that Arab Palestine will be an entity.

In Gaza on the 11th of December, "an Arab was shot dead by five Jews" apparently because he tried to stop the bombing they were about to carry out, as three of them were then blown up when the device they were carrying detonated. The same day saw a major anti-Jewish attack: "Arab attackers" killed nine people in "a convoy of Jewish buses on the Hebron Road" on the way to the Gush Etzion settlements.

The Irgun raided Tireh village on the 12th, killing thirteen Palestinians, and it was likely the Irgun as well that bombed and completely demolished a "Lebanese Arab" bus in Haifa, killing four and injuring thirty. Two Haganah "dressed as Arabs" set fire to two (Arab) buses and a car, and at midnight "a party of Jews" bombed "Arab premises" in Ramla, killing one.

Jerusalem was the scene of similar attacks, where "four Jewish youths hurled six grenades into two Arab taxicab offices, one café and the street outside." That evening, "Jews disguised as policemen and soldiers raided the Arab village of Shefat" on the outskirts of Jerusalem, bombing two houses.

The 13th of December began with the first of a series of four so-called "flying bomb" attacks by the Irgun. Two bombs thrown from a speeding taxi at Palestinians at a bus by the Damascus Gate killed seven immediately and wounded fifty-four.

Driving through central Jaffa, the militants threw a bomb into a cafè, killing six Palestinians, among them an eleven-year-old child, and wounding forty, including three children. The cafè and an adjoining shop were destroyed.

The Palestinian village of Yehudiya was next. Twenty-four Jews disguised as soldiers attacked the village with Bren guns, bombs, and hand grenades. Seven Palestinians were murdered, including a woman and children, and seven more seriously injured. As the *NY Times* reported it,

> Dressed in khaki uniforms and steel helmets the attackers, coming from the direction of Petah Tiqua, rolled into the village in four cars of British Army types. One group opened fire on villagers sitting outside a cafe while the rest of the invaders put time bombs against houses and threw hand grenades to discourage interference.

In the early the morning of the 14th,

> Jews threw two grenades at an Arab bus in Jerusalem. The bombs missed the bus and exploded on waste ground killing an Arab child. One passenger in the bus was injured.

A second Arab bus was ambushed and gutted in the Galilee that morning, the assailants leaving behind "a hat of Jewish manufacture" and more explosive material. Two days later, two sergeants walking in Zion Square (Jerusalem) were shot by Lehi; both died.

On a terrace overlooking Lake Hula stood Khisas, widely considered among the most beautiful of Palestinian villages. On the 18th of December, its mixed Christian-Muslim population became the target of Palmach militants under Yigal Allon, future IDF general and Israeli statesman. The onslaught began at about 9 PM, when two carloads of Haganah men drove through this northern village, blowing up houses along with their sleeping occupants, "burying the victims in the wreckage where their bodies were found only today by police searches," as the *NY Times* reported the next day. Fifteen Palestinians, five of them children under ten years of age, lay dead. "No shots were fired by Arabs in reply," Cunningham reported, describing the Haganah massacre as "no less than deliberate murder."

The Haganah justified the attack as defensive, a reprisal raid—but this claim was dismissed outright by the British military, as "the villagers did not use any firearms to defend themselves, and as far as is known, the village is not in possession of any." The British were correct: Zionist archives state that the massacre was undertaken by Allon for "experience." Khisas was only partially depopulated by the Zionist armies' 1948 purge, but on June 5 of the following year, three weeks after Israel's admittance to the UN, the IDF forced the village's remaining people onto trucks and dumped them in the wilderness.

With these post-181 attacks, the Jewish Agency and Haganah no longer feigned abhorrence of terror. When shortly after midnight on the morning of December 20 the Haganah launched a new attack, this time on the Palestinian village of Qazaza, the Haganah claimed in Lehi-fashion that it had killed more than the one casualty reported. Terror gang rivalry had, indeed, become a race for fanaticism, and so when the group Americans for Haganah held a rally in New York's Manhattan Center on December 23, it was disrupted by protesters accusing the militia of "appeasement."

On Christmas eve, the militants attacked four British soldiers leaving a café in Tel Aviv, killing two. The day after Christmas, a driver was shot dead at the English Girls School in Haifa, an escalation over the ineffective bomb a half year earlier. Ben-Gurion, addressing the Haganah, spoke of a "major offensive" to "greatly reduce the percentage of Arabs in the population of the new state."[483]

"The Jewish Agency's Hagana," Cunningham reported by telegram that month, has been

> responsible for severe attacks on Arab villages, which have caused considerable loss of life (including women and children) … Jewish terrorists have been responsible for unprovoked attacks on both Arabs and British Police and soldiers, yet, while ostensibly condemning such attacks, it is known that the Jewish Agency is cooperating with the terrorist leaders…[484]

Lehi as well was busy plunging Palestine into ethnic anarchy. In the words of a member of the 6th Airborne, the terror gang was making

> particularly bestial attacks on Arab villages, in which they showed not the slightest discrimination for women and children, whom they killed as opportunity offered.[485]

The second Irgun "flying bomb" attack hit the Damascus Gate on December 29.

> At 12.37 hours a green coloured taxi … containing a number of Jews … on reaching Damascus Gate the occupants threw an object from the taxi which exploded in the vicinity of a number of buses around which a large crowd of Arabs were standing, causing heavy casualties.

Three children aged 10-11 were among the eleven dead on the scene. Two policemen were killed "in the confusion following this outrage," and more of the thirty-two injured, including women and children, died soon afterwards.[486]

The Palestinian reaction to the Damascus Gate massacres was to set up road blocks at the old city under the supervision of the British, which was "recognized by the Government as a reasonable measure of self-defence on the part of the Arabs having regard to the indiscriminate outrages carried by the Irgun Zvei Leumi"—but the Jewish Agency seized on this defense against the attacks to claim that "1,800 members of their community inside the Old City were besieged, starved, and about to be massacred."

On December 29, the Irgun launched a seaborne attack on Jaffa. The ancient port city had for centuries been a hub of Palestinian life— culturally, commercially, politically—and so the architects of Partition could not easily have explained handing it over the Zionists. Settlements had however been established in the area, in particular the presumed capital of the new state, Tel Aviv. The UN considered solving the puzzle by connecting Jaffa to the rest of Palestine via a corridor, but this idea was abandoned because it would create "for the Jews the difficulty which it solved for the Arabs." And so Jaffa was orphaned as a small Palestinian island geographically within the Zionist state. No informed person in 1947 could have believed that the Zionists would respect the arrangement.[487]

Sir Hugh Dow, British Consul-General in Jerusalem, noted the disparity in international reaction thus:

> If, instead of the Jews seizing Jaffa, the Arabs had succeeded in establishing themselves in Tel Aviv, would the United Nations have agreed to the retention of Tel Aviv in an Arab State?[488]

"Provocation by the Jews" against the Palestinians, a British military report ending January 1 stated, "has continued during the past two weeks on an almost unprecedented scale."

The day after its attack on Jaffa (30th), the Irgun launched their third flying bomb attack, this time against about one hundred Palestinians seeking employment outside Haifa's oil refinery. The explosions killed six immediately and wounded about forty, many seriously.

Like the previous flying bombs, the specific purpose of this attack was, as the Hashomer Hatzair noted, to "provoke reprisals"—and this time, tragically, it did, quickly and indiscriminately against the refinery's Jewish employees, forty-one of whom died in the anti-Jewish rampage. Elsewhere that day, "an Arab government doctor was assassinated by Jews at Bethlehem," and an electrically detonated mine was used to kill two constables, nineteen and twenty years old, in Mahan Yehuda market.[489]

New Year's Eve began with the Irgun murder of a policeman outside Fink's Restaurant in Jerusalem. When four British men entered Tel Aviv's Park Hotel on Hayarkon Street to celebrate the new year, one was shot; his friends tried to rush him to the hospital, but their crashed jeep was found later. All had been shot.

It was the Jewish Agency's own Haganah that ushered in 1948 as the year of the precipitous ethnic cleansing of Palestine. Near Haifa, as the New Year struck and the corks popped in Tel Aviv, the militia massacred sixty Palestinians in Belad esh Sheikh, including many women and children, and attacked the Wadi Rushmiyya neighborhood, expelling non-Jews and blowing up their houses. According to Ilan Pappé, the Zionists conducted these two attacks in part to test the British reaction—and that reaction, to the Jewish Agency's satisfaction, was to "look the other way."

Both Jaffa and Jerusalem were targets on the first day of 1948. The Qatamon Quarter of Jerusalem was bombed by "approx 30 armed Jews, who placed charges and threw grenades," while the Irgun sped through Jaffa and fired at Palestinians sitting outside a café. The gang murdered two café-goers and wounded nine before crashing through a road block and vanishing into Tel Aviv.

The same day a "small party of Jews" placed a bomb inside a block of flats in the rear of Jaffa's Shell petrol station, demolishing a block of Palestinian homes.[490]

Claims that the United States was a major source for the bombs wreaking havoc in Palestine were vindicated on January 3. As crates bound for the settlements in Palestine were being loaded onto the freighter *Executer* at the docks at New Jersey, one marked "Used Industrial Machinery Parts" fell, breaking open and revealing its true contents: Cyclonite. There were twenty-five more crates like it. As described by the British military,

> The total consignment consisted of 65,000 lbs of Cyclonite TNT …
>
> In the warehouses from which the original consignment had

Jan
1948

come they [the police] found 5,200 combat knives, pig metal and machinery suitable for the production of arms … On the following Thursday and Friday, 110 tons of Cyclonite, also allegedly destined for the Jewish State, was confiscated in the New York counties of Ulster and Monmouth.[491]

The journalist Sam Pope Brewer—whose then-wife would run off with double-agent Kim Philby, son of John Philby who had tried with Weizmann to "purchase" Palestine—reported that because of the rising anti-Arab terror in Jaffa, road blocks had been set up at all the approaches to the city "for the special purpose of intercepting possible [Jewish] terrorists." The safeguard failed. On January 4, two men "dressed as Arabs" driving a truck loaded with oranges did not arouse suspicion as they entered Jaffa and headed down the street leading to the port. The "Arabs" turned their truck into an alley between the Barclays Bank and the Arab National Committee Building, parked, and were driven away in a waiting car. Bombs hidden within the orange crates detonated quickly, destroying the Old Serrai in Clock Tower Square. The blast "shook the city and smashed doors more than a mile away." Lehi claimed responsibility.

Fourteen people were known dead right away, and about a hundred wounded, and twelve more bodies were pulled from the rubble as relief efforts continued through the evening. The terror worked: "The local people," Brewer reported, "shaken by this outrage, are shooting at anybody with a suspicious appearance."

Any feigned distinction between the Jewish Agency and Lehi was left behind in 1947. It was not Lehi, but the Agency's Haganah that blew up the Semiramis Hotel in Qatamon the next day, January 5, killing twenty-six people, most from two Christian families, wounding scores, and indiscriminately blowing up private houses as they retreated. Among the dead was Manuel Allende Salazar y Travesedo, the Spanish vice-consul. The attackers, all wearing European clothes, first threw a grenade into the building as a diversion, then used the ensuing confusion to set the bomb, which exploded about a minute later.

Through a night of icy, torrential rains, British soldiers combed the ruins looking for survivors. The next morning, a young woman named Hala Sakakini recalled that

> All day long you could see people carrying their belongings and moving from their houses to safer ones in Qatamon or to another quarter altogether. They reminded us of pictures we used to see of European refugees during the war. People were simply panic-stricken.[492]

As rescue workers continued the search for survivors, the Haganah dynamited three houses in the village of Safad, north of the Sea of Galilee, killing fourteen Palestinians. The militia justified the attack by claiming that a "lieutenant" of the mufti was in one of the houses.

On January 7, eastern Christmas, a final survivor was extracted from the rubble of the Semiramis Hotel, trapped for thirty-six hours next to the body of her fifteen-year-old son.

British officials angrily confronted the Jewish Agency, impressing upon them that the Arabs had never organized an attack against any building containing women and children, in contrast to the Haganah and the other Jewish terror groups. They knew the hotel and dismissed as "without foundation" the Agency's claim that the hotel was a base for Arab militants. Zionist militias nonetheless pushed on, bombing fourteen more buildings until, as recalled by the Palestinian scholar and eye-witness Sami Hadawi, "5,000 Zionist 'fedayeen' made their last assault and occupied the quarter." All non-Jews were forced to evacuate.[493]

The fourth flying bomb hit on January 7. Using a Jewish Settlement Police armored vehicle, five Jews threw a parcel bomb packed with rivets as they sped past the Jaffa Gate. Fifteen Palestinians were killed on the spot, and forty Palestinians and British injured, some of whom are presumed to have died from their wounds. The attackers turned onto Mamillah Road and threw a second bomb while traveling at high speed. Now pursued by police, the car, "having apparently also caught the blast of the exploding bomb, came to a standstill against the wall of the Moslem cemetery." Inside the car were the grenades for thirteen more flying bombs.[494]

In Europe, fears of renewed Zionist terror were straining Allied resources. On January 6, the Counterintelligence Corps of the US Army warned the British of another Zionist attack on a Medloc train in Austria, to "wreak vengeance" for the imprisonment of a Jewish terrorist. Although additional precautions had already been enacted after the near-catastrophe of August 1947—three or four empty coaches or fully fitted freight wagons were being attached to the pilot engine on the Vienna sleeper train and a few other high-risk lines—the alert was met with heightened monitoring at both ends of the tunnel.

"Armed Jews raided Barclays Bank in Tel Aviv" on the 12th, topping up the war coffers by £15,000. A deadly bombing in London was averted on the 21st, when a bomb rigged to the door of the Arab Bureau was discovered before the door was opened.

Barely a month after the Truman Administration shoved through the Partition vote, it was overcome with buyer's remorse. Secretly, it proposed to Britain that the US would announce a change of heart if they, Britain, would cancel its planned exit and remain in Palestine as caretaker until after the US presidential election in November. British officials scoffed at the suggestion and US irresponsibility: Full-page Irgun ads in the US were predicting that Britain would not keep its word, Palestine had already fallen into chaos, and the UN could not afford to appear indecisive on this early important mission, as such wavering had fatally weakened the League of Nations.

Two months after the vote, Truman's conundrum became public: the *NY Times'* James Reston reported the

> conviction, widely held at the State and Defense Departments, that President Truman's decision to support the partition of Palestine was influenced by the political strength of pro-Zionist organizations in key political centers of this country.

Reston's sources predicted that Israel would not stop at its borders, but instead "once the Jewish independent state is established," it would seek US support for its "external policies."

Meanwhile, Britain's War Disposals Board sold the Jewish Agency twenty-one Auster aircraft, contrary to a ban on supplying arms to either side. Bevin's protests did nothing—he was told that a telegram from the Ministry of Supply suspending such sales "arrived too late."[495]

In early February, the Truman Administration tried another tactic to turn back the clock and undo Resolution 181. Secretary of Defense Robert Lovett told the British that the US had "developed doubts" as to the "constitutional validity" of Partition, and "made it pretty plain that [the] United States government were now having second thoughts on the whole matter." But his proposal that a Special Assembly be held to reconsider Partition "filled everyone here with horror" because US "vacillations" were discrediting the UN.[496]

Alexander Cadogan testified to the United Nations that he feared that ethnic mayhem was coming, an that "the Jewish story that the Arabs are the attackers and the Jews the attacked is not tenable…"[497]

It was perhaps partially in response to this that on February 2, the Jewish Agency distributed a *Memorandum on Acts of Arab Aggression* to the UN, beseeching the international community to intervene on its behalf against the alleged aggression. There were, to be sure, no Arab armies in Palestine (even the Arab Legion had been withdrawn), and there would not be for another three and a half months, after much of the Palestinian side of Partition was already occupied by the Zionist armies. Small "Arab Guerilla Bands" (as Cunningham called them) had tried to check Zionist advances but were quickly defeated and had instead "provided them [Zionists] with the excuse that they are merely defending themselves against Arab aggression."

Just as the Jewish Agency had used Biblical arguments in the lead-up to the UN decision the previous November, it now used Biblical arithmetic to argue the injustice of that decision: the memorandum charged that the area allotted to the Zionists (56.5% of Palestine) was a mere one-eighth of what had been "promised" them, seven-eighths forfeited to placate the "Arabs."[498]

Defeating Resolution 181's internationalization of Jerusalem was a priority for Ben-Gurion, and so on February 5 he ordered the Haganah to expel non-Jews from parts of Jerusalem and replace them with Jews. Those Jews who wanted no part of the population transfer were intimidated and, if that failed, forcibly loaded onto trucks and transferred. The work was swift: two days later, he congratulated the Mapai Council on the areas that were now "one hundred percent Jews," claiming that he had effectively returned the city to late Biblical times.[499]

Barely three years earlier, the US and Britain were at the forefront of the world's battle against acquisition of territory by force and ethnic depopulation. Both countries now watched as another racial-nationalist movement seized and depopulated territory—but instead of stopping it, they looked for ways to accommodate it. Still more than three months before the end of the Mandate, British and American officials not only declare that the Palestinians will never get the state they were promised, but express approval over it and explore ways to help it along—with ethnic cleansing implicit. The US administration was "happy" with the Zionists taking much of Palestine, and the British noted "certain advantages" in it for themselves.

Tellingly, they refer to the Palestinian land Jordan's Abdullah might get in his collusion with the Zionists as "the area of Palestine not under the control of the Jewish State," not as the Palestinian side of the Partition. The focus turned to finding ways to buy the complicity of Arab states on Israel's behalf. A "Memorandum by the Chiefs of Staff to the Minister of Defence" dated the 26th of February proposed that "the Southern and Eastern Arab States in Palestine should be incorporated with Transjordan, the Northern Arab State with Syria/Lebanon." By bribing neighboring states to accept the Israeli confiscation of Palestine, it was hoped to "bring a less disastrous outcome to present events."

Alec Kirkbride, British ambassador to Amman, agreed. Syrian opposition to what he euphemistically called the "consolidation of the Jewish State ... might be abated" if it were given some "territorial advantage" in the deal. Jaffa would of course go to Israel.

Among the few official voices of dissent was Sir Richard Ashton Beaumont, Consul in Jerusalem upon the declaration of the Israeli state. He reacted in unmasked indignation:

> It is disquieting to note ... with what equanimity you appear to
> accept the view that in order to settle the Arab-Jewish problem in

Palestine … we need not hesitate [to seduce two Arab states] with bribe of territorial advantage.

Yet for Sir John Troutbeck in Rhodes, "the difficulty" with the scheme was the opposite: that the Zionists might not be satisfied with it. He thought the bribes were too high, because "the north-eastern corner of Palestine, including the Huleh concession area, is a district to which the Jews are likely to attach very great importance." Indeed over the ensuing months it was Israel, not Syria or Lebanon, that seized the area.[500]

Since the end of World War II, many Jews resident in Palestine had been trying to leave for their homes in Europe, or for new homes in the United States or Australia, subject to "various forms of pressure" (as the Foreign Office put it) by the Zionists to remain in Palestine. Britain's imminent departure now made the Jewish Agency tighten its hold over Jews, announcing that it controlled "the exit of all Jewish persons between the ages of 17 and 40" regardless of their nationality. It claimed the right to conscript people by virtue of being Jewish, including the drafting of US citizens—this finally prompting a protest from the United States. Travel and ticket agencies, public places, and venues such as movie theaters, were monitored to catch "deserters." When the Haganah discovered that one Jewish family's eldest son was no longer in Palestine, it confiscated their house. Another Jewish family's son had gone to England; the Haganah took control of their house, forced the family to pay $4,000 (about $46,000 in 2022 dollars), and gave them six weeks to get the son back in Palestine, else an additional $8,000 and other penalties would be imposed.

In late February, about two hundred US citizens tried to board a ship in Haifa to begin their voyage home, but since they were Jews the Haganah invaded the pier and began throwing their passports into the sea to force them to remain. British marines stopped them.

In this claim of a Jewish "nationality" binding Jews to the coming Zionist state, the Jewish Agency was now more fanatical than Peter Bergson. Bergson publicly called himself "post-Zionist" and said that all Jews should now decide whether to become citizens of the

Hebrew Republic of Palestine (as he wanted to call the new state), *or* choose to be fully assimilated citizens of their home countries with no link to the new state.

> The Jewish Agency seeks to institutionalize the problem. Their proposed ghetto-like 'Jewish State' will only perpetuate the abnormality of the Jewish problem.

In pursuit of that ghetto, the Haganah set up recruiting centers in cities like Leeds, Manchester, Liverpool, Glasgow, and London. One was secretly established in London's Marks & Spencer.[501]

On February 22, explosions rocked Jerusalem's Ben Yehuda Street in one of the era's most iconic attacks against Jews. The attackers distributed a broadside from the neo-fascist "British League Palestine Branch," with language strikingly reminiscent of London's neo-Nazi *Protestant Vanguard*. MPs in Britain then received a pamphlet from the "British League," sent by airmail from Jerusalem, taking credit for the anti-Jewish terror attack and calling on the "nations of the world [to] arise and smite the Jews." Officials privately expressed suspicion that the actual bomber was a certain renegade Briton known to them.[502]

Lehi bombed the Cairo-Haifa train near Rehovot on leap day, killing twenty-four people immediately (apparently Palestinian civilians), and injuring sixty-one, six of whom soon succumbed to their wounds. The Salam Building was Lehi's next target: fourteen Palestinians were killed when the militia blew it up on March 3.[503]

In Europe, it was the Irgun that took credit for the bombing of Vienna's Park Hotel on March 19.

Targeting the British served no further tactical purpose by late 1947; yet it continued, terror without an apparent object. After the militants murdered eight more British personnel in Palestine and widened their reach to target Britons recovering in hospitals, the Jewish Agency grew concerned that the British "might even ultimately be driven to side with the Arabs in repulsing Jewish attacks." It deflected violence onto a so-called "Farran Group" within the British forces, alleged vigilantes led by the hated Major Farran.[504]

March 1948

In response to the Jewish Agency's February memorandum claiming Arab aggression, the Arab delegation to the UN distributed its own *Black Paper of the Jewish Agency and Zionist Terrorism*. It claimed that the Jewish Agency and the terror gangs worked together, and warned of their "totalitarian" methods.

> The Zionists have purposely and deliberately aggravated the [European Jewish] refugees' problem. They have exploited the miseries of the refugees to win world sympathy for Zionism [and have even formed] kidnapping rings for abducting children and taking them to Palestine.

The pamphlet described the methods by which Zionists indoctrinate Jewish youth, methods that "have molded a generation of Jewish fanatics," and how the Zionist terror organizations "rob, terrorize, blackmail and murder Jews."

Of that much, the Americans and British were well aware. However the memorandum went further, charging that the Zionists have "set up laboratories for bacteriological warfare." Yet this, too, was proven correct: Ben-Gurion's laboratory, the so-called "Science Corps of the Hagana," enabled his armies to infect Palestinian villages' wells with typhoid and dysentery in order "to make sure the Arabs couldn't return to make a fresh life for themselves in these villages," as a gang member who knew participants in the biological attacks would later explain it.

In early May, the Haganah injected typhoid into the aqueduct supplying water to the "Capri" spring that served Acre, causing an epidemic that expedited the ethnic cleansing and expropriation of this city that lay on the Palestinian side of the Partition. Vaccine was in short supply, and by early May the disease had spread to neighboring villages.

A then-secret telegram from Cunningham adds a mysterious layer to the question of *why* the typhoid vaccine was in short supply. In it, Cunningham complains of the apparently deliberate lethargy "by the Jewish bacteriologist" in obtaining the vaccine to contain the outbreak.

A small but significant feature of this campaign was the dilatory

and even obstructive attitude adopted by the Jewish bacteriologist of
the Health Department in making available from store the required
supplies of vaccine.

Whether the bacteriologist was a Haganah plant or acting on
personal initiative, the biological warfare against Acre "worked so
well," former gang member Giladi wrote, "that they sent a Haganah
division dressed as Arabs into Gaza" to launch a similar biological
attack there. Indeed on May 27, two Haganah operatives—now
soldiers of the two-week old Israeli state—were caught putting two
cans of bacteria, typhoid and dysentery, into Gaza's wells.[505]

The soon-to-be Israeli Defence Forces (IDF)

The "Jewish Army," with the Haganah at its core, was according
to British intelligence "based on the German organization in the
years 1935-36." Described by the CIA as "a ready-made army for
a Jewish state in Palestine," at the time of the Partition vote it
estimated Haganah membership at 70,000-90,000, with the ability
to mobilize 200,000 soldiers and enough modern weapons to arm
all of them. Fully 5,000 were permanently mobilized commando
troops (the Palmach). The Irgun and Lehi were estimated at 8,000
and 500 members respectively. Both the Haganah and the Irgun had
excellent intelligence, the latter having exceptional secrecy because
of its cell-based structure. New recruits (including from the US and
UK), Jewish DPs from Europe, and about 5,000 soldiers from the
Jewish Brigade completed the army.[506]

Yerachmiel Kahanovitch, a machine-gunner in the Hagana's elite
Palmach unit, described ethnic cleansing missions conducted in early
1948, months before Arab troops entered Palestine.

> We cleared one [Palestinian] village after another and expelled—
> expelled them, they fled to the Sea of Galilee … we shot, we threw
> a grenade here and there

and fired on them as they fled on boats. With Ben-Gurion's knowledge, Palmach Commander Allon instructed them to use axes rather

than bullets when possible "so that they won't hear it" at the British police station. Their orders were to "leave no trace."

> Yes, you march up to a village, you expel it, you gather round to have a bite to eat, and go on to the next village.[507]

Corroborating survivors' accounts, Kahanovitch testified that the Palmach killed anyone hiding in mosques or churches. Anti-tank weapons (PIATs) were used to exterminate those taking refuge inside a cave mosque :

> Let me tell you what it does—you make it like it was a beautiful painting by an artist. You think. He makes a hole about this big and inside everybody's crushed on the walls from the pressure it makes inside.[508]

Anyone attempting to escape was slaughtered. How many people were killed with one blast? "Plenty. [It was now] an empty hall [with] everyone on the walls." After Ben-Gurion gave the order to expel the survivors, it looked like "our [Jewish] refugees walking, from Germany." Palestinian refugees were killed for sport, since watching them on their forced march

> was boring ... There was a cow there that ran off and this guy tried to chase it and I shot them both.[509]

He spoke of non-Jews caught pretending to be Jews in order to stay safe—like non-Zionist Jews in the DP camps, a twist on the *Marranos* of post-1492 Spain. Some were executed, such as one doctor who "we thought this was a Jew, a Russian who came here, an idealist" who they then discovered not to be Jewish. When another non-Jewish doctor was exposed, they cut off his testicles. The ex-Palmach soldier alluded to further atrocities that he would not cite on the record.[510]

Rape, too, was a systemic weapon in Israel's 1948 ethnic cleansing of Palestine. The Israeli historian Benny Morris documented twelve cases of the rape of Palestinian girls by the IDF in 1948, but warned that these were "just the tip of the iceberg." Even if the girls survived— the soldiers sometimes murdered them, as well as their fathers or brothers—few cases were reported. Those that reached Ben-Gurion's notice were numerous enough to warrant mention in his diary every few days, yet he did not believe that any punishment was in order.[511]

Four years had passed since President Roosevelt's plan of new homes for those displaced by the war, including 300,000 between the US and UK, was thwarted by American Zionists (pages 135-136, above). Roosevelt's co-planner, Morris Ernst, had however not given up. He updated the plan to the present circumstances and met with Bevin on April 9 hoping to advance it.

April 1948

Bevin reminded him that he too had promoted freer immigration to Truman and the US Administration, with no response. Ernst confirmed this, and explained that the problem was the Zionists.

> It was really the question of the Jewish Agency. In their inner councils they had always held the view that if they allowed any diversion of Jews from Palestine and their settlement elsewhere, their attempts to raise money and to carry on their campaign from Palestine would be seriously affected. That was the truth of the matter.[512]

This staunch US support for Zionism left one enigma: Why were no US troops helping on-the-ground? Ernst explained that "American Jews were very much opposed" to US troops assisting the Zionists, because that staunch support would be harmed when American troops were "killed by Jewish terrorists."

The iconography of Deir Yassin
As Ernst and Bevin spoke in London on April 9, about 3600 km (2200 miles) away, the Irgun, in coordination with the Hagana, wiped out the Palestinian village of Deir Yassin.

Deir Yassin was not the first Palestinian village to be exterminated by the Zionist armies and was certainly not the last; but the terror inflicted on Deir Yassin took on iconic significance because of its high visibility in the Jerusalem environs, because the savagery was well documented and reported, and because the fate of Deir Yassin was used to convince Palestinians to leave. The Irgun boasted, surely accurately, that the terror it instilled hastened the evacuation of other Palestinian villages.[513]

As described by British intelligence, Deir Yassin was wiped out

> accompanied by every circumstance of savagery. Women and children were stripped, lined up, photographed and then slaughtered …

Those taken prisoner suffered "incredible bestialities." An early eye-witness was the head of the International Red Cross Delegation in Palestine, Jacques de Reynier. Arriving in the village, he described the Irgun soldiers:

> All of them were young, some even adolescents, men and women, armed to the teeth: revolvers, machine-guns, hand grenades, and also cutlasses in their hands, most of them still blood-stained. A beautiful young girl, with criminal eyes, showed me hers still dripping with blood; she displayed it like a trophy.

Forcing his way into some of the houses,

> Here the 'cleaning up' had been done with machine-guns, then hand grenades. It had been finished off with knives, anyone could see that … I heard something like a sigh. I looked everywhere, turned over all the bodies, and eventually found a little foot, still warm. It was a little girl of ten, mutilated by a hand grenade, but still alive … everywhere it was the same horrible sight … there had been 400 people in this village; about fifty of them had escaped and were still alive. All the rest had been deliberately massacred in cold blood for, as I observed for myself, this gang [the Irgun] was admirably disciplined and only acted under orders.

As described by a Palmach member, the survivors,

> some twenty-five men … were loaded into a freight truck and led
> in a 'victory parade,' like a Roman triumph, through the Mahaneh
> Yahudah and Zikhron Yosef quarters [of Jerusalem, then] taken
> to a stone quarry between Giv'at Shaul and Deir Yasin and shot
> in cold blood.

In response to the massacre, the British wanted to rout out the Irgun but feared that an on-the-ground confrontation would result in British deaths. Instead, they "arranged for aircraft to make a punitive attack on the village … to eject the terrorists from the village and punish those responsible for this vile crime."

But then they discovered that the Irgun had "been replaced by Hagana." Instead of outrage at the Jewish Agency's complicity or the removal of its militia from the village, "it was decided not to proceed with air operations in this case."

Four days after the massacre, the Irgun issued a press statement that read in part:

> We intend to attack, conquer and keep until we have the whole of
> Palestine and Transjordan in a Greater Jewish State. This attack is
> first step.

Israel's official Holocaust memorial, Yad va-Shem, borders the ashes of Deir Yassin.

Three days after the massacre, on April 12, the Haganah formally took the Irgun into its fold. Chief Rabbi Herzog—the same who conducted the removal of Jewish orphans from their homes two years earlier—was credited with brokering the marriage.[514]

In mid-April, the US was still prodding the UK to delay its departure from Palestine, but the British replied that it would be they who would die in the ensuing terror as a result of the US having bulldozed through the UN "a plan which represented the extreme demands" of the Zionists.

Truman's fudging on Partition brought pro-Zionist protests and rallied politicians to the cause. When the more extreme Zionists publicly condemned Reconstruction in Europe as an enemy of Zionism, others distanced themselves, though opposition to Reconstruction was the unadvertised Jewish Agency position.[515]

Thus Truman renewed his support for Partition having, according to US sources cited in British documents, "been persuaded that he must do obeisance, until election time, to the fund-raising powers of the Jewish community." In the early 1950s it would be revealed that Truman's obeisance extended to interfering in the judicial process when Israeli agents were accused (and convicted) of violating the Neutrality Acts.[516]

The Hagana, over which Ben-Gurion was effectively the Commander in Chief, was producing mortars they called the Davika, containing 60 pounds of explosives that it catapulted about 300 yards, and "barrel-bombs" filled with explosives, shrapnel, glass, and nails, designed to cause maximum casualties and terror in Palestinian villages.

Fear—psychological terror—was another potent weapon in the ethnic cleansing of Palestine. "Horror recordings" blared through loudspeakers warning those who remained that they would suffer the fate of Deir Yassin. Rumors of plagues were given credence by the Hagana's poisoning of wells, and a whispering campaign warned of preparations to use the atomic bomb on Arab villages.*

On the 21st of April the Zionist armies began a final ethnic cleansing of Haifa. Cunningham reported by telegram that heavy fighting began about midday, with

Jewish attacks on Arab outposts at Burj Hill and Prophets Steps and

---

* The Zionist narrative alleges that Arab authorities told the Palestinians, by radio broadcast and/or loudspeaker, to vacate the land, that the Palestinians obeyed, and thus forfeited any right to return. Such claims are, above all, nonsensical. All people have the unqualified right to leave their homes, whether during a conflict or peace, no matter who told them what—one need merely apply this claim to any other people or place to expose how ludicrous it is. Further, the allegations themselves are untrue. The historical record, as well as the testimony of living witnesses, shows that Arab leaders beseeched the population *not* to leave. For example, a report by the then Greek Archbishop in Galilee was used by the Israelis in books and in testimony to the UN to claim that the Palestinians were given evacuation orders (if that mattered). But the Archbishop himself put on record that his words meant something very different—indeed antithetical—to what he called the "concoctions and falsifications" of the Israeli "propagandists." See, e.g., Erskine B. Childers' "The Wordless Wish: From Citizens to Refugees," in Abu-Lughod, *Transformation*.

telephone exchange successful by night. Khoury House, Headquarters Palestine Railways, on fire and gutted with all records. Jewish forces have captured Salameh Building and positions Station Street–Burj Hill and are now closing in on Khamra Square. Fire in port caused by mortaring has been extinguished. Heavy firing continues with mortaring of Suq [market] area which is reported deserted.[517]

As the militias literally pushed the Palestinians into the sea and British landing craft evacuated survivors to Acre, some 3600 km (2200 miles)away in London the US ambassador spoke with Bevin. The "Jewish attitude," as the Ambassador phrased it, was "[w]hy should they cease hostilities when they had so many trained men and munitions, and were in a position to win, with their goal [all of Palestine] in sight?"

Morris Ernst, who was "opposed to any joinder of religion and state, or race and state," was in contact with Judah Magnes and was still trying to sway the Foreign Office to establish a single state. The "distressed Jews from Europe" would be settled in various parts of the world, including the US, France, and Palestine. A "joint Arab and Jewish Council of Ministers" would rule Palestine and promote an eventual constitution.

Bevin was still saying much the same: "If [the Jews] could be brought to see that the principle of one man one vote applied in Palestine to Arabs and Jews alike as much as anywhere else our difficulties might be solved."[518]

The US Ambassador also met with Prime Minister Attlee and his Foreign Minister on April 28, two weeks before the Israeli declaration of statehood. There was no disagreement among them that the aggression was coming from the Zionists ("the Jews"), and that no defensive action had been taken by Palestinians. Yet

United States policy was to allow no Arab country to help their fellow Arabs anywhere, but for the U.S. to assist the Jews to crush the Arabs within Palestine and to allow the slaughter to go on, and then to ask the British Government to restrain [Jordan's] Abdullah [who had merely dug trenches on his own territory but taken no action].

The Jews had disregarded all the appeals that had been made to them by the United Nations, the US Ambassador was reminded, and now threatened to attack Jerusalem. The Ambassador nonetheless stood by the Zionist position and warned that "if Great Britain maintained her present attitude [critical of the Zionists], the repercussions might be very serious"—presumably the ever-present threat of pulling the US' post-war loan.[519]

The militias attacked Saint Simeon Monastery and the Katamon area of Jerusalem on the night of April 29-30, and just before 7:00 in the evening on the 30th "two ambulances clearly marked with the Red Cross and proceeding to evacuate wounded from the area [were] heavily fired upon"—a scene to be repeated in modern times in Israel's attacks on Lebanon and Gaza. During the next few days, the British tried, but failed, to counter an Irgun offensive against the population of Jaffa.

"It should be made clear," Cunningham reported,

> that I.Z.L. [Irgun] attack with mortars was indiscriminate and designed to create panic amongst civilian inhabitants. It was not a Military operation.[520]

The British identified the mortars being used by the Zionists as their own—"British of Eley make"—a detail they noted to counter any claims that shells fired in Jerusalem from Nebi Samwil (which the Palmach was trying to capture) could be by Arabs because the devices were of British manufacture.

The scene in Jaffa was a repeat of Haifa: Zionist forces surrounded the Palestinians on three sides—the fourth being the sea—and the British, unable to stop them, rescued by landing craft those whom they could. Hoisting the Star of David over the town, the Irgun handed control over to the Hagana, which vowed not to "give an inch" on this city that lay on the Palestinian side of Partition. A half century later, the Israeli Ministry of Defence published a book that justified the ethnic cleansing of Jaffa by calling it "a festering cancer in the middle of the Jewish population."[521]

When Cunningham saw that the media were reporting the

Zionist's brutal ethnic cleansing as "Jewish military successes," he sent an angry telegram to British and US contacts. These "successes," he wrote, are in truth

> operations based on the mortaring of terrified women and children.

The settlers as a whole approved of what was being done on their behalf. There prevailed "among the Jews themselves a spirit of arrogance," as they boasted of their ability to dictate the fate of the Palestinians. "Jewish broadcasts," Cunningham added, probably referring to the Hagana's Kol Israel, "both in content and in manner of delivery, are remarkably like those of Nazi Germany." A week later he wrote that

> The Jews are still jubilant and still busy [with] their campaign of calculated aggression coupled with brutality…[522]

A British intelligence briefing, meanwhile, reported that

> the internal machinery of the Jewish State is now almost completely organised and includes staff for press censorship and all the equipment of a totalitarian regime, including a Custodian of Enemy Property to handle Arab lands.[523]

Thus Israel's confiscation of lands by ethnicity was built into the machinery of the state at birth. Painting imagery of a population gone berserk, the intelligence report described the fruits of decades of Zionist control over the settlers:

> In the Yishuv itself persecution of Christian Jews [converts] and others who offend against national discipline has shown a marked increase and in some cases has reached mediaeval standards.[524]

The entire ethnic cleansing of Palestine, whether by the Haganah, the Irgun, Lehi, or any collaboration thereof, was marked by atrocity for its own sake, beyond even the needs of the crime itself.

Pro-Zionist terror continues in the UK & US

A series of anti-British and anti-Arab bomb scares disrupted New York and London in the months leading to Israeli statehood. On February 23, two days after the thwarted "door bomb" on London's Arab Bureau, a larger device with what were described as "Jewish markings" was planted in a building partly occupied by the Colonial Office, fifty yards from Big Ben.[525]

A bomb scare closed London's Victoria Station on the evening of March 7. Ten days later, a New York bound British airliner, among whose passengers was the Assistant Secretary to the Foreign Office, received a radio message claiming that a bomb had been planted aboard it. As the pilot made an emergency U-turn to London, New York's Empire State Building received its third bomb threat: a woman called from the Gedney exchange (Brooklyn) and said that the building "is going to be blown up." The floors scoured by the police included the British Consulate General. At least five bomb threats were made to Arab offices during May, including the Syrian and Egyptian delegations to the UN, the Consul General of Lebanon, the Iraq Consulate, and the manager of the Arabic language newspaper *Al-Hoda*.[526]

The real bombs struck without warning. On the morning of May 3, Rex Farran, a twenty-five year old draughtsman, was in the family home in the West Midlands. His younger brother and grandmother were upstairs. When the postwoman delivered a package addressed to "R Farran," Rex took it to the living room. He probably lived long enough to see the volume of Shakespeare—hollowed out by Lehi to make it into a bomb.

Lehi had presumably intended to kill his brother, the infamous Roy Farran, and this is the version given in a 2005 interview with Yaakov Heruti, a Lehi operative who claims to have made and mailed the Shakespeare bomb with parts supplied from the United States. A different story was told by Lehi members to a *NY Times* correspondent in Paris four months after the murder: that the ambiguity of the initial was deliberate and Rex was indeed the target. "It would force him [Roy] to live with this memory always. We meant to torture him." This seems credible—the use of the initial was odd, and Lehi could have known that Roy was not then present at the address*.[527]

The day that Rex Farran was killed, twelve days before the end of the Mandate, an internal US State Department memorandum stated that

> the Jews will be the actual aggressors against the Arabs. However, the Jews will claim that they are merely defending [themselves]. In the event of such Arab outside aid the Jews will come running to the Security Council with the claim that their state is the object of armed aggression and will use every means to obscure the fact that it is their own armed aggression against the Arabs inside which is the cause of Arab counter-attack.[528]

Internal US security was a special concern. The CIA reported that Zionist operatives were impersonating both US military and American Airlines personnel, and that their clandestine air transport operations constituted a threat to the security of the United States.[529]

Since US citizens serving in the Zionist militias were breaking US law as it then stood, some senators were pushing through a bill to make serving in this foreign army legal. More remarkably, in early May the Irgun's American League for a Free Palestine brought together senators from both major parties in an attempt to sponsor a six-point initiative. Its goal was unprecedented: blanket US recognition, in advance, of Israeli sovereignty over any lands its militias could seize beyond Partition, even before the state existed.[530]

In London on the morning of May 11, Lieut. Gen. Sir Evelyn Barker received a cylinder of the type used for posting magazines, mailed locally. The wife of this former military commander in Palestine, and her maid, were both alert enough to notice an un-convincing W.H. Smith label, and what seemed excessive postage. Unwrapping the package carefully, she saw a rolled copy of the American magazine *News Review*, but stopped at the smell of an

---

* The author's FOI request to access TNA document MEPO 2/8766, "Murder of Francis Rex Farran by parcel bomb…" was denied by the British government.

odor resembling disinfectant and the sight of wires and black tape. This was not the first assassination attempt against Barker: Ezer Weizmann, a former RAF pilot and nephew of Chaim Weizmann (and like his uncle a future president of Israel) had already tried to assassinate him by mining the walkway to his house.

A new spate of letter bombs targeted British officials that spring. Among the recipients were Winston Churchill, the Lord Speaker, Ernest Bevin, Philip Noel-Baker, Oliver Stanley, Admiral Lord Fraser, and Anthony Eden. Eden carried his around in his briefcase for a full day thinking it was a Whitehall circular he could open later. A police alert reached him in time.[531]

The newer letter bombs were designed to explode in water in order to defeat the standard method of rendering them inert. Many now contained a packet of the poison sodium cyanide in an effort to assure death from an otherwise non-fatal wound. The main explosives sac of the letter bomb sent to Churchill was removed and detonated under controlled conditions; "it badly bent a ¼ [¾?] inch steel plate."[*]

Specialists determined that the detonators in the devices mailed from Italy in 1947-1948 were of US manufacture, among them Dupont, "enormous quantities" of which had been left behind in Italy by the Allied troops. Malfunctions, usually weakened batteries or broken contacts, had kept some from exploding.[532]

On May 14, 1948, in the final hours of the Mandate, the Palestinians of Haifa who had fled to Acre now faced the Zionist armies again as the Haganah overran this key city that, unlike Haifa, lay on the Palestinian side of Partition.[†] The Irgun, in concert, captured five more northern villages that were supposed to be in the Palestinian state. Even as the Declaration establishing the state

---

[*] In TNA, EF 5/12, "Statement of Dr. Watts" says "it badly bent a ¾ inch steel plate," whereas another document ("Letter Bombs," June 16, 1947), cites a ¼ inch plate.

[†] A public statement by Britain during the ethnic cleansing of Haifa mistakenly reported the figure of 35,000 Arabs in the city. In private, officials acknowledged that this was about half the correct number of about 70,000 Arab Christians and Muslims, but debated the risk of correcting it and drawing attention to the error, since "considerable damage may be done in the Middle East if any such obvious error on the part of our Information Service were exploited." See, among others, TNA, CO 537/3860, red "65," "63," letter from M.P. Preston dated May 6, letter from W.B. Osborne dated May 1.

of Israel that night failed to acknowledge any national border (it defined Israel geographically as the Biblical *Eretz-Israel*), the US Administration jumped on board with *de facto* recognition just after midnight, quickly followed by Iran (though it had voted against Partition). Russia jumped the queue to become the first nation to accord Israel *de jure* recognition on May 17.

President Truman's speedy recognition of Israel, Lehi bragged in a radio broadcast of June 3, was not "out of conviction," but because he "needed the Jewish vote"—though even if that "vote" were monolithic, the boast makes little sense demographically.[533]

June–
July
1948

In mid-June, the Foreign Office impressed upon Washington the necessity of establishing permanent borders, else "with the aid of American dollars," Israel would in due course "burst out of its frontiers and attempt to enlarge itself." The summer also brought renewed warnings from the CIA of "increased Israeli intransigence" and the "growing feeling of self-sufficiency and confidence on the part of the Israeli[s] which portends willingness to take matters into their own hands without being bound by the UN." The new state already regarded the United Nations as a nuisance, "deterring Israel from expanding" beyond its boundaries, whereas "the Arab states," the CIA reported, "appear to have been fairly conscientious in cooperating with the mediator and the UN."[534]

In early June, a newly-invigorated campaign against Britain was launched in the US by the "Sons of Liberty Boycott Committee," which named itself after a group from the American Revolution. Operating out of 106 West 70th Street, it financed full-page ads in New York denouncing Britain's (allegedly ongoing) "invasion of Israel." All good Americans, it said, will join the boycott of Britain, so that when London sees the resulting "red ink, [this] nation of merchants and bookkeepers" (this description of the British strangely one of Jewish stereotypes) will be made to stop "destroying Israel." Other ads by the organization continued the drive to deny European Recovery Program (Marshall Plan) funds to Britain, claiming that it was using the money to finance "Arab murder."

How to make sense of wasting effort and money on Britain after it had abdicated rule and effectively evacuated? The only practical

Left: Ben Hecht's advertisement, in the form of an open letter to the Zionist terror gangs, advocating further terror and admonishing the "rich Jews" who refuse to finance it. *New York Post*, May 14, 1947, and the following day in the *New York Herald Tribune*, exactly a year before Israel's declaration of statehood.
Right: The Irgun "Sons of Liberty and Boycott Committee", advertisement in the *NY Post and the Home News*, June 2 1948. (TNA, FO 371/68650)

explanation is as insurance against any British temptation to use its influence at the Security Council to contain Israeli aggression.

Whatever the reasoning, the calls for boycott were taken seriously. When the cigarette giant Philip Morris realized that some people perceived it as British (which it was until 1919), the company published a full-page ad assuring the public that it was American, illustrating a letter from the "Sons of Liberty" confirming that it was not a target of the boycott.[535]

Britain bought about nine million cases of citrus fruit from Palestine each year, half from Palestinian and half from Jewish growers. But so precipitously had the Zionists already stolen Palestinian farmers' land, orchards, and equipment, that alternative sources were considered, rather than implicitly "condoning [the crime and] enabling them to profit from their expulsion of the Arab inhabitants."[536]

In London, the bomb sent to Evelyn Barker led authorities to monitor the actions of one Monte Harris, a resident of 14 Gravel

Lane in East London who was associated with the Hebrew Legion (Irgun) and ran a grocery shop that he had inherited from his father. Suspicions were reinforced when on August 15 thick blue smoke filled the interior of his flat, forcing Harris to keep his door open to let it clear—and to invent an explanation to a concerned passer-by.

The police continued to monitor until on August 28 they arrested him, preventing "a wave of incendiarism and sabotage in England." Others with similar ideas were not caught: fires on two troopships that left Southampton about this time were believed to have been caused by parcel bombs set by Zionist extremists within Britain.[537]

British intelligence was also tracking Cyril Ross, Managing Director of the lucrative Oxford Street furrier Swears & Wells, who was thought to have been head of the Jewish Agency's spy network in the UK. This comprised informants "in every [UK] Government department of importance" as well as "contacts in the U.S. Embassy in London, who provided him [Ross] with U.S. secret reports."[538]

Peace plans, and assassination, of Count Folke Bernadotte

The UN named Folke Bernadotte, a Swedish diplomat who had secured the release of 30,000 Jews from German death camps, to mediate the chaos in Palestine. Although Bernadotte believed an Arab-Jewish union to be the best solution, the US Administration turned against the idea "due to violent American-Zionist opposition in the midst of a presidential election campaign," according to a then-classified 1949 National War College report.[539]

Bernadotte proposed a variation of Resolution 181 at the end of June, but the upheaval in Palestine rendered that plan obsolete. As he set about composing a second plan, he considered two tenets inviolable: the internationalization of Jerusalem and, especially, the unquestioned right of the refugees to return home.

> It would be an offence against the principles of elemental justice if these innocent victims of the conflict were denied the right to return to their homes while Jewish immigrants flow into Palestine…

Israel wanted neither. But whereas laws against ethnic cleansing could be ignored, UN stewardship of Jerusalem would be difficult to undo once established. And so both the Irgun and Lehi responded in early August with threats of terrorism in Europe, and Lehi with thinly-veiled threats against Bernadotte's life:

> We hereby warn the United Nations observers, Bernadotte's generals and all officials and soldiery who may be sent here to demilitarize Jerusalem and set up a non-Jewish administration—it cannot and will not be.[540]

More directly, on September 6 its *Bulletin* announced:

> The task at the moment is to oust Bernadotte and his observers. Blessed be the hand that does it.[541]

The British hoped to influence Bernadotte before he presented his revised plan. *Please destroy this telegram after perusal*, is the final (obviously unheeded) statement on a "top secret" British message of 9th September that "should be delivered orally" to Bernadotte regarding discussions with the Americans. Confirmation came the next day from Bernadotte's base in Rhodes: he had received the message and looked forward "to receive your views."

Those views were kept secret and all copies are said to have been destroyed, but they were surely some version of the privately discussed schemes to give most the Palestinian side of Partition to Israel and the remaining scraps to Egypt and Syria "in order to secure a sufficient measure of acquiescence," as the Foreign Office put it in a telegram sent on the 11th to British Middle East Office Cairo. The Palestinians are out of consideration altogether:

> The United Kingdom government conclude that the creation of a separate Palestinian Arab State would not be a satisfactory settlement of the Arab parts of Palestine.

Bernadotte not only retained the Palestinian state in his new peace plan, but put the Negev within it. US Secretary of State George

Marshall showed Bevin a document stating that the US would announce its approval in Paris at 3:00 PM on the 21st. But Bernadotte would not live that long, and the US decision was reversed.

Leaving his base in Rhodes on the 16th on an aircraft supplied by the UN, Bernadotte visited Beruit and Damascus, and on the 17th flew on to Palestine, landing at the airfield at Qalandiya in what is now the West Bank. His new plan was to have remained secret until being submitted to the General Assembly, but by this day, Ben-Gurion had already secured a copy through an American contact.

After a brief stop in nearby Ramallah, the Arab Legion sent an armed escort vehicle to see his three-car entourage safety as far as they could: to the threshold of the New City, the part of Jerusalem under Israeli control. Israel was fully informed of the Mediator's visit and was well aware that tensions were especially high. Yet Israel sent no escort.*

What would be Bernadotte's final stop was at an Agricultural School. While he was there, elsewhere in the new state, Israeli Major Bernard was asked by a man known to him by sight if it was true that Count Bernadotte had been murdered. There is no record of this having raised any concern.

The three-car entourage left the School at about 5 PM back to the YMCA, where Bernadotte was staying. They were stopped by an Israeli checkpoint where, some of his colleagues later testified, they were "manoeuvred in such a way that was later interpreted by them as a signal [to the assassins that Bernadotte] was seated in the third car," though this remains speculation.

After leaving the checkpoint they passed an armored car in which sat Israel's military governor in Jerusalem, Dr. Bernhard Joseph. They then overtook a break-down lorry (pickup truck) with three soldiers.

Upon reaching the crest of a hill, a jeep with four men blocked the road. They were now roughly 30-40 meters (100-130 ft) beyond

---

* Israeli denials of responsibility rest on the claim that Bernadotte had refused an escort, and eulogies to Bernadotte have inadvertently given credence to this when describing his courage. Bernadotte had not refused an escort; his position was that it was up to the local authorities to determine the appropriate security. The Arab Legion arranged security on its own initiative. Israel had offered none.

the lorry and 350 meters (1150 ft) from the checkpoint. Standing nearby were a girl of fifteen years, three boys of about 12, and a girl of eleven. Two of the boys asked the men in the jeep about their weapons. A couple that ran a shop in a nearby building called Tnuva was not in direct view but had seen the jeep about a hour earlier.

Three armed men jumped from the jeep, only the driver remaining. Two approached the first car. A Captain Hillman, addressing them through the front-right window, asked in Hebrew to be allowed to pass. The third gunman went straight to the third car, apparently knowing in advance that it contained Bernadotte in the rear seat.

Suddenly the front two gunmen shot out the tires of the first car, while the third put his weapon through the open left rear window of the third car and aimed at the Mediator, the right-most of three in the rear seat, firing an estimated twenty-seven rounds past General Lundström, killing Colonel Sérot in the middle seat as well. As the killers fled, neighborhood people—all potential witnesses—rushed to their windows or balconies to see what was happening.

The driver of the break-down lorry told the principal witness, the older girl, to say nothing to the police about what she had seen. That evening, leaflets were distributed in Jerusalem by an unknown "Fatherland Front" (*Hazit Hamoledeth*), claiming responsibility for the murders.

Thus four months into the Israeli state's quest for legitimacy, it suddenly faced the challenge, or opportunity, to demonstrate that it could respond to this most notorious of Zionist assassinations as a competent, responsible nation free of its terroristic genesis.

Israel falsely described the crime scene as "an isolated spot" and never cordoned it off. The Assistant Superintendent of Police who was assigned the case did not visit the scene until the following evening, and made no systematic analysis of the situation. In the interim, the girl saw a man arrive in a "Transport and Fuel Supply Service" car and take away a Sten gun that the one of the assailants had left on the ground.

The car in which Bernadotte was murdered was not examined until a week later—*after* it had been repaired—and the first car was never examined at all. The assassin had (deliberately?) left behind the barrel to his gun, but it was passed without precaution through a few officials' hands before being given to a lab for analysis, by which point any fingerprints that might have been left behind were useless. No serious attempt was made to identify the jeep, despite available clues, nor to identify the source of the Fatherland Front leaflets, nor the typewriter that typed them.

Lehi suspects were rounded up but appeared unconcerned, then turned their prison into a co-ed celebratory party scene. As *Time Magazine* reported it on October 18:

> Cold Beer. The Sternists threw open the door of the jail, disarmed the guards, directed traffic in the square where a great crowd had gathered. Some prisoners strolled off to the beach for a swim. Others relaxed with prison guards over coffee in a nearby café. Few showed any disposition to escape from the city. "If we left the jail for good," explained one Sternist, "it would only mean that we would have to go underground again."[542]

All the Lehi suspects were soon freed, and key members of the terror gang rose to positions in the Israeli government. Nathan Yellin-Mor, whose previous infamy rested with his overtures to the Nazis and his involvement in Lord Moyne's murder, ascended to the Knesset. Matityahu Shmuelevitz would join the staff of future PM Begin. Most remarkably, Lehi big-wig Yitzhak Shamir joined the Mossad and would eventually be elected Prime Minister of Israel—twice.

In response to the Swedish government's protests of Israeli inaction on the assassins, Israel submitted a report to the Security Council that went a step beyond the release of the suspects: it claimed that there was insufficient evidence even to attribute the murder to Lehi.[543]

Theory: Israel, not Lehi, murdered Bernadotte
The ultimate irony could be that Israel's leaders were on that point telling the truth—because it was they who arranged the assassination.

Beginning about a week after the murder, US and UK intelligence began reporting slightly varying versions of the same claim: that on the day of the assassination, the Czechoslovak Consul General in Jerusalem had issued visas and arranged travel for Lehi operatives to fly to Prague on a Czech aircraft under false names. In Prague they would get new papers and continue to Paris. A report dated September 26 from a source marked "Squib" also noted that a number of passports had recently been stolen, notably from the British Consulate at Haifa.

A different "top secret and delicate source" noted that the French, aware of the situation, were urgently requesting the false names used, so that the impersonators could be stopped, especially as it was feared they were heading to Paris to attack United Nations Organization personnel, and that the plans were somehow part of Soviet intrigue.

On October 6, US Ambassador Lewis Douglas told the British Charge d'Affaires that "the murderers of Count Bernadotte had been assisted to escape by the Czechoslovak Consul in Jerusalem. The latter had given the men false passports and arranged air passages for them in a Czech airline." Two days later, M.I.5 head Sir Percy Sillitoe received a report from M.I.6 stating the same, and that "the passports were made out in non-Jewish names."

These brief intelligence memos did not venture an answer as to how Lehi had the clout to involve the Czechs in the complicated escape, and with such secrecy.

The answer may come from the Belgium Consul-General M. Jean Niewenhuys, who was Chairman of the Truce Commission. "In the strictest confidence" the following August (1949), he related the following to Major V.P. Rich of the War Office:

> For about a year, source, whom I consider to be reliable, has been in secret communication with a certain Czech employee in the Czechoslovak Consulate-General in the New City [i.e., West Jerusalem]. This employee is said to be anti-communist and a fervent Catholic, which may explain the common link between source and subsource. About two days before the Bernadotte murder, subsource sent a message to Niewenhuys to keep away from Jerusalem for the next few days. He did not do this, but he thinks that the reason for the warning was that he, as Chairman of the Truce Committee,

was often seen about with Count Bernadotte. Some twenty four hours after the murder, the Czech employee met source secretly and gave him the following information. It appeared that the Czech Consul-General had been approached by Mr Shiloah of the Israeli Foreign Office and now Israeli delegate at Lausanne, about a week before the murder, to arrange Czech visas and air passage for seven Jews in a Czech air line for the late afternoon flight to Prague. The date requested coincided with the date of the murder. A request by the Czech Consulate to the French Consulate for further visas for France was refused.*

Further investigation was undertaken, after which

it was disclosed that these seven Jews were in fact members of the Stern Gang and that Shiloah, acting on behalf of the Israeli Government, was the organiser of the murder.

The reason Israel wanted Bernadotte dead was not just to prevent "the internationalisation of Jerusalem," but also to stop him from influencing world opinion against "Israel's expansionist plans."

Some time after the murder, "a senior member" of Lehi told the source that their organization was not responsible, "but that these seven [Lehi] members had been hired by the Government and handsomely paid." The original plan that they continue from Prague to Paris was abandoned "owing to the extremely strong precautions taken by the Paris police." The seven were believed to be back in Israel, as the body of one "recently washed ashore near Jaffa with a bullet hole in the back of his head," liquidated for an indiscretion about the affair.

The evidence all points to the Israeli state, not Lehi, as the assassin. Lehi could not have penetrated the Czech Consul-General and invisibly secured its cooperation in the complex arrangements. The assassins had awaited Bernadotte's arrival for at least an hour,

---

* Declassified by the British in 2005. "Shiloah" = Reuven Shiloah, who would become the first director of Mossad. "Lausanne" = Conference of 1949 to resolve disputes of 1948 war. From Major V. P. Ric of the Military Liaison Office, Jerusalem, to Major C. de B. deLisle of the War Office, TNA, FO 371/75266.

unbothered by Israeli checkpoints before or after. And Niewenhuys' source appears credible: s/he knew to advise him to stay away from Jerusalem (as he would normally join Bernadotte); details regarding the assassins' escape to Prague tally with US and UK intelligence, which s/he could not have known; nor could s/he have known that Shiloah, cited as the organizer, would soon create and direct the Mossad, infamous for assassinations.[544]

Israel's downing of an Arab Airways passenger plane

Six days after Bernadotte's assassination, September 23, an Arab Airways (Jordan) de Haviland *Rapide* passenger plane departed Beirut airport for Amman along a well-established flight path that followed the eastern shore of Lakes Hula and Tiberias (Sea of Galilee). Toward the southern end of Tiberias, at about eleven in the morning, the aircraft briefly crossed a segment of Israeli-held territory on which sat the settlement of Ein Gev—an outpost founded in 1937 as a fact-on-the-ground to counter the Peel Commission's proposal that placed the area in the Palestinian state.

As it did, an Israeli fighter plane attacked, disabling the plane's radio. The *Rapide's* pilot, S.G. Nowers, dived from 6,000 to 5,000 feet as he pointed the plane to the nearest Jordanian territory in an attempt to escape to safety. The Israeli fighter followed the small crimson passenger craft into Jordanian skies and attacked again, setting the *Rapide* ablaze and leaving Nowers no choice but to attempt an emergency landing.

Just as the burning passenger plane was about to skim a rocky field about 30 km (18.6 miles) from Israel, the Israeli pursuer attacked a third time. Three of the passengers jumped from the rear door in a desperate bid to survive the flames and the crash. The *Rapide* hit the ground at about 150 mph, rolled about 50 yards, nosed over and skidded to a stop. Nowers punched out the windshield, through which he and the two remaining passengers escaped before the fire reached the fuel tanks and the plane exploded.

The three people who jumped through the rear were dead: John Nixon of the BBC, David Woodford of the *Daily Telegraph*, and a man named Abou Aswad about whom nothing further is recorded. Among the three burned survivors was Dr. Ovid Sellers, Director of the American School of Archaeology in Jerusalem.

Ambassador Kirkbride arranged a Christian service and burial for Woodford and Nixon on a "dreary hillside" the next day, with coffins "knocked together in haste by a local carpenter." In a move that baffled him, the British government obligated Jordan—not Israel—to pay compensation to the dependents of the two British journalists.

Israel justified its downing of the unarmed passenger plane on the grounds that it had passed through airspace that it claimed as its own. Yet Israel had been making daily *armed* incursions over Jordan with impunity, and continued to do so well into the 1950s.

Like the fate of Bernadotte's assassins, the lack of any meaningful response to Israel's deadly downing of an unarmed passenger plane underscores the significance of statehood—had the same incident occurred a half year earlier, it would have elicited world outrage as an unprovoked act of international terrorism.[545]

Depopulated villages: pre, versus post-statehood

The same power of statehood over perception is seen in the stories of two Palestinian villages, Deir Yassin and Al-Dawayima (or Dawaymeh). In the body of world opinion, the extinction of Deir Yassin on April 9, five weeks before statehood, was terrorism, indeed it quickly became iconic of racist savagery. However, the bloodier massacre five and a half months *after* statehood, on October 28 in the village of Al-Dawayima is remembered as a military operation, when it is remembered at all. By that time there had, indeed, been "a number of incidents like Deir Yassin," as Yigael Yadin, IDF head of operations put it; but Israeli statehood now brought Zionism the newspeak of nation-states.[546]

Oct 1948

Whereas it was the Irgun that ravaged Deir Yassin, it was Israel's 89th Battalion that massacred Al-Dawayima. The soldiers approached the village on three sides (Plan Dalet), and "jumped out of the armoured cars and spread through the streets of the village firing promiscuously at anything they saw," as a survivor testified. In the words of one of the soldiers, his Battalion began shooting from the rooftops and

> we saw Arabs running about in the alleyways [below]. We opened fire on them … From our high position we saw a vast plain stretching eastward … covered by thousands of fleeing Arabs … [Our] machine guns began to chatter and the flight [of the refugees] turned into a rout.[547]

Acting under orders, the soldiers forced people into houses and then blew them up. Of those who escaped, some took refuge in the mosque, others hid in a nearby cave. The next day, the bodies of men, women, and children littered the streets. Sixty people who had taken refuge in the mosque lay dead. Eighty-five men, women, and children who had hidden in the cave had all been butchered. The hundreds murdered included 175 women and children. A soldier who participated in the attack testified that

> The children they [the Israeli soldiers] killed by breaking their heads with sticks. There was not a house without dead … One soldier boasted that he had raped a woman and then shot her. One woman, with a newborn baby in her arms, was employed to clean the courtyard where the soldiers ate. [Then] they shot her and her baby.[548]

The settlement Israel built over the ruins of Dawayima was given a name from Jewish antiquity to erase what had been exterminated: Amatzia, after King Amaziah of Judah.

The following day, October 29, the village of Safsaf, in the Galilee region, was the first to be leveled in so-called Operation Hiram. As recorded by an Israeli officer, the inhabitants had "raised the white flag" as the IDF attacked with two platoons of armored cars and a tank company from the 7th Brigade.

> 52 men were caught, tied them to one another, dug a pit and shot them. 10 were still twitching. Women came, begged for mercy. Found bodies of 6 elderly men. There were 61 bodies. 3 cases of rape

[including a] girl of 14 [from Safed], 4 men shot and killed. From one they cut off his fingers with a knife to take the ring.[549]

Others were left lying in a thicket, "among them a woman clutching her dead child." The people of two more villages, Ilabun and Faradia, "greeted the soldiers with white flags," upon which the soldiers "opened fire and after thirty people had been killed they started moving the rest on foot." Again in the village of Saliha, after raising a white flag the villagers were forced into a building which the Israelis then blew up—a method commonly used by them not just during 1948, but in Israel's post-statehood raids into the West Bank as well.

The Irgun's blueprint for depopulation was like the Hagana's. Also in the Galilee region, the militia "annihilated with a machine gun 35 Arabs who had surrendered to that company with a white flag in their hands," ordering peaceful residents, including women and children, "to dig a pit, then pushing them into it with long French bayonets and murdering all … shooting dead Arab children of about 13-14; [and] raping a girl, then stabbing her with a bayonet and thrusting a wooden stick into her body."

Palestinian villages both within Israel and beyond the Partition suffered similar fates, with orders that some must be "wiped out" coming directly from Ben-Gurion.[550]

Massive arms and other military equipment continued to flow illegally to Israel from the US, often by way of bribed Latin American dictatorships. Teddy Kollek was there toward the end of 1948; the British Intelligence Service believed that he was purchasing tanks and radar equipment, and establishing an espionage network. Sneh, former head of the Hagana, went to the United States in October and appealed to the public to stop the Bernadotte plan, claiming it would "rob the Jewish State of the possibility of existence." Most publicly, Begin—who laid blame for Bernadotte's murder with the United Nations for failing to give all of Palestine and Transjordan to the Zionists (therefore creating the need to do away with him) went to the US in November to garner support for the takeover of what remained of Palestine.[551]

The Irgun leader was received with great pomp in New York, a lavish motorcade escorting him through the garment district of Manhattan to an official welcome at City Hall. Mayor O'Dwyer joked about his being wanted as a terrorist, saying that in New York City the Police Department were singing for him. Begin railed against the assassinated Bernadotte for attempting to limit Israel's expansionism, railed against Albert Einstein for being among twenty-one academics accusing him of "openly preach[ing] the doctrine of the Fascist state," and accused the American Council for Judaism of antisemitism for its criticism of him. To cheering New York crowds, Begin openly preached violence to seize yet more territory:

> The fight is not yet over, and not yet has the aim of victory been achieved. We shall continue the fight … until the whole of [i.e., Biblical] Israel is liberated and the whole of our people are back in the country.

At New York's Diplomat Hotel, Begin spread the same message to two hundred youths aged ten to twenty-three years, all members of the militaristic youth group Brith Trumpeldor, standing in uniform at attention. He addressed a crowd in Carnegie Hall to the accompaniment of a small protest outside; his presence was also publicly condemned by several Christian and Jewish religious leaders. When the issue of Deir Yassin was raised, Begin countered that the villagers themselves were to blame.

As he spoke, the British Consulate-General in Jerusalem was reporting, wryly, that "the Arabs left in Palestine are having a very poor deal … Arabs left in the Jewish State have been dispossessed of their property, and many of the villages have been wantonly blown up or destroyed after being looted by the Jews." Israel was attributing the destruction to "hostilities," he reported, but "this explanation is obviously untrue." International observers on the scene from the Red Cross and elsewhere "have fully confirmed this wanton destruction by the Jews of Arab property."[552]

In Paris as in New York, Begin sought support to "finish the struggle for the liberation of all of Palestine," and back in Israel he rallied the public for an "undivided Fatherland." By campaigning for the conquest of the rest of Palestine, Begin quickly won fourteen seats in the Knesset for his new Herut Party in the nation's first elections. He denounced any "alignment with the United Nations," pushed for seizing the land to the Jordan, and warned of new terror should Jerusalem remain an international zone.[553]

A Security Council resolution to halt Egyptian-Israeli hostilities in the Negev was accepted by the Egyptian government, but (as recorded in Cabinet papers) "the Jewish authorities, so far from complying with them, retained their new positions and launched a second offensive against the Egyptians on December 22"; and in the north, refused to vacate Lebanese territory. Yet "despite the clear refusal of the Jewish authorities to comply," the Security Council "failed to act as required." Israel's impunity, the British said, was a result of the "reluctance of the United States Government to be associated with any measures which could be regarded as hostile" to Israel, and of the Israeli representative's success in confusing the public by deliberately mixing up two separate UN resolutions.[554]

Israel shoots down British planes

The Acting Mediator reported to the Security Council that Israel alone was to blame for the fighting in the south. There had been no acts of provocation on the Egyptian side, and Israel "entirely prevented the United Nations staff from observing the operations in southern Palestine. This was the culmination of the obstructive attitude" by Israel. Nor could the UN confirm reports received on December 29 that Israeli troops had invaded Gaza, because Israel blocked its observers.

As a result, Britain sent a reconnaissance flight on the 30th which found that Israeli forces were about twenty miles inside Gaza. Further reports confirmed this. "Fresh incursion in strength" by Israeli troops was sighted on January 6, and so the next morning Britain sent four Spitfire aircraft to investigate and photograph.

Jan–Feb 1949

Israel responded by shooting down all four of the British aircraft over Egyptian territory. Three of the four pilots who parachuted from their stricken Spitfires survived and were helped by local Bedouin, but two were then seized by the Israelis. The fourth was dead; according to a Bedouin eye-witness, he was machine-gunned after parachuting. Ben-Gurion ordered one of the British wrecks to be dragged onto Israeli-held territory, making it appear that the plane had violated its sovereignty.

Britain sent four more Spitfires to learn the fate of the others, now escorted by fifteen Tempest aircraft. Reaching as far as Rafah, they, too, were attacked by Israeli aircraft, whose gunners shot down one of the British Tempests, killing its pilot.

Two of the Israeli Air Force pilots involved in the Israeli attacks, Chalmers Goodlin and John McElroy, were US and Canadian citizens respectively, shooting down Allied aircraft in Israel's attempt to conquer land by force.[555]

Remarkably, Churchill defended Israel's downing of British aircraft and killing of his own servicemen, and when Bevin condemned the attacks, the famed wartime leader accused him of antisemitism. Churchill wrote that when the "Israelite aeroplanes"—his use of the Biblical term itself telling—launched the attack in which "two British pilots were killed … Ernest Bevin, being temperamentally anti-Semite, made the great mistake of backing Egypt against Israel." Churchill then specifically equates the new Zionist state with the Biblical realm—"I seem to have heard of it in bygone days"—dismisses objections to Israeli aggression and its blocking of UN access, and again calls Bevin "anti-Semitic" for criticizing Israel's actions. Ironically, in the same note, Churchill worries about "the powerful and possibly decisive Jewish vote" in New York.[556]

When in January 1949 Bevin tried to raise the issue of the Palestinian refugees in the House of Commons, the Israeli creation myth already dominated, and was already enforced by the militarization of the antisemitism smear.

"We cannot handle these problems unless we put ourselves in the other fellow's place," he insisted. There would be trouble in "this House" and perhaps beyond, if parts of Britain had been handed over "to another race, and the present inhabitants had been compelled to make way." He reminded his colleagues of the Arabs' importance in winning the recent war, and of their help in World War I.

Churchill—who in the case of Europeans a few years earlier wrote that "the violent driving of people from one territory to another, is one of the most horrible events in human history"—now dismissed the ethnically cleansed Palestinians as Arabs who had entered Palestine to benefit from the British Administration. Sidney Silverman, representative of the now-defunct Nelson and Colne constituency in Lancashire, went further: the Palestinians were not driven out by Israel at all, but by Bevin's own "agents on the spot," and the Israelis, "so far from driving anyone away, they did their utmost to persuade them to stay, and those who did stay were very well treated."

Bevin pressed on. "The fact is that 500,000 Arabs are gone [an early, significant underestimate]; and I do not think they walked out voluntarily … I am trying to make a balanced speech…"

But then the transcript is odd:

> However I cannot accept the position that when anybody mentions the Arabs he is—*[Interruption]*—

… with no further explanation. "Well, I will leave it at that," Bevin finished. "I will not use the phrase I was about to use," the forbidden phrase presumably being "accused of anti-Semitism."

He continued:

> The marvel to me is that the conscience of the world has been so little stirred over [the tragedy of the Palestinian refugees] … I hate the refugee problem; I think that the driving of poor innocent people from their homes, whether it is in Germany by Hitler, or by anybody else … is a crime.[557]

The Sinai-Gaza region where Israel downed the British planes was part of its larger plans to confiscate the entire south. Ben-Gurion promised to precipitously transform Beersheba, which lay on Palestinian side of Partition, into "a Hebrew town." In response to UN demands that Israel withdraw its illegal occupation, he instead promised to seize it through "the largest settlement programme that has ever been carried out in Palestine at one time," and laid out plans "to establish a chain of semi-military settlements in the whole of the conquered [i.e., Palestinian] area."[558]

And so it was in mid January 1949 that the prolific *New York Times'* war correspondent, Anne McCormick, already tolled the death-knell for any two-state solution. After describing how Israel "overstepped" the Partition and now "claim possession of territory they have conquered," she wrote that there is no Palestine, but rather "there is Israel and an overcrowded remnant of territory that is not and cannot be a state…"

"Israel will break the heart of its friends yet," the *Manchester Guardian* wrote when, on February 10, 1949, the new state declared an unconditional, general amnesty for Bernadotte's presumed murderers and "forty members of the Stern Gang in custody and many more in hiding"—even, the paper lamented, as they refused to renounce terrorism.

Cyril Marriott, British Consul-General in Haifa, wrote that Israeli leaders freed the Lehi suspects not just because they welcomed the crime, but also because they they feared "for their own skins" and "would not have been able to keep them prisoners." Knowing nothing of Belgium Consul-General Niewenhuys' evidence that the Israeli government was in fact the assassin, Marriott wrote in a government memo that "in fact I believe they connived at" Bernadotte's murder.[559]

An armistice agreement ending hostilities was signed on February 24. It explicitly stated that the cease-fire line agreed to—roughly what became known as the Green Line or, in later political parlance, the "1967 borders"—"is not to be construed in any sense as a political or territorial boundary." It was not a *de facto* legitimization of Israel's illegal conquest beyond the Partition, but temporary lines to end hostilities. Sharett's reaction was typical: now a Knesset member, he quickly disavowed any commitment even to the cease-fire line, saying that Israel's territory will be determined by "possession," not by Partition or any other plan.[560]

Kermit Roosevelt appraised the situation for the National War College in Washington in November of 1948. Americans do not realize the extent to which partition was refused acceptance as a final settlement by the Zionists in Palestine, [nor the conviction that they] must not only have all of Palestine, but Trans-Jordan, part of Syria and Lebanon, parts of Iraq and parts of Egypt as well.[561]

Scattered in the rubble of Partition was the credibility of the United States. Palestinians had looked with admiration to the US and its lofty principles of liberty and democracy, but that respect now lay shattered. Until now, one could

> talk to a farmer in a little Arab village in Palestine who has never seen an American, who has never had any contact with American life, and yet he has known over the last years that the people he has most admired in his Arab community, in his larger Arab community, were people who were trained at American schools and who told him what the American views on politics, on world order and on the dignity of human beings were.

Their shock at America's betrayal of those principles "is one of the most extreme forms of disillusionment I have seen anywhere in the world … tears would run down his face" when Palestinians realized what the United States had done.[562]

8

Impunity *sans frontières*

> "The Israeli leaders now state freely, though usually unofficially,
> their demand for an ever-increasing empire. Their present
> boundaries are regarded by them as only a beachhead."
> —*CIA report, eleven months after Israel declared statehood, the term*
> *"present boundaries" referring not to the borders Israel agreed to*
> *with Resolution 181, but to the Armistice Line, which included more*
> *than half the land designated for a Palestinian state and which was*
> *supposed to be temporary.* [563]

The year 1948 left in its wake nearly a million Palestinians purged by Israel because they are not Jewish and more than five hundred of their villages destroyed, crippling life even for those spared the immediate ethnic cleansing. This catastrophe—*nakba*—was for the Zionists "a miraculous simplification of our task," to quote Weizmann. Like Ben-Gurion, he pretended as though the deed had happened of its own accord through some inexplicable intervention of fate. The Israeli press openly applauded the ethnic cleansing of non-Jews, and the Israeli Foreign Ministry predicted that "natural selection" would reduce the refugees to "a human heap, the scum of the earth."[564]

The international community reassured those uprooted people of their unqualified right to return home, and in December (1948) the UNGA passed Resolution 194 which, despite odd language, reaffirmed it. Yet the world body did nothing as Israel in its early years killed roughly five thousand Palestinians for the attempt to go home.[565]

The new state's method was self-perpetuating, as it remains today: its blocking of the refugees' return home, its blanket theft of their property, and its continuing violence, all assured the threat that it would cite as the justification for further aggression and ethnic cleansing. "No resolution of the United Nations," British officials witnessing the upheaval predicted, will get the Israelis to return the Palestinian land they seized beyond Partition, "or prevent the expansion of the 'beach-head' they have already secured."[566]

MI5, however, suggested that Israel's need for *de jure* recognition would compel it to agree to fixed borders.

> The Americans and the Russians have so far recognised no more than the de facto State of Israel. The de jure State cannot exist until its boundaries are defined…[567]

This seemed obvious—no nation that refuses to state its claimed geographic limits could be formally recognized. Yet today, several decades after most of the world granted Israel *de jure* recognition, Israel is still expanding without national borders, while the Palestinians are called upon to recognize a state that occupies their land and refuses to state where, or if, it will stop.

A CIA report of March, 1949, warned of the consequences of this sovereignty without borders. Its prophetic title was "A Long-Range Disaster":

> The establishment of the State of Israel by force, with intimidation of Arab governments by the US and the USSR [means that] the Israeli battle-victory is complete, but it has solved nothing. If boundaries to an Israeli state, any boundaries, had been set and guaranteed by the Great Powers, peace might return to the area. On the contrary, we have actually a victorious state which is limited to no frontiers and which is determined that no narrow limit shall be set. The Near East is faced with the almost certain prospect of a profound and growing disturbance by Israel which may last for decades…[568]

Three months later, the CIA suggested that Israel's poor cooperation with efforts to bring a lasting peace, both at the Lausanne Conference and in talks with Syria and Jordan, was a tactic for continued expansion, and the US State Department as well warned of Israel's wild territorial designs.

The British rejected Israel's sincerity for peace, as it continued to violate the Armistice and was "laying claim to everything which they now [illegally] possessed [beyond Partition] and to the Gaza Strip as well."

Reuven Shiloah, the first director of Mossad, told the US that Israel would never relinquish any of the Palestinian land it had seized, and when British authorities in Tel Aviv pressed him on permanent borders, he replied instead that it would always be Israel's right to take more land as necessary. The "ingathering" was not complete, as Mapai argued with a favored messianic word—or in Moshe Dayan's more direct language, "we have not yet determined whether ... our existing borders [referring to the Armistice, not Partition] satisfy us...."[569]

For its first eighteen years officially, and longer in practice, Israel enforced martial law based on ethnicity—Jews were exempt. Non-Jews were required to get permits from the military government to leave their village for any reason, paralyzing all aspects of normal daily life—civilian, family, cultural, artistic, economic. Farmers or merchants barred from reaching markets because they are not Jewish had no choice but to sell their produce to Jewish merchants for considerably less; and when non-Jewish husbands and fathers did get "permission" to leave their village for work, they did so in constant fear of what Israeli soldiers or settlers might do to their families while they were away.[570]

Cyril Marriott was an on-the-ground witness in Haifa. "The Arab community is living in terror," he reported in early 1949,

> [Non-Jewish] workmen are only able to get to work if they produce identity cards at a given office where they have to leave them. A few hours later they are arrested for not having documents of identity. Numbers of young Arabs have recently disappeared ... Arab houses are daily invaded by armed Jews and Arab men are increasingly

afraid to go to work because of what may happen to their families in their absence...[571]

The "United Nations Assembly," Marriott warned, "should be aware of the barbarous nature of the country now applying for membership."

Yet despite its "barbarous nature" and defiance of the international body, on May 11 it was admitted to the United Nations. Israel mollified objections with promises of compliance, but reneged on those assurances twenty-four hours after admission to the world body. It moved government offices to Jerusalem immediately after the UN specifically forbade it (since Jerusalem does not lie in Israel), and continued to force out non-Jews from the land under its control.[572]

A ready-made state

Israel took over an intact, ready-made country—homes, assets, money, orchards, quarries, 10,000 acres of vineyards, 25,000 acres of citrus groves, 10,000 business establishments, olive groves, and machinery. Despite the massive infusion of foreign capital into Israel and its claims of "making the desert bloom," economic analysis demonstrates it was the Palestinians that saved the Israeli state from stillbirth.[573]

A few months after its establishment, the value of property Israel had stolen from the Palestinians was put at about £P50 million, and the Israel's theft of their financial assets was estimated at between £P4 million and £P5 million. When the UN ordered Israel to return the money to its owners, Israel replied that it would agree to do so if any Arab states blocking "Arab" [Palestinian] assets would also return them, "on a basis of equal and reciprocal compensation." Arab negotiators were happy to agree to this—but Israel then claimed that its wording obliged them to return only the *same amount* as what Arab nations had blocked. Only one Arab state had any such account, and the amount was small. The project was dropped. Today, Israel reaps vast financial benefits through the theft of Palestinian natural resources, and micro-control of the Palestinian economy, taxes, tourism, imports, and exports.[574]

The commonly cited figure of Palestinians ethnically cleansed in 1948—750,000—is misleadingly low (Eisenhower put it at 900,000), as it includes only those who were pushed over the Armistice Line *and* whose homes and fields lay entirely on the Israeli side of it. That Line was wild and irrational, as it was merely a cease-fire expediency and it lay entirely in Palestinian land. The Israeli side of the Armistice Line included more than half of the Palestinian side of Partition.

Eighty Palestinian villages were orphaned partly in what became the West Bank and partly in a newly-enlarged Israel, separating homes from farming and grazing lands. By 1952, one-quarter of the people in the West Bank who were *not* categorized as refugees were, according to a British report, "slowly starving" as a consequence of Israel's intransigence, "and a further substantial proportion are not far above the same level and may soon sink below it."[575]

The Palestine village of Qalqilya, which for generations had lived off its orange groves, is illustrative. Although the entire village lay on the Palestinian side of Partition, the Armistice Line fell between the villagers' homes on the Jordanian-occupied side and their groves on the Israeli-occupied side. The result was that "the people of Qalqiliya," in the words of Glubb, "are starving in their houses and can see their orange groves only three hundred yards from their houses."

> A great many of these wretched people are killed now picking their own oranges and olives just beyond the line … If the Jewish patrol sees him he is shot dead on the spot, without any questions.[576]

Nor does the refugee figure record those driven from their homes by the settlers but who remained in land under Israeli control. Israel continued to seize the property of non-Jews, and by April 1949, it had placed 150,000 Jewish settlers in stolen Palestinians' homes—not including the Palestinian homes commandeered by individual settlers under the protection of the state, as continues today in, for example, Hebron and East Jerusalem.

One such post-statehood ethnic cleansing campaign began in Haifa at six in the morning on April 7, 1949. Groups of about one hundred Israeli soldiers, all armed with Tommy (sub-machine) guns, went house-to-house commandeering homes of non-Jews as Israeli military police looked on, then faced "serious Arab baiting" after being forced from their homes. British witnesses informed the United

States, but hesitated to inform the UN Conciliation Commission for fear that "these unfortunate people [be] branded as British stooges" and render their situation even worse. Arab leaders, for the same reason, advised the villagers that protest would lead only to Israeli retribution. Many Palestinians ethnically cleansed from their homes, but not pushed over the Armistice Line, were used by the state for forced labor, sheltering in shacks or caves.[577]

Once Israel's UN membership was secured, the Israeli Air Force (IAF) began strafing West Bank refugees, killing men, women, and children, as well as their livestock. Seventy-six Israeli air violations over Jordan are recorded between December 12 1949 and October 22 1950. No Jordanian resistance was possible, as it then had no air force. Seven attacks are recorded in 1950 in which, to quote Glubb, "Israeli fighter aircraft machine-gunned farmers and shepherds (many of them women and children) and herds in the Hebron sector." The specter of Britain's defence treaty with Jordan made IAF strafing uncommon after 1950, though the IAF's harassing violations of West Bank airspace remained commonplace.[578]

Fear of ethnic violence by the state continued to dominate the lives of non-Jewish citizens of Israel. Not even the presence of UN observers could protect them from being rounded up by Israeli soldiers and forced into barbed-wire compounds in order to loot their homes—"spoiled of their gold items and of their money by the Jews," to quote one UN witness—before forcing them over the Armistice Line.[579]

Abu Gosh

One documented case is the village of Abu Gosh. The people of Abu Gosh had tried to make peace with the Zionist settlers during the Mandate, and indeed had provided them with assistance. Once the Israeli state was established, they too became victims of mass expulsion and disappearances. In an "Open letter to the Inhabitants of Israel," dated July 10, 1950, the villagers testified that the IDF had repeatedly

> surrounded our village [and] taken our women and children [and sent them into] the Negev Desert, where they met their deaths …

they rounded up our women, old people, children, the sick, the blind, and pregnant women, using force and blows [and took them] to an unknown destination, and we still do not know what has befallen them.[580] [see also Wadi Araba, pages 323-326, below]

Kafr Bir'im and Iqrit

The Israeli justice system was, and remains, a maze of official, administrative, and *de facto* discrimination designed to offer the illusion of consistency and redress. The histories of two Christian villages in the far north, Kafr Bir'im and Iqrit, offer a well-documented glimpse at the reality of non-Jewish citizens seeking its protection. During the Mandate, both villages had been known for their friendliness to Jewish settlers. In 1948 the villagers greeted the soldiers with fresh bread and salt when they arrived on their sweep across Palestine. When Israel nonetheless forced them from their villages because they were not Jews, they sought redress through the Israeli legal system. The IDF then bombed and leveled both villages.

Yet the villagers persevered through the Israeli courts, but were then informed that they could not return home due to what was called a "security" situation. Still they worked within the system, asking that the government preserve their title to their land so that when the alleged security issues were resolved, they could return home. Israel built Jewish-only towns on the ruins of their stolen villages.[581]

The hundreds of obliterated Palestinian villages had also to be obliterated metaphysically—erased from the map both figuratively and literally. Over their ashes, Israel planted fast-growing non-native trees or erected new villages with Biblically-suggestive names replacing their Arabic names. For the purpose, in July 1949 Ben-Gurion appointed Israel's first Governmental Names Committee, some of whose members would become important figures in Israel's narrative-driven state archaeology.[582]

The ethnic cleansing of Baghdad

Jews of North Africa and the Middle East were needed "as cannon and demographic fodder" for the state, in the words of Hanna Braun, a Haganah member involved with bringing them into Israel shortly after its founding. Until its ethnic cleansing of 300,000 more non-Jews from Palestine in 1967, Israel's most precipitous post-1948 ethnic cleansing was its destruction of the ancient Jewish community of Iraq, where Jews comprised one third of Baghdad's population until the Zionist purge.

As allegations of the horrific plight of Iraqi Jews circulated in early 1949, the British Embassy in Baghdad tried to sort truth from invention or spin. The general feeling was that "there is no reason to apprehend serious pogroms," as matters stood, but that "the establishment of the Israeli state has, of course increased it." The Embassy was very conscious of the "dual-loyalty" conundrum that Israel itself had created by claiming to be *the* state of *the* Jews—"British Jews who danced the Hora in the streets of London … about the hoisting of *our* flag" can not now be surprised when people take them at their word.

News of anti-Jewish Iraqi violence increased in the Israeli press in September, and in mid-October the Israeli government issued "gravely disquieting reports of a new wave of persecution against the Jewish minority in Iraq." The World Zionist Organization warned of coming pogroms, and soon the worst was confirmed—or so it appeared. The pogroms began by April 8, 1950, with a hand grenade thrown from a passing car into a popular café, Dar El-Beyda, accompanied by leaflets warning Jews to flee Iraq.

Such was the alleged emergency that Israel proposed transplanting the entire Iraqi Jewish community by airlift to the new state. The United Jewish Appeal called for "every understanding person in the United States" to donate money to the effort, stressing that they were "in a race against time" to rescue Jews who had not yet reached the safety of Israel.

The race seemed real: a series of bombings over fourteen months hit Baghdad's American Cultural Center and US Information Service Library, a Jewish-owned automobile company, and Jewish homes. The worst single attack was the bombing of Masouda Shem-Tov Synagogue on January 14, 1951, among whose victims was a twelve year old boy, electrocuted when a grenade felled a high voltage line.

The US Embassy in Baghdad found itself pressured by the Truman Administration to help facilitate the airlift to Israel, while at the same time it was receiving constant reports that the situation was being "artificially inflamed from without." The Iraqi government, meanwhile was, in the words of a CIA official present, "loathe to lose these Jews," who "formed the backbone of the civil service and merchant class," and so tried to create obstacles to limit their exodus.

Iraq's chief rabbi, a frequent visitor to the Embassy, was urging calm. But the anti-Jewish violence seemed to be the tragic confirmation of the warnings, and so despite his appeals Iraqis began forfeiting their ancient homeland by the tens of thousands to become settlers in the Israeli state.[583]

The airlift operation was called "Ali Baba," the character who learns the secret phrase *Open Sesame* in the *1001 Nights*, now opening the door to Israel. Nor was Zionism's obligatory Biblical association overlooked: they were the flight of 42,360 Jews from Iraq to Jerusalem two and a half millennia ago, when the Persian King Cyrus freed the Jews who had been exiled by Nebuchadnezzar.[584]

It materialized quickly—but strangely. In May, 1950, an exclusive contract for it went to a company called Near East Air Transport (NEAT), a previously unknown company that had two planes. NEAT began shipping Iraqi Jews to Israel on the 20th of the month, but its two aircraft were wholly inadequate to keep up with the exodus of people who were now stranded in Iraq after giving up their homes and citizenship. Yet after having roused the world to such an imminent threat that the funds had to be raised to evacuate them in "a race against time," Israel now insisted that no other airline take part in the allegedly urgent mass human migration.

In response to criticism, Israel used a phrase that the Jewish Agency would have railed against a few years earlier: it replied that there was a "regulated plan of absorption" of new immigrants, and this "regulated plan" happened to be "the capacity of the two aircraft provided by Near East Air Transport."

By September, the backlog of Jews waiting to leave Iraq had created a humanitarian catastrophe. In the words of a Jewish witness,

I can only add that thousands of them literally face starvation, having sold all their belongings and expended the last penny of it, in the expectation of an early departure. [NEAT has] proved utterly inadequate to cope with the situation.[585]

Even after "the onset of winter [further worsened] the sufferings of those Jews," Israel not only continued to forbid any assistance, but threatened that it would impound any aircraft that tried to help—as it had already done to two aircraft of Britain's Eagle Aviation Limited when they landed in Lydda bringing Jews from Tehran.

Why was Israel claiming a life-or-death crisis to save Iraqi Jews from massacre at the hands of their countrymen, yet threatening other countries not to help save them, even as the uprooting now left tens of thousands of them homeless, freezing, and starving? As long as Israel blocked any airline but NEAT, the money it sought was irrelevant: no amount of donations raised could help NEAT ferry the new refugees any faster.

Some premonition of what was going on in Iraq might have been seen in a series of bombings in the West Bank villages of Nablus and East Jerusalem in September (1950), which at first baffled the Jordanians, who suspected communists or fighters loyal to the ex-Mufti, but proved to be a covert Israeli sabotage and espionage operation.

And so it was with the Iraqi anti-Jewish violence. The Iraqi pogroms were exposed as an Israeli false flag operation to force Iraqi Jews to become human facts-on-the-ground for Israel's stolen land beyond Partition. NEAT turned out to be an Israeli outfit, founded jointly by El Al and the owner of Alaskan Airlines, its name designed to obscure identification. As a bonus, the "rescue" furthered the Israeli narrative of a world inhospitable for Jews.[586]

The scheme began to unravel in the summer of 1950 when an Israeli from Acre was recognized in Baghdad by a Palestinian refugee. His arrest led to others and, by June of 1951, to the exposing of the Iraqi operation. The police were led to a vast cache of arms, maps, and Zionist materials, including 426 hand grenades, 33 Tommy-guns, 186 pistols, 24,764 bullets, 97 machine gun magazines, and 32 daggers, all spread out among three Baghdad synagogues and two houses. Further arrests led to the trials of two accused bombers of what the police called the Shoura and Tnua terror organizations. In confiscated documents, one of the defendants had written that the café grenade that started the panic "had very good effect," and congratulated his colleagues on successfully defeating those Jews who had tried to counter the hysteria. The Zionist terror cell, training for which began at age thirteen, was held responsible for Iraq's bombings.

In response, the World Jewish Congress claimed the scandal was part of an anti-Jewish conspiracy and blamed the Muslim Brotherhood. But the Iraqi police were in contact with the US Embassy, a CIA official was present, and the British carefully monitored the proceedings, as well as the evidence, protocol, and even the quality of the special court's president.

British witness P.A. Rhodes reported that the trial was conducted fairly, that there was no evidence to support Israeli claims that the defendants were tortured or that there was any "irregular procedure" by the court. Nothing, he wrote, suggested that the two principal suspects "were anything but guilty of the charges preferred against them." The explosive devices used in the bombings matched those discovered in the underground caches, and the leaflets warning Jews to flee were written with a typewriter found with the suspects. Among the documents was a letter from Yigal Allon, who would become chief of staff of the IDF and Israeli Foreign Minister, expressing satisfaction that he had been able to transfer arms into Iraq.[587]

The two principal conspirators were sentenced to death. Fifteen of twenty-one accomplices were given sentences as long as life imprisonment, and as short as (in the case of three girls) five months, including time already spent in detention. Six defendants were found not guilty.

In Israel, crowded, dismal refugee camps greeted the approximately one hundred twenty thousand ex-Iraqi Jews ethnically cleansed by Israel, their situation made all the worse when hundreds of their tents were destroyed by a particularly strong mid-December gale. For the sake of the settler state, Zionism had within two years destroyed a vibrant Jewish community dating back two and a half millennia.[588]

When the "false flag" Lavon affair broke a few years later (pages 350-352, below), the Israeli Defense Minister commented that the method had first been tried in Iraq. Teddy Kollek, who was close to then-PM Ben-Gurion, defended the ethnic cleansing of Iraqi Jews by arguing that it was "better for a country to be homogeneous."

The US was not amused. "It was one thing," State Dept official George McGhee remarked, "to take Jews from all over the world who were in distress, but it was another matter entirely to attempt to create circumstances which would stimulate immigration of Jews from areas where they were living in peace." Thus when Israel next set its sight on the Jews of Iran, State Dept official G. Lewis Jones warned Israel that the US State Dept "would not favor a deliberately generated exodus there along the lines of the ingathering from Iraq." Israel refuses to release documents relating to the operation.[589]

Purge of North African Jews

Israel also turned to North Africa's Jewish communities to quench its need for ethnically-correct settlers. As described by Haganah member Hanna Braun, sent to Eliat in 1952 to process arriving Arab Jews and teach them Hebrew, the North African immigrants had not abandoned their homes because of persecution, but as a result of propaganda, intimidation, and false-flag "Arab" terrorism. A punitive Israeli exit tax and loss of original citizenship kept many from returning home once the deceit was exposed. Since these were not European Jews, they "were sprayed with DDT at the port of entry and then crammed into extremely primitive reception camps," shipped to the army for three years, then settled in the frontier regions with their lesser infrastructure and greater risk of violence across the Armistice Line.[590]

Perhaps the most extreme form of official Israeli racism against non-Europeans Jews was its mass kidnapping of Mizrahi (Middle Eastern) newborns. The infants were taken from their mothers and given to Ashkenazi couples, while their parents were told that the child had died. However suspicious the circumstances surrounding their newborn's disappearance and supposed death, the parents could prove nothing, and the practice persisted through Israel's first decade.

Bitter resentment against their uprooting and treatment led Mizrahi Jews to form a resistance group named the Black Panthers.

What did you do, Ben-Gurion? victims railed in song.

> *Would that we had come riding on a donkey and we hadn't arrived here*
> *yet! Woe, what a black hour it was! To hell with the plane that brought*
> *us here!*

The consummate cynicism of Israel's uprooting of Middle Eastern
and North African Jews from their homelands is that the Israeli
state now uses its ethnic cleansing of both Jews and Palestinians as
a racial settling of scores. The former balanced out the latter—the
same injustice having been committed against both "races," the logic
goes, the Palestinians have no grievance.[591]

Two years in: the Palestinian lands, and Israel

Ambassador Kirkbride visited the northern West Bank village of
Nablus in the summer of 1950 and described the situation there as
"gloomy indeed." Its most cultivable land had been taken by Israel,
and commodities now had to be imported through Beirut at great
expense. Malaria was increasing, and the refugees were crowded
into unfit tents that offered little protection against the winter.
Nonetheless, there was calm and order in the West Bank, or as Glubb
described it, "the appearance of normality."

> Crime statistics are lower than in the days of the Mandate—
> apparently in contrast to Israel which seems to be suffering from a
> crime wave. The low incidence of crime in Arab Palestine is especially
> remarkable in view of the great fall in the standard of living since
> Mandate days and the presence of tens of thousands of homeless
> refugees.[592]

Gaza was more horrific still. As described by a Quaker aid worker,
the people of the Gaza Strip

> who owned fields [that are now] in no-man's land … have, from
> sheer desperation, plowed … as close to the Jewish lines [Armistice,
> not Partition] as it was possible to go … In doing so, they braved

the very determined efforts of the Jews [who have] shot and killed
various men, women, cows, sheep, camels, donkeys, and so forth.[593]

Another Quaker witness spoke of the "wretched cave, tent or hovel"
that the displaced "have called home" since their expulsion. The IDF
itself was blunt: it had "condemned to complete extinction" those it
had made refugees in Gaza, and the Red Cross reported that about
ten children were dying every day from hunger and cold.

Desperate, some refugees risked a nocturnal crossing to Hebron
(West Bank), passing charred animal carcasses that were a constant
reminder that they might get blown up by land mines even before
risking Israeli soldiers. Those who survived were greeted in Hebron
by a somewhat less horrific situation and a typhus epidemic. In one
incident of May, 1950, recorded without further explanation, "two
Egyptian aircraft arrived unannounced at Kolundia [Kalandia, West
Bank] and dumped two loads of destitute [Gazan] refugees on the
runway."

In the north, more stories of desperation: non-Jews ethnically
cleansed by Israel into southern Lebanon "had to brave IDF fire
when they crossed the lines to forage for food" in what had been
their homeland—these the words of an Israeli settler.[594]

The Kingdom of Israel
Neither Lehi nor the Irgun continued to exist as such, but some Lehi
veterans formed a new terror group, the Kingdom of Israel (or Tzrifin
Underground), supplementing their ranks with sixteen-to-eighteen
year olds who were raised with the gang's heroic myths.

When in 1953 some of its members were caught and put on trial,
twenty-seven year old Zeev Yevin, son of the writer and historian
Yehoshua Yevin, was among those who told the court he had been
raised to believe in a "Kingdom of Israel." The defendant charged
with bombing the Soviet legation in Tel Aviv was ex-Lehi member
Yaacov Heruti, who had served in the military police and was the
son of the president of Israel's Supreme Military Court. He claimed
to have created the Shakespeare volume that killed Rex Farran. Even
the Lehi veterans could be young: on trial also was 24-year-old Yaffa

Dromi, who as a teenager had been a Lehi radio announcer.

The Kingdom's repertoire included the bombing of the Czech Consulate (December 5, 1952) and Soviet Legation (February 9, 1953), and two attempts on the life of Konrad Adenauer (March 28 and June 24, 1952). On April 16, 1953, as the violinist Jascha Heifetz exited a taxi at Jerusalem's King David Hotel after a performance, he was attacked with an iron pipe by an unidentified Kingdom of Israel member for having programmed Richard Strauss' violin sonata. Heifetz suffered an injured right wrist, causing him to cancel a Tel Aviv concert scheduled for the following day. As Heifetz maintained that he would perform whatever music he wished, Kol Radio received a telephone warning that he would be killed unless he left Israel.

The gang was also suspected in an attempt to burn the Russian Minister's car, throwing a hand grenade into the Czechoslovakian legation, and burning shops that sold non-Kosher meat. Convicted Kingdom of Israel operatives were briefly imprisoned: repeating history, Israel commuted their sentences.

The name *Irgun* did pop up now and then, for example in England on the morning of July 25, 1952, when Harold MacMichael, targeted by a letter bomb five years earlier, received a new threat to his life, "day or night, walking or sleeping," signed "I.Z.L." But although a British report that year described the Irgun as "still very much a force," there is little evidence of it beyond a brand franchise, a glamorous, nostalgic identity to affix to individual initiatives of extra-state terror.[595]

Aside from some Kingdom of Israel vigilantism along the West Bank Armistice Line, these vestiges of Mandate-era terror militias were short-lived and uninvolved with the new state's expansionism. That expansionism was the charge of the Israeli military, whose recruits were taken on training patrols into Palestinian territory in order to "overcome their conscience," as the marginalized peace group Agudat Ihud put it, and to get accustomed to killing. When parents who heard about the nature of the training their children were getting asked Agudat Ihud to bring their complaints to the government anonymously, Ben-Gurion, whose diary proves that he himself ordered such missions, dismissed the accusations as "imaginary and without foundation."[596]

Israel's expulsions of non-Jews continued "at the whim of the Israeli police or District Administration," as Kirkbride put it, and by making life so miserable that it is "impossible for any Arab to contemplate spending a lifetime under Israeli rule." But if stories of abuse "reduced the earlier determination of the refugees to go home," it did not stop them. Many tried, despite risking beatings, torture, rape, and murder. In mid-1949, an IDF intelligence officer spoke of the "hundreds" of Palestinians attempting to return home to the villages of Western Galilee (which by UN Resolution 181 was Palestine, not Israel) that were rounded up and "liquidated by military order"—tied to a tree and shot in the head being one documented method. In his study of declassified Zionist archives, Benny Morris determined that

> Israeli troops more or less routinely beat captured infiltrators [people attempting to return home], sometimes torturing them, and occasionally raped and/or murdered them.[597]

This continued with impunity because of "the pervasive attitude among the Israeli public that Arab life was cheap," and that the

> killing, torturing, beating, and raping of Arab infiltrators was, if not permitted, at least not particularly reprehensible…[598]

Statehood did not end the rape of Palestinian girls and women by Israeli soldiers, such as one early documented case that began on August 22, 1949. Israeli soldiers machine-gunned dead a Bedouin man for sport as he fled in fear, unarmed, up a sand dune, killed six of the Bedouins' camels, and kidnapped a girl whose age was estimated to be between ten and (more likely) fifteen. They took her to the IDF camp, stripped her naked, and forced her to stand under a water pipe while the men rubbed her body with soap. Three soldiers then raped her. After the Sabbath meal, the platoon commander got involved: he ordered soldiers to cut her hair and wash what was left in kerosene, and for her again to be displayed under the shower pipe. The girl was then gang-raped over a period of three days, at times leaving her unconscious. Pecking order was decided by the commander: Squad A on day one, Squad B on day two, Squad C on day three.

When they finished, they dug her grave right in front of her eyes before shooting her.[599]

In 2003 this atrocity surfaced in the Israeli and British press, reported as though it were a dark secret newly unearthed, a regrettable aberration of the fledgling state, terrible but singular. As would become a pattern, the state insulated itself by passing blame onto the war's Jewish survivors: these were IDF soldiers, yes, but they were World War II DPs, and thus they were something apart, of "low professional and moral level," as it was reported—yet the elite Palmach and "cultured officers" were specifically cited by soldiers as eager participants in such crimes. Israel's final violence against the girl was the exploitation of her memory for the state's ritual absolution, burying its sin in the Negev along with its victim, name unknown.[600]

In 1950, Ben-Gurion still referred to an IDF battalion as "prone to" raping and murdering Arab girls. On March 16 of that year, three Palestinian children, two girls and a boy, were kidnapped from the Gaza Strip by Israeli soldiers. The soldiers gang-raped both girls, then murdered all three children. When the villagers responded to the atrocity with an ambush on an IDF car, Israel mortared the village.

We do know the name of a 26 year old woman kidnapped and blindfolded by an Israeli patrol five months later, on August 15: Khadija bint Suleiman. Khadija was picking fruit in her family's own grove, but which the Armistice Line had orphaned onto the Israeli side. Held at the Israeli police station in Abu Gosh, she was beaten and raped by four Israeli constables. When both the Red Cross and UNRWA confirmed the charge, Israel accused the ICRC of disseminating "anti-Israel propaganda" and called for the removal of the Red Cross representative.[601]

Another organization with which Israel was frequently at odds was the Mixed Armistice Commission (MAC), created by the United Nations to supervise the truce that ended the 1948 war. Composed of separate organizations for each of Israel's four *de facto* (but not actual) borders—Lebanon, Syria, Jordan, and Egypt—each of the five countries had a representative, and UN observers monitored the borders and investigated complaints. Records demonstrate that complaints were given a fair hearing and investigators were thorough, though the MAC had no power of enforcement. One of the early issues the MAC investigated became known as the Wadi Araba incident.

The Wadi Araba incident

In the first days of June, 1950, eighty-seven half-dead naked men and boys as young as seven began turning up on the western frontier of southern Jordan, the Wadi Araba desert region to the south of the Dead Sea. They were the survivors of about one hundred twenty "infiltrators" seized by Israel in various parts of the land under its control and marched into this desert to their likely deaths. Approximately thirty-four of the victims perished, among them at least two girls, one who did not survive the desert and another who the IDF shot dead when she attempted to escape.[602]

Israel had conducted such forced marches during its 1948 ethnic cleansing, in which children and the elderly in particular perished. The Wadi Araba expulsion was exceptional, however, in that many of the victims survived when found by Bedouin and Arab Legion patrols, and that their stories were documented and corroborated. Two years into Israeli statehood, these accounts offer an unparalleled examination of Palestinian "infiltrators," who they were, their motivations, how Israel dealt with them, and how Israeli media reported it. Since they were arrested over a wide area and over a period of several months, we can assume that they are a representative sampling of such people. Three chroniclers interviewed the survivors: a representative from the International Red Cross, a Belgian observer from the MAC, and a correspondent from The *Observer* (UK). Fifty-one survivors are accounted for in forty-nine interviews by these three observers. The survivors' stories closely corroborated.[603]

In late May, the prisoners were collected into a camp at Katra (near Rehovot)—"a concentration camp in Israel run on Nazi lines," as Kirkbride described the facility. All were suffering from extreme malnutrition; many had been tortured. Early on the morning of Wednesday, May 31, they were blindfolded and loaded onto two trucks, with no water or other supplies, and driven south under Israeli soldier escort fore and aft. Later that day they reached a military camp which they surmised was near Beersheba. An Israeli woman from a southern kibbutz witnessed their arrival:[604]

> Two large trucks arrived, packed with blindfolded Arabs [men, women, children] … The way the Arabs were crowded together [on the trucks] was inhuman … Those of us standing nearby had witnessed no bad behaviour on the part of the Arabs, who sat frightened, almost one on top of the other. [Then one or more of the soldiers] jumped up and began to … hit [the Arabs] across their blindfolded eyes and when he had finished, he stamped on all of them and then, in the end, laughed uproariously and with satisfaction at his heroism…

"I ask," the woman from the kibbutz finished, "does this not remind us exactly of the Nazi acts towards the Jews?" Having already endured the long drive in the heat, the prisoners asked for water. The Israeli soldiers brought water and—the Palestinians' blindfolds now removed so that they could see—"poured it away on the ground in front of the Arabs." None of the roughly sixty people in each of the two trucks were allowed to descend, not even "to relieve nature."

Blindfolded again, they were trucked several more hours. About midnight, blindfolds removed, they found themselves at "completely uninhabited desert." The soldiers ordered them to walk into it. As summarized from the interviews,

> The general direction indicated to them seemed to be south-east. They were told that anyone who ran north would be shot. This procedure was then applied, the men being taken forward in groups of four. As each party ran off into the darkness, bursts of fire were opened on them by the Jews.[605]

The interviewers described the spot as "one of the hottest, wildest and most utterly desolate areas in the world," and "is infested by snakes, wolves and hyenas, so that the missing persons may well have been eaten by wild animals." The post nearest to where they were released was Dhahal, about ten miles away, but none of them found it in under 36 hours since it lay east-north-east. "Others walked 25 to 28 miles and climbed a range of mountains 3000 feet high, before arriving at inhabited country in the vicinity of Shobek."[606]

All were weak from hunger and extreme thirst. Many were suffering from torture, including beatings, whipping, teeth smashed off by rifle butts, hearing loss from beatings on the ears, and fingernails torn out. Some adults who collapsed along the way had to be abandoned by those still conscious in order to save the children among them.

Yet the Wadi Araba incident might have slipped by little noticed had the journalist Philip Toynbee not been passing through Amman and heard of the survivors. The *Observer* published his shocking account in which Toynbee, who had been a supporter of Zionism, now compared the Israeli regime to Nazi Germany.[607]

Who were these "infiltrators"?

All but four of the survivors who were interviewed (these representing 42.5% of those pushed into the desert) had been ethnically cleansed by Israel and were attempting either to reach the West Bank from Gaza, or to reach their homes in an attempt to rejoin their families or retrieve property (hidden cash or grain). For all but four, starvation resulting from the ethnic cleansing was the common driving force: fathers or sons hoping to save their starving families. For two of the remaining four, the desert march was itself their ethnic cleansing. They had escaped the 1948 purge. The last two were chance outsiders, a man from Sudan making a pilgrimage to Hebron, and a student at Al-Azhar University in Cairo en route to his home in Tira to get money to complete his studies.*

After Toynbee's exposé, the *Jerusalem Post* repeated the government denial. These infiltrators posed a grave threat to Israel, yet they had been well treated. Still with three hours before sunset, they had been released to an Arab Legion post directly in front of

---

* The author's summary of the individual interviews is available at paldocs.net.

them. But as Israel denied everything publicly, it placated US unease by claiming that an investigation was in progress—and indeed, an internal Israeli memo advised the government simply to "promise an inquiry in order to settle things down."[608]

The systematic expulsion of non-Jews continued: 5,548 people were known to have been pushed over the Line in the half year ending January, 1951, or one every forty-seven minutes. Atrocities were white-washed by the government to the extent of forging victims' statements, and "the brutality," Glubb noted, "is too general to be due only to the sadism of ordinary soldiers." For example, when on the night of October 20, 1950, IDF soldiers seized and tortured seven Palestinians in the (predominantly Christian) town of Jish in upper Galilee, some suffering severe injuries, they did so under the leadership of the local military governor.[609]

The Yalu village incident, November 2, 1950

"I came from Deir Ayyub and live with my family in Yalu village. Yesterday morning my son Ali, my daughter Fakhriyeh, and my niece Khadijeh went to the southern side of Yalu to gather wood." So began the translated testimony of thirty-two year old Mohamad Ali Mohamad, a native of Deir Ayyub ethnically cleansed by Israel two years earlier, now a refugee in Yalu. Mohamad's son Ali was twelve years old; his daughter Fakhriyeh, ten.

As recounted by the niece, eight-year-old Khadijeh,

> After sunrise my cousin Ali and his sister Fakhriyeh … and I went to the old Legion trenches to the south of Yalu to gather wood. While we were collecting wood below the trenches, I saw someone looking at us. I could only see the upper part of him, I mean his head and shoulders. I called to my cousin Ali "This is a Jew", and I ran away.

Bullets raced past her as she ran, one hitting her in the leg. Her father, Mohamad's younger brother Abd El Hamid Ali, heard them:

> I heard shots about 200 yards from my house. I got up to see what was the matter, and [my daughter] Khadijeh saw me. She was crying

and shouting and had a bullet in her left leg above the knee. I found
out from her that she had been collecting wood with her cousins Ali
and Fakhrieh to the south of Yalu and that the Jews had come on
them there. She had escaped ...

He ran the direction of the two children while Khadijeh ran to tell
her uncle, their father, and was then attended to with iodine. Both
brothers now stood on a hilltop at the south end of Yalu from where
they could see the children in the distance, being taken away by
twelve Israeli soldiers.

The younger brother:

> I looked southwards from the top of the hill and saw about 12 Jews
> north of Deir Ayyub. The distance between us was about 400 yards;
> I could see the two children Ali and Fakhrieh with them, and they
> all went to the village school south of the main road.

It need not even be said that the men's instinct was to race to save
the children from the soldiers—but both knew without question
that they would not live to reach them, that the very attempt would
instead further endanger them. All they could do was watch and hope.

The younger brother continued:

> There near the olive grove I saw them place the two children and
> stand to the north of them. Then I heard about seven shots [and] I
> saw the two children fall to the ground when they were shot at.[610]

Even now, their only chance of reaching the bodies was to keep
vigil for an opportunity to avoid the Israel soldiers. To quote from
the formal report:

> It is indicative of the terror which the Israel Army have infused into
> the Arab civilians living near the demarcation line, that no one, not
> even the children's father and uncle who witnessed the crime, dared
> to go down the hillside to where the bodies lay, until dusk ... they
> had to go down a hill-side to the wadi-bed, a distance of about half-

a-mile in full view of the Israel Army post at Bab El Wad, close to
the main road … only a few hundred yards from the Israel troops;
and to climb that exposed hill-side again burdened with the bodies
of the two children.

They found Ali dead, with two bullets in his head and neck. Fakhriyeh
had been shot four times but was still breathing. The uncle carried
the boy's body back, while Mohamad carried his daughter, who was
brought to a hospital in Ramallah.*

There she made a statement to the authorities:

> This morning I went with my brother Ali and my cousin Khadijeh
> to Yalu lands to gather wood. Suddenly six armed Jews came upon
> us. Khadijeh ran away. They shot at her but I don't know if they hit
> her or not. They caught me and my brother Ali and took us down
> to the Wadi near Yalu and near our village. There they shot us with
> their stens … After that the Jews left us and went away by the road.
> I remained near my brother all day till my uncle Abd El Hamid Ali
> and my father Mohamad Ali and other people came. They brought
> us away. I don't know what happened after that.

Fakhriyeh died at six o'clock the next morning.

Only a tiny fraction of Israeli atrocities were witnessed by outsiders. Like Wadi Araba, this was an exception: it was witnessed and
corroborating testimony by two of the victims was recorded by the
authorities—*and* the atrocity hit the British press, saddling Israel
with another public relations problem. Questions were raised in the
House of Commons, and the British Zionist establishment's denials
convinced few (Israel briefly tried the story that the children had
been caught in cross-fire).

Yalu village itself was attacked less than three months later, on
January 29 1951, by about sixteen Israeli soldiers descending on

1951

---

* The author has relied on the witnesses' actual testimony in British archives rather
than the Arab Legion report, which appears to inadvertently confuse a few details,
e.g., that the children were shot in the ditch where they were discovered, as well as
Fakhriyeh's age.

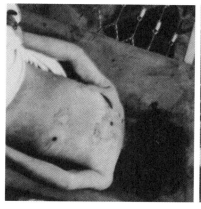

The bodies of of ten-year-old Fakhriyeh and twelve-year old Ali, murdered execution-style by the Israel Defense Forces on November 2, 1950 near Yalu village. [TNA, FO 371/82209].

the village from two directions while attacking with gunfire and grenades. In 1967 Israel ethnically cleansed and leveled Yalu, and Israel's Canada Park now stands on its ruins and those of neighboring Deir Ayyub and Beit Nuba.[611]

Sharafat

The Tulkarm area was invaded by Israeli soldiers on the night of February 2, and the following day the IDF killed three Palestinians in an attack on Saffa. The attacks then grew bolder. On the night of February 7, the soldiers invaded Sharafat, near Jerusalem, and blew up two houses, killing thirteen and wounding five. Twelve of those killed were women and children, and more than half were under fifteen.

When a special MAC meeting was called the next day to address the Sharafat massacre, the Israeli representative insisted that it be put at the bottom of the list of outstanding matters and walked out when this was not agreed to. The UN Information Officer confirmed that the attack was carried out by the Israeli army with Israeli army equipment, but that "in view of the Israeli delegation's attitude there was no likelihood of M.A.C. being able to do anything in the matter."

Next, Beit Nuba and Emmaus—like Yalu, depopulated by Israel sixteen years later—were attacked, but successfully defended by the

National Guard. The village of Falma, however, was too small to have either police or National Guard. "In the small hours of the morning of February 9," an Israeli patrol slipped about two kilometers inside Jordanian territory and attacked the small village. As reported by the Arab Legion,

> Failing apparently to achieve any bloodshed, they then knocked down the door of a house and threw in a handgrenade, killing a man, his son and daughter, who were asleep in bed.

The targets were apparently random, and no explanation was offered.[612]

The Sharafat massacre followed "a period of mounting attacks against Arab villages," as the *Manchester Guardian* reported. The paper, which had for years been staunchly pro-Zionist, now suggested that Israel was engaged in a "deliberate terroristic policy" against the Palestinians, whereas *Haaretz* defended the attacks even as it acknowledged that the victims were innocent. Most tellingly, the liberal Israeli paper claimed that events perhaps justified "the ultimate acquisition by Israel of Arab Palestine"—that is, that Israel should annex the West Bank and Gaza. When Israel did precisely that in 1967, it ethnically cleansed much of Sharafat to build Gilo settlement, and as Gilo expanded, it further destroyed Sharafat's non-Jewish homes, vineyards, and orchards to make way. [613]

A week after Sharafat, Jordanian officials, hoping to establish frontier cooperation, met in Jerusalem with Israel's General Mordechai Maklef, a veteran of notorious Operation Hiram and soon to become Israeli Chief of Staff. When Maklef blamed the troubles on infiltrators, the Jordanian representatives asked for more information. In response, the General "waved his arm in a noble gesture and said he was prepared to forgive us." Similarly, when at a MAC meeting the Israeli representative was asked why they made their allegations difficult for the MAC to investigate, he answered that since the Arabs knew what they did, why should Israel have to give any details?[614]

The investigative journalist Colin Reid published an analysis of Israel's interaction with the MAC in January (1951). His conclusions mirrored those of British government documents which he could not have seen. "As a matter of policy," he found, "details were not published or reported to the authorities. Only the charge was reported, and often too late to follow up." Israel constantly varied its claims, no two statements coinciding, with even the place names changing, so that a single claim appeared to be many claims. The allegations were filed as much as five months after the alleged incidents, and accompanied by artificial complaints of Palestinian aggression so as to "considerably obscure the issue" to the press. Allegations never bore any date of origin or filing, rarely indicated the date of the act complained of, and were submitted in batches. In concert with these methods, Israel subjected Palestinian charges to "skillfully constructed procedural obstruction."[615]

On April 2, an Israeli patrol attacked four unarmed Palestinians collecting brushwood near Hebron; two escaped, but the bodies of the other two, aged eighteen and sixty-two, were later recovered by the MAC and IRC investigators. The IDF had cut off their sexual organs, skinned their buttocks, stabbed their sides with bayonets, and fired Sten gun rounds into their skulls.[616]

In the north, Israel was illegally draining Lake Hula and continued to do so in defiance of the UN and threat of US sanctions, both of which had proven impotent. Ben-Gurion, in New York in May (1951), reiterated Israel's refusal to address the Palestinian land it had stolen beyond the Partition, and stated that it would take all the demilitarized zones as well.

For a moment, it appeared that Israel had finally gone too far when it pirated aircraft parts from a US vessel, prompting the State Department to withhold arms exports. But this was quickly reversed: the US Congress instead prepared an unconditional grant of $150m to Israel, leading US Secretary of Labor Maurice Tobin, then in Israel, to propose that the grant at least be contingent on Israel abiding by UN Resolutions. This, too, failed.[617]

Idna, the target of several earlier attacks, was invaded again on the 23rd of May. Khirbet Najjar, two kilometers (1.24 miles) inside the West Bank, was attacked on July 11 by six to eight Israeli soldiers who threw grenades into a house, killing an eight-year-old girl and wounding her brother and mother. An Israeli patrol penetrated to the south-eastern end of the Dead Sea on September 25 and blew up a house in Ghor Safi village, killing a twelve-year-old girl and her mother as they slept inside, and wounding a boy and two women.[618]

Eastern Christmas Eve in the village of Christ's birth, 1952

A tragedy unfolded at the end of 1951 which, like the Wadi Araba incident, illustrates the Israeli state's need for a perceived external threat and the manipulation of news and information. It demonstrates, further, how Israel's need for a crime to confirm to its political constructs can mean that it must deliberately fail to solve the crime. It began with the rape and murder of a young Israeli woman from the town of Malha.

On December 4, eighteen-year-old Lea Festinger disappeared. Twenty-two days later, her body was discovered in a cave. There were no tracks, as rains had flooded the area, no evidence, and no suspects. "Arab infiltrators" were, however, automatically blamed. Similarly, when on the night of December 30 a woman in Jerusalem was murdered, the "notoriously overworked and understaffed" Israeli police blamed "Arab infiltrators" because someone claimed to have seen "men in torn khaki clothes" in the area.

Yet Israel's ongoing domestic violent crime, including rape, was so rampant that when Lea Festinger's body was discovered, even the *Jerusalem Post* warned against using "infiltrators" as scapegoats:

> Murder, rape and robbery in Israel have taken on alarming proportions. By no means all the incidents can be blamed on infiltrators or remnants of war psychosis among either immigrants or old timers … we are faced with a political situation in which no crime is too crude or pathological to be exploited.[619]

"Intolerance," as a British report noted, "explodes into violence with appalling ease in Israel." Nonetheless, Jordan, aware that West Bankers were the presumed suspects, immediately asked Israel "for any evidence they might have about the murderer so that steps could be taken." Israel replied that there "was no need for Arabs to bother with evidence," since "we have our own methods of dealing with this sort of thing."[620]

Those "methods" came on the night of Eastern Christmas Eve, January 6: three attacks surrounding Bethlehem, timed to coincide with the start of the great midnight procession to the Church of the Nativity in this predominantly Christian area and the site of Christ's birth.

As one Israeli patrol blew up a house near Beit Jala, about two kilometers west of Bethlehem, another bombed two houses one kilometer north of Bethlehem, near the Greek Orthodox monastery of Mar Elias. A third IDF patrol crossed three kilometers (1.85 miles) of no man's land in the Latrun Salient and opened fire on the village of Imwas. (Fifteen years later, Imwas would be leveled on the orders of Yitzhak Rabin).

It happened that some British MPs had come for the Christmas Eve procession, and so there were early outside witnesses to the carnage. The MAC's US Commander E. H. Hutchison was there as well: "No person could live long enough," he wrote, "to become calloused to such a sight" of massacred men, women, and children.[621]

Israeli leaflets, printed on pink paper by cyclostyle, were scattered in Beit Jala and Mar Elias, announcing that the attacks were in retaliation for the rape and murder of the Jewish girl on December 4. The leaflets were identical except for the name of the accused village.[622]

Israel frames its Christmas Eve victims

Israel, to be sure, had never named any suspects for Lea Festinger's murderer, and had still not named a single suspect when at the next MAC meeting the Jordanian representative put on record the names of the Christmas Eve victims. Upon presenting the Committee members with the names of the dead, an extraordinary fraud took place openly, but for which the MAC could do nothing:

> Some minutes after the occupants of the demolished houses were named in the MAC by the Jordan representative, one of the Israeli representatives left the room and returned with a slip of paper on

1952

Above: Bethlehem area, Eastern Christmas morning (January 7), 1952.
Victims of the Christmas Eve massacre are pulled from the rubble.

Below: cyclostyle leaflet scattered at Mar Elias framing that village for the
murder of Lea Festinger, the same as those left at Beit Jala except for the
name of the village. [TNA, FO 371/98490]

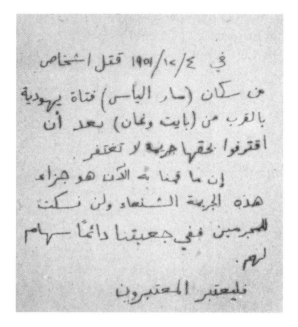

which were written three names, allegedly those of the Jewish girl's murderers: they were those of the householders just previously named by Jordan as the victims of the assault. The Senior Israeli delegate then said: "We have the names of the people who carried out [the rape and murder], but I did not want to pass them on before."[623]

And so Israel posthumously framed three of its Christmas eve victims for Lea Festinger's rape and murder. Spreading the lie to the media, Israel announced that the houses blown up on Christmas Eve "appeared to be inhabited by the three infiltrators whose names were given [by Israel to] the Jordanian delegation as responsible." As would happen again whenever Israeli aggression required framing a particular area or village for a particular crime, the fraud meant that the actual murderer had to remain free. Even the attempt to solve the crime would lay bare the official lie.

As for the soldiers responsible for the Christmas Eve massacre, Ramati, the Israeli representative, refused to do anything, telling the MAC that the Armistice agreement only provides for prevention. The MAC chairman suspected that the Christmas eve atrocities were "intended to provoke Arab hostilities which would be capitalised abroad by the Israelis."[624]

A week after the Bethlehem massacre, on January 13th, a father and son working on the lands of Cremisan, the area near Bethlehem known for its wine, were seized by nine IDF soldiers, "taken into the Israel area, and butchered." Five days later, three villagers working a vegetable plot (on the Israeli side, but under agreement) were murdered in similar fashion, "marched a few hundred metres further into Israel [i.e., to make them 'infiltrators'] and gunned down at point-blank range." The same formula was used in the murder of two more villagers the next day. Between February and May, thirty-nine Israeli attacks on the West Bank were recorded, involving the murder of civilians, including farmers asleep in their field, the targeting of UN observers, theft of livestock, and kidnappings.[625]

On May 7, about a kilometer inside Jordanian territory between Qaffin and Nazlot Issa, an Israeli patrol of about thirty-two soldiers opened fire on harvesters at a range of about 200 yards, among them a sixty-year-old woman too feeble to run. On the night of May 20, an Israel patrol laid a delayed-action mine against a house on the outskirts of Qaffin village (northwest Palestine). When it exploded at about 1:30 in the morning, a sixteen-year-old boy and two children aged five and six were killed outright, and a baby of one and a half years died while being extracted from the rubble. The father was asleep in his field, having left the teenage son to take care of the family in his absence. As in distant Bethlehem, leaflets were again left behind announcing that the bombing was retribution for the murder of a Jewish girl.

A senior Belgian UN observer joined those warning that Israel was attacking in order to create a war:

> Jews are deliberately working up the tension and the shooting with a view to provoking the Arab Legion to retaliate and then blaming us and starting up the war again.[626]

Mt. Scopus and the "barrel" incident

Relations between Israel and the United Nations reached a crisis in June of 1952 over Mt. Scopus, an area in northeast Jerusalem that lay on the Palestinian side of the Armistice Line but which Israel occupied. The UN tolerated Israel's occupation of Mt. Scopus with the stipulation that it not be militarized. Israel, however, was digging trenches along the hill, defying UN demands that it stop, and was smuggling in weapons.

It was caught on June 4, when one of its convoys heading for Mt. Scopus was stopped at the UN border crossing at the Mandelbaum Gate, and a UN guard dipped a test rod into one of the oil drums it was transporting. The rod struck a "heavy object concealed beneath." As the drum was removed from the truck to be checked, the Israeli driver pretended to have engine trouble, pushed the truck to make it roll toward the Israeli check post, jumped in, and escaped with the rest of the evidence.

After much deliberation, it was agreed that the impounded barrel would be opened on June 20 at half past noon, in front of international observers and representatives from Israel and Jordan.

For safekeeping until then, it was rolled into the bathroom of the MAC headquarters and locked.

That meeting, however, never took place. As described by US Commander Hutchison, at noon on the appointed day,

> the door of the MAC office burst open and three Israeli officers, with pistols drawn and escorted by two enlisted men who were holding Thompson sub-machine guns at the ready, marched into the room.[627]

The Israelis commandeered the UN office, prevented the examination of the barrel, replaced the MAC's key to the bathroom with their own, kept guard over UN personnel and answered the UN's phones. The MAC itself now hijacked by Israel, MAC personnel kept vigil by the door, taking turns throughout the night to prevent any action going unwitnessed. Israel's next move was its smokescreen: it issued an *Aide Memoire* requesting "the immediate replacement of the United Nations Personnel involved in this disreputable incident."

A new date was set—July 10—to open the barrel, now with the presence of Israel's friend, US General William Riley, Commander of the UN Truce Supervision Organization. With Riley in charge, Israel had no objections to proceeding. When as before the rod struck a significant object inside the barrel, to everyone's astonishment Riley declared that it would be returned to Israel unopened—"against violent opposition by [MAC chairman Colonel] de Ridder and Sloan and against the views of almost his whole staff." As Hutchison explained, Riley's action made the entire peace-keeping endeavor meaningless, since Israel's violations carried no risk. Foreseeing the barrel incident "win" as another watershed in Israeli intransigence, the British in Jerusalem warned the Foreign Office that "the Israeli use of force has thus paid handsome dividend and I fear the consequences may be far-reaching."[628]

Describing Israel's occupation of Mt. Scopus as "a dangerous anomaly," officials wrote in despair of their inability "to bring the Israelis to heel." Some advocated the suspension of UN convoys to Mt. Scopus until Israel cooperated, but this, too, was not pursued because of the surety that Israel would respond with force. In the words of Commander Hutchison—who by his own account had gone to the Middle East pro-Israel—"had the Jordanians been guilty of these deeds, Israel would have spelled them out in banner headlines from Baghdad to Fresno."[629]

Israel's ethnic cleansing of Palestinians continued both by force and by making "it so uncomfortable for its remaining Arabs," as the CIA reported in late 1952, "that eventually they will all try to emigrate." Among those methods, Bedouin were forced to sign "requests" to move to Jordan, under the threat of expulsion to un-productive desert if they refused. In another method, witnessed by Hutchison, the IDF broke and ignited benzene-filled beer bottles over the humps of their camels, burning the animals alive in order to make even the hides unsalvageable.

Moshe Dayan stuck to the script of an existential threat: According to Kollek, Dayan had his soldiers chase Bedouin in jeeps, firing at them and killing several in order to provoke them to attack army patrols—which "was what Dayan was looking for," giving him the "reason" to wage a "mopping up campaign." The violent commandeer-ing of Palestinian homes by Jewish Israelis continued with impunity as well, Israel maintaining that it "cannot evict a Jew from a house" once he has gone inside it, no matter the circumstances.[630]

Mt. Scopus, again

The stranger-than-fiction intrigue of Mt. Scopus continued on the night of December 13, 1952, when Israeli soldiers were caught running an arms cache past the border. They fled, leaving behind six US Army manpacks filled with 1,000 rounds of rifle ammunition, 2,000 rounds of stengun ammunition, six 81mm mortar shells, six 2" mortar shells, three 90-volt dry batteries, twenty-four hand grenades, and a tin of detonators—all destined for Mt. Scopus. Twice during the night, the Israelis attempted to retrieve the arms, but were driven back.

Throughout the next day (December 14), the MAC tried to contact Israeli authorities, but were continually told that no one "was available" to speak to them. The ritual obfuscation came the following day, when Israel filed what Hutchison described as "perhaps the most ridiculous allegation received during the history of the [MAC] mission": the culprits were not Israeli, but "Jordanian marauders" who had stolen ammunition from an Israeli army dump and wounded an Israeli soldier.

To the MAC's credit, it nonetheless took the allegation seriously, and had the Israelis submit evidence and walk the investigators through the alleged events. After the Israeli claim proved farcical and the MAC condemned Israel for the breach of the Armistice, Israel responded by launching an international campaign against Chairman de Ridder. Soon, de Ridder needed a bodyguard. The harassment continued, and although de Ridder stood firm, the UN did not. Under what Hutchison referred to as Israel's constant pressure on the UN, he was eventually removed from his position.

The Israeli "smokescreen of words" was described by John Wilson upon leaving the British delegation in Tel Aviv in mid-1953. Israeli officials have built up "a sickening jargon … the air is thick with propaganda … Misleading stories and press campaigns are worked up [and] censorship stifles the dissemination of honest news." Several observers noted how the Israeli state, following in the footsteps of the Jewish Agency, conjured such hysteria with its manipulation of the news that it found itself having to take action against the threats it had invented.[631]

Five years of Israeli terror against those it made refugees finally produced the inevitable, and it would seem intended, result: Palestinian reprisal raids were now a threat. As Glubb put it, "Jewish terrorism made the infiltrator into a gunman":

> [T]he infiltrators are the dispossessed … The creation of a vast horde—nearly a million—of dispossessed, who four years after the battle are still wholly prevented from returning to their lands and villages now lying fallow or given over to Israeli immigrants, [the separation of villages from their fields], all these are Israel's doing; and they have created a landless, and a depressed community of almost ungovernable proportions on the fringes of Israel.[632]

Yet few infiltrators were armed even as late as the Suez Crisis, and fewer still crossed the Armistice with the intent to cause harm.

Typical infiltrators, according to the British ambassador to Jordan, Geoffrey Furlonge, were hungry refugee children risking their lives to steal.

Consistent with expansionist goals, Israel appeared to exacerbate the desperation as the opportunity offered. In Qalqilya (West Bank) there were several impoverished families near the Armistice Line who depended on a single cistern which, according to the MAC, lay well within a twenty-yard uncertainty of the Armistice Line. Once the Line was set more clearly, the cistern ended up three yards into the Israeli side. Israel did not use the cistern, but for the families Israel had displaced, its water meant survival, and so the MAC asked that they be allowed to access it. Israel refused. Any Arab who tried to make the extra few steps to the water, its representative assured the MAC, would be shot dead.

Israeli raids into the West Bank continued. Two IDF paratrooper companies were sent to Idna (Hebron area) and Falama on the night of January 22 with orders blow up houses and kill their inhabitants, but were intercepted by National Guardsmen, though a repeat attack against Falama six days later was more successful. On February 25 an IDF patrol murdered five shepherds, the youngest age thirteen, mutilated their bodies and stole their flock of 177 sheep.[633]

Jerusalem "maneuvres"

April 22 brought what became known as the "Jerusalem incident," in which both the Jordanians and the Israelis accused the other of initiating a bloody sunset encounter along the Armistice Line.

Two pieces of evidence pointed to Israel. One, it was learned that Israel knew there would be such an incident. The "lady friend" (as the British Consul described her) of an Israeli soldier stationed at an advanced post happened to be employed at a French convent on the border. The day before the incident, April 21, he warned her not to go to the convent's garden the next day because "there were going to be manoeuvres." She alerted the Mother Superior.

Two, Israeli fire was from the first moment coordinated over a wide area. "Judging by his own military experience," a senior investigating officer explained, he could not understand "how such widespread and simultaneous firing by the Israelis took place unless there had been a pre-set time or signal," that is, unless the Israelis were the initiators of the violence.

The UN reached no verdict on culpability, contrary to the views of the British General Consul in Jerusalem, the United Nations staff, and both the US and British consuls in Amman, for whom the evidence pointed wholly to Israel.

According to Ambassador Furlonge, Israel escaped blame because of General Riley—the same who saved Israel in the "barrel incident" the previous summer—having "resorted to the suppression of evidence" in withholding from the UN such information unfavorable to Israel. It was, according to Glubb, again General Riley who stepped in for Israel to block any investigation of an alleged May 17 attack on the village of Beit Sira.[634]

Three days after Beit Sira, small parties of Israelis penetrated into the West Bank and attacked five villages in the Tulkarm area. According to the British in Amman and Nablus, they "laid mines at doors and windows of a house and then lobbed hand-grenades through the windows and directed machine-gun fire at the doors."

An attack the next night (May 21) on the village of Jaba provides a concise example of Israel's pattern of obfuscation. After Israel blew up a house in Jaba, near Jerusalem, killing a woman and child, it refused to allow the MAC to investigate, dismissing the attack as an internal matter for Jordan. In response, de Ridder proposed modifying MAC procedure "to permit UN observers to investigate incidents, although the one party may not agree that incident is a breach of armistice agreement." This would of course be equally binding on both parties, but although Jordan agreed, Israel refused. Next, Israel alleged an attack by Palestinians which it had never previously cited but that it now dated at about the same time as its own attacks on Tulkarm and Jaba, thus "balancing" the situation. Despite the suspect circumstances, the MAC was fully ready to investigate and Jordan was fully prepared to cooperate. But Israel then refused the MAC's procedure for investigating the very accusation it had used (and obviously invented) to obfuscate investigation of its own attack—and there the matter ended.

Among continuing attacks, four Palestinian villages were targeted on four successive nights, May 20-23, and Palestinians already reduced to hiding in West Bank caves were killed on May 24.[635]

Throughout these years, Israel exerted control of news and information to keep its public sheltered in the belief that they were the victims. In June the British Consulate in Jerusalem again complained of the mythology constituting news in Israel. The Israeli government

> has created a situation in which no ordinary Israeli can learn the truth about border incidents. The only picture available … is approximately the reverse of the truth.

As for the Arab press in Jordan, while it "is not notable for accuracy," on the whole it presents "a substantially reliable picture" of the border incidents," if only because "Jordan is generally the innocent party."[636]

The pattern continued. The MAC judged that there was no evidence to link two murders in Beit Jibrin on August 8 to West Bank infiltrators, but Israeli "reprisals nevertheless followed swiftly." Three days later, on the night of August 11-12, Israel forces attacked Wadi Fukin, Surif, and Idna using demolition mines, bangalore torpedoes, 2-inch mortars, machine-guns, and small arms. As reported by UN investigators, "bullet-riddled bodies near the doorways and multiple bullet hits on the doors of the demolished houses indicated that the inhabitants had been forced to remain inside until their homes were blown up over them."

Unit 101 and Gaza

The Israeli Air Force's strafing of Gaza resumed in July (1953), and it was this summer that Israel's elite terror militia, Unit 101, began its raids. On August 28, the young Ariel Sharon (then Scheinerman) led Unit 101 in an attack against the Bureij refugee camp in Gaza in an alleged search for "infiltrators," but what the MAC described as "an appalling case of deliberate mass murder." Using automatic weapons, hand grenades, and incendiary bombs, forty-three men, women, and children whom Israel had ethnically cleansed five years earlier were killed, and twenty-two seriously injured.

Israel's smokescreen to the Gaza refugee camp massacre came three days later, when Tel Aviv radio reported terrible news: "Arabs" had attacked UNRWA warehouses in Gaza. The story served its purpose, but it was a fabrication—that it was "entirely without foundation" came directly from the acting director of UNRWA, Leslie Carver.[637]

After the MAC dismissed Israeli claims that the Israeli village of Ahiezer, near Lydda, was attacked by infiltrators on September 7 (1953), four IDF patrols nonetheless crossed into the West Bank in retaliation. They attacked a shepherd, stole his flock, and kidnapped a twenty-five year old Palestinian woman who was collecting firewood.

The fate of the woman remains unknown. When the MAC demanded that she be freed, Israel replied that she had suddenly died. To demands that her body be returned to her family, Israel replied that she had already been buried.[638]

Israel's ongoing activity in the south at this time, though less visible, would ultimately prove more decisive. A CIA report dated September 20 summarized:

> In the past two weeks, Israeli troops have made almost daily armed incursions into the neutral zone and attacked Arab bedouin settlements. Moreover, the insistence of UN observers that the Israelis leave the zone has apparently been ignored … [it is] apparently a deliberate move on the part of the Ben-Gurion government to gain control of the El Auja [demilitarised] zone.[639]

Qibya

October of 1953 began relatively quietly. The MAC condemned Israeli ambushes on October 10 and rejected an Israeli claim of an attack on the 11th for lack of evidence. However, when on the 13th a grenade was thrown into a house in the Israeli town of Yehud, killing a woman and two of her children, the Jordanians themselves acknowledged the possibility that the murderers had come from the West Bank. Glubb immediately flew to Jerusalem and met with Hutchison. They arranged for the Israelis and their tracking dogs to follow the tracks wherever they may lead. The bloodhounds, however, lost the scent in Rantis, due east of Yehud.[640]

The following evening, October 14, Sharon's Unit 101 invaded the West Bank village of Qibya, using the well-proven maneuver of surrounding the village on three sides, as had been used two months earlier in the August attack on Wadi Fukin.

Sixty-nine Palestinians were murdered, half of them women and children. Forty-five houses were blown up, along with the village water reservoir and school. Twenty livestock were killed.

The soldiers had "advanced into the village … killing all civilians found in houses [and after each] house was dealt with, engineers blew it up," as the Arab Legion reported it, though in some cases it appeared that the victims had simply been forced to remain in their homes while they were bombed. The roads to Budrus and Shuqba were mined, and both villages were shelled. UN observers who reached the scene about midnight reported that

> about 10 PM Israeli forces, estimated conservatively at 3 companies or 400 men, moved on the village of Qibya … Forces used demolition bombs, Bangalore torpedoes, hand grenades, automatic weapons and incendiary bombs. Persons attempting to escape were machine-gunned.[641]

For Hutchison, it was "difficult to describe the wanton destruction that had taken place."

> An Arab woman [was] perched high on a pile of rubble. Here and there between the rocks you could see a tiny hand or foot protruding. The woman's stare was blank … she was sitting on the pile of rock that held the lifeless bodies of her six children. The bullet riddled body of the husband lay face down in the dusty road behind her.[642]

Sharon had obeyed Central Command's orders, which were

> to attack and temporarily to occupy the village, carry out destruction and maximum killing, in order to drive out the inhabitants of the village from their homes.

Qibya village, the morning of October 15, 1953, searching for bodies under the rubble of houses bombed by Israel Defense Forces during the night. [TNA, FO 371/104790]

Qibya quickly became Israel's worst public relations scandal, and so in a special broadcast, Ben-Gurion—who had approved the operation—emphatically denied "the false and fantastic tale" that Israeli soldiers committed the massacre. "We have examined the facts in detail," and can categorically state that "not a single unit, not even the smallest, was absent from its barracks." Instead, addressing his nation and the world, Ben-Gurion framed Holocaust survivors for the slaughter.[643]

As with previous attacks, Israel retroactively vilified the victims: Qibya, Israeli media announced, was "a nest of marauders." This, too, was a lie: the village had not once figured into the MAC files, or in any incident, since the Armistice was signed four and a half years earlier. When investigations by the American Consulate and US Embassy contradicted Ben-Gurion, the Israeli Foreign Minister blamed the United States for a lack of friendship. The US, he charged, was encouraging "Arab appetites."[644]

The US, already alarmed by Israel's continued obstruction of UN personnel and refusal to suspend its illegal diversion of the upper Jordan, described Israel's behavior as "shocking" and "was so disturbed about a whole series of Israeli incidents along the Arab frontiers" that President Eisenhower held up $30 million allocated to Israel for the first six months of 1954, and "urgently" considered Security Council action in consideration of "the inefficiency of past representations to the Israeli government."

This was short-lived. As Benny Morris described it, Israel then "promptly and successfully mobilized the pro-Israel lobby in Washington," which caused US officials to grow concerned about its "effect on General Eisenhower's and the Administration's political future." New York Mayor-elect Robert F. Wagner joined Zionist groups in smearing as antisemites anyone who called for an investigation into Qibya, while Ben-Gurion claimed persecution: "If it is difficult to be a Jew," he said in response to condemnation of the massacre, "then it is even more difficult to be a Jewish state." Ben-Gurion then linked this "difficulty" to "something that happened two thousand years ago in this very country," which the *NY Times* assumed to be a reference to the birth of Christ.[645]

Israel made two attempts to counter outrage over Qibya with alleged anti-Israeli attacks—but the attacks had to be from the West Bank for the tactic to be effective. The first came eleven days later and was almost certainly staged. The second came five months later and was real, but doubtfully had anything to do with the West Bank: the so-called Scorpion's Pass massacre.

On the morning of October 25, an empty Israeli freight train was derailed by an explosive device. Immediately, Israel lodged a "sharp protest against this new Jordanian aggression," and wanted Britain to "reprove Jordan for this latest act of violence [as it was] swift to react to the Kibya incident." The Israeli press stressed how fortunate it was that the "infiltrators" happened to hit an empty train rather than a crowded passenger train.

The train bombing, however, was almost surely a false flag operation. There was no evidence to link it to the West Bank, and in the words of Ambassador Furlonge, "we all here remain firmly of the opinion that the whole thing was a frame-up on the part of the Israelis, who staged it themselves."[646]

Like Deir Yassin in 1948, Qibya may have been calculated to destroy any hope among Palestinians that they could ever regain normalcy as long as they were on land wanted by Israel. In Qibya's wake, Israel heightened the psychological terror by continuing military exercises with live ammunition right at the Armistice Line, stray bullets hitting Palestinian villages such as Budrus, all to the accompaniment of the IAF's menacing airspace violations. None of this was in response to any Jordanian action.

The British ambassador to Israel, Francis Evans, suspected that Israel was also now encouraging Jewish settlers (i.e., in the lands near the Armistice on the Israeli side) to attack Palestinians and then say they had no control over them—this foreshadowing settler attacks in the West Bank and East Jerusalem today.[647]

It is unclear whether surveillance hiking teams, like those of the Mandate period, continued on a small scale. In late 1953, three Israeli men and two women were caught by Jordanian police, then killed when they attempted to escape. They carried maps, compasses, and army type water bottles, but no identification papers. Israel claimed they were tourists en route to Petra, yet did not raise this incident with the MAC, nor explain why Israeli "tourists" would have thought they could roam freely through Jordan when the reverse would have meant an IDF execution on the spot.[648]

Mount Scopus, which Israel was now arming by airdropping the weapons by parachute, flared to the fore again on the 1st of November (1953). When a time bomb destroyed part of the eight-inch diameter pipe that was Arab Jerusalem's only water pipeline, Mount Scopus was where the tracks led UN observers until Israel blocked them from proceeding further. The British on the scene suspected that the sabotage was intended to provoke Palestinians to attack Mt. Scopus.[649]

More raids filled the night of December 21-22. A party of about four Israelis "blasted open door of house selected apparently at random and murdered women inside with automatic fire [and then] murdered two unarmed Arabs running to the scene" to help. Two more homes were sprayed with bullets, but the occupants had escaped. Near Tarqumiya, a Bedouin village was attacked with Sten guns, submachine guns, and a grenade.

Israel's balancing allegation came on December 28: It announced that an Arab had murdered an Israeli "engaged in marking the demarcation line." A meeting was immediately arranged for 17:00 hours at the scene of the alleged murder. The UN representative and the Jordanian delegate were present and waited two hours for the Israeli representative, who failed to come. The meeting was set again for the next day, but the UN and Jordanian representatives again waited in vain for the Israeli representative. At a MAC meeting on December 30, the Israeli representative, asked why he twice failed to show up at the meeting arranged to examine his own allegation, replied that he was both times "unavoidably late."[650]

The Scorpion's Pass massacre

The era's most infamous attack against Israeli civilians occurred on the night of March 16-17, 1954. An Israeli bus on an unscheduled run from Eilat to Tel Aviv was barbarously attacked while traveling through Scorpion's Pass (Ma'ale Akrabim) in the Negev. Eleven people were murdered; three survived.

Israel seized on the atrocity, as Hutchison put it, to "wipe the Qibya massacre from the Israeli slate"—but it could only do so if the murderers came from the West Bank or Jordan, rather than from Gaza or the southern Negev, as was far more likely. Israel however immediately insisted that the West Bank was to blame, and its military delegate handed Hutchison the names and locations of the culprits, with the odd instructions that it not be given to the MAC, claiming to doing so would "delay the proceedings." Hutchison and Glubb nonetheless accommodated him and within a half hour launched a massive search. Just before midnight, failing even to find anyone who recognized the names, they widened the scope.

As they searched, Israel manufactured a media coup that would "make the MAC look ridiculous unless the vote went to Israel," as Hutchison put it. The headline of the morning's *Jerusalem Post* and a second front-page article were fabrications, with fabricated citations, planted to create the "fact" that the murderers were from the West Bank, and that the MAC knew this.

Now armed with the Israeli public's manufactured belief, Israel put "intolerable pressure" on the MAC chairman that a vote blaming Jordan be concluded immediately, without investigation—PM

1954

Sharett threatening the chairman that "he would not like to see the press the following day" if the commission did not do as instructed. Jordan, meanwhile, made available trackers, officers, and an airplane for the search, sent forces to the adjacent Jordanian area, and offered a large monetary reward for information.[651]

No determination was immediately made by the MAC—all possibilities, including the West Bank, remained open. The MAC having failed to heed Israel's blackmail to frame the West Bank, Israel quit and launched a campaign of intimidation against Hutchison who, like de Ridder before him, soon needed a bodyguard. It blocked UN personnel and tracking dogs from circling the area of the crime, and when a solitary piece of evidence, a skull cap that fit the description given by one of the survivors, was discovered to the west of the crime scene (indicating assailants from Gaza or the Negev), an Israeli watcher took it and planted it to the east, in order to implicate the West Bank.

The CIA reported that there was no evidence to support the Israeli contention, and four independent sources cited a Black Hand Gang, formed by Bedouin who had been the victims of Israeli violence, as the likely perpetrators. As with the murder of Lea Festinger, Israel's need to affix blame by way of political necessity, meant that the actual murderers must never be found. The Scorpion's Pass massacre, like the murder of Lea Festinger, remains unsolved.[652]

At about midnight on March 28-29, an Israeli force of about 200 men penetrated 3.5 km (2.2 miles) east of the Armistice Line and attacked the West Bank village of Nahalin, killing nine and wounding fourteen. Reminiscent of the Mandate gangs' habit of targeting first responders, the soldiers hid a grenade and a prepared charge of TNT that blew up an Arab Legion vehicle rushing to the scene. UN investigators were there within three hours, but the Israeli representative failed to attend the MAC meeting called about the incident, despite several attempts to secure his participation.

In a confidential memo from the British Consulate-General in July 1954, T. Wikeley voiced "doubts regarding the sincerity of Israeli protestations for peace ... until the boundaries of Israel have reached the Jordan."

> [These doubts] have been strongly reinforced by the disgusting
> manner in which the United Nations Truce Supervision Organisation
> is being treated by the Israel Military authorities and in the Israel
> press … Far from pointing to a desire for peace, this can most
> easily be interpreted as an indication of a wish to stop unwelcome
> investigations which U.N. observers are constantly making, or trying
> to make, along the Israel frontier … the repeated Israeli requests for
> a peace meeting with Jordan are no more than a tactical manoeuvre
> aimed at the Security Council…[653]

"It is the deliberate intention of the Israelis," concluded British
Lt.-Col R. J. Gammon in reporting one of the continuing IDF
mortar attacks on the West Bank, "to provoke the Arab Legion
into crossing the frontier in retaliation," and "in this they may well
succeed." US intelligence as well continued its bleak assessment of
Israeli intentions.[654]

The Lavon Affair

When on July 2, 1954, bombs exploded inside the post office in
Alexandria, the Egyptian government's ability to control terrorism
was thrown into doubt. Whether the attacks were by the Muslim
Brotherhood, as some claimed, or the Communists, as others alleged,
Egypt was obviously not stable, and the British, who were considering
withdrawing their military from the region, now had second thoughts.

Matters worsened twelve days later as bombs exploded inside US
cultural centers in both Alexandria and Cairo. The events bolstered
Defense Minister Lavon's case when at a news conference on July 19
he warned that Israel must act aggressively to defend itself from its
neighbors—and, significantly, that Israel's borders (Armistice Line)
"should not be regarded as unchangeable."[655]

On July 23, the Egyptian bombers targeted cinemas in Cairo and
Alexandria, and a railroad yard in Alexandria. But then the nascent
wave of terror abruptly ended: As one of the bombers neared the
next target, the British-owned Rio Cinema in Alexandria, his device
exploded prematurely. Soon, thirteen men and one women were in
custody, charged with espionage and terrorism against Egyptian,

American, and British civilian targets, including a cinema, library, and an American educational center. Egypt was now certainly foremost in Lavon's thoughts, because the suspects were neither Communists nor Islamic radicals, but Jews and Israelis. The bombings—by Israel's Unit 131, created in 1948 to conduct sabotage and "black propaganda"—were what the CIA called a "sabotage operation against US and UK installations," a bungled false-flag operation that soon became known by Lavon's name*.[656]

Egypt's arrests ignited charges of anti-Semitism. The Political Director of the World Jewish Congress warned the British government that he feared large-scale anti-Jewish campaigns in Egypt, and others warned of a wave of pogroms. Rabbi Nahum, chief rabbi of the Jewish communities in Egypt, responded with the following statement:

> I consider it my duty to declare that there is no racial terror against our communities in Egypt. On the contrary, and especially under the present regime [Nasser], the Egyptian authorities have repeatedly shown their sympathy for Egyptian Jews.[657]

Much the same was reported by T. W. Garvey from the British Embassy in Cairo. "Anti-Semitism as known in Europe had no real parallel" in Egypt, and "successive Egyptian governments and this one in particular, made a special point of religious toleration." Nonetheless the Israeli government pressured Britain to intervene to free the suspects and to "mobilize the support of world opinion" against the Egyptians. A guilty verdict, Israel warned, could "provoke extremely violent reactions in Israel."

The typical view of the Western public was that expressed by the *Manchester Guardian*: the accusations against the defendants were too outrageous to be plausible. "What conceivable benefit could Israel have gained," it asked, from bombing American and British facilities?[658]

---

* Lavon's signature was allegedly forged on the orders authorizing the false flag operation, which was code-named Operation Susannah. TNA FO 371/151273, declassified in September, 2013, states that the Head of Military Intelligence who submitted the plan to Lavon, Benyamin Givli, was then Israel's Military Attaché in London. The document also records an alleged 1960 Israeli attempt to assassinate Egyptian president Nasser.

The answer to that, however, soon became clear. In the blunt words of the CIA, Israel staged "Arab" bombings "to embitter relations between Egypt and the West." Domestically, Israel used its strict news censorship to keep its denials credible, and did not admit the Affair to its own citizens for a half century. In 2005, it honored the operatives at a Jerusalem ceremony and bestowed certificates of appreciation upon three who were still alive. Israel's archives relating to the operation remain secret.[659]

Israel was "determined to get revenge," as Kollek put it, against Egypt for its execution of two of the Lavon Affair bombers. The pretexts came the following February 23 and 25, 1955, when maps and documents were stolen from an Israeli military facility, and a bicyclist was murdered near Tel Aviv, which Israel blamed on infiltrators from Gaza. With this scorecard in hand, Israel staged a brutal attack against Gazan civilians on February 28, the bloodiest against the coastal strip since the 1948 war.[660]

Israel's pretexts failed to explain the massacre, and so Ben-Gurion concocted an official lie to quell the international condemnation. An Egyptian patrol, the new story went, had ambushed an IDF patrol inside Israeli territory, and so in self-defense the Israeli unit had chased the Arabs back into Gaza. The soldiers were ordered to repeat the story to UN observers if questioned. Privately, Sharett doubted that anyone would believe it, and he was correct: "the pretence deceived no one and was at once abandoned," as the British Embassy in Tel Aviv put it. For the first time, both the US and the USSR voted to censure Israel.[661]

Israeli troops attacked Beit Liqya (near Ramallah) on the 1st of September (1954), and on the 11th, the Sabbath, settlers from a Herut (ex-Irgun) settlement just west of the Line went up a hill and fired on ten children 10-13 years of age who were swimming in a reservoir near Wadi Fukin, roughly 300 meters inside the West Bank. Two boys were severely injured, one in the stomach, the other in the head. This was likely the settlers' own initiative, but Israel took no action against them. In the background, expulsions of non-Jews from Israel and frequent IAF violations continued.[662]

When the US Ambassador approached Sharett about Israel's

continued intransigence, he replied with the extraordinary statement that no Palestinian had been fully engaged in agriculture, and that therefore Israel had the right to keep the land. In a premonition of 1967, members of the Israeli delegation in Beirut told a British counterpart that Israel was preparing to attack the Arab states in order to expand its territory. The timing depended on [1] preparing their armed forces; [2] predicting the reaction of the US and UK; and [3] then "luring the Arab Legion" to attack Israeli territory to provide pretext.[663]

Syrian passenger plane hijacking

The morning after the trial for the Lavon Affair bombers began in Cairo, December 12, 1954, a Syrian passenger plane left Damascus on a routine, scheduled flight to Cairo. It flew west over Lebanon, and once it was well over the Mediterranean, it turned south. A US businessman onboard estimated that they were about 70 miles offshore when, without warning, Israeli fighter planes intercepted the aircraft and forced it to land in Lydda—an air piracy "without precedent in the history of international practice," the State Department informed Sharett. (In fact, this was not the first time Israel forced down a passenger plane. In June 1950, it did so to an Arab Airways passenger *Rapide* en route to Egypt over the Negev.)

Israel claimed that the plane was intercepted over its sovereign territory in Acre (actually Palestinian, but seized in 1948), roughly 60 kilometer (37 miles) south of where, according to the American witness, it crossed the coast on its westward course from Damascus. Common speculation at the time was that Israel wanted the passengers as hostages to secure the release of five Israeli soldiers whom Syria had just captured in the Golan Heights changing batteries in Israeli bugs on Syrian telephone lines.[664]

In December, a young Israeli man and woman infiltrated Jordan to the southeast of the Dead Sea. When by February 1955 they had failed to return, UN observers asked local Bedouins' assistance. The UN/Bedouin team found their bodies, but no clue as to what had happened.

1955

In response, an Israeli military patrol penetrated 15-20 kilometers (9-12 miles) inside the West Bank, kidnapped six random Bedouin, brought them to the Israeli side and murdered five of them, four with knifes, one with firearms. One was sixteen years old. They sent the sixth back to announce that the five were executed in revenge for the two Israeli "tourists." Israel gave wide publicity to the (unsolved) murder of the two yet, as before, inexplicably did not file a complaint with the MAC "on which UN observers can initiate their normal investigations." Ben-Gurion prevented the soldiers from being tried for the Bedouins' murders, and Lt.-Col R. J. Gammon speculated that this tactic—"abduction of isolated peasants near the border and their subsequent murder on Israeli territory"—was replacing the tactic of fewer, larger attacks on West Bank soil.[665]

British plans to invade Israel and/or Egypt

British officials hoped never to have to make good on the defense treaty they maintained with Jordan, avoiding the issue by parsing words: was Israel "attacking" Jordan, or merely "raiding" it? The military nonetheless took the defense pact seriously, in part because a destabilized Jordan would invite Soviet intrigue.

In early 1954, as the Lavon operatives planned their bombings, the British developed secret plans to destroy the entire Israeli Air Force, as well as key Israeli military and communication installations, in order to stop Israeli aggression. In preparation, Britain moved one armored squadron, consisting of about 20 tanks and 100 men, from the Suez area to supplement its small garrison at Aqaba.[666]

A summary of plans dated April 27, 1955 read:

> Neutralise the Israeli Air Force using all the planned reinforcements and operating from the following bases Nicosia Abu Sueir Fayid Amman and Mafraq. Conduct operations against military targets in Israel in particular centres of communications and oil installations.[667]

Britain had been giving military aid to Israel even as it protested Israeli crimes and soul-searched its obligation to come to the West Bank's defense. Only in October 1953 did it acknowledge to itself

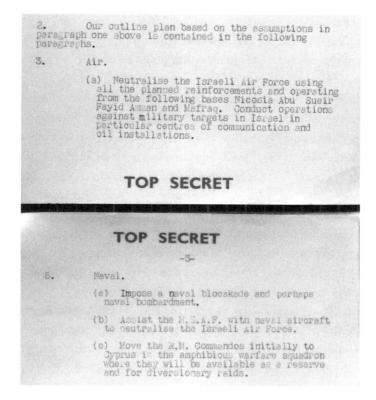

2.   Our outline plan based on the assumptions in
paragraph one above is contained in the following
paragraphs.

3.   Air.

    (a)   Neutralise the Israeli Air Force using
all the planned reinforcements and operating
from the following bases Nicosia Abu Sueir
Fayid Amman and Mafraq. Conduct operations
against military targets in Israel in
particular centres of communication and
oil installations.

TOP SECRET

TOP SECRET

-3-

5.   Naval.

    (a)   Impose a naval blockade and perhaps
naval bombardment.

    (b)   Assist the M.E.A.F. with naval aircraft
to neutralise the Israeli Air Force.

    (c)   Move the R.M. Commandos initially to
Cyprus in the amphibious warfare squadron
where they will be available as a reserve
and for diversionary raids.

Extracts from a document dated April 27, 1955, from G.H.Q.
Middle East Land Forces, to the Ministry of Defence, London,
regarding British plans to attack Israel. The M.E.A.F. is the Middle
East Air Force, a Royal Air Force contingent in the eastern
Mediterranean. [TNA, PREM 11/945]

that "Israel's military strength was at least partly due to our assistance"
and speak of discontinuing that aid.[668]

Military force was also being considered to stop Israeli aggression against Gaza, and Israeli maneuvers inside the UN's El Auja
demilitarized zone, a turtle shell shaped area whose bottom was
the Egyptian border. The area was in fact integral to Gaza and was
supposed to be Palestinian, but what we know today as the Gaza
strip was all that remained after 1948.[669]

In April 1955, the US State Department advised the British
Foreign Office that the UK "should consider urgently what action
we should be prepared to take if Israel made a deliberate attempt
to alter her existing frontier with Egyptian occupied territory [the

Gaza Strip]," the *we* suggesting joint US-UK action against Israel. Four months later, the Foreign Office indeed proposed enlisting the help of the United States in an attack on Israel to halt its aggression against Gaza.[670]

By 1955, Israel was treating the DMZ as its sovereign territory. It built a military camp (which it called a kibbutz) and planted minefields (which it called "non-military"). Egypt had no such militarization of the DMZ nor claimed it as its territory. It had however placed cement markers in the south, indicating its view of the (imprecise) Egyptian-DMZ border. After some back-and-forth, on November 2, Israeli soldiers took over the DMZ's UN compound and wiped out the Egyptian post, massacring about fifty Egyptians. Hoping to repeat its earlier success in commandeering Mt. Scopus, Israel forced out the UN peacekeepers, who continued their work as best they could from Gaza.[671]

Finally, to create what the CIA called "a rise in war fever," on December 27 all Israeli newspapers carried an alarming report—"inspired by the Israeli army," in the CIA's judgment—that predicted a considerable increase in Arab military strength and warned of Israel's increasing vulnerability. Israel further inflamed the "fever" by moving personnel and vehicles to the Negev for what it called "maneuvers" to be held in January or February 1956. All news was spun as bad news: When General Glubb, long a thorn in Israel's side, was dismissed from his post in March, the Israeli press now warned that the "threat to Israel, with Glubb's departure, has increased ominously."[672]

1956

Ironically, the bungled Lavon Affair ultimately influenced the course of events roughly as intended—if circuitously. Israel's massacre in Gaza on February 28, in retribution for Egypt's execution of two of the Lavon terrorists, was the spark that ignited the Gazan powder keg that Israel had created—what the CIA at the time called "more than 200,000 Palestinian Arab refugees, deeply embittered and frustrated after more than six years in camps," and whom the United Nations had failed to protect "against Israeli attacks." Gazan refugees rioted against the Egyptian regime for its inability to defend them, Nasser stopped secret peace talks he was holding with Israel, the British and Americans stopped their "Project Alpha" initiative to bring a lasting peace, Fedayeen groups formed and attacked southern Israel, and these in turn provided Israel's pretext for its next occupation of Gaza in which hundreds more civilians were killed. Pressure on Nasser to purchase weapons heightened, and unable buy them from the US, he concluded an arms deal with Czechoslovakia.

"It is no flight of fancy," Britain's Ambassador in Israel observed in 1956, "to suggest that Israel, by her attack on Gaza in February [28, 1955], was herself responsible for Egypt's decision in August to accept Communist arms."

The US feared Soviet influence in the region and was furious at Nasser (though Israel had bought arms extensively through Czechoslovakia). His hopes for a US loan to build a high dam at Aswan now looked all but dead, contributing to his decision to nationalize the Suez Canal. When on July 26, 1956, Nasser announced this move, he sealed his fate. His relationship with the West was poisoned, and regime change was the solution: PM Eden looked to military action to oust him.[673]

Thus Britain, instead of attacking Israel to defend Jordan or Egypt, joined with Israel and France against Egypt in Operation Musketeer, creating the war known as the Suez Crisis. Yet Britain's seemingly antithetical options—destroying Israel's military, versus joining forces with it against Egypt—were kept alive simultaneously. These remarkable instructions were written by the Chiefs of Staff Committee (October 1956):

> If these operations [British neutralizing of Israeli Air Force and communications] are ordered while Musketeer [British-Israeli-French attack against Egypt] is still held in readiness they [attacks against Israel] will take priority and consequent delay to Musketeer will be accepted.[674]

Musketeer was to be launched on September 15 but was postponed "due to political factors," while top British military figures continued to discuss logistics and circulate plans for a British attack on Israel. If the attack against Israel was commenced, squadrons in Malta, Germany, and Cyprus that were in place for Musketeer would be used, but without compromising their readiness for Musketeer should it be enacted afterwards.[675]

Nor the opposite: if Musketeer were launched, Britain might still attack Israel afterwards. The seemingly irreconcilable contradiction is caught in this instruction from the Ministry of Defence on October 18, a scant eleven days before Israel invaded Egypt in step one of Musketeer:

> We are advising Ministers that once Musketeer is launched we should avoid all hostilities with Israel until after Egypt had capitulated or until we could dispose our maximum air effort against Israel.[676]

Among the many twists that the British had to weigh was the possibility that during Musketeer, Jordan were to support Egypt. Britain would then be obligated to attack Jordan, at the same time it was preparing to attack Israel in *defense* of Jordan once its British-Israeli-French invasion of Egypt was concluded. And since both the British and the French had bases in Cyprus used for Musketeer, a British post-Musketeer attack on Israel could mean that the French would be hit as well as the British by Israel.[677]

Meanwhile, Israel's harassing airspace violations by its military planes continued, as did its ground incursions. About twenty Palestinians were killed in a raid on Hebron on September 11, and about ninety lay dead after an assault against Qalqilya on the night of October 10. But renewed Jordanian requests for British protection following the Qalqilya attack were moot. The collusion among Israel, France, and Britain was formalized in the secret Protocol of Sèvres between October 22 and 24. Two days later, on the 26th, British ambassador J. Nicholls was meeting with Ben-Gurion, nervous that rumors of the deal "were far more dangerous to us than to Israel." On October 29, Israel invaded Egypt. Musketeer had begun.[678]

Kafr Qasim

This first move in the new conspiracy to destabilize Egypt was accompanied by one of the better documented Israeli massacres against non-Jews within Israel (rather than cross-Armistice into

Palestine). Israel had maintained a 6:00 PM curfew on the village of Kafr Qasim (since non-Jews were under martial law), but that day decided to make it earlier because of the invasion of Egypt. At 4:45 PM the villagers were informed that the curfew was now 5:00, effective immediately. Many of the villagers were out in the fields and could not possibly be informed of the change and be back in fifteen minutes. Over the next hour, twenty-two children aged eight to seventeen, six women (one of whom was pregnant), and nineteen men were shot dead by Israeli soldiers as they returned home from the day's labor.

Post-Suez
After the Suez Crisis, Israeli forces remained in Gaza and began the large-scale execution of civilians and soldiers. According to the UN's figures, within the first three weeks of its occupation of Gaza the Israeli military killed 447-550 civilians "in cold blood and for no apparent reason," in the words of the head of the Egyptian-Israeli Mixed Armistice Commission (EIMAC). Between 49 and 100 more refugees were killed when Israel seized Rafah in the first two days of November, and a few hundred people, about half of whom were refugees from 1948, were executed by Israeli troops upon capturing Khan Yunis on November 3.

1957+

When Israel cited Palestinian "fedayeen activity" to justify its occupation and assault on Gaza, the US Eisenhower Administration "derided" Israel's explanation; in response, the *Jerusalem Post*, which the CIA considered to reflect the voice of the government, accused the United States of being "singularly unfriendly … a crystallization of [US] policy against Israel."

Israel used the attack against Egypt to seize the Sinai, which it intended to annex. For Eisenhower, the celebrated general of World War II, Israel had finally gone too far. He threatened to stop US underwriting of Israel if it refused to vacate the Sinai, and unlike all such US threats before and after, this one time, this one president did not back down. Privately, Administration figures like Secretary of State Dulles were warning that Israel was effectively running US foreign policy. The pressure on Eisenhower to yield to Israel was so great that on February 20 1957, he appeared on national television to explain what in any other situation would not need explanation: why a nation should not be permitted to seize and annex land by force of arms, or to impose conditions on its own withdrawal.

Ben-Gurion stood fast as well, telling the world that Eisenhower's demands "place me under great moral pressure … as a man and a Jew, the pressure of the justice for which my people were fighting." Israel, Ben-Gurion suggested, was the victim of discrimination "because we are few, weak and perhaps isolated." Ultimately, with face-saving diplomacy, Israel withdrew.[679]

From Suez to Oslo

Suez was big news because it was action. The suffocating choke-hold under which Israel has held Palestinians since 1948 is instead static, and thus falsely interpreted as peace by the outside world. It is normalized violence festering until Israel's next major move.

That came a decade after Suez. With the Six Day War of 1967, Israel seized the rest of Palestine and ethnically cleansed three hundred thousand more non-Jews, all with the same impunity as in 1948. No informed person was surprised by this: the conquest of river-to-sea was always Israel's plan, simply a matter of the right opportunity. Nor was it unexpected that Israel again exploited the Old Testament and Judaism to depict the crime as not merely heroic, but messianic.

Israel's assault on the United States' SS *Liberty* was different. On the fourth day of the war, Israel launched a sustained attack on the US vessel in international waters, killing thirty-four US citizens and wounding 171.*

---

* Though much has been written about the *Liberty* incident, in the absence of a formal Congressional inquiry I defer to a 2004 report to Congress by an independent committee of high-ranking US military figures. They concluded "that there is compelling evidence that Israel's attack was a deliberate attempt to destroy an American ship and kill her entire crew... [It is] the only instance in American naval history where a rescue mission was cancelled when an American ship was under attack... [but] due to the influence of Israel's powerful supporters in the United States, the White House deliberately covered up the facts of this attack from the American people [and due to Israeli pressure] this attack remains the only serious naval incident that has never been thoroughly investigated by Congress ... the official cover-up [is] without precedent in American naval history." For full text and signatories, Congressional Rec Vol 150, No. 130.

The reason for the attack is disputed, but theories fall into one or both of two categories. One, akin to Israel's downing of British planes in January 1949, was to prevent snooping into its activities. The other is that it was to appear as an attack by Egypt, a Lavon-esque false-flag attempt to bring the US into the war. Whatever the reason, the Johnson Administration accepted the Israeli explanation that the attack was an error: that despite repeated aerial surveillance of the ship, its military attacked the *Liberty* for two hours by both air and sea thinking it was an Egyptian vessel. Twenty-four years later, the Secretary of State at the time of the attack, Dean Rusk, wrote of Israel's "error" claim: "I didn't believe them then, and I don't believe them to this day."

Nor does the "error" theory explain why Rusk's boss recalled rescue aircraft minutes after being dispatched. That US military assistance for the stricken *Liberty* and its injured survivors was 40 minutes away, but the Johnson Administration instead left them abandoned in the crippled vessel for seventeen hours.[680]

As the *Liberty* survivors were sidelined, Israel treated the newly-occupied lands as its own. After the new ethnic cleansing, it segregated those who remained into three bantustans it itself created*—Gaza, the West Bank, and East Jerusalem—and assigned identification cards accordingly. There was a pecking order, what Israel treated as akin to heaven, purgatory, and hell: East Jerusalem, the West Bank, and Gaza.

The ethnic purification of East Jerusalem was at the top of Israel's priorities. Non-Jewish historic sites were razed, and a minefield of race laws began evicting non-Jewish Jerusalemites to the West Bank. If parents were assigned different IDs, the spouse with the Jerusalem ID would have to self-ethnically-cleanse to the West Bank—else live apart, leading to the break-up of families. The determination for non-Jews with Jerusalem IDs to remain in the city was strong, not just because it was their home, but because Israel's determination to ethnically cleanse it was obvious.

---

* East Jerusalem is part of the West Bank according to the Armistice. Gaza is physically separated from the West Bank, but this is the result of Israeli expropriation of Palestinian land in 1948; legally, it remains part of a single Palestinian territory. Using these as three distinct geo-political entities was an Israeli construct.

Gaza was the basement with a one-way door in. Anyone it had assigned a Gaza ID caught in the West Bank was arrested and forced into the enclave, permanently severed from the life s/he had known.

After the 1967 war, more UN Resolutions, now pale ghosts of their 1948-1949 ancestors, were passed and ignored. The stranglehold on Palestine and Palestinians tightened, and the violent, static "peace" returned once more. The "temporary" 1949 Armistice Line, orphaning more than half of the Palestinian side of Partition to Israel, became the so-called "1967 borders." When in 1980 Israel announced that it had formally annexed East Jerusalem, explicit Security Council Resolutions condemned the move and, fully aware of Israel's history, warned that its obvious rush to create a *fait accompli* by new "facts on the ground" would be in vain. But Israel ignored the UN ultimatum about ignoring UN ultimatums, and these Resolutions as well quickly joined the graveyard of their ancestors.

And therein lies the irony of successive international demands on Israel: Israel is rewarded for its crimes. Rather than being held to account, every new aggression is met with weaker demands than the previous unenforced rulings. With each newly-emasculated ruling, their impotent predecessors are forgotten, giving Israel the difference. The clock is restarted regarding non-compliance, until the next, ever weaker and unenforced ruling incrementally lowers the bar of what is, futilely, demanded of the state.

A half century of Israeli intransigence was the starting point for the Trojan horse known as the Oslo Accords, sold as the basis for negotiations to lead to two states. Yet Oslo proved to be another windfall for Israel as it exploited the Accord's provision for semi-legitimacy in the West Bank to further its river-to-sea annexation, cementing apartheid as the nature of the state itself.

Even Oslo's creation of the Palestinian Authority, sold as an embryonic government toward a never-defined Palestinian state, ultimately serves Israel. It acts as a fig-leaf to hide Israeli apartheid by serving to "explain" why non-Jews in the occupied lands can not vote in Israeli elections. It is Israel's subcontractor for day-to-day affairs and political repression, keeping Israel's hands clean of both. And it is an additional source of money for Israel, since foreign aid to the PA merely saves Israel the expense of its own occupation, an economic windfall on top of its exploitation of Palestinian trade, taxes, tourism, and resources.[681]

Over the decades to the present, the circumstances and personalities changes, but the psyche and inertia of a settler movement determined to regain an imagined, ethnically-pure land to which it claims messianic entitlement, remains ever-constant.

9

Postscript: What now?

The previous chapters document the Zionist movement's imposition of European ethnic nationalism upon the land and people of Palestine, cloaked in mythology and narrative.

History would be a pointless exercise, an abdication of responsibility, if after a conscientious examination of the evidence we feign moral neutrality over what it tells us. And so, having done my best in the previous pages to document *what* happened to Palestine and *why* it happened, the question is: What now? How do we make this history, *history*?

We must begin by acknowledging that we, the so-called West—the USA, the UK, Europe, Australia, Canada—are not mere observers. After defeating fascism in Europe eight decades ago, we nurtured and defended Israel's own brand of blood-and-soil nationalism. We then knowingly misdiagnosed the resulting catastrophe as a conflict, and have ever since knowingly mis-prescribed a peace process as the cure.

Conflict and peace process assume a *dispute* between two empowered sides, each with grievances and bargaining chips. Ethnic cleansing, apartheid, and the acquisition of territory by force are not disagreements to be mediated. They are crimes to be stopped.

Israel has always held all the power: militarily, politically, and of the narrative. Palestinians have no army to defend their land, no navy to defend their waters, no air force to defend their skies. Palestinians have nothing to leverage, no chips to bargain away, nothing with which to negotiate, not even a true elected government to represent them.

Perhaps the most powerful part of the misdiagnosis in terms of public understanding is the seemingly ubiquitous juxtaposition of "Israel versus the Palestinians" or "versus the Arabs." This is so well-ingrained in society that it is repeated endlessly without any thought—but what it tells us, is false.

The reason Israel holds millions of human beings under various levels of apartheid, the reason it keeps millions more languishing in refugee camps, is not that they are Palestinian, not that they are Arab.

It is, rather, strictly because they are not Jewish. If they were Jewish, whether Palestinian or Arab or anything else, they would be welcomed and given a generous subsidy to move in from whatever part of the world they live and take over a house whose owner was expelled because s/he is *not* Jewish.

Nothing in the history of Zionism, of the Israeli state, or the so-called conflict can be understood divorced from this.

By framing the dispute in terms of Israel vs the Palestinians, and 1967 borders vs settlements, we are led to envision some sort of political squabble, an endlessly complicated border dispute which the Palestinians are endlessly unwilling to settle.

This misdiagnosis nurtures another myth: the idea of a cycle of violence. The violence in Israel-Palestine is linear, not cyclical. Israel's territorial expansion and ethnic cleansing are the forward violence, not the result of a cycle, and continue no matter what the Palestinians do in response to it.

Finally, our misdiagnosis suggests that the nature of the disease is *occupation*. Leaving aside that the word is tossed about without a clue as to what those invoking it mean geographically, the word is a distraction, conveying little of the actual nature of the disease. "Occupation" is of course territorial, a strategy toward confiscating all of Palestine. But Israel's occupation of Palestine is also an occupation of the people themselves.

As Palestinians live it, the occupation is there to dehumanize you, to erase you and subsume your cultural iconography as its own. It is to suffocate your achievement at every turn, to break your will and convince you that neither you nor your children will lead normal lives as long as you live on land it wants and as long as you claim to have ever existed as who you are.

This occupation decides whether your children may pursue their dreams, whether a musician may perform or an athlete may compete. It decides whether *it* will block your child from accepting the scholarship s/he was awarded at the prestigious university abroad. It decides whether you will visit your family, and whether you will marry the person you love.

It, not you, decides what of your own history you can be taught, and who may enter and leave your country. It can, and has, calculated just how much caloric intake will keep you dependent and compromised but not visibly starving. It alone decides what aspects of your life *it* will decide.[682]

This thing called the occupation decides whether you or your loved one will receive cancer treatment. It decides whether you may see your sick parent or spouse or child before s/he dies. After *it* decides *no*, *it* decides whether you will attend the funeral.

Israel's occupation means that you are powerless to protect your family. At its own pleasure, *it* will invade your home at four in the morning, trash it and march your child off to some undisclosed dungeon. *It* blows up your family house, makes you pay *it* for the trouble, and has the media parrot *its* story explaining why.

To know the word occupation as Palestinians live it, you must come to fear that which a free person would most cherish: It is to fear that your child might grow up with enough self-dignity as to stand up for her or his rights. It is to fear this because you know that s/he might be shot dead for it in a raid on the refugee camp the lords of this "occupation" have put you in. It is to wonder if the soldier that violates your home at will is the one living in your own home, the home that you have never seen because you, too, were born in the camp.

Occupation as Palestinians live it is to know that if in self-defence under international law you capture and humanely treat that invading soldier, the occupation would have it spun it as an act of terror. *Occupation* is also to know that you and the several thousand civilians like you languishing in Israeli prisons, hundreds of children among you, instead serve to "prove" the existential threat that is Israel's ever-present narrative. Kidnapped on Palestinian land, many tortured and held indefinitely without charge, your very imprisonment is proof that you are to blame—the more in prison, the more the proof.

Thus what we call the Israeli occupation of Palestine is in truth the crime of genocide, as defined by the UN Convention on the Prevention and Punishment of the Crime of Genocide, a definition endorsed by the United States Holocaust Museum, among others.*

In an effort to bring their plight to the world's attention through an act of non-violent protest, Palestinians in Gaza organized a Great March of Return (2018-19) in which hundreds made a symbolic attempt to approach the Israeli fence enclosing them—that is, a symbolic walk toward the homes from which they were ethnically cleansed, and to the rest of their own country. About two hundred of them, including children and medics, were shot dead by Israeli snipers on the other side of the fence. About 9200 more were injured by the soldiers, a high proportion crippled or otherwise permanently impaired.

If the media were to report the scene simply and accurately, headlines would read something like this:

People trying to return home continue to be shot
dead by Israeli snipers because they are not Jewish

There is nothing interpretive here. People are trying to return to what is home by international law, by what Israel claimed to have agreed

---

* "Genocide means any of the following acts committed with intent to destroy, in whole or in part, a national, ethnical, racial or religious group, as such: (a) Killing members of the group; (b) Causing serious bodily or mental harm to members of the group; (c) Deliberately inflicting on the group conditions of life calculated to bring about its physical destruction in whole or in part; (d) Imposing measures intended to prevent births within the group; (e) Forcibly transferring children of the group to another group." –*Convention on the Prevention and Punishment of the Crime of Genocide, Approved and proposed for signature and ratification or accession by General Assembly resolution 260 A (III) of December 9, 1948; Entry into force: January 12, 1951, in accordance with article XIII.*

in order to be accepted by the UN, and above all by any measure that would be applied anywhere else (anyone who doubts this should try reversing the ethnicities)—and the single reason Israel kills them is the single reason Israel locked them up in Gaza three-quarters of a century ago: because they are anything other than Jewish. That Israel presents them to the world as a threat is Israel's own doing.

The "Jewish state"?

But Israel insulates itself with the most powerful weapon in its arsenal: its hijacking of Jewish identity, codified through its unassailable brand *Israel* and mantra *the Jewish State*. By marketing itself as the regeneration of the otherworldly "Israel" born in Western civilization's core Creation text, state+Jews become synonymous, enabling Israel to spin criticism of its crimes not just as an attack on Jews, but an attack on our collective cultural womb.

We are told that there are many states with religion-based associations—Christian states, Muslim states, Buddhist states, Hindu states—and that Israel is "the only Jewish state." The inference of this claim, that Israel is just like other nations with state religions, is absurd, and the difference is fundamental.

First, Israel has no state religion, Judaism or otherwise. Israel, rather, has a state *race*, what it treats, defines, and exploits in racial terms. That, not religion or even cultural tradition, is Israel's meaning of "the Jewish state."

Secondly, for states with an official religion, that officialness extends to their borders and stops. Such states neither claim exclusivity on the religion, nor to have any claim on co-religionist citizens of other countries.

Israel is the opposite. Israel is "the only Jewish state" not in the sense that there happen to be no others, but because by Israel's construct there *can be no other*. Its claim over Jews is global; it claims to be *the* Jewish state, not simply *a* Jewish state.

This nation-state adaptation of tribalism, in which the state is part of the DNA of an ethnic identity, bears no relation to states with a national religion, and is unknown in the modern world, with two exceptions: Israel, and common bigots.

Everyday racists blame individuals by virtue of perceived synonymity with some ethnicity or nationality or "type." Thus, as but one example, during the spread of Covid19 in the United States, "Asian-looking" people were attacked because the virus came from China. "They" caused Covid.

Israel does precisely this to Jews, but in reverse, in order to use Jews as a human shield. Just as the bigot made "Asian-looking" people into China, Israel made Jews into *it*. What Israel does, "the Jews" did, and so to accuse Israel is to libel Jews *as Jews*—that is, antisemitism.

Israel thus wields the triptych "the Jewish state" as a talisman. Other states may deflect criticism of their crimes by "hiding behind the flag," accusing dissenting *citizens* of being unpatriotic to the *state*. Israel instead hides behind the *ethnicity*, free of borders, accusing dissenting voices anywhere of being traitorous to the *ethnicity*.

If this is Israel's most powerful weapon, it is also its Achilles' heel, Zionism's fatal flaw, and in my view will ultimately cause Zionism to fail of its own accord. Traditional antisemitism, for all its horrors, is powerless to harm the integrity of Jews or Judaism, powerless to make its libels true. Israel and Zionism—if we accept them at their word—succeed. If we accept their claims on Jewish identity, then we are the common racist blaming Jews, because they are Jews.

Israel's defenders, meanwhile, tolerate and even celebrate true anti-Jewish bigots, because they are invariably avid supporters of Zionism and the state—and are invariably critics of Israel's critics. This is all the more tragic given the rise in neo-fascism and the true threat it poses against Jews and anyone else perceived as an *Other*, that Zionism excuses if not supports.

The dependence on a never-ending existential threat

The Gaza strip best illustrates Israel's dependence on an ever-assured perceived threat. In response to Israel's siege and attacks, Hamas and fringe groups launch rockets over the Armistice Line, usually toward Israeli towns like Sderot (which is actually the Palestinian village of Najd, seized and ethnically cleansed by Israel in 1948), but occasionally reaching further. Western media reverse cause and effect, and depict Israel's siege as though it were the Caspian Gates keeping out the barbarian hordes.

The siege of Gaza began in 1948, fifty-eight years before the 2006 election of Hamas which Israel now uses to justify it. It served then the same singular purpose it serves today: to block people of the wrong ethnicity from returning home.

Although to the eye the Gaza fence seems benign compared to the towering cement Wall in parts of the West Bank, it is far more impenetrable and deadly. Israeli snipers and militarized remote-controlled towers murder on sight any in Gaza who approach it, so that a wide swath of Gaza's best farmland lies barren, a death trap. Similarly on the west, Gazan fishermen are attacked by Israeli patrols if they attempt to reach Gaza's most fertile fishing grounds, while the nearer waters are contaminated by sewage as a result of Israel's destruction of Gaza's sewage treatment plants and blocking of their repair. Israel's sponsor states hear little about this; but when in response, Hamas or fringe groups fire rockets over the Armistice Line, it is reported as an unprovoked attack against which Israel has the right to respond.

On the day of the 2008 US presidential election, Israel launched an unprovoked attack against Gaza, the date chosen to ensure that the attack would be off the Western news radar. After Israel received in exchange what it wanted—rockets fired over the Armistice Line—it announced the Palestinian "terror attack" to the world and "defended" itself by killing about 1400 of the very people it holds captive in the enclave, and wounding thousands more.

In the wake of this so-called Cast Lead operation, Israel left behind precisely what its siege is allegedly in place to prevent: a vast stockpile of explosives *inside* Gaza, in the form of its own unexploded ordnance (UXOs).

For the UN and bomb disposal organizations, this was an emergency: children happening upon them may be blown up, and the live mines, bombs, and unspent white phosphorus were there for the taking.

Yet for fourteen months, Israel steadfastly blocked UN bomb experts from neutralizing this huge stockpile of explosive devices

A child plays amidst destruction in the southern Gaza strip following Israel's "Cast Lead" attacks, 2009 (Photo © Tom Suárez)

that Israel itself put there. It did not merely do nothing (which in itself would have begged explanation), but actively *prevented their destruction*, insuring that they would be taken by Hamas and, more dangerously for Israel, fringe groups—as, of course, happened.

Even after Israel's interference landed the first batch of bombs into Hamas' hands, it still blocked bomb disposal personnel from rendering the materials harmless. Nor did it relent when five more tons of its UXOs disappeared into the hands of unidentified militant groups. And so it was as if scripted when white phosphorus, which had burned people alive when it rained down on Gaza from Israeli aircraft, was now blasted by the militants over the Armistice Line (without casualty). *Terrorists fired 2 phosphorus shells into Israel*, as the *Jerusalem Post* headline read.

For the *BBC*, for the *New York Times*, for *Haaretz*, not even this Machiavellian episode of manufactured threat elicited any hint of journalistic curiosity. When, fourteen months after Cast Lead, Israel finally stopped blocking the UN Mine Action Service and related organizations from destroying whatever UXOs remained, their readers were given the impression that the bomb disposal agencies somehow just hadn't gotten around to the job, but it was now undertaken at Israel's initiative for the benefit of the people of Palestine.[683]

The summer of 2014 was twice as barbaric as Cast Lead. Called "Protective Edge," it caused roughly the same human carnage as the 9/11 terror attack in the United States. The 9/11 attacks have become iconic of Evil itself—as well they should—yet this massacre, the justification for which was as obscene as that of the 9/11 terrorists, was applauded by the US Congress.[684]

And so, the question: What now?

Israel controls the lives of the twelve million people in historic Palestine, from the Jordan River to the coastal waters of the Mediterranean Sea. It also dictates the lives of millions more in Jordan, Lebanon, and Syria, who languish in sixty-eight refugee camps so that Israel can pursue its goal of ethnic purity.

Israel has been given seven decades of opportunity to demonstrate that it is a responsible state. It is time to say it: Israel is a failed experiment toward an illegitimate end, not merely a state in need of reform. The problem won't be fixed simply by rewinding to 1990s Oslo or to June 1967 or May 1948. It will be fixed only by acknowledging the truth of all that has happened since 1917, and by canceling the apartheid and the ethnic cleansing the UN set in motion under Zionist and US pressure in November 1947.

Apartheid must give way to what the UN would have decreed in 1947 had it honored its own principles: a single state of all its people, rooted in secularism, democracy, equality. All people river-to-sea must be equal citizens in a shared society, including Israel's Jewish citizens, all of whom had since 1948 enjoyed institutional racial privilege.

Above all, equality by definition means the absolute right of all refugees to return. Apartheid has not ended if its foremost victims are now told that equality does not apply to them since, precisely due to that apartheid, they are not physically present, while the people who ethnically cleansed them, remain. The moment Israel physically blocked the refugees from returning home, the refugee camps became Israeli internment camps, paid for by the international community.*

Israel was born by the wholesale hijacking of Palestine. It wasn't just the land itself; it was uncountable Palestinian businesses, orchards, assets, factories, homes, schools, villas, hospitals, equipment, industries, and export trades, all stolen by Israel and its settlers. What we call the Israeli state was an entire, intact country; the Zionists simply hung their own shingle on its door.[685]

Yet our nations, while claiming to be the beacons of enlightened values and democracy, treat the idea of democracy and equality in Israel-Palestine as radical, unthinkable—even, yes, antisemitic.

Israel's sponsor states repress us, their own citizenry, in its service. In Europe, in the United Kingdom, the United States, Canada, and Australia, a state of fear on the subject permeates society, academia, and well beyond. This fear extracts obedience from anyone whose life situation or livelihood could be destroyed, as the fate of those who disobey invariably demonstrates. Most insidiously, we have been taught to self-censor on behalf of Israel, because self-censorship leaves no trace.

The United States gives nearly four billion dollars a year to Israel. Yet the economic drain pales next to the pro-Israel repression the US imposes on US citizens. Anti-boycott loyalty oaths to Israel are mandatory in many states for work or services involving the state. School teachers, newspapers, and ordinary businesses have been forced to sign these pledges, and after a devastating hurricane a Texas city, following state law, required residents seeking government disaster relief to sign a loyalty pledge to Israel†.[686]

---

* Dr. Salman Abu Sitta of the Palestine Land Society (plands.org) has studied the land and populations to set the logistical groundwork for the return of the refugees.

† As of 2021, 35 US states have passed bills and executive orders penalizing the boycott of Israel. Re: disaster relief, Dickinson, Texas, in line with state law, clause 11 for flood relief is typical of general US anti-BDS clauses: *Verification not to Boycott Israel. By executing this Agreement below, the Applicant verifies that the Applicant: (1) does not boycott Israel; and (2) will not boycott Israel during the term of this Agreement.*

One hardly need point out how extraordinary, how surreal this is. That we as a nation have not been shocked by it and demanded that it end is our failing. We cannot blame Israel—whatever the reason for our self-harm on Israel's behalf, no amount of Israeli lobbying or political strong-arming can actually force us to comply.

Like the Palestinians in the West Bank, we in Israel's benefactor nations live behind a towering Israeli wall. But whereas the West Bank wall is of cement, our wall is a towering vacuum keeping out the truth of what is being done in our name and with our money, our political power, and our moral integrity. Israel can not stop us from tearing it down.

One state of all its people, with a warm welcome home for the refugees, would finally make this book and all like it, history.

Tom Suárez, January 2022

Bibliography

Abu El-Haj, Nadia, *Facts on the Ground: Archaeological Practice and Territorial Self-Fashioning in Israeli Society*, [University of Chicago Press, 2002]

Abu-Lughod, Ibrahim (ed.), *Transformation of Palestine* [Northwestern University Press, 1987]

Anglo-Palestinian Club, *Palestine 1917-1944. Pamphlet No. 2. A Review by Sir Wyndham Deedes, The Hon. R. D. Denman, M.P., Mrs. E. Dugdale, Victor Gollancz, S.S. Hammersley, M.P. Sir Andrew McFadyean* [The Narod Press, London]

Arab Higher Committee, *Palestine The Arab Case, Being a statement made by the Delegation of the Arab Higher Committee before the first committee of the General Assembly of the United Nation's Organization on 9th May, 1947* [Cairo, Costa Tsoumas & Co., 1947]

Arab Higher Committee Delegation for Palestine, *The Black Paper on the Jewish Agency and Zionist Terrorism, memorandum to The United Nations Delegations. Submitted by The Arab Higher Committee Delegation for Palestine* 4512 Empire State Building, New York, NY. 12 March 1948. Copy examined: BL.

Bailes, Jon (ed.), Aksan, Cihan (ed), *Weapon of the Strong: Conversations on US State Terrorism* [Pluto, 2013]

Baumel, Judith Tydor, translation Dena Ordan, *The "Bergson Boys" and the Origins of Contemporary Zionist Militancy* [Syracuse University, 2005]

Bell, Bowyer, *Terror out of Zion: Irgun Zvai Leumi, LEHI, and the Palestine Underground, 1929-1949* [St. Martin's 1977]

Ben-Yehuda, Nachman, *Political Assassinations by Jews: A Rhetorical Device for Justice* [SUNY Press, 1993]

— *The Masada Myth: Collective Memory and Mythmaking in Israel* [University of Wisconsin Press, 1996]

Benziman, Uzi, *Sharon: An Israeli Caesar* [London: Robson Books, 1987]

Bishop, Patrick, *The Reckoning: Death and Intrigue in the Promised Land* [Kindle edition, HarperCollins, 2014]

Black, Edward, *The Transfer Agreement: The Dramatic Story of the Pact Between the Third Reich and Jewish Palestine* [Dialog Press, 2009]

Black, Ian, and Morris, Benny, *Israel's Secret Wars: A History of Israel's Intelligence Services* [Grove Press, 1992]

Burt, Leonard, *Commander Burt of Scotland Yard, by Himself.* [Heinemann, 1959]

Braun, Hanna, *Weeds Don't Perish*, Garnet Publishing, 2011. Also the author's conversation with Ms. Braun in London in 2007.

Brenner, Lenni, *Zionism in the Age of Dictators* [Croom Helm, 1983 / Kindle, Amazon Digital, 2015]—*51 Documents: Zionist Collaboration with the Nazis* [Barricade Books, 2010]

[British government], *Palestine Pamphlet Terrorist Methods With Mines and Booby Traps.* Headquarters, Chief Engineer, Palestine and Transjordan. December 1946.

Central Intelligence Agency, *The Consequences of the Partition of Palestine, ORE 55, 28 November 1947 Copy No. 35.*

Cesarani, David, *Major Farran's Hat: The Untold Story of the Struggle to Establish the Jewish State* [Da Capo Press, 2009]

Chomsky, Noam, *Fateful Triangle: The United States, Israel, and the Palestinians* [South End Press, 1999]

Clarke, Thurston, *By Blood and Fire: The Attack on the King David Hotel* [Hutchinson, 1981]

Cohen, Michael, *Churchill and the Jews, 1900-1948* [Frank Cass, 2003]

Cohen, Stuart A., "A Still Stranger Aspect of Suez: British Operational Plans to Attack Suez," in *The International History Review*, Vol. 10, No. 2, May, 1988

— *English Zionists and British Jews: The Communal Politics of Anglo-Jewry, 1895-1920*, Princeton University Press, 1982

Davis, Uri, *Apartheid Israel* [Zed Books, 2003]

Dieckhoff, Alain, *The Invention of a Nation.* [Columbia University Press, 2003]

Dreyfus, Laurence, *Wagner and the Erotic Impulse*, [Harvard University Press, 2010]

Ehrlich, Mark Avrum, Encyclopedia of the Jewish Diaspora: Origins, Experiences, and Culture, Vol 1 [ABC-CLIO, 2008]

Elkins, Caroline (ed.), and Pedersen, Susan (ed), *Settler Colonialism in the Twentieth Century: Projects, Practices, Legacies* [Routledge, 2005]

Ernst, Morris, *So Far So Good* [New York, Harper & Brothers, 1948]

Eveland, Wilbur Crane, *Ropes of Sand, America's Failure in the Middle East* [W W Norton & Co, 1980]

Feldman, Ilana, Governing Gaza [Duke University, 2008]

Filiu, Jean-Pierre, *Gaza: A History* [Comparative Politics and International Studies, Oxford University Press, Kindle Edition, 2014; translated by John King]

Fischbach, Michael R., *Records of Dispossession: Palestinian Refugee Property and the Arab-Israeli Conflict* [Columbia University Press, 2003]

Frantz, Douglas, & Collins, Catherine, *Death on the Black Sea* [HarperCollins, 2003]

Friedmann, Robert R. (ed), *Crime and Criminal Justice in Israel: Assessing the Knowledge Base Toward the Twenty-First Century* [State University of New York Press, 1998]

Gallagher, Nancy, *Quakers in the Israeli–Palestinian Conflict: The Dilemmas of NGO Humanitarian Activism* [American University in Cairo Press, 2007]

Gat, Moshe, *The Jewish Exodus from Iraq, 1948-1951* [Routledge, 1997]

Giladi, Naeim, *Ben-Gurion's Scandals: How the Haganah and the Mossad Eliminated Jews.* [Dandelion Enterprises, 2006]

Golani, Motti, *Palestine Between Politics & Terror* [Brandeis University, 2013]

Gorny, Joseph, *The British Labour Movement and Zionism, 1917-1948* [Rutledge, 1983]

Greenfield, Murray, and Hochstein, Joseph, *The Jews' Secret Fleet: The Untold Story of North American Volunteers who Smashed the British Blockade.* [Gefen Publishing, 2010]

Grodzinsky, Yosef, *In the Shadow of the Holocaust: The Struggle Between Jews and Zionists in the Aftermath of World War II.* [Common Courage Press, July 1, 2004]

Grossman, Avraham, *Pious and Rebellious: Jewish Women in Medieval Europe.* [University Press of New England, 2004]

Herzl, Theodor, *Diaries of Theodor Herzl* [Grosset & Dunlap, 1962]

— *Zionist Writings. Essays and Addresses. Volume 1: January 1896–June, 1898.* Translated by Harry Zohn [NY, Herzl Press, 1973]

Hirst, David, *The Gun and the Olive Branch: The Roots of Violence in the Middle East* [Nation Books, 2003]

Hope Simpson, Sir John, Palestine. *Report on Immigration, Land Settlement and Development. Presented by the Secretary of State for the Colonies to Parliament by Command of His Majesty.* October, 1930.

Hughes, Matthew, *Britain's Pacification of Palestine: The British Army, the Colonial State, and the Arab Revolt, 1936–1939* [Cambridge, 2020]

Hutchison, Elmo Harrison, *Violent truce: A military observer looks at the Arab-Israeli conflict, 1951-1955* [Calder, 1956]

Institute for Palestine Studies, Arab Women's Information Committee, *Who Are the Terrorists? Aspects of Zionist and Israeli Terrorism* [Beirut: 1972]

Irgun Zvai Leumi, *Official Report of the Proceedings at a Conference between Representatives of the United Nations Special Committee on Palestine and of the Irgun Zvai Leumi, held in Palestine on 24 June, 1947. Published by the Diaspora Headquarters of the IRGUN ZVAI LEUMI By Authority of the High Command in Eretz Israel.* Copy examined, TNA, FO 371/61866. [Typewritten, not printed.]

Jeffries, J.M.N., *Palestine: The Reality* [1939; facsimile, Delhi, 2015]

Jewish Agency for Palestine, *Memorandum on Acts of Arab Aggression to Alter by Force the Settlement on the Future Government of Palestine Approved by the General Assembly of the United Nations, submitted to the United Nations Palestine Commission by the Jewish Agency for Palestine.* [Lake Success, New York, February 2, 1948. Copy examined: BL]

Jewish Legion, *Report of the Conference between Representatives of the United Nations Special Committee on Palestine and the Commander and Two Other Representatives of the Irgun Zvai Leumi.* [London: Published by the Jewish Legion, November, 1947] [Copied examined: TNA, KV 5/39]

Kapeliouk, Amnon, "New Light on the lsraeli-Arab Conflict and the Refugee Problem and Its Origins," in *Journal of Palestine Studies*, Vol. 16, No. 3, Spring, 1987.

Karmi, Ghada, *In Search of Fatima* [Verso, 2009]

— *Married to Another Man: Israel's Dilemma in Palestine* [Pluto, 2007]

Kesaris, Paul (ed), Dobrosky, Nanette (compiler), *A Guide to the Microfilm Edition of U.S. State Department Central Files Palestine, United Nations Activities, 1945-1949* [University Publications of America, 1987]

Khalidi, Thabet, *The Rising Tide of Terror or Three Years of an "Armistice" in the Holy Land.* [Ministry of Foreign Affairs, Amman, 1952]

Khalidi, Walid, *All That Remains: The Palestinian Villages Occupied and Depopulated by Israel in 1948* [Institute for Palestine Studies, 2006]

— "Revisiting the UNGA Partition Resolution," *JPS*, XXVII, no.1 (Autumn 1997), 5-21.

Kirkbride, Alec, *From the Wings: Amman Memoirs 1947-1951* [Routledge, 1976]

Kister, Joseph, *The Irgun the Story of the Irgun Zvai Leumi in Eretz-Israel* [Ministry of Defence Publishing House, 2000]

Koestler, Arthur, *Promise and Fulfilment Palestine 1917-1949* [Macmillan, 1949]

Kolsky, Thomas, *Jews Against Zionism: The American Council for Judaism, 1942-1948* [Temple University Press, 1992]

Kranzler, David, *Holocaust Hero: The Untold Story of Solomon Schonfeld, an Orthodox British Rabbi* [Ktav Pub Inc, 2003]

Lavie, Smadar, *Wrapped in the Flag of Israel: Mizrahi Single Mothers and Bureaucratic Torture* [Berghahn Books, 2014]

Lazin, Fred A., "Refugee Resettlement and 'Freedom of Choice'–The Case of Soviet Jewry," Center for Immigration Studies [June 2005]

Lilienthal, Alfred M., *What Price Israel?* [Infinity Publishing, 2004]

Maov, Zeev, *Defending the Holy Land: A Critical Analysis of Israel's Security and Foreign Policy* [University of Michigan Press, 2006]

Masalha, Nur, *Expulsion of the Palestinians, the Concept of "Transfer" in Zionist Political Thought, 1882-1948* [Institute for Palestinian Studies, 1992 /2001]

Maxwell, ex-Sergeant Max, "An Explosive Situation," [personal account of the bombing of the Mallnitz train on August 12, 1947]. Accessed online January 20, 2012; and subsequent email exchanges with Mr. Maxwell.

Medoff, Rafael, *Militant Zionism in America: The Rise and Impact of the Jabotinsky Movement in the United States, 1926-1948*. [University of Alabama Press, 2006]

Menuhin, Moshe, *The decadence of Judaism in our time* [Beirut Institute for Palestine Studies, 1969]

Morris, Benny, *The Birth of the Palestinian Refugee Problem, 1947-1949* [Cambridge University Press, 1989]

— *The Birth of the Palestinian Refugee Problem Revisited* [Cambridge University Press, 2004]

— *Israel's Border Wars, 1949-1956: Arab Infiltration, Israeli Retaliation, and the Countdown to the Suez War* [Oxford: Clarendon Press, 1993]

— *Righteous Victims: A History of the Zionist-Arab Conflict, 1881-1998* [Vintage ed, 2011]

— *1948: A History of the First Arab-Israeli War* [Yale, 2009]

Morris, Ira R.T., & Smith, Joe Alex, *"Dear Mr. President ..." The Story of Fifty Years in the White House* [Julian Messner, 1949]

Murray S. Greenfield & Joseph Hochstein, *Jews Secret Fleet* [Gefen, 1996]

Nasr, Kameel B., *Arab and Israeli Terrorism: The Causes and Effects of Political Violence* [McFarland & Company, 2007]

Neff, Donald, *Fallen Pillars: U.S. Policy Towards Palestine and Israel Since 1945* [Institute for Palestine Studies, 2002]

Nicosia, Francis R., *The Third Reich and the Palestine Question* [Transaction Publishers, 2000]

Pappé, Ilan, *The Idea of Israel: A History Of Power and Knowledge* [Verso, 2014]

— *Out of the Frame* [Pluto, 2010, Kindle]

— *The Ethnic Cleansing of Palestine* [Oneworld Publications, 2007]

— *The Making of the Arab-Israeli Conflict 1947-1951* [I.B. Tauris, 1992]

— *A History of Modern Palestine* [Cambridge University, 2008]

Pedahzur, Ami, and Perliger Arie, *Jewish Terrorism in Israel* [Columbia University Press, 2011]

Pedahzur, Ami (ed.), and Weinberg, Leonard (ed), *Religious Fundamentalism and Political Extremism* [Frank Cass, 2004]

Polkehn, Klaus, "The Secret Contacts: Zionism and Nazi Germany, 1933-1941," in *Journal of Palestine Studies*, Vol. 5, No. 3/4 (1976), 54-82

Pragnell, F. A., *Palestine Chronicle, 1880-1950: Extracts from the Arabic Press Tracing the Main Political and Social Developments* [Pragnell Books, 2005]

Quigley, John, *Palestine and Israel: A Challenge to Justice* [Durham and London: Duke University Press, 1990]

Qumsiyeh, Mazin B., *Popular Resistance in Palestine: A History of Hope and Empowerment* [Pluto Press, 2006]

Rabinovich, Itamar, and Reinharz, Jehuda (eds), *Israel in the Middle East: Documents and Readings on Society, Politics, and Foreign Relations, Pre-1948 to the Present* [Brandeis University, 2007]

Reinharz, Shulamit, and Schor, Laura S., *The Best School in Jerusalem: Annie Landau's School for Girls, 1900-1960* [HBI Series on Jewish Women, Brandeis University,2013]

Rhett, Maryanne A., *The Global History of the Balfour Declaration: Declared Nation* [Routledge, 2015]

Robinson, Shira N., *Citizen Strangers: Palestinians and the Birth of Israel's Liberal Settler State* [Stanford University Press, 2013

Rogan, Eugene, *The Arabs: A History* [Basic Books, 2011]

Rokach, Livia, *Israel's Sacred Terrorism: A Study Based on Moshe Sharett's Personal Diary and Other Documents* [Assn of Arab-American University Graduates, 1985]

Roosevelt, Kermit, *The Arab Position on Palestine*, Presented at the National War College, Washington, DC, 24 November, 1948

— *Partition of Palestine: A Lesson in Pressure Politics*, The Institute of Arab American Affairs, NY, February, 1948

Rose, John, *The Myths of Zionism* [London: Pluto Press, 2004]

Ryan, Joseph L, "Refugees Within Israel: The Case of the Villagers of Kafr Bir'im and Iqrit," in *Journal of Palestine Studies*, Vol. 2, No. 4, Summer, 1973, 55-81

Said, Edward, *Orientalism* [Vintage Books, 1979]

Sand, Schlomo, *The Invention of the Jewish People* [Verso, 2009]

Scott, James M., *The Attack on the Liberty: The Untold Story of Israel's Deadly 1967 Assault on a U.S. Spy Ship* [Simon & Schuster, 2009]

Schwartz, Ted, *Walking with the Damned* [New York: Paragon, 1992]

Segev, Tom, *One Palestine, Complete: Jews and Arabs Under the British Mandate* [Picador, 2001]

Sharett, Moshe, The 1953 Qibya Raid Revisited: Excerpts from Moshe Sharett's Diaries Introduced by Walid Khalidi and Annotated by Neil Caplan. In *Journal of Palestine Studies,* XXXI, no. 4 (Summer 2002), pages 77-98.

Shlaim, Avi, "The Protocol of Sèvres, 1956: Anatomy of a War Plot," in *International Affairs*, 73:3, 1997, 509-530

Sitkowski, Andrzej, *UN Peacekeeping: Myth and Reality* [Praeger, 2006]

Sprinzak, Ehud, *Brother Against Brother: Violence and Extremism in Israeli Politics from Altalena to the Rabin Assassination* [Free Press, 1999]

Smith, Charles, *Palestine and the Arab-Israeli Conflict: A History with Documents* [Bedford/St. Martin's, 2010]

Stein, Kenneth W., "The Jewish National Fund: Land Purchase Methods and Priorities, 1924-1939," in *Middle Eastern Studies*, Volume 20 Number 2, 190-205, April 1984.

Sternhell, Zeev (translation D. Maisel), *The Founding Myths of Israel* [Princeton University Press, 1999]

Strawson, John, *Partitioning Palestine Legal Fundamentalism in the Palestinian-Israeli Conflict*. [Pluto, 2010]

Tamari, Salim, (ed.), Jerusalem 1948: The Arab Neighbourhoods and Their Fate in the War. [Inst for Palestine Studies, 2002]

Teveth, Shabtai, *Ben-Gurion and the Palestinian Arabs: From Peace to War* [Oxford University Press, 1985]

Tomes, Jason, *Balfour and Foreign Policy: The International Thought of a Conservative Statesman* [Cambridge University Press, 1997]

Veracini, Lorenzo, *Israel and Settler Society* [Pluto, 2006]

Wagner, Steven, "British Intelligence and the Jewish Resistance Movement in the Palestine Mandate, 1945-46," in *Intelligence and National Security*, Volume 23, Issue 5, 2008, 629-657

Walton, Calder, *Empire of Secrets: British Intelligence, the Cold War, and the Twilight of Empire* [Overlook, 2013]

Weizmann, Chaim, *The Letters and Papers of Chaim Weizmann, Series B, Papers, Volume II, December 1931-April 1952*; Edited by Barnet Litvinoff [Transaction Books, 1984]

Wendehorst, Stephan E. C., *British Jewry, Zionism, and the Jewish State, 1936-1956* [Oxford University Press, 2011]

Wilson, Major-General Dare, *With 6th Airborne Division in Palestine 1945-1948* [Gale and Polden Ltd, 1949 /Kindle, 2008]

Wistrich, Robert S., *From Ambivalence to Betrayal: The Left, the Jews, and Israel* [Studies in Antisemitism, University of Nebraska Press, 2012]

Zertal, Idith, *Israel's Holocaust and the Politics of Nationhood* [Cambridge University Press, 2005]

End Notes

BL = British Library
CIA = Central Intelligence Agency (US)
JTA = Jewish Telegraphic Agency
LOC = Library of Congress (Washington, D.C.)
NYT = New York Times
TNA = The National Archives (Kew)
ZOA = Zionist Organization of America

TNA WO 169/4334, contains a Glossary of Hebrew Terms

Introduction

1   TNA, FO 1093/330.

2   TNA, CAB 24/28/0063, p3. Bentwich was criticized for the remark by members of the Universities of Oxford, Cambridge, and London.

3   For an analysis of Zionism's settler colonialism, see Robinson, *Citizen Strangers*. For similarities to traditional settler ventures, see, e.g., Veracini, *Israel and Settler Society*. See Bibliography for works by Lilienthal, Menuhin, and Pappé.

4   Regarding the common use of "terrorism" for violence against the military, for example, the bombings of the 1995 Oklahoma City bombing and the 1983 Beirut US Marine compound bombing, which were government and military targets respectively, are usually referred to as terrorism.

5   Virtually all Zionist leaders subscribe to all these justifications against democracy, but specific mention in this book includes Weizmann claiming that "Arabs"are inferior people and so do not deserve a vote he and Begin arguing that all Jews are, by blood, "nationals" of Palestine; all, including Ben-Gurion, arguing that Jews were a majority in a vast Biblical realm, and that this gives alleged descendants the right to "return"; and Ben-Gurion arguing explicitly (and all others at least implicitly) that the Zionist state is not bound by the norms governing any other nation. International Humanitarian Law prohibits "acts of terrorism" against persons not or no longer taking part in hostilities. https://www.icrc.org/eng/resources/documents/faq/terrorism-faq-050504.htm (accessed Mar 2, 2015). The US Joint Chiefs of Staff definition: Terrorism is the unlawful use of violence or threat of violence, often motivated by religious, political, or other ideological beliefs, to instill fear and coerce governments or

societies in pursuit of goals that are usually political. (Joint Publication 3-26, Counterterrorism, 24 October 2014). For further discussion on definitions of "terrorism" (no variation of which would affect this book's working definition), see Cihan and Bailes, Introduction to *Weapon of the Strong*; Richard P. Stevens, "Zionism as a Phase of Western Imperialism," in Abu-Lughod, *Transformation*, 40-41; TNA, FO 608/99, 281-295, esp 287-288; Jewish Legion, *Report of the Conference...*; FO 1093/330, after 48, 12; UNSCOP A/364/Add.2 PV.19 (7 July 1947). Many Zionist leaders distrusted democracy even within the Jewish community. It was for Ben-Gurion an enemy in the "building of Eretz Israel by the Jewish people"; he and others argued that Zionists knew what was best for Jews and thus did not require their majority support (see e.g., the Begin "conference" with the UNSCOP committee in the present book, in TNA, KV 5/39, and Sternhell, *Founding Myths*, 190-191).

6   TNA, FO 371/91715, 29; for more Zionist settler analogy to European colonization of America, e.g., NYT, Jan 27 1947; The Israeli state's claim on language enables its Ministry of Defense to publish a book glorifying even the most ghastly terrorism of the Mandate period (Kister, *Irgun*). For CNN obligating reporters to refer to Israeli settlements as "Jewish neighborhoods," Robert Fisk, "CNN caves in to Israel over its references to illegal settlements," The *Independent*, Sept 3 2001.

7   Regarding "Arab Jews," for an excellent personal and historical account, see Massoud Hayoun's *When We Were Arabs: A Jewish Family's Forgotten History* [The New Press, 2019].

8   Benny Morris, *Revisited*, 5-6, argues that while "the evidence for pre-1948 Zionist support for "Transfer" really is unambiguous," the ethnic cleansing of 1948 was not "tantamount to a master plan." This argument defies the unequivocal deliberateness and years of planning behind what happened, and fails to explain why, if it was not the "plan," Israel to this day steadfastly blocks the refugees' return. Morris, indeed, "bemoans the fact that the job was left unfinished" (2004 interview, "Survival of the fittest," Ari Shavit, in *Haaretz*, January 8, 2004, haaretz.com/survival-of-the-fittest-1.61345 retrieved June 16, 2014. For Palestinian agricultural and industrial productivity expanding markedly in the nineteenth century, before Zionist presence, see e.g., Smith, *Palestine*, 22-23.

9   Regarding the far more lenient treatment of Jews, the opposite claim was (and is) sometimes made, apparently based on a *Jewish Chronicle* report from 11 February 1944 alleging a few cases in which Arabs received lesser sentences than Jews had for the same charges. These specific cases involved possession of pistols and bullets. See TNA, FO 371/40126, "Discrepancies between sentences awarded in Palestine to Jews and Arabs for similar offences." A telegram 299 commented on the "circumstances of the cases in question."

10   TNA, CAB 129/21/0009, Cabinet / Palestine / Memorandum by the Secretary of State for Foriegn Affairs / C.P. (47) 259, esp 5 ('52 stamped at upper right) (18 September, 1947).

11   One may find a two or three percent disparity in published percentages for the Partition. The reason is that Resolution 181 established an international zone comprising Jerusalem and Bethlehem, and so some figures tally Israel and Palestine combined as slightly short of 100%, while others, such as that quoted herein, exclude it, dividing the remainder; *NYT*, 19 Jan 1949, 10 Jan 1949. For Britain's claim that it bore no responsibility to keep peace Palestine when it decided to end the Mandate, see e.g., FO 800/487, 55.

12   For extending terms of classified Zionist documents, see e.g., Barak Ravid, "State archives to stay classified for 20 more years, PM instructs," in *Haaretz*, July 28, 2010; Hagar Shezaf, "Burying the Nakba: How Israel Systematically Hides Evidence of 1948 Expulsion of Arabs", *Haaretz* July 5 2019.

13   Re: "Arab", although British reports usually used the generic "Arab," one clear example of the deliberate use of "Palestinian" is seen in a report about the bombing of the King David Hotel in July of 1946, which uses the term "Palestinian" employees, rather than the usual "Arab" employees, to account for nearly half of the fatalities; TNA, WO 275/58, 6 Airborne Division, Intelligence Summary No. 3 (to 26 July 46). Also "Coat Bomb and Explosive Prosthesis: British Intel Files Reveal How the Zionist Stern Gang Terrorized London" in *Haaretz*, Dec 2, 2017.

14   Eduard Bernstein, see Robert S. Wistrich, Ambivalence to Betrayal [Un of Nebraska, 2012] p147.

15   Ben-Gurion quote, NYT, 8 Jan 1937; this was to the Peel Commission, and his use of the word "mandate" in regard to the Bible was a play on the British *Mandate*; Also, e.g., Jewish right to take Palestine "is based on the ancient mandate of the Bible" in TNA, WO 275/121, Appendix A, The Voice of Israel.

16   For Weizmann, CO 537/1711, 29; for Lehi, Pedahzur & Perliger, *Jewish Terrorism*, 11; Weizmann warned Churchill in 1946 that failure to accede to Zionists' demands for ethnicity-based minority rule in Palestine would mean the "destruction of the Third Temple," thus "destroying the last hope of hundreds of thousands of Jews throughout the world." Ben-Gurion, singing "the song of Moses and the Children of Ancient Israel," spoke of IDF conquests that "will become a part of the third kingdom of Israel" and of "IDF divisions [who] extended a hand to King Solomon" (Sand, *Invention*, 108). Judaism and the Bible are invoked even for the names Israel assigns its wars; Genesis, the Biblical six days of Creation, is invoked in the name "Six Day War" (1967 war; Rabin chose the name. See Michael Oren, *Six Days of War*, 309 [Ballantine, 2003]); more recently, "Cast Lead," Israel's 2008-2009 attacks against Gaza, refers to a Hanukkah festival; and "Pillar of Cloud," its 2012 assault against Gaza, is a reference to the Biblical Exodus; Moshe Dayan equated the Suez War with the Exodus, and the 1948 and 1967 wars with the conquest of Canaan (Sand, *Invention*, 112); Zertal, *Israel's Holocaust*, 93; Congressional Record, 1922 House of Representatives, June 30, 1922B, *National Home in Palestine for the Jewish People, cont. Pages 9809-.9820.*

17 Quote by former Arkansas Senate majority leader, Bart Hester, in Alan Leveritt, "We're a Small Arkansas Newspaper. Why Is the State Making Us Sign a Pledge About Israel?", in NYT, Nov 22 2021.

18 Ilan Pappé addresses the "selling" of Israel in his *The Idea of Israel: A History of Power and Knowledge* (Verso, 2014).

19 Herzl, *Diaries* (Lowenthal), 412, 407; Herzl, *Jewish State*; For same principle espoused by Weizmann, see CO 733/443/18, MS "25 To JS MacPherson" in upper left; See also Weizmann comment in CO 733/443/18, E 2399/87/31, verso, regarding psychological value of Palestine as Jewish settler state; Herzl pushing for Jewish settlement in the Sinai, FO 78/5479; Post-World War I Cyprus still proposed as part of a "Greater Palestine," see FO 608/99, letter from David Treitsch.

20 Herzl, *Diaries*, 283 (in Jerusalem in 1898).

21 Dr. Paul Nathan's Trip to the East, The *Hebrew Standard*, Nov 1 1907; Nathan, see NYT, 18 Jan 1914 & Feb 1 1914.; Landau, Reinharz /Schor, Best School, 92-93. Criticism of him, "The Struggle for the Hebrew Language in Palestine", Actions Committee of the Zionist Organization, 1914; Regarding the fight between adopting Hebrew or Yiddish, etc., as the settlers' "native" tongue, also see Dieckhoff, *Invention of a Nation*, ch 3.

22 For Jacob Melnik, see *The Jewish Transcript*, Seattle, 11 Feb 1938, and after the appeal, Evening Telegraph & Post, Dundee, Jan 30 1939, Nottingham Evening Post, Jan 30 1939; a comprehensive account is in The Kentucky Jewish Chronicle, Feb 25, 1938; see also The *Palestine Post*, Jan 27 & Oct 7 1938, Jan 20 1939; led to reform, Jan 23 1939. Grossman, *Pious and Rebellious*, 68; Irgun/Torah, KV 5/40, Principles of Hebrew Freedom Mov't.

23 Special Committee on Palestine Verbatim Record of the Nineteenth Meeting, Held at the Y.M.C.A. Building Jerusalem, Palestine, Monday, 7 July 1947; Ben-Gurion also applied ethnicity arguments to the Palestinians: at his UN testimony, he argued that since the Palestinians are "Arabs," and "there were already many lands with 'Arabs,'" that therefore "they" (the "Arabs") already had sovereign land and didn't need Palestine; Regarding medieval mapmakers, depending on the geographer and, ultimately, on the viewer, *mappaemundi* could represent a spherical earth, where Palestine formed the central vantage point; or a flat earth, in which case Palestine's middle-earth location was literal. For PEF, Abu El-Haj, *Facts on the Ground*; Begin, Irgun Zvai Leumi, *Official Report*. The Palestine Exploration Fund's Biblical mind set is evident even into the Mandate period; see e.g., TNA, CO 1071/305, *Report on his Britannic Majesty's Government on the Administration Under Mandate of Palestine and Transjordan for the year 1924*, 5.

24 Ben-Gurion, "The Redemption," *Der Yiddisher Kempfer*, 39, 16 Nov 1917 (Quoted from Zertal, 93); For Meinertzhagen, TNA, FO 608/99, 510.

25 Israel, Law of Return, 2nd amendment, 1970, section 4.a. "Jewish" nationality most recently reaffirmed in 2013; see *Haaretz*, Supreme Court rejects citizens' request to change nationality from "Jewish" to

"Israeli," 3 Oct 2013; The Israeli government does not recognize an Israeli citizenship. (See Jonathan Ofir, "Israelis Don't Exist," in *Mondoweiss*, 25 March 2016). Regarding the Jewish Brigade and Jewish "nationality," see TNA, WO 193/68, Minute Sheet 35, MS, verso Israel has, in a few test cases precipitated by individuals to contest the state on this issue, denied citizenship to a Jew who has converted to another religion and legally challenged his Israeli identity on that account. For an analysis of the various genetic theories being flaunted since the mid nineteenth century regarding blood descent and the Jewish "race," see Sand, *Invention*, esp ch 5.

26 Masalha, *Expulsion,* 7; Erskine B. Childers, "The Wordless Wish: From Citizens to Refugees," in Abu-Lughod, *Transformation*, 166; Richard Crossman, Palestine Mission: A Personal Record (1947), 159, quoted in Quigley, *Challenge*, ch 3; Rothschild, TNA FO 608/99, 218; at a meeting with British officials on March 22, 1919; For early Palestinian resistance, Qumsiyeh, *Resistance*, 41.

27 Ahad Ha'Am, see Menuhin, *Decadence*, 63-64; and many others.

28 Traveller was Laurence Oliphant in 1882, in the Plain of Esdraelon; see Quigley, Challenge, ch 1. Yitzhak Epstein, The Hidden Question, lecture delivered at the Seventh Zionist Congress in Basel in 1905, published 1907. Translation quoted from the Balfour Project; "tin-can settlement" quoted from Quigley, who cites Richard Crossman, *Palestine Mission: A Personal Record* (1947), 159.

29 *London Standard*, 6 Sep, 1897, 5.

30 Cohen, *English Zionists and British Jews*, 83-84; also *Cheltenham Chronicle and Gloucestershire Graphic*, 12 Sep 1903. East Africa was the immediate target site in 1903.

31 Herzl, *Zionist Writings.* 167; also *The World*, October 15, 1897, quoted from Dreyfus, *Wagner,* 165-166.

32 Reagan, see, e.g., Lazin, *Refugee Resettlement…*;Today, Israeli global "ownership" of Jews can be seen, for example, in its blocking of Jews of any nationality from entering the Arab old city of Hebron in the Palestinian West Bank (e.g., in November, 2014 the author, entering the old city to teach violin, was detained by two IDF soldiers for refusing to deny that he is Jewish, and was freed only by stating that he is Christian).

33 TNA, CAB 24/28/0063, 2; CAB 24/4/0014, 7. For support of Zionism among Nazis, see e.g., Nicosia, *Third Reich,* 19-21.34 Edgar Suares, TNA, FO 141/476.

35 1905 Aliens Act. For quotes, Tomes, *Balfour and Foreign Policy*, 201; Cohen, *Churchill and the Jews*, 19.

36 TNA, FO 492/30, p10.

37 Samuel memorandum, TNA, CAB 37/123/43.

38 Edgar Suares, TNA, FO 141/476.; Suares had also written to author and cultural Zionist Israel Zangwill. Both Suares in Alexandria, and one A. Alexander "representing the Jewish Committe in Cairo" were raising

funds for relief work in Palestine, but Alexander clearly distrusted Suares and refused to channel the funds through him. While not spelled out, the impression is that Alexander intended the money as actual relief work, whereas Suares channeled it to the Zionist movement (FO 141/805).

39   TNA, FO 800/176, Letter from Paris dated March 12, 1916.

40   For Malcolm, TNA KV 2/3171 and FO 371/45383. Letter to Weizmann dated 18 June 1948.; also, for claimed influence in Balfour Declaration, see his letter in the NYT, Dec18 1947.

41   TNA CAB 24/4/0014, 4; CAB 21/58; CAB 24/28/0063, 3; CAB 24/4/0014, 2; CAB 21/58; See also Bentwich quote from 1909 commingling Jews and nationality; the original proposed clause would have guaranteed "the rights and political status enjoyed in any other country by such Jews who are fully contented with their existing nationality and citizenship." Regarding the Zionists' attempt to have the Balfour Declaration read "re-establishment" rather than "establishment," in 1935 the British government's unabashedly pro-Zionist report on Palestine and Trans-Jordan referred to the "re-settlement" of the "Jewish people" in Palestine (TNA, CO 1071/310, 19).

42   Montefiore, TNA CAB 21/58, 80-81; Montagu, on Jewish nationalism, FO 800/99, 412-414, letter to Eric Drummond, August 3, 1916; on Jewish superiority in Palestine, letter to Robert Cecil, 1st Viscount Cecil of Chelwood, Sep 1917, CAB 24/27/0093, "Memo on British Government's Anti-Semitism", submitted on August 23, 1917 (also CAB 21/58, 218; Montagu re French, CAB 21/58, 206; James A. Malcolm, twelve-page typewritten document entitled "Origins of the Balfour Declaration Dr. Weizmann's Contribution," London, 1944, The British Museum, reprinted by the Institute for Historical Review, 1983; TNA, KV 2/3171, letter from Malcolm to Weizmann, 18 June, 1948.

According to Jeffries (Palestine), Lloyd George claimed that Britain "gave" Palestine to the Zionists in payment for influencing the US' participation in the war, and for Weizmann's acetone method, though Jeffries disparages the acetone claim, noting that Weizmann's method was impractical and not widely used.

43   Weizmann, CAB 24/4/0014, 5. For Sykes and Wolff, FO 141/805, April 28 1917.

44   Cabinet meeting of 3 Sept 1917, see TNA, CAB 23/4, large 25, 80; CAB 24/30/6.; T. E. Lawrence, letter to Sir Mark Sykes, 9 Sep 1917; TNA, CO 733/272/12.

45   TNA, CAB 23/4, large 25, 80; Proskauer, FO 800/486, 137; Strawson, *Partitioning Palestine*, 33; A further benefit of Zionism proposed in 1917 was to counter "Jewish pacifists and socialist propaganda in Russia" (FO 141/805); Rabbi Herz letter, CAB 21/58, 60-61; Wilson response, CAB 21/58, 215; for Rothschild-Weizmann letter of 3 Oct 1917, FO 371/61783, penciled "59" upper right.

46   TNA, FO 608/99, 106, 475-484; As reported by British Major-General Thwaites in February of 1919, Weizmann "wants to be able to give an

assurance to the Jews throughout the world [that] a Jewish country will be established in, say, one or two years [i.e., by 1921]."

47   TNA, FO 608/99, 106, 114, 153; The new term "Jewish Commonwealth" apparently originated with the American Jewish Congress. Regarding Weizmann's meeting with Thwaites, a MS annotation questions whether Weizmann was misunderstood, but the demand as related by Thwaites is consistent with what Weizmann consistently expressed privately.

48   *ibid*, 104.

49   *ibid*, 513; for Meinertzhagen's antisemitism, see e.g., Segev, *Complete*, 95.

50   For Meinertzhagen, TNA, FO 608/99, 514; Britain did not release the Meinertzhagen document because it presumed that Britain would be the Mandatory power in Palestine, which was not yet legally official; Sir Erle Richards, among many others, explicitly states that no Jewish state was promised and indeed would be contrary to pledges given to Arabs (4 Feb 1919); FO 608/99, 15; Weizmann quote, FO 608/99, 281-295.

51   TNA, FO 608/99, 286-288, 281-283, obvious typos corrected.

52   TNA, CAB 21/58, 18; CO 730/153/5, type-written page beginning Sir S. Wilson, and MS page preceding it; CO 730/153/5, early MS pages.

53   Anti-Zionist prohibition, TNA, FO 608/99, 192, 196 and others; Weizmann, FO 608/99, 103; Rothschild, FO 608/99, 214, 217 (at a meeting with British officials, 21 Mar 1919); Jaffa governor, Segev, *Complete*, 87; Christian-Muslim exclusion, Abu-Lughod, *Transformation*, 58; regarding the prohibition of anti-Zionist articles, even Emir Faisal, for his own political calculations, wanted them stifled (see FO 608/99, 196); According to Jeffries (*Palestine*, 312), attempts to stifle the native Arabic led Jaffa Municipality to pass a by-law making Arabic compulsory on all signboards (in addition to Hebrew and English), but the Zionist Commission intervened and forced the cancellation of the Jaffa by-law.

54   NYT, 5 March, 1919; Kahn's letter delivered on 4 March. Composed by Rev. Dr. Henry Berkowitz, of Philadelphia, Mr. Max Senior, of Cincinnati, and Professor Morris Jastrow, Jr., of the University of Pennsylvania.

55   TNA, FO 608/99, 218, at a meeting with British officials on 22 March 1919.

56   Said, *Orientalism*, Vintage Books,1979; Jaffa Moslem Christian Committee, Mar 1919, TNA, FO 608/99, 222, 235.

57   TNA, FO 608/99, stamped "271" (Balfour) & "273" (Weizmann).

58   Editor & Publisher, V.55, No. 27 (Dec 2, 1922.); NYT, Dec 3 1922. Typo in original, "The word is askew…" Introduction by Mideast correspondent William Ellis. Also see Smith, *Arab-Israeli Conflict*, 81-82; King-Crane Report, section E, 3. 1919; In March 1947 a British Intelligence Newsletter condensed parts of George Antonius' book The Arab Awakening, which claimed that "nobody really knows" what happened to the King-Crane Report after it was handed to the Secretariat of the US Delegation in Paris by August 28, 1919, (UK War Office in 1947, WO 261/566, Fortnightly Intelligence Newsletter No. 37, 1–14 Mar 47).

59 King-Crane Report, E, 3. Most people in the region wanted independence. US stewardship was second choice, British stewardship third.

60 TNA, FO 608/99, 486-488. Report by H. D. Watson, Major-General, Chief Administrator, 16 August, 1919.

61 Report by Sd Major J. N. Camp, 12 Aug 1919, Jerusalem. Ironically, neither realized that it was ultimately for defense against the Zionist settlers, not against the Palestinians, that the British would send more troops.

62 TNA, FO 608/99, 511-513.

63 King-Crane Report; Segev, *Complete*, 119.

64 J.M.N. Jeffries, *Palestine the Reality*, p368, 333, 359, for the quotes of Louis Bols, the boasts of Weizmann in the selection of Samuel, and general contemporary reporting about the surrounding events.

65 TNA, FO 608/100, letter from Weizmann to E. Forbes-Adams, July 23 1919. Stamped "368". See also Suárez, "'One Palestine, complete' was no joke", in *CounterCurrents*, July 15 2020.

66 Weizmann, *Daily Express*, Nov 1922, in Falastin, 3 Nov 1922, quoted from Palestine Chronicle. TNA, CAB 24/127/13, August 1921. Churchill, CAB 95/14; de Hahn, Ben-Yehuda, *Assassinations*, 66-67, 137-140; & Segev, *Complete*, 210.

67 Churchill quoted from: Official Records of the Second Session of the General Assembly, Supplement No. 11 Untied Nations Special Committee on Palestine, Report to the General Assembly, Volume 1; Cabinet report, 1923, CO 733/58, 321.

    TNA, CAB 24/263/24, & Matthew Hughes, *Britain's Pacification of Palestine: The British Army, the Colonial State, and the Arab Revolt, 1936–1939* (Cambridge 2020).

68 Regarding Sir Ellis Kadoorie, the author examined Kadoorie's original will in Kew, FO 917/2315; TS 27/175, letter by J.E. Shuckburgh from Downing Street, 24 May, 1923; TS 27/198; Protests at Kadoorie funds used for non-Jews, The *Palestine Post* Jan 2 1933; For Agricultural School land transferred to JNF, see *Palestine Post* Feb 24 1936; "Mrs. Bertha Guggenheimer Leaves $125,000 Bequests," JTA, March 14, 1927. The fund's administrator was Stephen Wise, then acting president of New York's Jewish Institute of Religion; for Zionist reaction, see Segev, *Complete*, 390-391. The *Palestine Post* of January 26 1934 reported that of five Guggenheimer playgrounds, the one in Jerusalem had fifty percent "Arabs, Armenians and others." The first Guggenheimer playground was 1925 (*Palestine Post*, Nov 11 1938). See also notice of her death, with mention of playgrounds, *Jewish Daily Bulletin*, Mar 7 1927. For Weizmann & Syria, TNA, CO 537/866.

69 At the time (1895), Herzl wrote in context of a proposed Zionist colony in Argentina. *Diaries*, vol. 1 88, 90. For Ben-Gurion, see Erskine B. Childers, "The Wordless Wish: From Citizens to Refugees," in Abu-Lughod, *Transformation*, 168. Labour, *ibid*, 174, and Gershon Shafir, in Elkins /Pedersen, *Settler Colonialism*, 41-46. Other techniques, such

as pouring gasoline on Arabs' produce, further starved out the native population (see, e.g., Pappé, *Ethnic Cleansing*). Traditional Jews and Sabbath, *Falastin*, 25 Mar 1924, in *Palestine Chronicle*. Jew Agency Constitution and race laws, summarized in the Hope Simpson report. Also see John Ruedy, "Dynamics of Land Alienation," in Abu-Lughod, Transformation, 130.

70 For JNF, see e.g., Stein, "The Jewish National Fund," 190-205; Hope Simpson, ch 5.

71 Hope Simpson, ch 1.

72 French, Lewis, "Supplementary Report on Agricultural Development and Land Settlement in Palestine," Director of Development, Jerusalem, April 20, 1932; Archer Cust, TNA CO 733/283/12, penciled 43, 45, 50-51; field mice, Hope Simpson, ch 1. Lewis French, *Supplementary Report on Agricultural Development and Land Settlement in Palestine*; TNA, CO 733/272/12 (Parkinson quote from verso of penciled "11").

73 Weizmann, TNA, CAB 24/263/0020, 6; TNA, CO 733/250/1, penciled "2", "9"; regarding Zionists' refusal to work with Palestinians, see also reference in *Report on his Britannic Majesty's Government on the Administration Under Mandate of Palestine and Transjordan for the year 1926*, 60, which cites strikes stemming from "the refusal of Jewish labourers to work with Arabs" (TNA, CO 1071/306).

74 Weizmann & Mussolini, *Papers*, Feb 17 1934; TNA, KV 5/31, 143a.

75 On July 24 1933 the pro-Zionist Board of Deputies of British Jews voted 110 to 27 against boycotting German goods (JTA, July 25 1933); for 27th of March protests, NYT, Mar 28 1933; effect of boycott on German economy, Black, p264; Toscanini, NYT, June 8 1933.

76 Business interests also led some German Jews even to refute claims that the Nazis were ill-treating Jews; see Nadan Feldman, "The Jews Who Opposed Boycotting Nazi Germany," *Haaretz*, 20 Apr 2015.

77 It is not universally accepted that Arlosoroff was murdered for Haavara (see Ben Yehuda, 140-3; JTA, Vol. 1 No. 117, December 24 1935, p4,5,8,9; 42.8% figure from JTA, May 25 1936 Nicosia, *Third Reich*, ch 3, and 50, 53, 63; Black, *Transfer Agreement*; Brenner, *51 Documents*; Polkehn, "Secret Contacts," 72. When on 8 September 1939 Haavara announced its closing, it had transferred US $35 million, which is about $600m in 2016 dollars, using the value of 1936 dollars (see Jewish Telegraphic Agency, 10 Sept 1939); Brenner, *Age of Dictators*, Kindle 2559-2561; My thanks to Joseph Massad, Professor of Modern Arab Politics and Intellectual History, for his email correspondence regarding the Brenner reference, May 2016.

78 Brenner, *51 Documents*, 115-118; Nicosia, *Third Reich*, 62; It is not clear to what extent Polkes was operating independently or representing the Hagana. Brenner, quoting the custodian of the Haganah records, said the files on Polkes are closed "because it would be too embarrassing" (*51 Documents*, 111, 117). There is inconsistency in records as to whether Polkes went with Eichmann to Egypt, or met him there again after traveling separately.

79 Report of the Palestine Royal Commission, Chapter XXII.

80 NYT, 8 Jan 1937 (note error in Ben-Gurion quote, where (as quoted) he refers to the Basel program of 1897 as being forty years before the Balfour, Declaration (1917), when he obviously meant before the present (1937); Interestingly, a year earlier, Weizmann told the Cabinet that he did not remember using the phrase "there would be the Jewish National Home" and wanted it omitted from the record. TNA, CAB 24/263/0020, 6.

81 Ben-Gurion, *Palestine Royal Commission Notes of Evidence.*

82 Segev, *Complete*, 403-404; Morris (*Righteous*) translation: "This is more than a state, government and sovereignty—this is national consolidation in a free homeland."

83 For the 1933 news photo, TNA, CO 733/333/8; Morris, *Righteous*, ch 4 (During the first six months of 1936, approximately two hundred Palestinians, eighty Jews, and twenty-eight British personnel died); NYT 27 Oct 1946.

84 TNA, reference to mayor of Nablus, demolitions, CO 733/316/11, 3-6. See also Wasif Jawhariyyeh, *Storyteller of Jerusalem: The Life and Times of Wasif Jawhariyyeh, 1904-1948* [Olive Branch, 2013], 228-229; CAB 24/263/24; Cafferata, hostages, see Hughes, *Pacification*, 215; Charles Anderson, "When Palestinians Became Human Shields: Counterinsurgency, Racialization, and the Great Revolt (1936–1939)", in *Comparative Studies in Society and History* 2021, 63(3), 625–654. Manchetser Regiment quote from Hughes, 342; TNA, CO 537/2303, penciled "12"; red "49"; ADM 116/3690, "Report of Proceedings "Malaya" No. 04895/9"; "Report of Proceedings "Malaya" No. 04967/9"; CO 733/316/11, letter, penciled "Dear Eddie" (red "6"), p3; statement by F.A. Buckley, No. 04895/9. The demolition operation began at 16:45 on Thursday, 25 August, 1938. "Minesweepers" were not abolished until January 1940 (see TNA, WO 169/148, Notes on G.O.C.'s Conference Held at Force Headquarters on 19 Jan 40, 4); Harakevet Journal 21, June 1993, 21:2; TNA CO 733/366/4.

85 Palestinian terrorism, TNA, MS, N. Ollerenshaw, CO 733/477/3, 196-205; Zionist terror, CAB 67/4/17/0001, 1; War Cabinet, Palestine, W.P. (G.) (40) 17, Jan 1940, 3; for example of Irgun records, see pages 66-67, above.

86 Morris, *Righteous*, K location 3174; Both Morris, and (contemporary) *Falastin* (in *Palestine Chronicle*), date the Ramataeem attack on 17 April (and the *Falastin* identifies it as a Friday, which would be the 17th), though the Irgun's dating in Kister (*Irgun*) is the 16th; TNA, CAB 67/4/17; Kister, *Irgun*, 246.

87 A British War Cabinet Report dated January, 1940, cites an incident of October 5, 1939, in which 43 armed and uniformed Irgun were caught, and a large cache of weapons and explosives discovered in a nearby settlement, as Britain's first confirmation of the Irgun as a specific organization; This may have made it bureaucratically official, but British records well before this date cite the Irgun by name and as responsible for terror attacks; TNA, CAB 67/4/17; Kister, *Irgun*, 246.

88   TNA, CO 733/370/11, especially Dispatch No. 383 Reference No. K/50/38; Kister, *Irgun*, 249; NYT, 12 Apr 1938.

89   Kister, *Irgun*, 251; Pedahzur & Weinberg, *Religious Fundamentalism*, 100-101; By 1939, more than 60 terror attacks against Palestinian civilians are known. Hoffman, *Anonymous*, records the April 21 attempted bus attack and claims that the bombers intended to blow up a bus whose passengers included certain "Arabs" who, the bombers claimed, were responsible for an attack against Jews. Even if the claim of guilty Palestinians on that bus were correct, and even if one forgets the majority of the victims would have been innocent passengers, Hoffman's position is untenable, as the bombers then targeted a different bus after failing to hit the first. (k1736 etc); Bell, 42.

90   TNA, ADM 116/3690, No. 191/9862; see also beginning (unnumbered) pages.

91   Falastin, 7 July 1938, in *Palestine Chronicle*.

92   TNA, ADM 116/3690, No. 191/9862; see also beginning (unnumbered) pages.

93   NYT, 9 July 1938; Kister, *Irgun*, 251 (which cites an attack at the Jaffa Gate at 10 July, but this is presumably a misdating for July 8).

94   TNA, ADM 116/3690, SECRET. H.M.S. "REPULSE" at Haifa, 3oth July, 1938. For Tel Aviv attack, Hoffman, *Anonymous*, k1896, cites a bombing in Tel Aviv on 23 July 1938 in which twenty-three Jews were injured.

95   TNA, KV 5/34, 10AB; Bell, *Terror*, 42-43; Kister, *Irgun*, 252.

96   TNA, FO 919/5 (loose), is a telegram dated July 15, 1938, sent to London by Lipman Schalit (who apparently was attending the Conference), which says that Roosevelt could grant five years' quota to German Jewish emigrants to be used right away, without going through Congress; Ben-Gurion quote, Rose, *Myths*, 145; Brenner, *51 Documents*, 149 & 159 n23; "If I knew that it would be possible to save all the [Jewish] children in Germany by bringing them over to England, and only half of them to Eretz Israel, then I would opt for the second alternative"; Braun (*Weeds*, 66) states that Ben-Gurion expressed this "more than once"; Segev, *Complete*, 394, for Ben-Gurion; Segev also notes 1930s Zionists' "tendency to see the Jews of Europe as 'human material' necessary to establish the state, rather than seeing the state as a means to save the Jews"; BoD, see the JTA July 11 1938; ZOA, see the JTA July 5 1938. Hanna Braun, conversations, London, 2007.

97   TNA, FO 608/99, 277-288.

98   TNA, FO 371/68649, 43, Conversation with US Amb (E 4887/1078/G).99   Jabotinsky was active in the US in 1926 (see Medoff, *Militant Zionism*, 5-6).

100   Lehi "Pro-Axis," TNA, KV 5/34, 430x, "C.O. file 75969 (7a)"; FO 371/40125, Inward Telegram 372; For Nazi collaboration, see also Rogan, *The Arabs*, 248, and Brenner, *51 Documents*; Exploiting Britain's vulnerability during the war, see Yellin-Mor, MS letter, in Brenner, *51*

Documents, 307; This differed from Ben-Gurion's plan only in that Ben-Gurion advocated striking right after D-Day, rather than during the war. Jabotinsky & Mussolini, *B'nai B'rith Messenger*, 6 April 1973, p78-79, regarding then-newly uncovered correspondence.

101 Weizmann, *Papers*, in Litvinoff , 39; Lehi, TNA, KV 5/34, 7a; Jerusalem Agreement, KV 5/31, 143a; WO 275/121, "The Stern Group." See also Yossi Melman, "Undermining the Underground,"in *Haaretz*, June 3 2011, citing twenty-two clauses in the Jerusalem Agreement (last accessed Dec 13 2021), and which identifies the go-between as Moshe Rothstein.

102 Targeting anyone in uniform is implicit in most relevant TNA documents; see also Ben-Yehuda, *Assassinations*, 190; Regarding most targets of assassination were Jewish, the numbers demonstrate this, and also see Friedmann, *Crime*, 162.

103 TNA, KV 5/34, 72A; FO 371/23244. There was continuing violence against civilians, both Palestinians and Jewish settlers, during early 1939, not all clearly political. For a detailed record, see e.g., MacMichael's reports in FO 371/23244; FO 371/23245, 14-15.

104 White Paper related violence, FO 371/23245, 15, 20; FO 371/23244, 83, 85, 88, 89, 109; on 18 May in Tel Aviv, Revisionists and Hapoel (sports association) stoned one another; NYT, "Twenty–Five Hurt in Palestine Riot," 18 May 1939.

105 TNA, FO 371/23244, 109, 110; FO 371/23245, 17, 18; Rex Cinema, KV 5/34, 54a; FO 371/23245, 18, says "a third bomb failed to explode" (instead of half failed). In Bethlehem's Ghirass Cultural Centre, among a series of old photographs, are two showing an explosion at the "Riex movie," with the date 1946. The author could not corroborate an attack on the Rex Cinema in 1946.

106 TNA, FO 371/23244, 115, 131, 135; Communications sabotage, see also Bell, *Terror*, 48.

107 TNA, FO 371/23244, 131, 135 (which records a "Jewess arrested placing time bomb near central prison Jerusalem" on 9 June 1939, but this is also probably the same as the attempted attack on the Arab market); Jewish origin of bombs, "Time-Bomb in Basket," the *Times*, 10 June 1939.

108 TNA, FO 371/23244, 141, 142, 146, 152 (which cites the 10 June attack in Tiberias, with some ambiguity as to whether the seven dead is (as it seems) just from that land mine attack, or includes the day's other attacks).

109 TNA, FO 371/23244, 141, 142, 146, 148, 154; Regarding the execution of five villagers of Belad es Sheikh (Balad esh Sheikh), a Telegram from the High Commissioner of June 14 1939, in FO 371/23244, states only that "the village headman reported that the perpetrators were Jews," as this was before the Zionist gang confirmed that they had done it; "More Terrorism in Palestine," the *Times*, 16 June 1939.

110 TNA, FO 371/23244,156, 167; The 19 June market attack is surely the one cited in Kister (*Irgun*) as 20 June, and that Hoffman (*Anonymous*) refers

to (k2209) but does not date. The British same-day report is certainly the correct dating.

111 TNA, FO 371/23245, 21, 22, 23; FO 371/23244, 109, 110, 115, 131; FO 371/23244 141, 142, 146, 148, 154, 156, 167, 173, 177, 181, 184; WO 169/148; For an example of Palestinians working to capture Palestinian gangs, FO 371/23244, 138; "Jewish Terrorism in Palestine," the *Times*, 26 June 1939; British documents record instances of Palestinian villagers working together to capture remaining Palestinian gang leaders, with no parallel effort of the Jewish settlements; For a record of the "background" ongoing (lessening) Palestinian and (increasing) Jewish violence during 1939, see TNA, FO 371/23244 and FO 371/23245.

112 Irgun record of attacks, TNA, KV 5/34, 10AB. It is here cross-checked with Irgun records from the Israeli state (Kister, *Irgun*, 254-256). A slight variation of the British record is preserved in TNA, FO 1093/330, "Notes on Illegal Jewish Organizations," 8.

113 Bell, *Terror*, 42, 48; Kister, Irgun, 256-257 (in which the Irgun claims six victims on July 20), 259; TNA, FO 371/23244, 246, 253; WO 169/148, "Secret High Grade Cipher Message," red "3a" at upper-right; FO 371/23245, 2 (which dates the failed cricket bombing at August 6), 6, 36, 38, 110; KV 5/34, 10AB (8); CO 733/415/4, 20-24; Ben-Yehuda, *Assassinations*, 155-156; Bell, *Terror*, 48; Pedahzur & Weinberg, *Religious Fundamentalism*, 99-102; the audience at the failed cricket match bombings (5 Aug) were "men women and children of the European community"; for Irgun interview, KV 5/34, CO 733/415/4, 11-13, 15 Aug 1939; the Irgun member interviewed gave his name as Yardany. RE: British reports about July 1-2, and resumption of attacks, TNA, FO 371/23245, 24, 25; FO 371/23244, 179, 186, 190, 198, 213; "Jewish Terrorism Another Bomb Outrage in Jerusalem," the *Times*, 7 Jan 1939; Bell, *Terror*, 48; Pedahzur & Weinberg, *Religious Fundamentalism*, 99-102; A British corporal was murdered because he "was a trickster in the pay of the Jewish Agency … the second traitor to be done away with," TNA, KV 5/34. The British apparent duplications of the July 3 & 4 Irgun records: On July 3 another Arab café was blown up, killing one Palestinian and injuring thirty-five. Early the next morning, "two Jews threw a bomb into an Arab truck near Rehavia quarter of Jerusalem … the Jews escaping to Rehavia," and another Palestinian was shot "by an unknown Jew" in Jerusalem.

114 For a show of Jewish Agency cooperation with enlistment, see TNA, WO 169/148, "Supplementary Summary 1," which is then qualified "Summary of Intelligence," 18th Sept 1940, 2.

115 TNA, WO 169/183, Weekly Progress Report (up to 24 Feb 40); Lydda Area, Intelligence Summary, week ending 24 Feb 1940; week ending 16th March 1940.

116 TNA, WO 169/183, Weekly Progress Report (up to 9th March 1940); the Jewish constable was not expected to survive and was too injured to make a statement, but the British attributed the assassination to retribution for the arrest of the Histadrut officials (Intelligence Summary week ending 16th March 1940); Weekly Progress Report up to 23 March, & 30 March,

1940: TNA, WO 169/183, Weekly Progress Report (up to 9 March 1940); Lydda Area, Intelligence Summary, week ending 24 Feb 1940; Intelligence Summary, week ending 3 May.

117 TNA, WO 169/183, Weekly Progress Report (up to 9th March 1940); Lydda Area, Intelligence Summary, week ending 24 Feb 1940; Intelligence Summary, week ending 3 May; Letter from the High Commissioner, October 16, 1939; KV 5/34, 10AB.

118 TNA, WO 169/148, "Political Situation"; "Situation Report," "128a" in pencil upper-right; *Pum*, see TNA, WO 169/183, Weekly Progress Report (up to 11th May, 1940); the soldier assassinated on 11 May was AMPC, 401 Auxiliary Military Pioneer Corps; note that Ben-Yehuda (*Assassinations*, 161) cites three Haganah assassinations in May, 1940, with one on the 11th perhaps being a duplication. Regarding Czech military service, TNA, WO 169/183, Intelligence Summary, week ending 3 May; For Axis attacks, see WO 169/148, "Secret 104 196" and subsequent pages.

119 *Patria*, CO 733/446/4, Letter to MacMichael, signed Alan Rose, A.J. McNeil, L.J. Edwards, 3; Hoffman (*Anonymous*) omits this attack and cites the less deadly King David Hotel bombing in 1946 as the most deadly terror attack to that time.

120 TNA, WO 169/148, "War Diary," 14 December, 1940; Arthur Koestler, *Promise and Fulfilment*, New York, The Macmillan Company, 1949, 60; Regarding spinning incident in relation to the Masada, see Meir Chazan, "The Patria Affair: Moderates vs. Activists in Mapai in the 1940s," in *The Journal of Israeli History*, Vol.22, No.2 (Autumn 2003), 61–95 [Frank Cass, London]; regarding Masada in the "Israel of the Bible," the Masada is not mentioned in the Bible, but the alleged event was recorded by Josephus during the period of "Biblical" Israel. All modern sources noted (e.g., Wikipedia, last accessed 6 June 2016), state that the Hagana's responsibility for the bombing was not established until conceded by alleged bomber Mardor in 1957. Although the British were uncertain of the bombers' identity in their initial investigation, the Hagana's responsibility was soon established (e.g., TNA, CO 733/457/12, Intelligence Summary No. 8/45, 3-4). British reaction, TNA CO 733/446/4, letter from Mac Michael, C.S.499; TNA, CO 733/457/12, Criminal Investigation Department, Jerusalem, 24 April, 1945, Secret Document, 3-4; CO 733/457/12, Jewish Affairs, Terrorism, Intelligence Summary No. 8/45, esp 3-4; CO 733/446/4, red "10.2.41", begins "I am sorry to have delayed...." There was opposition from the British command to allowing the *Patria* survivors to remain, based on the fear that "it will be spread all over the Arab world that Jews have again successfully challenged decision of British Government," CAB 66/13/48/0001. The British committee investigating the tragedy was unsure "whether the loss of life was due to the saboteurs having bungled, or whether they were callously prepared to risk killing a number of the passengers in order to sink the ship" to prevent temporary safe haven for them in Mauritius.

121 The advertisements for the *Struma* "read like a summer camp brochure", Frantz & Collins, *Black Sea*, 78; TNA FO 371/32662, penciled "127";

Giladi (*Scandals*) says 769 passengers, Frantz & Collins (likely the more accurate source) says 781; Both British records and Frantz & Collins, 216, state that Britain refused them entry because they were nationals of a country at war with Britain, proceeding direct from enemy territory. Giladi insinuates that the Jewish Agency had 25,000 entry permits available but refused to use them for the *Struma* passengers. The author found no evidence of this in the British archives (see FO 371/32662, 97, verso, although Robert Weltsch also spoke of the Jewish Agency's refusal to consider any non-Palestine means to save the refugees; See TNA, FO 371/32662, 66 for British explanation of refusal to admit Struma's passengers; For British attempt to admit children aged 11-16; see *ibid*, 96; See also CO 733/446/11, CO 733/449/34; The cause of the sinking was hotly disputed, but recent research, and the recovery of the wreck, convincingly point to a Russian torpedo as the cause (Frantz & Collins, *Black Sea*).

122 For Robert Weltsch on the Jewish Agency and Zionist leaders, 1942 TNA, WO 169/4334; WO 169/4334, Appendix "A" to Weekly Intelligence Summary week ending April 8 1942; for Haganah against Allied recruitment, see e.g. WO 169/4334, week ending 10 June 42; Jabotinsky and Trumpeldor, among others, were lobbying for a segregated "Jewish" army by 1914 (WO 32/11352).

123 See Giladi, *Scandals*; TNA, FO 1093/330, Lehi's Communique No. 21/41, dated 1 August, 1941, 3; CO 733/420/19 (released as a result of the author's F.O.I. request), also cites new evidence for the Mufti's close involvement with the Italian fascists in 1940; on November 16 of 1940, S.E.V. Luke noted that "possible action against [the Mufti] was discussed with the Secretary of State a few days ago, [and] it was decided that the only really effective means of securing a control over him would be a military occupation of Iraq"; the same day, H.F. Downie stated that "We may be able to clip the Mufti's wings when we can get a new Government in Iraq. F.O. [Foreign Office] are working for this." For Zionist move to get Iraqi Jews to move to Palestine, see FO 371/98767, Special Court Judgement in Zionist Activity Case, in *The Iraq Times*, 20 Dec 1951; British refusal to declassify 1941 archive about Iraq, email correspondence with the National Archives.

124 FO 1093/330, "Notes on Illegal Jewish Organizations" (11).

125 TNA, FO 1093/330, Note of Meeting Held of New Court, St. Swithin's Lane, E.C., on Tuesday, September the 9th, 1941 at 2:30 p.m.

126 Regarding Zionism's need to confine Jewish settlement to Palestine alone, in 1940 Sharret allegedly deflected criticism by saying that he welcomes all plans for Jewish colonization in countries other than Palestine because any such endeavor is doomed to fail (TNA, WO 169/148, "Situation Report," 2). Kister, *Irgun*, 256-257 (in which the Irgun claims six victims on July 20), 259; TNA, FO 371/23244, 221, 246, 253; FO 371/23245, 2 (which dates the failed cricket bombing at August 6), 6, 36, 38, 110; Interview, 15 Aug 1939; the man gave his name as Yardany; KV 5/34, CO 733/415/4, 11-13; KV 5/34, 10AB (8); CO 733/415/4, 20-24; Ben-Yehuda, *Assassinations*, 155-156; for Irgun Biblical justification, TNA,

KV 5/34, 10AB. Explosions alerted the British to one Irgun contingent undergoing military-style drills on 18 November, comprised of thirty-four men aged sixteen to twenty-five, and two women aged seventeen and eighteen. Irgun drill was at Mishmar Hay Yarden Colony–WO 169-148, High Grade Cipher Message, blue "38a" at top. Irgun, KV 5/34, blue "8c".

127 Bell, *Terror* (73) states that Lehi's "electronically [sic? electrically?] detonated bomb blasted across the road—and missed." In the same year, Lehi attempted, but failed, to assassinate Alan Saunders, a British official, for his role in sending illegal immigrants to Mauritius; Lehi assassinated one of its first members, Abraham Wilenchik, after his release from British detention; Some say he had given information in exchange for his release, but others maintain that he tried to quit the gang, and his murder was a warning to other members that "only death would release from the organization" (See Ben-Yehuda, *Assassinations*); TNA, WO 169/4334, High Grade Cipher ref 35a; Weekly Intelligence Review No. 9; CO 733/439/20, verso of leaf with MS "2"; TNA, CO 733/457/9 38, verso; TNA, CO 733/439/20, No. 580 Secret; WO 169/4334, Weekly Intelligence Review No. 14; Hoffman, *Anonymous*, K2526.

128 TNA, WO 169/4334, Weekly Intelligence Report no. 21; G.S.I. Palestine Base & L of C 1-30 April 1942.

129 TNA CO/733/439/20, Cypher Telegram No. 523.Note that at least three different versions of the attempted assassination of McConnell exist; Ben-Yehuda, *Assassinations* (172), citing Eliav and Haaretz, says that the bomb was rigged to the car's back wheel, that the servant backed the car out of the garage for McConnell, and the device exploded as intended, save for the wrong victim; Bell, *Terror* (73) claims that "the Arab" had "seized the opportunity to curry favor" with his boss by opening the car door for him, and "as he swept open the door with a grand gesture ... a small package tumbled in front of him [and] McConnel [sic] was left "standing over his shattered corpse"; The author has dismissed Bell's account as an ethnically condescending embellishment; and has opted for the British account over Ben-Yehuda's (in principle credible) account because it relies on Lehi's operative Eliav, but the British, not Lehi, were the ones on the scene after the explosion; WO 169/4334, High Geade Cipher ref 13a; Weekly Intelligence Reviews No. 22, 24; G.S.I. Palestine Base & L of C 1-30 April 1942; 1-31 May 1942; also the *Times*, 24 April 1942.

130 TNA, CO 733/444/17, FO 371/68697, Ref. 3/315/48; for Proskauer, FO 800/486, 137A.

131 TNA, KV 5/34, 15a.

132 Previously cited US Intelligence Report; for "Propagation of Hebrew", WO 169/4334, Weekly Intelligence Reviews No. 27, p2.

133 TNA, WO 169/4334, Weekly Intelligence Review, week ending 17 June 42; The Palestine Post, June 28 1942, p3.

134 Yourgrau quote from *Old and New Questions in Physics, Cosmology, Philosophy, and Theoretical Biology Essays in Honor of Wolfgang Yourgrau*, Ed Alwyn Van Der Merwe, Plenum Press (1983).

Also Adi Gordon, "German Exiles in the >Orient< / The German-language Weekly Orient (Haifa, 1942-1943) between German Exile and Zionist Aliya", in *Placeless Topographies Jewish Perspectives on the Literature of Exile* Ed. Bernhard Greiner (2003), p149-159.

135 TNA, WO 169/4334, G.S.I. HQ Palestine … 1-30 Sept 1942, Summary no. 11; G.S.I. Palestine Summary No. 10; Weekly Intelligence Review No. 39; for disillusionment with Mufti, WO 169/4334, Weekly Intelligence Review No. 9, ending 21 Jan 42; CO 733/420/19, declassified in July 2014 as a result of the author's F.O.I. request, cites new evidence for the Mufti's close involvement with the Italian fascists as well (1940). There were signs that the Mufti, whose meeting with the Nazis is still used to smear the Palestinians, was at this time (1942) losing support. As one once-ardent follower explained, the struggle was for independence, not replacing one oppressor with another.

136 TNA, WO 169/4334, G.S.I. HQ Palestine, Summary No. 12 (1-31 Oct 1942); Weekly Intelligence Summary No. 40; the author assumes that the 4 Oct meeting cited in this document is not the same as the similar (but undated) meeting cited in the September Summary no. 11 in the same folder (WO 169/4334), whose coverage ended 30 September; Weizmann, conversation with Isaiah Berlin, on or about May 18, 1943 (CO 733/443/18, E 2399/87/31, verso, and otherwise untitled "Copy").

137 TNA, WO 169/4334, Weekly Intelligence Review No. 42 week ending 25 Nov 42; Summary No. 14.

138 TNA, WO 169/4334, Weekly Intelligence Review No. 6, week ending 1 Jan 1942; CO 733/443/21, letter from Elias N. Koussa; Palestinian enlistment figure quoted in Khalidi, and in Kimberly Katz and Salim Tamari, *A Young Palestinian's Diary, 1941-1945: The Life of Sami 'Amr*, 31 [University of Texas Press, 2010].

139 TNA FO 371/40129, Cypher Telegram No. 117; CO 733/458/13, Outward Telegram No. 117; FO 1093/330, Extract From Security Summary Middle East No. 131; *ibid*, Most Secret, Ref No.C.S.573/1, red "31", esp 2. Sabotage training was also sought clandestinely from the Allies; for example two ex-S.O.E. agents (Special Operations Executive, a WWII espionage and sabotage unit against the Axis powers) on leave on Denmark were "approached by some Jews who wanted them to give instruction in sabotage methods." (They were "of a pretty tough variety, although one of them like Bach and the other Nietsche.") See TNA, KV 4/467, 294 Liddel Diaries, entry August 13, 1946.

140 Kranzler, Untold Story, especially 95-97; Also The *Jewish Chronicle*, letter to the editor,

141 As Idith Zertal has written, Zionists' associating themselves with Jews struggling in the Warsaw ghetto trivialized the reality of life under Nazi occupation; Zertal, *Israel's Holocaust*, 26-29, 35; "We fought here and they fought there," in the words of a Palmach commander in Palestine. Edelman, *The Ghetto Fights*, published by The Bund, Warsaw, 1945.

142 Zertal, *Israel's Holocaust and the Politics of Nationhood*, 29-30; for Eliezer Livneh quote, at a symposium in 1966, Polkehn, *Secret Contacts*, 54; Lilienthal, *What Price*, 29; Brenner, *51 Documents*, 211-212.

143 Brenner, *51 Documents*, 212. Brenner states that Yehuda Bauer, in his *From Diplomacy to Resistance*, explains Gruenbaum's behavior this way: Gruenbaum had no hope of saving European Jews and thought the money would be wasted, but had to "go through the motions" of trying.

144 TNA, CAB 66/37/25, 14; FO 371/45377, 84; FO 371/45377, pencil "84"; also see KV 2/1435, "1642", esp verso; FO 1093/330, red "44", Inner Zionist General Council and Non-Cooperation; Dr. Senator is described as a non-Zionist. Marcus Retter, 5 Feb 1993. Stephen Wise's press conference was November 24 1942.

145 TNA FO 1093/330, Following upon the High Commissioner's; *ibid*, letter from Robert Scott to "My dear Boyd," unnumbered, "MOST SECRET 21st January 1942" at top.

146 TNA, KV 5/33, 37a, 38a, 35a (10 pages) London, "from our Palestine representative on the Jewish situation, as viewed by him." The report is dated 28 May 1943 but is said to be from observation in January. Also see FO 1093/330, Latest Aspects of the Palestine Zionist-Arab Problem, 6; for charge against Hunloke, see Nigel West, *The A to Z of Sexspionage*, Scarecrow Press (2009), 132-133 (Hunloke was cleared).

147 TNA, FO 1093/330, The Jewish Situation, The Hagana; CO 733/458/13, "Dr. Altman" (red "21", etc).

148 Moshe Arens quote from foreword in Baumel, *Bergson Boys*, xii; TNA, KV 2/2251, 25305/PS; CO 733/458/13, Extract from a memorandum submitted for pre-censorship by Mr. Gershon Agronsky; FO 371/40129, letter dated 4.9.43. The friend was J. H. Dayag, 3 Antolsky St. (*sic* Antokolsky), Neveh Bezalel, Jerusalem.

149 *ibid.*; TNA, FO 371/40129, letter dated 4.9.43; extra comma in original: "...San Francisco, Houston, (Texas) and..."

150 *ibid.*

151 Memo from the National Headquarters of the Committee for a Jewish Army, Feb 27 1942, p4. Dorothy Thompson, e.g., NY Post, June 16 1941; George Sokolsky, e.g., The Sun, July 14 1942. The author also examined various Committee documents in the collection of The Berman Jewish Policy Archive (BJPA), Stanford University. Dorothy Thompson was however vilified by Lehi for her pro-British anti-Soviet sympathies (KV 5/31, Lehi *Bulletin*, following 159z.

152 TNA, FO 371/40129, penciled "16", Robert Scott, Acting Chief Secretary; (written "organizers," not the British "organisers"); Capitalization "HER" original. Cited in WO 208/1705, penciled "68", cited as appearing in NYT, 30 April 1943; the author did not see this ad on the NYT's online resource for this date, but the transcript is specific and other full-page NYT political advertisements have definitely been omitted online; For Jewish Authority connection, KV 2/1435, "1642"; FO 371/40129, penciled

"11", January 3, 1944; CO 733/457/5, Note on Visit to the United States, 3; Biltmore Program.

153 PICME (British Political Intelligence in the Middle East) WO 208/1705, P.I.C. Paper No. 35; TNA WO 208/1705, An Estimate of the Possibility that the Jews in Palestine May Use Force in 1944 to Achieve Their Political Aims (pencil "46"); Similarly, in Apartheid South Africa, opponents of the racial system were smeared as anti-Christian (see, e.g., Davis, *Apartheid*, 4-5).

154 War Cabinet, CAB 66/37/46, 2.

155 TNA, FO 1093/330, red "48"; *ibid*, Latest Aspects of the Palestine Zionist-Arab Problem (In the original, one typo: "find themselves *in* anachronism"); *US Office of Strategic Services Foreign Nationalities Branch Files 1942-1945* (Congressional Information Service, 1988) lists two reports by this name, INT-18JE-242 (July 19) and INT-18JE-251 (July 25); the Kew document cited here would appear to be an earlier draft than either; String-bound between red "48" & "46" when examined.

156 TNA, FO 1093/330, *ibid*.

157 TNA, FO 1093/330, *ibid*.

158 TNA CO 733/456/2, Fortnightly Report ending 31 Jan 1944, "IV"; KV 5/36, *Herut*, no. 59, July, 1946; TNA, FO 371/45377, 84, Running Diary of Political Developments in Palestine; the 1943 campaign to prevent Jewish-Gentile friendships was launched in September. Also see Sand, 291.

159 TNA, KV 5/39, Report of Conference, 2; also note FO 371/40126, Inward Telegram 695, in which in May 1944 MacMichael reports the feeling in Palestine that the war was merely an "irksome complication" to nationalist aims.

160 TNA, FO 371/40125, Inward Telegram No. 217; CO 733/443/18, red "60"; *ibid*, red "30.8.43", verso, others; *ibid*, red "50"; Weizmann allegedly claimed to have gotten Roosevelt's promise to guarantee the funds. Shertok (Sharett) was also involved *ibid*, letter to Hayter/Campbell/Wright; Churchill confirms that he was the origin of the plan *ibid*, red "5", red "6"; Also see Monroe, *Philby of Arabia*, 221-225; CO 733/443/19, Weizmann to S. Welles, 13 Dec 1943; *ibid*, Aide Memoire, Riyiadh, 20 Aug 1943.

161 Ben-Gurion, TNA, WO 208/1705, red "16A"; CO 733/456/6, Extract from Middle East telegram 0/72248; FO 371/40125, penciled "32"; CO 733/456/2; CO 733/458/13, Intelligence Summary No. 3/44; CO 733/457/9, Summary of Terrorist Outrages, 1944; CO 733/456/6, Inward Telegram, MS 143. Also CO 733/456/2, Fortnightly Report Jerusalem District ending 15 Feb 1944; For Latrun, TNA FO 1093/330, red "51"; FO 371/40125, penciled "33", & Inward Telegram 238.

162 TNA, CO 733/456/6, Inward Telegram No. 238; FO 1093/330, "Palestine, Jewish Terrorism"; CO 733/456/6, Inward Telegram No. 205; CO 733/456/2, Fortnightly Report Jerusalem District ending 29 Feb 1944; Fortnightly Report Jerusalem District ending 15 Feb 1944; Kister, *Irgun*,

257 February, 1944; Bell, *Terror*, 113; CO 733/457/9, Summary of Terrorist Outrages, 1944; KV 5/34, "Jewish Newsletter No. 10"; FO 371/40125, penciled "34", & Inward Telegrams 217, 238; Also FO 1093/330, "places must be known to many" at top.

163 The *Times*, Feb 19 1944; TNA, WO 208/1705, P.I.C. Paper No. 35, 4; NYT April 1944; TNA FO 371/40130, letter from Rachel Yarden (MS "64" at top); for White Paper as anti-Bible, e.g., CO 733/456/2, Jerusalem Fortnightly Report for the Period 16–31 October, 1944; and *ibid*, 1–15 September, 1944, Chief Rabbi Herzog; "writing on wall," WO 193/68, MO/5 Loose Minute Sheet 305 (January, 1944).

164 Kister, *Irgun*, 112; TNA, CO 733/456/6, Inward Telegram No. 207; CO 733/456/2, Fortnightly Report Haifa District ended 15 Fed 1944; CO 733/456/6, Extract from Middle East Telegram 0/72248; FO 371/40125, Inward Telegrams 217, 257; CO 733/456/6, MS "18"; CO 733/456/6, MS "2" with date 13.2.44, and following page; *ibid*, Inward Telegram No. 205; CO 733/456/6, penciled "133"; *ibid*, typewritten "(7) Paragraph 1" under MS notes; CO 733/456/6, MS red "9", "8", "24". Note that CO 733/457/9, Summary of Terrorist Outrages, and FO 371/40125, Inward Telegram No. 217, date the murder of Green and Ewer at Feb 14-15, while other sources cite a day earlier, probably due to a day difference between the attack and their succumbing to the wounds; CO 733/457/9, Summary of Terrorist Outrages, 1944; CO 733/458/13, Extract from HC Pal tel 258; CO 733/456/2, Fortnightly Report Haifa District ended 29th Feb 1944; CO 733/456/2, Extract from Middle East Telegram 0/77252; *ibid*, Inward Telegram No. 257; CO 733/456/6, MS "120"; CO 733/456/2, Fortnightly Report Jerusalem District ended 29 Feb 1944; CO 733/456/2, Fortnightly Report Lydda District ended 29 Feb 1944; CO 733/456/6, MS "56", Extract from telegram No. 384; FO 371/40125, Inward Telegram 269; Also see Bell, *Terror*, 114; CO 733/456/2, Fortnightly Report for Haifa District ended 29 Feb 1944; FO 371/40125, penciled "52"; Kister, *Irgun*, 258.

165 NYT, Feb 26, 1944; TNA, CO 733/457/5, as reported in 1944 by a contact called "Y 32," R. C. Catling, "Notes on Visit to the United States," p6. Also Brenner, *51 Documents*, 198; CO 733/457/5, Telegram No. 784 ("C.S. 679/7" at top); the inclusion of non-Zionist Jews in the governing bodies of the Jewish Agency after 1929 similarly served to bring it new sources of revenue; see Abu-Lughod, *Transformation*, 132; and TNA, CO 733/457/5, R. C. Catling, "Notes…".

166 Regarding the "hiking groups" that were part of military gathering intelligence about Palestinian villages and population prior to 1948, my thanks to Dr. Rona Sela for sharing her knowledge via email correspondence and a meeting in Tel Aviv, November, 2012. This information was published in Rona Sela, *Made Public—Palestinian Photographs in Military Archives in Israel* (Israel: Helena Publishing House, 2009); TNA, CO 733/456/2, Fortnightly Report Jerusalem District ended 15 Feb 1944; FO 371/40125, Inward Telegram 340; Pappé, in JPS, 11-13; See also the Haganah operations chief's acknowledgment of a "map in which the strategic character of every Arab village, and the quality of its inhabitants, were indicated" (Erskine B. Childers' "The Wordless Wish:

From Citizens to Refugees," in Abu-Lughod, *Transformation*, 178); Pappe, *Ethnic Cleansing*, 18-22; Quigley, *Challenge*, ch 3 (who does not connect the simulated attacks with the hikers); FO 1093/330, "Palestine, the Jewish Defense Forces" (penciled "22"), 5-6. Centers cited are "Aylet es Shahar" and "Ain Aaaron near Ain Geb."

167 Restaurant, TNA CO 733/456/2, Fortnightly Report Jerusalem District ended 15 March 1944, 2; CO 733/456/6, typewritten "(7) Paragraph 1" under MS notes; CO 733/456/2, Fortnight Report Lydda District ended 14 March 1944; *ibid*, Fortnightly Report Haifa ended 31 Mar 1944; CO 733/456/6, Inward Telegrams 3384, 362, 340; Note that in CO 733/456/6, blue leaf with type-written "2nd March" at top, the murder of a Jewish CID is cited on March 15, which to avoid the risk of duplication I have assumed to be the same as cited elsewhere on Mar 13; However, CO 733/456/7, Inward Telegram No. 1586, cites two British police killed on Mar 15, hence I have assumed that at least one is not a duplication; FO 371/40125, Inward Telegram 362; CO 733/457/9, Summary of Terrorist Outrages, 1944; media clippings in CO 733/456/6, e.g. "Bomb Outrages in Palestine," News Chronicle, the *Times*, Mar 25 1944; Bell, *Terror*, 115-117; Kister, *Irgun*, 258.

168 TNA, CO 733/457/5, Extract From Top-Secret Telegram No 409 from Palestine dated 2 April 1944; CO 733/456/6, Inward Telegram No. 372, esp verso; *ibid*, Inward Telegram No. 363; also FO 371/40125, Inward Telegram No. 363, 372; MacMichael proposed that the Agency has "a real chance of saving their face before the world" by "handing over the guilty," which it had the power, but not the will, to do.

169 TNA, CO 733/457/5, "Extract From Top-Secret Telegram No 409 from Palestine Dated 2.4.44"; CO 733/456/2, Fortnightly Report Nablus District ended 30 Nov 1944; CO 733/456/3, Fortnightly Report Jerusalem District ended 31 Jan 1945; CO 733/457/12, Intelligence Summary No. 8/45, esp 3; On April 2, addressing a fund-raiser to bring Jews to Palestine (only to Palestine); CO 733/456/6, JTA Bulletin Vol XXV. No. 80; *ibid*, penciled "17" upper right; *ibid*, red 40; see also KV 5/34, O.F. 608/1; Jewish Agency agreed to "help" fight terrorism if the British would agree to give it 25 to 50 anonymous firearms permits, and then it would conduct an investigation autonomously; the Agency would share limited information of its choosing with the police, who would have to agree not to search settlements for illegal arms; CO 733/456/6, "221522" at top next to "Most Secret Cipher Telegram"; *ibid*, "436585" at top next to "Most Secret Cipher Telegram"; For transcript of discussion among Mapai leaders regarding cooperation with British, see CO 537/1814, "Speech Delivered by Eliezer Kaplan… 22.10.46"; Anglo-Palestinian Club, *Pamphlet No. 2*, 1944.

170 TNA, CO 733/458/13, Palestine Censorship, red "57", 3-4. CO 733/456/2, Fortnightly Report, Jerusalem, end 31 July 1944; Fortnightly Report, Gaza, end 15 May 1944 (for McGeagh); FO 371/40126, Inward Telegram 695; this telegram from MacMichael states that some segments of the Yishuv were nervous about the Labour Party motion, as it gave the public the impression that there was no available space left in Palestine. Public protestations from Zionist spokespeople that they did not want to

expel the Arabs is consistently contradicted behind closed doors. Labour Declaration, Dec 1944, 43d annual conference.

171 TNA, FO 371/40125, Inward Telegram 409, 431, 448, Cypher Telegram 214749, 223481; CO 733/456/2, (Haifa District) Fortnightly Report for the period May 1–April 15, 1944; CO 733/456/7, Inward Telegram No. 1586;
CO 733/456/6, JTA Bulletin Vol XXV. No. 80, 3; *ibid*, Palcor Bulletin, 3 April 1944, 3; CO 733/456/2, Fortnightly Report Lydda District ended 15 April 1944.

172 TNA, CO 733/456/6, Inward Telegram No. 448; CO 733/456/7, Inward Telegram No. 1586, esp verso; CO 733/456/2, Fortnightly Report Haifa District ending 31 May 1944; *ibid*, Fortnightly Report Lydda District ending 15 May 1944; CO 733/456/6, Inward Telegram No. 591; Kister, *Irgun*, 258.

173 TNA, CO 733/456/6, Inward Telegram No. 639; which puts a question mark by the "17th May" date; but the subsequent events (2:30 AM on the 18th) support that date. Police at the nearby Ramallah police station, who had heard the explosion, arrived followed the sound and found the Arabs that had been targeted. The assailants had left behind a small amount of gelignite. This attack is briefly cited in Bell, *Terror*, 120; CO 733/456/6, red MS "Extract from HC Pal tel 695 Sec. of 29.5.44" and "78"; FO 371/40125, Inward Telegram 591; CO 733/456/2, Fortnightly Report Jerusalem District ended 15 July 1944; CO 733/456/7, Inward Telegram No. 875; *ibid*, "Terrorist Activities," red "109" upper left; For Arab identity, see CO 733/456/7, Inward Telegram No. 930, verso; In Kister, *Irgun*, 258, the Irgun identifies one destroyed building as the Jaffa District Intelligence Command, which I have assumed to be the same the Kew records' District Police Headquarters; Bell, *Terror*, 120; CO 733/456/7, Inward Telegram 1586; FO 371/40126, Inward Telegram 695, 875, 930.

174 TNA, CO 733/456/2, Fortnightly Report, Lydda, end 15 July 1944; Fortnightly Report, Jerusalem, end 15 July 1944.

175 TNA, CO 733/456/2, Fortnightly Report, Jerusalem, end 31 July 1944; FO 371/40126, Inward Telegram 814; CO 733/456/6, penciled "102".

176 TNA, WO 193/68, "81E"; For Jewish Brigade, CAB 66/51/44; Sternhell, *Founding Myths*, 31; Segev, *Complete*, 393, quoting from Ben-Gurion, *Memoirs*, vol III, 24, 38, 41, 64, 85; FO 1093/330, red p "7", esp 2. Since the beginning of the war, as the Nazis were overrunning Poland and the darkest days of European Jewry were dawning, Ben-Gurion opposed a general conscription of Jews to fight Hitler, as this would detract from what he called "Zionist considerations." Future PM Sharett, addressing Jewish recruits as the war raged two years later, spoke of Jewry's "tragic alliance with Britain in this war" (that the fight against the Axis had put them on the same side as the British), and stressed that they would later use British military training to make the people of Palestine "reckon with us."

177 Regarding the Jewish Brigade and Jewish "nationality," see TNA, WO 193/68, Minute Sheet 35, MS, verso Israel has, in a few test cases precipitated by individuals to contest the state on this issue, denied

citizenship to a Jew who has converted to another religion and legally challenged his Israeli identity on that account; WO 193/68, penciled 118, SD2/6005; CAB 66/27/12; WO 193/68, penciled "305", blue MS notes at bottom and verso; FO 1093/330, Latest Aspects of the Palestine Zionist-Arab Problem, esp 7; *ibid*, "No. 1541 Most Secret" from MacMichael, verso; "The extreme Zionists contemplate the use of armed force for the attainment of their objectives. They have already large quantities of illegal arms. What they need is training [and the Hagana,] whose threat, already formidable, would be strengthened by the existence of an official Jewish army." CAB 66/27/12; WO 193/68, Army Secretariat, Reference W.P. (44) 344. A.C.S. /B/969; CO 733/456/2, Fortnightly Report Nablus District ended 30 Nov 1944.

178 TNA, WO 193/68, Weizmann, letter 9 February, & War Office comments, Minute Sheet No. 305, Jan 30 1944. War Cabinet dated 4 March, 1942. TNA, FO 371/32662, penciled "93", "101"; Cohen, NYT, "A Zionist Army?," Jan 26 1942.

179 TNA, FO 371/40127, Inward Telegram 1081. Ben-Gurion speech in Haifa, August 21, 1944. TNA, CO 733/457/4; As example of Ben-Gurion against Partition, WO 208/1705, red "16A", among many others; TNA, CO 733/456/2, Fortnightly Report Nablus District ended 30 Nov 1944; Fortnightly Report Jaffa District ended 30 Nov 1944; NYT, Jan 22 1942; The idea of a "Jewish army" to establish an ethnicity-based national identity dates back at least to 1914; in January 1917, Joseph Trumpeldor petitioned the British government for the establishment of a Jewish Regiment in language that took the concept of a Jewish "nation" for granted. See TNA, WO 32/11352, red "3A" at top; FO 371/32662, penciled "76"; Ben-Yehuda, *Assassinations*, 120; Grodzinsky, 50, etc.

180 TNA, CO 733/457/3, "Report on the attempt to assassinate the High Commissioner of Palestine"; TNA, CO 733/457/3, Inward Telegram No. 994; TNA, CO 733/456/2, Lydda District Fortnightly Report ended 15 Aug 1944. MacMichael had already survived several assassination attempts. Among the assailants' unspent weaponry discovered nearby was a US grenade. One of the British reports states that it was the driver who was shot in the lung, but I have gone according to MacMichael's statement in FO 371/40126, Inward Telegram 984. The A.D.C. was a Major Nicholls.

181 Sir Harold MacMichael decided in 1943 that as result of "severe disorders" upon search at Ramat Hakovesh that no further searches of Jewish settlements would be made. See e.g., TNA, CO 733/456/8, penciled 14 upper-right; CO 733/456/9, light penciled "99" at top, letter from Sgd John A. Rocke, 4 November, 1945; CO 537/3854, Intelligence Summary No. 2/46, 2; FO 371/45377, Running Diary of Political Developments in Palestine (MS "82" at top); CAB 158/1, "Annex Organisation of Illegal Immigration"; FO 371/40127, Inward Telegram 1081.

182 TNA, CO 733/456/7, red no. 111, 113, 114; FO 371/40127, Inward Telegram 1051; FO 371/40127, Inward Telegrams 1235, 1238; Bell, *Terror* (120) cites Irgun attacks on March 23 on CID barracks in Jaffa,

Abu-Kabir, and Neve Shaanan. I have assumed these are the same I have cited.

183 TNA, KV 5/34, Inward Telegram 1051; FO 371/40127, penciled "20" top-right; Inward Telegram 1288; CO 733/456/2, Lydda Fortnightly Report ended 31 Aug 1944; Kister, *Irgun*, 258.; KV 5/34, Inward Telegram No. 1051; CO 733/456/2 Lydda Fortnightly Report end 31 Aug 1944; CO 733/456/2, Nablus Fortnightly Report, end 30 Nov 1944, *ibid*, Haifa Fortnightly Report, end 30 Sept 1944; CO 733/457/9, red "38"; NYT, Sept 29 1944; Kister, *Irgun*, 259. TNA, also records this theft. For Al Capone quote, see Segev, *Complete*, 475; bands of Jewish youth, TNA, CO 733/456/2, Lydda District Fortnight Report ending 15 August 1944; rumors of Partition, Lydda District Fortnight Report ending 31 August 1944.

184 TNA, for War Office, CAB 95/14; KV 5/34; CO 733/456/2; WO 208/1705, penciled "9"; WO 208/1705, 17A; Ramat Hakovesh is cited as the "recent experience"; this a reference to the extreme reaction of the settlers to the British attempt to search that settlement in November of 1943. Also see WO 208/1705, P.I.C. Paper No. 35.

185 TNA, WO 208/1705, No. 1259; Weizmann, FO 371/40129, 98A.

186 TNA, WO 208/1705, Cipher Telegram 1259; CO 733/457/9, "Important Notice" with MS "4" in upper right; also FO 371/40127, Inward Telegrams 1300, 1299, 23, 1282.

187 TNA, WO 208/1705, Cipher Telegram 1259, from the Officer Administering Government (O.A.G.).

188 TNA, WO 208/1705, Cipher Telegram 1259; CO 733/456/2, Jerusalem Fortnightly Report, 16-31 Oct., 1944.

189 CO 733/457/9, Inward Telegram 1245 (also in FO 371/40127); TNA, CO 733/456/2, Lydda District Report Fortnight ended 30 Sept 1944.

190 TNA, WO 208/1705, "An Estimate of the Possibility that the Jews in Palestine May Use Force in 1944 to Achieve their Political Aims," 4 (C. D. Quilliam, 15 Feb 44).

191 September, 1944. TNA, CO 733/456/2, Gaza District Fortnightly Report No. 138; For Zionist and Israeli tactic of creating a threat against which to defend itself, see Postscript; CO 733/456/2, Jerusalem Fortnightly Report, ended 31 Oct 1944.

192 The scale of these terror attacks made it "sufficiently evident," a secret telegram to the Secretary of State for the Colonies read, that they were "not attributable to an isolated small gang of terrorists, but are planned and executed by a formidable organization, which is able to command a considerable force of well armed men." TNA, CO 733/457/9, "No. 1245"; TNA, CO 733/456/2, Lydda Fortnightly Report Ended 30 Sept 1944; TNA, CAB 67/4/17/0001, 3.

193 Hikers, TNA, CO 733/456/2, Nablus Fortnightly Report ending 31 Oct 1944; CO 733/456/4 Nazareth Fortnightly Report, ended 31 Oct 1945, 2.

194 For records in Kew regarding Moyne, see e.g. CO 733/456/2, CO 733/457/13, and especially FO 141/1001, which contains the statements of the witnesses.

195 House of Lords Debate, 9 June 1942, vol 123 cc179-210.

196 Ben-Yehuda, *Assassinations*, 207; CIA, N-193, "American Zionists Intercede with Egyptian Authorities on Behalf of Moyne Assassins," 9 Feb 1945, declassified Feb 2002.

197 Jewish Agency, TNA, CO 537/1711, 112; TNA, CO 537/1712, "Jewish Agency and Haganah Anti-Terror Campaign"; *ibid*, MS "121"; *ibid*, 118; Also Ben-Yehuda, *Assassinations*, 210, who refers to it as "settling scores." For claimed cooperation, see TNA, CO 537/1814 "Report on a meeting of I.Z.C. Held on 29.10.46". TNA, KV 3/41, Zionist Subversive Activities, 22; also KV 2/1435 333B; CO 537/1711, "Cooperation by the Jewish Agency"; For Fishman and Gruenbaum, TNA, CO 733/457/9, "Jewish Reaction to the assassination of Lord Moyne," 4-5; NYT, "Churchill Warns Jews to Oust Gangs," 18 Nov 1944; Postage stamps, Ben-Yehuda, *Assassinations*, 210. For Herzog, Kister, *Irgun*, 121.

198 TNA, CAB 66/37/46, 2.

199 CIA, N-193, "American Zionists Intercede with Egyptian Authorities on Behalf of Moyne Assassins," 9 Feb 1945, declassified Feb 2002.

200 Ben-Gurion, TNA, WO 208/1705, red "16A"; CO 537/1715, 262/10/5/GS, esp 6; FO 1093/330, "Sir W. Battershill" at top, verso, suggests that Roosevelt did not think Palestine was the best solution for the problem of Jewish DPs, and Colonel Hoskins states that Roosevelt favored a Jewish-Christian-Muslim trusteeship, but felt the Zionists would not agree; CO 733/443/19, "Palestine Question" (red "77A"); CO 733/456/3, to Chief Secretary, 21 Apr 1945; WO 208/1705 16A, "Note No. 1" (red "16A"); CAB 66/37/46; CO 733/457/14, letter from Liddell to Eastwood (red "1"); CAB 66/37/46, p2; WO 208/1705 , "Note No. 1" (red "16A"); CO 733/457/12, Intelligence Summary No. 8/45, esp 3, re "The Time Factor in Zionism."

201 TNA, FO 371/40127, 75156/151E/44, letter dated 8 September 1944; Inward Telegram 977; CO 733/457/5, Catling, "Note on Visit to the United States. Sept. 29–Oct. 10 1944", esp 2; *ibid*, John Harington, "Top Secret" to Cecil, 8 Dec 1944 (red "36"); *ibid*, Agenda, red "35"; *ibid*, Telegram No. 784 (red "34"); CO 537/1720, C.S.728/11 (red "4"), contains samples of propaganda in which "imaginary atrocities were painted in glaring colours," collected during an attempt to search settlements to June 29, 1946, e.g.: *Children and old people, men and women—pregnant—cripples and invalids were beaten up cruelly with rifle butts, bayoneted, maltreated and hit on all parts of their bodies until they fell unconscious. All were dragged over the ground and the stones or loaded like cattle on trucks... Suckling babies were torn from their mothers arms in cold blood ...children were being carried away ... their cries being heard from a distance...*"; See also *ibid*, "Copy Statement," for similar from the Yishuv's leaders, indistinguishable from what the Irgun or Lehi were printing. CO 733/457/14, MS, begins "Jacob Meridor" (red "1945"); *ibid*, letter from Liddell to Eastwood (red "1"); letter, 3 May 1945 (red "2").

202 TNA, CO 733/456/3, Fortnightly Report, Haifa, ending 15 May 1945; *ibid*, Fortnightly Report, Lydda, ending 15 May 1945; for May 13, Hoffman, *Anonymous*, k4491; TNA, KV 5/34, Cipher Telegram 21.5.45 (MS "49A"); *ibid*, 45AC; CO 733/456/8, Palestine Outrages 1945 (red "49"); re hiking parties, CO 733/456/3, Fortnightly Report, Samaria (Nablus), end 15 May 1945; CO 733/456/8, Palestine Outrages 1945 (red "49"); KV 5/34, Cipher Telegram 21.5.45 (blue "49A"); CO 733/456/3, Fortnightly Report, Galilee, end 31 May 1945; *ibid*, Fortnightly Report, Lydda, end 31 May 1945; CO 733/456/8, Palestine Outrages 1945 (red "49"); Kister, *Irgun*, 260-261.

203 Shertok, TNA, FO 371/45377, Inward Telegram H.C.757; CO 537/1715, chart, "30. Aug 45" upper left; Weizmann, CAB 95/14, 210-211, 216; KV 5/29, Interview No. 8 with Kollek, ref DSO/P/13576; *ibid*, Extract from … Palestine Summary No. 47; Kollek in London, quoted from KV 2/2261, 236; for British flirting with Kollek as source, also KV 2/2263 & KV 2/2264.; also see Palmach, CO 537/1715, "Memorandum", for relationship of the Jewish Agency to the Hagana and Kol Radio.

204 TNA, CO 733/456/8, Palestine Outrages 1945 (red "49"); The battery "aligned in the direction of the King David" surely corresponds to the statement by Teddy Kollek that an Irgun mortar had been discovered near a YMCA (KV 5/29, interview, paper dated 3 months later [15.9.45]).

205 TNA, KV 5/34, Extract Relating to O.F. 608/1 (blue MS "57B"); CO 733/456/8, begins "This Telegram should," dated 25.8.45; *ibid*, letter, G.H. Hall to Earl Winterton, MP, 15 Nov 1945. Some records cite Constable Hill, but Wilde is correct.

206 TNA, CO 733/456/8, letter, signed Francis James Bloor, Frederick John Popkins, R.L. Creese, dated 12.10.45.

207 Kister, *Irgun*, 261; TNA, KV 5/29, "Command Announcement" MS "81a"; All four piers had been mined, but two charges exploded. CO 733/456/8, red "29"; *ibid*, red MS "23.7.45" upper right, begins "(24). This telegram"; *ibid*, Palestine Outrages 1945 (red "49").

208 Former Congressman and Senator from Iowa, Guy Gillette. JTA, Aug 2, 1945; TNA, KV 3/56, "Jewish illegal immigration to Palestine" ("96c"), 20; KV 5/29, Inward Telegram 1149; Regarding the explosives theft on Aug 13, contradictory report from interview with Kollek, saying gang found no detonators—see KV 5/29 ("54B" upper right) verso; *ibid*, Jew Shot in Zichron Yaacov (MS "50B"); *ibid*, Inward Telegram 1149; CO 733/456/8, Palestine Outrages 1945 (red "49"); See JTA, Aug 23 1945.

209 TNA, CO 733/456/4, Gaza Fortnightly Report No. 160. Item 199 refers to "a separate report [that] has been submitted to you on the subject" of hiker, but which the author has not been able to locate. The Nablus report was based on "tour" to "Masherik", presumably referring to an area east of Nablus; *ibid*, Fortnightly Report, Nablus, ending 30 Sep 1945.

210 Sept 1945 boycott of Britain, see e.g., reference in TNA, FO 371/61770, full-page newspaper ad. Palestine Discount Bank, Sept 2 '45, KV 5/29, "Command Announcement" MS "81a"; *ibid*, "Extract," Defense Security Office, DSO/B/2/5 (2 sides); *ibid*, Interview with Kollek ("54B" upper

right); CO 537/1814, letter, HL. Brown to T Smith, P.F. 46863/B3a/ HLB.

211 TNA, KV 5/29, "Command Announcement" MS "81a" ("Zichon Moshe" Street in document).

212 TNA, KV 5/29, "Extract," Defense Security Office, DSO/B/2/5 (2 sides); CO 733/456/8, Palestine Outrages 1945 (red "49") (The British records lists the Sept 28 incident as an "outrage" (terror attack) and specifies one of the three assailants as having been identified as a Jew.)

213 TNA, KV 5/36, & WO 261/562, *Palestine: Statement of Information Relating to Acts of Violence;* Also Hoffman, *Anonymous,* k4839. Weizmann, FO 371/45796/12, letter, Sept 20 1945; the Foreign Office commentator was John S. Dent.

214 TNA, FO 371/45383, Inward Telegram No. 1531; Magnus, WO 261/571, Fortnightly Intelligence Newsletter No. 54.

215 JTA, July 3 1946, suggests that Athlit doubled as a prison, which the British deny, though it may have been used at times to detain people (see WO 275/38 Operation at Givat Haim, 26th Nov 1945); TNA, CO 733/456/4, Fortnightly Report 1-15 Oct 1945 (there is no explanation for the presence of the Christian woman in the clearing camp); FO 371/45381, Outward Telegram 1572; Inward Telegram 1433; FO 371/45383, Inward Telegram 1531; CO 537/1715, "Illegal Zionist Armed Forces in Palestine and the Complicity of the Jewish Agency," esp Appendix to Part I, & penciled page 6; CO 733/456/8, Palestine Outrages 1945, esp "6th Oct"; *ibid,* letter from G.H. Hall, red "69".

216 Kister, *Irgun,* 261; Lord Gort, TNA, FO 371/45381, Inward Telegeam 1441, 1440; CO 733/456/4, Jaffa District, Report 16-31 Oct 1945; *ibid,* Gaza Fortnightly Report No. 160; CO 733/456/8, "Palestine Outrages 1945,"
red "49", verso; Azzam Bey, KV 5/29, 59A; FO 371/45383, Inward Telegram 1531.

217 TNA, FO 371/45382, penciled "233", "Note of a Verbal Report made to the Secretary of State by Mr. R. Newton … 17th October, 1945."

218 TNA, *ibid,* ("Note of a Verbal Report…"); CO 733/456/4, Fortnightly Report ending 15 Oct 1945, verso; CO 733/456/4, District Report, Jaffa, 16-31 Oct 1945, Ref S/7/38 ("sabateurs" in the document).

219 TNA, CO 733/456/8, Palestine Outrages 1945, verso, and Inward Telegram 1566; Kol Israel, see Statement of Information Relating to Acts of Violence (WO 261/562 and others); CO 733/456/4, Fortnightly Report ending 31 Oct 1945; A train carrying stone was also fired on near Tantura; see CO 733/456/8; CO 733/456/8, Cipher Telegram, 351075 red "54"; *ibid,* Cipher Telegram, 350892; *ibid,* Inward Telegrams 1549, 1566; repeated in FO 371/45383; According to Kister (*Irgun,* 128) the attacks of 31 Oct 1945 were not coordinated among Irgun-Lehi-Palmach, but were independent, unknown to each other, timed for the Balfour Declaration anniversary. Egged bus documents, CO 733/456/10, Summary of Documents Seized at Birya Settlement on 27.2.46. See also: CO 733/457-11, Inward Telegram 1549; CO 537/1715, "Illegal Zionist

Armed Forces in Palestine and the Complicity of the Jewish Agency,"
esp Part II; *ibid*, red "48", No. 5 (1 Nov 1945); *ibid*, "(b) Kol Israel
Broadcasts..."; *ibid*, "No. 5" 1 Nov 1945 "To London from Jerusalem".
British Foreign Secretary Ernest Bevin met with Weizmann and Sharett
in London on November 2. Pressing them about the attacks, Weizmann
blamed the British, saying that they had "encouraged the spark which
had set off the charge," falsely framing the sabotage as the unofficial
acts of individuals. Bevin countered that "every one of these outrages
had been carefully planned and kept secret so that they should operate
simultaneously." Bevin meeting, see TNA, FO 800/484, 46.

220 KV 5/39, Jewish Legion, *Report of the Conference*; FO 371/45387, Inward
Telegram 1710, 2; FO 226/306, Army Signal In, No. GI/63977.

221 TNA, CO 733/457/11, after red "10"; Outward Telegram 3 Nov 1945;
Wagner, 21 June, 1946, FO 371/52530, Cable and Wireless Limited,
stamped 21 June 1946, penciled "76"; Sharett speech June 19 1946, TNA,
FO 371/45378, penciled "55"; FO 371/45378, marked "No. 743", British
Embassy, Washington, D.C., July 1, 1945; CO 733/457/11, Outward
Telegram, 3 Nov re No. 1549; *ibid*, letter by Bevin about meeting with
Weizmann and Sharett, 2 Nov 1945.

222 TNA, CO 537/1715, "Illegal Zionist Armed Forces in Palestine and the
Complicity of the Jewish Agency," esp 3-4; CO 733/456/4, Report for
Period 1-15 Nov 1945, esp 2; CO 733/456/9, Inward Telegram 1625; *ibid*,
Inward Telegram "Not numbered" (red "86"); FO 226/306, Telegram, No.
509, 15 Nov; *ibid*, Army Message In, GO/63204; FO 371/45386, Inward
Telegram (unnumbered, penciled "141"); WO 275/38, Events in Tel Aviv
on 15.11.45; NYT, Nov 15 1945; Kister, *Irgun*, 261.

223 TNA, CO 733/456/9, Inward Telegrams 1677, 1680; *ibid*, Inward
Telegram "Not numbered" (red "88"); some repeated in FO 371/45386;
CO 733/456/4; Fortnightly Report ending 30 Nov 1945, and others; CO
537/1715, "Illegal Zionist Armed Forces in Palestine and the Complicity
of the Jewish Agency," esp Part II; FO 371/45387, Inward Telegram,
1680; CO 733/456/9, various cables, penciled 68-74, Outward Telegram
1906; FO 371/45386, Meyer Levin, NY Post, Nov 20 1945.

224 TNA, FO 1093/508, "Top Secret" / begins "Ben Gurion returned,"
esp p6 (in the original, "succeed" is "suceed"); FO 371/45382, penciled
"233", "Note of a Verbal Report made to the Secretary of State by Mr.
R. Newton ... 17th October, 1945"; KV 2/1435, "1642" (typo in original:
"...Americans on he lines that...." Zionism's need to assure and exploit
perpetual anti-Semitism did not go unrecognized, for example being
satirized by the cartoonist David Low, whose output condemned fascism
in its various incarnations. He satirized Zionism's need for antisemitism
in a cartoon published in the *Evening Standard* on 22 Nov 1946. A man
standing on a street corner is being observed by two Zionist terrorists
hiding in the shadows. "What, he's not anti-Semitic?" one exclaims,
obviously troubled. "We'll soon alter that." In another *Evening Standard*
cartoon (3 Jan 1947), labeled "The Dark Mirror," Low shows a Zionist
terrorist looking at himself in a mirror. His reflection is a monster labeled
"Anti-Semitism."

225 Embassy quote, July, 1945 FO 371/45378.

226 TNA, CO 733/456/4, Chief Secretary 26 Nov 1945, signed A.N. Law; *ibid*, Fortnightly Report ending 15 Nov 1945; TNA, KV 2/1435, 67191 CIRCUS 51a; KV 3/347; FO 371/45387, various cables to Bevin.

227 Kister, *Irgun*, 262; TNA, CO 733/456/9, Inward Telegrams 1840, 1845; *ibid*, Outward Telegram, 2063; CO 537/1715, "Part II–The Outrages," penciled 5-8; The Irgun cites an attack on Army Camp in north Tel Aviv on Dec 27 as its first naval action. Attacks that day on what it called Intelligence Headquarters in Jerusalem and in Jaffa were said to be a collaborative effort with Lehi (Kister, 131, 262), also confirmed by pamphlet bombs dropped on 2 Jan 1946; CO 733/456/10, Palestine Situation / Terrorist Outrages (red "6"); Inward Telegrams 27, 26; regarding charges of pervasive antisemitism and fascism among British personnel cited, e.g., by Hoffman (*Anonymous*), see CO 733/456/10, Cypher letter from Washington to Jerusalem, red "2", Inward Telegram 21, and cypher message about US radio commentator Walter Winchell.

228 CO 537/1715, "Illegal Zionist Armed Forces in Palestine and the Complicity of the Jewish Agency," esp Part II; CO 733/456/4, Fortnightly Report through 31 Dec 1945; CO 733/457/11, Inward Telegram 1840; CO 733/456/9, Inward Telegram 1840; NYT 4 Jan 1946; NYT, 31 Dec 1945; CO 537/3854, Intelligence Summary No. 2/46, esp "ONLY SO Proclamation"; Note total casualties unclear, but one (incomplete?) tally recorded ten people were killed and twelve wounded in one day; CO 733/456/9, esp Inward Telegram 1845; CO 733/456/10, Palestine Situation / Terrorist Outrages (red "6"); Kister, *Irgun*, 262; The Palestinian telephone operator killed in the 27 Dec 1946 attack was Coustandi Eissa Ghaneim.

229 TNA, CO 733/457/11, Cabinet 1 (46); CO 537/1711, Co-operation by the Jewish Agency in suppression of terrorism, esp 4-5; press clippings; KV 3/56, Outward Telegram 1414. Regarding JA refusal to use the post-White Paper quota of 1500 a month, see Churchill's letter, FO 800/484, MS, 8, item 3; WO 275/38, Incident in Tel Aviv Monday 31 Dec 45; WO 169/23031, Monthly Summary No. 4, Jan 46; No. 7, Apr 46, p4; Appendix B 21.4.46.

230 TNA, KV 2/1435, 67191 CIRCUS 51a; Moshe Sneh was a proactive advocate for seeking support from the Soviet Union.; Ben-Gurion "reassurance" was according to Circus.

231 Regarding Sneh's overtures to Soviet sponsorship, TNA, KV 2-1390; TNA, CO 537/1715, 75156/151/J.B. (red "77"), page "D" at top. This particular document is undated. Most dated documents from the cache are from late 1945, but in any event this document and the penciled annotation can not be later than the summer of 1946. Also see TNA, KV 4/467, for Jewish Agency terror link.

232 Plan of action is from "B.L." (translated from the Hebrew) dated Dec 19 1945. TNA, CO 537/1715, 75156/151/J.B. (red "77"), esp 2,3,5; *ibid*, Inward Telegram 1279: News reports misquoted the letters and made the Haganah appear more cooperative; That Zionism would require force, not political argument, was commonly expressed, e.g. Mr. Golomb of the

Histadruth Executive in July of 1942 (See CAB 66/37-46, 2). Having the Jewish National Fund purchase land was at odds with the Irgun's belief that the entire region belonged to Jews by right and did not have to be purchased back.

233 NYT 27 Oct 1946.

234 TNA, CO 537/1715, letter, C.W. Baxter to T. Smith (red "82"); CO 733/457/12, Criminal Investigation Dept, Jewish Affairs. Terrorism, esp 3-4. The threat of using terrorism to stop Jews from leaving Palestine was expressed by saying the Hagana's sinking of the Patria would be eclipsed to intimidate Jews in Palestine against leaving (see Kew, CO 733/457/12, Criminal Investigation Department, Jerusalem, 24 April, 1945, Secret Document, 3-4); Ben-Gurion quote, Segev, *Complete*, 471, quoting from CZA S25/6090; Zertal eloquently points out that for these people just freed from unspeakable horror, then put into a new totalitarian environment, there was no such thing as free will or free choice.

235 The sole post-Holocaust survey of DPs' wishes, before substantial Zionist intervention in the camps, was conducted in Dachau among 2,190 Jewish survivors. Fifteen percent expressed a desire to emigrate to Palestine. The rest wanted to return home or emigrate to the US (Grodzinsky, 41). This same opinion is voiced by several independent first-hand sources, among them Ernst (*So Far So Good*, 171).

236 TNA, FO 1093/508, "Top Secret / Ben Gurion returned to Palestine...," esp 6-7; Grodznski 60, 129-130; TNA, KV 3/41, "Zionist Subversive Activities," (blue "7a"), esp p8; KV 3/437, draft of address, "We have been considering...," (blue "100[N?]") esp third page. An example of an Irgun pamphlet printed in several languages and disseminated in the camps, such as one distributed at the DP camp in Linz Bindermicht, US Zone of Austria: It implored Jewish youth to fight to take "our homeland in its historical frontiers ... the state of Erez-Izrael must be given back to the Jewish nation, as the Almight promised the Jewish people." With the phrase "ki kecha ulezerache nattati et haaretz hazot". KV 5/38, "Subject: Jewish Pamphlet," penciled "323". In KV 3/41 there is a note that many Jewish DPs were in UNRRA camps, not Zionist-run camps; however, the influence of the Zionist remains the same, and other documents suggest strong Zionist influence even in the UNRRA camps. Regarding Churchill-Truman correspondence, FO 800/484 MS 9.

237 Grodzinsky, *Shadow*, 76-77 (September 1945); Bergen-Belson was also called Hohne Camp by MI5's 1946 report. TNA, KV 3/56, Report on a Tour of M.I.5 Liaison Officer in France, Germany, Austria and Italy between 5 September, 1946 and 8 October 1946, esp 4,6; violence against DPs, Grodzinsky, *Shadow*; pro-Zionist conditioning in camps also cited in TNA, CO 537/1705, letter, W.H.B. Hack, Mar 20 1946.

238 NYT, Feb 18 1946, which quotes 90% wanting to go to Palestine; for 100%, see Morris, *1948*, 46.

239 TNA, FO 371/75340, Policy of HM Government in Relation to Palestine 1945-1948 (52A), esp 3; Re US coercion, see also Lord Moyne's comments to the War Cabinet, 10 Dec 1943, in CAB 95/14, 31.

240 TNA, KV 3/56, Report on a Tour of M.I.5 Liaison Officer in France, Germany, Austria and Italy between 5 September, 1946 and 8 October 1946, esp 4,6; CAB 158/1, Annex, Organisation of Illegal Immigration.

241 NYT Feb 25 1946; Grodzinsky, *Shadow*; also mentioned in The *Palestine Post* Mar 31 1946 & Aug 26 1946. TNA, CO 537/1705, account by "a usually reliable source" of Chief Rabbi Herzog's report to the Vaad Leumi Executive; Grodzinsky, *Shadow*.

242 *ibid*; Note quoted extract reads "with 1,000-500 children" but the latter number is surely a typo for "1,500").

243 *ibid*.

244 *ibid*.

245 *ibid*; Herzog's view of assimilation is also clear in his scathing condemnation of Reform Judaism: "[Reform Judaism] is a malignant growth eating away at the very vitals of what is holiest and dearest to Israel and jeopardising the continuity of our great God-inspired history. Reform inevitably leads to assimilation, and it has been aptly described as a back-door way to total apostasy from Judaism." (Quoted from *The Jewish Post* (Indiana), 7 June 1946, quoting *London Jewish Chronicle*).

246 TNA, CO 537/1705; Gutch, letter Oct 21 1946; Smith, letter, Nov 18 1946. There appear to have been two contemporaries named John Gutch with British military careers, causing some confusion; the present Gutch was best known in his day for his career in the Solomon Islands.

247 One of the children "rescued" from his adoptive home was Yossi Peled, former IDF general and politician. Grodzinsky (*Shadow*, 50) cites an interview with him, his sister, and the daughter of their Belgian adoptive family, in which both of the Peled children's parents are said have perished in the Holocaust. The present author noted that the Wikipedia entry on Yossi Peled (accessed 9 May, 2013, again 17 May, 2014) states that Peled's mother survived the death camps and that it was she, with the Jewish Brigade's help, that "reclaimed" him, and then they made *aliyah*. The Wikipedia entry appears to be based on Peled's profile in the Israel Ministry of Foreign Affairs (accessed as above). The author contacted Prof Grodzinsky, who replied that he can produce the source with Yossi Peled's sister's testimony, and that Peled's story is well-known in Israel and does not include his mother. Prof Grodzinsky stated: "Further, the Wikipedia version raises a question: if his mother reclaimed him, how did he end up without her at kibbutz Negba? He was in the kibbutz by himself." Prof Grodzinsky found a web page that "fixes" this part of the story, placing his mother with him in the kibbutz. He also found that the Likud party's website (in Hebrew, no longer accessible), had stated that "Peled was raised as a Christian child up to age 8, at which point his mother arrived with soldiers of the Jewish Brigade to return him to the bosom of Judaism." The present author also noted that Wikipedia and the IMFA date his birth at 1941, raising the additional question as to why the mother wait four years after the end of the war before retrieving her children. *My thanks to Professor Grodzinsky for his kind assistance.*

248 Grodzinsky, *Shadow*, 94, 51, 90-91. The cited example of contact forbidden with surviving family is the orphanage in Selvino, northern Italy. TNA, CO 537/1705/0003; Eliyahu Dobkin, TNA CO 537/1705, report dated 18 May 1946.

249 Ernst, *So Far So Good*, 173; TNA, FO 800/487, 110, 211.

250 Lilienthal, *What Price*, 26-27; Regarding Roosevelt's quip about Wise, the President worried that Wise might pass by Joseph Proskauer, president of the American Jewish Committee and influential critic of Zionism, outside his office; Menuhin, *Decadence*, 96; Ernst, *So Far So Good*, 176-177. See also TNA, FO 800/487, 110.

251 TNA, KV 5/29, "69C"; *ibid*, DSO/P/2131/D.3. ("Lochmei Herut Israel"); FO 1093/508, red "64"; CO 537/1709, C.S. 731; The British, aware that Jews were being murdered if they were suspected of working with the British against terror, tightened the small pool of individuals privy to their identities. The caution was vindicated when documents seized in a raid of the Jewish Agency included records of the Agency's spies. TNA, CO 537/1715, "Top Secret: Memorandum" begins "following are further," see item 4.

252 In correspondence with the British, Sharett presented new arguments, not cited in 1944, as to why the Brigade should not be disbanded. See, e.g., TNA, CO 537/1821, letter, Shertook to Bevin; CO 537/1821, MS page with penciled "5" upper left, begins *immigration and the recent seizure*; *ibid*, Loose Minute to SD2/7580'A', & *ibid*, penciled "27 End".

253 TNA, CO 537/1820, Palcor Bulletin, 3 Jan 1946, 3, 5; CO 733/456/10, Inward Telegram 45, 55; 51; Outward Telegram 95; WO 275/73, chart 31 Oct /1 Nov; KV 5/34, blue "70d", blue "73c"; According to Circus (MI6), "a large number of Palmach men" reportedly joined in the attack; CO 537/1709, C.S. 731; CO 537/ 1715, "Top Secret: Memorandum" begins "following are further," see item 4.

254 TNA, CO 537/1715, "Illegal Zionist Armed Forces in Palestine and the Complicity of the Jewish Agency," esp Part II; CO 733/456/10, 330/169/ GS; Inward Telegram 95; Outward Telegram 118; Kister, *Irgun*, 262; NYT Jan 20 1946.

255 *ibid*.

256 TNA, CO 733/456/10, 75156/151A; CO 537/1715, "Illegal Zionist Armed Forces in Palestine and the Complicity of the the Jewish Agency," esp 16; Kister, *Irgun*, 132, 262; for yarn theft, TNSAA, WO 169/23031, Monthly Summary No. 4, Jan 46; The radar station at Mount Carmel was also known as the RAF Experimental Station in Haifa.

257 Kister, *Irgun*, 262; TNA, WO 169/23031, Monthly Summary No. 5, Feb 1946; CO 733/456/10, Inward Telegrams 220, 214; KV 5/35, O.F.608/1 "IZL and LHI," 6; CO 537/1715, chart, "20 Feb 46" upper left; KV 5/30 Statement Relating to Acts of Violence, esp 7; also summarized in CO 733/456/10, "Extract from Palestine Tel. 349…" (red "36").

258 TNA, CO 733/456/10, Cypher Telegram marked D.T.O. 161330B (red "21"); Inward Telegram 260; "Extract from Palestine Tel. 349…"

(red "36"); Ben-Yehuda, *Assassinations*, 217-218; TNA, KV 5/29, OF 85/22(1)B.1.B.; *ibid*, "78a"; *ibid*, Extract "68b"; KV 2/3428 (leaf 13A for connection with Manchester paper).

259 TNA, KV 5/29, 373/2/1/GS; CO 537/1715, Statement Relating to Acts of Violence; CO 733/456/10, Inward Telegram 614, Inward Telegram 289; British record cite attacks at three separate locations: Shafr Amr, Kfar Vitkin, and Sarona; See also NYT Feb 22 1946; CO 537/1715, "Illegal Zionist Armed Forces in Palestine and the Complicity of the Jewish Agency," esp 16-22; CO 733/456/10, Inward Telegrams 289, 301, 311, 319, & "Extract from Palestine Tel. 349..." (red "36"); CO 537/1715, Top Secret: Memorandum, begins "Following are further," esp 2; WO 169/23031, Monthly Summary No. 5, Feb 1946.

260 Cunningham, in a telegram dated 19 February; TNA, CO 537/1711, Inward Telegram 281; Already in the early 1950s, British records speak of Israel's government using the country's media to create mass hysteria of an alleged threat, then finding itself forced to take action against that "threat," lest it lose credibility. This is repeated quite explicitly, e.g., in 1956 (see FO 371/121692, report from British Embassy, Tel Aviv, February 20, 1956, 2).

261 NYT 23 Feb 1946, Masada, the youth organization of the ZOA, announced the campaign at their eleventh annual national convention.

262 Kister, *Irgun*, 132, 262-263; TNA, CO 537/1715, Statement Relating to Acts of Violence, 7, cites seven aircraft destroyed and eight damaged; another report says seven aircraft destroyed and fifteen damaged; I have used the figures in TNA, CO 537/3854, MS.11750 /AOC.215 Feb 26, as it seemed to be the final British tally. WO 275/34, Appendix A in "General Report on Terrorist Activities in 6 Airborne Divisional Area in 1946"; the NYT cites fourteen aircraft destroyed, eight damaged beyond repair (NYT 27 Feb 1946); TNA, CO 733/456/10, Cipher Telegram 363920; *ibid*, Inward Telegram 320; CO 733/456/10, Official Communiqué (penciled "52"); Summary of Documents Seized at Birya Settlement on 27 February 46, and subsequent pages through "79"; Inward Telegram 352.

263 TNA, CO 733/456/10, Extract from Palestine Tel. 349 (red "36"); CO 537/1715, "Top Secret / Illegal Zionist Armed Forces in Palestine and the Complicity of the Jewish Agency," esp 8; CO 537/1821, 92275/1/ SD1a; ibid, penciled "27 End"; Kister, *Irgun*, 263; NYT 7 Mar 1946; CO 733/456/10, Inward Telegrams 376, 502; According to WO 275/73, chart, "31 Oct 1 Nov" (1945), the railway station at was bombed on 27 Mar, without casualty or damage; for a list of minor incidents for March 1946, see WO 169/23031.

264 TNA, WO 275/73, chart 1; CO 733/456/10, Inward Telegrams 542, 546; KV 5/35, 104AB; *ibid*, 101z; WO 169/23031, Monthly Summary No. 7, Apr 46, p4; Kister, *Irgun*, 263.

265 TNA, CO 733/456/10, Inward Telegram 613, 614; WO 275/73, chart, "31 Oct / 1 Nov" (1945); WO 275/34, Appendix A in "General Report on Terrorist Activities in 6 Airborne Divisional Area in 1946" cites an attack on the "3 CON DEPOT armoury," which I have assumed to be the

same attack as on the Army Convalescent Depot. This report estimated 20 "armed Jews" rather than 10-15 for the second Nathanya attack.

266 TNA, CO 73/456/10, Inward Telegram, 664; According to WO 275/34, "General Report on Terrorist Activities in 6 Airborne Divisional Area in 1946," Appendix A, the Tel Aviv station bombing was a diversionary tactic for the police station attack; Kister, *Irgun*, 263.

267 TNA, KV 5/29, Inward Telegram 687; *ibid*, "Mourning Notice"; CO 537/3854, 75156/151; *ibid*, Cypher Telegram, IZ 2315; *ibid*, Outward Telegram, 739; WO 169/23031, Monthly Summary No. 7, Apr 46; CO 733/456/10, Attack on Airborne Car Park TEL AVIV 25 Apr 46; Appendix with Statements; Outward Telegram 739; Inward Telegram 687; for minor incidents see WO 169/23031, Diary of Events–April 1946.

268 HMS *Chevron*, TNA, CO 733/456/10, Inward Telegram 737, 749.

269 TNA, KV 5/30, "Extract," DSO/B/2/5, "97z", verso & following; WO 169/23031, Monthly Summary 8, May 1946; WO 275/34, Appendix "A" 613/A/GSI; WO 275/73, chart, "31 Oct / 1 Nov"; CO 733/456/10, Inward Telegram 847; Kister, *Irgun*, 263.

270 TNA, CO 733/477/3, Main Terrorist Incidents; CO 733/456/10, Inward Telegram 935; KV 5/35, DSO/B/2/5, Rescue by the LHI, 6; WO 169/23031, Monthly Summary 9, June 1946; Re clinic incident, some documents say Irgun (KV 5/30, O.F. 606/1 "96B"), but Lehi is surely correct (KV 5/30, B.3.a., 92a); Israel Eldad, *The Road to Full Redemption* p3,5,37; and *Temple Mount In Ruins* (1951), both translated from Hebrew. KV 5/35, blue "91ZA", etc; *ibid*, blue "96"; WO 169/22957, Report on the Train Sabotage on 10 June 46; WO 275/73, chart "1 Nov 45"; CO 733/456/11, C.S. 759 (red "86").

271 TNA, CO 733/456/11, Report, C.S. 759, red "86"; WO 275/73, chart, "11 Jun 46"; KV 5/30, press clippings; CO 537/1712, "135" upper right; KV 5/38, 162a; WO 169/22957, red "J58" at top, and North Palestine Dist Weekly Int Review No 11.

272 TNA, KV 5/34, 112a; said to be an "unconfirmed report" of a Haganah meeting on March 13 1946; in original, "...he be a Jew or otherwise," in pencil corrected to "be he." First comma added to transcript.

273 Bevin's quotes from the NYT, June 13 1946; reaction, NYT June 14; Wagner, FO 371/52530, Cable and Wireless Limited, stamped 21 June 1946, penciled "76".

274 TNA, CO 733/477/3, Main terrorist incidents 1 June 1946 -6 Mar 1947; CO 733/456/11, pencil 131 red 86; *ibid*, red "89", 22 August, 2946 [sic]; *ibid*, "128" upper right; *ibid*, "Acts of Sabotage," penciled "99" (one Bedouin was stabbed and seriously wounded); FO 371/52530, Inward Telegram 985, 987; WO 169/22957, North Palestine Dist Weekly Int Review No 11.

275 TNA, FO 371/52530, Inward Telegram not numbered but penciled "70"; FO 371/52530, Cipher Telegram (373476 at top), Inward Telegram 987; WO 169/22957, North Palestine Dist Weekly Int Review No 11; CO 537/1711, red "112"; *ibid*, letter, Weizmann to Churchill, April 14, 1946,

esp 2. According to Weizmann, Sharett had the Haganah carry out the June 16-17 1946 attacks to give the British a "kick in the pants" while he, Weizmann, continued to reassure the British that "a Jewish Palestine" is "the surest of all available bulwarks for British power in this part of the world."

276 TNA, for Gottgetreu, KV 5/34, "80a"; CO 537/3854, SF.209/Palestine/ Supp/B3a/JCR (red "20"); KV 5/35, JTA, "98W" (The JTA reported attack as Irgun, but British believed it was Lehi, seems to be confirmed in CO 537/3854 red "20", and MS annotation KV 5/35 JTA blue "97"; WO 169/22957, Incidents night 17/18 Jun; CO 537/1715, Statement Relating to Acts of Violence, p8; FO 371/52530, Inward Telegram 989; for other attacks of June 17-18, see WO 169/22957, Outline report of incidents night 17/18 June 46; KV 5/35, "Kol Israel Broadcast Gives Reasons For Attacks"; document found with Shertok re June 17 1946, CO 537/1715, red "69".

277 TNA, CO 733/456/11, 106; Kidnapped officers, see also WO 169/22957, J81, & North Palestine Dist Weekly Int Review No 11; KV 5/35, 97B (JTA Bulletin); *ibid*, "O.F.608/1", IZL and LHI, esp 6; CO 733/477/3, Main Terrorist Incidents; CAB 129/10/0/0038; FO 371/52530, Inward Telegram 992; CO 537/1711, Inward Telegrams 1100, 993; KV 5/35, 98W (Attack on Haifa Railway Workshops); CO 537/1711, 1071 (red "49"); *ibid*, Inward Telegram 993; WO 275/58, 6 Airborne Division, Intelligence Summary No. 1 (27 Jun–11 Jul 46); kidnapped officers' release, WO 275/58, 6 Airborne Division, Intelligence Summary No. 1 (27 Jun–11 Jul 46); my description of the wooden box as coffin-like is based on several British reports describing a box used at the scene of the kidnappings in which stretchers were seen hidden and which was believed used for the abductions. The men were believed to have been held at 9 Salameth Road, Givat Moshe Qtr, Tel Aviv.

278 TNA, CO 537/1715, 262/10/5/GS, Criminal Investigation Dep't, esp 7,11,12; Kolsky, *Jews Against Zionism*, 143-144.

279 Regarding knowledge of Committee discussion, KV 2/1435, letter, Kellar to Smith, 229a.

280 Insurance fraud, TNA, KV 5/30, 107 (DSO/P/20054/S.1.); WO 169/23031, Monthly Summary 9, June 1946; Re insurance & diamonds, see also WO 275/79, 317 Airborne Field Security, Report No. 44, week ending 9 Sep 47. Diamond firms with British insurance were targeted, and after receiving the insurance money the owner would repurchase the merchandise from the gangs; WO 275/58, 6 Airborne Division, Intelligence Summary No. 1 (27 Jun–11 Jul 46).

TNA, KV 2/1435, 229a.

281 The Palestine Post, March 18 1946.

282 TNA, FO 371/67813B, Z 6069, Jewish terrorism in Italy.

283 TNA, KV 5/37, "Extract from MITROPA"; The leaflets mentioned were taken at Bad Gastein. The document cites a "Bagola" branch of the Irgun, of which the author found no further trace but the name apparently (?)

from Ilo Bagola, an African-American Christian said to have joined the Zionist cause in the early twentieth century.

284 TNA, KV 5/36, 107x (Irgun posters); *ibid*, Palestine Statement of Information Relating to Acts of Violence; WO 261/562, Historical Record July–Sep 1946.

285 TNA, WO 261/562, Historical Record July–Sep 1946. Op Agatha; WO 275/27; WO 275/29, Operation Agatha, Instruction No. 68; CO 537/1711, *HQ Palestine and Transjordan Operation Agatha 29 June–1 July 1946*, 3-5; *ibid*, Inward Telegram 1056; Telegram from Prime Minister To the President of the United States; Draft Oral Statement ... (60th Conclusions: Minute 3, 20 June, 1946); *ibid*, Inward Telegram 1007; The British records refer to leakage from an Operation Broadside, which appears to have been another name for Agatha. Broadside was a "theory, then widespread in the Yishuv and repeated in Israeli historiography," of a large-scale plan (Motti Golani, *Palestine between Politics and Terror, 1945-1947*. Brandeis University Press, 2013, 92-93). For the pamphlet *Palestine Statement of Information Relating to Acts of Violence*, see TNA, CO 537/1715, WO 261/562.

286 TNA, CO 537/1711, *HQ Palestine and Transjordan Operation Agatha 29 June–1 July 1946*, p12, 5; WO 275/29, Operation Agatha, Instruction No. 68, 2; CO 537/1715, Telegram No. 1130 / no. 1077 Case Against Jewish Agency; *ibid*, From High Commissioner No. 1038. Some documents alluded to a previously unknown terror group called Kotzer, which the British thought was named for the initial letters of the Hebrews words meaning "Military Reserve Group"; Wise and Truman, see FO 371/52563, letter from Secretary of State James F. Byrnes to Wise, October 24, 1946, and accompanying correspondence from Wise.

287 TNA, CO 537/1711, *HQ Palestine and Transjordan Operation Agatha 29 June–1 July 1946*, esp 10-11 (note "the childrens [sic] see-saw"); CO 537/1712, "Jewish Agency Policy".

288 TNA, CO 733/456/11, Inward Telegram 1175; WO 275/58, 6 Airborne Division, Intelligence Summary No. 2 (12 Jul–19 Jul), & No. 1 (27 Jun–11 Jul 46). For specific reference to pressure against Czechs joining the Czech Army, see e.g., WO 169/148, Summary of Intelligence, 8 June 1940, section 75.

289 TNA, WO 275/58, 6 Airborne Division, Intelligence Summary No. 4 (up to 9 Aug 46).

290 Rogan, *The Arabs*, 250 (and many others); TNA, KV 5/36, 110b; 113 (DSO/P/18281/14/P2); 112 (O.F.608/1/B.3a/JCR) re claim that between 10-11 the morning of the bombing, the Irgun informed all Jewish institutions of a more aggressive stance; Cunningham quote, FCO 141/14292, letter to Creech Jones, 30 October 1946; WO 261/562, The Attack on the King David Hotel (which includes "diversionary bombing"); WO 275/33A, "Translation of One of the Documents Found in Meir Garden on 30 July 46"; Somewhat clarified in CO 537/1715, Inward Telegram 1257; KV2 2251, 25a; KV 5/30, Summary of a letter from D.S.O. Palestine ref. DSO/P/S1; KV 5/36, 112z; 114 (Irgun Zvai Leumi); Irgun *Communique*, also intercepted

message, KV 5/36. Among the leads given the British after the King David attack, one ex-corporal named Jewson identified four individuals who he claimed were involved with terrorism, including the pilot of a training plane and a former doctor of philosophy in Vienna who now extorted money for the Hagana. The following appeared in a special edition of *Falastin* (in *Palestine Chronicle*) on 22 July 1946: *All the employees of the second grade utterly condemn that appalling campaign which was directed at the general secretariat in Jerusalem and which as a result many of its members met their death with many of their companions of the employees of the first grade while they were carrying out their duties with all loyalty. The association has no doubt that all members of the public will express the most heartfelt sympathy at this dark hour to the families of the victims who were killed by the most repulsive act of barbarity that can be described. Under these circumstances the association offers with a wounded heart its deep condolences to the families of the victims and to His Excellency the head of the government works this momentous calamity.* For modern vigilante groups, see e.g., Sheera Frenkel, Vigilantes Patrol For Jewish Women Dating Arab Men, NPR, October 12 2009. TNA, CO 537/1715, "58"; See also unlikely claim about Begin & the Knesset of on 18 Oct 1950, KV2 2252, "100a".

291 TNA, WO 275/58, 6 Airborne Division Intelligence Summary No. 4 (through 9 Aug 46); KV 5/36, Extract GI/33879; KV 2/1435, 264c; Mr. Ted Steel, interview with the author in Knighton, Wales, August 3, 2014; a friend of his, Hilda, was a sergeant in charge of the ATS girls (Auxiliary Territorial Service); CO 537/3854, red "2A.J. Kellar" in upper left; CO 537/3854, "Top Secret & Personal … 21.1.46"; A rumor was spread that the British knew of the King David attack in advance; see CO 733/478/2, red "31", where a misquoted British officer may have been the gossip's origin. For an improbably detailed reconstruction of alleged warning calls, see Clarke, *By Blood and Fire*, which presents a moment-to-moment record of the alleged caller's precise movements and thoughts. The author also met a man in East Jerusalem in 2016 who was related by marriage to the person allegedly making the calls. For record of the Irgun's fake bomb scares around the time of the King David bombing, see, e.g., TNA, WO 275/121.

292 E.g., Hoffman (*Anonymous Soldiers*) cites the King David attack as the most deadly to that time. It is also said that the neighboring Post Office and French Consulate received warning calls; this is true, but they were received after the main explosion. TNA, WO 261/562, The Attack on the King David Hotel.

293 TNA, KV 2/1435, Robertson to Smith, 264C; For Iltyd Clayton, CO 733/478/2, letter from Cairo, 26 July 1946; CO 733/478/2, 112A (eight dots at end in original).

294 TNA, WO 261/562, Historical Record July–Sep 1946 Op Shark; WO 275/31; WO 275/32; Cesarani, *Hat*, 41; CIA Documents; KV 5/30, Press section; Counterfeiting equipment and counterfeit bonds, Jewish Virtual Library, accessed June 15 2014; KV 5/37, Kellar to Smith, 126B; TNA, KV 5/36, Herut No. 59. Begin avoiding identification during Shark, KV 5/36, "124". Palestine Potash Company, CO 537/1715, pencilled "7"; KV

5/35, Extract from report forwarded by D.S.O. Palestine re Jewish affairs, DSO/P/17478/P2. Capitalization original; WO 261/562. TNA, WO 275/58, Intelligence Summary No. 3, … up to 26 July 46.

295 *ibid.*; CO 537/1711, "3. Situation in Palestine"; TNA, CO 733/456/11, red "73"; CO 537/1711, C.O.S. 534/6; *Palestine Statement of Information Relating to Acts of Violence*, Colonial Office, July, 1946. Its most damning evidence was intercepted Agency telegrams and broadcasts by Kol Israel. The case was further supported by printed materials: the Irgun's Herut, Lehi's Hamaas, and the Eshnav of the Jewish Resistance Movement (a Hagana-Irgun-Lehi alliance). TNA, KV 5/36, Statement of Information Relating to Acts of Violence; WO 261/562, Historical Record July–Sep 1946.

296 TNA, CO 733/456/10, Inward Telegram 737; CO 733/456/11, red "73"; CO 537/1711, C.O.S. 534/6; *ibid*, letter, L.G. Hollis to PRIME MINISTER; *ibid*, Cypher Telegram, 972/CIC 4 May; CO 537/1711, "3. Situation in Palestine," "Annex II," "Enclosure to Annex II"; *ibid*, for Ben-Gurion directing the Hagana, upper left "Top Secret 95"; *ibid*, letter, Weizmann to Churchill, April 14 1946.

297 TNA, WO 275/31; WO 275/32; Cesarani, *Hat*, 41; CIA Documents; KV 5/30, Press section; Counterfeiting equipment and counterfeit bonds, Jewish Virtual Library, accessed June 15 2014; KV 5/37, Kellar to Smith, 126B; TNA, KV 5/36, Herut No. 59. The Anglo-American loan was approved in July despite American Zionists' attempts to stop it (Medoff, *Militant Zionism*, 143-144). Wise was the only prominent Zionist not openly opposing the loan. See also FO 800/485, 159.

298 TNA, WO 275/73, chart, "11 Jun 46"; KV 5/36, 115z; KV 3/56, Outward Telegram, 1414.

299 TNA, HO 45/25586.

300 TNA, KV 3/56, Outward Telegram (no marking); KV 5/36, Extract, JTA, OF.608/1; WO 275/121, Periodical Intelligence Review, Period Ended 29 Aug 1946; CO 733/456/11, Cipher Telegram, 42257G(0)4, & Inward Telegram 1355; CO 537/2292, Inward Telegram 1400, & letter, Glutch to Smith, C.S. 728. Some sources (e.g., Wikipedia) date the Empire Rival attack at August 22; British records state that the charges were placed at 22:45 on the 21st. Haganah responsibility, WO 275/58, Intelligence Summary No. 6, 6; For HMG policy bringing illegal immigrants to Cypus, see WO 261/562, "G Branch," Historical Record July–Sept 1946 Illegal Immigration. For reasons that the author could not determine, the exact timing of the announcement commuting the death sentences was crucial, and the British took measures to insure that word did not leak out early; KV 5/38, "Jewish Interest in Atomic Fission."

301 TNA, KV 3/437, 46A, media reports; Medoff, *Militant Zionism*, Ch. 8; NYT Nov 11 1946; TNA, FO 800/486, 106, 128; PM quote: Dr. Nahum Goldmann made the proposals on behalf of the Agency. TNA, FO 800/485, 194 (No. 1218). This document refers also to telegrams 606 & 607, which the author has not been able to locate. Re Golda Meir and Jewish Agency's instance on global control of Jewish presence at the London Conference, see interview transcript in WO 261/562.

302 TNA, KV 5/30, media reports; FO 371/52560, Outward Telegram 1683; NYT 11 Sep 1946; Haifa-Kantara Line bombings 8-9 Sept were reported as between Rehovoth and Bir Yaacov (destroyed in three places), between Kfar Jinnis and Ras El Ain, and near Qalqilya. CO 733/456/11, Inward Telegram 1453 (Tarshiha is "Acretarshiha," Qalqilya is "Kalkiliya"); *ibid*, Letter to Alec Kirkbride (E 8911/4/31); WO 275/73, chart, "1 Nov 45" upper left; chart, 9 Sept 46; WO 261/562, Terrorist Activities from 8 Sep–30 Sep.

303 TNA, KV 5/30, media reports; Letter to Trafford Smith, 120B; CO 733/477/3. KV 5/37, Cipher Telegram 58248/G(0); CO 733/456/11, Inward Telegram 1466. British documents record a very different account of Sergeant Martin's assassination than that in Bowyer Bell (167) and cited by Ben-Yehuda (*Assassinations*, 225). That account has the assassins posing as tennis players who kill Martin as he walks past the court. According British documents, three Jews in a Buick car drove up to Martin, two exited the car while the driver remained at the wheel, and fired seven shots, five bullets hitting Martin in the back. Instead of dying on the spot as per the Zionist account, British records have him surviving for two hours, dying in the hospital. Bowyer Bell's dating the assassination at 10 August is surely in error. Yitzhak Shamir = Itzhak Yazernitzky-Shamir.

304 TNA, CO 733/456/11, Inward Telegram 1496; KV 5/37, Inward Telegrams 1487, 1455; Cipher Telegram 380587; Inward Telegram 1466; blue 136B; blue 133D; WO 261/562, Terrorist Activities from 8 Sep–30 Sep; CO 733/477/3, HO 45/25586, *Jewish Struggle*; Perhaps these four Arab deaths from the bank robberies were confused with those from the train incident of the same day?; NYT Sep 14 1946; Bevin & Byrnes, TNA, FO 800/486, 123; WO 275/121, Periodical Intelligence Review Period Ended 8th October 1946.

305 TNA CO 733/456/11, Inward Telegram 1552, 1528, 1599; KV 5/37, Cypher Telegram blue 136; *ibid*, Inward Telegram 1528; WO 275/73, chart, "8/9 Sept" upper left; "18/19 Feb" upper left; WO 275/121, Periodical Intelligence Review Period Ended 8th October 1946. WO 261/658, Intelligence Summary No. 12, up to 4 Oct 46; CO 733/456/11 puts the Haifa-Kantara line bombing on Sep 24 (night of the 23-24) Irgun records cite the 23rd Kister, *Irgun*, 265); WO 261/647, HQ South Palestine District, Intelligence Summary No. 16, period ending 29 Sep 46; KV 5/37, Secret Telegram Received in Cipher 136; Inward Telegram 1528; CO 733/477/3, Main Terrorist Incidents during the Period 1 June–6 March 1947; KV 5/30, Inward Telegram 1603; dogs, see WO 261/647, HQ South Palestine District, Intelligence Summary No. 16, period ending 29 Sep 46; FO 371/52560, Inward Telegram 1599 cites 50 lbs explosives in the 29 Sept 1946 Haifa oil dock incident, though another British report estimated 40 lbs; Inward Telegram 1603.

306 NYT 26 Sep 1946; Bevin, TNA, FO 800/486, MS "123" at upper right.

307 TNA, FO 800/486, 16.

308 TNA, WO 275/121, also WO 261/564, "Text of an address given by a Jew before an audience at a dominion club".

309 *Ibid.* (Text of an address…); The speaker cited the case of Australia: "No greater betrayal of the tortured Jews of Europe is it possible to imagine than the refusal by the Political Zionists of Australia to accept the generous offer of the Australian government to open its shores." As regards Zionist interference with the emigration of Jewish DPs to Australia, Klaus Neumann, in *Across the Seas—Australia's Response to Refugees: A History* (Black, 2015), states that many Jewish leaders were against Jewish immigration "either because they feared the emergence of anti-Semitism or because they were committed Zionists."

310 TNA, WO 261/562, "G Branch," Historical Record July–Sept 1946, Intelligence Newsletter 34 June–7 July [1946]; and others; WO 275/121, Periodic Intelligence Review, Period Ended 12 Sept. 1946.

311 TNA, KV 5/30, 128z "Terrorist Methods"; WO 275/58, and WO 261/656, Intelligence Summary No. 12 (to 4 Oct 46); WO 261/647, Intelligence Summary No. 17, ending 28 Oct 46.

312 TNA, WO 275/121, Periodical Intelligence Review Period Ended 8th October 1946; *ibid*, Monthly Air Letter No. 1. October–1946; L.H.I. Bulletin No. 1, Nov 1946; TNA, CO 733/456/11, Inward Telegram 1634 (also in FO 371/52560); CO 537/1814, P.F.93,666/B.3.a/DJS; KV 5/37, "Notes on a Conversation between the D.S.O. and Z on 7 October 1946"; CO 733/456/11, Inward Telegram 1634; WO 275/58, Intelligence Summary No. 13 (to 11 Oct 46).

313 TNA, KV 5/30, Inward Telegram 1647; CO 733/456/11; WO 261/564, Summary of Major Incidents During the Quarter Ending 31 Dec 46; WO 261/656, Road Mining Incidents in Division Area since 16 Jun 46; FO 371/52560, Inward Telegram 1647; Kister, *Irgun*, 265; L.H.I. Bulletin, No. 1, Nov 1946.

314 TNA, CO 733/457/12, Inward Telegram 1441; CO 733/477/3, Main Terrorist Incidents during the Period 1 June–6 March 1947; WO 261/564, Summary of Major Incidents During the Quarter Ending 31 Dec 46; Ben-Yehuda, Assassinations, 227-230; CO 733/456/11, Inward Telegram 1958; WO 275/73, chart, "8/9 Sept" upper left (places time at night of 21st-22nd); FO 371/52563, C.S. 421, No. 1563; WO 275/58, Intelligence Summary No. 15 (to 25 Oct 46), No. 14 (to 18 Oct 46); some duplication in WO 261/656; WO 261/647; Intelligence Summary No. 17, period ending 28 Oct 46; L.H.I.-Bulletin, no. 1, Nov 1946, 10; TNA, WO 27/121, Monthly Air Letter No. 1. October–1946; FO 371/52563, Inward Telegram 1767; WO 261/564, Fortnightly Intelligence Newsletter No. 27.

315 TNA, FCO 141/14286, Telegram No. 2078, 1803, 1676; FO 371/52563, Inward Telegram 2078; Gillette's ads on the 23rd, see FO 371/52563, letter from the British Embassy in Washington, 25 October 1946.

316 Silver, NYT Oct 27 1946. Some works cite what is claimed to be Silver's actual quote about refugees at the 49th ZOA Convention, wrongly attributing it to this NYT article; The author could find no source for the alleged quote, "…are we again, in moments of desperation, going to confuse Zionism with refugeeism, which is likely to defeat Zionism? Zionism is not a refugee movement." Also TNA, WO 275/58,

Intelligence Summary 22 (to 13 Dec 46); for Silver claiming the Agency to be representative body of all Jews, see e.g., NYT, 27 Jan 1947.

317 Regarding the Lehi attack on the 29th near Wilhelma, the *NY Times* reported what was likely the same attack, "some miles north of Tel Aviv"; NYT Oct 31 1946; L.H.I.-Bulletin, no. 1, Nov 1946, p10-11; TNA, WO 27/121, Monthly Air Letter No. 1. October–1946; CO 537/1712, OF.607/1/Link/B.3a/HPC; KV 5/31, 138; FO 371/52563, Inward Telegram 1777; L.H.I.-Bulletin, no. 1, Nov 1946, p11; Kister, *Irgun*, 265; TNA, CO 733/456/11; CO 733/456/11, Inward Telegram 1777; See *Palestine Pamphlet*, 17, for seventeen injured; WO 275/79, 317 Airborne Field Security Section, Report No. 1, for the week ending 5 Nov 1946.

318 TNA, CO 733/456/11, Inward Telegram 1780; WO 275/121, Monthly Air Letter No. 1. October–1946; Ben-Yehuda, *Assassinations*, (242) says the attack commenced at 2:00, not 3:00. The NYT account (31 Oct 1946) cites three Jews in the taxi when apprehended, not four that Ben-Yehuda cites as captured. The document in WO 27/121 cited herein states that three men were arrested but that "the girl seems to have escaped"; FO 371/52563, Inward Telegram 1780. A slightly different account of the 30 Oct attack is found in WO 261/564, Historical Record Oct-Dec 1946, Attack on Jerusalem Station on 30 Oct 46. It has Constable Smith leaving the first suitcase outside without destroying it, the second suitcase exploding and killing him, then the first exploding outside, and after that the third suitcase (inside).

319 TNA, FO 371/60786, From Rome to Foreign Office, No: 1618; KV 5/38, 158A; NYT, Nov 1 (report that a passer-by was too injured to be questioned), & Nov 5 1946; Kister, *Irgun*, 191; A newsreel (unidentified) from the time states that two people were killed in the Rome bombing. TNA, FO 371/60786, ZM 3734 No. 1649 ("Ineretz" [sic, "in Eretz"]).

320 TNA, FO 371/60786, ZM 3734 (3684, & No. 1652).

321 TNA, CO 537/2295, "Your telegram No. 2017 paragraph 2." Sanctuary in Vatican City was said to be the goal of the suspect killed while escaping.

322 TNA, CO 537/2295, "28.12.46" upper right; The suspect who was killed was Israel Epstein; some documents note that Italian police believed there was insufficient evidence to bring him to trial, but he was being held, apparently, for extradition back to Palestine; CO 537/1729, Appendix I, "The National Military Organisation in Palestine"; FO 371/67796, British Embassy Rome, 37/199/47; FO 371/102121,British Legation Tel Aviv WT1651/1; *Daily Express*, 18 , April 1952; JTA, 21 April 1952; NYT, 18 April 1952.

323 L.H.I.-Bulletin, no. 1, Nov 1946, 9; TNA, KV 5/38, Cipher Telegram G(0)1 73795; *ibid*, Inward Telegram, 1783; WO 275/58, Intelligence Summary No. 16 (to 1 Nov 46); HO 45/25586, *The Jewish Struggle*, No. 1, Dec 1945. The author was a student of Felix Galimir and has tried without success to find record of his experiences in Mandate Palestine.

324 TNA, FO 371/61865, Cairo to Foreign Office No. 331; letter to Mr. Mayhew, "Barc., Dec. 5th, 1946"; KV 3/437, 46A, 45A, 44A; Sneh, FO

371/52563, letter from the British Embassy in Washington, dated 26
October 1946, and note to Trafford Smith, dated 31 October, 1946.

325 TNA, WO 261/658, Extract from Notice Issued by the Stern Group; KV
5/38, Cipher Telegram G(0)1 73795; FO 371/52563, Inward Telegram
1783; CO 733/456/11, Inward Telegrams 1793, 1783; the *Times*, Nov 19
1946; FO 371/52563., Inward Telegram 1803.

326 TNA, FO 371/52563, Inward Telegrams 1795, 1815, 1826; CIA
documents; TNA, WO 275/79, 317 Airborne Field Security Section,
Report No. 1, for the week ending 5 Nov 1946; CO 733/456/11, Inward
Telegram 1795, 1805, 1815; WO 275/73, chart, "9 Sept 46"; KV 5/38,
Inward Telegrams 1805, 1826, 1815; *ibid*, 162a, 1556; CO 733/477/3,
Main Terrorist Incidents during the Period 1 June–6 March 1947; WO
275/73, chart, "9 Sept 46"; WO 275/58, Rail Sabotage in Divisional Area
Since 7 Nov 46. Note that the L.H.I.-Bulletin, no. 1, November, 1946,
p11 claims that Lehi cut cables on the 6th, but I have assumed it is the
same as the British report of the 5th. *Falastin*, in *Palestine Chronicle*, 4 Nov
1946. What I assumed to be Petah Tiqva is written as "Sht Ha Tiqua".

327 TNA, KV 5/31, "136b"; *Palestine Pamphlet Terrorist Methods With Mines
and Booby Traps*, 5; Note that the two Palestinians killed on 3 Nov was
reported as two people killed "on Arab land."

328 TNA, WO 275/79, Capt. J. Linklator, 317 Airborne Field Security
Section, Report No. 1, for the week ending 5 Nov 1946.

329 TNA, CO 733/456/11, Inward Telegrams 1841, 1854; WO 275/121,
Air Headquarters Levant, Monthly Air Letter–November 1946; L.H.I.-
Bulletin, no. 1, Nov, 1946, p11. Also NYT Nov 12 1946; FO 371/52563,
Inward Telegram 1854; KV 5/38, 160c, etc; WO 275/79, 317 Airborne
Field Security Report No 2, week ending 12 Nov 46; WO 275/73, chart,
"9 Sept 46" upper left; The *New York Times* reported "Three Zionists drove
up in a black police-type truck..." (NYT 12 Nov 1946).

330 TNA, CO 733/456/11, Inward Telegram, 1854 (One further attack on
Nov 11 was thwarted); Kister, *Irgun*, 266; WO 275 73, chart, "11 June 46"
upper left; *ibid*, chart, "8/9 Sep" upper left; *ibid*, "11 Nov 46" upper left;
Daily Herald, FBI, Irgun files, News Chronicle, Nov 11 1946; L.H.I.-
Bulletin, no. 1, telegraph wires on the 11th, 11; the Rosh Ha'Ayin attack
is report by Kister and does not appear to be a duplication of the "El Ain"
attack recorded the previous day.

331 Lehi, L.H.I.-Bulletin, no. 1, Nov 1946, 7; TNA, CO 733/457/13,
S.F.57/2/11(2)/B.1.B/JCR, red "10"; for Nakam, see e.g. Jonathan
Freedland, Revenge, The Observer, July 2008.

332 TNA, FO 371/61761, Wichita Beacon, 14 Nov 1946; For the forming of
Political Action Committee for Palestine, see NYT, 13 Feb 1946.

333 TNA, CO 733/456/11, Inward Telegram 1871, 1876, 1926, 1904, 1898;
FO 371/52563, Inward Telegrams 1871, 1876, 1886, 1898; "Times,
19.11.46"; Illustrated London News, Jan 11 1947; WO 275/73, chart,
"11 Nov 46" at upper left; Lehi claims it cut telegraph wires on the 11th
(L.H.I.-Bulletin, no. 1, Nov 1946, p11); FBI, *Irgun*; Lehi's report of
what appears to be the same 13 Nov attack cites the death of the two

policemen, but not the four Arab civilians (L.H.I.-Bulletin, no. 1, Nov 1946, 11, item 25); WO 274/79 Airborne Field Security, Report No. 3, week ending 19 Nov 46; KV 3/437, 63c; Nov 13, Six Palestine Officers Killed in Ambushing of Railway Patrol, Washington Evening Star, 13 Nov 1946; CO 733/477/3, "Main terrorist incidents during the period 1 June, 1946–6 March, 1947," esp penciled "220"; WO 275/121, Monthly Air Letter–November 1946; NYT, 18 Nov 1946; Kister, *Irgun*, 267; *Falastin*, in *Palestine Chronicle*, 19 Nov 1946.

334 Kister, *Irgun*, 267; TNA, CO 733/456/11, Inward Telegram 1931A; WO 275/73, chart, "11 Nov 46" at upper left cites a mine discovered at Ras Al Ein on November 19, blown up *in situ*; I have omitted it to avoid risk of duplication; NYT, Nov 20 1946; TNA, FCO 141/14286, Telegram No. 1858.

335 TNA, CO 733/456/11, Inward Telegrams 1938, 1958, 1986, 2015; *ibid*, DTO 210920B; CO 733/477/3, penciled "220"; WO 275/121, Monthly Air Letter–November 1946; KV 5/31, 137a, 136b; KV 5/38, 166c; CO 537/1712, OF.607/1/Link/B.3a/HPC; What I have cited as Petah Tiqva appears as "Sht Ha Tiqua" in the MS WO 275/73, chart, "11 Nov 46" at upper left; NYT, Dec 1 1946.

336 TNA, CO 733/456/11, red "163"; These letters held by the National Archives are presumably those that Segev (*Complete*, 482) says Kollek saw while in London.

337 TNA, FO 371/61768, letter, Mrs. W Talhouse, 21 Feb 47.

338 TNA, KV 5/31, "136b"; NYT, Dec 5, 1946; TNA, CO 537/1712, Anti-Partition Feeling in Palestine; FCO 141/14286, Cunningham, Telegram No. 1769 (1727).

339 *Palestine Pamphlet Terrorist Methods With Mines and Booby Traps*. Headquarters, Chief Engineer, Palestine and Transjordan. December 1946.

340 L.H.I.-Bulletin, no. 2, Dec, 1946, 14; TNA, WO 275/75, Report No. 5, p2; CO 733/456/11, Inward Telegram 2032; FO 371/61761, penciled "197"; CO 733/477/3, penciled "220". The British pamphlet was *Palestine Pamphlet Terrorist Methods With Mines and Booby Traps*; WO 275/121, Section II, Terrorist Activities.

341 TNA, WO 261/647, Report–252 Field Security Section 7 Dec 46, and others; CO 733/456/11, Inward Telegram 2050; FO 371/61761, penciled "196", "197"; WO 261/648 (the single sheet in this folder had been extracted from WO 261/647 and relates to the 5 Dec '46 attack); CO 733/477/3, penciled "220" (this document states that the truck, rather than the taxi, ran over the island regarding the Dec 5 incident); WO 275/121, Section II, Terrorist Activities, which is more detailed but somewhat ambiguous in referring to the occupants of "the other two vehicles" (i.e., one taxi and one truck) being booby-trapped after the explosion from the crashed taxi, then stating that both taxis were destroyed *in situ*, leaving the truck unexplained. Another slight variation to the incident is in WO 261/564, Report on Incidents in Jerusalem 5-6 Dec 46; *ibid*, The Stern Group attack on HQ South Palestine District, Sarafand 5 Dec 46;

Regarding Syrina, the first relief to reach the DPs stranded on Syrina was the Greek destroyer Themistocles; FO 371/52563, Inward Telegram 2133.

342 TNA, FO 371/52563, Inward Telegram 2023; WO 261/564, Fortnightly Intelligence Newsletter No. 30; NYT, 13 Dec 1946; TNA, CO 733/456/11, Inward Telegrams 1496, 2213; WO 275/121, Section IV–Political Affairs. The children were kidnapped for an alleged theft of arms. Note that on 10ᵗʰ December Cunningham (FO 371/52563, Inward Telegram 2078) comments that there had been no terror attack for four days due to the Zionist Conference in Basle that began on the 9ᵗʰ, but omits that at least one was intended, the failed terror attack of the 8ᵗʰ; FO 371/52563, Inward Telegram 2133.

343 WO 275/79, 317 Airborne Field Security Section, Report No. 7, week ending 17 Dec 46.

344 TNA, WO 275/79, 317 Airborne Field Security Section, Report No. 7, week ending 17 Dec 46; WO 275/58, Intelligence Summary No 53 (to 20 Dec 46); No. 22 (to 13 Dec 46); Report No. 8, week ending 24 Dec 46; WO 261/659 (only two sheets in folder).

345 For "Jews are not Zulus," see TNA, WO 275/58, Intelligence Summary 25, 8-9; WO 275/58, Intelligence Summary No. 24; CO 733/477/3, penciled "221". Date of incident obliterated by punch hole; subsequent incident is 26.12.46; NYT, Jan 5 1947; TNA, WO_261-657 (the single sheet in the folder had been extracted from WO 261/656 and relates to the floggings of 29 Dec '46); CO 733/456/11 (repeated in FO 371/61761), Inward Telegram 2213 (When the Irgun attacked the Ottoman Bank in Jaffa on the 13th, the British caught one of the participants, a sixteen year old boy. He was given 18 lashes ("strokes of the cane," as a manuscript note clarifies), an extreme punishment of a child that boomeranged with the Irgun's retaliatory caning of British military men.); NYT, Jan 1 1947; "We would have been greatly disappointed," a spokesman for the US' Political Action Committee for Palestine said, "if the kidnapping and floggings had not been carried out." For any new flogging of a gang member, the Irgun promised, a British officer would be assassinated.

346 TNA, KV2 2251, "The I.Z.L. and the Jewish Agency," verso. Litvinoff, Weizmann's papers, Paper 9, p40.

347 TNA, KV 3/41, "Notes on the security situation in Palestine…" ("Top Secret Cream" in bold red); CO 537/1712, "Berl Locker on Rabbi Aba Hillel Silver"; FO 371/61865, "Zionist Advertisements in US Press"; ACJ, see NYT, 14 Feb 1947.

348 TNA, WO 275/58, Intelligence Summary No. 30 (up to 16 Feb 47).

349 TNA, WO 275/34, "Report on the Incidents Night 2/3 Jan 47."

350 TNA, CO 733/477/3, Main terrorist incidents … 1 June, 1946–6 March 1947; NYT 3 Jan 1947; TNA, WO 275/34, Report on Incident evening 2 Jan 47; WO 275/34, "Report on the Incidents Night 2/3 Jan 47"; FO 371/61761, Inward Telegram No. 22; WO 275/79, 317 Airborne Field Security, Report No. 10, week ending 7 Jan 47, Appendix "B"; WO 261/656, Report on Flamethrowers used by Terrorists on 2 Jan 1947 During the Attack on Citrus House MR12941634.

351 TNA, CO 733/477/3, Inward Telegram 22; CO 733/477/3, Main terrorist incidents … 1 June, 1946–6 March 1947, p3; WO 275/121, Monthly Air Letter—January 1947. Some incidents of Jan 2 have not been cited here to avoid the risk of duplication, as it is not always clear whether similar incidents are variant reports of a single incident.

352 TNA, WO 275/34, Report on Incident evening 2 Jan 47; TNA, WO 275/34, "Report on the Incidents Night 2/3 Jan 47"; WO 275/58, Intelligence Summary No. 25; NYT 3 Jan 1947.

353 TNA, WO 275/34, "Third Incident" ("-2-"); CO 733/477/3, Inward Telegram 22; WO 275/58, Intelligence Summary No. 25 (repeated in WO 261/656).

354 TNA, WO 275/58, Intelligence Summary No. 26 (to 10 Jan 1947); Kister, *Irgun*, 268; TNA, CO 733/477/3, Inward Telegram 31, 35; FO 371/61761, penciled "228", "233". On 6 Jan 1947, A heavy utility police vehicle was stolen in Tel Aviv on the 11th, the driver dragged from the vehicle and held captive. Levin, KV 5/31, Jewish Standard, Jan 3 1947.

355 TNA, CO 733/478/1, *Daily Telegraph* 27 Jan 1947 quotes a figure of £200,000; the pound was worth just over US \$4; FO 371/67796, Amended Distribution (18/2/47); Telegram, Rome to Foreign Office 22 Jan 1957; CO 537/2295, Amended Distribution (18/1/47).

356 TNA, CO 733/477/3, Bomb explosion District Police Headquarters 12 January, 1947 ("318"); Cipher Telegram 391390; L.H.I.-Bulletin, no. 3, January, 1947, 15; CO 537/2285, Inward Telegram 94074 G(O)I; FO 371/61761, penciled "239"; WO 275/121, Monthly Air Letter–January 1947; pamphlet, *For the Record*.

357 TNA, WO 275/79, various; Haganah employ female spies, see KV 2/2261, 33; re sex workers, 317 Airborne Field Security Section, Report No. 11, week ending 14 Jan 47, & No. 26, ending 29 April; Wiretapping, see Airborne… Report No. 23, week ending 8 Apr 47.

358 TNA, WO 261/566, The Kidnapping of Mr. H.A.I. Collins and Judge Windham; CO 733/477/3, Inward Telegram 177 (which says "H.A.I. Collins"); Irgun confirms reason for kidnappings, see WO 275/79, 317 Airborne Field Security, Report No. 16, week ending 18 Feb 47; CO 733/478/1, Daily Sketch 29 Jan 1947; WO 275/121, Monthly Air Letter, January, 1947.

359 TNA, CO 733/478/1, *News Chronicle* 29 Jan 1947 ("35"); CO 537/2285, *Evening Standard* 30 Jan 1947; *The Star* 30 Jan 1947. For Gruner not having applied to Privy Council, WO 261/566, Fortnightly Intelligence Newsletter No. 34.

360 TNA, CO 733/477/3, Inward Telegram 177.

361 TNA, CO 733/478/1, News Chronicle 28-1-47; meeting of January 20, 1947. CO 537/2285, "Cable and Wireless," from Cunningham to S. of S. Colonies (2 pages). CO 537/2285, 142/67/GS 23 Jan 1947, attachment, 2-3.

362 TNA, WO 261/573, "Government of Palestine indictment of Jewish Agency as a result of outrages." Typo in the original: "political interate."

363 TNA, CAB 128/9/0/0022, 145; CO 537/2285, 142/67/GS, 7 Jan; No.C.S.759; 142/67/GS, 23 Jan; Inward Telegrams 239, 299; Plenum meetings of the Va'ad Leumi in which cooperation in the fight against terror was refused is cited for 20 January and 5 February, but it is not clear whether the Feb 5 is the same cited elsewhere as 3 Feb; Archbishop of New York, Dr C. F. Garbett, in *Diocesan Leaflet* for February, 1947. Safad, TNA, WO 275/34, "Third Incident" ("-2-").

364 TNA, CO 733/478/1, the *Times*, 27 Jan 1947 (red "5" at top); CO 733/478/1, *Daily Telegraph*, January 28, 1947.

365 TNA, CO 733/478/1, (red "5" at top).

366 NYT, 8 Feb 1947; TNA, FO 371/61761, penciled "201", verso; NYT 15 Feb 1947; Heyd is "Heydt" in the document; KV 2/1435, typed "459", "460"; Lebanon, see also KV 2/1435, "460" at top, and KV 2/1435, typed "460" (page begins "I think you will…").

367 TNA, WO 275/79, 317 Airborne Field Security, Report No. 15, week ending 11 Feb 47; WO 261/660, Report on illegal immigrant ship "Merica." Broken bottle and tins would also be used by passengers of the *Runnymede Park*, suggesting that this was taught on the ships; WO 275/58, Intelligence Summary No. 34 (up to 14 Mar 47), No. 35 (up to 21 Mar 47). A contrasting immigration enterprise was the Abril, a German-built converted motor yacht owned by a US shipping company. The ship was well supplied, well-endowed with all American equipment, clean, and its cargo of immigrants acquired in Bouc (southern France) were cooperative. They possessed faux landing documents issued in Paris by Bergson's Hebrew Committee for National Liberation.

368 Hashomir Hatzair Gazette, 12 Feb 1947; TNA, WO 275/121, Air Headquarters Levant, Monthly Air Letter, February, 1947; CO 733/477/3, Inward Telegrams 372, 379 (also in FO 371/61768); CO 733/477/3, Inward Telegram 322; WO 275/73, chart, 18/19 Feb upper left; WO 261/660, Intelligence Summary No. 30, No. 31, No. 32; WO 275/79, 317 Airborne Field Security, Report No. 17, week ending 25 Feb 47; WO 261/566, Fortnightly Intelligence Newsletter No. 36 (15–28 Feb 47); NYT, Feb 21 1947; CO 733/477/3, Inward Telegrams 381, 444, 446, 448; continuing sabotage of oil pipelines, see WO 275/79, 317 Airborne Field Security Section, Report No. 13, week ending 28 Jan 47, & Report No. 18, week ending 4 Mar 47, & No. 20, 18 Mar. Re: pipelines sabotaged at Endor village, Wadi Malka, Haifa, the pipeline attack dated by the author as on the night of the 19th is dated by Hoffman (*Anonymous*) on the night of the 20th, but this is doubtful, as the event is recorded in the NYT on the 21st; Most sources cite third floor or Barclays Bank, while WO 261/566, Summary of Major Incidents, cites the second floor; for Gruner's sister, WO 275/58, Intelligence Summary No. 30 (up to 16 Feb 47).

369 TNA, WO 275/79, 317 Airborne Field Security, Report No. 18, week ending 4 Mar 47.

370 United Zionists-Revisionists, see TNA FO 371/61770. For Irgun "hell," TNA, FO 371/61866, Irgun, "To the People and the Youth!"; "besieged

garrison," CAB 129/17/0/0009, 60; TNA, CO 733/477/3, Main terrorist incidents during the period 1 June, 1946–6 March 1947 (penciled "222").; Inward Telegrams 451, 454, 462; WO 261/566, HQ British Troops in Palestine & Transjordan G Branch … Incidents in Jerusalem 1-2 Mar 47; Pikovsky's printing press was at 6, Keren Kayemeth Street (see also incident in TNA, CO 537/3856, Summary of Events, 1 February, 1948).

371 TNA, CO 733/477/3, Inward Telegrams 451, 454, 462; Outward Telegram 437; sheet marked "(4) 222"; CO 537/3854, Inward Telegram 453; CO 733/477/3, "Main Terrorist Incidents during the Period 1 June, 1946–6 March 1947," 3; WO 275/79, 317 Airborne Field Security, Report No. 18, week ending 4 Mar 47; WO 275/58, Intelligence Summary No.33; WO 261/566, Summary of Major Incidents; Hoffman, *Anonymous*, K8404: Kister, *Irgun*, 269. Casualty figure for the attacks of March 1 vary, likely because of people dying of their wounds after the initial reports; I have used the times of the various attacks to avoid duplication of the same attack described differently by different sources. For Jewish witness to the March 1 Haifa attack, see WO 275/79, Report No. 18, week ending 4 Mar 47, Para 8(g); and Report No. 54, week ending 19 Nov 47, 4-5.

372 TNA, WO 275/79, 317 Airborne Field Security, Report No. 18, week ending 4 Mar 47; WO 275/58, Intelligence Summary No.33; CO 733/477/3, Inward Telegrams 473, 484, 491; *ibid*, penciled "222" upper right; also in FO 371/61770; NYT, Mar 5 1947; WO 27 4/79, 317 Airborne Field Security, Report No. 19, week ending 11 Mar 47; WO 261/660, Intelligence Summary No. 33, WO 275/79, 317 Airborne Field Security, Report No. 18, week ending 4 Mar 47, & Report No. 19, week ending 11 Mar 47; WO 261/566, Summary of Attacks by Armed Jews…

373 TNA, boycott, FO 371/61770, penciled "212", and FO 371/68650; London terror cell, KV 3/441, S.F.218/UK/Link.

374 TNA, KV 3/441, "Part 1 (A)" (blue 9A); The British were at a loss to explain how the Colonial Club bomb was planted, and indeed had at first not realized that the explosion was from a bomb.

375 Cesarani 83-86, TNA, KV 3/41, Zionist Subversive Activities (7a), p11-12; Walton, *Empire of Secrets*, 79; KV 3/439, Jewish Terrorist Activities in Britain (219z), KV 3/438 157a. Levstein, KV 2/4362, sheet (torn) after 43A.

376 TNA, CO 733/477/3, Inward Telegrams 506, 512, 753; CO 733/477/3, Inward Telegram 517; Kister, Irgun, 270.

377 NYT, Mar 9 1947; CO 537/2270, "Secondment of Army Officers to Palestine Police"; For dating of previous, see CO 537/2270, letter to Eric Speed, red "7".

378 TNA, CO 733/477/3, Inward Telegram 533, 542.

379 TNA, CO 733/477/3, Inward Telegram 533, 542; NYT, 15 Mar 1947; TNA, CO 733/477/3, Inward Telegram 545; WO 261/566, Fortnightly Intelligence Newsletter No. 37 (1–14 Mar 47); WO 275/73, chart, 18/19 Feb upper left; TNA record says three charges explode on the oil pipeline near Haifa, and the Haifa-Kantara line blown up near Rehovoth. The Irgun also records demolishing the oil pipeline in the Haifa area on Mar

14 (Kister, *Irgun*, 270); WO 275/79, 317 Airborne Field Security, Report No. 20, week ending 18 Mar 47; WO 275/58, Intelligence Summary No. 34; TNA, WO 261/660, Intelligence Summary No. 34, which suggests that the oil pipeline attack of March 14 was the work of the Hagana, unaware that the Irgun would take credit. Regarding the two trains blown up on March 13 1947, the brief account in Inward Telegram 545 in FO 371/61770 switches a couple of the details.

380 Kister, *Irgun*, 270; TNA, WO 275/79, 317 Airborne Field Security, Report No. 20, week ending 18 Mar 47; CO 733/477/3, Inward Telegram 577; WO 261/660, Intelligence Summary No. 35; CO 537/2285, Bucharest to Foreign Office No. 264; The Irgun denied responsibility for the Press room bombing (FCO 141/14286, Telegram No. 648, item 7, and WO 275/79, 317 Airborne Field Security, Report No. 20, week ending 18 Mar 47; WO 275/58, Intelligence Summary No. 35 (up to 21 Mar 47); WO 261/660, Intelligence Summary No. 34, No. 36.

381 TNA, CO 733/477/3, Inward Telegrams 600, 679, 577, 689; WO 275/58; WO 275/79, 317 Airborne Field Security, Report No. 22, week ending 1 Apr 47.

CO 733/477/3, Inward Telegram 689 states that in Tel Aviv on March 28, "six Jewish youths armed with sticks" killed a police corporal", but it was unclear whether the motivation was political and so I have not cited it in the main text.

382 TNA, CO 733/477/3, Inward Telegram 696, 734; for misdated(?) claim by the Irgun, see Kister, 270.

383 Kister, 270; TNA, CO 733/477/3, Inward Telegrams 696; Kister, *Irgun*, 271; TNA, CO 733/477/3, Inward Telegrams 699, 700; CIA; L.H.I.-Bulletin, no. 5, June, 1947, 16 (not numbered); WO 275/79, 317 Airborne Field Security, Report No. 22, week ending 1 Apr 47; Morris, *1948*, 39.

384 TNA, CO 733/477/3, penciled 228, 227, 226, 225 (N. Ollerenshaw.) Underline original. A widow's MS letter is preserved in CO 733/477/4, penciled "150".

385 TNA, CO 733/477/3, MS notes, 15156/151A, penciled 196-205.

386 TNA, WO 208/1705, 5397 cipher 16 Jan ("18a"); ADM 116/3690, "Report of Proceedings 'Malaya' No. 04895/9" for reports of Arab assistance, and non-assistance.

387 NA CO 733/477/3, letter 75156/151A/47; CO 537/3854, Despatch No. 24.

388 TNA, CO 733/477/3, Inward Telegram 721; Kolsky, p160-162. American Jewish Conference Bulletin April 4, 1947. Lilienthal, *What Price*, 28; A year later, one month and three days after Israel's declaration of statehood, a much different Displaced Persons Act passed which limited Jewish immigration.

389 TNA, WO 275/79, 317 Airborne Field Security, Report No. 22, week ending 1 Apr 47, which states the Galilee attack of 1 Apr was carried out by 3 Lehi members dressed as Arabs; CO 733/477/3, Inward Telegrams 725, 734; FO 371/61866, Outward Telegram 549; Inward Telegram 579;

WO 275/79, 317 Airborne Field Security, Report No. 23, week ending 8 Apr 47; for ship bombings also NYT April 5 1947.

390 TNA, KV 5/4, "The Betar Organisation." The Betar premises were at 20 Heathland Road, Stoke Newington, N. 16; CO 733/478/1, Outward Telegram 184; Tom Segev, "A British Memoir On Dov Gruner," *Haaretz*, May 2, 2008. At writing, Gruner's execution is commonly placed at April 19, but this is surely wrong. He was executed on the 16th. Outward Telegram in CO 537/2295, red "10", dated the 16th at 12:35 PM states that he "and three other Jews were executed in Palestine this morning, at 8 a.m. local time," and other British records corroborate this; one indicates that Jewish shops closed in protest on 17 April, after the execution (FO 371/61773, Cypher, penciled "70"); and an Airborne Field Security report state that he was transferred to Acre on 15 April and hung "four hours after the week began," in context meaning Wednesday the 16th (WO 275/79, 317 Airborne Field Security, Report No. 25, week ending 22 Apr 47).

391 TNA, KV 3/438 152a; Burt, *Commander Burt*; Cesarani, *Hat*, 86-87; Yinon Royhman, "What connects Molotov, Lehi underground?" ynetnews.com 11.05.06. KV 3/441; EF 5/12, begins "On 15th April 1947, a time bomb"; "Outrage, June 1947, Postal Packets";* KV 3/41, p 11 begins "More spectacular." For security after the Dover House bombing, see CAB 21/2567, "Establishment Department Notice"; "Instructions to Doorkeepers"; 1460/1/47 Security; For idea that bomb was not meant to go off, and that Eliav was wanted for the King David Hotel bombing, see KV 3/441, 2a; and KV 3/438 131b. (* This document refers to a bombing by Zionist terrorists in London on April 16 ("outrage at Dover House on 16/4/47," but this is surely an error for the 15th.)

392 L.H.I.-Bulletin, no. 5, June, 1947, 15 (underline original). TNA, FO 371/61865, Letters from British Consulate-General Chicago, April 17, 1947; British Embassy, Athens, 3 March, 1947; British Embassy Buenos Aires, 24 February, 1947; WO 275/79, 317 Airborne Field Security Section, Report No. 25, week ending 22 Apr 47; British Embassy Santiago; Note in French from the Irgun to British Counsel; FO 371/61866, British Embassy, Bogata, 29th April, 1947; "From Addis Ababa to Asmara," "E4054".

393 TNA, CO 733/477/3, Inward Telegram 825, 829, others in same collection; also in FO 371/61773. Red Cross depot, see britishforcesinpalestine.org/events47.html, accessed 14 Mar 2016; events 16 April, *Falastin* quoted from *Palestine Chronicle*, 17 April. Regarding the No. 61 Field Dressing Station attack, the Irgun claimed it also bombed the camp headquarters.

394 Witness to the April 22 train bombing, Major OG Plowman, RAPC, source: britishforcesinpalestine.org accessed Dec 10 2021.

395 TNA, CO 733/477/3, Inward Telegrams 841, 852; CO 537/2285, Inward telegram 845. Original: "...detonated the [sic] mines..."; FO 371/61773, Inward Telegram 851; CO 733/477/3, Inward Telegram 834.

396 TNA, CO 733/477/3, Inward Telegrams 829, 841, 834, 877. In original: "...detonated the [sic] mines..."

397 TNA, CO 733/477/3, Inward Telegrams 841, 852, 857; also in FO 371/61773; WO 275/79, 317 Airborne Field Security Section, Report No. 26, week ending 29 Apr 47.

398 CIA documents; TNA, CO 733/477/3, Inward Telegram 863, 856, 841; Lehi Bulletin 5, June 1947, p16 (not numbered).

399 TNA, CO 733/477/3, Inward Telegrams 874, 864, 1045, 1050, 901 (901 also in FO 371/61776); Lehi Bulletin 5, June 1947, p16 (not numbered).

400 TNA, CO 733/477/3, Outward Telegrams 911, 903; MS notes penciled "126"; CO 537/3854, Despatch No. 24; FO 371/61771, Inward Telegram 919, 921.

401 TNA, CO 537/3854, typewritten letter to "Sir T. Lloyd" from "TS" (probably Trafford Smith of the Colonial Office). The US loan to Britain's war-ravaged economy was the context of British fear of offending the Zionists.

402 TNA, CO 733/477/3, 146,145; 118, 969, 962, 937 (which states three cases of "armed Jews" setting fire to shops); copies of same documents found in FO 371/61776; WO 275/73, chart, "18/19 Feb" at upper left; WO 275/121, Air Headquarters, Levant, Monthly Air Letter—June, 1947; WO 275/121, Current Palestine Affairs, Section III; NYT, May 19 1947; May 15 1947.

403 TNA, CO 733/477/3, Inward Telegrams 969, 988; WO 275/73, chart, "11 Nov 46" upper left; The destination of the civilians' train was listed as "614 AOD"; identity of 614 AOD as being near Haifa taken from http://cosmos.ucc.ie/cs1064/jabowen/IPSC/php/place.php, accessed 8 December 2013; WO 275/79, 317 Airborne Field Security, Report No. 29, week ending 20 May 47. I have omitted the murder of a plain-cloth Palestinian constable in Haifa on 19 May, probably while attempting to make an arrest, because the British were unsure of the identity of the assailant (FO 371/61776, Inward Telegram 1007).

404 New York Post, 14 May 1947.

405 Douglas, TNA, FO 371/61754, penciled "414"; Medoff, *Militant Zionism*, 196-198.

406 E.g., for Baruch Korff's American Political Action Committee for Palestine. TNA, CO 967/103, "357d"; Ads, e.g., June 30 and October 7, 1947. FO 371/61866, OF.85/19/B.3.a/HLB; TNA, CO 967/103, letter,"357e"; letter, "C.S. 679/7". The Palestine Relief Committee operated out of an office at 123 West 44th Street in New York City. "It does seem to us fantastic," the British complained from Jerusalem, "that the Americans, while associating themselves with appeals for peace in Palestine, should allow" the terror organization to openly fund-raise.

407 TNA, CO 733/478/3, "Anti-Terror League, Palestine"; CO 537/1712, O.F.85/11/B.3.a./PS. The author could find no mention of this Anti-Terror League in the published literature. An internet search (10 May 2015) reveals only a listing in St Antony's College (Oxford), Middle East Centre, Jerusalem and the East Mission Collection, Box 70, 70/2.

408 TNA, WO 275/79, 317 Airborne Field Security, Report No. 29, week
ending 20 May 47; CO 733/477/3, Inward Telegrams 988, 1018, 1007
(also in FO 371/61776); KV 3/438, 157a.

409 Kister, *Irgun*, 272; WO 275/79, 317 Airborne Field Security, Report No.
31, week ending 3 June 47; TNA, CO 733/477/3, Inward Telegrams
1050, 1053, 1088, 1094 (also in FO 371/61776); WO 275/73, chart,
"11 Nov 46" upper left. The Irgun records (in Kister) what appear to be
these same attacks all on June 3.

410 TNA, KV 3/56, "Organisation of Illegal Immigration"; For Jewish
Democratic Front, FO 1071/39, Foreign Office 22 May 1947, MS "36" at
top; see also Ehrlich, *Encyclopedia of the Jewish Diaspora*, 962.

411 TNA, KV 3/56, SF.215.B3A.DJS, 5, 22; WO 275/79, 317 Airborne Field
Security, Report No. 30, week ending 27 May 47; Report 31, week ending
3 June 47.

412 TNA KV 3/439, Jewish Terrorist Activities in Britain (blue "219z"); KV
3/438, 157a; KV 3/441, "9a".

413 *ibid*; also Yinon Royhman, "What connects Molotov, Lehi underground?"
ynetnews.com 11.05.06; TNA, KV 2/4362; Knut also appears as Knout,
Knuth. There are disparate dates for Lazarus' move to Israel and to
Beersheva, from 1951 to 1953. For family background, I have relied on a
work in Russian by Vladimir Lazaris, "Three Women" [Tel Aviv, 200], as
cited and translated in Wikipedia's entry on Ariadna Scriabin; Gilberte's
dissociation from Lehi after Bernadotte's murder is mentioned in, e.g.,
symphonette.co.il/en/holocaust-remembrance ("Brandot" = Bernadotte)
(both accessed Oct 31 2021; ynet re-accessed).

414 TNA, EF 5/12, "Outrage June, 1947, Postal Packets"; A piece of the
original carbon paper used to obscure the bomb mechanism is preserved
in this folder in TNA. Two months after the letter bomb, MacMichael
received a threatening message type-written on an American anti-British
cartoon mailed from Los Angeles. Cartoon was from a Drew Pearson
article. Regarding the letter bomb thrown in the pail of water, accounts
differ as to whether the secretary or the MP threw it into the water.

415 NYT, June 7 1947; TNA, EF 5/12, "Outrage June, 1947, Postal Packets";
Letter, Ref 865,258/35; Cesarani, *Hat*, 117-118; Walton, *Empire of Secrets*,
80; Kenya bomb may have been brought by the bomber, not mailed there.
TNA, CO 537/2297, letter from H.L. Brown, red "6" upper right; another
from Brown, red "1".

416 Ira Morris, 229-230. Lehi is said to be the origin of the anti-Truman
letter bombs, but the author was unable to find any confirmation of this.

417 Kadima Building, see NYT June 18 1947; CO 537/2366, "Appendix
"B" Translation of Handwritten documemets [sic] ..."; "allowd" and
"inportnce" [sic] in the transcript; also "questions as also." After their
mission the "Theater" spies proved useful in a "stitching group," perhaps
to do with processing their data. The publisher and the author would
be very interested to learn if any of the women who were the "Theater
spies" are known to be alive and can be contacted. For association with

JA's liaison officers, FCO 141/14284 [F]rom the High Commissioner for Palestine, No. 169, 9th July, 1947, 2, item 5.

418 Regarding secrecy of Irgun-UNSCOP, meeting is merely "alleged" in TNA CO 537/2303, red "49" upper right, 2; FO 371/61866, Letter, Ministry of Defense, 1 October 1947; KV 3/439, Metropolitan Police, 257c; KV 5/39, Jewish Legion, *Report of the Conference...*; Note also allusion to meeting as a rumor, in FCO 141/14286, Telegram, No. 1283, item 3. Regarding BEGIN's BIBLICAL GEOGRAPHY, "Dan" is usually identified as Tell el Kadi, now northern Israel and southern Lebanon.

419 TNA, CO 733/477/3, Telegram 1088 & 1094; WO 275/73, penciled circled "3" in upper left. WO 275/121, Air Headquarters Levant, Monthly Newsletter, June, 1947, 6; WO 275/79, 317 Airborne Field Security, Report No. 32, week ending 10 Jun 47.

420 TNA, WO 275/121, Air Headquarters Levant, Monthly Newsletter, June, 1947, 6,7,8; FCO 141/14284, Monthly Report for June, 1947, from the High Commissioner for Palestine; WO 275/79, 317 Airborne Field Security, Report No. 33, week ending 17 Jun 47; The Irgun (Kister, p272) dates the Haganah discovery of its tunnel at June 19; See also TNA, FO 371/61776, Inward Telegram 1170 (Haganah agent misspelled "Zev Werber").

421 Regarding the attack in Jordan Book Shop, what is surely the same incident is dated 19 June in TNA, WO 275/121, Air Headquarters Levant, Monthly Newsletter, June, 1947, 8; I have trusted the dating in FO 371/61776, Inward Telegram 1200; Haifa English Girls School, WO 275/79, 317 Airborne Field Security, Report No. 34, week ending 24 Jun 47.

422 TNA, WO 275/121, Air Headquarters Levant, Monthly Newsletter, June, 1947, 8; CO 733/477/3, Inward Telegrams 1116, 1119, 1140, 1181, 1200, 1232 (some also in FO 371/61776); FCO 141/14284, Telegram, No. 1226 (from the High Commissioner), p2, and No. 1283, p1; KV 3/439, Jewish Terrorist Activities in Britain (blue "219z"), esp 5.

423 "Hanover Trial Linked to Zionist Terrorism," NYT, Sep 4 1947; TNA, WO 275/79, 317 Airborne Field Security, Report No. 35, week ending 1 Jul 47; CO 733/477/3, Inward Telegram 1242 & 1250 (also in FO 371/61776); WO 275/73, chart starting "29 June 47" in upper left; also WO 275/121, Air Headquarters Levant, Monthly Newsletters; WO 275/121, Air Headquarters Levant, Monthly Newsletter, June, 1947, p9.

424 TNA, KV 3/41, "Zionist Subversive Activities," blue "7a", esp 9-10; MI5 reported that terror activity in Austria was greater than in Germany, but less was known about it.

425 CO 537/2302, statement by W.N. Gray, Inspector General regarding an account by Assistant Inspector General of Police, Bernard Fergusson, of a confession by Farran.

426 TNA, FCO 141/14284 Telegram, "No. 1283 Top Secret Immediate"; Zertal, 46; TNA, WO 208/1705, P.I.C. Paper No. 35, 3-4; CAB 129/12/0/0020, p4; KV 2/1435, typed "460" ("Zionists of the stamp of BEN GURION," a British correspondence wrote, are "humanitarians only

for the purpose of propaganda."); Gort and Newton, FO 371/45382, "234" (but not penciled); FCO 141/14284.

427 Zertal, 48; TNA, KV 2/1435, 548a; Normally, Britain sent would-be immigrants to facilities in Cyprus or Mauritius, but the Exodus passengers were returned to southern France, from where they had embarked; refused to land there, then to the British Zone of Germany.

428 Zertal, 50, 178. For Israeli theft of Holocaust survivor funds, see Norman Finkelstein, *The Holocaust Industry* [Verso, 2000]. Survivor quote from Daniel Gordis, "What Israel Owes Holocaust Survivors," *Bloomberg*, 16 Apr 2015. Recent reports claim that some newborns of Holocaust survivors were stolen and sold by the state, this allegedly occurred both in Israel and in the DP camps in Cyprus. See "Dozens of Ashkenazi Babies Mysteriously Disappeared During Israel's Early Years," *Haaretz*, 12 Aug 2016.

429 This account was published in the *Daily Telegraph & Morning Post* on October 3, 1947, without authorization. Transcript consulted is in TNA, WO 275/64, Fortnightly Intelligence Newsletter No. 52, 8-11 (also in WO 261/571). Meyerson, see FCO 141/14286, Telegram (Cunningham), No. 1572, 23.8.47, 2, item 8.

430 TNA, CO 537/2303. One Kew document cites the date as July 10, but another on the 12th, as does Kister's listing of Irgun records 272, and this squares with the day of the week (Thursday) in 1947. The kidnapping presumably happened in the early hours of the 13th. TNA, CO 537/2303, 330/364/GS ("55" upper right), 14 pages. The pamphlet, *For the Record*, misdates the abduction as 17 July.

431 TNA, CO 733/477/3, Inward Telegrams 1351, 1378, 1361 (also in FO 371/61776); also see FCO 141/14284, Monthly report for July, 1947. One of the two constables shot on July 19 in Haifa did not die immediately, but succumbed to his wounds later.

432 TNA, WO 275/121, Monthly report for July, 1947, and Section III.

433 KV 3/41, "Zionist Subversive Activities," blue "7a"; CAB 21/2567, E75/19; KV 3/439, Jewish Terrorist Activities in Britain (blue "219z"); KV 3/438 178a. Grenade and detonator figures vary slightly.

434 KV 3/439, Jewish Terrorist Activities in Britain (blue "219z"), 4, 8; KV 2/3171; KV 3/438, blue "180", etc; KV 2/3779, at top: "PF.93044", type begins "B.4.d report on movements"; KV 2/3779, at top: "PF.93044", type begins "B.4.d report on movements"; *ibid*, "Northoit Airport / Metropolitan Police," dated 25 Jan 1948; KV 3/438 178a.

435 TNA, FO 371/61776, Inward Telegram 1384; WO 275/79, 317 Airborne Field Security, Report No. 37, week ending 22 Jul 47; FO 371/61776, Inward Telegram 1384; CO 733/477/3, Inward Telegram 1398 (also in FO 371/61783); FCO 141/14284, Monthly report for July, 1947, and Section III.

436 Headline from NYT, July 24 1947; Casualty figures quoted in CIA Documents On Truman & Zionist Terrorism and http://www.jewishvirtuallibrary.org/jsource/History/brits.html (accessed 15 Sept

2012, again March 13 2016 at http://www.jewishvirtuallibrary.org/
jsource/History/timeline.html#brits2). Donald Neff cites sixty-five deaths
(Hamas: A Pale Image of the Jewish Irgun And Lehi Gangs, WRMEA,
May/June, 2006); Giladi, *Scandals*, 76-77; FCO 141/14284, C.S. 699,
No. 212, 9th September, 1947, 4; The *Empire Lifeguard* was used once
after the attack to transport 500 (elsewhere: 485) Jewish orphans from
Cyprus. These and other orphans the British did not count as part of the
quota. Citing no casualties: NY Times; Greenfield & Hochstein, *Jews
Secret Fleet*, 114; Moshe Nachshon, "This is the Way it Was," palyam.org/
English/IS/Nachshon_Moshe, retrieved 15 Mar 2016. Regarding the
number of immigrants on the *Empire Lifeguard*, the allegedly first-hand
account of Moshe Nachshon says 750 immigrants (which was Britain's
monthly quota), while other contemporary sources, such as the JTA Daily
News Bulletin of 24 July says 300, as does the non-contemporary book
by Greenfield & Hochstein. Retribution for the Exodus debacle was the
alleged motivation for bombing the vessel, though preparations for the
bombing long predated the Exodus' Haifa landing. The bombing forced
the British to stop using its own ships to transport Jewish immigrants to
Palestine.

437 TNA, CO 733/477/3, Inward Telegrams 1398, 1412, 1423 (also in FO
371/61783). Police car was also targeted on July 24 1947; WO 275/79,
317 Airborne Field Security, Report No. 38, week ending 29 Jul 47.

438 Kister, *Irgun*, 194; TNA, CO 733/477/3, Inward Telegram 1431 (also
in FO 371/61783); WO 275/86, "Sabotage of Cables"; WO 275/121,
Monthly report for July, 1947, and Section III.

439 Kister, *Irgun*, 276; TNA, CO 733/477/3, Inward Telegrams 1438, 1448,
1451, 1477 (also in FO 371/61783).

440 TNA, CO 537/2303, 330/364/GS at upper left, total 14 pages; CO
537/3854, Outward Telegram 1708; Some sources, e.g., NYT, 1 Aug 1947,
say one of the two bodies was booby-trapped, while others, e.g., author's
interview with Ted Steel, and WO 275/121, Section III, say both bodies
were booby-trapped.

441 CIA docs; TNA, WO 275/121, Current Palestine Affairs, 2; HO
45/25586, begins "'Jewish Struggle' had now reached 7 issues";
ibid, "Metropolitan Police," "1 Jauary [194]7"; *ibid*, "Extract from
Parliamentary Debates, 29.3.45, Coles 1522-3"; *ibid*, "Lesse's Bureau of
Anti-Jewish Information"; *Christian Patriots*: Copies examined in BL;
NYT, 1 Aug 1947. In Palestine, the "reports of increasing anti-Semitism
in Britain" allowed the scandals of Jewish terrorism to be "relegated to the
background," British intelligence noted; *Falastin*, 31 July 1947, quoted
from *Palestine Chronicle*; Retaliation was not, the Irgun announced, the
reason for the hangings of the two sergeants; the executions were a
"normal" action of the of the Irgun "court."

442 NYT, Aug 14 1947; Kister, *Irgun*, 194, & 275 (where Sacher is "British
Officers Club"); TNA, KV 3/41, "Zionist Subversive Activities," blue "7a",
esp 9-10; FO 371/64126, "C10934"; KV 3/438. Kister, *Irgun*, 274; TNA,
CO 733/477/3, Inward Telegram 1501 (also in FO 371/61783); WO

275/79, 317 Airborne Field Security, Report No. 39, week ending 5 Aug 47.

443 TNA, CO 733/477/3, Inward Telegrams 1502, 1511, 1517 (also in FO 371/61783).

444 *ibid*, Inward Telegram 1517. An accomplice in the Ajami incident escaped.

445 TNA, CO 733/477/4, Inward Telegram 1525 (also in FO 371/61783); WO 275/121, Current Palestine Affairs, 6 (which dates the Aug 9 attack as Aug 7); NYT, 10 Aug 1947.

446 *ibid*, Inward Telegram 1537 (also in FO 371/61783); the Hawaii café is spelled "Hawari", and is called "the Gan Hawaii night club" in WO 275/121, Current Palestine Affairs, 2; See also The *Palestine Post*, 12 August 1947, p1; FCO 141/14284, C.S. 699, No. 212, 9th September, 1947, 2-3; From High Commissioner for Palestine, No. 1651; C.S. 699/2 No. 1572; WO 275/79, Airborne Security Report 40.

447 TNA, CO 733/477/4, Inward Telegram 1547, 1554, 1559 (also in FO 371/61783); WO 275/79, 317 Airborne Field Security, Report No. 40, week ending 12 Aug 47.

448 TNA, FO 1020/2279, "Statement on Oath by P/267936 Cpt. R. Wilson."

449 TNA, FO 1020/2279, Investigation-Department of the Landesgendarmeriekommando/Carinthia, Klagenfurt, Aug. 17th, 1947.

450 TNA records cite 130 men + 40 women aboard the Medloc train, while the NYT quoted 175 people on the train, so I have assumed five were crew: NYT, 14 Aug 1947; TNA, FO 371/64126, "C10934/10522/3"; TNA, FO 1020/2279, letter from explosives expert Franz Kubicek, 13 Aug 1947; *ibid*, "Statement on Oath by P/267936 Cpt. R. Wilson," esp 2; TNA, FO 1020/1774, penciled "21A"; FO 1020/2279; NYT, Sep 4 1947; NYT, 16 Aug 1947; KV 3/41, "Zionist Subversive Activities," blue "7a", esp 9-10; ex-Sergeant Major Bob Maxwell, "An Explosive Situation," in *The Rose & The Laurel, Journal of the Intelligence Corps*, 1995. Since the bomb could not be hidden on the trestle itself, the saboteurs had opted for firm ground between two sets of trestles rather than risk discovery. The partial explosion hit the outside track, thus pushing the train inward.

451 TNA, FO 371/64126, "C10934" appears to date a Velden attack August 15 [unclear]; the "5" should be a "3" (it is not a second attack); NYT Aug 14 1947; NYT 17 Aug 1947; NYT 20 Aug 1947.

452 TNA, FO 1020/1774, "Note by Brigadier Waghorn. Bombing of Medloc 'C'"; Letter, Schmidt, blue "51A" upper right; Minutes of Meeting, "30B" upper right. Efforts were made to replace the coal-hungry pilot trains with lighter draisines where possible, or electric locomotives where there were steep gradients.

453 NYT, Aug 14 1947; Kister, *Irgun*, 194, & 275 (where Sacher is "British Officers Club"); TNA, KV 3/41, "Zionist Subversive Activities," blue "7a", esp 9-10; FO 371/64126, C10934; CIA docs; TNA, CO 537/1814, "Speech Delivered by Eliezer Kaplan … 22.10.46."

454 The idea of boycotting Jewish citrus crop was encouraged by Henry Gurney, Chief Secretary to the Palestine Mandate. TNA, CO 537/2303, red "29", "30", black "7" for UK cash advances on citrus.

455 *ibid*, Inward Telegrams 1547, 1554, 1559, 1570.

456 TNA, CO 733/477/4, Inward Telegrams 1537, 1566 (also in FO 371/61783).

457 "Irgun Denounces Killing of Arabs," *The Daily Worker*, Aug 18 1947; TNA, WO 275/121, Current Palestine Affairs, 2, which states that the Hagana's Aug 15 attack in Petah Tikvah was in retaliation for the Aug 10 café attack allegedly by Arabs, and that the Haganah apologized for the murdering the wrong people; *ibid*, p6; CO 733/477/4, Telegram 1570; FCO 141/14284, C.S. 699, No. 212 9th September, 1947; C.S. 699/2 No. 1572; In Zurich, the General Zionist Council met and, "under the pretext of avoiding civil war" among the Yishuv (as a British report put it), did "their best to block effective counter-terrorist action."

458 TNA, CO 733/477/4, Inward Telegrams 1570, 1579 (also in FO 371/61783); Thomas Reynolds, "Hagana Warns Irgun to Desist," Chicago Sun, 9 Nov 1947; NYT, June 12 1947.

459 Regarding beginnings of anti-Jewish Palestinian violence, possible exception is the August 10 café attack (perpetrators unknown, but based on precedent it may have been a Zionist attack to jump-start ethnic violence); TNA, CO 733/477/4, Inward Telegrams 1576, 1579, 1592, 1598, 1605, 1632, 1689, 1717; WO 275/121, Current Palestine Affairs, p2; FCO 141/14284, C.S. 699/2 No. 1572, p1-2; for a list of incidents of violence between Palestinians and Jewish settlers during this period, see WO 275/121, Jewish-Arab Incidents. Regarding Lehi threats against Jewish civil servants, on the night of 4 Sept the gang warned twenty Jewish members of the staff of the Income Tax Department in Tel Aviv to quit their jobs; for arms cache, see also KV 3/447, 276, 278.

460 TNA, FO 371/61915, letter, "Inverchapel"; *ibid*, letter, penciled "22"; NY Sun, June 24 1947; the *Times*, Sep 9 1947; TNA, KV 3/41, Zionist Subversive Activities, 11; Martinski and Korff, KV 2/4363, 14a opposition to Korff, e.g., The Detroit Jewish News, April 11 1947, p14; NYT Sep 9 1947; Cesarani, *Hat*, 117, 151.

461 TNA, KV3/439, MS note dated 23 Aug '47. The word "the" in "the Colonial office" is surmised, as it is punched through; 3 Sep 1947 postal bomb, TNA, KV 3/439, 220B.

462 TNA CO 733/477/4, Inward Telegram 1717; WO 275/83, "Minutes of a Meeting Held in the Refinery Superintendent's Office ... 15th September 1947." The Irgun reference in Kister, *Irgun*, 275, for this day simply states "Three fuel containers blown up during curfew in Haifa"; CO 733/477/4, Inward Telegram 1808; WO 275/64; Fortnightly Intelligence Newsletter No. 51, 4-6. (of the two police murdered in the chase after the bank robbers, one was reported killed, the other as "not expected to recover." The author could find no further record of the alleged "Lameri" branch of the Hagana; FCO 141/14284, No. 1850.

463   NYT, Sep 30 1947; TNA, WO 275/64, Fortnightly Intelligence
      Newsletter No. 52, 4 (repeated in WO 261/571).

464   TNA, CO 733/477/4, Inward Telegrams 1842, 1836; *ibid*, Colonial
      Office Telegram No. 1827; Kister, *Irgun*, 275; TNA, WO 275/64,
      Fortnightly Intelligence Newsletter No. 52, p5; WO 275/73, "Railway
      Sabotage," 1947; for the military advocating using "armed Jews," "thugs,"
      and "murderers" instead of "terrorist," because it "invests the individuals
      concerned with a certain amount of glamor," see WO 275/86, "Stern and
      Irgun" (red "40").

465   TNA, CO 537/3854, 330/424/GS. The number of rounds is based on
      the expended cartridges recovered by the British in the morning; Irgun-
      Lehi meeting, KV 5/39, 200z; Military report, WO 275/64, Fortnightly
      Intelligence Newsletter No. 52, 4; American Consulate, see WP 275/64,
      Fortnightly Newsletter No. 53, p2; Irgun banners, *ibid*, 5; WO 261/571,
      Fortnightly Intelligence Newsletter No. 54, 6.

466   TNA, WO 275/79, 317 Airborne Field Security, Report No. 54, week
      ending 19 Nov 47; Report No. 42, week ending 26 Aug 47; Content of
      sex workers' spying forms based on a questionnaire confiscated from an
      Irgun member that was believed to be similar to that given the women.

467   TNA, WO 261/573, 1 March 1948, "Government of Palestine indictment
      of Jewish Agency as a result of outrages," 2.

468   TNA, CO 733/477/4, Inward Telegrams 2071, 2139; Early reports
      about the oil workers say that one survived the attack, but from later
      correspondence it is clear that he died within a few days; The brother
      of one of the murdered oil workers wrote to Parliament asking what so
      many others had: why was Britain so powerless against Jewish terrorism?
      The reason, an MP replied, was again "the constant refusal of the Jewish
      community and their organizations to afford them any measure of
      co-operation." TNA, CO 733/477/4, Inward Telegram No. 2150; *ibid*,
      red MS "2426" at top; Regarding the four oil workers, another report
      identified the cinema as the May Cinema (WO 275/79, 317 Airborne
      Field Security, Report No. 54, week ending 19 Nov 47); Nov 20, WO
      261/571, Fortnightly Intelligence Newsletter No. 55 (8-21 Nov 1947), 1,
      6; CO 733/477/4, 75156/151A/47; *ibid*, 75156151A/47; CO 733/477/4,
      Inward Telegram No. 2155; Leaflets from Tel Aviv, KV 3/439; Hebrew
      Legion, KV5/11, "100" at top; *Aliyah*, WO 275/79, 317 Airborne Field
      Security Section Report No. 54 for the week ending 19 Nov 47; Lehi
      "school," TNA, WO 261/571, "Search for Stern Gang School". Note
      that the sentence "some three hundred carefully selected young Jews,
      earmarked and trained for service with HAGANA" continues to the
      page end "and that most......." but the next page (3) is missing from the
      National Archives; KV 3/447, 320c; also 313z, according to which at the
      Lehi school incident, one girl was killed, three men and two girls seriously
      injured, one girl captured unhurt.

469   Weizmann & Mussolini, Rome, Feb 17 1934; *Papers*, 9, p38.

470   Under Secretary of State Sumner Welles, quoted in Quigley, *Challenge*,
      ch 4; also Roosevelt, *Partition of Palestine a Lesson in Pressure Politics*. Ben-
      Gurion quote, Morris, *Birth* (1989) 24; CIA, *Consequences*, 8-9; Roosevelt,

Arab Position, 9; For earlier discussion of Arab and Jewish cantons in a single state, see CO 733/283/12. Also see CAB 95/14 for a collection of related Partition papers.

471 TNA, CAB 129/21/0009, Cabinet / Palestine / Memorandum by the Secretary of State for Foriegn Affairs / C.P. (47) 259, esp 5 ("52" stamped at upper right) (18 September, 1947).

472 Cadogan, TNA, CAB 129/21/0/0009, 4. Foreign Office, 18 September, 1947; Quigley, *Challenge*, ch 3; Ben-Gurion to Amos, new, critical translation used. See JPS Responds to CAMERA's Call for Accuracy: Ben-Gurion and the Arab Transfer," in Journal of Palestine Studies Vol. XLI, No. 2 (Winter 2012), 245–250. Also also Shabtai Teveth, 188; Brenner, *51 Documents*, 117.

473 TNA, FO 1093/330, "Outlines of Zionist Policy," especially ch 2, "Jewish State." See also FCO 141/14284, Monthly Report for June, 1947, 1, item 2 suggesting the same tact regarding statehood, Partition, and land allocation when the UN deliberated Palestine's fate.

474 TNA, CO 733/456/3, Fortnightly Report, Jerusalem, end 15 Dec 1944; FO 371/45376, Inward Telegram 1768, 3.

475 Begin & Partition, e.g., TNA, KV 5/37, blue "136b"; Tel Aviv Mayor, CO 537/1712, "Top Secret / Jewish Agency Policy," 3; Hashomer Hazair, *ibid*, also Penkower, Monty Noam, *Decision on Palestine Deferred: America, Britain and Wartime Diplomacy, 1939-1945*. [Routledge, 2002]; FO 371/45376, Memorandum by the S of S, 6th page, penciled "65" and containing points 18, 19, 20.

476 *Jewish Standard*, TNA, KV 5/39, A. Abrahams, "Irgun and Partition."

477 Jewish Struggle, TNA, HO 45/25586; ZOA, see NYT Oct 27 1946; TNA, KV 5/31, Bulletin of the Fighters for the Freedom of Israel; *ibid*, Palestine The I.Z.L. and the Jewish Agency, (vi), (vii), (viii).

478 TNA, FO 371/75344, "Brief for UN Political Dept on Item 18...," 2; FCO 141/14284, No. 1992.

479 TNA, CAB 129/16/0049, p3 UN, A_364_Add.2 PV.19, 7 July 1947; Arab Higher Committee, *Palestine The Arab Case*, 26; Roosevelt, *Arab Position*, 4-5; Husseini, WO 261/571, Fortnightly Intelligence Newsletter No. 56; Alon's statement is widely quoted, e.g., Abu-Lughod, *Transformation*, 178-179.

480 CIA, *The Consequences of the Partition of Palestine, CIA, ORE 55, 28 November, 1947*; TNA, FCO 141/14286, telegram 2285, including for Tel Aviv mayor,; FCO 141/14284, Monthly Report for November, 1947 (No. 295); WO 275/79, 317 Airborne Field Security, Report No. 56, week ending 3 Dec 47; WO 261/571, Fortnightly Intelligence Newsletter No. 56, 5,6,7, and Partition of Palestine after Newsletter No. 56, and 317 Airborne Field Security, The UNO Decision; WO 275/79.

481 For Israeli provocation to elicit a response against which it must defend itself by aggression, see also Ilan Pappé, *Ethnic Cleansing*, especially chapter 4. which draws on Zionist archives unavailable to this author; also Zeez Maoz, *Defending the Holy Land*, and the Postscript to this

book; Kapeliouk, *New Light on the Israeli Arab Conflict*, 17; British report, see TNA, Fortnightly Intelligence Newsletter No. 57, 2; Cunningham, FCO 141/14284, telegram No. 2413; WO 261/571, Partition of Palestine; Agency refusal to move to Tel Aviv, FCO 141/14284, No. 2345. Palestinian anti-Jewish violence is commonly said to reemerge on November 30, since it was the day after Resolution 181's passage and the UN precedent of a Zionist state (there was also Jewish anti-Arab violence that day). It was however in mid-August, with UNSCOP's announcement of its recommendations, that a Zionist state was widely understood as inevitable, and that the beginnings of this violence date, as cited in chapter 6, page 226.

482 TNA, WO 261/571, Resume of the major acts of Arab and Jewish violence during the period 5-19 Dec 1947; WO 275/64, Fortnightly Intelligence Newsletter No. 57, 2-3; also in WO 261/571.

483 Haifa bus attack, TNA, FCO 141/14284, telegram No. 2413, 2; WO 275/31, Illegal Appropriation of Land Appx "B" to 3 Para Bde; CO 733/477/4, Inward Telegram 2509; NYT Dec 13, 20, 21, 24, 13 1947; Pappé, *Cleansing*, 57; For British report on Khisas attack, WO 275/64, Fortnightly Intelligence Newsletter No. 58, 6; For Khisas, also see Khalidi, *All That Remains*, 465-6; for Abdullah and prediction of no Palestinian state, WO 261/571, Fortnightly Intelligence Newsletter No. 57, 6 Dec–18 Dec 47, esp 2; CO 733/477/4, Inward Telegram 2426, 2397, 2409, & others; KV 3/447, Inward Telegram 14th December, 1947 ("not numbered"); Quigley, *Challenge*, ch 5; pamphlet, *For the Record* dates the café attack as Christmas eve, whereas TNA documents say the 25th. For the issue of Zionist provocation in December 1947 with the specific purpose of igniting a civil war from which the new Israeli state would have to "defend" itself through ethnic cleansing, land confiscation, and ethnically-selective martial law, see, e.g., Pappe, *Ethnic Cleansing*, especially ch 3; and Amnon Kapelionk. "New Light on the Arab-Israeli Conflict and Refugee Problems and Its Origin," in *Journal of Palestine Studies* 16, no. 3 (Spring 1987): 16–24.

484 TNA, CO 733/477/4 penciled "34", Inward Telegram, To the Secretary of State for the Colonies; "cooperating" is corrupt but intent clear; pages out of order in Kew but identity of quoted page seems clear.

485 Wilson, *6th Airborne*, kindle 2640-2641.

486 TNA, Pappé, *Cleaning*, 59; Also TNA, KV 5/39, "203a" re Hashomer and Haifa; NYT Dec 31 1947; NYT Dec 30 1947; UN A_AC.21_SR.16 21 Jan 1948; TNA, CO 537/3855 Inward Telegram 2525; *ibid*, Summary of Events, 29 Dec 1947 (red "1").

487 Res 181 placed Jaffa as an Arab enclave separated from the rest of Arab Palestine; See TNA CAB 128/6/0/0009 219; UN, A_AC.21_SR.16 21 Jan 1948, Summary Record of Sixteenth Meeting of the United Nations Palestine Commission; Pamphlet, *For the Record*; TNA, KV 5/39, blue "203a".

488 TNA, FO 800/487, Hugh Dow, telegram, September 1 1948.

489 Provocation, see TNA, WO 275/64, Fortnightly Intelligence Newsletter No. 58, 1; WO 275/83, 317 Airborne Field ... Report on CRL Massacre; Pappé, *Cleaning*, 59; Also TNA, KV 5/39, "203a" re Hashomer and Haifa; NYT 31 Dec 1947; NYT 30 Dec 1947; For British reaction to Damascus Gate roadblocks, Summary Record of Sixteenth Meeting of the, United Nations Palestine Commission, 21 January 1948 (UN A_AC.21_SR.16 21); TNA CO 537/3855 Inward Telegram 2525; *ibid*, Summary of Events, 29 Dec 1947 (red "1"); WO 275/83, Report on Rioting at GRL Refinery on 30 December 1947. Benny Morris (Revisited), while acknowledging that "what Arabs did to Jews was barely relevant" in regard to "how and why the Palestinian refugee problem came about" (7), begins the post-181 descent into chaos with an Arab attack against two buses the day after the vote (30 Nov), then effectively jumps to 1948 (65) having mentioned nothing of Zionist provocation that was calculated to cause the civil war.

490 NYT, 5 Jan 1948; Pappé, *Cleansing*, 59-60; NYT 7 Jan 1948; NYT 5 Jan 1948; UN, A_AC.21_SR.16 of 21 Jan 1948; Krystal dates the attack January 4, but most sources say the night of January 5-6. See also Karmi, *Fatima*, 86-89, who mentions the torrential rains that night; Jerusalem Quarterly... Qatamon, 1948 The Fall of a Neighborhood. Quoted from Krystall, "The De Arabization of West Jerusalem." Attacks of Dec 31 & Jan 1, see WO 275/64, Fortnightly Intelligence Newsletter No. 57, p7-8. About the timing of the Haganah attacks on Balad esh Sheikh and Wadi Rushmiyya, Pappe dates these as roughly simultaneous on Dec 31, whereas British records places Balad esh Sheikh at 01:00 on Jan 1. I thus felt it safe to assume that they occurred on the night of the 31st-1st, just around midnight; WO 275/64, Fortnightly Intelligence Newsletter No. 58; The Balad esh Sheikh massacre, as reported by the British, "was carried out simultaneously from two sides by a party of 32 [Hagana]. A gang of 12 took up positions and opened fire from the hills to the West of the village, while a second group numbering some 20 persons entered the village from the South, firing SMGs and throwing grenades."; Pamphlet, *For the Record*. Straight-forward, detailed record of early 1948's daily anti-Jewish and anti-Arab carnage can be found in TNA records, for example CO 537/3855 and WO 261/573. The history of the 1948 war itself is beyond the scope of this book, except to cite civilian terror's evolution into the arsenal of the Israeli state.

491 TNA, WO 275/64, Fortnightly Intelligence Newsletter No. 59, 6.

492 TNA, KV 5/39, blue "203a"; NYT, Jan 5 1948; Pappé, Cleansing, 60; Kim Philby was John Philby's son; NYT 7 Jan 1948; Kister, 202; NYT 5 Jan 1948; UN, A_AC.21_SR.16 of 21 Jan 1948; Krystal dates the attack January 4, but most sources say the night of January 5-6. See also Karmi, *Fatima*, 86-89, who mentions the "howling, icy wind" and "torrential rain" that night; Jerusalem Quarterly... Qatamon, 1948 The Fall of a Neighborhood. Quoted from Krystall, "The De Arabization of West Jerusalem". Attacks of Dec 31 & Jan 1, see Fortnightly Intelligence Newsletter No. 57, 7-8; CO 537/3855, Summary of Events—4 Jan 1948; The attack on the "Old Serrai" completely destroyed the Social Welfare Offices. WO 261/573, Fortnightly Intelligence Newsletter No. 59, 5,

which claims that the Semiramis Hotel attack was not authorized by the Agency.

493 NYT 7 Jan 1948; Re Semiramis, Ghada Karmi, who lived in Qatamon at the time of the bombing, also dismisses the Hagana's claim. She writes that "Arab journalists were in the habit of staying at the Semiramis and it was a well-known meeting place for activists of all political persuasions" (Karmi, *Fatima*, 89); NYT, 27 Feb 1957.

494 TNA, CO 537/3855, WO 275/58, Summary of Events, 7 January, 1948.

495 Re new Mallnitz threat, the "vengeance" was alleged to be for the imprisonment of one Gonsior Henoch; See TNA, FO 1020/1774, Cipher Telegram INT/B/1106, 6 Jan 1948; FO 371/68648, letter from Hector McNeil to S of State; James Reston, NYT 27 Jan 1948; Also see TNA, FO 371/68648; Barclays Bank, KV 3/447, 328; Bomb at Arab Bureau in London, *Falastin*, Jan 24 1948; Wash. to F.O. No. 422. British reports place the Arab Bureau bomb at January 21, whereas *Falastin* reported the 23rd. (KV 3/440, 277A); Sales of Auster aircraft, FO 800/487, 91, etc.

496 TNA, FO 371/68648, Inward Telegram to Commonwealth Relation Office (No. 121).

497 UN, A/AC.21/SR.16, 21 Jan 1948; for the reaction in the Zionist press of the Semiramis bombing, see TNA, WO 275/64, Fortnightly Intelligence Newsletter No. 59, p9.

498 Jewish Agency, *Memorandum on Acts of Arab Aggression*; TNA, FCO 141/14286, Cunningham telegram 1119.

499 Krystall, "De Arabization of West Jerusalem"; Tamari, Salim, (ed.), *Jerusalem 1948*, ch 4, esp 94-95; Morris, *Birth*, 52.

500 TNA, FO 800/487; Kirkbride, Telegram 693; Beaumont, telegram of September 16, p262; FO 371/68648, Cypher 816 (penciled "43"); *ibid*, Telegram, UK Delegation to UN, No. 462, p2; FO 371/82703, Monthly Situation Report for the Jordan, Dec 1949, 2; CIA, *Possible Developments* (the Zionists will try to "set up a Jewish state in all of Palestine and Transjordan"); CIA, *Aims of the Revisionists*; TNA, FO 371/68649, Telegram No. 5459; For early mention of Abdullah deal, see WO 261/571, Fortnightly Intelligence Newsletter No. 57, 6 Dec–18 Dec 47. Britain as well hoped to get something out of the spoils of Palestine. The Chiefs of Staff had been hoping for Jordan to get "the southern Arab portion of Palestine" so that it could "provide a base for Great Britain in the Middle East," but it was again Israel that seized most of the south. Two years later, a secret British report reaffirmed that in already early 1948 it had been "assumed that Jordan would absorb the eastern part of Arab Palestine"—no Palestinian state.

501 Re "various forms of pressure," TNA, FO 371/61914, FO to Jedda (penciled "7"); NYT 8 Mar 1948; NYT 9 Mar 1948; 1948; 2014 dollar conversion based on dollartimes.com; Peter Bergson, letter to the NY Herald Tribune, Dec 4 1947 (examined in TNA, KV 2/2956); Haganah set up recruiting centers, see Wendehorst, *British Jewry*, 263.

502 Posterity has laid blame on British irregulars and Arabs for the Ben Yehuda attack; a document preserved in TNA, alleging to be by investigators hired by the Jewish Agency and Va'ad Leumi, categorically dismissed any Arab involvement, putting all blame on the British, probably wrongly and for strategic reasons; TNA, CO 537/3858, "Report of the Committee" (red "66"), esp p6; For pamphlet, *ibid*, "The British League Palestine Branch".

503 TNA, CO 733/477/5, Inward Telegram 834; All the victims appear to have been Arab civilians. Both the *Times*, 2 Mar 1948, and UN Palestine Commission Daily News Summary 23, 1 Mar 1948, describe the victims as British military, apparently in error, as the British telegram in TNA citing the dead specifically states that British military personnel "were not (repeat not) injured."; Salam Building, NYT 4 Mar 1948.

504 NYT 23 Mar 1948; Kister, *Irgun*, 277; KV 5/31, Extract OF 606/1, "159z", spelled "Farren [sic] Group," but as the "Farran Group" by the Irgun, e.g., KV 3/440, 278ab, Irgun letter, p3; Regarding Roy Farran, the present author interviewed an acquaintance of Major Farran from the late 1940s in Palestine, Ted Steel, who did not believe the murder charge; while Cesarani's account, *Major Farran's Hat*, is fairly incriminating.

505 Arab Higher Committee Delegation for Palestine, *The Black Paper*, dated 12 March, 3. Distribution of pamphlet reported by NYT May 14 1948. For "Science Corps of the Hagana," see Pappé, *Ethnic Cleansing*, 100-101. For bacteriologist, TNA, FCO 141/14286, Telegram, No. 1293, 8.5.48, 2, item 5. For article reporting typhoid outbreak in Acre, NYT, 6 May 1948. Morris, *Revisited*, states that the Acre epidemic may have been the result of poor sanitary conditions resulting from the displacement of people, but health officials determined that the infection was water borne, not due to crowded or unhygienic conditions. Further dispelling Morris' contention, roughly the same number of Palestinians and British soldiers were infected, and there was no outbreak in the more dire conditions in other Arab cities. Naeim Giladi, the source quoted herewith for the biological attacks, was with the terror organizations and records the use of bacteriological warfare in Acre, Gaza, and in the depopulating of Palestinian villages; See AMEU, *The Link*, Volume 31, Issue 2, April-May, 1998, and Giladi, *Scandals*. Some reports use the word "typhus" when "typhoid" is surely what is meant; my thanks to Prof. Francis Manasek for this correction.

506 CIA, *Consequences*, 14; TNA, WO 261/571, Fortnightly Intelligence Newsletter No. 54, 8 Nov 1947; Haganah secrecy and the assassination of suspected informants, WO 275/121, "What's What," item 5; TNA (ibid) mentions the need of interning all Germans in Jaffa and the Enclosed Colonies, "especially the women."

507 Transcript of videoed interview of Yerachmiel Kahanovitch, filmed in Kibbutz Degania, 23 July 2012. He was part of Operation Broom and Operation Dani. English translation by Ami Asher. Published in *Zochot*. Accessed October 18, 2012.

508 *ibid*.

509 *ibid*.

510 *ibid.*

511 Rapes in 1948, see Morris, *Revisited*, and his interview with Ari Shavit, "Survival of the Fittest." Pappé, *Ethnic Cleansing*, 209; Ben-Gurion "forgiveness" of rape, Ofer Aderet, "State Archive Error Shows Israeli Censorship Guided by Concerns Over National Image", *Haaretz*, Jan 5 2022.

512 Ernst and Bevin, TNA, FO 800/487, 110. When Ernst "talked to people over there about what Britain had done in the spite of the attack by his fellow Jews upon us, they had scarcely believed it."

513 UN Palestine Commission Daily News Summary 23; NYT, 13 Apr 1948; Kapeliouk, *New Light on the Israeli Arab Conflict*, 17.

514 British intelligence report is in the Weekly Intelligence Appreciation of April 17; TNA KV 5/39, blue 214a; FCO 141/14286, Telegram (from Cunningham), No. 1023; Davis, *Apartheid*, 21-22, 25. Irgun press statement, TNA, CO 733/477/5, 148, telegram 933; For British plan to attack Irgun in Deir Yassin by air, FO 371/68504, 17-18; See also FO 371/68504, 17-18. Using the coordinates of 31°47'8.5"N , 35°10'40.7"E for Deir Yassin, the Yad va-Shem structure lies 1.25 km from what was the village's center.

515 TNA, FO 371/68649, Dept notice from British Emb, Ref 3/144/48, esp 2; *ibid*, Draft Brief for SS for Discussion with PM and Minister of Defense on April 15, and *Aide-Memoire*.

516 TNA, FO 371/68649, R.H. Hadow to P. Mason (UN), 2 May, 1948; FBI, Americans for Haganah Incorporated.

517 Morris 1989, p200 note 4. TNA FO 371/68504, e.g. Inward Telegram 1076 and others. Former BBC correspondent and United Nations senior civil servant, Erskine B. Childers, in Lughod, 182, states that another Haganah method of attack was to place explosives around Palestinian houses at night as people slept, drenching wooden parts in petrol, then igniting it by gunfire from a distance. While Childers and Lughod were both credible, the author was unable to corroborate this tactic independently.

518 TNA FO 371/68649, E5020, penciled "54" & "55"; Bevin, FO 800/487, FO 371/68649, 43.

519 TNA, FO/371 68649, Record of Conversation PM and SS with US Ambassador 28 Apr 1948 (penciled "110").

520 TNA, CO 537/3861, Inward Telegram 1232.

521 NYT 2 May 1948; Kister, 202.

522 TNA, FCO 141/14286, Cunningham telegrams 1119 (8 May 48), 1211 (30 May 48).

523 TNA, FCO 141/14286, No. 1119, "My telegram No. 1023," Weekly intelligence appreciation, 2.

524 *Ibid.*

525 TNA, KV 3/440, 277A, and follow-up 278A; Home Office experts described the Feb 23 Colonial Office device as a "home-made incendiary." There was a fake bomb planted by the Colonial Office on 20 August 1947, what the Office described as a "nose-thumbing" gesture in support of Palestinian (Zionist) terror. (See NYT 20 Aug 1947).

526 NYT, 8 Mar 1948; 18 Mar 1948; 22 May 1948; 21 May 1948.

527 Cesarani, 193. TNA EF 5/12, "The Star, Poison Bomb Secrets Out"; KV 3/440, 302a; KV 3/440 299g; Yossi Melman, The Heruti Code, Haaretz, Jan. 13, 2005; NYT, Sept 18 1948.

528 Neff, *Pillars*, 65.

529 CIA, Clandestine Air Transport Operations (DOC_0000655104).

530 Erskine B. Childers' "The Wordless Wish: From Citizens to Refugees," in Abu-Lughod, *Transformation*, 187, 182; Quigley, *Challenge*, ch 10; TNA, FO 371/68649, British Emb doc 3/175/48, penciled 136, esp 3; Morris, *Birth* (1989), 200 note 4; TNA, FO 371/68649, penciled 33, 136-137; Ben-Gurion himself gave orders to ethnically cleanse villages, though even three decades later, in 1979, the Israeli government barred Yitzhak Rabin, a commander in 1948, from stating this (NYT 23 Oct 1979).

531 TNA, EF 5/12, Daily Telegraph, 12 May 1948; NYT 12 May 1948; Segev (*Complete*, 480) writes that Barker himself, not his wife or the maid, noted the rigged envelope; the author has trusted TNA docs; TNA, EF 5/12, "Statement of Dr. Watts," p2; *ibid*, "To the Superintendent" from Surray Constabulary, 13 May 1948. The Lord Speaker is written as "Lord Chairman of the House of Lords".

532 TNA, EF 5/12, news clippings; Some published reports (e.g., *Daily Mail*) stated that it is the sodium cyanide that cause the devices to explode in contact with water, but this is incorrect; sodium cyanide does not explode in water (my thanks to Prof. Francis Manasek for this correction); *ibid*, note that "Statement of Dr. Watts," 2, says "it badly bent a ¾ inch steel plate," whereas "Letter Bombs," 16 June 1947, cites a ¼ inch plate.; *ibid*, letter to Dr. Watts (upper right 292,569), MS doc beginning "Telephone message," cite the Atlas Powder Company (Wilmington, Delaware), Dupont, and Hercules Powder Company; *ibid*, letter, Venizia Giulia Police Force (red "1"); *ibid*, CRDD Reference X12/123, "Outrage, June 1947, Postal Packets," esp 5.

533 TNA CO 537/3860, red "68", "56", "50"; NYT 15 May 1948; *Declaration of the Establishment of the State of Israel*; Kapeliouk, *New Light on the Israeli Arab Conflict*, 3; Herzog, re Hagana-Irgun merger, TNA, FCO 141/14286, Cunningham telegram 1119; KV 5/31, Stern Gang Broadcasts ("168A"); Ernst FO 800/487, 198.

534 TNA, FO 371/68650, Telegram 6612 (penciled "125"); CIA, Possible Developments from the Palestine Truce, 31 Aug 1948 (DOC_0000258353).

535 TNA, FO 371/68650, Telegram 6612 (penciled "125"); Halt ERP funds to Britain, e.g., NY Post and the Home News, June 2 1948, in FO

371/68650. CIA, Possible Developments from the Palestine Truce, 31 Aug 1948 (DOC_0000258353).

536 Cabinet memorandum, CAB 129/29/0018, 5.

537 TNA, CRIM 1/1951 (for arrest, "Copy Charge," 8); Cesarani, *Hat*, 199-200; Walton, *Empire of Secrets*, 94; Canberra Times, 16 Dec 1948.

538 TNA, KV 2/3171, The Activities of Mr. Cyril ROSS (dated May, 1949, attachment to CD/99 of 31.3.50); and others, e.g., 22a; 20a contains transcripts of intercepted phone calls that included reference to "Daniel," the same name Sneh contacted in an intercepted telegram in 1946; and reference to the fear of blackmail, and (separately) de Beers (presumably the diamond firm).

539 Colonel W.W. O'Connor, Israel Problems and Viability, The National War College, Oct 28 1949, p3; declassified Dec 6 1967.

540 TNA, KV 5/31, press clippings, esp Daily Telegraph.

541 Lehi, Daily Press Bulletin No. 37, Sept 6 1948. See TNA FO 371/68696, penciled "18".

542 TNA, Marshall, Bevin, and aborted US announcement of approval for Bernadotte's plan, FO 492/12. Finding of an examination of a report submitted by the Israeli government on the assassination of Count Folke Bernadotte [o]f Wisborg / submitted by Maths Heuman Chief Prosecutor of the Realm (translated from the Swedish, in TNA FO 371/82623). The celebratory situation in prison is from Time Magazine Oct 18 1948 ("ISRAEL: Who's in Charge Here?"). Also cited in Schwartz, *Walking With the Damned*, 305-6, though Schwartz does not cite his sources.

543 TNA, FO 371/75266, report dated 3 May 1949. Bernadotte plan, CAB 129/29; Newspaper report, KV 5/32, 217a; Jerusalem, *ibid*, 222a.

544 TNA, FO 371/75266, "Top Secret" letter from Major V. P. Ric of the Military Liaison Office, Jerusalem, to Major C. de B. deLisle of the War Office, on the 13th of August 1949, "in the strictest confidence." Note the cable to the F.O. in TNA KV 5/31, 199B, stating the Fatherland Front is composed Lehi and Irgun, "but is beyond the control of either." Early reports of flights to Prague, KV 5/31, 192c, 194a, 195a, 196a, 198a. See also Suárez, "Did Israel, not Lehi, murder UN Mediator, Folke Bernadotte, in 1948?", in *Middle East Monitor*, Oct 19 2022.

545 UN, S/1098, "Attack on Arab Airways Commercial Aircraft," Letter dated 29 November 1948 from the Acting Mediator Addressed to the Secretary-general Transmitting a Report on Truce Violation by Jewish Forces on 23 September 1948.; Kirkbride, *From the Wings*, 108-110 (in his somewhat embellished account of the attack, he states that the Israeli fighter was 9 miles inside Jordan, perhaps referring to the second, rather than the third, attack).

546 Morris, *Revisited*, 4, 469-470; FO 371/111104; letter T. Wikeley, R1091/160, esp p2.

547 Pappé Ethnic Cleansing 196; UN Conciliation Commission for Palestine, The Dawaymeh Massacre, 14 June 1949, testimony of Hassan Mahmaud Ihdeib, the Mukhtar of the village; Morris, *Border*, 469.

548 UN Conciliation Commission for Palestine, The Dawaymeh Massacre, 14 June 1949; Morris, *Revisited*, 469-470.

549 From documents uncovered by historian Tamar Novick; from notes by Mapam Central Committee member Aharon Cohen based on a briefing given in November 1948 by Israel Galili, former Haganah chief of staff. Also reported by Benny Morris. Quoted from Hagar Shezaf, "Burying the Nakba: How Israel Systematically Hides Evidence of 1948 Expulsion of Arabs," in Haaretz, Jul. 5, 2019. Adam Raz, "Classified Docs Reveal Massacres of Palestinians in '48—and What Israeli Leaders Knew", Haaretz Dec 9 2021.

550 Officer in Op Hiram was Yosef Nahmani; Morris, Revisited, 500; Zertal, 171. For Mikunis, see Adam Raz, "Classified Docs Reveal Massacres of Palestinians in '48—and What Israeli Leaders Knew," *Haaretz*, Dec 9 2021; Ben-Gurion orders, Ofer Aderet, "State Archive Error Shows Israeli Censorship Guided by Concerns Over National Image", *Haaretz*, Jan 5 2022.

551 Ricky-Dale Calhoun, "Arming David: The Haganah's illegal arms procurement network in the United States 1945-1949," in Journal of Palestine Studies Vol. XXXVI, No. 4 (Summer 2007), 22–32; TNA, KV 2/2264, Extract, "202b," (surname misspelled "Koller"); *ibid*, "S.F.76/Palestine/4/B3a/MCSP (blue "190a[?]"; these state that British Secret Intelligence Service reported that Teddy Kollek, according to sources of "unknown reliability," purchased a million dollars of radar equipment which was shipped to Israel by way of Mexico, but the US authorities stopped the same path for fifty tanks he had bought. Unable to get them to Israel, he sold them to China and, having come to the notice of the FBI, returned to Israel; KV 2/1390, W.1239, "192a"; KV 5/40, "Statement by Mr. Menachem Begin…19th Septembre[sic], 1948, esp p2.

552 TNA, KV 2/2251, "76c," "76b," "77w," "77y"; FO 371/68512, MS "38 upper right. FO 371/68697, letter, ref 3/315/48, 3 December, 1948; KV2 2251, 78a; NYT, Nov 27 1948; NYT, Dec 3 1948; NYT, Dec 4 1948. Note that NYT article with photo of Begin in motorcade is misdated as Nov 28 in KV 2/2251.

553 Begin, TNA, KV 5/40, Voice of Jerusalem (blue "266a").

554 TNA, FO 371/75340, "74-75" in upper right. British report, preliminary memo from Harold Beeley to Bernard Burrows suggests their (and probably especially Beeley's) authorship.

555 TNA, CAB 129/32-0010, 69; PREM 8/1251, "Historical memorandum … Since 1945," esp 8; FO 371/75402, Draft Statement re 5 RAF planes, & more; FO 371/75400, Cypher MS.10019, etc; TNA, FO 371/75402 Cypher Telegram No. 99. See also FO 800/487, 293-295; For an analysis and history of the spitfire downings more favorable to Israel, see Zeev Tzahor, "The 1949 Air Clash Between the Israeli Air Force and the RAF", in *Journal of Contemporary History*, Vol. 28 (1993), 75-101; regarding the two Allied pilots cited in the Israeli attacks over the Sinai in January 1949, Churchill, referring to the incident in 1952, cites three: "…

contained three pilots who had fought for us in the Battle of Britain" (FO 800/811).

556 Churchill vs Bevin on IAF downing of British planes was during Churchill's second term as Prime Minister. TNA, FO 800/811, "Prime Minister's Personal Minute," M512-52, October 19, 1951.

557 TNA, FO 492/12, and FO 492/30, House of Commons, Jan 26, 1949, The National Archives (Kew), FO 492/12, No. 3, Policy of His Majesty's Government in Palestine and the Middle East, extracted from House of Commons debate, 26th January, 1949. The Churchill quote of that meeting is on page 6; the post-war quote about people driven from their homes is in his letter to Truman, Sept 16 1945, FO 800/484. The Bevin quote, as well as the "Interruption", page 7. Joan Peters, From Time Immemorial; Alan Dershowitz, The Case for Israel; for World Zionist Organization, Segev, One Palestine, Complete, p300)]

558 FO 371/75377, Jeru to FO (pencil "3"); PREM 8/1251, "Historical memorandum … Since 1945," esp 6; While the British Cabinet expressed continued bewilderment at the Security Council's refusal to take action against Israel's invasion, the US was supporting Israel's admission to the United Nations even as it was "simultaneously refusing to comply" with the Security Council.

559 Manchester Guardian, 12 Feb 1949; TNA, FO 371/75192, Haifa to F.O. no. 262, penciled 3; KV 3/.447, 29a; FO 371/75192, Haifa to F.O. no. 262, penciled 3.

560 NYT, 19 Jan 1949; Jan 10 1949; TNA, FO 371/75344, Cipher No. 611; Sharett, e.g. at the Knesset 15 June 1949.

561 Kermit Roosevelt, *The Arab Position* (address to National War College), Nov 24 1948.

562 Roosevelt, *Arab Position*, 3. The CIA reported the same American fall from grace in Iraq during this time. Through the end of World War II, "U.S. ideals of democracy, observed both on the American and the world stage, created a confidence in the United States as the one world power which would abide by the principles of right and justice." But its betrayal of those principles made America "the most hypocritical of nations." (CIA, National Intelligence Survey, Iraq, Jan 1951, declassified Oct 2005.)

563 CIA, "A Long-Range Disaster," Information Report, Mar 1949 (declassified date illegible on pdf examined, DOC_0000107452).

564 For Weizmann, Fischbach 8; Israeli Foreign Ministry, Quoted from Kapeliouk, *New Light on the Israeli Arab Conflict*. "The [Palestinian] refugees will find their place in the diaspora. Those who can resist will live thanks to natural selection, the others will simply crumble. Some of them will persist, but the majority will become a human heap, the scum of the earth and will sink into the lowest levels of the Arab world." Israel State Archives, Ministry of Foreign Affairs, Files-refugees, no. 2444/19. For Israel's claim, after its 1967 conquests, that Jordan is Palestine, see TNA, FCO 93/3271.

565 Pappé, *Idea of Israel*, 38, or Kindle 635; For "infiltration" to retrieve belongings, e.g., TNA FO 371/111101, The Star in the East, 10; FO 371/98492, Israel Respects an Armistice, 3.

566 TNA KV 2/1435, typed "460" (page begins "I think you will...").

567 TNA J. C. Robertson, May 19, 1948, KV 2/1435, PF.46863 (592, 593, 594) (One error in Robertson's statement: Russia had already accorded Israel *de jure* recognition); Also see Cabinet report CAB 129/32/0010, 63.

568 CIA, Information Report, Along Range Disaster, Mar 1949, 2 (declassified date illegible on pdf examined, DOC_0000107452).

569 CIA, Review of the World Situation as it Relates to the Security of the United States, 13 June, 1949, 13-14 (DOC_0000215472), declassified July 1998; TNA FO 371/75350, Minute of Meeting With Mr Lewis Jones of US Embassy; FO 371/75350, E8707, stamped "148"; KV 5/40, Reports on Possible Developments (blue "284"); FO 371/75344, Tel Aviv to F.O. Sir K Helm No. 655; FO 371/91376, British Legation Tel Aviv EE1084/6; Rabinovich-Reinharz 97-98.

570 Quigley, *Challenge*, ch 14; Even when martial law was lifted in name in 1966, non-Jewish areas remained "closed" and thereby under near-military control.

571 TNA FO 371/75192, Haifa to F.O., E4575, penciled 11, 2 (8 April 1949).

572 TNA FO 371/98484, Palestine Question Before the UN ME 105/52 es 1, 8 (unnumbered); Pappé, Making of the Arab-Israeli Conflict. Rationalizations for admitting Israel to the UN despite its intransigence ranged from France's, whose representative argued, without apparent irony, that perhaps Israel might cooperate if admitted; to the United States', that the Assembly itself was not directly concerned with compliance (even though it is a condition of membership).

573 John Ruedy, "Dynamics of Land Alienation," in Abu-Lughod, *Transformation*, esp 134-136.

574 TNA, FO 800/487, 241. Regarding value of £P, a 100 pound note was equivalent to 40 months wages of a skilled worker in Palestine (wikipedia. org/wiki/Palestine_pound, accessed 5-27-13); UN General Progress Report and Supplementary Report of the United Nations Conciliation Commission for Palestine Covering the Period from 11 December 1949 to 23 October 1950, Chapter III, point 35 etc (A/1367/rev.1); Quigley, *Challenge*, ch 12.

575 TNA, FO 371/104778; FO 371/91387; FO 371/91386; Morris, *Border Wars*, 4, 36, 37; For Eisenhower figure on refugees, see The *Times*, "U.S. Willing to Guarantee Arab-Israel Borders," 27 Aug 1955, quoting Dulles, speaking "with the authority of the President."

576 TNA FO 371/91385, E1091/23.

577 TNA FO 371/75192, Haifa to F.O., No. 507, penciled E6; *ibid*, Jewish squatters, penciled "7"; Quigley, *Challenge*, ch 12-13; Pappé, *Idea*, 288.

578 TNA, FO 371/104791, Notes and Jordan–Israel Border Relations June 1952 to October 1953 (which includes summaries of earlier years), 13;

secret report by Sir John Bagot Glubb, 15 Oct, 1949, FO 371/75344; Morris, *Border*, 191.

579 Morris, *Border*, 149, 146-147. IDF records confirm such thefts; see e.g., Morris, 151; TNA, FO 371/82209, Appx G.

580 Israeli Ministry of Foreign Affairs, Abu Ghosh–The Saga of an Arab Village, 1 June 2000; Morris, *Border*, 149, 146-147, 151-152.

581 Ryan, *Refugees*, 55-81. See also Quigley, *Challenge*, ch 12-13.

582 El-Haj, *Facts on the Ground*, 91-94.

583 NYT 18 Oct 1949, 26 Jan 1951; Giladi, *Scandals*, ch 4; Regarding Iraq, Giladi is largely corroborated in Eveland, *Ropes of Sand*, 48-49; Also Quigley, *Challenge*, ch 2; For Haganah member in Eliat, Braun, *Weeds*, 82-83, and the author's conversions with Ms. Braun in London, 2007; TNA, CO 733/420/19. A temporary suppression of Zionist material in Iraq following the 1929 disturbances in Palestine was cited as antisemitism. The 19 Oct 1934 issue of *The Jewish Chronicle* claimed that "the Iraqi Jewish population is living in a state of perpetual fear," CO 733/275/4, 39. Re: news from Iraq, e.g., *Palestine Post* letter Sept 19 1949, p4, "More than 120,000 Jews are held hostages," one letter in the Palestine Post warned, "thousands … thrown into the notorious prisons" and subjected to "savage and barbarous treatment." Signed only "Jew from Iraq" because "you can imagine the fate of my parents" should the writer's identity be revealed.

584 NYT 22 May 1950; NYT 20 Jan 1951.

585 TNA CO 67/373/8, stamped "4"; NYT May 22 1950; The flights were routed via Cyprus because Iraq would not allow direct flights to Israel; CO 67/373/8, British Legation, 1572/31/50; *ibid*, "Enclosure No. 1 in Henry Mack's Despatch No. 230"; TNA CO 67/373/8, letter from Moshe D. Shohet, "Committee for the Renunciation of Nationality and Departation" [sic].

586 TNA FO 371/82703, Monthly Situation Report, Jordan, for Sept 1950, British Legation Amman, esp 2; Morris, *Border*, 198; According to one of the operatives, the Zionist movement even paid some Iraqi newspaper "large payoffs" to publish anti-Jewish propaganda demanding that Jews be expelled (Giladi, *Scandals*, 200); TNA, CO 67/373/8, letter by Moshe Shohet, stamped 35-37; See *ibid*, letter, Henry Mack, stamped 58-61, for movement from Iraq through Iran to Israel. For N.E. Air Transport, see also Moshe Gat, *Exodus from Iraq*, 88 (TNA documents also cite the Alaskan Airlines link).

587 Hirst, *Gun and Olive Branch*, 282-283; TNA, FO 371/91692, penciled E133; FO 371/98767, Q1571/2; ibid, The Baghdad Trials (4pp); *ibid*, EQ1571/20; ibid, The *Iraq Times*, penciled 101; letter from P.A. Rhodes, 26 Jan 52 (penciled "110"); Eveland, *Ropes of Sand*, 49.

588 TNA, FO 371/98767, Q1571/2; ibid, The Baghdad Trials. Synagogues with arms caches were Masooda Shantobe, Hakham Hestel, Ezra Daood, plus the house of Eliahu Gurgi Abid, and another house in Faraj Alla Wahbi's quarter. NYT June 30 1951; Dec 17 1951; Dec 18 1951. Figure of 120,000 Iraqi Jews who fled to Israel is derived from "a leading Iraqi Jew who was a Director-General of the Iraqi Ministry of Finance" (FO

371/98767, letter from P.A. Rhodes, 8 Feb 1952); 5000 were said to be left.

589   Mordechai Ben-Porat quote from the blurb to his book *To Baghdad and Back: The Miraculous 2,000 Year Homecoming of the Iraqi Jews* (Gefen Books, 1998): "Between the years 1949 and 1952, over 130,000 Jews immigrated to Israel from Iraq, thanks largely to the efforts of emissaries from Israel and activists of the "Halutz" Movement in Iraq. This astounding Zionist accomplishment, known as Operation Ezra and Nehemiah, gave a final and glorious curtain call to the ancient Babylonian exile"; TNA, FO 371/98767, EQ 1571/18 (penciled "117"); Eveland, *Ropes of Sand*, 48-49, and Naeim Giladi, *Scandals*, ch 7-8; McGhee, see "Memorandum of Conversation, by the Assistant Secretary of State for Near Eastern, South Asian, and African Affairs (McGhee)," 11 June, 1951, Foreign Relations of the United States 1951, vol. 5, 707, at 710 (1982); Jones, see "Memorandum of Conversation by the Director of the Office of Near Eastern Affairs (Jones)," August 2, 1951, Foreign Relations of the United States 1951, vol. 6, 813, at 815 (1982); both quoted in Quigley, *Challenge*, ch 12. See also Suárez, "Iraqi Jews in 1950: the 'race against time' vs Near East Air Transport", in *Mondoweiss*, Aug 26 2023.

590   For Haganah member in Eliat, Braun, *Weeds*, 82-83, and the author's conversations with Ms. Braun in London, 2007; for reports on "Oriental" Jews in Israel in 1982, after the election of Begin, see TNA, FCO 93/3191; Protest song excerpted from Hirst, *Gun and Olive Branch*, 290.

591   For a summary of what is known about the state's kidnapping of non-Ashkenazi babies, see Jonathan Cook, "The shocking story of Israel's disappeared babies," in *Al Jazeera*, 5 Aug 2016, who draws from Shoshana Madmoni-Gerber's book, *Israeli Media and the Framing of Internal Conflict: The Yemenite Babies Affair* [Palgrave Macmillan; 2009]. One rationalization offered for the kidnappings of the newborns was to give them to Holocaust survivors unable to have children due to the emotional trauma they had suffered; but even if this argument had any merit, it is contradicted by the fact that Holocaust survivors themselves were victims of a similar scheme. Some had their babies stolen by state institutions and sold, and were similarly told that their child had died (see Endnote 428). Israel's use of its injustice against North African and Middle Eastern Jews to justify its injustice against the Palestinians has been known for some time, but was made an official device in 2012 (see, e.g., Judy Malz, "In Bid to Counter Palestinian Efforts, Israeli Diplomats Told to Raise Issue of Jewish Refugees," in *Haaretz*, 11 Sep 2012).

592   For Kirkbride, TNA FO 371/82706, T1017/1, esp 4 (July 1950); see also FO 371/75455, and FO 371/75344, Secret report by Glubb, 15 Oct 1949.

593   Morris, *Border*, 31.

594   Morris, *Border*, 43; TNA FO 371/82703, Monthly Situation Report for May 1950, British Legation Amman, esp 2; Red Cross figure cited in *Falastin* 28 Feb 1949 (in *Palestine Chronicle*), in Filiu, *Gaza*, 70, and Gallagher, *Quakers*, 64; Typhus, see Palestine Chronicle, 28 Feb 1949 (in *Palestine Chronicle*).

595   TNA, KV 5/41, J.C. Gove, blue 318a; Kent County Constabulary, blue 316a; Pedahzur & Weinberg, *Religious Fundamentalism*, 31-33, 175,176;

Yossi Melman, Inside Intel Time Bomb, in *Haaretz*, August 13, 2009; JTA, July 13 1953 & Sept 9 1953.; NYT, April 18 1953. According to the JTA, Heifetz' attacker aimed for this violin case, and the wrist injury was the result of protecting the violin, which would have been a Stradivarius, Tononi, or Guarneri del Gesù.

596 Pedahzur 31, 176; Benziman, *Israeli Caesar*, 54-55. Some sources (e.g., Benziman, *Israeli Caesar*, 55) state that Unit 101 was composed entirely of kibbutzim and settlers, with no ex-Mandate militants, but Morris (Border Wars) cites an ex-Palmach member in Unit 101's raid of Bureij on Aug 28 '53; Morris, 239-241; for Agudat Ihud see also Morris, *One State, Two States*, Yale, 2009, 48-50; When some parents who heard of the "training" their sons were getting asked Agudat Ihud to bring their complaints to the government, Ben-Gurion dismissed the accusations as "imaginary and without foundation." His diary proves that he himself ordered such missions. Curiously, in the early 1950s Israeli officials told the American consul general in Jerusalem that the "Israeli terrorists" (i.e., rogue groups, not the IDF) are responsible for some of the trouble and might be trying to precipitate war between Israel and Jordan, though this defense is not cited later in the MAC meetings. The claim is recorded by the CIA: CIA-RDP79T00975A001100590001-4.pdf. The same documents claims that Glubb suspected the Stern Gang in attacks in 1953, but this is probably a reference to the Kingdom of Israel.

597 TNA FO 371/82706, T1017/1, From a report by Alec Kirkbride, British ambassador to Amman, visiting "West Jordan" (Palestine). See also FO 371/75455; Morris, *Border*, 167. It should be clarified that not only were the "infiltrators" people attempting merely to return to their own homes, but they were not even infiltrators according to the Armistice terms, which specified that it must involve "warlike acts or acts of hostility" (TNA, FO 371/104779, ERL091/82, 2).

598 Morris, *Border*, 166-167.

599 According to a soldier eye-witness, the Bedouin man had a rifle which he deliberately threw to the ground at the sight of the soldiers, and ran in fear. The soldier who gunned him down simply recorded that he was "armed" (See *Haartez*, article cited below).

600 Transcript of videoed interview of Yerachmiel Kahanovitch, filmed in Kibbutz Degania, July 23, 2012. He was part of Operation Broom and Operation Dani. English translation by Ami Asher. Published in Zochot, Accessed October 18, 2012. For "cultured officers," Morris, *Border*, 470; for rapes in 1948, see Morris, *Revisited*, and his interview with Ari Shavit, "Survival of theFittest." Pappé, *Ethnic Cleansing*, 209. For media reports, Chris McGreal, "Israel learns of a hidden shame in its early years," in The Guardian, 4 Nov 2003, and Aviv Lavie, Moshe Gorali, "I saw fit to remove her from the world," Haaretz, Oct. 29 2003.

601 Ben-Gurion's diary, in Morris, *Border*, 167-168; For rapes in 1948, see Morris, *Revisited*, and his interview with Ari Shavit, "Survival of the Fittest"; Morris, *Border*, 470; Pappé, *Ethnic Cleansing*, 209; FO 371/104791, Notes on Jordan–Israel Border Relations June 1952 to October 1953; FO 371/91385, E1091/7; FO 371/82209.

602 Toynbee, in his *Observer* piece, cites the daughter of a mason who was arrested with his daughter, the latter "shot dead while trying to escape." She thus appears not to be the same girl cited in other testimony, who "died on the way" (i.e., perished in the desert). FO 1018/70, "To: O.C. Police, Amman".

603 TNA FO 371/91387, letter, M.T. Walker, 15 June 1951, S103/5/33/51; Forced marches, see NYT Oct 23 1979; Three folders in TNA contain the Wadi Araba files, duplicated: FO 624/191, FO 905/111, and FO 1018/70.

604 TNA FO 371/82703, Monthly Situation Report, Jordan, June, 1950; Morris, *Border*, 147-148. (The eye witness from the kibbutz witnessed most likely this incident, else a similar mass expulsion with a month).

605 Morris, *Border*, 147-148; TNA FO 1018/70, Incident in the Wai Araba, 1-2.

606 TNA, FO 1018/70, Incident in the Wai Araba, 1-3.

607 *The Observer*, 11 June, 1950, "A Tragic Change of Role"; Morris, *Border*, 161, 163. Philip Toynbee was the son of the historian Arnold Toynbee, but unlike his father had been a supporter of Israel.

608 "Infiltrators Not Maltreated Army Declares," June 15 1950. TNA FO 1018/70, Incident in the Wai Araba, Appendix II; Morris, *Border*, 161, 163.

609 TNA, FO 371/91385, E1091/1; see also FO 371/82703, Monthly Situation Report Oct 1950; for fabricating victims' statements, see Morris, *Border*, 150. The soldiers accused the men in Jish of "buying smuggled shoes."

610 TNA, FO_371-104791, penciled 75, or Notes on Jordan-Israel Border Relations, June 1952 to October 1953, 13; FO 371/98492, penciled 71; FO 371/82703, Monthly Situation Report Nov 1950, esp p2; Yalu victims' statement in FO 371/82209.

611 TNA, FO 371/98490, penciled 56; Quigley, *Challenge*, ch 16; Morris, Border, 169.

612 TNA, FO 371/91385, Sharafat and Falama Atrocities; Fourteen telegraph were rigged with delayed action explosives, but four did not explode; *ibid*, E1091/8, E1091/18; FO 371/104791; Morris, *Border*, 194; TNA, FO 371/98492, penciled 71. Azmi Nashashibi, Chairman of the Jordan delegation to the MAC, claimed that Ramati had been well-known as a member of Lehi and after statehood became a member of the radical Expansionists. The author could not confirm this. See TNA, FO 371/91385, E1091/17, E1091/19; FO 371/91385, E1091/10; The Jerusalem Post published a letter from several associates of Hebrew University strongly criticizing their government's behavior. See FO 371/91385, To The Editor of the Post, etc.

613 TNA FO 371/91385, Appendix "A," Sharafat admitted to be a "reprisal"; *ibid*, E1091/13.

614 TNA FO 371/91386, letter from Glubb to Kirkbride, 17 Feb 1951; FO 371/91385, E1091/23 (letter from Glubb, 8 Feb 51).

615 TNA, FO 371/91385, E1091/1; Regarding "balancing" complaints, see FO 371/104791, Note on Jordan–Israel Border Relations June 1952 to October 1953. For example, in early 1953, Israel flew numerous air sorties over the whole of Jordan's lines of communication. Each time Israel did so, it filed a complaint alleging that Jordan—whose fleet consisted of a small number of passenger aircraft and unarmed Austers—had violated Israeli airspace.

616 TNA, FO 371/98490, penciled 56; *ibid*, photographs of the atrocities stored. Morris, *Border*, 171, while confirming the murder of both, cites the mutilation and "15 sten gun rounds" for the older man without specifying the methods against the 18 year old.

617 TNA, FO 371/91715, R10345/2 (4pp); FO 371/91383, E1083/358; CIA, SE-13, 24 Sept 1951, p20; R10345/9, letter, P.S. Stephens; R10345/10, letter, J.E. Chadwick.

618 TNA, FO 371/75344; FO 371/98492, penciled 71-72; FO 371/75344 cites two girls and the mother in the Ghor Safi attack; one of the wounded may have died later, but the author has used the lesser figure.

619 TNA, FO 371/98490, "Reprisal on the Innocent," 2 (penciled 24); J Post, *ibid*, penciled 35, 101 (Jan 4, 1952).

620 TNA, FO 371/98490, penciled 104; Israeli murder rate based on Israeli State Yearbook for 1952: TNA, FO 371/104791, Jordan–Israel Border Relations June 1952 to Oct 1953, p7 (penciled 69); FO 371/75344, Secret report by Glubb, 15 Oct 1949; FO 371/91387, E1091/54, p2; FO 371/98490, report by A.R. Walmsley, 9 Jan 1952, 1091/1/52.

621 TNA, FO 371/98490, "Reprisal on the Innocent," penciled 23-28; Morris, *Border*, 204, and the previous TNA document, whose details differ slightly but without real contradiction; Hutchison, 14 ("no person could live long enough to become calloused to such a sight").

622 The leaflets left at the scenes of the Christmas Eve massacres were in rough Arabic, printed on pink paper by cyclostyle. The same leaflet, for the same crime, was printed separately for two villages, Beit Jala and Mar Elias. Translation follows: *On December 4, 1951, people from the residents of Beit Jala* [or *Mar Elias* on the leaflets left in that village] *killed a Jewish girl near Bayt Waghan after they had committed a crime which cannot be forgiven. What we've done now is the punishment of that horrible crime and we will not stay silent as we always have* [literally] *arrows for them. May the listeners listen.* [Translation Rawan Yaghi.] TNA, FO 371/98490.

623 TNA, FO 371/98490, penciled p "26"; see also *ibid*, E 1091/3.

624 Benny Morris (*Border*, 61 etc), has a confused account of the Christmas Eve attacks. He states that Lea Festinger's murderer(s) was the so-called (Arab) Mansi gang, because "on 8 January 1952, Israel passed their names to the Jordanian authorities," unaware of the document that exposes this fraud (TNA, FO 371/98490, penciled "26"). Yet elsewhere he states that the Mansi gang were not among the bombing's victims, though the names passed back to the MAC were specifically of Christmas Eve victims—that was the whole point. Western diplomats never accepted Israel's post-facto claim, the US consul-general for example noting that Lea Festinger's

Israeli boyfriend had never been cleared of suspicion (Morris, *Border*, 204); FO 371/98490, E1091/2.

625 TNA, FO 371/104791, Note on Jordan-Israel Border Relations June 1952 to October 1953, esp 14; Morris, *Border*, 171; TNA, FO 371/98492, penciled 84-86.

626 TNA, FO 371/98492, Appx "B," p2, penciled 72, and others; Appx "C" contains an Israeli Army response, as quoted in Haaretz, much of it demonstrably false; FO 816/179, MS letter, 10301/31A, 10pp; For a different view re tactic of provocation, FO 371/111104, 1033/231/54.

627 TNA, FO 371/98493, E1091/83; Hutchison, 25

628 TNA, FO 371/98492, Cypher, No. 127, penciled 97-98. Regarding Riley's pro-Israel bias, see also FO 371/82209, letter from Hugh Dow, 4th Nov 1950.

629 TNA, FO 371/98492, E1091/58, esp 2; *ibid*, "Secret—Jerusalem—Barrel"; To justify commandeering the UN office, Israel claimed that it lay on the Israeli side of the Line, which was irrelevant (the international status and inviolability of the UN office was implicit in the agreements) and ironic, since the UN and Jordan had accommodated Israel by allowing it access to its facilities there. See Kirkbride, *From the Wings*, 101, on the Jordanians agreeing to Bernadotte suggestion that they allow the Mt of Olives to be UN administered, and how after his assassination "in some mysterious manner" the Israeli police guard allowed there to prevent looting changed to be a company of Israeli infantry when the Armistice was signed.

630 CIA, Current Intelligence Bulletin, 23 Oct 1952, declassified Oct 2003 (RDP79T00975A000900110001-9); TNA, FO 816/179, 10301/124, esp p2; Camels, see Hutchison, captions between 136-137; Morris, *Border*, 229; Hanna Braun served under Dayan and wrote that he would "boast freely of his fear-striking tactics" (*Weeds*, 80).

631 TNA, FO 371/104735, 10117/2/53, penciled 34-37; FO 371/104791, penciled 80; FO 371/104785, R1091/273; R1091/277; FO 371/98493, E1091/84; FO 371/104791, Note on Jordan-Israel Border Relations June 1952 to October 1953, esp 11-12; UN, Security Council, S_PV.630 27 Oct 1953. Regarding the repeatedly documented IDF policy of Palestinians being forced to remain in their homes as they were blown up, the opposite is stated in Thomas Mitchell, in *Israel's Security Men* (McFarland & Co., 2015). Mitchel writes that the Israeli soldiers called for people to vacate their houses and only afterwards "discovered" that "some 69 had remained." The same claim is made in Samuel Katz, *Israeli Elite Units since 1948*, 10. Regarding the Israeli government's control of the domestic media, and thus of its population's beliefs and attitudes, see Ilan Pappé's *Israel Out of the Frame* [Pluto, 2010].

632 UN, Security Council, S/PV.630, 27 Oct 1953; Morris, *Border*, 51; TNA FO 371/104791, "Note on Jordan-Israel Border Relations June 1952 to October 1953," p2; Syrian border, e.g., TNA, FO 371/104788, penciled 14-20, 27. Few "infiltrators" armed, see Morris, *Border*; children crossing the line, see British Ambassador Geoffrey Furlonge, TNA, FO 371/104779, letter, March 9, 1953.

633 Hutchison 120-121; TNA, FO 371/104785, R1091/278; For ongoing Syrian border clashes, FO 371/104788, penciled 14-20, 27; Morris (who states that very few "infiltrators" crossed with the intent to do harm), *Border*, 172, 213; TNA, FO 371/104782, R1091/168; hiding in caves, R1091/169.

634 TNA, FO 371/104781, 1062/126, letter to the Foreign Office from the British Consulate in Jerusalem, dated 11 May, 1953; British Embassy, Amman, Despatch No. 62; British Embassy, Tel Aviv, 20th May, 1953; also see Cypher/OTP No. 274; Beit Sira, FO 371/104781, Cypher/OTP No. 69, May 22, 1953.

635 TNA, FO 371/104781, Cypher/OTP No. 273, No. 65, No. 64, No. 66; FO 371/104782, Mr. Walmsley, ER1091/168, 24 May 24 1953, and ER1091/169, 25 May, 1953.

636 TNA, FO 371/104784, letter from A.R. Walmsley, 8 June 1953.

637 Morris, *Border*, 191-192, 240; Benziman, *Israeli Caesar*, 50, 56-57; TNA, FO 371/104786; FO 371/104788, "ISUM 134," penciled 8; Telegram, penciled 63. Unit 101 was composed principally of Israelis from the kibbutzim and settlement movement, not ex-members of the pre-state gangs. The Israeli resumption of strafing of Gaza in July 1953 based on US Colonel T.M. Hinkle.

638 Report by Glubb, 15Oct 1949, TNA FO 371/75344; FO 371/104788, "ISUM 135", penciled 14, and others.

639 CIA, Current Intelligence Bulletin, 20 Sept 1953, declassified July 2004 (RDP79T00975A001300080001-8).

640 TNA, FO 371/104791, "Note on Jordan-Israel Border Relations June 1952 to October 1953," p12; Khalidi-Caplan, Sharett Diary, 81; Hirst, *Olive Branch*, 307.

641 TNA, FO 371/104790, penciled 11-12; FO 371/104788, penciled 29; *ibid*, penciled 106.

642 Benziman, *Israeli Caesar*, 53; Hirst, *Olive Branch*, (who says Qibya dead is 66) 307-308; Alternate translation of Ben-Gurion speech, FO 371/104789, penciled 153; Hutchison (who estimated 250-300 well-trained soldiers), 163, 44.

643 Morris, *Border*, 245; Hirst, *Olive Branch*, 307-308; Benziman, *Israeli Caesar*, 54–55; TNA, FO 371/104789/1091/408. Zertal (*Israel's Holocaust*, 176-178) also notes the framing of Holocaust survivors.

644 TNA, Report by Sir John Bagot Glubb, 15th Oct, 1949, FO 371/75344; Sharon later claimed that he had thought the houses were empty; For infiltration, Morris, *Border*, 245; CIA, Current Intelligence Bulletin, 21 Oct 1953, declassified Dec 2003 (RDP79T00975A001300340001-9).

645 TNA, FO 371/104788, R1091/353; *ibid*, R1091/364; FO 371/104790, Foriegn Ministers' Conference (with US Secretary of State John Dulles); Morris, *Border*, 250; NYT, Oct 26 1953, Oct 19 1953; Eveland, *Ropes of Sand*, 75-77, who cites Britain's Archbishop of York as one victim of the "anti-Semitism" smear for raising the issue of Qibya.

646 Benziman, *Israeli Caesar*, 56-57, Morris, *Border*, 240; TNA, FO 371/104789, penciled "120", "202", "203"; FO 371/104779, R1091/82; FO 371/104789, penciled "120", "168", "202"; FO 371/104791, Notes on Jordan–Israel Border Relations.

647 TNA, FO 371/104788, R1091/365, penciled "150"; *ibid*, R. Makins, penciled "143"; FO 371/104791, penciled "81", & others; *ibid*, letter, A.R. Moore, penciled "88"; NYT, 19 Oct 1953.

648 TNA, FO 371/104788, "ISUM no. 133", penciled "10"-"11".

649 TNA, FO 371/104791, R1091/452c, R1091/447.

650 TNA, FO 371/104791, R1091/471; FO 371/111098, HQ Arab Legion Intelligence Summary No. 150, p2; *ibid*, No. 151, p2.

651 CIA, Current Intelligence Bulletin, 23 Mar 1954, declassified Sep 2003 (RDP79T00975A001500090001-5); That Jordanians were not responsible was subsequently supported in CIA, Current Intelligence Bulletin, 4 Apr 1954, declassified Sep 2003 (RDP79T00975A001500210001-1); Morris, *Border*, 294-300; UN, Security Council S//3252 (19 June 1954); Hutchison, *Violent Truce*, 47-54; TNA FO 371/111098.

652 Hutchison, *Violent Truce*, 47-54; TNA, FO 371/111101, R1091/77, 1032/87/54, and others; among Israel's misrepresentations noted by Hutchison, Dayan claimed that the Scorpion's Pass attack was political (=West Bank) because the victims were not robbed, but this, according to Hutchison, was a fabrication, that the victims had clearly been robbed.

653 TNA, FO 371/111098, Incidents Report 163, p5; Incidents Report 164 (which cites an ambush on the vehicle rather than land mine); UN Sec Council s/3251; TNA, FO 371/111104, R1091/160, letter by T. Wikeley, British Consulate-General Jerusalem, July 20, 1954.

654 TNA, FO 371/111104, R/1091/172, and R1091/178. Fabrication, in a report filed about an incident he witnessed near Sheikh Mathkoor in Hebron District on August 13 of 1954; Israeli soldiers crossed the Armistice Line in the Hebron District on August 13 of 1954, murdered one Palestinian with a 2" mortar, and presumably kidnapped another who had taken refuge in a cave; *ibid*, Extracts from Colonel Gammon's Frontier Report; CIA, *National Intelligence Estimate Number 36-54 Probable Developments in the Arab States* (declassified Sep 1997); This September CIA National Intelligence Estimate remarked on Arab countries' overtures to improving relations with Israel and finding solutions, but "the Israelis have not, however, shown a like tendency to reasonableness and compromise."

655 TNA, FO 371/108548, E1571/1(c); Morris, *Border*, 317; Black-Morris, *Secret Wars*, 107-110; CIA, Current Intelligence Bulletin, 22 July 1954, declassified Oct 2003 (RDP79T00975A001600500001-8).

656 CIA, Central Intelligence Bulletin, 15 Dec 1964, declassified May 2005 (RDP79T00975A008000360001-3); Some sources cite twelve men and one women arrested by Egypt when the Lavon Affair broke, but the figure of fourteen people is cited in, e.g., TNA, FO 371/108548, E/1571/9.

657 TNA, FO 371/108548, E1571/1; "Confidential Mr. Barnett Janner"; "YZEP V EGYPT"; Wikipedia's entire entry on Rabbi Nahun relies on a single, online source by Victor D. Sanua, who suggests that much of the Rabbi's words against Zionism were imposed on him by the Egyptian government. British source makes no reference to this, and the Egyptian Jewry had a long history of opposition to Zionism, cited by Zionist leaders themselves.

658 TNA, FO 371/108548, E/1571/9; E1571/2; E1571/3; E1571/19/a.

659 CIA, Central Intelligence Bulletin, 15 Dec 1964, declassified May 2005 (RDP79T00975A008000360001-3); CIA, Current Intelligence Bulletin, 1 Sept 1954, declassified Jan 2004 (RDP79T00975A001700560001-1); "Israel honors 9 Egyptian spies," Reuters, Mar 30 2005; Barak Ravid, "State archives to stay classified for 20 more years, PM instructs," in *Haaretz*, July 28 2010 (the Lavon Affair is specifically cited).

660 TNA FO 371/151273, declassified in September, 2013; Rabinovich and Reinharz, *Israel in the Middle East*, 114-115; Morris, *Border*, 324.

661 Morris, *Border*, 327; TNA, FO 371/121692, John Nicholls, letter from British Embassy, Tel Aviv, No. 24 (1013/56), p2.

662 TNA, FO 371/111106; The victims were taken to the hospital in Bethlehem, but there is no further word on them. Morris, *Border*, 312 n132, says that the attackers were from the Mevo Beitar cooperative.

663 Sharett, TNA, PREM 11/945, 24. Israeli delegation in Beirut TNA, FO 371/111106, Sir Stewart Crawford reported this from the British Middle East Office in Beirut, via letter by Sir Edwin A. Chapman to P. S. Falla, October 12 1954.

664 Nasr, 51, cites the first known hijacking as having taken place in Peru in 1931. NYT, Dec 29 1954, Dec 15 1954, Dec 14 1954, Dec 13 1954. Also Chomsky, *Triangle*, 77. For the June 1950 incident, FO 371/82703, Monthly Situation Report for the Jordan for the month of June, 1950, 2.

665 TNA, FO 371/115898, Press Release No 60; Morris, *Border*, 384, who acknowledges that the murdered bedouin had nothing to do with the deaths of the hikers, but does presume, without indicating why, that bedouin were responsible.

666 For parsing of the legal obligation to come to Jordan's defense, see e,g. TNA, FO 371/111101; CIA, Current Intelligence Bulletin, 28 January 1954.

667 CIA, Current Intelligence Bulletin, 28 Jan 1954, declassified Jan 2004 (CIA-RDP79T00975A001400350001-7); TNA, PREM 11/945, IZ 4753.

668 TNA, FO 371/104789, Secret From Amman to Foreign Office, October 24, 1953.

669 See CIA, Current Intelligence Bulletin, 20 Sep 1953, declassified July 2004 (CIA-RDP79T00975A001300080001-8); Sitkowski, *UN Peacekeeping*, 46-48.

670 TNA, PREM 11/945, letter, "Action in the Event of Israeli Aggression"; AIR 8/1895, TS 47304 415/3; AIR 8/1895, "Israeli Aggression–United States Assistance PJ (55)54(Final)".

671 TNA, FO 371/115905 / FO 371/104788; FO 371/121692, John Nicholls, letter from British Embassy, Tel Aviv, No. 24 (1013/56), 4,6; Morris, *Border*, 357-359.

672 For "rise in war fever," see CIA, Current Intelligence Bulletin, 30 Dec 1955, declassified Mar 2004 (CIA-RDP79T00975A002300390001-3); Such reports, according to the CIA, were "inspired by the Israeli army"; CIA, Current Intelligence Bulletin, 8 Mar 1956, declassified Jan 2003 (CIA-RDP79T00975A002400430001-7); Sitkowski, *UN Peacekeeping*, 46-48.

673 For Project Alpha, Morris, *Border*, 330; CIA, Current Intelligence Bulletin, 6 Mar 1955, declassified Sep 2002 (RDP79T00975A001900270001-1); Cohen, 264; TNA, FO 371/121692, John Nicholls, letter from British Embassy, Tel Aviv, No. 24 (1013/56), p3-4, who also wrote that "There is no reason to doubt Colonel Nasser's assertion that the raid [of February 28] convinced him that Israel's intentions were aggressive … and that this led him in the end to the now notorious arms deal with Czechoslovakia."

674 TNA, DEFE 6/39, Annex to J.P.(56) Note 9, "33" at top right.

675 TNA, DEFE 6/39, Note by General Sir Charles Keightley, who was C-i-C of Musketeer; *ibid*, Aid to Jordan in the Event of Israeli Aggression Note by the Directors of Plans, "30" at top right; ibid, "32" at top right; FO 371/121535, From: Ministry of Defence, London, to G.H.Q. Middle East Land Forces (Main). Commander-in-Chief, Mediterranean, 18th October, 1956; escalation of attacks and counter-attacks, see also FO 371/121773.

676 TNA, FO 371/121535, VJ 1192 118.

677 TNA, AIR 8/1895, "Exclusive for C.A.S.—from CINC" ("27" at top); DEFE 6/39, Aid to Jordan in the Event of Israeli Aggression Note by the Directors of Plans, "30" at top right.

678 Morris, *Border*, 397-398, suggests that perhaps talk of the attack on Israel was kept alive to the end because Britain could not reveal its contradictory arrangements with Israel and France; but as quoted herein, top secret British documents that had no need for any such pretense continued to deal seriously with the raid on Israel. For US correspondence regarding Suez, see TNA, FO 371/121794; British records, see e.g. WO 32/21899; Jordanian request after Qalqilya, FO 371/121535, "Aid to Jordan". See also Stuart A. Cohen, "A Still Stranger Aspect of Suez". J. Nicholls meeting with Ben-Gurion, FO 391/121803, letter, Nov 26 1956.

679 Morris, *Border*, 408-409, Khan Yunis, UN figures record "some 135 local residents" and "140 refugees"; TNA, FO 371/121776, VR1091/158; CIA, Intelligence Bulletin 30 Dec 1956 (RDP79T00975A002900130001-5); Neff, *Pillars*, 99; NYT, 22 & 24 Feb 57.

680 Regarding the *USS Liberty*, see CIA report 3403-67, dated 9 Nov '67, for the theory that the attack was ordered by Moshe Dayan. Theories for the attack include keeping the US from knowing Moshe Dayan's plans to seize the Golan Heights, hiding an Israeli massacre of Egyptians in the Sinai, and blaming the attack on Egypt in order to drag the US into the war. See also Scott, *Attack on the Liberty*. For Dean Rusk, *As I Saw It*, Penguin, 1991, p388.

681 Regarding Israel and foreign aid to the Palestinians, see also Jonathan Cook, "Study: At least 78% of humanitarian aid intended for Palestinians ends up in Israeli coffers," *Mondoweiss*, 8 March 2016.

682 For caloric intake, see e.g. Amira Hass, 2,279 Calories per Person: How Israel Made Sure Gaza Didn't Starve, Haaretz, Oct 17 2012. School room desks, books, pasta, and shampoo without conditioner have been among the lengthy list of items Israel blocks from entry into Gaza. The list frequently changes. See e.g., Amira Hass, "Israel bans books, music and clothes from entering Gaza," *Haaretz*, 17 May 2009; Gisha (Legal Center for Freedom of Movement), Restrictions on the transfer of goods to Gaza: Obstruction and obfuscation, Jan 2010; "UN agency calls on Israel to lift book blockade of Gaza schools," UN News Center, 10 Sep 2009; "Israel: Stop Blocking School Supplies From Entering Gaza," Human Rights Watch, 11 Oct 2009.

683 Suárez, Thomas, "UXOs: Did Israel deliberately arm Hamas?," in *Mondoweiss*, 13 Dec 2010; also Email correspondence between the author and a United Nations Mine Action Service Officer, March, 2010.

684 The 2014 Israeli attack (Protective Edge) killed 2200-2400 people, roughly 24% fewer than the 2977 killed on 9/11 [Wikipedia, accessed 29 Jan 2019.] not counting the 19 hijackers), and nearly 11,000 injured, roughly double the injuries of 9/11. About a third of the injured in Protective Edge were children, including one thousand left permanently disabled by the Israeli attacks. White phosphorous into Israel, *Jerusalem Post*, 15 September, 2010.

685 See e.g., John Ruedy, "Dynamics of Land Alienation," in Abu-Lughod, Transformation, esp 134-136. Re: refugees, Suárez, "Palestinians remain holed up in internment, not 'refugee', camps", *Middle East Monitor*, Aug 2 2023.

686 Among many others, A Texas Elementary School Speech Pathologist Refused to Sign a Pro-Israel Oath, Now Mandatory in Many States—so She Lost Her Job, The Intercept, Dec17 2018. Disaster relief, for example, BBC, "Texas city requires Israel pledge for hurricane relief," Oct 20 2017; The Independent, "Texas city refuses to give people hurricane aid unless they pledge not to boycott Israel," Oct 20, 2017.

Index